SCT 100 Introduction to Microcomputers,

Chattahoochee Technical College

VISTA edition

David Beskeen I Carol Cram I Jennifer Duffy
Lisa Friedrichsen I Elizabeth Eisner Reding

CENGAGE
Learning™

Australia • Brazil • Japan • Korea • Mexico • Singapore • Spain • United Kingdom • United States

CENGAGE
Learning™

SCT 100 Introduction to Microcomputers
VISTA edition
Chattahoochee Technical College

David Beskeen I Carol Cram I Jennifer Duffy
Lisa Friedrichsen I Elizabeth Eisner Reding

Executive Editors:
 Maureen Staudt
 Michael Stranz

Senior Project Development Manager:
 Linda DeStefano

Marketing Specialist:
 Sara Mercurio
 Lindsay Shapiro

Senior Production / Manufacturing Manager:
 Donna M. Brown

PreMedia Supervisor:
 Joel Brennecke

Rights & Permissions Specialist:
 Kalina Hintz
 Todd Osborne

Cover Image:
 Getty Images*

© 2009 Cengage Learning
Source: MICROSOFT OFFICE 07 ILLUS INTRODUCTORY PREMIUM VIDEO Ed., BESKEEN/CRAM/DUFFY, 2009 Course Technology

For product information and technology assistance, contact us at
Cengage Learning Customer & Sales Support, 1-800-354-9706

For permission to use material from this text or product,
submit all requests online at **cengage.com/permissions**
Further permissions questions can be emailed to
permissionrequest@cengage.com

ISBN-13: 978-1-111-06671-0

ISBN-10: 1-111-06671-X

Cengage Learning
5191 Natorp Boulevard
Mason, Ohio 45040
USA

Cengage Learning is a leading provider of customized learning solutions with office locations around the globe, including Singapore, the United Kingdom, Australia, Mexico, Brazil, and Japan. Locate your local office at:
international.cengage.com/region

Cengage Learning products are represented in Canada by Nelson Education, Ltd.

For your lifelong learning solutions, visit **www.cengage.com/custom**

Visit our corporate website at **www.cengage.com**

Printed in the United States of America

Preface

Welcome to *Microsoft Office 2007—Illustrated Introductory, Premium Video Edition*. If this is your first experience with the Illustrated series, you'll see that this book has a unique design: each skill is presented on two facing pages, with steps on the left and screens on the right. The layout makes it easy to learn a skill without having to read a lot of text and flip pages to see an illustration.

This book is an ideal learning tool for a wide range of learners—the "rookies" will find the clean design easy to follow and focused with only essential information presented, and the "hotshots" will appreciate being able to move quickly through the lessons to find the information they need without reading a lot of text. The design also makes this a great reference after the course is over! See the illustration on the right to learn more about the pedagogical and design elements of a typical lesson.

About the Videos

This book comes with nearly 150 video tutorials that map to the lessons in the Word, Excel, Access, PowerPoint, and Integration units in the book. Here are some of the benefits of using the videos with the book:

- **Brings the book content to life.** Each five-minute video maps to a two-page lesson in the text. Visual learners who resist reading textbooks will be more engaged and will gain a deeper understanding of the skills and why they are important.

- **Improves skill retention.** Watching a video before performing the steps in a lesson helps students understand what they are doing when they actually perform the steps. This rich learning experience helps students retain skills longer.

Each two-page spread focuses on a single skill.

Concise text introduces the basic principles in the lesson and integrates a real-world case study.

UNIT D
Word 2007

Dividing a Document into Sections

Dividing a document into sections allows you to format each section of the document with different page layout settings. A **section** is a portion of a document that is separated from the rest of the document by section breaks. **Section breaks** are formatting marks that you insert in a document to show the end of a section. Once you have divided a document into sections, you can format each section with different column, margin, page orientation, header and footer, and other page layout settings. By default, a document is formatted as a single section, but you can divide a document into as many sections as you like. You insert a section break to divide the document into two sections, and then format the text in the second section in two columns. First, you customize the status bar to display section information.

STEPS

QUICK TIP
Use the Customize Status bar menu to turn on and off the display of information in the status bar.

1. **Right-click the status bar, click Section on the Customize Status Bar menu that opens (if it is not already checked), then click the document to close the menu**
   The status bar indicates the insertion point is located in section 1 of the document.

2. **Click the Home tab, then click the Show/Hide ¶ button ⁊ in the Paragraph group**
   Turning on formatting marks allows you to see the section breaks you insert in a document.

QUICK TIP
When you insert a section break at the beginning of a paragraph, Word inserts the break at the end of the previous paragraph. A section break stores the formatting information for the preceding section.

3. **Place the insertion point before the headline QST Launches New Tours to South Africa, click the Page Layout tab, then click the Breaks button in the Page Setup group**
   The Breaks menu opens. You use this menu to insert different types of section breaks. See Table D-1.

4. **Click Continuous**
   Word inserts a continuous section break, shown as a dotted double line, above the headline. The document now has two sections. Notice that the status bar indicates the insertion point is in section 2.

5. **Click the Columns button in the Page Setup group**
   The columns menu opens. You use this menu to format text in one, two, or three columns of equal width, or to create two columns of different widths, one narrow and one wider. To create columns with custom widths and spacing, you click More Columns on the Columns menu.

QUICK TIP
When you delete a section break, you delete the section formatting of the text before the break. That text becomes part of the following section, and it assumes the formatting of that section.

6. **Click Two**
   Section 2 is formatted in two columns of equal width, as shown in Figure D-3. The text in section 1 remains formatted in a single column. Notice that the status bar now indicates the document is four pages long. Formatting text in columns is another way to increase the amount of text that fits on a page.

7. **Click the View tab, click the Two Pages button in the Zoom group, scroll down to examine all four pages of the document, press [Ctrl][Home], then save the document**
   The text in section 2—all the text below the continuous section break—is formatted in two columns. Text in columns flows automatically from the bottom of one column to the top of the next column.

TABLE D-1: Types of section breaks

section	function
Next page	Begins a new section and moves the text following the break to the top of the next page
Continuous	Begins a new section on the same page
Even page	Begins a new section and moves the text following the break to the top of the next even-numbered page
Odd page	Begins a new section and moves the text following the break to the top of the next odd-numbered page

Word 80 Formatting Documents

Hints as well as troubleshooting advice, right where you need it—next to the step itself.

Tables are quickly accessible summaries of key terms, toolbar buttons, or keyboard alternatives connected with the lesson material.

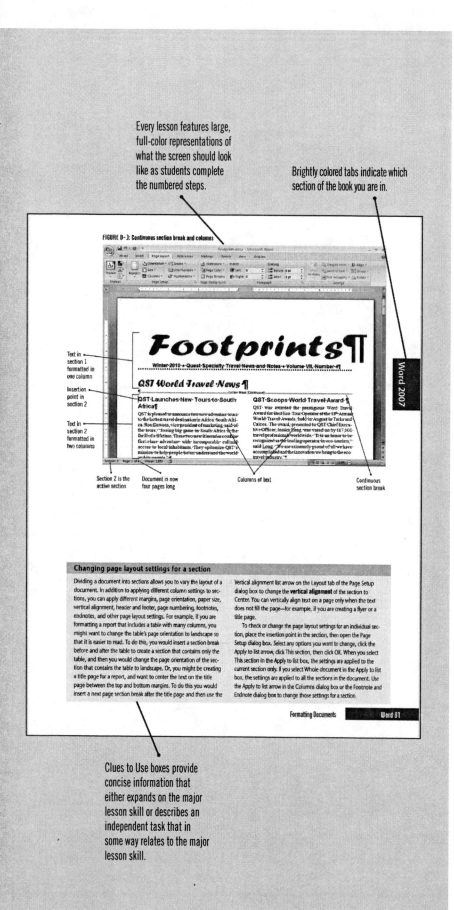

Every lesson features large, full-color representations of what the screen should look like as students complete the numbered steps.

Brightly colored tabs indicate which section of the book you are in.

FIGURE D-3: Continuous section break and columns

Text in section 1 formatted in one column

Insertion point in section 2

Text in section 2 formatted in two columns

Section 2 is the active section

Document is now four pages long

Columns of text

Continuous section break

Changing page layout settings for a section

Dividing a document into sections allows you to vary the layout of a document. In addition to applying different column settings to sections, you can apply different margins, page orientation, paper size, vertical alignment, header and footer, page numbering, footnotes, endnotes, and other page layout settings. For example, if you are formatting a report that includes a table with many columns, you might want to change the table's page orientation to landscape so that it is easier to read. To do this, you would insert a section break before and after the table to create a section that contains only the table, and then you would change the page orientation of the section that contains the table to landscape. Or, you might be creating a title page for a report, and want to center the text on the title page between the top and bottom margins. To do this you would insert a next page section break after the title page and then use the

Vertical alignment list arrow on the Layout tab of the Page Setup dialog box to change the **vertical alignment** of the section to Center. You can vertically align text on a page only when the text does not fill the page—for example, if you are creating a flyer or a title page.

To check or change the page layout settings for an individual section, place the insertion point in the section, then open the Page Setup dialog box. Select any options you want to change, click the Apply to list arrow, click This section, then click OK. When you select This section in the Apply to list box, the settings are applied to the current section only. If you select Whole document in the Apply to list box, the settings are applied to all the sections in the document. Use the Apply to list arrow in the Columns dialog box or the Footnote and Endnote dialog box to change those settings for a section.

Formatting Documents   Word 61

Clues to Use boxes provide concise information that either expands on the major lesson skill or describes an independent task that in some way relates to the major lesson skill.

• **Ensures that students get the help they need.** The videos provide help any time of the day or night! With ten hours of private instruction packed into the nearly 150 videos, students can watch each video—again and again—until they understand.

• **Provides support for distance learning and ESL students.** Having the Video Companion as a tool provides extra support for online students and for students who speak English as a second language. Watching the videos is like having a personal instructor at their side to keep them engaged and motivated. All videos contain closed captioning to meet accessibility standards.

• **Available in many delivery options.** Students can access the videos on the DVD-ROM packaged with the book or over the Web as streaming video. Videos are also available for use in Learning Management Systems including Blackboard, WebCT, and Angel.

Other Enhancements

This new edition also includes the following new material:

• **Capstone Projects:** New section includes ten capstone projects—two each for Word, Excel, Access, PowerPoint, and Integration. Each project requires a variety of skills covered in all of the units for that application.

• **SAM Projects.** Twelve SAM Projects are included in a bonus section at the end of the book. Students can complete these SAM Projects, submit them online, and almost instantly receive a detailed report that reviews what they did right and what they did wrong. (Purchase of SAM Projects pin code required.)

• **Covers Windows Vista and Windows XP.** This book includes two units on Windows Vista and two units on Windows XP (in the Appendix). This ensures that your students get the operating system coverage that's right for them.

Assessment & Training Solutions

SAM 2007: ASSESSMENT & TRAINING AND PROJECT GRADING SOLUTIONS

SAM 2007 now contains Assessment, Training, and Projects assignments. Instructors may choose to assign any or all of these assignment types based on the needs of the course. The SAM system includes robust reporting, classroom management, section management, and scheduling to help instructors manage their classes with ease. The newest addition to the SAM family is SAM Projects. SAM Projects is live-in-the-application grading software that enables students to complete projects in Word, Excel, and PowerPoint 2007 and have them graded instantly. SAM Projects assesses a student's ability to connect skills and complete tasks in the context of real-world projects. SAM Projects evaluates whether or not a student can complete a document, spreadsheet, or presentation, allowing them to solve a problem or make a sound business decision. This tangible experience prepares today's learners for success in the workplace. Designed to be used with the Illustrated series, SAM 2007 includes built-in page references so students can print helpful study guides that match the textbooks used in class.

STUDENT EDITION LABS

Our Web-based interactive labs help students master hundreds of computer concepts, including input and output devices, file management and desktop applications, computer ethics, virus protection, and much more. Featuring up-to-the-minute content, eye-popping graphics, and rich animation, the highly interactive Student Edition Labs offer students an alternative way to learn through dynamic observation, step-by-step practice, and challenging review questions.

DISTANCE LEARNING CONTENT (OR CONTENT FOR ONLINE LEARNING)

Course Technology has partnered with Blackboard, the leading distance learning solution provider and class-management platform today. In addition to providing content for Blackboard and WebCT, Course Technology provides premium online content for multiple learning management system platforms. To access this material, simply visit our password-protected instructor resources available at www.cengage.com/coursetechnology. The resources available for download may include topic reviews, case projects, review questions, test banks, practice tests, custom syllabi, and more. For additional information or for an instructor username and password, please contact your sales representative.

COURSENOTES

Course Technology's CourseNotes are six-panel quick reference cards that reinforce the most important and widely used features of a software application in a visual and user-friendly format. CourseNotes serve as a great reference tool during and after the student completes the course. CourseNotes for Microsoft Office 2007, Word 2007, Excel 2007, Access 2007, PowerPoint 2007, Windows Vista, and more are available now!

Instructor Resources

The Instructor Resources CD is Course Technology's way of putting the resources and information needed to teach and learn effectively into your hands. With an integrated array of teaching and learning tools that offer you and your students a broad range of technology-based instructional options, we believe this CD represents the highest quality and most cutting edge resources available to instructors today. Many of these resources are available at www.cengage.com/coursetechnology. The resources available with this book are:

- **Instructor's Manual**—Available as an electronic file, the Instructor's Manual includes detailed lecture topics with teaching tips for each unit.

- **Sample Syllabus**—Prepare and customize your course easily using this sample course outline.

- **PowerPoint Presentations**—Each unit has a corresponding PowerPoint presentation that you can use in lecture, distribute to your students, or customize to suit your course.

- **Figure Files**—The figures in the text are provided on the Instructor Resources CD to help you illustrate key topics or concepts. You can create traditional overhead transparencies by printing the figure files. Or you can create electronic slide shows by using the figures in a presentation program such as PowerPoint.

- **Solutions to Exercises**—Solutions to Exercises contains every file students are asked to create or modify in the lessons and end-of-unit material. Also provided in this section, there is a document outlining the solutions for the end-of-unit Concepts Review, Skills Review, and Independent Challenges. An Annotated Solution File and Grading Rubric accompany each file and can be used together for quick and easy grading.

- **Data Files for Students**—To complete most of the units in this book, your students will need Data Files. You can post the Data Files on a file server for students to copy. The Data Files are available on the Instructor Resources CD-ROM, the Review Pack, and can also be downloaded from www.cengage.com/coursetechnology. In this edition, we have included a lesson on downloading the Data Files for this book, see the inside back cover of this text.

Instruct students to use the Data Files List included on the Review Pack and the Instructor Resources CD. This list gives instructions on copying and organizing files.

- **ExamView**—ExamView is a powerful testing software package that allows you to create and administer printed, computer (LAN-based), and Internet exams. ExamView includes hundreds of questions that correspond to the topics covered in this text, enabling students to generate detailed study guides that include page references for further review. The computer-based and Internet testing components allow students to take exams at their computers, and also saves you time by grading each exam automatically.

CourseCasts Learning on the Go. Always Available...Always Relevant.

Our fast-paced world is driven by technology. You know because you are an active participant—always on the go, always keeping up with technological trends, and always learning new ways to embrace technology to power your life. Let CourseCasts, hosted by Ken Baldauf of Florida State University, be your guide into weekly updates in this ever-changing space. These timely, relevant podcasts are produced weekly and are available for download at http://coursecasts.course.com or directly from iTunes (search by CourseCasts). CourseCasts are a perfect solution to getting students (and even instructors) to learn on the go!

COURSECASTS

Custom Contents

SCT 100 Introduction to Microcomputers

Read This Before You Begin

Frequently Asked Questions

What are Data Files?

A Data File is a partially completed Word document, Excel workbook, Access database, PowerPoint presentation, or another type of file that you use to complete the steps in the units and exercises to create the final document that you submit to your instructor. Each unit opener page lists the Data Files that you need for that unit.

Where are the Data Files?

Your instructor will provide the Data Files to you or direct you to a location on a network drive from which you can download them. Alternatively, you can follow the instructions on the next page to download the Data Files from this book's Web page.

What software was used to write and test this book?

This book was written and tested using a typical installation of Microsoft Office 2007 on a computer with a typical installation of Microsoft Windows Vista.

The browser used for any steps that require a browser is Internet Explorer 7.

Do I need to be connected to the Internet to complete the steps and exercises in this book?

Some of the exercises in this book assume that your computer is connected to the Internet. If you are not connected to the Internet, see your instructor for information on how to complete the exercises.

What do I do if my screen is different from the figures shown in this book?

This book was written and tested on computers with monitors set at a resolution of 1024 × 768. If your screen shows more or less information than the figures in the book, your monitor is probably set at a higher or lower resolution. If you don't see something on your screen, you might have to scroll down or up to see the object identified in the figures.

The Ribbon—the blue area at the top of the screen—in Microsoft Office 2007 adapts to different resolutions. If your monitor is set at a lower resolution than 1024 × 768, you might not see all of the buttons shown in the figures. The groups of buttons will always appear, but the entire group might be condensed into a single button that you need to click to access the buttons described in the instructions. For example, the figures and steps in this book assume that the Editing group on the Home tab in Word looks like the following:

1024 × 768 Editing Group

Editing Group on the
Home Tab of the
Ribbon at 1024 × 768

If your resolution is set to 800 × 600, the Ribbon in Word will look like the following figure, and you will need to click the Editing button to access the buttons that are visible in the Editing group.

800 × 600 Editing Group

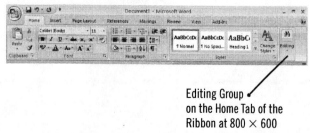

Editing Group
on the Home Tab of the
Ribbon at 800 × 600

800 × 600 Editing Group Clicked

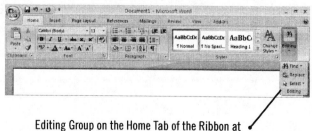

Editing Group on the Home Tab of the Ribbon at
800 × 600 is selected to show available buttons

Important Notes for Windows XP Users

The screenshots in this book show Microsoft Office 2007 running on Windows Vista. However, if you are using Microsoft Windows XP, you can still use this book because Office 2007 runs virtually the same on both platforms. There are a few differences that you will encounter if you are using Windows XP. Read this section to understand the differences.

Dialog boxes

If you are a Windows XP user, dialog boxes shown in this book will look slightly different than what you see on your screen. Dialog boxes for Windows XP have a blue title bar, instead of a gray title bar. However, beyond this superficial difference in appearance, the options in the dialog boxes across platforms are the same. For instance, the screen shots below show the Font dialog box running on Windows XP and the Font dialog box running on Windows Vista.

FIGURE 1: Dialog box in Windows XP

FIGURE 2: Dialog box in Windows Vista

Alternate Steps for Windows XP Users

Nearly all of the steps in this book work exactly the same for Windows XP users. However, there are a few tasks that will require you to complete slightly different steps. This section provides alternate steps for a few specific skills.

Starting a program

1. Click the **Start button** on the taskbar
2. Point to **All Programs,** point to **Microsoft Office,** then click the application you want to use

FIGURE 3: Starting a program

Saving a file for the first time

1. Click the **Office button**, then click **Save As**
2. Type a name for your file in the File Name text box
3. Click the **Save in list arrow**, then navigate to the drive and folder where you store your Data Files
4. Click **Save**

FIGURE 4: Save As dialog box

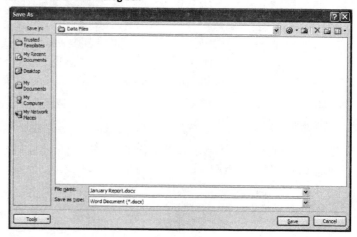

Opening a file

1. Click the **Office button**, then click **Open**
2. Click the **Look in list arrow**, then navigate to the drive and folder where you store your Data Files
3. Click the file you want to open
4. Click **Open**

FIGURE 5: Open dialog box

Using SAM Projects

SAM Projects is live-in-the-application autograding software that lets you complete projects in Word, Excel, and PowerPoint 2007 and have them graded instantly. This is a huge benefit to you because you can complete your SAM Projects homework, submit it to the SAM Projects site, and instantly receive a detailed report stating what you did correctly and where you made mistakes. There are 12 SAM Projects that practice the Word, Excel, and PowerPoint skills presented in the units in this book. These SAM Projects are nearly identical to the Independent Challenge 1 exercises in these units with a few small changes (which are necessitated by the software). Note that you can only use SAM Projects if you purchased a SAM Projects access code with your textbook. This bonus section includes the exact instructions for each of the SAM Projects for the Word, Excel and PowerPoint units in this book. The first four lessons cover some basic tasks you need to perform to get started with SAM Projects.

OBJECTIVES

Create a SAM User Profile

Join a section

Understand the process of using
   SAM Projects

Understanding SAM Projects reports

Instructions for :

- Word SAM Projects
- Excel SAM Projects
- PowerPoint SAM Projects

Creating a SAM User Profile

In order to use the SAM system (and specifically SAM Projects), you must have a username and password. You set these up yourself by creating a SAM user profile via the SAM login page. ▨▨▨ In this lesson, you set up a user profile and establish a username and password.

STEPS

1. **Be sure you are connected to the Internet, start Internet Explorer, type http://sam2007.course.com in the address bar, then press [Enter]**

   The SAM login page opens in the Internet Explorer window, as shown in Figure SP-1. You use this page to login if you already have a username and password or to create a SAM user profile if you do not.

> **QUICK TIP**
>
> If you have already created a SAM user profile, type your username and password in the appropriate text boxes, then skip to the next lesson.

2. **Click New user**

   A new page opens that contains an area for entering your Institution Key. See Figure SP-2. An **Institution Key** is an 8-digit code that uniquely identifies your school. Your instructor will provide you with your school's Institution Key.

3. **Type your school's Institution Key in the Institution Key field, then click Submit**

   A dialog box appears, asking you to verify that you have entered the correct Institution Key for your institution.

4. **Verify that the Institution Key matches the one for your school, then click OK**

   If your institution is using the key code version of SAM 2007, then a page opens after step 4 that requests your 18-digit key code. You can find this key code inside the flap of the SAM 2007 card you received when you purchased your textbook(s).

5. **If requested to do so, enter your 18-digit key code exactly as printed, then click Save; if you do not see this screen, skip this step**

   The SAM user profile screen opens, as shown in Figure SP-3, containing fields for entering your information, including your name, address, and e-mail address.

6. **Enter your information in all of the required (*) fields, including a secret question and answer that will be used for security purposes should you ever forget your password**

> **QUICK TIP**
>
> If you see incorrect information in any of the fields, click Revise to go back to the previous screen, make your edits, then click Save.

7. **Click Save**

   The Profile Confirmation page opens and displays the information that you entered on the user profile page.

8. **Verify that all of the information on the user profile page is accurate, then click Confirm**

   The SAM 2007 TERMS and CONDITIONS page opens and displays the terms of the end user license agreement.

9. **Read the terms of the agreement fully, scrolling as you go, then click I Agree to accept the terms and conditions**

   The SAM Welcome screen appears, where you will begin each SAM session. See Figure SP-4.

FIGURE SP-1: SAM Login screen

Click to set up a new user profile

FIGURE SP-2: Entering your Institution Key

Type your school's Institution Key here

FIGURE SP-3: MY PROFILE screen

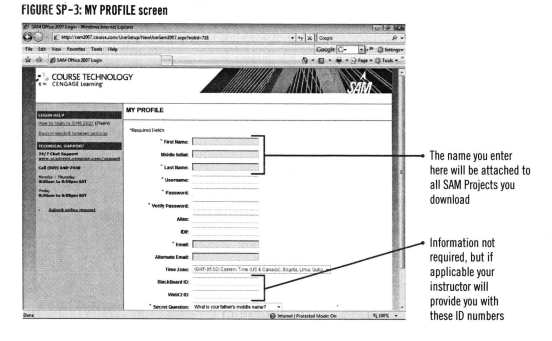

The name you enter here will be attached to all SAM Projects you download

Information not required, but if applicable your instructor will provide you with these ID numbers

FIGURE SP-4: The SAM Welcome Screen

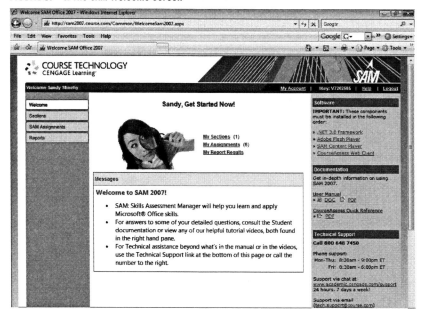

Joining a Section (Class)

In order to access SAM Projects, you must first join a section (or a class). Once you have joined, then you will be able to access specific SAM Projects that your instructor has assigned for your section. In this lesson, you join a section, which allows you to see which assignments your instructor has assigned.

STEPS

1. Click Sections on the left navigation pane

The MY SECTIONS page opens, similar to the one shown in Figure SP-5. Each section you join is listed in the Records area of this page. Notice, because you have not yet signed up for a section, no sections are listed on your screen.

> **QUICK TIP**
>
> If you want to limit the list, use the Instructor list arrow to select a specific instructor and list only the sections associated with that instructor.

2. Click Join a Section in the upper-right corner

The MY SECTIONS page changes, as shown in Figure SP-6. The All Sections box in the lower-left corner of the page shows sections you can join. The My Sections box will list sections you join. Your screen lists different sections—those specific to your school—than those shown in Figure SP-6.

3. Click the section listed in the All Sections box that you want to join, then click the right arrow button next to the All Sections box

The section you clicked is now in the My Sections box to the right of the All Sections box. To join more sections, simply repeat step 3.

4. Click Save, then click OK in the dialog box that opens

Now that you have joined a section, you can retrieve the assignments scheduled for your section.

> **QUICK TIP**
>
> If you have joined more than one section, you can view the assignments for a different section, by clicking the Section list arrow, clicking the name of the section you want to view the assignments for, then clicking the Search or the Refresh Screen button.

5. Click SAM Assignments on the left navigation pane

The MY SAM ASSIGNMENTS screen opens. This page lists all the assignments that your instructor has assigned for the section you joined. Figure SP-7 shows an example a MY SAM ASSIGNMENTS page; yours will look different.

FIGURE SP-5: Example of a MY SECTIONS page

Sections taught by all instructors this user has joined

Click to join a section

Click to select a specific instructor and display only sections associated with that instructor

FIGURE SP-6: Joining a section

Available sections for all instructors appear here; click to select a section

Click the left arrow button to remove a selected section from My Sections

Click to select a specific instructor and display only sections associated with that instructor

Click the right arrow button to add a selected section to My Sections

Any section you join will appear in this box

FIGURE SP-7: Example of MY SAM ASSIGNMENTS screen

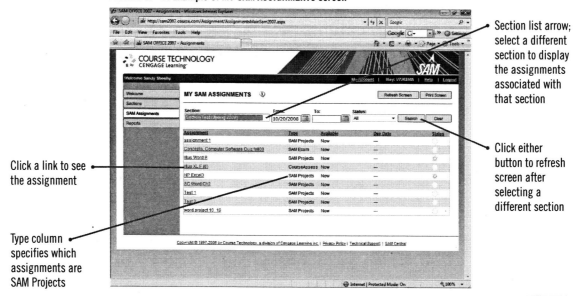

Click a link to see the assignment

Type column specifies which assignments are SAM Projects

Section list arrow; select a different section to display the assignments associated with that section

Click either button to refresh screen after selecting a different section

Understanding the Process of Using SAM Projects

Before you begin a SAM Project, make sure that you are ready. To determine whether you are ready or not, you can review the instructions, which include the skills covered, for any SAM Project. If you think you can do all the steps, than you are probably ready. If your instructor assigns SAM Projects as homework (and not as a test) you might be allowed to try a SAM Project multiple times. ▆▆▆ In this lesson, you learn the key steps for obtaining the instructions, downloading a SAM Project, and then submitting your completed project for grading.

STEPS

TROUBLE

If you are not ready to do the project, click Close.

QUICK TIP

Before completing a project, review these instructions to see which skills are covered in the project.

1. **Click the link in the Assignment column on the MY SAM ASSIGNMENTS page for the SAM Project assignment you want to complete**

   The Assignment Details dialog box opens, as shown in Figure SP-8. This box gives you information about the SAM Project you selected, including how many submissions are allowed and how many remain.

2. **Read the Assignment Details dialog box, then if you are ready to proceed click OK**

   The MY SAM ASSIGNMENTS page opens, as shown in Figure SP-9. Your page will differ depending on what assignment you clicked. Notice that the MY SAM ASSIGNMENTS page has three parts to it as follows:

   - **Instructions.** The first step in completing a SAM Project is downloading the instructions (or steps) you will need to follow in order to complete the project. *Note*: You will *not* have to download these instructions for the SAM Projects that map to this book because the pages that follow these lessons contain the instructions for each of those SAM Projects. However, if your instructor assigns a different SAM Project as a test or another homework assignment, you will need to download the instructions for that assignment.

   - **Start Files.** The second step in completing a SAM Project is downloading a start file. The start file appears as a link in the Start Files section of the MY SAM ASSIGNMENTS page. To download a start file, click the filename link in the Start Files section, then save the file to a location you will remember. *Important note*: You must be signed in via your SAM user profile to download this starting file. The username you entered in your SAM user profile is attached to the start filename and to the completed project filename. *Do not* let someone else download this starting file using his or her SAM user profile or the wrong name will be associated with the file. The username will also appear in the footer of each project you complete. After you download the start file, you open it and then follow the instructions for that SAM Project to complete it. Note that the very first step in every SAM Project is to rename the start file to a specified new name so that your changes will be saved as a solution file that you will submit for grading.

   - **Grade Submission.** When you complete all the steps in a SAM Project, the third and final step is to submit your file for grading. To do this, click the Browse button, navigate to the drive and folder where your solution file is stored. Double-click the filename, then click Submit.

FIGURE SP-8: Assignment Details dialog box for one assignment

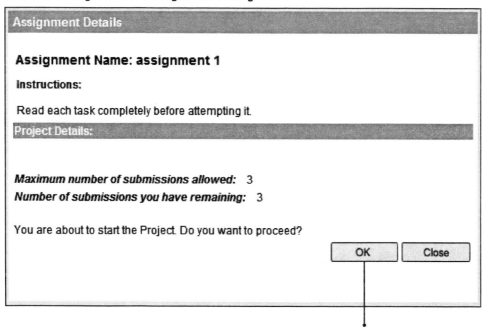

Click OK to open the Assignment
page for the selected assignment

FIGURE SP-9: MY SAM ASSIGNMENTS page for one assignment

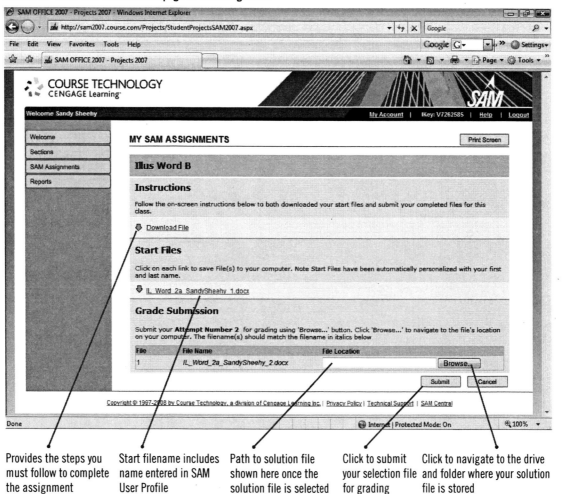

Provides the steps you
must follow to complete
the assignment

Start filename includes
name entered in SAM
User Profile

Path to solution file
shown here once the
solution file is selected

Click to submit
your selection file
for grading

Click to navigate to the drive
and folder where your solution
file is stored

SAM Projects

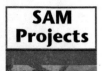

Understanding SAM Projects Reports

Very soon after you submit a SAM Project for grading, you can generate a report that provides a score and also gives detailed feedback on which steps you performed correctly and which ones you performed incorrectly. ⬛⬛⬛ lesson, you learn how to generate a report.

STEPS

1. **Be sure the path to your solution file appears in the File Location box in the Grade Submission section of the MY SAM ASSIGNMENTS page, then click Submit**

2. **Click Reports on the Navigation pane**

   The MY REPORTS screen opens, which lists all the assignments you have completed. You can generate reports for all assignments in the list. Figure SP-10 shows an example of a MY REPORTS screen; yours will look different.

3. **Click the assignment for which you want to see a report, click the Report Type list arrow, then click Download Submitted Projects**

4. **Click the Download link at the far right of your screen, then click Open in the File Download dialog box that opens**

   A new window opens and displays a detailed report. See Figure SP-11 for an example of a report generated for a student named Sandy Sheehy. Sandy's score is displayed in the bar at the top; detailed feedback on each step in the SAM Project named IL Word Case 2A that she completed is provided.

5. **Review the report, then close the report window without saving changes to the report**

   You can also generate other types of reports for your completed assignments. For instance, you can create a Study Guide report that shows you all the steps in the Project and where that skill is covered in the book. Figure SP-12 shows an example of a Study Guide report.

FIGURE SP-10: MY REPORTS screen

Report Type list arrow; click to display a menu of report types

List of completed assignments; click an option button to select that assignment

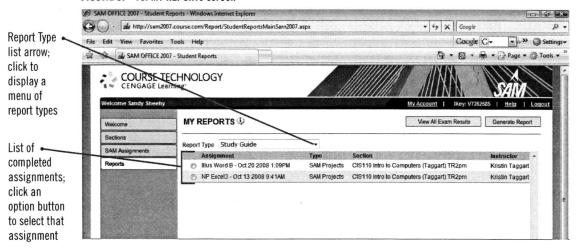

FIGURE SP-11: Downloaded SAM report

Username and assignment filename

Score appears here

Incorrect steps are marked and feedback tells you what you did wrong

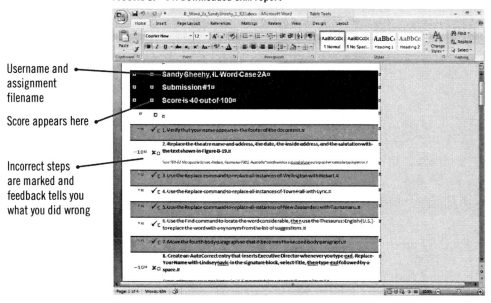

FIGURE SP-12: Example of a SAM Project Study Guide

Understanding Essential Computer Concepts

Computers are essential tools in almost all kinds of activity in virtually every type of business. In this unit, you will learn about computers and their components. You will learn about input and output, how a computer processes data and stores information, how information is transmitted, and ways to secure that information. Finally, you will learn about system and application software. Quest Specialty Travel is expanding its North American offices and just purchased Sheehan Tours, an established travel agency in Boston, Massachusetts. Sheehan Tours has been in business for over 40 years and has a large customer base. Unfortunately, its computer system is tremendously outdated. Its office contains a hodgepodge of computer equipment, most of which has been purchased used. The office staff still carries data between computers on floppy disks, and only one computer is connected to the Internet. Kevin O'Brien, the manager of the New York office, has been sent to the new Boston office to help them switch to Quest's business practices. He has already ordered and installed new computer equipment. His next task is to teach the staff how to use the new equipment.

OBJECTIVES

Investigate types of computers

Examine computer systems

Examine input devices

Examine output devices

Investigate data processing

Understand memory

Understand storage media

Explore data communications

Learn about networks

Learn about security threats

Understand system software

Understand application software

Investigating Types of Computers

A **computer** is an electronic device that accepts information and instructions from a user, manipulates the information according to the instructions, displays the information in some way, and stores the information for retrieval later. Computers are classified by their size, speed, and capabilities. ▰▰▰▰ Most of the staff at Sheehan Tours do not know anything about computers except for the ones that sit on their desks, so Kevin decides to start with a basic explanation of the types of computers available.

Machines dedicated primarily to playing games, such as the Xbox and PlayStation, are also computers.

The following list describes various types of computers:

- **Personal computers** are computers typically used by a single user, for use in the home or office. Personal computers are used for general computing tasks such as word processing, manipulating numbers, working with photographs or graphics, exchanging e-mail, and accessing the Internet.

- A personal computer is available as a **desktop computer**, which is designed to sit compactly on a desk; as a **notebook computer** (also referred to as a **laptop computer**), which is small, lightweight, and designed for portability; or as a **tablet PC**, which is also designed for portability, but includes the capability of recognizing ordinary handwriting on the screen. Figure A-1 shows a notebook computer. Desktop personal computers can be purchased for as little as $300, but high-end notebooks can cost more than $3500. A notebook computer with similar capability is usually more expensive than a desktop computer, and tablet PCs are generally more expensive than notebook computers. Many computer users spend between $800 and $1500 when purchasing a new personal computer.

- **Hand-held computers** are small computers that fit in the palm of your hand. Hand-held computers have more limited capabilities than personal computers.

  - **PDAs (personal digital assistants)** are generally used to maintain an electronic appointment book, address book, calculator, and notepad. See Figure A-2. High-end PDAs are all-in-one devices that can send and receive e-mails and make phone calls.
  - **MP3 players** are hand-held computers that are primarily used to store and play music, although some models can also be used to play digital movies or television shows.
  - Cell phones are another type of hand-held computer. In addition to being used to make telephone calls, cell phones store contact information. Many cell phones can take and store digital photos and video and play and store music. Most cell phones have additional capabilities such as built-in calculator programs. High-end cell phones can also perform many of the same functions as a PDA.

- **Mainframe computers** are used by larger businesses and government agencies to provide centralized storage, processing, and management for large amounts of data. The price of a mainframe computer varies widely, from several hundred thousand dollars to several million dollars.

- The largest and fastest computers, called **supercomputers**, are used by large corporations and government agencies when the tremendous volume of data would seriously delay processing on a mainframe computer. A supercomputer, like the one shown in Figure A-3, can cost tens of millions of dollars.

Understanding terminals

When an organization uses mainframes or supercomputers, each user inputs processing requests and views output through a **terminal** or a **terminal emulator**. A terminal has a keyboard for input and a monitor for output, but processes little or no data on its own. A terminal emulator is a personal computer, workstation, or server that uses special software to imitate a terminal so that the PC can communicate with the mainframe or supercomputer for complex data processing.

FIGURE A-1: Notebook computer

FIGURE A-2: PDA

FIGURE A-3: Supercomputer

Understanding Essential Computer Concepts

12

Examining Computer Systems

A **computer system** includes computer hardware and software. **Hardware** refers to the physical components of a computer. **Software** refers to the intangible components of a computer system, particularly the **programs**, or lists of instructions, that the computer needs to perform a specific task. Kevin explains how computers work and points out the main components of a computer system.

The following list provides an overview of computer system components and how they work:

- The design and construction of a computer is referred to as its **architecture** or **configuration**. The technical details about each hardware component are called **specifications**. For example, a computer system might be configured to include a printer; a specification for that printer might be a print speed of eight pages per minute or the capacity to print in color.

- The hardware and the software of a computer system work together to process data. **Data** refers to the words, numbers, figures, sounds, and graphics that describe people, events, things, and ideas. Modifying data is referred to as **processing**.

- In a computer, processing tasks occur on the **motherboard**, which is located inside the computer and is the main electronic component of the computer. The motherboard is a **circuit board**, which is a rigid piece of insulating material with **circuits**, electrical paths, on it that control specific functions. See Figure A-4. The motherboard contains the following processing hardware:

  - The **microprocessor**, also called the **processor** or the **central processing unit (CPU)**, consists of transistors and electronic circuits on a silicon **chip** (an integrated circuit embedded in semiconductor material). See Figure A-5. The processor is mounted on the motherboard and is responsible for executing instructions to process information.
  - **Cards** are removable **circuit boards** that are inserted into slots in the motherboard to expand the capabilities of the motherboard. For example, a sound card translates the digital audio information from the computer into analog sounds that the human ear can hear.

- The data or instructions you type into the computer are called **input**. The result of the computer processing input is referred to as **output**. The computer itself takes care of the processing functions, but it needs additional components, called **peripheral devices**, to accomplish the input, output, and storage functions.

  - You use an **input device**, such as a keyboard or a mouse, to enter data and issue commands. **Commands** are input instructions that tell the computer how to process data. For example, you might want to center the title and double-space the text of a report. You use the appropriate commands in the word processing program that instruct the computer to modify the data you have input so the report text is double-spaced and the report title is centered.
  - Output can be in many different forms, including reports, documents, graphs, sounds, and pictures. Computers produce output using **output devices**, such as a monitor or printer.
  - The output you create using a computer can be stored either inside the computer itself or on an external storage device, such as a DVD. You will learn more about storage devices later in this unit.

FIGURE A-4: Motherboard

FIGURE A-5: Microprocessor (front and back views)

Comparing microprocessor speeds

How fast a computer can process instructions depends partially on the speed of the microprocessor, which is determined by its clock speed, word size, and cache size, and whether it is single or dual core. **Clock speed** is measured in **megahertz (MHz)**, millions of cycles per second, or in **gigahertz (GHz)**, billions of cycles per second. **Word size** refers to the amount of data that is processed at one time. Finally, a **dual-core processor**, one that has two processors on a single chip, can process information up to twice as fast as a **single-core processor**, one with one processor on the chip.

Examining Input Devices

Before a computer can produce useful information, people must get data into the computer. This is accomplished by using input devices. In a typical personal computer system, you input data and commands by using an input device such as a keyboard or a mouse. Computers can also receive input from a storage device. You will learn about storage devices later in this unit. ▰▰▰▰ As Kevin explains peripheral devices to the Sheehan Tours staff, they ask several questions about input devices. For example, one person doesn't understand the difference between a mouse and a trackball. Kevin continues his explanation with a discussion of various input devices.

There are many types of input devices, as described below:

- One of the most frequently used input devices is a **keyboard**. The top keyboard in Figure A-6 is a standard keyboard. The bottom keyboard in Figure A-6 is **ergonomic**, which means that it has been designed to fit the natural placement of your hands and should reduce the risk of repetitive-motion injuries. It also has several additional keys programmed as shortcut keys to commonly used functions.

- Another common input device is a **pointing device**, which controls the **pointer**, a small arrow or other symbol on the screen. Pointing devices are used to select commands and manipulate text or graphics on the screen.

  - The most popular pointing device for a desktop computer is a **mouse**, such as the one shown on the left side in Figure A-7. An ordinary mouse has a rolling ball on its underside, and an optical mouse has a tiny camera on its underside that takes pictures as the mouse is moved. You control the pointer by moving the entire mouse. A mouse usually has two or more buttons for clicking commands. A mouse might also have a **scroll wheel** that you roll to scroll the page on the screen and that may function as one of the buttons.

  - The **trackball**, such as the one shown on the right side in Figure A-7, is similar to a mouse except that the rolling ball is on the top side and you control the movement of the pointer by moving only the ball.

  - Notebook computers are usually equipped with a touch pad or a pointing stick. See Figure A-8. A **touch pad** is a touch-sensitive device that you drag your finger over to control the pointer. The buttons are located in front of the touch pad. A **pointing stick** is a small, eraser-like device embedded among the typing keys that you push up, left, right, or down to move the pointer. Two buttons equivalent to mouse buttons are located in front of the spacebar.

- A **scanner** is a device that transfers the content on a piece of paper into memory. To do this, you place a piece of paper on the glass, a beam of light moves across the glass similar to a photocopier, and stores the image or words on the paper as digital information. You can scan a document or a photo and save it as an image file, or you can scan a document and have the text "read" by the scanner and saved in a document file for editing later.

- Microphones are another type of input device. You can use them to record sound for certain types of files, or, if you have the voice-recognition software, you can use them to input data and commands.

- Input devices can be connected to the computer with cables or wirelessly. Wireless input devices connect to the computer using infrared or radio frequency technology, similar to a remote control for a television.

Using assistive devices

People with physical impairments or disabilities can use computers because of advances in making computers accessible to everyone. For example, people who cannot use their arms or hands instead can use foot, head, or eye movements to control the pointer. People with poor vision can use keyboards with large keys for input, screen enlargers to enlarge the type and images on the monitor, or screen readers to read the content of the screen aloud. Computers are being developed that can be controlled by a person's thoughts, that is, the brain's electromagnetic waves.

FIGURE A-6: Keyboards

Editing keypad

Function keys

Main keyboard

Traditional keyboard

Numeric keypad

Ergonomic keyboard

FIGURE A-7: Personal computer pointing devices

Mouse   Trackball

FIGURE A-8: Notebook pointing devices

Touch pad   Pointing Stick

Examining Output Devices

As stated earlier, output is the result of processing data; output devices show you those results. The most commonly used output devices are monitors and printers. ▰▰▰ Kevin continues his discussion of peripheral devices with an explanation of output devices.

Output devices are described below:

- The **monitor** displays the output from a computer.

  - The monitor shown on the left in Figure A-9 is a **flat panel monitor**, a lightweight monitor that takes up very little room on the desktop. Most flat panel monitors use **LCD (liquid crystal display)** technology, which creates the image you see on the screen by manipulating light within a layer of liquid crystal. A **CRT (cathode ray tube) monitor**, shown on the right in Figure A-9, uses gun-like devices that direct beams of electrons toward the screen to activate dots of color to form the image you see on the screen. CRT monitors require much more desk space than flat-panel display monitors.

  - Monitor **screen size** is the diagonal measurement from one corner of the screen to the other. In general, monitors on desktop computers range in size from 15" to 30", whereas monitors on notebook computers range in size from 12" to 20".

  - Most monitors have a **graphics display**, which divides the screen into a matrix of small dots called **pixels. Resolution** is the number of pixels the monitor displays. Standard resolutions range from 640×480 to 1600×1200. If your screen is small, a 1600×1200 resolution will make the objects on the screen too small to see clearly. **Dot pitch (dp)** measures the distance between pixels, so a smaller dot pitch means a sharper image. A .28 or .26 dot pitch is typical for today's monitors.

  - To display graphics, a computer must have a **graphics card**, also called a **video display adapter** or **video card**. The graphics card is installed on the motherboard, and controls the signals the computer sends to the monitor.

- A **printer** produces a paper copy, often called **hard copy**, of the text or graphics processed by the computer. There are three popular categories of printers: laser printers, inkjet printers, and dot matrix printers.

  - **Laser printers**, like the one shown on the left in Figure A-10, are popular for business use because they produce high-quality output quickly and efficiently. In a laser printer, a temporary laser image is transferred onto paper with a powdery substance called **toner**.

  - **Inkjet printers**, such as the one shown on the right in Figure A-10, are popular printers for home use. These printers spray ink onto paper and produce output whose quality is comparable to that of a laser printer.

  - **Dot matrix printers** transfer ink to the paper by striking a ribbon with pins. A 24-pin dot matrix printer produces better quality print than a 9-pin. Dot matrix printers are most often used when a large number of pages need to be printed fairly quickly or when a business needs to print multi-page continuous forms.

- Speakers, like speakers on a sound system, allow you to hear sounds from the computer. Speakers can be separate peripheral devices attached to the computer, or they can be built in to the monitor.

- Like input devices, output devices can be connected to a computer using cables or a wireless connection.

FIGURE A-9: Monitors

Flat panel monitor   CRT monitor

FIGURE A-10: Printers

Laser printer   Inkjet printer

Investigating Data Processing

In order to understand how data is processed in a computer, you first need to learn how the computer represents and stores data. All data and programs are stored as files. A computer **file** is a named collection of stored data. An **executable file** contains the instructions that tell a computer how to perform a specific task; for instance, the files that are used while the computer starts are executable. A **data file** is created by a user, usually with software. For instance, a report that you write with a word processing program is data, and must be saved as a data file if you want to access it later. Kevin gives a basic description of how information is represented inside a computer.

DETAILS

The following information will help you understand data processing:

- The characters used in human language are meaningless to a computer. Like a light bulb, the computer must interpret every signal as either "on" or "off." A computer represents data as distinct or separate numbers. Specifically, it represents "on" with a 1 and "off" with a 0. These numbers are referred to as **binary digits**, or **bits**.

- A series of eight bits is called a **byte**. As Figure A-11 shows, the byte that represents the integer value 0 is 00000000, with all eight bits "off" or set to 0. The byte that represents the integer value 1 is 00000001, and the byte that represents 255 is 11111111.

- A **kilobyte** (**KB** or simply **K**) is 1024 bytes, or approximately one thousand bytes. A **megabyte** (**MB**) is 1,048,576 bytes, or about one million bytes. A **gigabyte** (**GB**) is 1,073,741,824 bytes, or about one billion bytes. A **terabyte** (**TB**) is 1,024 GB, or approximately one trillion bytes.

- Personal computers commonly use the ASCII system to represent character data. **ASCII** (pronounced "ASK-ee") stands for **American Standard Code for Information Interchange**. Each ASCII number represents an English character. Computers translate ASCII into binary data so that they can process it.

  - The original ASCII system used 7 bits to represent the numbers 0 (0000000) through 127 (1111111) to stand for 128 common characters and nonprinting control characters. Because bits are usually arranged in bytes, the eighth bit is reserved for error checking.

  - Extended ASCII uses eight bits and includes the numbers 128 (10000000) through 255 (11111111) to represent additional characters and symbols. Extended ASCII was developed to add codes for punctuation marks, symbols, such as $ and ©, and additional characters, such as é and ü, that were not included in the original 128 codes.

  - Most computers use the original ASCII definitions, but not all computers use the same definitions for Extended ASCII. Computers that run the Windows operating system use the set of Extended ASCII definitions defined by the American National Standards Institute (ANSI). Figure A-12 shows sample ASCII code with ANSI standard Extended ASCII characters.

FIGURE A-11: Binary representation of numbers

Number	Binary representation
0	00000000
1	00000001
2	00000010
3	00000011
4	00000100
5	00000101
6	00000110
7	00000111
8	00001000
⋮	⋮
253	11111101
254	11111110
255	11111111

FIGURE A-12: Sample ASCII code representing letters and symbols

Character	ASCII Code	Binary Number
(space)	32	00100000
$	36	00100100
A	65	01000001
B	66	01000010
a	97	01100001
b	98	01100010
?	129	10000001
£	163	10100011
®	217	11011001
é	233	11101001

Understanding Memory

In addition to the microprocessor, another important component of personal computer hardware is the **memory**, which stores instructions and data. Memory is different from permanent storage in a computer. Your computer has five types of memory: random access memory, cache memory, virtual memory, read-only memory, and complementary metal oxide semiconductor memory. ▰▰▰▰ Kevin realizes that most of the Sheehan Tours staff don't understand the difference between memory types, so he explains the different types of memory.

DETAILS

Types of memory include the following:

- **Random access memory** (**RAM**) temporarily holds programs and data while the computer is on and allows the computer to access that information randomly; in other words, RAM doesn't need to access data in the same sequence in which it was stored. For example, if you are writing a report, the microprocessor temporarily copies the word processing program you are using into RAM so the microprocessor can quickly access the instructions that you will need as you type and format your report. The characters you type are also stored in RAM, along with the fonts, graphics, and other objects that you might use. RAM consists of chips on cards that plug into the motherboard.

  - Most personal computers use **synchronous dynamic random access memory** (**SDRAM**), which is synchronized with the processor to allow faster access to its contents.
  - RAM is sometimes referred to as **volatile memory** or **temporary memory** because it is constantly changing as long as the computer is on and is cleared when the computer is turned off.
  - **Memory capacity**, sometimes referred to as **storage capacity**, is the amount of data that the computer can handle at any given time and is measured in megabytes or gigabytes. For example, a computer that has 512 MB of RAM has the capacity to temporarily store more than 512 million bits of data at one time.

- **Cache memory**, sometimes called **RAM cache** or **CPU cache**, is a special, high-speed memory chip on the motherboard or CPU itself that stores frequently accessed and recently accessed data and commands.

- **Virtual memory** is space on the computer's storage devices that simulates additional RAM. It enables programs to run as if your computer had more RAM by moving data and commands from RAM to the hard drive and swapping in the new data and commands. See Figure A-13. Virtual memory, however, is much slower than RAM.

- **Read-only memory** (**ROM**) is a chip on the motherboard that has been prerecorded with data. ROM permanently stores the set of instructions that the computer uses to check the computer system's components to make sure they are working and to activate the essential software that controls the processing function when you turn the computer on.

  - ROM contains a set of instructions called the **BIOS** (**basic input/output system**), which tells the computer to initialize the motherboard, how to recognize the peripherals, and to start the boot process. The **boot process** is the set of events that occurs between the moment you turn on the computer and the moment you can begin to use the computer. The set of instructions for executing the boot process is stored in ROM.
  - ROM never changes and it remains intact when the computer is turned off; therefore, it is called **nonvolatile memory** or **permanent memory**.

- **Complementary metal oxide semiconductor** (**CMOS**, pronounced "SEE-moss") **memory** is a chip installed on the motherboard that is activated during the boot process and identifies where essential software is stored.

  - A small rechargeable battery powers CMOS so its contents are saved when the computer is turned off. CMOS changes every time you add or remove hardware on your computer system.
  - CMOS, often referred to as **semipermanent memory**, changes when hardware is added or removed, but doesn't empty when the computer is shut off.
  - Because CMOS retains its contents when the computer is turned off, the date and time are stored there.

FIGURE A-13: How virtual memory works

1. Your computer is running a word processing program that takes up most of the program area in RAM, but you want to run a spreadsheet program at the same time.

2. The operating system moves the least-used segment of the word processing program into virtual memory on disk.

3. The spreadsheet program can now be loaded into the RAM vacated by the least-used segment of the word processing program.

4. If the least-used segment of the word processing program is later needed, it is copied from virtual memory back into RAM. To make room, some other infrequently used segment of a program will need to be transferred into virtual memory.

Upgrading RAM

One of the easiest ways to make a computer run faster is to add more RAM. This enables the computer to access instructions and data stored in RAM very quickly. The more RAM a computer has, the more instructions and data can be stored there. Currently, you can buy from 64 MB to 1 GB RAM cards, and usually, you can add more than one card. You need to check your computer's specifications to see what size RAM cards the slots on your motherboard will accept.

Understanding Storage Media

Because RAM retains data only while the power is on, your computer must have a more permanent storage option. As Figure A-14 shows, a storage device receives data from RAM and writes it on a storage medium, such as a CD. Later the data can be read and sent back to RAM to use again. Kevin explains the types of storage media available. He starts with magnetic storage because almost all computers have a hard disk.

The types of storage media are discussed below:

- **Magnetic storage devices** store data as magnetized particles on mylar, a plastic, which is then coated on both sides with a magnetic oxide coating. Common magnetic storage devices are hard disks, tape, and floppy disks.

  - A **hard disk** is the most common type of magnetic storage media. It contains several magnetic oxide-covered metal platters that are usually sealed in a case inside the computer.
  - **Tape** is another type of magnetic storage media. Tape storage is much too slow to be used for day-to-day computer tasks; therefore, tapes are used to make backup copies of data stored on hard disks. Tape provides inexpensive, though slow, archival storage for large companies who need to back up large quantities of data.
  - A **floppy disk** is a flat circle of magnetic oxide-coated mylar enclosed in a hard plastic case; a floppy disk can store 1.44 MB of data. Floppy disks are sometimes called 3½" disks because of the size of the hard plastic case. The floppy disk has almost become obsolete, and most personal computers are now manufactured without a floppy disk drive.

- **Optical storage devices** are polycarbonate discs coated with a reflective metal on which data is recorded using laser technology as a trail of tiny pits or dark spots in the surface of the disc. The data that these pits or spots represent can then be "read" with a beam of laser light.

  - The first standard optical storage device available for personal computers was the **CD** (**compact disc**). One CD can store 700 MB of data.
  - A **DVD**, though the same size as a CD, currently stores between 4.7 and 15.9 GB of data, depending on whether data is stored on one or two sides of the disc, and how many layers of data each side contains. The term *DVD* is no longer an acronym, although it was originally an acronym for *digital video disc* and later was sometimes updated to *digital versatile disc*.
  - New formats of optical storage include Blu-ray Discs and HD-DVD, which are capable of storing between 15 and 50 GB of data. They are used for storing high-definition video. Different companies support each format and it remains to be seen if one dominates the market.

- **Flash memory** is similar to ROM except that it can be written to more than once. **Flash memory cards** are small, portable cards encased in hard plastic to which data can be written and rewritten. They are used in digital cameras, handheld computers, video game controllers, and other devices.

- A popular type of flash memory is a **USB flash storage device**, also called a **USB drive** or a **flash drive**. See Figure A-15.

  - USB drives for personal computers are available in a wide range of sizes; they currently range from drives capable of holding 32 MB of data to drives capable of holding 16 GB of data. They are becoming more popular for use as a secondary or backup storage device for data typically stored on a hard disk drive.
  - USB drives plug directly into the USB port of a personal computer; the computer recognizes the device as another disk drive. The location and letter designation of USB ports varies with the brand and model of computer you are using, but the physical port may be on the front, back, or side of a computer.
  - USB flash storage devices are about the size of a pack of gum and often have a ring that you can attach to your key chain.

A storage device receives information from RAM, writes it on the storage medium, and reads and sends it back to RAM

DVD drive

Storage medium

Storage device

Retrieve (read)

Store (write)

RAM

FIGURE A-15: Flash storage device

Erasing and rewriting on CDs and DVDs

CD-ROM stands for **compact disc read-only memory**. CDs that you buy with software or music already on them are CD-ROMs—you can read from them, but you cannot record additional data onto them. In order to record data on a CD, you need a **CD-R (compact disc recordable)** or **CD-RW (compact disc rewritable)** drive and a CD-R or CD-RW disk. On CD-ROMs, data is stored in pits made on the surface of the disk; when you record data on a CD-R or -RW, a laser changes the reflectivity of a dye layer on a blank disk, creating dark spots on the disk's surface that represent the data. On a CD-R, once the data is recorded, you cannot erase or modify it, but you can add new data to the disk, as long as the disk has not been finalized. In contrast, you can re-record a CD-RW. CD-R disks can be read by a standard CD-ROM drive or a DVD drive; CD-RW disks can be read only by CD-RW drives or CD-ROM drives labeled "multi-read." Recordable DVD drives are also available. As with CDs, you can buy a DVD to which you can record only once, or a rewritable DVD to which you can record and then re-record data. Recordable and rewriteable DVDs come in several formats; for example, recordable DVDs are available as DVD-R and DVD+R. Make sure you know which type of DVD your DVD drive uses. Newer DVD drives are capable of reading from and writing to both -RW and +RW DVDs and CDs, as well as DVDs with two layers.

Exploring Data Communications

Data communications is the transmission of data from one computer to another or to a peripheral device. The computer that originates the message is the **sender**. The message is sent over some type of **channel**, such as a telephone or coaxial cable. The computer or peripheral at the message's destination is the **receiver**. The rules that establish an orderly transfer of data between the sender and the receiver are called **protocols**. The transmission protocol between a computer and its peripheral devices is handled by a **device driver**, or simply **driver**, which is a computer program that can establish communication because it contains information about the characteristics of your computer and of the device. █████ The Sheehan Tours staff will use their computers to connect to the computers at the Quest headquarters in California as well as to surf the Internet, so Kevin next explains how computers communicate.

DETAILS

The following describes some of the ways that computers communicate:

- The data path between the microprocessor, RAM, and the peripherals along which communication travels is called the **data bus**. Figure A-16 illustrates the data bus that connects a printer to a computer.

- An external peripheral device must have a corresponding **port** and **cable** that connect it to the computer. Inside the computer, each port connects to a **controller card**, sometimes called an **expansion card** or **interface card**. These cards plug into electrical connectors on the motherboard called **expansion slots** or **slots**. Personal computers can have several types of ports, including parallel, serial, SCSI, USB, MIDI, and Ethernet. Figure A-17 shows the ports on one desktop personal computer.

  - A **parallel port** transmits data eight bits at a time. Parallel transmissions are relatively fast, but they have an increased risk for interference. A **serial port** transmits data one bit at a time.

  - One **SCSI** (**small computer system interface**, pronounced "scuzzy") **port** provides an interface for one or more peripheral devices at the same port. The first is connected directly to the computer through the port, and the second device is plugged into a similar port on the first device.

  - A **USB** (**Universal Serial Bus**) **port** is a high-speed serial port which allows multiple connections at the same port. The device you install must have a **USB connector**, a small rectangular plug, as shown in Figure A-18. When you plug the USB connector into the USB port, the computer recognizes the device and allows you to use it immediately. You can connect multiple devices to a single USB port by "daisy chaining" them or by using a hub. USB flash storage devices plug into USB ports. For most USB devices, power is supplied via the port, so there is no need for extra power cables.

  - The port for a sound card usually includes jacks for speakers and a microphone, which are designed to work with a **MIDI** (**Musical Instrument Digital Interface**, pronounced "middy") **card**.

  - You can connect to another computer, a LAN, a modem, or sometimes directly to the Internet using an **Ethernet port**. Ethernet ports allow data to be transmitted at high speeds.

- An internal peripheral device such as a hard disk drive may plug directly into the motherboard, or it may have an attached controller card.

- Notebook computers may also include a **portable computer card** (**PC Card**). PC Cards are credit card-sized cards that plug directly into the PC Card slot and can contain additional RAM, a fax modem, or a hard disk drive (similar to a USB flash storage device).

QUICK TIP

Typically, a printer that is near the computer is connected to a parallel port, and the mouse, keyboard, and modem are connected to serial ports.

QUICK TIP

FireWire is another standard for transferring information between digital devices similar to USB.

FIGURE A-16: Components needed to connect a printer to a computer

Controller card

Motherboard

Printer port

Cable

Port

Expansion slots

Rear view of printer

Rear view of system unit

FIGURE A-17: Computer ports and connections

Power connection

Keyboard port

Mouse port

Audio connection

Monitor port

FireWire port

USB ports

Network port

Speaker and microphone connections

Phone line connection

FIGURE A-18: USB connector

Learning about Networks

A **network** connects one computer to other computers and peripheral devices, enabling you to share data and resources with others. There are a variety of network configurations; however, any type of network has some basic characteristics and requirements that you should know. ▓▓▓▓ Kevin continues his discussion of how computers communicate with an explanation of networking.

DETAILS

Types of networks are described below:

- Each computer that is part of the network must have a **network interface card** (**NIC**) installed. This card creates a communications channel between the computer and the network. A cable is used to connect the NIC port to the network.

- **Network software** is also essential, establishing the communications protocols that will be observed on the network and controlling the "traffic flow" as data travels throughout the network.

- Some networks have one or more computers, called **servers**, that act as the central storage location for programs and provide mass storage for most of the data used on the network. A network with a server and computers dependent on the server is called a **client/server network**. The dependent computers are the **clients**.

- When a network does not have a server, all the computers essentially are equal, and programs and data are distributed among them. This is called a **peer-to-peer network**.

- A personal computer that is not connected to a network is called a **standalone computer**. When it is connected to the network, it becomes a **workstation**. You have already learned that a terminal has a keyboard and monitor used for input and output, but it is not capable of processing on its own. A terminal is connected to a network that uses mainframes as servers. Any device connected to the network is called a **node**. Figure A-19 illustrates a typical network configuration.

- In a **local area network** (**LAN**), computers and peripheral devices are located relatively close to each other, generally in the same building.

- A **wide area network** (**WAN**) is more than one LAN connected together. The Internet is the largest example of a WAN.

- In a **wireless local area network** (**WLAN**), computers and peripherals use high-frequency radio waves instead of wires to communicate and connect in a network. **Wi-Fi** (short for **wireless fidelity**) is the term created by the nonprofit Wi-Fi Alliance to describe networks connected using a standard radio frequency established by the Institute of Electrical and Electronics Engineers (IEEE). Wi-Fi is used over short distances to connect computers to a LAN.

- A **personal area network** (**PAN**) is a network that allows two or more devices located close to each other to communicate or to connect a device to the Internet. In a PAN, devices are connected with cables or wireless.

  - **Infrared technology** uses infrared light waves to beam data from one device to another. The devices must be compatible, and they must be positioned close to each other with their infrared ports pointed at each other for this to work. This is the technology used in TV remote controls.

  - **Bluetooth** uses short range radio waves to connect a device wirelessly to another device or to the Internet. The devices must each have a Bluetooth transmitter, but unlike infrared connections, they can communicate around corners or through walls.

- **WiMAX** (short for **Worldwide Interoperability for Microwave Access**), another standard defined by the IEEE, allows computer users to connect over many miles to a LAN. A WiMAX tower sends signals to a WiMAX receiver built or plugged into a computer. WiMAX towers can communicate with each other or with an Internet service provider.

Workstation

Server

Printer

Workstation

Your local workstation

Understanding telecommunications

Telecommunications means communicating over a comparatively long distance using a phone line or some other data conduit. When it is not possible to connect users on one network, telecommunications allows you to send and receive data over the telephone lines. To make this connection, you must use a communications device called a modem. A **modem**, which stands for *modulator-dem*odulator, is a device that connects your computer to a standard telephone jack. The modem converts the **digital**, or stop-start, **signals** your computer outputs into **analog**, or continuous wave, **signals** (sound waves) that can traverse ordinary phone lines. Figure A-20 shows the telecommunications process, in which a modem converts digital signals to analog signals at the sending site (modulates) and a second modem converts the analog signals back into digital signals at the receiving site (demodulates). Most computers today come with a built-in 56 K modem and/or NIC (network interface card). 56 K represents the modem's capability to send and receive about 56,000 **bits per second** (**bps**). Actual speed may be reduced by factors such as distance, technical interference, and other issues. People who want to use a high-speed connection either over phone lines, such as a **DSL** (**digital subscriber line**), or over a cable connection, usually need to purchase an external DSL or cable modem separately.

FIGURE A-20: Using modems to send and receive data

Analog signal

Digital signal

Digital signal

Sending site

Modem

Modem

Receiving site

Concepts

UNIT
A

Concepts

Learning about Security Threats

Security refers to the steps a computer owner takes to prevent unauthorized use of or damage to the computer. Once a computer is connected to a network, it is essential that the computer be protected against possible threats from people intent on stealing information or causing malicious damage. Kevin explains how important it is to be vigilant about keeping the office computers secure and reviews ways to do this.

DETAILS

Several types of security threats are discussed below:

- **Malware** is a broad term that describes any program that is intended to cause harm or convey information to others without the owner's permission.

QUICK TIP

Some specific types of viruses are called worms; another type is a Trojan horse. Antivirus software usually protects against both types.

  - Unscrupulous programmers deliberately construct harmful programs, called **viruses**, which instruct your computer to perform destructive activities, such as erasing a disk drive. Some viruses are more annoying than destructive, but some can be harmful, erasing data or causing your hard disk to require reformatting. **Antivirus software**, sometimes referred to as **virus protection software**, searches executable files for the sequences of characters that may cause harm and disinfects the files by erasing or disabling those commands. Figure A-21 shows the screen that appears after AVG Anti-Virus Free Edition finished scanning a computer.

QUICK TIP

Adware is software installed with another program usually with the user's permission that generates advertising revenue for the program's creator by displaying targeted ads to the program's user.

  - Some software programs contain other programs called **spyware** that track a computer user's Internet usage and send this data back to the company or person that created it. Most often, this is done without the computer user's permission or knowledge. **Anti-spyware software** can detect these programs and delete them.

- A **firewall** is like a locked door on a computer. It prevents other computers on the Internet from accessing a computer and prevents programs on a computer from accessing the Internet without the computer user's permission. A firewall can be either hardware or software.

  - A hardware firewall provides strong protection against incoming threats. A **router**, a device that controls traffic between network components, usually has a built-in firewall.

  - Software firewalls track all incoming and outgoing traffic. If a program that never accessed the Internet before attempts to do so, the user is notified and can choose to forbid access. There are several free software firewall packages available. Figure A-22 shows an alert from Zone Alarm, a software firewall.

- Criminals are getting more aggressive as they try to figure out new ways to access computer users' personal information and passwords.

  - A Web site set up to look exactly like another Web site, such as a bank's Web site, but which does not actually belong to the organization portrayed in the site, is a **spoofed** site. The site developer creates a **URL** (address on the Web) that looks similar to a URL from the legitimate site. Usually, spoofed sites are set up to try to convince customers of the real site to enter personal information, such as credit card numbers, Social Security numbers, and passwords, so that the thief collecting the information can use it to steal the customer's money or identity.

QUICK TIP

Never click a URL in a phishing message. Open your browser and type the URL of the organization into the Address or Location bar instead.

  - **Phishing** refers to the practice of sending e-mails to customers or potential customers of a legitimate Web site asking them to click a link in the e-mail. The link leads to a spoofed site where the user is asked to verify or enter personal information.

  - Sometimes a criminal can break into a **DNS server** (a computer responsible for directing Internet traffic) and redirect any attempts to access a particular Web site to the criminal's spoofed site. This is called **pharming**.

FIGURE A-21: Completed antivirus scan

FIGURE A-22: Security alert from a software firewall

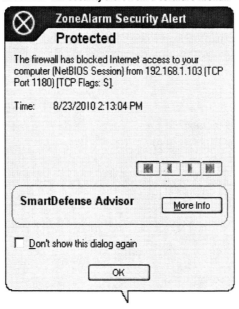

Protecting information with passwords

You can protect data on your computer by using passwords. You can set up accounts on your computer for multiple users and require that all users sign in with a user name and password before they can use the computer. This is known as **logging in**. You can also protect individual files on your computer so that people who try to open or alter a file need to type the password before they are allowed access to the file. Many Web sites require a user name and password in order to access the information stored on it. To prevent anyone from guessing your password, you should always create and use strong passwords. A **strong password** is at least eight characters of upper and lowercase letters and numbers. Avoid using common personal information, such as birthdays and addresses.

Understanding System Software

Sometimes the term software refers to a single program, but often the term refers to a collection of programs and data that are packaged together. **System software** helps the computer carry out its basic operating tasks. Before Kevin describes the various types of software that people use to accomplish things like writing memos, he needs to describe system software.

The components of system software are described below:

- System software manages the fundamental operations of your computer, such as loading programs and data into memory, executing programs, saving data to disks, displaying information on the monitor, and transmitting data through a port to a peripheral device. There are four types of system software: operating systems, utilities, device drivers, and programming languages.

- An **operating system** allocates system resources, manages storage space, maintains security, detects equipment failure, and controls basic input and output. **Input and output**, or **I/O**, is the flow of data from the microprocessor to memory to peripherals and back again.

  - The operating system allocates system resources so programs run properly. A **system resource** is any part of the computer system, including memory, storage devices, and the microprocessor, that can be used by a computer program.

  - The operating system is also responsible for managing the files on your storage devices. Not only does it open and save files, but it also keeps track of every part of every file for you and lets you know if any part is missing.

  - While you are working on the computer, the operating system is constantly guarding against equipment failure. Each electronic circuit is checked periodically, and the moment a problem is detected, the user is notified with a warning message on the screen.

  - Microsoft Windows, used on many personal computers, and the MAC OS, used exclusively on Macintosh computers, are referred to as **operating environments** because they provide a **graphical user interface** (**GUI**, pronounced "goo-ey") that acts as a liaison between the user and all of the computer's hardware and software. Figure A-23 shows the starting screen on a computer using Microsoft Windows Vista.

- **Utilities** are another category of system software that augment the operating system by taking over some of its responsibility for allocating hardware resources.

- As you learned earlier in the discussion of ports, device drivers handle the transmission protocol between a computer and its peripherals. When you add a device to an existing computer, part of its installation includes adding its device driver to the computer's configuration.

- Computer **programming languages**, which a programmer uses to write computer instructions, are also part of the system software. The instructions are translated into electrical signals that the computer can manipulate and process.

Icon (You might see additional icons on your screen)

Recycle Bin

Gadgets (small programs; you might see additional or different gadgets on your screen)

Start button

Taskbar

Quick Launch toolbar

Examining Windows Vista hardware requirements

Windows Vista, the successor to Windows XP, requires more memory and hard drive space and a faster processor than Windows XP. To take full advantage of all of the features and capabilities of Windows Vista, you need a computer with a 1 GHz processor, 1 GB of RAM, a DirectX 9 graphics processor, 128 MB of specialized graphics RAM, and a 40 GB hard drive with at least 15 GB of available space. To run Windows Vista without all of its features, you need a computer with an 800 MHz processor, 512 MB of RAM, a graphics processor that is DirectX 9 capable (most computers come with this type of graphics processor), and 20 GB hard drive with at least 15 GB of available space. Keep in mind that these are the minimum recommendations. To prevent your computer from slowing to a crawl, you should consider upgrading the amount of RAM and the processor speed.

Concepts

Understanding Application Software

Application software enables you to perform specific computer tasks. Some examples of tasks that are accomplished with application software are document production, spreadsheet calculations, database management, and giving presentations. Now that the Sheehan Tours staff understands operating systems, Kevin describes some common application software.

Typical application software includes the following:

- **Document production software** includes word processing software, desktop publishing software, e-mail editors, and Web authoring software. All of these production tools have a variety of features that assist you in writing and formatting documents, including changing the **font** (the style of type). Most offer **spell checking** to help you avoid typographical and spelling errors, as shown in Figure A-24.

- **Spreadsheet software** is a numerical analysis tool. Spreadsheet software creates a **worksheet**, composed of a grid of columns and rows. You can type data into the cells, and then enter mathematical formulas into other cells that reference the data. Figure A-25 shows a typical worksheet that includes a simple calculation and the data in the spreadsheet represented as a simple graph.

- **Database management software** lets you collect and manage data. A **database** is a collection of information stored on one or more computers organized in a uniform format of records and fields. A **record** is a collection of data items in a database. A **field** is one piece of information in the record. An example of a database is the online catalog of books at a library; the catalog contains one record for each book in the library, and each record contains fields that identify the title, the author, and the subjects under which the book can be classified.

- **Graphics** and **presentation software** allow you to create illustrations, diagrams, graphs, and charts that can be projected before a group, printed out for quick reference, or transmitted to remote computers. You can also use **clip art**, simple drawings that are included as collections with many software packages.

- **Photo editing software** allows you to manipulate digital photos. You can make the images brighter, add special effects to the photo, add additional images to a photo, or crop the photo to include only relevant parts of the image.

- **Multimedia authoring software** allows you to record digital sound files, video files, and animations that can be included in presentations and other documents.

- **Information management software** keeps track of schedules, appointments, contacts, and "to-do" lists. Most e-mail software allows users to add all the information about contacts to the list of e-mail addresses. In addition, some software, such as Microsoft Outlook, combines a contact list with information management components, such as a calendar and to-do list. The main screen of Microsoft Outlook is shown in Figure A-26.

- **Web site creation and management software** allows you to create and manage Web sites. They allow you to see what the Web pages will look like as you create them.

Understanding object linking and embedding (OLE)

Many programs allow users to use data created in one application in a document created by another application. **Object linking and embedding (OLE)** refers to the ability to use data from another file, called the **source**. **Embedding** occurs when you copy and paste the source data in the new file. **Linking** allows you to create a connection between the source data and the copy in the new file. The link updates the copy every time a change is made to the source data. The seamless nature of OLE among some applications is referred to as **integration**.

FIGURE A-24: Spell checking a document

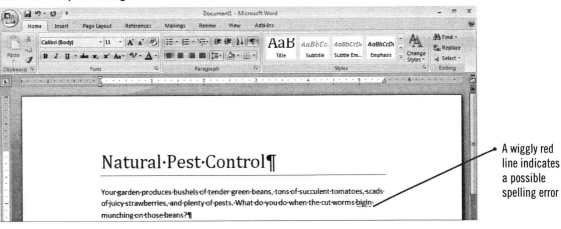

A wiggly red line indicates a possible spelling error

FIGURE A-25: Typical worksheet with numerical data and a graph

Cell B5 contains result of calculation performed by spreadsheet software

Graph

FIGURE A-26: Information management software

Practice

▼ CONCEPTS REVIEW

Label each component of the desktop personal computer shown in Figure A-27.

FIGURE A-27

1. Which component do you use to point to items on the screen?
2. Which component displays output?
3. Which component is used to enter text?
4. Which component processes data?
5. Which component transmits audio output?

Match each term with the statement that best describes it.

6. **configuration**
7. **byte**
8. **RAM**
9. **hard disk**
10. **expansion slot**
11. **server**
12. **spyware**
13. **operating system**
14. **font**

a. Software that allocates resources, manages storage space, maintains security, and controls I/O

b. The style of type

c. The design and construction of a computer

d. Magnetic storage media that is usually sealed in a case inside the computer

e. Series of eight bits

f. A computer on a network that acts as the central storage location for programs and data used on the network

g. A program that tracks a user's Internet usage without the user's permission

h. A slot on the motherboard into which a controller card for a peripheral device is inserted

i. Temporarily holds data and programs while the computer is on

Select the best answer from the list of choices.

15. **Which one of the following would not be considered a personal computer?**
    a. Desktop
    b. Notebook
    c. Mainframe
    d. Tablet PC

16. **The intangible components of a computer system, including the programs, are called _____.**
    a. software
    b. hardware
    c. price
    d. peripherals

17. **What part of the computer is responsible for executing instructions to process information?**
    a. Card
    b. Processor
    c. Motherboard
    d. Peripheral device

18. **What are the technical details about each hardware component called?**
    a. Configuration
    b. Circuits
    c. Specifications
    d. Cards

19. **Keyboards, monitors, and printers are all examples of which of the following?**
    a. Input devices
    b. Output devices
    c. Software
    d. Peripheral devices

20. **Which of the following is a pointing device that allows you to control the pointer by moving the entire device around on a desk?**
    a. Mouse
    b. Trackball
    c. Touch pad
    d. Pointing stick

21. **In order to display graphics, a computer needs a monitor and a _____.**
   a. parallel port
   b. network card
   c. graphics card
   d. sound card

22. **What do you call each 1 or 0 used in the representation of computer data?**
   a. A bit
   b. A byte
   c. An ASCII
   d. A pixel

23. **Another way to refer to 1024 bytes is a _____.**
   a. byte
   b. kilobyte
   c. megabyte
   d. binary

24. **Which of the following is a chip installed on the motherboard that is activated during the boot process and identifies where essential software is stored?**
   a. RAM
   b. CMOS
   c. CPU cache
   d. ROM

25. **Which of the following is space on the computer's storage devices that simulates additional RAM?**
   a. Cache memory
   b. Virtual memory
   c. Read-only memory
   d. Volatile memory

26. **Which of the following permanently stores the set of instructions that the computer uses to activate the software that controls the processing function when you turn the computer on?**
   a. RAM
   b. CMOS
   c. CPU cache
   d. ROM

27. **Which of the following storage media is not a magnetic storage device?**
   a. Hard disk
   b. Floppy disk
   c. DVD
   d. Tape

28. **The transmission protocol between a computer and its peripheral devices is handled by a _____.**
   a. channel
   b. data bus
   c. driver
   d. controller card

29. **Which of the following is the data path between the microprocessor, RAM, and the peripherals?**
   a. Data bus
   b. Data channel
   c. Data port
   d. Cable

30. The computer that originates a message to send to another computer is called the _____.
   a. channel
   b. sender
   c. receiver
   d. driver

31. A personal computer that is connected to a network is called a _____.
   a. desktop
   b. workstation
   c. terminal
   d. PDA

32. Which of the following acts as a locked door on a computer?
   a. Antivirus software
   b. Firewall
   c. DNS server
   d. Spyware

33. A _____ consists of connected computers and peripheral devices that are located relatively close to each other.
   a. LAN
   b. WAN
   c. WLAN
   d. PAN

34. The term that describes networks connected using a standard radio frequency established by the IEEE is _____.
   a. WiMAX
   b. WAN
   c. WLAN
   d. Wi-Fi

35. A Web site set up to look exactly like another Web site, such as a bank's Web site, but which does not actually belong to the organization portrayed in the site, is a _____ site.
   a. malware
   b. phished
   c. spoofed
   d. served

▼ INDEPENDENT CHALLENGE 1

This Independent Challenge requires an Internet connection. In order to run the newest software, many people need to upgrade their existing computer system or buy a brand new one. What do you do with your old computer when you purchase a new one? Most municipalities have enacted laws regulating the disposal of electronics. Research these laws in your city and state and write a brief report describing them.

   a. Start your browser, go to your favorite search engine, then search for information about laws regarding the disposal of electronics in your city and state. Try finding your city's Web site and searching it for the information, or use **electronics disposal laws** followed by your city name as a search term and then repeat that search with your state's name in place of your city's name.
   b. Open each Web site that you find in a separate tab or browser window.
   c. Read the information on each Web site. Can some components be thrown away? Are there laws that apply only to monitors?

▼ INDEPENDENT CHALLENGE 1 (CONTINUED)

Advanced Challenge Exercise

- Search for organizations to which you can donate your computer.
- How do these organizations promise to protect your privacy?
- Can you take a deduction on your federal income tax for your donation?

d. Write a short report describing your findings. Include the URLs for all relevant Web sites. (*Hint*: If you are using a word processor to write your report, you can copy the URLs from your browser and paste them into the document. Drag to select the entire URL in the Address or Location bar in your browser. Right-click the selected text, then click Copy on the shortcut menu. Position the insertion point in the document where you want the URL to appear, then press [Ctrl][V].)

▼ INDEPENDENT CHALLENGE 2

This Independent Challenge requires an Internet connection. New viruses are discovered on an almost daily basis. If you surf the Internet or exchange e-mail, it is important to use updated anti-virus software. Research the most current virus threats and create a table listing the threats and details about them.

a. Start your browser, go to Symantec's Web site at **www.symantec.com**, then click the Latest Threats link. (If you don't see that link, type **threat explorer** in the Search box on the page, then click the link to Threat Explorer in the list of search results. On the Threat Explorer page, click the Latest tab.)

b. Click links to the first five latest threats.

c. Open a new word processing document and create a table listing each virus threat, a description of what each virus does, how widely it is distributed (the Wild value), and how damaging it is (the Damage Level value).

d. In your browser, go to the Security Advisor on CA's Web site at **www3.ca.com/securityadvisor**, and then click the Virus Information Center link. If any of the first five latest virus threats are different from the ones on the Symantec site, add them to your table. (*Hint*: After you click a virus name, check the "Also known as" list.)

e. For any viruses that are already in your table because they were on the Symantec site, read the CA description to see if there is any additional information describing how the virus could damage your system. Add this information to your table.

f. Save the word processing document as **Latest Threats** to the drive and folder where you store your Data Files.

▼ INDEPENDENT CHALLENGE 3

This Independent Challenge requires an Internet connection. One of the keyboards shown in this unit is an ergonomic keyboard. Ergonomics is the study of the design of a workspace so that the worker can work efficiently and avoid injury. The U.S. Occupational Safety and Health Administration (OSHA) has developed guidelines that describe a healthy computer work environment. Research these guidelines and evaluate your workspace.

a. Start your browser, and then go to **www.osha.gov/SLTC/etools/computerworkstations**.

b. Read the information on the main page. Follow links to descriptions of the best arrangement for equipment you use when working on a computer. (*Hint*: Look for the Workstation Components link, and point to it to open a submenu of links.)

c. Locate and print the checklist for evaluating your workspace. (*Hint*: Click the Checklist link, then click the View/Print the Evaluation Checklist PDF link. A new tab or window opens and the checklist opens in Adobe Acrobat Reader, a program that displays PDF files. If a dialog box opens telling you that you need to install Acrobat Reader to continue, ask your instructor or technical support person for help.)

d. Using the checklist, evaluate each of the conditions listed. If a condition does not apply to you, write N/A (not applicable) in the Yes column.

▼ INDEPENDENT CHALLENGE 3 (CONTINUED)

Advanced Challenge Exercise

- Use the OSHA Web site or a search engine to research repetitive motion injuries to which computer users are susceptible.
- Evaluate your risk for at least three common injuries.
- On the OSHA checklist, note what injury or injuries each applicable item or behavior will help prevent.

▼ REAL LIFE INDEPENDENT CHALLENGE

You are buying a new desktop computer. You want the computer to run Windows Vista and Microsoft Office 2007, and you want to make sure you are protected against security threats. You would like a large flat panel monitor and you need a printer. However, you have a limited budget, and can spend no more than $800 for everything (all hardware and software).

a. To help you organize your information, create the table shown in Figure A-28.

FIGURE A-28

	Your Requirements	Computer Retailer #1	Computer Retailer #2	Computer Retailer #3
Windows Vista (Edition)				
Office 2007 (Edition)				
Brand of computer				
Processor (brand and speed)				
RAM (amount)				
Video RAM (amount)				
Hard disk (size)				
Monitor (type and size)				
Printer (type and speed)				
Speakers				
Antivirus software				
Firewall (software or router with built-in firewall)				
System price				
Additional costs				
Total price				

b. Decide which edition of Windows Vista you want, Windows Vista Home Basic, Windows Vista Home Premium, Windows Vista Business, or Windows Vista Ultimate, and enter it in the Your Requirements column of the table. To read a description of the available editions, go to www.microsoft.com and search the Microsoft Web site for information about the Windows Vista Editions.

c. Research the hardware requirements for running the edition of Windows Vista you selected. Search the Microsoft Web site again for the minimum and recommended hardware requirements for running Windows Vista.

d. Decide which edition of Office 2007 you want and enter it in the first column of the table. Search the Microsoft Web site to find a description of the software included with each edition of Office 2007, and then search for the hardware requirements for running the edition of Office 2007 that you chose. If necessary, change the hardware requirements in the table.

e. Research the cost of your new computer system. To begin, visit local stores, look at advertisements, or search the Web for computer system retailers. Most computer retailers sell complete systems that come with all the necessary hardware, an operating system, and additional software already installed. In the Computer Retailer #1 column of the table, fill in the specifications for the system you chose. If any item listed as a minimum requirement is not included with the system you chose, find the cost of adding that item and enter the price in the table. Repeat this process with systems from two other retailers, entering the specifications in the Computer Retailer #2 and Computer Retailer #3 columns.

f. If the system you chose does not come with a printer, search the Web for an inexpensive color inkjet printer.

g. If the system you chose does not come with antivirus software, search the Web for the cost, if any, of an antivirus software package. Make sure you look up reviews of the package you chose. Decide whether to purchase this software or download a free one, and enter this cost in the table.

h. If you decide you need a router with a built-in firewall, search the Web for the price of one. Enter this information in the table.

i. Total the costs you entered in the table for the various items. Is the total cost $800 or less? If not, revisit some of the items. Can you get a less expensive printer? Do you need to downgrade to a less expensive monitor? Likewise, if you are under budget, upgrade a part of your system. For example, if the system you chose meets only the minimum requirements for running Windows Vista, see if you can afford a system that will be able to run Windows Vista with all of its features. Or perhaps you can afford to upgrade the monitor to a larger, flat panel monitor. Reevaluate your choices if necessary and try to get your total cost close to $800.

j. Submit your completed table to your instructor.

Getting Started with Windows Vista

Microsoft Windows Vista, or **Windows**, is an **operating system**—software that manages the complete operation of your computer. When you start a computer, Windows sets it up for use and then displays the **desktop**—a graphical user interface (GUI) that you use to interact with Windows and the other software on your computer. The Windows desktop displays **icons**, or small images, that represent items such as the Recycle Bin and Computer. When you open a program or document, Windows displays the program or document in a rectangular-shaped work area known as a **window**. Windows helps you organize **files** (collections of stored electronic data, such as text, pictures, video, music, and programs) in **folders** (containers for files) so that you can easily find them later. Windows also keeps all the computer hardware and software working together properly. As a new Oceania tour guide for Quest Specialty Travel (QST), you need to develop basic Windows skills to keep track of all the tour files on your company laptop computer.

OBJECTIVES

Start Windows Vista

Use a pointing device

Start a program

Move and resize windows

Use menus, toolbars, and

    keyboard shortcuts

Use dialog boxes

Use scroll bars

Use Windows Help and Support

End a Windows Vista session

Note: If you are using Microsoft Windows XP, then you should not read these units. Instead, turn to the Windows XP units in the back of the book.

Starting Windows Vista

When you start your computer, Windows steps through a process called **booting** to get the computer up and running. During this time, you might need to select your user account and enter your password. This information identifies you to Windows as an authorized user of the computer and helps keep your computer secure. After booting is complete, Windows displays the Windows desktop. The desktop, shown in Figure A-1, provides a way for you to interact with Windows Vista and to access its tools. The desktop appears with preset, or **default**, settings; however, you can change these settings to suit your needs. The image that fills the desktop background is called **wallpaper**. The desktop contains an icon for the Recycle Bin, which stores deleted files and folders. The desktop also displays **gadgets** (mini-programs for performing everyday tasks, such as a Clock) on the **Sidebar**. The **taskbar**, the horizontal bar at the bottom of the screen, displays information about open programs, folders, and files. You click the **Start button** on the left side of the taskbar to start programs, find and open files, access Windows Help and Support, and more. The **Quick Launch toolbar**, located on the taskbar, includes buttons for showing the desktop when it is not currently visible, switching between windows (the work areas for open programs), and starting the Internet Explorer Web browser. Table A-1 identifies the default icons and elements found on a desktop. Your supervisor, Nancy McDonald, Oceania's tour developer, asks you to become familiar with Windows Vista and its features before your upcoming tour.

STEPS

1. **If your computer and monitor are turned off, press the Power button on the front of the system unit, then press the Power button on the monitor**

   After your computer starts, you see either a **Welcome screen** with icons for each user account on the computer or the Windows desktop. If you see the Welcome screen, continue with Step 2. If you see the Windows desktop, compare it to the one shown in Figure A-1, then continue with Step 4.

2. **If necessary, click the icon for your user account**

   If you use a password with your user account, Windows prompts you for the password. If not, continue with Step 4.

3. **If prompted for a password, type your password in the Password box, then click the Next button**

   After Windows verifies your password, you see the Windows desktop. See Figure A-1. Your Windows desktop may look slightly different.

   TROUBLE
   If you don't know your password, ask your instructor or technical support person. If you don't use a password, leave the Password box empty and click the Next button

4. **If the Welcome Center opens, click the Close button** ✖ **in the upper-right corner of the Welcome Center window**

TABLE A-1: Common desktop components

desktop element	icon	allows you to
Recycle Bin	🗑	Store folders and files you delete from your hard drive(s) and restore them
Windows Sidebar (or Sidebar)		View the current time on a clock, view a slide show, and more
Taskbar		Switch between open programs, folders, and files; and resize windows
Notification area		Check the time, adjust the volume of your speakers, connect to the Internet, check problems identified by Windows Vista, and more
Quick Launch toolbar		Show the desktop, switch between windows, and open the Internet Explorer Web browser
Start button	⊕	Start programs, search for files, open documents, view pictures, listen to music, play games, get help, and more

FIGURE A-1: Windows Vista desktop

Icon

Wallpaper (background image)

Quick Launch toolbar

Start button

Gadgets on the Sidebar

Taskbar

Notification area

Using Windows Vista with Aero

Some editions of Windows Vista support **Windows Aero**, a new graphical user-interface feature that enhances the transparency (referred to as **translucency**) of the Start menu, taskbar, windows, and dialog boxes, as shown in Figure A-2. These transparency features also enable you to locate content by seeing through one window to the next window. **Windows Flip** allows you to display a set of thumbnails or miniature images of all open windows. **Windows Flip 3D** allows you to display stacked windows at a three-dimensional angle to see even more of the content of all open windows. Likewise, **live taskbar thumbnails** display the content within open, but not visible, windows, including live content such as video. These features provide three different ways to quickly view, locate, and select windows with the content you need. To view these effects, your version of Windows Vista and your computer's hardware must support the use of Windows Aero.

FIGURE A-2: Windows Aero features

Translucent Start menu

Translucent window frame and borders

Live thumbnail

Live taskbar thumbnail for a minimized window

Using a Pointing Device

The most common way to interact with your computer and the software you are using is with a **pointing device**, such as a mouse, trackball, touch pad, or pointing stick, as shown in Figure A-3. If touch input is available on your computer, you can also use an onscreen **touch pointer** to perform pointing operations with a finger. As you move your pointing device, a small arrow or other symbol on the screen, called a **pointer**, moves in the same direction. Table A-2 illustrates common pointer shapes and their functions. You press the left and right buttons on the pointing device to select and move objects (such as icons and desktop windows); open programs, windows, folders, and files; and select options for performing specific tasks, such as saving your work. Table A-3 lists the five basic ways in which you can use a pointing device. Pointing devices can work with your computer through a cable or through a wireless connection that transmits data using radio waves. ▰▰▰ You'll practice using your pointing device so you can work more efficiently.

STEPS

QUICK TIP

Left-handed users can change the Button configuration setting in the Mouse Properties dialog box to switch the primary and secondary (left and right) mouse buttons.

1. **Locate the pointer on the desktop, then move your pointing device**

   The pointer moves across the Windows desktop in the same direction as you move your pointing device.

2. **Move the pointer so the tip is directly over the Recycle Bin icon** 🗑

   Positioning the pointer over an item is called **pointing**. The Recycle Bin icon is highlighted and a **ToolTip**, or label, identifies its purpose.

3. **With the pointer over** 🗑**, press and release the left button on your pointing device**

   Pressing and releasing the left button, called **clicking** or **single-clicking**, selects an icon on the desktop or in a window and selects options and objects within a program. In this case, the Recycle Bin icon is selected.

TROUBLE

If the Recycle Bin window opens, you may have pressed the left button twice. Click the Close button in the title bar to close the window.

4. **With** 🗑 **still selected, press and hold down the left button on your pointing device, move your pointing device to another location on the desktop, then release the left button**

   A copy of the Recycle Bin icon moves with the pointer. When you release the left button on your pointing device, the Recycle Bin is placed on the desktop in a different location. You use this technique, called **dragging**, to move icons and windows.

5. **Drag** 🗑 **back to its original desktop location**

6. **Position the pointer over** 🗑**, then press and release the right button on your pointing device**

   This action, called **right-clicking**, opens a shortcut menu, as shown in Figure A-4. A **shortcut menu** lists common commands for an object. A **command** is an instruction to perform a task, such as renaming an object. If a command is dimmed, such as "Empty Recycle Bin," it is not currently available for you to use.

QUICK TIP

When a step says "click," use the left button on your pointing device. When it says "right-click," use the right button.

7. **Click the desktop background**

   The shortcut menu closes and Windows selects the desktop background.

8. **Point to** 🗑**, then quickly press the left button on your pointing device twice and release it**

   Quickly clicking the left button twice is called **double-clicking**, which opens a window or a program. In this case, the Recycle Bin window opens to display any folders and files deleted from the hard disk.

QUICK TIP

Be sure to hold your pointing device still as you double-click.

9. **Click the Close button** ❌ **in the upper-right corner of the Recycle Bin window**

   The Recycle Bin window closes. Every window has a Close button; clicking it is the fastest way to close a window.

FIGURE A-3: Common pointing devices

Mouse

Trackball

Touch pointer

Touchpad

Pointing stick

FIGURE A-4: Shortcut menu

Selected object

Dimmed command is unavailable

Command

Shortcut menu

TABLE A-2: Common pointer shapes

shape	name	description
⬉	Normal Select	Points to an object and chooses a command
◯	Busy	Indicates that Windows or another program is busy and you must wait before continuing
⬉◌	Working in Background	Indicates that Windows or another program is busy and the computer's response time is slower, but you can still perform other operations
I	Text Select (also called I-Beam)	Identifies where you can type, select, insert, or edit text
⬏	Link Select	Identifies a link you can click to jump to another location, such as a Help topic or a Web site

TABLE A-3: Basic pointing device techniques

technique	what to do
Pointing	Move the pointing device to position the tip of the pointer over an object, option, or item
Clicking	Quickly press and release the left button
Double-clicking	Quickly press and release the left button twice
Dragging	Point to an object, press and hold the left button, move the object to a new location, then release the left button
Right-clicking	Point to an object, then quickly press and release the right button

Starting a Program

From the Start menu, you can open programs or software products on your computer. In addition to other software that you purchase and install on the computer, Windows Vista includes a variety of programs, such as Windows Calendar, Windows Mail, Windows Movie Maker, and Windows Photo Gallery. Windows also comes with **accessories**, which are simple programs to perform specific tasks, such as the Windows Calculator accessory for performing quick calculations. Table A-4 describes the organization of the Start menu. ▨▨▨ Because you need to develop QST tour proposals and brochures with photographs of exotic Pacific islands, you want to try the Windows Photo Gallery.

You can also press the Windows logo key to open or close the Start menu.

1. **Click the Start button ⊕ on the taskbar**
    The Start menu opens, as shown in Figure A-5. From the left pane, you can start programs installed on your computer. From the right pane, you can open specific folders, open Windows tools, change Windows settings, get Help and Support, and shut down Windows. Some of the options on your Start menu will differ.

2. **Point to All Programs**
    The All Programs menu opens in the left pane, with an alphabetical listing of the programs installed on your computer followed by groups of related programs, such as Accessories. See Figure A-6. Your list of programs will differ.

If you see an Info Pane on the right side of the window, close it by clicking the Hide Info Pane button.

3. **Click Windows Photo Gallery on the All Programs menu**
    The Windows Photo Gallery window opens, displaying thumbnails of images in the Sample Pictures folder on your computer. See Figure A-7. A **thumbnail** is a smaller image of the actual contents of a file that contains a picture. Windows also displays a Windows Photo Gallery button on the taskbar for the now open Windows Photo Gallery.

4. **Leave the Photo Gallery window open for the next lesson**

TABLE A-4: Start menu components

component	description
Pinned Items List	Contains the two programs commonly used for a Web browser and e-mail: Internet Explorer and a version of Microsoft Outlook; you can change these two programs and you can add other programs to this list
Recently-opened Programs List	Lists programs you have recently opened so you can quickly return to them.
All Programs	Displays a list of programs installed on your computer
Search Box	Quickly locates programs, folders, and files, and shows the search results in the left pane of the Start menu
User Folders	Provides quick access to your Documents, Pictures, Music, and Games folders, plus the folder for your user account (your username at the top of the right pane)
Windows Tools	Search quickly locates programs, folders, and files Recent Items displays the names of up to 15 files you recently opened Computer opens a Windows Explorer window and shows the drives and other hardware on your computer Network provides access to computers and other hardware on your network Connect To shows your Internet and network connections
Settings & Help	Control Panel provides tools for viewing and changing Windows settings and installing hardware and software Default Programs lets you specify the programs and program settings you prefer to use Help and Support opens the Windows Help and Support Center to provide you with assistance and Help information
Power & Lock Buttons	Power button puts your computer to sleep (your computer appears off and uses very little power) Lock button locks your computer (a security measure for when you are not using the computer), and displays shut-down options

FIGURE A-5: Start menu

Pinned items list

Recently-opened programs

Power, Lock, and Lock menu buttons

User account icon

Your important folders

Windows tools, settings, and Help

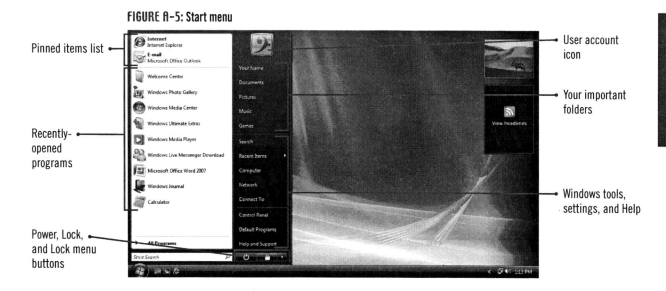

FIGURE A-6: All Programs menu

Installed programs (your list will differ)

FIGURE A-7: Windows Photo Gallery window

Thumbnail of an image

Taskbar button for Windows Photo Gallery window

Moving and Resizing Windows

Each program you start opens in its own window. As you work, you will invariably need to move and resize windows so that you can see more of one window or view two or more windows at the same time. To resize a window, you use the **resizing buttons**—Maximize 🔲, Restore Down 🗗, and Minimize 🗕—in the upper-right corner of the window. To adjust a window's height or width (or both), you drag a window border or window corner. To move a window, you drag its **title bar**—the area across the top of the window that displays the window name or program name. If you open more than one program at once, you are **multitasking**—performing several tasks at the same time—and each program appears in a different window. The **active window** is the window you are currently using. An **inactive window** is another open window that you are not currently using. As you examine photos for a new tour brochure, you need to move and resize the Windows Photo Gallery window.

STEPS

QUICK TIP

You can also maximize or restore down a window by double-clicking its title bar.

1. **If the Windows Photo Gallery window does not fill the desktop, click the Maximize button 🔲 in the upper-right corner of the Windows Photo Gallery window**

    The Windows Photo Gallery window is maximized. A **maximized window** fills your desktop and you cannot see its borders. After you maximize a window, the Maximize button changes to a Restore Down button.

2. **Click the Restore Down button 🗗 in the upper-right corner of the Windows Photo Gallery window**

    The Windows Photo Gallery window returns to its previous size and position on the desktop. The window borders are visible, and the Restore Down button changes to a Maximize button.

3. **Click the Minimize button 🗕 in the upper-right corner of the Windows Photo Gallery window**

    The Windows Photo Gallery window is still open, just not visible. See Figure A-8. A **minimized window** shrinks to a button on the taskbar. You can use this feature to hide a window that you are not currently using, but may use later.

4. **Click the Windows Photo Gallery taskbar button**

    The Windows Photo Gallery window returns to its original size and position on the desktop.

5. **Drag the title bar on the Windows Photo Gallery window to the upper-left corner of the desktop**

    The Windows Photo Gallery window is repositioned on the desktop.

6. **Position the pointer on the right border of the Windows Photo Gallery window until the pointer changes to ⟺, then drag the border left**

    The width of the Windows Photo Gallery window narrows. See Figure A-9. To widen the window, you drag the right window border to the right. To decrease or increase a window's height, you drag the bottom border up or down.

7. **Position the pointer on the lower-right corner of the Windows Photo Gallery window until the pointer changes to ⬊, then drag down and to the right**

    Both the height and width of the window change.

8. **Right-click the Windows Photo Gallery taskbar button, then click Close on the shortcut menu**

    The Windows Photo Gallery window closes.

FIGURE A-8: Minimized window

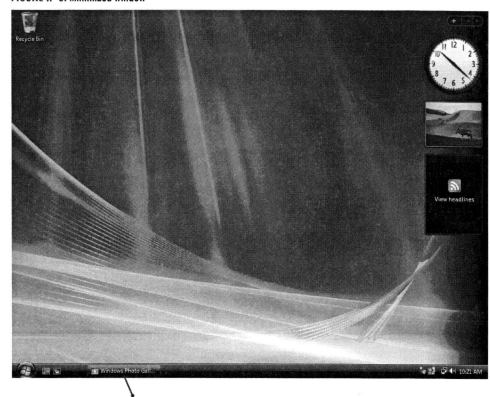

Windows Photo Gallery
is open, but not visible

FIGURE A-9: Restored down window being resized

Title bar

Close button

Maximize button

Minimize button

Side border adjusts the window's width

Corner adjusts the window's height and width

Using Menus, Toolbars, and Keyboard Shortcuts

A **menu** displays a list of commands you use to accomplish a task. Menus organize commands into groups of related tasks. In some program windows, you open menus from a **menu bar** located below the window's title bar. At other times, you open menus from a **toolbar**, a set of buttons you can click to open menus or select common commands that may also be available from a menu bar. Some menu commands and toolbar buttons have a **keyboard shortcut**, which is a key or a combination of keys that you press to perform a command. ▓▓▓ As you prepare for your first tour, Nancy recommends that you examine the Slide Show gadget and the Windows Photo Gallery.

STEPS

TROUBLE
If you don't see the Sidebar, click the Start button, point to All Programs, click Accessories, then click Windows Sidebar. If you still don't see the Sidebar, click the Windows Sidebar icon in the taskbar Notification area.

1. **Point to the Slide Show gadget on the Sidebar, resting the pointer on the displayed image**

   The Slide Show toolbar appears at the bottom of the slide show image, and the Slide Show gadget toolbar appears to the right of the Slide Show gadget. See Figure A-10. The left border of the Sidebar is now visible.

2. **Click the View button ▨ on the Slide Show toolbar**

   The Windows Photo Gallery window opens and displays an enlarged view of the image displayed in the Slide Show gadget. The title bar identifies the filename of the image and the name of the open program. A toolbar appears below the title bar, with options for working with the image.

3. **Click the File button ▣ File ▾ on the toolbar**

   The File menu lists commands related to working with the files. See Figure A-11. A keyboard shortcut appears to the right of some commands.

4. **Click Exit**

   The Windows Photo Gallery window closes.

5. **Point to the Slide Show gadget on the Sidebar, then click ▨ on the Slide Show toolbar**

   The Photo Gallery Viewer window opens again.

6. **Click the Play Slide Show button ▣ on the Slide Show toolbar at the bottom of the window**

   Windows Photo Gallery displays a full-screen slide show of each image in your Sample Pictures folder, one at a time.

QUICK TIP
"Esc," an abbreviation for "Escape," is a standard keyboard shortcut for canceling an operation or backing up a step.

7. **Press [Esc]**

   The slide show stops and you return to the Windows Photo Gallery window.

8. **Press and hold [Alt], press and release [F4], then release [Alt]**

   The Windows Photo Gallery window closes. The keyboard shortcut [Alt][F4] closes any active window.

FIGURE A-10: Windows Sidebar

Add Gadget button

Slide Show gadget

View button

FIGURE A-11: File menu

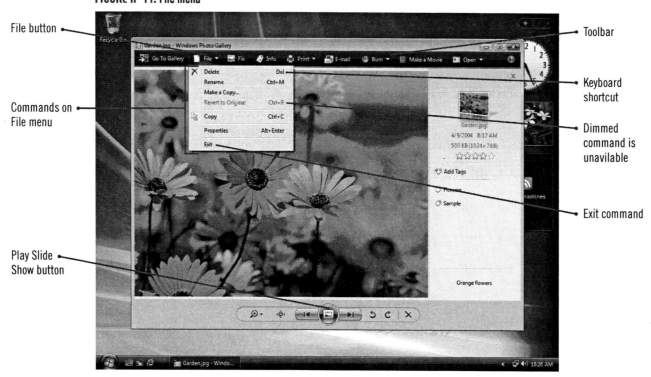

File button

Commands on File menu

Play Slide Show button

Toolbar

Keyboard shortcut

Dimmed command is unavilable

Exit command

Using keyboard shortcuts

Keyboard shortcuts allow you to work more quickly and efficiently because you can keep your hands on the keyboard rather than moving between the keyboard and your pointing device. Many programs use the same keyboard shortcuts for common operations, such as [Ctrl][O] for opening a file and [Ctrl][S] for saving a file. Taking the time to learn the keyboard shortcuts for the actions you perform frequently will improve your productivity. Keyboard shortcuts are shown on menus with a plus sign separating the keys you need to press at the same time, such as Ctrl+S for saving a file. Remember, you do not press the plus sign when you use a keyboard shortcut

Using Dialog Boxes

When you select a command from a menu or toolbar, the program may perform the operation immediately. Or, it may open a **dialog box**, a type of window in which you specify how you want to complete the operation. Although dialog boxes are similar to a window, they do not contain Maximize, Minimize, and Restore Down buttons, and you usually cannot resize a dialog box. Figure A-12 shows a Print dialog box with two **tabs**—General and Options—that separate groups of settings into related categories. Dialog boxes provide different ways to select options. Table A-5 lists common types of options found in dialog boxes. ⬛️ You want to review the Sidebar default settings to determine whether they meet your needs while you work.

1. **Right-click the background of the Sidebar under the last gadget, then click Properties**

   The Windows Sidebar Properties dialog box opens, as shown in Figure A-13. **Properties** are characteristics or settings of a component of the graphical user interface. The first setting in the dialog box is a check box for starting the Sidebar whenever Windows starts. A **check box** turns an option on (checked) or off (unchecked). You click the check box to change the option's status. As you can see from the check mark in the Start Sidebar when Windows starts check box, it is already turned on.

2. **Click the Sidebar is always on top of other windows check box**

   A check mark is added to the check box, which sets the Sidebar to remain visible when you open a window.

3. **In the Arrangement section, click the Left option button**

   You click one **option button** to select from several options. In this case, you clicked the option button to display the Sidebar on the left side of the desktop. You can select only one option button for a setting. The "Display Sidebar on monitor" button is a **drop-down list button** that you click to open a list that shows one or more options to choose. The **link** at the bottom of the Maintenance section opens a Help topic about how to customize the Sidebar. At the bottom of the dialog box are **command buttons**, which you click to complete or cancel any changes you make in the dialog box. Clicking OK closes the dialog box and applies the settings you selected. Clicking Apply applies the settings you selected, but keeps the dialog box open for additional changes. Clicking Cancel leaves the settings unchanged and closes the dialog box.

In a dialog box, pressing [Enter] is the same as clicking OK; pressing [Esc] is the same as clicking Cancel.

4. **Click Cancel**

   The dialog box closes without changing any of the settings for the Sidebar.

FIGURE A-12: Print dialog box

FIGURE A-13: Windows Sidebar Properties dialog box

TABLE A-5: Typical elements in a dialog box

element	description
Check box	A box that turns an option on when checked or off when unchecked
Collapse button	A button that shrinks a portion of a dialog box to hide some settings
Command button	A button that completes or cancels an operation
Drop-down list button	A button that displays a list of options from which you can choose
Expand button	A button that extends a dialog box to display additional settings
Link	A shortcut for opening a Help topic or a Web site
List box	A box that displays a list of options from which you can choose (you may need to adjust your view to see additional options in the list)
Option button	A small circle you click to select only one of two or more related options
Slider	A shape you drag along a bar to select a setting that falls within a range, such as between Slow and Fast
Spin box	A text box with up and down arrows; you can type a setting in the text box or click the arrows to increase or decrease a setting
Text box	A box in which you type text (such as a password)

Using Scroll Bars

When you cannot see all of the items available in a window, list box, or drop-down list box, you must **scroll**, or adjust your view. Scrolling is similar to taking a picture with a camera. You move the camera to select a view of a landscape in front of you. If you move the camera to the right or left or up or down, you see a different part of that same landscape. When a window on your computer contains more items than it can display at once, scroll bars appear so you can adjust your view in the window. **Scroll bars** are vertical and horizontal bars that appear along the right and bottom sides of a window when there is more content than can be displayed within the window. At each end of a scroll bar are **scroll arrow buttons** for shifting your view in small increments in either direction. Within each scroll bar is a **scroll box** you can drag to display a different part of a window. You can also click in a scroll bar on either side of the scroll box to shift your view in larger increments. Instead of using a pointing device to scroll, you can also use keyboard shortcuts to scroll, which can be faster. Table A-6 summarizes different ways to scroll. ▰▰▰▰ For each QST tour, you work with a large variety of files. To locate your files, and to view different pages within each file, you use scroll bars. You will practice scrolling using a Windows Vista accessory called Paint—a graphics program.

STEPS

1. **Point to the Slide Show gadget on the Sidebar, then click the View button ▦ on the Slide Show toolbar**

   An image from your Sample Pictures folder appears in the Windows Photo Gallery window.

2. **Click the Open button on the toolbar, then click Paint**

   The image opens in a Paint window for editing. Paint is one of the Windows Vista accessories.

   TROUBLE

   If you don't see scroll bars, drag the lower-right corner of the Paint window up and to the left until both scroll bars appear.

3. **If the Paint window fills the desktop, then click its Restore Down button ▣**

   Because of the large size of the image, you can see only a portion of it within the window. However, Paint displays scroll bars on the right and bottom of the window so you can adjust your view. See Figure A-14. Your image and view may differ.

4. **Click the down scroll arrow in the vertical scroll bar**

   The window scrolls down to show another part of the image, and part of the image has now scrolled out of view.

5. **Drag the vertical scroll box slowly down the window to the bottom of the vertical scroll bar**

   The window view changes in larger increments, and the bottom part of the image is visible at the bottom of the window.

6. **Click the vertical scroll bar between the scroll box and the up scroll arrow**

   The view moves up approximately the height of one window.

7. **Click the right scroll arrow in the horizontal scroll bar three times**

   The window keeps scrolling right to show other views onto the image.

   TROUBLE

   If a dialog box opens asking if you want to save changes to the image, click Don't Save.

8. **Click the Close button ▣✕ on the Paint title bar**

   The Paint window closes.

9. **Click ▣✕ on the Windows Photo Gallery title bar**

   The Windows Photo Gallery window closes.

FIGURE A-14: Scroll bars

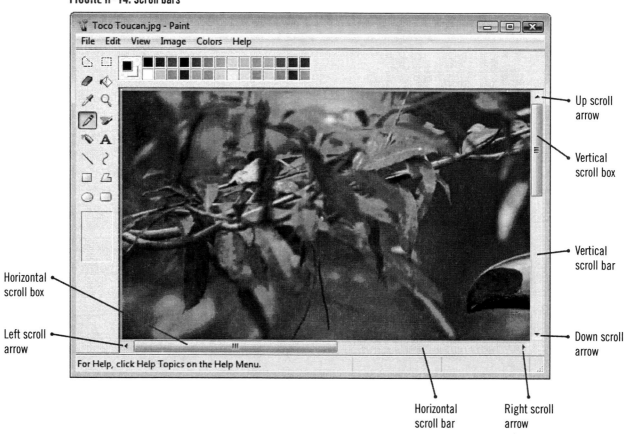

Up scroll arrow

Vertical scroll box

Vertical scroll bar

Horizontal scroll box

Down scroll arrow

Left scroll arrow

Horizontal scroll bar

Right scroll arrow

TABLE A-6: Using scroll bars

to	do this with the mouse
Move down a small increment or one line	Click the down scroll arrow at the bottom of the vertical scroll bar
Move up a small increment or one line	Click the up scroll arrow at the top of the vertical scroll bar
Move down about one window's height	Click between the scroll box and the down scroll arrow in the vertical scroll bar
Move up about one window's height	Click between the scroll box and the up scroll arrow in the vertical scroll bar
Move up a large distance	Drag the scroll box up the vertical scroll bar
Move down a large distance	Drag the scroll box down the vertical scroll bar
Move left or right a small distance	Click the left or the right scroll arrow in the horizontal scroll bar
Move to the left or right one window's width	Click between the scroll box and the left or right scroll arrow in the horizontal scroll bar
Move left or right a large distance	Drag the scroll box in the horizontal scroll bar to the left or right

Using Windows Help and Support

When you need assistance or more information about how to use Windows, you can use Help and Support. After you open Help and Support, you can browse Help by first selecting a general category, such as "Windows Basics," then a narrower category, such as "Desktop fundamentals," and finally a specific Help topic, such as "The desktop (overview)." Or, you can select a topic from a table of contents. You can also search Help and Support using one or more descriptive words called **keywords**, such as "Windows Sidebar gadgets," to obtain a list of search results for all the Help topics that include the word or phrase. In certain places within Help and Support, you can use Windows Media Player to watch video clips called Windows Vista demos that provide an overview of Windows features and how to use them. ▰▰▱ Because you often use the Sidebar and Windows Photo Gallery as a tour guide, you decide to review the information in Windows Help and Support on these two Windows features.

STEPS

TROUBLE

If the Help and Support dialog box opens, asking you if you want to get the latest online content, click No. If a warning appears that you have lost your connection to the Windows Help and Support Web site, you are not connected to the Internet. Continue with the remaining steps.

1. **Click the Start button ⊕ on the taskbar, click Help and Support, then click the Maximize button ⬜ if the window doesn't fill the desktop**

   The Windows Help and Support window opens and fills the desktop. Figure A-15 identifies the various types of Help options. Table A-7 explains the purpose of the buttons on the Help toolbar in the upper-right corner of the window.

2. **Under Find an answer, click the Windows Basics icon**

   Windows Help and Support displays categories of Help topics about basic Windows features.

3. **Under Desktop fundamentals, click Windows Sidebar and gadgets (overview)**

   The Windows Sidebar and gadgets (overview) Help topic explains what the Sidebar is, how it works, why you would use it, and how to work with gadgets—including adding, removing, and organizing gadgets.

4. **Click in the Search Help text box, type edit my digital photos, then click the Search Help button ⌕**

   A list of search results appears for the keywords you specified. As shown in Figure A-16, the 30 best results for editing digital photos are listed.

QUICK TIP

If you click a topic under "In this article," the window automatically scrolls to that topic.

5. **Click Working with digital pictures in the list of Help topics**

   This Help topic explains how to get pictures from a camera into your computer—just what you need as a tour guide.

6. **In the second paragraph, click flash memory card (shown in green)**

   The definition of a flash memory card and how you can use this device appears.

7. **Click the Close button ⊠ in the upper-right corner of the Windows Help and Support window**

   The Windows Help and Support window closes.

Using Windows Online Help

Windows Vista Help and Support provides answers on how to use basic and advanced Windows Vista features. You can get additional help from the Microsoft Windows Help and How-to Web site. On this Web site, you can find more information about basic and advanced Windows Vista features, view "how-to" videos, get help from other people in Windows Vista online discussion groups, read up-to-date articles on changes in Windows Vista, and get online support from Microsoft technical support staff. To open the Windows Online Help and Support Home page, click Windows Online Help in the Find an answer section of the Windows Help and Support window.

FIGURE A-15: Windows Help and Support window

Back button

Forward button

Help category

Home button

Options button

Ask button

Browse Help button

Print button

Online Help

FIGURE A-16: Search results

Search keywords

Search results

Search Help button

Search Help text box

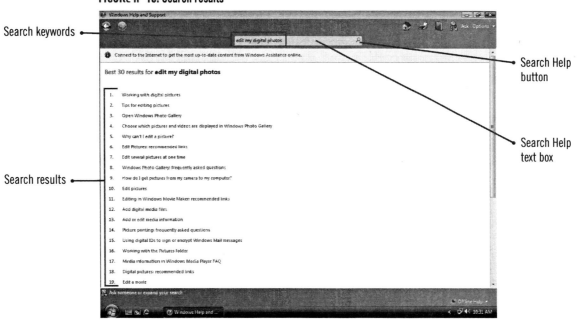

TABLE A-7: Windows Help and Support toolbar buttons

button icon	button name	purpose
	Back	Takes you back to previous Help topic(s)
	Forward	Returns you to Help topic(s) you just left (available only after you click the Back button)
	Home	Opens the Help and Support starting page
	Print	Prints a Help topic
	Browse Help	Displays a list of Help topics to browse
	Ask	Provides additional resources and tools for finding Help information
	Options	Lists options for printing, browsing Help, adjusting the Help text size, searching a Help topic page, and changing Help settings

Ending a Windows Vista Session

When you finish working on your computer, you should save and close any open files, close any open programs, close any open windows, and shut down Windows. As shown in Table A-8, there are various options for ending your Windows sessions. Whichever option you choose, it's important to shut down your computer in an orderly manner. If you turn off the computer while Windows Vista is running, you could lose data or damage Windows Vista and your computer. If you are working in a computer lab, follow your instructor's directions and your lab's policies and guidelines for ending your Windows session. ███ You have examined the basic ways in which you can use Windows Vista, so you are ready to end your Windows Vista session.

STEPS

1. **Click the Start button 🪟 on the taskbar**

   The Start menu has three buttons for ending a Windows session—the Power button, the Lock button, and the Lock menu button.

QUICK TIP

Some keyboards have Log Off and Sleep keys that you can press to perform these operations.

2. **Point to the Lock menu button ▶**

   The Lock menu lists all the shut-down options. See Figure A-17.

3. **If you are working in a computer lab, follow the instructions provided by your instructor or technical support person for ending your Windows Vista session; if you are working on your own computer, click Shut Down or the option you prefer for ending your Windows Vista session**

   After you shut down your computer, you may also need to turn off your monitor and other hardware devices, such as a printer, to conserve energy.

FIGURE A-17: Shut down Windows Vista options

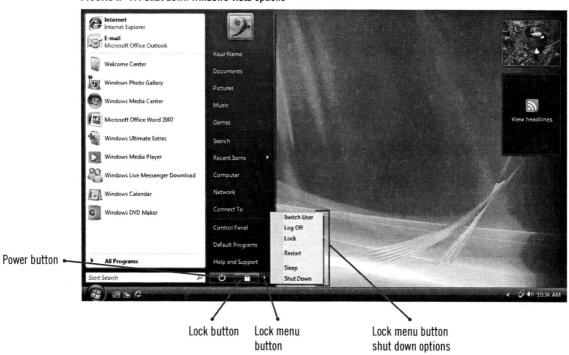

Power button

Lock button   Lock menu button

Lock menu button shut down options

TABLE A-8: Options for ending a Windows Vista session

option	description	click
Shut Down	Completely shuts down your computer.	Start button, Lock menu button, Shut Down
Log Off	Closes all windows, programs, and documents, then displays the Welcome screen.	Start button, Lock menu button, Log Off
Restart	Shuts down your computer, then restarts it.	Start button, Lock menu button, Restart
Switch User	Locks your user account and displays the Welcome screen so another user can log on.	Start button, Lock menu button, Switch User
Lock	Locks your user account, then displays the Welcome screen.	Start button, Lock button, OR Start button, Lock menu button, Lock
Sleep	Saves your work, turns off the monitor, then reduces power consumption to all hardware components in your computer so it appears off.	Start button, Power button, OR Start button, Lock menu button, Sleep
Hibernate	Saves your work, then turns off your computer.	Start button, Lock menu button, Hibernate

Getting Started with Windows Vista

Practice

▼ CONCEPTS REVIEW

Identify each of the items labeled in Figure A-18.

FIGURE A-18

Match each statement with the term it describes.

12. A desktop object that displays buttons for open programs and windows
13. A desktop object that represents a program or Windows tool
14. A type of window that opens after you select a menu command so you can specify settings for completing the operation
15. A Windows component for adjusting your view within a window
16. The workspace within which you work with a program

   a. dialog box
   b. taskbar
   c. scroll bar
   d. window
   e. icon

Select the best answer from the list of choices.

17. **Operating system software is software that:**
   a. Interferes with your use of a computer.
   b. Manages the operation of a computer.
   c. Performs a single task, such as connecting to the Internet.
   d. Creates documents, such as a resume.

18. **When you right-click a pointing device such as a mouse, Windows:**
   a. Opens a Windows tool or program.
   b. Moves an object, such as a desktop icon.
   c. Opens a shortcut menu.
   d. Deletes the object.

19. **What portion of a window displays the name of the program you opened?**
    a. Title bar
    b. Menu bar
    c. Toolbar
    d. Scroll bar

20. **You use the Maximize button to:**
    a. Restore a window to its previous size and location.
    b. Expand a window to fill the entire desktop.
    c. Temporarily hide a window.
    d. Scroll through a window.

21. **When you put a computer to sleep, Windows:**
    a. Completely shuts down the computer.
    b. Provides an option for switching users.
    c. Restarts your computer.
    d. Reduces power to the computer and its hardware.

▼ SKILLS REVIEW

1. **Start Windows Vista and view the desktop.**
    a. Turn on your computer, select your user account or enter your user name, then enter your password (if necessary).
    b. Identify and list as many components of the Windows Vista desktop as you can without referring to the lessons.
    c. Compare your results to Figure A-1 to make sure that you have identified all the desktop objects and icons.

2. **Use a pointing device.**
    a. Point to the Recycle Bin icon and display its ToolTip.
    b. Double-click the Recycle Bin icon, then restore down the Recycle Bin window if it is maximized.
    c. Drag the Recycle Bin window to the upper-left corner of the desktop, then close the window.

3. **Start a program.**
    a. Open the Start menu.
    b. Display a list of all programs.
    c. Start Windows Calendar.

4. **Move and resize windows.**
    a. If the Windows Calendar window is maximized, restore down the window.
    b. Adjust the height and width of the window in one operation.
    c. Maximize, minimize, then restore the Windows Calendar window.

5. **Use menus, toolbars, and keyboard shortcuts.**
    a. Open the View menu on the menu bar, then choose Month to display a calendar for the current month.
    b. Use the View button on the toolbar to display a calendar for the current day.
    c. In the mini-calendar in the Navigation pane on the left, click the date for the next day to view its schedule.
    d. Use the keyboard shortcut [Alt][F4] to close Windows Calendar.

6. **Use dialog boxes.**
    a. If you do not see the Sidebar on the desktop, open the Start menu, display the All Programs menu, and then choose Windows Sidebar from the Accessories menu (or click the Windows Sidebar icon in the Notification area).
    b. Right-click the Clock gadget, then click Options to view settings for the Clock gadget.
    c. Under the preview of a clock, use the Next button to advance through the eight options for viewing the Clock.
    d. Use the Previous button to return to the first (default) view for the Clock gadget.
    e. Click the Cancel button to close the Clock dialog box without making any changes to the settings.

7. **Use scroll bars.**
    a. From the Start menu, open Windows Help and Support and maximize the window (if necessary).
    b. Open the Windows Basics Help topic.
    c. Use the down scroll arrow in the vertical scroll bar to examine other Help topics.
    d. Use the up scroll arrow in the vertical scroll bar to view previously displayed Help topics.
    e. Use the scroll box in the vertical scroll bar to view the last Windows Basics Help topic.

8. **Use Windows Help and Support.**
    a. Open "The Start menu (overview)" Help topic.
    b. Read the information about the Start menu in the first two paragraphs (through the bulleted list).
    c. Use the Search Help box to locate help on gadgets.

Getting Started with Windows Vista

   d. Open the Help topic entitled "Windows Sidebar and gadgets (overview)."

   e. Under "In this article," click "Adding and removing gadgets" to jump to this Help topic.

   f. Click "To add a gadget to Sidebar" (shown in blue) to view the steps for this process, then click the "To remove a gadget from Sidebar" (shown in blue) to view the single step for this process.

   g. Close the Windows Help and Support window.

9. End a Windows Vista session.

   a. If you are working in a computer lab, follow the instructions provided by your instructor for using the Start menu to log off the computer, restart the computer, put the computer to sleep, or shut down the computer completely. If you are working on your own computer, use the Start menu to choose the shut-down option you prefer.

▼ INDEPENDENT CHALLENGE 1

You work as a teacher for ABC Computer Mentors. You need to prepare a set of handouts that provide an overview of some of the new desktop features in Windows Vista for individuals enrolled in an upcoming class on Computer Survival Skills.

   a. Open Windows Help and Support, then open the Windows Basics Help topic.

   b. Open the Using menus, buttons, bars, and boxes Help topic under Desktop Fundamentals.

   c. Use the vertical scroll bar to read the entire Help topic.

   d. Prepare a handwritten list of 10 new features that you learned about working with menus, buttons, bars, and boxes. Use the following title for your list: Using Menus, Buttons, Bars, and Boxes

   e. Close Windows Help and Support, write your name on your list, and submit it to your instructor.

▼ INDEPENDENT CHALLENGE 2

You are a freelance photographer who takes photographs for magazine covers, articles, newsletters, and Web sites. You want to evaluate how the Windows Photo Gallery can be used to make simple changes to digital photos.

   a. Open Windows Help and Support and search for tips on editing pictures in Windows Photo Gallery.

   b. After reading the Tips for editing pictures Help topic, prepare a handwritten summary with the title Tips for Editing Pictures, listing the recommended workflow for editing pictures in Windows Photo Gallery. (*Hint:* Use the first figure in the Help topic on the recommended workflow in Photo Gallery to identify the four steps.)

   c. Use Windows Help and Support to search for information on how to remove red eye from a picture.

   d. Add to your summary a short paragraph that describes red eye and how you can correct this problem with Windows Photo Gallery.

   e. Close Windows Help and Support, write your name on your summary, and submit it to your instructor.

▼ INDEPENDENT CHALLENGE 3

As a marketing analyst for Expert AI Systems, Ltd., in Great Britain, you contact and collaborate with employees at an Australian branch of the company. Because your colleagues live in a different time zone, you want to add another clock to your Sidebar and customize it to show the time in Australia. This way, you can quickly determine when to reach these employees at a convenient time during their workday hours.

   a. If Windows does not display the Sidebar on the desktop, use the All Programs menu or the Windows Sidebar icon in the Notification area to display the Sidebar.

   b. Use Windows Help and Support to search for information on how to customize the Windows Sidebar and how to change an individual gadget's options.

   c. Use this Help information to view the settings for the Clock gadget on the Sidebar, then try each setting.

   d. Click Cancel to close the Clock dialog box without changing the settings.

▼ INDEPENDENT CHALLENGE 3 (CONTINUED)

Advanced Challenge Exercise

- Point to the Gadgets toolbar at the top of the Sidebar, then click the Add Gadget button.
- Double-click the Clock gadget in the Add Gadgets dialog box, then close the Add Gadgets dialog box.
- Drag the new copy of the Clock gadget and place it below the last gadget on the Sidebar.
- Right-click the new Clock gadget, then click Options on the shortcut menu to view settings for the new Clock.
- Choose a different view for the clock and, in the Clock name text box, type **Australia**.
- Click the Time Zone list arrow to display a list of different time zones, then click the time zone for Canberra, Melbourne, and Sydney. (*Hint:* You want the GMT+10:00 time zone near the bottom of the list of time zones.)
- Add a check mark to the "Show the second hand" check box to enable this feature.
- Click OK to close the Clock dialog box.
- Right-click the new Clock gadget, then click Close Gadget on the shortcut menu to restore your Sidebar to its original state.

e. Prepare a handwritten summary entitled **Using Clock Gadgets** that describes what settings you examined and how you might use them in your daily life.

f. Write your name on your summary and submit it to your instructor.

▼ REAL LIFE INDEPENDENT CHALLENGE

In preparation for an upcoming convention to present new products produced by your company, Continental Saunas, Inc., you decide to prepare a slide show using the Windows Photo Gallery.

a. Open Windows Help and Support, then search for Help information on viewing your pictures as a slide show.

b. Read the Help information, studying the features of the Slide Show Controls toolbar and slide show themes.

c. Open the Photo Gallery Viewer from the Slide Show gadget on the Sidebar.

d. Use the Play Slide Show button to view a slide show of the photos in your Pictures folder.

Advanced Challenge Exercise

Note: To view the Slide Show Controls toolbar as well as certain themes and transitions, your computer must have a graphics card capable of displaying these features and special effects.

- After the slide show starts, move your pointing device to display the Slide Show Controls toolbar.
- Use the Slide Show Controls toolbar to perform the following operations during the slide show. Note the default setting for specific buttons, which options you choose, and what they do so that you can prepare a short written summary for co-workers who might use the Windows Photo Gallery for slide shows.
- Use the Themes pop-up list button to select and view other themes (or presentation formats) for slide shows. Note the default theme, try at least three other themes, then restore the default theme.
- Use the Slide Show Settings button to change the slide show speed and examine the Shuffle and Loop options, then restore the default slide show speed and Shuffle or Loop option.
- Use the Previous and Next buttons to view the previous and next image.
- Use the Exit button to end the slide show.

e. Prepare a one-page handwritten summary titled **Photo Gallery Slide Show** that describes what you have learned about the Windows Photo Gallery and how you might use it in your daily life.

f. Write your name on the summary and submit it to your instructor.

▼ VISUAL WORKSHOP

After returning from a Quest Specialty Travel tour, you want to print a copy of a digital photo to promote an upcoming trip. Use the skills you have learned in this lesson to print a copy of a digital photo:

- Use Windows Help and Support to search for information on how to print a picture using Windows Photo Gallery.
- Use the Slide Show gadget to open the Windows Photo Gallery, then choose the option to print a 4 x 6 inch copy of the image on letter-size paper, as shown in Figure A-19.
- Write your name on the printed copy and submit it to your instructor.

FIGURE A-19

Understanding File Management

You use Windows Vista to access the drives where you store your folders and files. Each **drive** on your computer is a physical location for storing files. Most people store their files on the computer's hard disk drive and keep duplicate copies on other drives, such as a USB flash drive. The **hard disk** is a built-in, high-capacity, high-speed storage medium for all the software, folders, and files on a computer. When you create a document or other types of data with a program, you save the results in a file, which consists of stored electronic data such as text, a picture, a video, or music. Each file is stored in a folder, which is a container for a group of related files such as reports, correspondence, or e-mail contacts. As a tour guide for Quest Specialty Travel (QST), you want to better understand how you can use Windows Vista to manage the files you need for proposing, planning, organizing, and documenting QST tours.

OBJECTIVES

Manage folders and files

Open the Computer window

Create and save documents

Open the Documents folder

Copy files

Open, edit, and print files

Move and rename files

Search for files

Delete and restore files

Managing Folders and Files

Most of the work you do on a computer involves using programs to create files, which you then store in folders. Over time, you create many folders and files and save them on different storage media. The process of organizing and finding your folders and files can become a challenge. It is helpful to develop a strategy for organizing your folders and files; these tasks are referred to as **file management**. Windows Vista provides a variety of file management tools to assist you in these tasks. ▄▄▟▛ As a QST tour guide for destinations in the South Pacific, you work with many types of files. You want to review how Windows can help you track and organize your files.

You can use Windows Vista to:

> In an office, a paper *file* refers to a manila folder that contains documents printed on paper, whereas a paper *folder* commonly refers to a hanging folder in which you place printed documents or manila folders that contain printed documents.

- **Create folders for storing and organizing files**

  Folders provide a location for your important files and help you organize them into groups of related files so that you can easily locate a file later. You give each folder you create a unique, descriptive **folder name** that identifies the files you intend to place in the folder. A folder can also contain other folders, called **subfolders**, to help organize files into smaller groups. This structure for organizing folders and files is called a **file hierarchy** because it describes the logic and layout of the folder structure on a disk. Windows Vista provides the Documents folder in which you create folders and subfolders for saving your files on your hard disk drive. Most programs automatically open and use the Documents folder when you save or open files. Figure B-1 illustrates how you might organize your tour folders and files within the Documents folder. Windows Vista provides other folders dedicated to specific types of files, such as the Pictures folder for image files; the Music folder for music or sound files; the Contacts folder for e-mail addresses and other contact information, including names, addresses, and phone numbers; and the Favorites folder for Internet shortcuts to your preferred Web sites. Figure B-2 shows the standard folders that Windows Vista creates for each user.

- **Rename, copy, and move folders and files**

  If you want to change the name of a folder or file, you can rename it. For example, you might change the name of the "French Polynesia Tour Proposal" file to "French Polynesia Tour" after your supervisor approves the tour. If you need a duplicate of a file, you can copy it. For example, you could make a copy of the "French Polynesia Tour" file, rename the copy to "Fiji Islands Tour Proposal," then modify the file's content for a new tour location. You can also move a folder or file to another folder or disk and physically change its location.

- **Delete and restore folders and files**

  Deleting folders and files you no longer need frees up storage space on your disk and helps keep your files organized. Folders and files deleted from your hard disk are moved to a Windows folder called the Recycle Bin. If you accidentally delete an important folder or file, or if you change your mind and want to restore a deleted folder or file, you can retrieve it from the Recycle Bin. Folders or files deleted from a removable disk, such as a USB flash drive, are permanently removed and cannot be retrieved with Windows.

- **Locate folders and files quickly using Instant Search**

  Instant Search helps you quickly locate a folder or file if you forget where you stored it. If you can provide part of the folder or file name—or some other fact about the item, such as the author's name—Instant Search can easily locate it and save you a lot of time and effort.

- **Use shortcuts to access frequently used files and folders**

  As your file structure becomes more complex, a file or folder you use often might be located several levels down the file hierarchy and require multiple steps to open. To save time, you can create shortcuts on your desktop to the files and folders you use frequently. A **shortcut** is a link that gives you quick access to a folder, file, or Web site. As shown in Figure B-2, Windows uses shortcuts to folders that contain sample files, such as pictures, music, and videos. Also, each program listed on the All Programs menu is a shortcut to the actual program stored elsewhere on your computer.

FIGURE B-1: Sample folder and file hierarchy

FIGURE B-2: Default user folders in Windows Vista

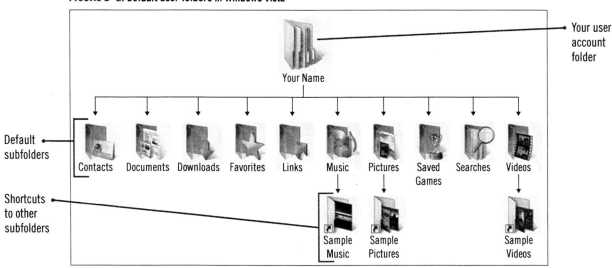

Organizing your folders and files efficiently

Good planning is essential for effective file management. First, identify the types of files you work with, such as images, music, and reports, then determine a logical system for organizing your files. The Pictures and Music folders are good places to store images and music. The Documents folder is the most common place to store all of your other files. Within each folder, use subfolders to better organize the files into smaller groups. For example, use subfolders in the Pictures folder to separate family photos from vacation photos, or to group them by year. In the Documents folder, you might group personal files in one subfolder and business files in another subfolder, then create additional subfolders to further distinguish sets of files. For example, your personal files might include subfolders for resumes, letters, and income tax returns, to name a few. Your business files might include subfolders for clients, projects, and invoices. You should periodically reevaluate your folder structure to ensure that it continues to meet your needs.

Opening the Computer Window

The **Computer window** shows the drives on your computer organized into two groups—Hard Disk Drives and Devices with Removable Storage. A **device** is a hardware component in your computer system. **Removable storage** refers to storage media that you can easily transfer from one computer to another, such as DVDs, CDs, or flash drives. **USB flash drives** (also called pen drives, jump drives, keychain drives, and thumb drives) are a popular removable storage device because of their ease of use and portability. When you attach a USB flash drive to a computer, a new drive icon appears under Devices with Removable Storage. To distinguish one drive from another, each drive has a unique **drive name** that consists of a letter followed by a colon, such as C: for the hard disk drive. Table B-1 lists examples of different drive types. Table B-2 lists commonly used terms to describe the storage capacities of different types of disks. ▄▄▄ Before you plan your next tour, you want to see what types of drives are available on your computer.

STEPS

1. **Start your computer and** Windows Vista, **logging onto your computer if necessary**

QUICK TIP

The **Navigation Pane** contains links to your personal folders, including the Documents, Pictures, and Music folders.

2. **Click the Start button** ⊕ **on the taskbar, click Computer on the right side of the Start menu, then click the Maximize button** ▭ **if the Computer window does not fill the desktop**

   The Computer window opens, displaying icons for the hard disk drive and removable storage devices on your computer. Your computer may have more than one hard disk drive or other types of removable storage. You may also see icons for other types of hardware, such as a scanner or digital camera.

TROUBLE

If the Details Pane is hidden, click the Organize button on the toolbar, point to Layout, then click Details Pane.

3. **Under Hard Disk Drives, click the your hard disk drive icon**

   As shown in Figure B-3, the **Details Pane** at the bottom of the Computer window shows a friendly name for your hard disk drive (such as Local Disk), its actual drive name (C:), the total size or total storage capacity, the amount of free space, and a horizontal bar that shows the storage space already being used on the hard disk drive. When you select the hard disk drive (or some other drive), the options on the toolbar change to ones available for that drive.

4. **Click the Close button** ▣ **on the Computer window title bar**

   The Computer window closes.

TABLE B-1: Drive names and drive icons

drive type	drive icon	friendly name	drive name	referred to as
floppy disk drive	🖫	3½ Floppy	A:	drive A
hard disk drive	🖴	Local Disk	C:	drive C
CD drive	💿	CD-RW Drive, CD-R Drive, or CD-ROM Drive	next available drive letter; for example, D:	drive D
DVD drive	📀	DVD-RW Drive, DVD-R Drive, or DVD-ROM Drive	next available drive letter; for example, E:	drive E
USB flash drive	🖾	[varies with drive]	next available drive letter; for example, F:	drive F

Understanding File Management

FIGURE B-3: Computer window

Address Bar

Navigation Pane

Details Pane

Toolbar

Friendly name

Drive name

Drive icon

TABLE B-2: Disk storage capacity terms

term	equals approximately	example	storage space
byte	one character of storage space on disk or in RAM (memory)	A simple text file with the phrase *To-Do List*	10 bytes; count all the characters in the phrase including the hyphen and the blank space between the two words (10 characters = 10 bytes of storage space)
kilobyte (KB or K)	one thousand bytes	A file with a 10-page term paper (approximately 3500 characters per page)	35 KB (approximately 35,000 bytes)
megabyte (MB or M)	one million bytes (or one thousand kilobytes)	512 MB USB flash drive	512 MB (approximately 512 million bytes)
gigabyte (GB or G)	one billion bytes (or one thousand megabytes)	350 GB hard disk	350 GB (approximately 350 billion bytes)
terabyte (TB or T)	one trillion bytes (or one thousand gigabytes)	1 TB hard disk drive	1 TB (approximately one trillion bytes)

Displaying the Computer icon on the desktop

By default, the Computer icon does not appear on the desktop. You can display the Computer icon on the desktop so you can open the Computer window in one step rather than from the Start menu, which involves several steps. To add the Computer icon to your desktop, click the Start button, right-click Computer, then click Show on Desktop. You can now quickly open the Computer window by double-clicking the Computer icon on the desktop. You can repeat these steps to remove the Computer icon from the desktop.

Understanding File Management

Creating and Saving Documents

Windows comes with easy-to-use programs called Accessories. For example, you can use the WordPad Accessory to create simple text documents such as a letter or to-do list. Any document you create with WordPad (or another program) is temporarily stored in your computer's **RAM (random access memory)**. Anything stored in RAM is lost when you turn off your computer or the power fails unexpectedly. Before you close a document or exit WordPad, you must create a permanent copy of the document by saving it as a file on a disk. You can save files in the **Documents folder** on your local hard disk drive (drive C) or on a removable storage device such as a USB flash drive. When you name a file, choose a **filename** that clearly identifies the file contents. Filenames can be no more than 255 characters, including spaces and can include letters, numbers, and certain symbols. ▰▰▰ You want to use WordPad to create a to-do list for your next tour, then save the file to the Documents folder. The To-Do List is shown in Figure B-4.

1. **Click the Start button ⊕ on the taskbar, point to All Programs, click Accessories, then click WordPad**

   The WordPad window opens with a new, blank document. Table B-3 identifies the components of the WordPad window. In the document window, a blinking **insertion point** indicates where the next character you type will appear.

   QUICK TIP

   If you make a typing mistake, press [Backspace] to delete the character to the left of the insertion point.

2. **Type To-Do List on the first line, then press [Enter] three times**

   Each time you press [Enter], WordPad inserts a new blank line and places the insertion point at the beginning of the line.

3. **Type the text shown in Figure B-4, pressing [Enter] at the end of each line**

   TROUBLE

   If the Documents folder is not displayed, click Documents in the Navigation Pane.

4. **Click File on the menu bar, click Save As, then click the Browse Folders button in the Save As dialog box**

   The Save As dialog box expands to show the contents of the Documents folder, as shown in Figure B-5.

5. **Click Document.rtf in the File name text box to select it, then type To-Do List**

   TROUBLE

   If a Confirm Save As dialog box asks if you want to replace a file with the same name, click Yes.

6. **Click Save in the Save As dialog box**

   WordPad saves the document in a file named "To-Do List" in the Documents folder and closes the Save As dialog box. The title bar displays "To-Do List.rtf"—the filename you entered followed by the file extension .rtf. A **file extension** identifies the type of file. Each program assigns a file extension to files you create, so you only need to enter a name for the file. Depending on how Windows is set up, you may not see the file extensions.

7. **Click the Close button ▧ on the WordPad title bar**

FIGURE B-3: Components of the WordPad window

component	used to
Title bar	Display the name of the open document and program
Menu bar	Display menu names with commands for performing operations on a document and its contents and for specifying program settings
Toolbar	Display buttons for common menu commands, such as saving and printing
Format bar	Display buttons for formatting, or enhancing, the appearance of a document
Ruler	Mark a document's width in ⅛ths of an inch (also shows one-inch marks)
Document window	Display all or part of the open document
Status bar	Display simple Help information and tips

Understanding File Management

FIGURE B-4: WordPad document

Temporary filename

Program name

Insertion point

Toolbar

Format bar

Ruler

Document window

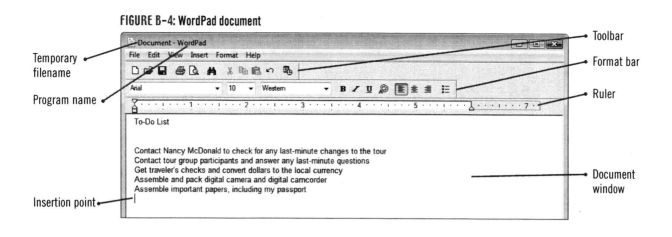

FIGURE B-5: Save As dialog box

Current folder

Folders in the current folder (yours will differ)

Navigation Pane

Temporary filename

Type of file

Using the Address Bar in the Save As dialog box

The **Address Bar** shows your current location in the computer's file hierarchy as a series of links separated by arrows. In Figure B-5, this series of links appears as an icon followed by "Your Name" (your user account folder name) then Documents. If you click the leftmost arrow in the Address Bar, you can use the drop-down list that opens to switch to the desktop, the Computer window, or other system folders. If you click the arrow after your user account name, you can use the list that opens to switch to any of your user account folders, such as Contacts, Music, Pictures, and Videos. If you click the arrow after Documents, you can use the list that opens to switch to a subfolder in the Documents folder, as shown in Figure B-6.

FIGURE B-6: Address Bar drop-down menu

Address Bar

Address Bar arrow displays a drop-down list of subfolders within the Documents folder

Subfolders in the Documents folder

Opening the Documents Folder

The Documents folder is the most common place to store files you create or receive from others. From the Documents folder, you can examine your files, organize them into subfolders, or perform other common file management tasks such as renaming, copying, moving, or deleting a folder or file. ▰▰▰▰ You store all your QST tour files in the Documents folder on your computer. You want to organize the files in your Documents folder before you copy them to a USB flash drive.

STEPS

1. **Click the Start button ⊛ on the taskbar, then click Documents**

   The Documents window opens and displays your folders and files, including the To-Do List.rtf file. Table B-4 identifies the components of the Documents window.

   TROUBLE
   If your view did not change, Windows Vista is already set to Large Icons view.

2. **Click the Views button arrow on the toolbar, then click Large Icons**

   Like some of the other views, Large Icons view displays folder icons with different icons for the types of files (such as a text document) contained in a folder or a **live view** of the actual content in files.

   QUICK TIP
   The Layout option on the Organize menu controls whether to display the Details, Preview, and Navigation panes.

3. **If you do not see the Preview Pane on the right side of the window, click the Organize button on the toolbar, point to Layout, then click Preview Pane**

   The **Preview Pane** shows the actual contents of the selected file, such as the WordPad file, without starting a program. Preview may not work for some types of files.

4. **Click the To-Do List.rtf file icon**

   The Preview Pane shows the actual contents of your To-Do List file, and the Details Pane lists information about the file itself, including the dates it was created and last modified, and its size. See Figure B-7.

5. **Leave the Documents window open for the next lesson**

TABLE B-4: Components of the Documents window

component	used to
Back button	Go back to previously viewed folders
Forward button	Return to the folders you just left
Address Bar	Display the name of the current folder and navigate to a different folder
Search box	Locate files or folders in the current folder
Toolbar	Perform common tasks on a folder or its contents (such as changing the view or e-mailing a file)
Navigation Pane	Navigate to another folder
File list	Display the subfolders and files in the current folder
Details Pane	View information about the folder or file you select in the File list
Preview Pane	View the actual content within some types of files

Understanding File Management

FIGURE B-7: Documents window

Forward button
Back button
Address Bar
Navigation Pane
Files list (shows folders and files in Large Icons view)

Search box
Toolbar
Preview Pane
Details Pane

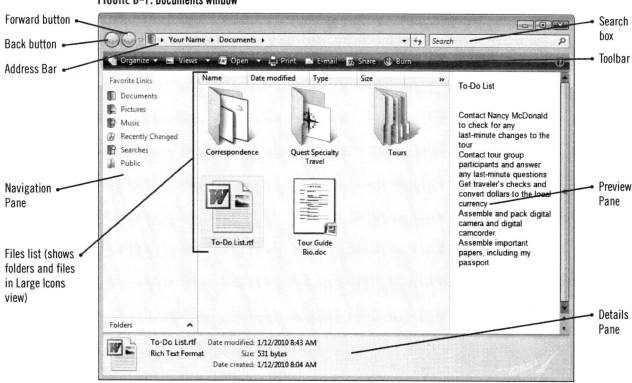

Changing views in a window

The Views button provides seven ways to display the folders and files in a window. Extra Large Icons, Large Icons, and Medium Icons views display rows of folder and file icons at different sizes, with their names displayed under the icon. Small Icons view displays rows of even smaller folder and file icons with the folder or filename to the right of the icon. List view displays columns of very small folder or filename icons with the names to the right of the icon. Tiles view is similar to Small Icons view, but displays larger icons and also lists the type of folder or file and the file size. Details view is similar to List view, but displays columns with the folder or filename, the date and time that a folder or file was modified, the type of folder or file, the size of files, and any tags assigned to a file. A **tag** is a word or phrase that reminds you of a file's content. You can use the Views button slider bar to scale icons to your preferred size between Small Icons and Extra Large Icons.

Understanding File Management

Copying Files

You can copy a file, a group of files, or a folder from one disk drive to another or from one folder to another. When you **copy** a file, the original file stays in its current location and a duplicate of the file is created in another location. This feature lets you make a backup of your important files. A **backup** is a copy of a file that is stored in another location. If you lose the original file, you can make a new working copy from your backup. You can use the Send To menu to quickly copy a file from the Documents folder to another disk drive. You want to copy your To-Do List.rtf file to your USB flash drive so you can work with the file as you travel.

STEPS

TROUBLE

If you are using a different storage device, insert the appropriate disk and substitute that device whenever you see USB flash drive in the steps.

1. **Attach your USB flash drive to your computer or to a cable connected to your computer, then, if the AutoPlay dialog box opens, click the Close button ⊠**
   Your USB flash drive is ready to use.

2. **Right-click the To-Do List.rtf file icon, then point to Send To on the shortcut menu**
   A list of the available drives and locations where you can copy the file appears on the shortcut menu, as shown in Figure B-8. The options on your Send To menu will differ.

QUICK TIP

If you hold down [Shift] while you click a Send To option, Windows moves the file to that disk; it does not make another copy

3. **Click the USB flash drive option**
   Windows copies the To-Do List.rtf file to your USB flash drive. There are now two copies of the same file stored in two different locations.

4. **Click the first Address Bar arrow ▶ on the Address Bar, as shown in Figure B-9, then click Computer**
   The contents of the Computer folder appear in the window.

5. **Double-click the USB flash drive icon**
   The contents of your USB flash drive, including the To-Do List.rtf file you copied to this disk, appear in the window. See Figure B-10.

6. **Click the Close button ⊠ on the Removable Disk window title bar**

Using the Send To menu

You can create a shortcut on the desktop to any folder or file you use frequently with the "Desktop (create shortcut)" option on the Send To menu. The Compressed (zipped) Folder option on the Send To menu creates a new compressed file using the same filename, but with the .zip file extension. For example, compressing To-Do List.rtf creates a new file named To-Do List.zip. Before you send a file by e-mail, especially a large file, it is a good idea to **compress** it, which makes the file smaller in size.

FIGURE B-8: Send To menu

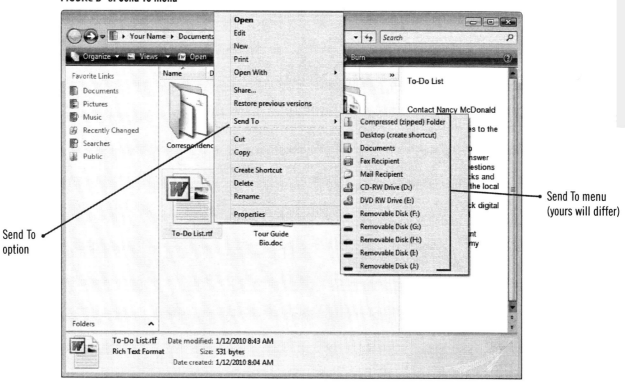

Send To option

Send To menu (yours will differ)

FIGURE B-9: Navigating with the Address Bar

Address Bar arrow displays a drop-down list of locations

Switches to the Computer window

FIGURE B-10: Removable Disk window

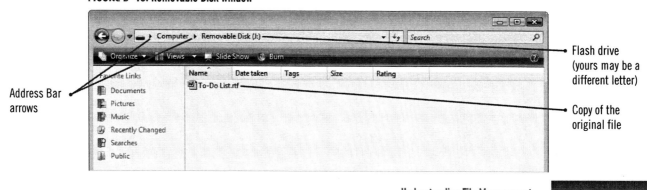

Address Bar arrows

Flash drive (yours may be a different letter)

Copy of the original file

Opening, Editing, and Printing Files

Sometimes you create new files, as you did in the previous lesson. But often, you want to change a file that you or someone else already created. After you open an existing file stored on a disk, you can **edit**, or make changes, to it. For example, you might want to add or delete text, or change the **formatting** or appearance of the text. After you finish editing, you usually save the file with the same filename, which replaces the file with a new copy that contains all your most recent changes. If you want to keep the original file, you can save the edited file with a different filename; this keeps the original file without the edits and creates a new copy of the file with the most recent changes. When you want a **hard copy**, or paper copy of the file, you need to print it. ▓▓▓▓ You need to add two items to your To-Do List, so you want to open and edit the file you created in WordPad, then print the To-Do List.

STEPS

1. **Click the Start button ⊕ on the taskbar, point to All Programs, click Accessories, then click WordPad**

   The WordPad program window opens.

2. **Click the Open button 📂 on the WordPad toolbar, click Computer in the Navigation Pane, then double-click your USB flash drive icon**

   The Open dialog box displays the contents of your USB flash drive. See Figure B-11. You may see additional files.

QUICK TIP
You can also open a file by double-clicking it in the Open dialog box.

3. **Click To-Do List.rtf in the File list, then click Open in the Open dialog box**

   The Open dialog box closes and the To-Do List.rtf file appears in the WordPad window.

4. **Click at the beginning of the last blank line in the To-Do List, then type the two additional lines shown in Figure B-12, pressing [Enter] after each line**

5. **Click the Save button 💾 on the WordPad toolbar**

   WordPad saves the edited To-Do List.rtf file under the same filename on your USB flash drive.

QUICK TIP
You should always use Print Preview before you print to save time and effort as well as toner ink and paper.

6. **Click the Print Preview button 🔍 on the WordPad toolbar**

   Print Preview displays a full-page view of your document, as shown in Figure B-13, so you can check its layout before you print. Dotted lines separate the area on the page reserved for the document and the blank space reserved for the left, right, top, and bottom margins. If you need to make additional edits, click the Close button on the Print Preview toolbar (not the title bar), make your changes, then use Print Preview to check the document again before printing.

7. **Click the Print button on the Print Preview toolbar**

   Print Preview closes and the Print dialog box opens, so you can verify the print settings.

8. **Click Print in the Print dialog box, then retrieve your printed copy from the printer**

9. **Click the Close button ✖ on the WordPad title bar**

   WordPad closes.

Comparing Save and Save As

The File menu has two save options—Save and Save As. When you first save a file, the Save As dialog box opens (whether you choose Save or Save As) so you can select the drive and folder where you want to save the file and enter its filename. If you edit and save a previously saved file, you can save the file to the same location with the same filename, you can change the location or filename, or you can do both. Save updates the file stored on disk using the same location and filename without opening the Save As dialog box. Save As opens the Save As dialog box so you can save an updated copy of the file to another location or with a new filename.

Understanding File Management

FIGURE B-11: Open dialog box

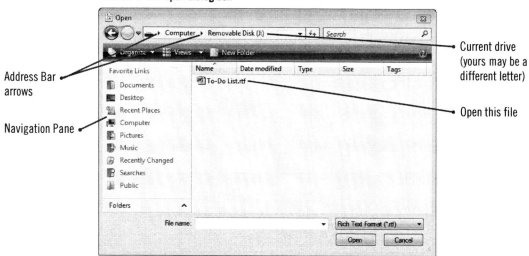

Address Bar arrows

Navigation Pane

Current drive (yours may be a different letter)

Open this file

FIGURE B-12: Edited To-Do List file

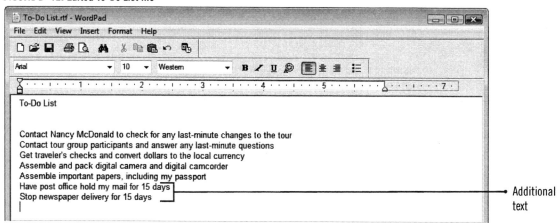

Additional text

FIGURE B-13: Print Preview

Closes the document and WordPad

Closes Print Preview, but not the document

Top margin

Left margin

Right margin

Bottom margin

Understanding File Management

Moving and Renaming Files

You can move a file, a group of files, or a folder to another location such as a different folder on the same drive or a different drive. When you **move** a file, the original file is stored in a different location. One of the fastest ways to move a file is with **drag and drop** (which uses a pointing device to drag a file or folder to a new location). You may also need to rename a file, giving it a name that more clearly describes the file's contents and how you intend to use the file. ◆◆◆◆ You want to move the To-Do List.rtf file to a new folder and rename it so you can update the list for your next tour.

STEPS

1. **Click the Start button ⊕ on the taskbar, click Computer, then double-click your USB flash drive icon**
   The contents of your USB flash drive appear in the Computer window.

2. **Click the Views button arrow on the Computer window toolbar, then click Large Icons**
   The larger icons make it easier to work with folder and file icons as you move and rename files.

3. **Click the Organize button on the Computer window toolbar, then click New Folder**
   Windows creates a new folder named "New Folder," as shown in Figure B-14. The folder name is highlighted so you can type a more descriptive folder name.

4. **Type French Polynesia Tour as the folder name, then press [Enter]**
   Windows changes the name of the folder.

TROUBLE
If you cannot type a name for the new folder, press [F2] (the Rename key), then repeat Step 4.

5. **Click the white background of the window, point to the To-Do List.rtf file, press and hold the left button on your pointing device, drag the To-Do List.rtf file icon on top of the French Polynesia Tour folder, then pause**
   As shown in Figure B-15, a smaller transparent copy of the To-Do List.rtf file icon appears over the French Polynesia Tour folder and a ToolTip describes the type of operation.

6. **Release the left button on your pointing device**
   The To-Do List.rtf file moves into the French Polynesia Tour folder.

7. **Double-click the French Polynesia Tour folder**
   The Address Bar shows the name of the open folder, French Polynesia Tour. The To-Do List.rtf file appears in this folder.

8. **Click the To-Do List.rtf file icon, click the Organize button, then click Rename**
   The first part of the filename is highlighted so you can type a new name for the file.

9. **Type Tour Preparation as the new filename, then press [Enter]**
   Windows renames the file. See Figure B-16.

10. **Click the Close button ▣ on the title bar**

FIGURE B-14: Creating a new folder

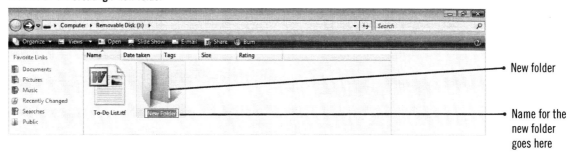

New folder

Name for the
new folder
goes here

FIGURE B-15: Moving a file using drag and drop

To-Do List file
dragged on
top of the new
folder

New folder name   Move arrow   ToolTip describes what
will happen to the file

FIGURE B-16: Renamed file

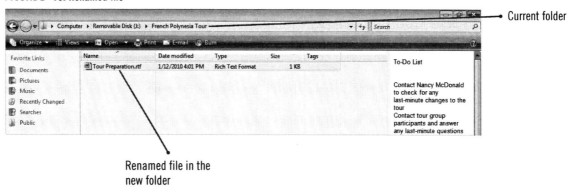

Current folder

Renamed file in the
new folder

Using drag and drop to copy and move files

If you drag and drop a file to a folder on the same drive, Windows moves the file into that folder. However, if you drag and drop a file to a folder on another drive, Windows copies the file instead. If you want to move a file to another drive, hold down [Shift] while you drag and drop. If you want to copy a file to another folder on the same drive, hold down [Ctrl] while you drag and drop.

Searching for Files

After creating, saving, deleting, and renaming folders and files, you may forget where you stored a particular folder or file, its name, or both. **Instant Search** helps you quickly find a folder or file on your computer. You must specify **search criteria** (one or more pieces of information that help Windows identify the file you want). You can search using all or part of the filename, a unique word in the file, or the file type such as document, picture, or music. Instant Search finds items only in your user account, not in other user accounts on the same computer. The **Boolean filters** shown in Table B-5 allow you to specify multiple criteria so that you have a greater chance of finding what you need quickly. When you use the Boolean filters AND, OR, and NOT, you must type them in uppercase so they work properly. ◼◼◼ You want to quickly locate the copy of the To-Do List for your next tour.

STEPS

1. **Click the Start button ⊕ on the taskbar, then click in the Start Search box**

QUICK TIP

Searches are not case sensitive, so you can use uppercase or lowercase letters when you type search criteria.

2. **Type To**
   The search results on the left side of the Start menu are organized by categories, as shown in Figure B-17. Your search results will differ; however, all of the search results will have the characters "To" somewhere in the name of each item in the search results. Under Files, you may see two listings for To-Do List.rtf. One is the file in your Documents folder. The other is a shortcut to the original file on the flash drive that you renamed. Windows Vista keeps a list of shortcuts to files you have used recently, even if that file no longer exists.

QUICK TIP

If you type "To-Do List" with quotation marks, Instant Search finds the To-Do List.rtf file and any shortcut or other files with the same name.

3. **Type -Do List after the word "To", then press [Spacebar]**
   The additional text you typed narrows the search results, as shown in Figure B-18. Now you see documents with "To," "Do," and "List" in the filename.

4. **Under Files, click To-Do List.rtf**
   The To-Do List.rtf file opens in Microsoft Word, WordPad, or another program that works with Rich Text Format files.

5. **Click the Close button ▣ in the program window's title bar**

TABLE B-5: Boolean filters

Boolean filter	example	how it works
AND	tour AND proposal	Finds all files that contain the word *tour* and the word *proposal*; the two words may or may not be located next to each other
OR	tour OR proposal	Finds all files that contain the word *tour* or the word *proposal* (or both)
NOT	tour NOT proposal	Finds all files that contain the word *tour* but not the word *proposal*
" " (quotation marks)	"tour proposal"	Finds all files that contain the exact phrase *tour proposal*

Understanding File Management

FIGURE B-17: Search results

Start Search box with search criterion

Search results show items that contain "To" (yours will differ)

FIGURE B-18: Narrowed search results

Search found the file with the To-Do List

Search criteria

Search results (yours will differ)

Performing more advanced searches

If you want to search all your personal folders for a file, use the Start Search box on the Start menu. If you want to locate a file in a specific folder and all its subfolders (such as the Documents folder), open the folder and use the Search box in the folder. If you want to locate all files that have the same file extension (such as .rtf), type the file extension as your search criteria. If you want to locate files created by a certain person, use the first name, last name, or first and last name as your search criteria. If you want to locate files created on a certain date, type the date (for example, 7/9/2010) as your search criteria. If you remember the title in a document, type the title as your search criteria. If you have created e-mail contacts in your Contacts folder, you can type the person's name to find his or her e-mail address.

Deleting and Restoring Files

If you no longer need a folder or file, you can **delete** (or remove) it. If you delete a folder, Windows removes the folder as well as everything stored in it. Windows places folders and files you delete from your hard disk drive in the Recycle Bin. If you later discover that you need a deleted file or folder, you can restore it to its original location as long as you have not yet emptied the Recycle Bin. Emptying the Recycle Bin permanently removes the deleted folders and files from your computer. By deleting files and folders you no longer need and periodically emptying the Recycle Bin, you free up valuable storage space on your hard disk drive and keep your computer uncluttered. Be aware that files and folders you delete from a removable disk drive, such as a USB flash drive, are immediately and permanently deleted and cannot be restored by Windows. If you try to delete a file or folder that is too large for the Recycle Bin, Windows asks whether you want to permanently delete the file or folder. Choose Yes to delete the file or folder, or choose No to cancel the operation. ⬛⬛⬛ You have the updated copy of the To-Do List.rtf file stored on your USB flash drive, so you want to delete the copy in the Documents folder.

STEPS

1. **Click the Start button 🔘 on the taskbar, click** Documents, **then click the** To-Do List **file in the Documents folder**

   After you select a folder or file, you can delete it.

QUICK TIP

You can also quickly delete a selected folder or file by pressing [Delete] or [Del].

2. **Click the** Organize **button on the toolbar, then click** Delete

   The Delete File dialog box opens so you can confirm the deletion, as shown in Figure B-19.

3. **Click** Yes

   The file moves from the Documents folder into the Recycle Bin.

4. **Click the Minimize button 🔲 on the Documents window title bar and examine the Recycle Bin icon**

   The Recycle Bin icon contains wads of paper if the Recycle Bin contains deleted folders and files. If the Recycle Bin icon does not contain wads of paper, then it is empty and does not contain any deleted files or folders.

5. **Double-click the Recycle Bin icon 🗑**

   The Recycle Bin window opens and displays any deleted folders and files, including the To-Do List.rtf file, as shown in Figure B-20. Your Recycle Bin's contents may differ.

QUICK TIP

Windows keeps track of the original location of deleted subfolders and files so it can restore them later, recreating the original folder structure as needed.

6. **Click the** To-Do List.rtf **file to select it, then click the** Restore this item **button on the Recycle Bin toolbar**

   The file returns its original location and no longer appears in the Recycle Bin window.

7. **Click the Close button ❎ on the Recycle Bin title bar, then click the** Documents **taskbar button**

   The Recycle Bin window closes, and the Documents window opens. The Documents window contains the restored file. You decide to permanently delete this previous version of the To-Do List file.

8. **Click the** To-Do List **file, press** [Delete], **then click** Yes **in the Delete File dialog box**

   The To-Do List moves from the Documents folder to the Recycle Bin.

9. **Click the Close button ❎ on the Documents window title bar, then end your Windows session**

FIGURE B-19: Delete File dialog box

File that will be deleted

FIGURE B-20: Recycle Bin folder

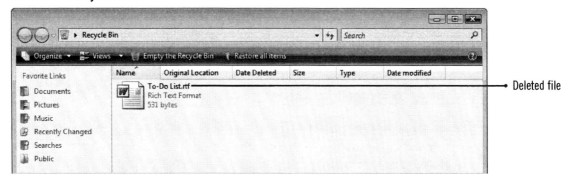

Deleted file

Emptying the Recycle Bin

If you are certain that you no longer need any of the deleted files and folders in your Recycle Bin, you can empty it. If the Recycle Bin folder is open, click the Empty the Recycle Bin button on the toolbar. If it is closed, right-click the Recycle Bin icon on the desktop, then click Empty Recycle Bin on the shortcut menu. In the Delete Multiple Items dialog box, choose Yes to confirm that you want to permanently delete all the items in the Recycle Bin, or choose No to cancel the operation.

Practice

▼ CONCEPTS REVIEW

Label each of the elements of the window shown in Figure B-21.

FIGURE B-21

Match each statement with the term it best describes.

11. A container for related files
12. A link that provides quick access to a folder, file, or Web site
13. One or more pieces of information for locating a folder or file
14. Organizing and managing folders and files
15. The name that you assign to a file to identify its contents

   a. file management
   b. filename
   c. folder
   d. Search criteria
   e. shortcut

Select the best answer from the list of choices.

16. One billion bytes of storage space on a disk is referred to as a:
   a. Kilobyte.
   b. Megabyte.
   c. Gigabyte.
   d. Terabyte.

17. To save a previously saved file with a new filename, you use the:
   a. Save command on the File menu.
   b. Save As command on the File menu.
   c. Save or Save As command on the File menu.
   d. Save button on the program's toolbar.

18. The blinking vertical bar in the WordPad application window is called the:
   a. Insertion point.
   b. Pointer.
   c. Ruler.
   d. Shortcut.

19. After you copy a file, you have:
   a. Only one copy of the file.
   b. A duplicate copy of the file in a different location.
   c. Moved the orginal file to a new location.
   d. Deleted the file.

20. **After you move a file, you have:**
    a. A backup copy of that file.
    c. The orginal file in a different location.
    b. A duplicate copy of the file in a different location.
    d. Deleted the file.

21. **When you delete a file from your hard disk drive, Windows:**
    a. Puts the deleted file in the Recycle Bin.
    c. Stores a duplicate copy of the file in the Recycle Bin..
    b. Permanently deletes the file from the hard disk drive.
    d. Moves the file to a removable disk.

▼ SKILLS REVIEW

1. **Manage folders and files.**
   a. Assume you manage a small travel agency. How would you organize your business files using a hierarchical file structure?
   b. What icon can you place on your desktop to quickly locate your flash drive where you store copies of important files?
   c. What shortcuts would you place on your desktop for easier access to your business files?

2. **Open the Computer window. (If possible, use a different computer than you used for the lessons.)**
   a. Attach your USB flash drive to your computer.
   b. Open the Computer window from the Start menu.
   c. Note the types of drives on this computer, their friendly names, and their actual drive names. Note the drive name assigned to your USB flash drive.
   d. Select the hard disk drive icon, then view the information in the Details Pane about the hard disk drive's total size and free space.
   e. Close the Computer window.

3. **Create and save documents.**
   a. Open WordPad from the All Programs menu.
   b. Type Oceania Tours as the title, followed by one blank line.
   c. Type your name, followed by two blank lines.
   d. Use WordPad to create the following list of current Oceania tours.
      Current Tours:
      1. French Poynesia
      2. Fiji Islands
      3. Pitcairn Islands
      4. Tonga
      5. Niue
      6. Tokelau
   e. Save the WordPad file with the filename Oceania Tours in the Documents folder.
   f. View the full filename in the WordPad title bar, then close WordPad.

4. **Open the Documents folder.**
   a. Open the Documents folder from the Start menu.
   b. If necessary, use the Views button to change the folder view to Large Icons.
   c. Click the Oceania Tours.rtf file.
   d. If necessary, use the Organize menu to display the Preview Pane.
   e. View the contents of the Oceania Tours.rtf file in the Preview Pane.

5. **Copy files.**
   a. Right-click the Oceania Tours.rft file, point to Send To on the shortcut menu, then send a copy of the WordPad file to your USB flash drive.
   b. Use the Address Bar to change to the Computer window, then to your USB flash drive window.
   c. Verify you successfully copied the Oceania Tours.rtf file to your USB flash drive, then close the USB flash drive window.

6. **Open, edit, and print files.**
   a. Open WordPad from the Start menu.
   b. Open the WordPad file named Oceania Tours.rtf from your USB flash drive (not from your Documents folder).

Understanding File Management

c. Click at the beginning of the blank line after the last current tour, then add the names of two more tours on two separate lines: **Palau** and **Tuvalu**.

d. Save the edited WordPad file.

e. Use Print Preview to display a full-page view of the document.

f. Print the Oceania Tours.rtf document and retrieve your printed copy from the printer, then close WordPad.

7. Move and rename files.

a. Open a Computer window, then display the contents of your USB flash drive.

b. If necessary, change your folder view to Large Icons.

c. Use the Organize menu to create a new folder and name it **Oceania Tours**.

d. Use drag and drop to move the Oceania Tours.rtf file into the new folder.

e. Open the new folder and verify the move operation.

f. Use the Organize menu to rename the moved WordPad file as **Current Oceania Tours**.

g. Close the folder window.

8. Search for files.

a. From the Start menu, enter **Oceania** in the Search box as the search criteria.

b. Examine the Search results, then open the original Oceania Tours.rtf file.

c. Close the program window.

9. Delete and restore files.

a. Open the Documents folder from the Start menu.

b. Select and delete your original WordPad file with the name **Oceania Tours.rtf**.

c. Minimize the Documents window, then open the Recycle Bin.

d. Select and restore the file named **Oceania Tours.rtf** that you just deleted, then close the Recycle Bin window.

e. Use the Documents taskbar button to redisplay the Documents window.

f. Verify Windows restored the file named Oceania Tours.rtf to the Documents folder.

g. Select and delete this file again, then close the Documents window.

h. Submit the printed copy of your revised WordPad document and your answers to Step 1 to your instructor.

▼ INDEPENDENT CHALLENGE 1

To meet the needs of high-tech workers in your town, you have opened an Internet café named Internet To-Go where your customers can enjoy a cup of fresh-brewed coffee and bakery goods while they check e-mail. To promote your new business, you want to develop a newspaper ad, flyers, and breakfast and lunch menus.

a. Connect your USB flash drive to your computer, if necessary.

b. Create a new folder named **Internet To-Go** on your USB flash drive.

c. In the Internet To-Go folder, create three subfolders named **Advertising**, **Flyers**, and **Menus**.

d. Use WordPad to create a short ad for your local newspaper that describes your business:

- Use the name of the business as the title for your document.
- Write a short paragraph about the business. Include a fictitious location, street address, and phone number.
- After the paragraph, type your name.

e. Save the WordPad document with the filename **Newspaper Ad** in the Advertising folder.

f. Preview and then print your WordPad document.

▼ INDEPENDENT CHALLENGE 2

As a freelance writer for several national magazines, you depend on your computer to meet critical deadlines. Whenever you encounter a computer problem, you contact a computer consultant who helps you resolve the problem. This consultant asked you to document, or keep records of, your computer's current settings.

a. Connect your USB flash drive to your computer, if necessary.

b. Open the Computer window so that you can view information on your drives and other installed hardware.

▼ INDEPENDENT CHALLENGE 2 (CONTINUED)

c. Open WordPad and create a document with the title **My Hardware Documentation** and your name on separate lines.

d. List the names of the hard disk drive (or drives), devices with removable storage, and any other hardware devices, such as a digital camera, installed on the computer you are using. Also include the total size and amount of free space on your hard disk drive(s). (*Hint:* If you need to check the Computer window for this information, use the taskbar button for the Computer window to view your drives, then use the WordPad taskbar button to return to WordPad.)

e. Save the WordPad document with the filename **My Hardware Documentation** on your USB flash drive.

f. Preview your document, print your WordPad document, then close WordPad.

▼ INDEPENDENT CHALLENGE 3

As an adjunct, or part-time, instructor at Everhart College, you teach special summer classes for kids on how to use and create computer games, compose digital art, work with digital photographs, and compose digital music. You want to create a folder structure on your USB flash drive to store the files for each class.

a. Connect your USB flash drive to your computer, then open the Computer window to your USB flash drive.

b. Create a folder named **Computer Games**.

c. In the Computer Games folder, create a subfolder named **Class 1**.

Advanced Challenge Exercise

- In the Class 1 folder, create subfolders named **Class Outline** and **Hands-On Lab**.
- Rename the Class Outline folder to **Class Handouts**.
- Create a new folder named **Interactive Presentations** in the Class 1 subfolder.

d. Close the Class 1 folder window.

e. Use WordPad to create a document with the title **Photocopying** and your name on separate lines, and the following list of items that you need to photocopy for the first class:

Class 1:

Class 1 Topics & Resources

Hands-On Lab Assignment

On Your Own Exercise

Interactive Presentation Slides

f. Save the WordPad document with the filename **Photocopying** in the Class 1 folder. (*Hint:* After you switch to your USB flash drive in the Save As dialog box, open the Computer Games folder, then open the Class 1 folder before saving the file.)

g. Preview and print the Photocopying.rtf file, then close WordPad.

h. Draw a diagram of your new folder structure on the printed copy of your WordPad document.

▼ REAL LIFE INDEPENDENT CHALLENGE

This Real Life Independent Challenge requires an Internet connection. You want to open a small specialty shop for pottery, stained glass, handcrafts, and other consignments from local artists and craftspeople. First, you need to search for information on the Internet about preparing a business plan so that you can obtain financing from your local bank for the business.

a. Using the Start Search box on the Start menu, enter **Preparing a Business Plan** as the search criteria, then click the Search the Internet button in the Search Results pane.

b. From the list of Search results, locate a Web site that contains information on how to write a business plan.

c. Start WordPad and create a document in which you summarize in your own words the basic process for preparing a business plan. Include a title and your name in the document. At the bottom of your document, list the URL of the Web site or sites from which you prepared your WordPad document. (*Note:* You should not copy the exact content of a Web site, but instead summarize your findings in your own words because many sites copyright the content on their Web site. If you want to determine what content at a Web site is copyrighted and the conditions for using that content, scroll to the bottom of the Web site and click the link that covers copyright use and restrictions.)

d. Preview and print your WordPad document, then save the document on your USB flash drive.

▼ VISUAL WORKSHOP

As a technical support specialist at Advanced Robotic Systems, Ltd., in Great Britain, you need to respond to employee queries quickly and thoroughly. You decide that it is time to evaluate and reorganize the folder structure on your computer so you can quickly access the resources required for your job. Create the folder structure shown in Figure B-22 on your USB flash drive. As you work, use WordPad to prepare a simple outline of the steps you follow to create the folder structure. Include your name in the document, preview and print the document, then submit it to your instructor.

FIGURE B-22

Getting Started with Internet Explorer 7

Files You Will Need:

No files needed.

In this unit, you learn how to use the Internet Explorer 7 browser to find information on the World Wide Web (WWW or the Web). You will learn how to navigate to sites on the Web, how to navigate from one Web page to another, and how to search for information on the Web. You will also learn how to print Web pages and how to get helpful information about using Internet Explorer. You need to connect to the Internet to complete this unit. At Quest Specialty Travel (QST), the tour developers for each region have decided to provide laptop computers with mobile Internet technology to all tour guides. Guides can then use the Internet to research the latest information on local weather, events, and news while traveling with the groups. Each computer will have Internet Explorer 7 installed as the browser. Your job is to train the guides to use the Internet Explorer 7 browser and teach them how to take advantage of the information on the Internet during their tours.

OBJECTIVES

Understand Web browsers

Explore the browser

View and navigate Web pages

Use tabbed browsing

Save favorite Web pages

Print a Web page

Search for information

Get Help and exit Internet Explorer

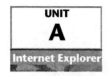

Understanding Web Browsers

The **World Wide Web** (the **Web** or **WWW**) is the part of the Internet that contains linked Web pages. **Web pages** are documents that can contain text, graphics, sound, and video. **Web browsers (browsers)** are software programs used to access and display Web pages. You must use a browser to view Web pages that are on the Web. Browsers, such as Microsoft Internet Explorer, Opera, FireFox, and Netscape Navigator, make navigating the Web easy. When you view Web pages with a browser, you click words, phrases, or graphics called **hyperlinks**, or simply **links**, to connect to and view other Web pages. Links on a Web page can also open graphics files or play sound or video files. This unit features **Internet Explorer**, a popular browser that is part of the Microsoft Windows operating system. Figure A-1 shows a Web page from the U.S. government's White House Web site. ▓▓▓▓ The tour developers have asked you to become familiar with Internet Explorer 7 and the Web so you can teach the guides how to find information for their tours. You discuss the features and benefits of using Internet Explorer.

DETAILS

- **Display Web pages**

  You can access Web sites from all over the world with a Web browser. A **Web site** is a group of Web pages focused on a particular subject. Web sites exist for individuals, businesses, museums, governments, charitable organizations, and educational institutions. There are Web sites for the arts, music, politics, education, sports, and commerce—for any topic, interest, or endeavor in the world. The QST tour guides can use the Web to get up-to-date information about the places they are touring. They can get maps and directions, explore shopping areas, find out about special events, determine currency conversion rates, get weather forecasts, read news, and view photographs.

- **Use links to move from one Web page to another**

  You can click the hyperlinks on a Web page to get more specific information about a business, city, or organization. For example, if a museum is on the tour, a guide can visit the Web site for the museum and click links to view different Web pages that describe current exhibits, visiting hours, or special tours.

- **Play audio and video clips**

  A Web browser can play audio and video clips if it has been configured to do so and your computer has the appropriate hardware, such as speakers. In their research, tour guides might find Web pages that include video clips of historic buildings, shopping trips, local stories and customs, or other information about a region.

- **Search the Web for information**

  A **search engine** is a special Web site that quickly searches the Internet for Web sites based on words or phrases that you enter. Tour guides can take advantage of search engines to look for Web sites that focus on a country, government, or region of travel, or on a specific topic of interest.

- **Save a list of favorite Web pages**

  You can save a list of links to Web pages that you might need to visit again, such as a page for a specific museum, city, or map. Internet Explorer makes it easy to compile a list of your favorite Web sites that is quickly accessible when you want to view those Web sites later. Tour guides can save pages for historic sites or museums for each city they visit with their groups.

- **Print or save the text and graphics on Web pages**

  If you want to keep a hard copy of the information or images you find on the Web, you can simply print the Web page, including any graphics. You can also save the text or graphics on a Web page or copy the information temporarily to the Clipboard, where it is available for pasting into other programs. Tour guides can print maps or informational paragraphs from the Web to hand out to the groups.

- **E-mail Web pages**

  If you want to share a Web page with a colleague, you can e-mail the link or the page directly from the browser window to another person who is set up for e-mail. The person receives the page or link to the page as part of an e-mail message.

FIGURE A-1: A sample Web page

The Internet, computer networks, and intranets

A **computer network** is the hardware and software that makes it possible for two or more computers to share information and resources. An **intranet** is a computer network that connects computers in a local area only, such as computers in a company's office. Users can dial into intranets from remote locations to share company information and resources. The **Internet** is a network of connected computers and computer networks located around the world. The Internet is an international community; Web pages exist from nearly every country in the world. There are over 200 million users worldwide currently connected to the Internet through telephone lines, cables, satellites, and other telecommunications media. Through the Internet, these computers can share many types of information, including text, graphics, sound, video, and computer programs. Anyone who has access to a computer and a connection to the Internet through a computer network or modem can use this rich information source.

The Internet has its roots in the U.S. Department of Defense Advanced Research Projects Agency Network (ARPANET), which began in 1969. In 1986 the National Science Foundation formed NSFNET, which replaced ARPANET. NSFNET expanded the foundation of the U.S. portion of the Internet with high-speed, long-distance lines. By the end of the 1980s, corporations began to use the Internet to communicate with each other and with their customers. In 1991, the U.S. Congress further expanded the Internet's capacity and speed and opened it to commercial use.

The World Wide Web was created in Switzerland in 1991 to allow links between documents on the Internet. The first graphical Web browser, Mosaic, was introduced at the University of Illinois in 1993, leading to the development of browsers such as Netscape Navigator and Internet Explorer. With the boom in the personal computer industry and the expanding availability of inexpensive desktop machines and powerful, network-ready servers, many companies were able to join the Internet for the first time in the early 1990s. The Web is now an integral component of corporate culture, educational institutions, and individuals' personal lives. The Web is used daily for commerce, education, and entertainment by millions of people around the world.

Internet

Exploring the Browser

Internet Explorer is a Web browser that connects your computer to the Web through an Internet connection. The browser lets you view, print, and search for information on the Web. You can customize elements of the window. You can choose to view the buttons on the toolbar with or without their corresponding text labels, with large icons, or with text labels on the right. You can also choose whether or not to display the menu bar. Typically, after Internet Explorer is installed, its icon appears on your Windows desktop and the Quick Launch section of the taskbar. You can double-click the desktop icon or click the Quick Launch icon to start Internet Explorer. ▰▰▰▰ Before you show the tour guides how to view Web pages and navigate from one page to another, you need to become more familiar with the components of the Internet Explorer browser window.

STEPS

QUICK TIP

If you use a modem and a telephone, follow your normal procedure to establish an Internet connection.

1. **Locate the Internet Explorer icon 🅔 on your Windows desktop**

   The location of the Internet Explorer icon shown in Figure A-2 might vary on different computers. You can start Internet Explorer by clicking the Start button on the taskbar, pointing to All Programs, then clicking Internet Explorer. Some computers have the Internet Explorer icon "pinned" to the Start menu, so you can click the Start button on the taskbar, then click Internet Explorer. You might also start Internet Explorer by clicking the Internet Explorer button on the Quick Launch toolbar.

TROUBLE

If an Internet Connection Wizard dialog box opens at any point, you either need to connect to the Internet or enter your Internet settings. Ask your technical support person for assistance.

2. **Double-click the Internet Explorer icon 🅔 on the Windows desktop, then if necessary, click the Maximize button 🔲 on the Internet Explorer title bar to maximize the program window**

   Internet Explorer opens and displays your home page. A **home page** is the first Web page that opens every time you start Internet Explorer. The term "home page" also applies to the main page that opens when you first go to a Web site. Figure A-3 shows the Quest Specialty Travel home page. Your home page may be different. Look at the home page on your screen and compare the elements described, using Figure A-3 as a guide.

The elements of the Internet Explorer browser window include the following:

- The **title bar** contains the name of the Web page currently displayed in the Web browser's active tab window.
- The **Address bar** displays the address of the Web page currently opened in the active tab. The **Uniform Resource Locator (URL)**, or the Web page's address, appears in the Address box on the Address bar after you open (or load) the page. If you click the Address box list arrow, you see a list of addresses you have recently entered in the Address box. The Address bar also has buttons to refresh a page, to stop the loading of a Web page, and to move forward and back from one Web page to another.
- The **Search box** is used along with the Address bar to help you search for Web sites about a particular topic. You can enter a keyword or words in the Search box, then click the Search button. Click the Search list arrow to specify the search engine to use. When the search is complete, a list of related Web sites opens in a search results Web page.
- The **menu bar** provides access to most of the browser's features through a series of menus.

QUICK TIP

To display toolbars, such as the menu bar and Links bar, click the Tools list arrow on the Command bar, click Menu Bar or point to Toolbars and then click the name of the bar you want to display.

- The **Links bar** is a convenient place to store links to Web pages that you use often. You can add a link to the Links bar by dragging the Internet Explorer icon that precedes the URL in the Address bar to the Links bar. Links placed in the Links bar are also found in the Links folder on the Favorites menu.
- The **Command bar** provides buttons for options, such as printing Web pages, adding Favorites, and searching for information on the Internet. Many commonly used commands available on menus are more quickly accomplished using the toolbar buttons. Depending on the programs installed on your computer, you may have additional buttons.
- The **Favorites Center** is used to store and organize the links to the Web pages that you want to revisit often. To open the Favorites Center, you click the Favorites Center button on the Command bar.
- The **browser window** is the specific area where the current Web page appears.

QUICK TIP

Click the tab for a Web page to display that Web page in front.

- The **tabs** identify the current Web page or pages open in the browser. **Tabbed browsing** allows you to open more than one Web page at a time in a browser window.
- The **vertical scroll bar** appears along the right side of a page if the page is longer than the window's viewable area. The **scroll box** indicates your relative position within the Web page.

FIGURE A-2: Starting Internet Explorer

Icon on desktop

Program pinned to Start menu

Icon on Quick Launch toolbar

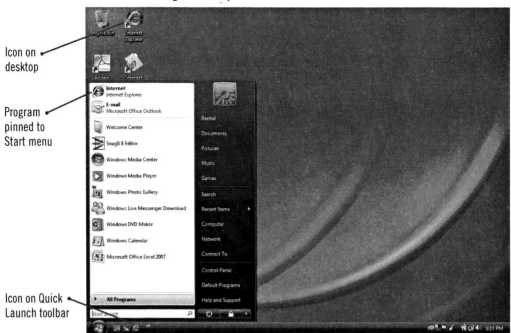

FIGURE A-3: Elements of the Internet Explorer window

Title bar with name of Web page

Address bar with URL

Favorites Center Button

Menu bar (closed by default)

Status bar

Search box

Links bar

Command bar

Tabs for tabbed browsing

Scroll box

Browser window

Vertical scroll bar

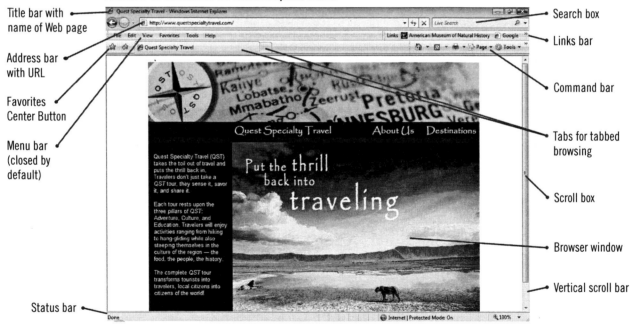

Understanding the status bar

The status bar performs several functions. It displays information about your connection progress whenever you open a new Web page. It notifies you when you connect to another Web site. As the page loads, it identifies the percentage of information transferred from the Web server to your browser and then displays "Done" when the page is loaded. The status bar displays the Web addresses of any links on the Web page when you move your mouse pointer over them. When the phishing filter is active, the status bar identifies the status of the filter. The Zoom Level button is also located on the status bar. The status indicator, a green bar, is animated while a new Web page loads. You can hide or display the status bar by clicking View on the menu bar and then clicking Status Bar, or by right-clicking the Command bar and then clicking Status Bar.

Viewing and Navigating Web Pages

Moving between Web pages located at different addresses is simple with hyperlinks. **Hyperlinks** enable you to navigate to, or open, another location on the same Web page or to jump to an entirely different Web page. You can follow these links to obtain more information about a topic by clicking a linked word or phrase. In addition to links on Web pages themselves, you can use the navigation tools in Internet Explorer to move around the Web. You can navigate from page to page using the Forward and Back buttons, as well as the Home button. If you click the Recent Pages button to the right of the Forward button or the Address box list arrow on the Address bar, you see a list of recently viewed Web pages. You can click the name of the page you want to view. ▰▰▰▰ You look at the Library of Congress Web site for information for a tour traveling to Washington, D.C.

STEPS

1. **Click anywhere in the Address box on the Address bar**

   The current address is highlighted; any text you type replaces it.

TROUBLE

If the Microsoft Phishing Filter dialog box opens, you can turn on the filter, turn off the filter, or decide whether to turn it off or on later.

2. **Type www.loc.gov, then press [Enter]**

   After a few seconds, the home page for the Library of Congress opens in the browser window, as shown in Figure A-4, and the status bar displays "Done". Web pages change frequently. The Web page you load may look different from that shown in the figure. After you press [Enter], Internet Explorer automatically adds the "http://" protocol to the beginning of the address you type. If you have typed a specific address in the Address bar previously, the AutoComplete feature recognizes the first few characters you type. A list opens below the Address box containing the addresses in which the typed letters appear; you can click the URL in the list to open the page rather than complete the typing of the URL. As the page is loading, the status bar displays the connection process. The page contains both pictures and text, some of which are hyperlinks.

3. **Place your mouse pointer on the Visitors link in the Resources for section**

   When you place the pointer on a hyperlink, the pointer changes to 🖑 and the URL for the hyperlink appears in the status bar. A ScreenTip may also appear, giving you more information about the linked page.

4. **Click the Visitors link**

   The Visitors page opens in your Web browser window, as shown in Figure A-5. The name of the Web page appears on the front tab in the browser window. A Web page icon appears to the left of the Web page name.

QUICK TIP

Move the pointer over the Back or Forward button to display a ScreenTip showing which page will appear when the button is clicked.

5. **Click the Back button 🔙 on the Address bar**

   The Web page that you viewed, the Library of Congress home page, opens in the browser window.

6. **Click the Forward button ➡ on the Address bar**

   The Forward button opens the Visitors page in the browser window again.

7. **Click the Home button 🏠 on the Command bar**

   Clicking the Home button opens the home page designated for your installation of Internet Explorer. Click the Refresh button 🔄 on the Address bar to update a page that may have changed.

QUICK TIP

If you change your mind or if a page takes too long to load, you can click the Stop button on the Address bar to stop a new Web page from loading.

8. **Click the Recent Pages button 🔽 to the right of the Forward button ➡ on the Address bar, then click The Library of Congress**

   The Recent Pages button displays a list of the last few pages that you visited.

FIGURE A-4: Home page for the Library of Congress

Back button

Forward button

URL

New Tab tab

Visitors link

FIGURE A-5: Visitors Web page at the Library of Congress Web site

Name of Web page on the tab

Stop button

Refresh button

Home button

Setting the Home Page

When you click the Home button on the Command bar, the page that is specified as the home page opens in your Web browser window. Each time you start Internet Explorer, the first page that appears is your home page. When you install Internet Explorer, the default home page might have been the Welcome to MSN.com home page at the MSN Web site. You can easily select a different home page to open each time you start Internet Explorer. Simply go to the page that you want to be your home page, click the Home button list arrow on the Command bar, then click Add or Change Home Page to open the Add or Change Home Page dialog box. See Figure A-6. When the dialog box opens, select the option that identifies how you want to set the Web page as your home page. If you have more than one tab open, you will see all these options. You can also click Tools on the menu bar,

then click Internet Options to open the Internet Options dialog box. Click the General tab if necessary, click the Use current button in the Home page area to specify the current page as your home page.

FIGURE A-6: Add or Change Home Page dialog box

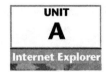

Using Tabbed Browsing

Tabbed browsing allows more than one Web page to open within the same browser window. Each window appears on a separate tab. This method for organizing Web pages while browsing makes navigation between Web pages fast and simple, and minimizes the number of windows you need open on your desktop as you browse the Web. You can open several Internet Explorer windows at the same time, each with its own series of Web pages accessible by tabs. You can also change the default settings for tabbed browsing: for example, you can have several pages open automatically for a Web site on several tabs, or you can bypass the tab settings to open pages in their own windows. Figure A-7 shows an Internet Explorer window with several pages from the Library of Congress Web site open in tabs. Table A-1 describes buttons that are available on the Command bar and the Address bar. ▓▓▓▓ You want to show the tour guides how tabbed browsing will allow them to more easily compare events in a location by viewing the Web pages in one browsing session.

STEPS

1. **Type www.usa.gov in the Address bar, then press [Enter]**
   The Web page for the U.S. government opens. It is on the front tab in the browser window.

> **TROUBLE**
> If someone has clicked the Don't show this page again check box on the about:Tabs page, you will see a Web page rather than the Welcome to Tabbed Browsing page.

2. **Click the New Tab tab in the browser window**
   The about:Tabs Web page appears as a new tab in the browser window, as shown in Figure A-8.

3. **Click the Close Tab button in the Welcome to Tabbed Browsing tab**
   The usa.gov Web page is in the browser window.

4. **Right-click the State Government link, click Open in New Tab on the menu, then click the State and Territorial tab to display the Web page**

5. **Right-click any state link, click Open in New Tab on the menu, then click the state tab**
   Using tabbed browsing, you now have three Web pages open in one browser window.

6. **Position the mouse pointer over each tab to display the ScreenTip for each**
   Each ScreenTip tells you the name and URL of the Web page in the tab.

7. **Click the Quick Tabs button 🁣 to the left of the tabs**
   Thumbnail images of open tabs appear in Quick Tabs view, as shown in Figure A-9.

8. **Click the Close Tab button for the second and third thumbnails in Quick Tabs view, then click the USA.gov tab**
   Quick Tabs view closes and the USA.gov tab is open in the window.

TABLE A-1: Internet Explorer 7 buttons

button name	button	description	button name	button	description
Back	⬅	Opens previous page	Add to Favorites	☆	Opens Add to Favorites menu and dialog box
Forward	➡	Opens next page	Print	🖨	Prints current Web page
Recent Pages	▾	Displays list of recently viewed pages	View Feeds on this page	🔊	Adds current RSS Feed to Favorites Center
Stop	✕	Stops loading new page	Page	Page ▾	Provides Page options
Refresh	⟳	Refreshes the contents of current page	Help	?	Displays Internet Explorer Help window
Home	🏠	Opens the home page	Tools	Tools ▾	Opens a menu of commands to manage settings for the Pop-up Blocker, Phishing Filter, Windows Update, and browsing history
Search	🔎	Searches for Web sites based on a keyword	Research	🔳	Opens Research task pane
Favorites Center	☆	Opens Favorites Center			

FIGURE A-7: Tabbed browsing

Tab list

New Tab tab

Three tabs open in one browser window

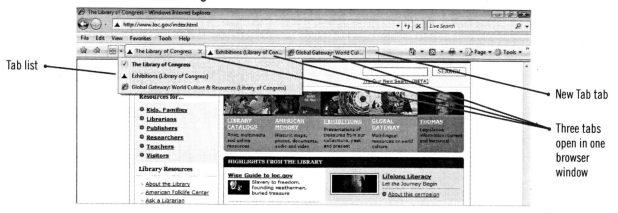

FIGURE A-8: New page in a second tab

Quick Tabs button

Close Tab button

Information about tabbed browsing

FIGURE A-9: Quick Tabs view

Three open Web page thumbnails

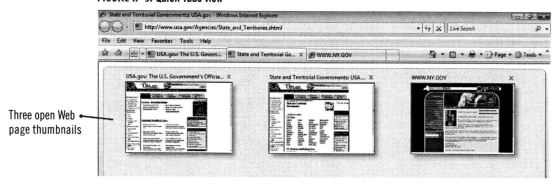

Internet

Exiting options when you have multiple tabs open

When you finish looking at Web pages using Internet Explorer, you may find that you have several tabs open. When you exit Internet Explorer and you have more than one tab open, a dialog box appears asking if you want to close all the tabs. If you want the same tabs to open the next time you start Internet Explorer, click Show Options, click Open these the next time I use Internet Explorer, then click Close Tabs.

Saving Favorite Web Pages

The **Favorites Center** allows you to create your own list of frequently visited Web pages, or **favorites**. When you find a Web page that you know you will want to revisit, add the site address to the Favorites Center. You can then access the site by clicking a link in the Favorites Center. After you add a Web page to the Favorites Center, you can automatically access that page by clicking the Favorites Center button on the Command bar, by clicking Favorites on the menu bar and then clicking the link, or by clicking the icon on the Links bar if available. ▨▨▨▨ The tour guides will want to be able to revisit some travel site Web pages without having to write the URLs on a sheet of paper and typing the URLs in the Address bar each time.

STEPS

1. **Click the Address bar, type www.nps.gov/brca, then press [Enter]**
   The home page for Bryce Canyon National Park opens, as shown in Figure A-10.

QUICK TIP

Web pages change frequently. The PHOTOS & MULTIMEDIA link may be in a new location on the page.

2. **Click the PHOTOS & MULTIMEDIA link, read the information, then click the Back button ⬅ on the Address bar**
   This site offers information for adventure travelers. You want to save the link in the Favorites Center.

3. **Click the Add to Favorites button ⬚ on the Command bar, then click Add to Favorites**
   The Add a Favorite dialog box opens, as shown in Figure A-11. The Add a Favorite dialog box shows the folders in which you can place the URL for the Bryce Canyon Web page. The name of the Web page appears in the Name text box, and the Favorites folder is selected by default. You can change the default page name by typing a new name in the Name text box.

4. **Click Add**
   The name and URL are added to the Favorites Center and the Favorites menu.

5. **Click the New Tab tab, type www.nps.gov/yell in the Address bar, press [Enter], click the New Tab tab, type www.nps.gov/zion in the Address bar, then press [Enter]**
   You opened new tabs for Yellowstone National Park and Zion National Park.

6. **Click the Add to Favorites button ⬚ on the Command bar, click Add Tab Group to Favorites, type National Parks Tour West in the Tab Group Name text box, then click Add**
   You added all the open tabs in the window to a tab group in the Favorites Center.

QUICK TIP

The most recently added favorites appear at the bottom of the Favorites list.

7. **Close the second and third tabs, then click the Home button ⬚ on the Command bar to return to your home page**

8. **Click the Favorites Center button ⬚ on the Command bar**
   The Favorites Center opens. You see a list of Favorites, including the Bryce Canyon National Park favorite you just added and the National Parks Tour West tab group you added, listed as a folder.

QUICK TIP

Click the arrow to open all links in the group, each in its own tab.

9. **Click National Parks Tour West to open the list of links associated with that Folder, then click the Bryce Canyon National Park link in the Favorites Center**
   The Bryce Canyon home page opens in your Web browser window.

Understanding URLs

Every Web page has a unique address on the Web, also known as the **URL** for the page. Browser software locates a Web page based on its address. All Web page addresses begin with "http," which stands for Hypertext Transfer Protocol, the set of rules for exchanging files on the Web. This is followed by a colon and two forward slashes. Most pages begin with "www" (which indicates that the page is on the World Wide Web), followed by a dot, or period, and

then the Web site's name, known as the **domain name**. Following the domain name is another dot and the top-level domain, such as com (for commercial sites), edu (for educational institutions), or org (for organizations). The **top-level domain** tells you the type of site you are visiting. After the top-level domain, another slash and one or more folder names and a filename might appear.

FIGURE A-10: Bryce Canyon National Park home page

Favorites Center button

Add to Favorites button

PHOTOS & MULTIMEDIA link

FIGURE A-11: Add a Favorite dialog box

Creating and organizing favorites

Once you add a Web page to your Favorites Center, returning to that page is much easier. To keep your Favorites Center list manageable, only add pages that you expect to visit again. You can organize your list of favorites by placing them into folders by category. For example, you may want to create folders according to your interests, such as sports, cooking, and travel. You may want to create folders in which each member of a household can place his or her own favorites. Favorites can be listed individually or placed in folders in the Favorites Center or on the Favorites menu. To add a folder to your Favorites Center, click Add to Favorites on the Command bar, then click Organize Favorites. The Organize Favorites dialog box opens, as shown in Figure A-12. Click the New Folder button to add a new folder to the list of folders and favorites. You can move a favorite to a specific folder by clicking the favorite, clicking the Move button, and then selecting the folder or creating a new folder in which to add the favorite you want to move. You can also drag and drop a favorite into a folder, and you can rename favorites and folders. Information about a selected favorite appears below the list.

Links stored in the Links folder appear on the Links bar in the browser window. The Favorites Center also stores the links for RSS feeds and keeps the history of all Web pages visited.

FIGURE A-12: Organize Favorites dialog box

Internet

Printing a Web Page

When you print a Web page, its text and any graphics appear on the printed page. Internet Explorer provides ways to shrink text so that the contents of a Web page fit on one page. You can also adjust margins, change the page orientation, change headers and footers, and adjust the print space to best meet your printing needs. The options in the Print dialog box allow you to specify print options such as the number of copies and the page range. With Internet Explorer, you can preview a Web page prior to printing by using Print Preview, which is helpful because some Web pages are lengthy and you may only want to print the pages that have the information relevant to your task. You show the tour guides how to print a copy of a Web page so they can provide the information as handouts to the tour guests.

STEPS

QUICK TIP

To have your name appear on the printed page, type your name in the Header or Footer text box.

1. **Click the Address box on the Address bar, type www.nps.gov, press [Enter], then click the HISTORY & CULTURE link**

   The History & Culture page for the National Park Service opens.

2. **Click the Print button list arrow 🖨 ▾ on the Command bar, then click Page Setup**

   The Page Setup dialog box opens. You can change the page size, margins, and orientation. You can also edit the footers and headers. By default, the current URL and the date and time are printed on the page, so people can see the URL and visit the Web site if they want to.

QUICK TIP

To print a Web page without previewing the page or changing any settings, click the Print button on the Command bar.

3. **Click Cancel, click the Print button list arrow 🖨 ▾, then click Print Preview**

   The Print Preview window opens. See Figure A-13. The default setting in the Change Print Size box is Shrink to Fit, which indicates that the Web page width will be adjusted to fit the width of one printed page. The Turn headers and footers on or off button on the toolbar determines whether the headers and footers are visible on the printed page.

4. **Click the Landscape button 🄰 on the toolbar, then click the Portrait button 🄰 on the toolbar**

   You confirm that Portrait orientation is best for the handout. If there are multiple pages to print, you can click the Show multiple pages list arrow on the toolbar and then click the number of pages that you prefer to view at once.

5. **Click the Print Document button 🖨 on the toolbar**

   The Print dialog box opens, as shown in Figure A-14. Table A-2 explains printing options in more detail.

6. **Make sure 1 appears in the Number of copies text box, then click the Current Page option button in the Page Range area**

   These settings indicate that one copy of the current Web page will print using the default printer.

TROUBLE

If your computer is not connected to a printer or if an error message appears, ask your technical support person for assistance.

7. **Make sure that your computer is connected to a printer and that the printer is turned on and contains paper, then click Print**

   The Print dialog box closes, and one copy of the current Web page prints.

Copying information from a Web page

You can select text on a Web page and use the Copy and Paste commands to use the same information in another program, such as Microsoft Word or other Office programs. You can also save a graphic image from a Web page by right-clicking the image, clicking Save Picture As on the shortcut menu, then specifying where to save the image. If you just need to copy an image, click the Copy command on the shortcut menu. Using the Copy command saves the text or image to the Clipboard.

Keep in mind that the same laws that protect printed works generally protect information and graphics published on a Web page. Do not use material on a Web page without citing its source and checking the site carefully for any usage restrictions.

FIGURE A-13: Print Preview window

Click to turn headers and footers on or off

1 Page View

Drag to adjust margins

Shrink To Fit on one page

Header

Footer

FIGURE A-14: Print dialog box

The printers listed in your Print dialog box will differ

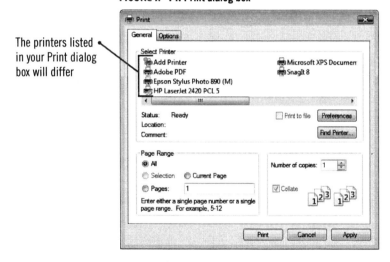

TABLE A-2: Printing options

option	tab	description
Select Printer	General	Displays information about the name, status, type, and location of the printer
Page Range	General	Choose to print current page, all pages, a range of pages, or a selection
Number of copies	General	Indicates the number of copies of each page to print and their sequence
Print all linked documents	Options	Opens and prints each document referenced by a link on the current page
Print frames	Options	In a Web page containing frames, allows you to print frames as laid out, only the selected frame, or all frames individually
Print table of links	Options	Prints links in a table at the end of the document
Orientation	(Depends on printer)	Allows you to specify landscape or portrait page orientation

Searching for Information

A vast and ever-increasing number of Web pages and other information sources are available through the Internet. A search for information using Internet Explorer's **Address bar** is based on criteria or **keywords**, which are words related to the topic for which you are searching. To search using the Address bar, you can enter a keyword or words in the Search box, then click the Search button to start the search. The **Search box** enables you to search in two ways: It can provide a list of links similar in content or topic to the Web page you are currently viewing, or you can use the Search box to search for information based on keywords. If you use Web **search engines** such as Windows Live, MSN Search, Google, or Yahoo! to locate information, the result is a list of links to Web sites related to your search topic. You can click one of the links in the list to go quickly to a site. You decide to show the tour guides how to look for adventure travel information by searching with the browser.

STEPS

QUICK TIP

Each search engine differs slightly in the way it formats information, the way it records the number of Internet sites in the database, and how often it updates the database.

1. **Click the Address bar, type www.google.com, then press [Enter]**

   The Google home page opens in the browser window. Google is a commercial company that runs a search engine. Search engines such as Yahoo!, Google, Ask, and Lycos routinely use software programs to methodically catalog, or crawl, through the entire Internet and create huge databases with links to Web pages and their URLs. When you enter a keyword or phrase, the search engine examines its database index for relevant information and displays a list of Web sites.

2. **Type adventure travel in the Search box, then click Google Search**

   Your search results appear as a list of links to related Web sites with a description of each site.

3. **Click any link to view a Web page, click the Back button ⟵ twice on the Address bar to return to the Google home page, then click the New Tab tab to open a new tab**

4. **Click the Search list arrow 🔎 ▾ on the Address bar**

   The default search engine for Internet Explorer 7 is Live Search. If another search engine is listed, such as Google, you can use that as well. You decide to investigate online photo-sharing, since tour guests like to exchange photos.

5. **Click Change Search Defaults**

   See Figure A-15. The Change Search Defaults dialog box is used to set another Web site as the default.

QUICK TIP

Topic searches, which limit the search to a specific subject such as travel, science, or history, are available through Web sites such as Expedia.com, About.com, and Wikipedia.com.

6. **Click Cancel in the Change Search Defaults dialog box, click in the Search box on the Address bar, type share photos online, then click the Search button 🔎 on the Address bar**

   The Web is searched on the keywords you entered using the default search engine. As shown in Figure A-16, your search results appear as a list of related Web sites in the Live Search Web page in the tab of the browser window. You can click any hyperlink to open a Web page or a list of Web pages relating to a specific category.

7. **Examine the results list by scrolling up or down, then right-click a hyperlink of your choice and click Open in New Tab**

   The related page containing information about a Web site that you can use to share photographs opens in the browser window. You want to compare these results with those of another search engine.

8. **Click the Google tab, type share photos online in the Google Search box, then click Google Search**

   You can click between the tabs to compare results and click the different Web pages to find the information.

9. **Review the list of results, press and hold [Ctrl], then click any hyperlink**

   The Web page opens in a new tab. You can click the tab to view the Web page. Based on your search, you see that there are many different Web sites with information about online photo-sharing.

10. **Close all open tabs except the first tab, then click the Home button 🏠**

    Your home page appears in the browser window.

FIGURE A-15: Change Search Defaults dialog box

FIGURE A-16: Search results

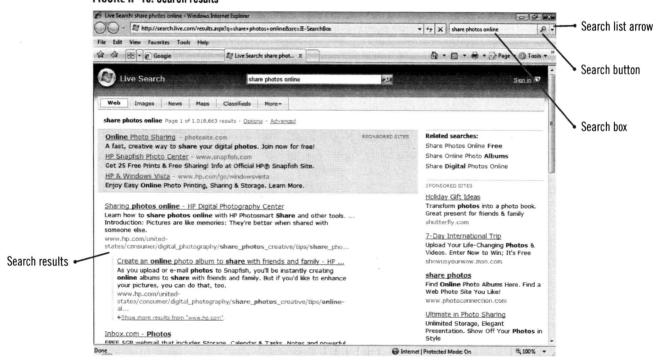

Search list arrow

Search button

Search box

Search results

Blocking pop-ups

Pop-ups are windows that open on your screen as you visit Web sites, generally to advertise products you may or may not want. Often they are annoying, so you might choose to block them. Internet Explorer comes with a built-in Pop-up Blocker. Click Tools on the Command bar, point to Pop-up Blocker, then click Turn Off Pop-up Blocker to turn it off if you want pop-ups, or click Pop-up Blocker Settings to open the Pop-up Blocker Settings dialog box to permit pop-ups from specific Web sites. You can also control notifications and set the filter level. Notifications will play a sound or show the Information Bar if a pop-up is blocked. Filter levels can be set to Low, Medium, or High.

Getting Help and Exiting Internet Explorer

Internet Explorer provides a Help system with information and instructions on various features and commands. ▰▰▰ While demonstrating Internet Explorer, you were asked about the purpose of the Phishing Filter on the status bar. **Phishing** is an illicit activity where people send you fraudulent Web sites to gather your personal information for possible illegal purposes. You decide to demonstrate the Help system to the tour guides by finding out more about phishing and privacy protection as you use Internet Explorer.

STEPS

TROUBLE

If the Help button is not visible, click the More button ⯆ on the Command bar, then click Help.

1. **Click the Help button 🔵 on the Command bar, then click Contents and Index**

   The Windows Help and Support window opens. You can type a keyword in the Search Help text box, or you can click links to access several Help features. The buttons at the top of the Window provide various avenues into the Help System. Refer to Figure A-17.

2. **Click the Browse Help button**

   The Contents page shows a list of common options.

3. **Click the Home button 🏠, type phishing in the Search Help text box, press [Enter], click Phishing Filter: frequently asked questions in the results list, then maximize the window if necessary**

   As shown in Figure A-18, the links in the Windows Help and Support window provide a list of frequently asked questions. Each question is a link to the answer.

QUICK TIP

Click Show All to display all the answers at once, then scroll as needed to read all the text.

4. **Click one question link and read the information**

   The question expands to reveal the answer to that question about phishing.

5. **Click the Close button ❌ in the upper-right corner of the Help window**

   The Help window closes. When you are ready to exit Internet Explorer, you can click the Close button in the upper-right corner of the browser window or click Close on the File menu. You do not need to save files before you exit.

6. **Click Add to Favorites ⭐ on the Command bar, click Organize Favorites, select each Favorite or Folder that you added in this unit, click Delete, click Yes in the confirmation dialog box, then click Close to close the Organize Favorites dialog box**

7. **Click the Close button ❌ on the title bar**

   The Internet Explorer browser window closes. If you have more than one tab open, you will see a dialog box like the one shown in Figure A-19, confirming that you want to close all tabs.

8. **If you connected to the Internet by telephone line, follow your normal procedure to close your connection**

Viewing sites in other languages

The Web is an international forum; as you surf the Web, you may find sites that display text in the native language of the country where the site originates. If you are a native English-speaking person, most Web sites have an English link somewhere on the site's home page that you can click to display the site in English.

FIGURE A-17: Windows Internet Explorer Help window

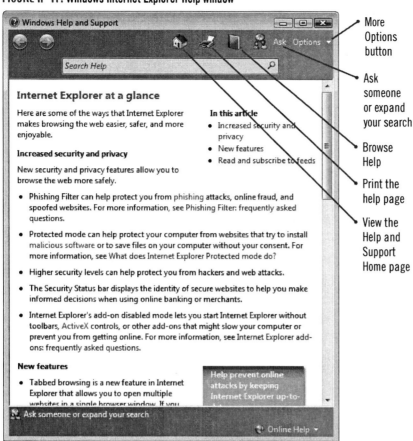

More Options button

Ask someone or expand your search

Browse Help

Print the help page

View the Help and Support Home page

FIGURE A-18: Phishing Filter FAQs

FIGURE A-19: Closing multiple tabs

Saving or sending a Web page

Before exiting Internet Explorer, you may want to save a copy of the current page or send someone a copy of the page. If you want to use the menu bar, you can click File on the menu bar to open the File menu and access the Save and Send commands. If you want to use the Command bar, you can click the Page button list arrow to see the Save and Send commands. By selecting the Save As command, you can save the complete Web page, including any graphics—or just the text from the page—in a file on your computer. If you want to send the complete page to someone, use the Send Page By E-mail command, and then use your e-mail program to address and send the message to the intended recipient. If you want to send the Link only, not the whole page, use the Send Link by E-mail command.

Practice

If you have a SAM user profile, you may have access to hands-on instruction, practice, and assessment of the skills covered in this unit. Log in to your SAM account (http://sam2007.course.com/) to launch any assigned training activities or exams that relate to the skills covered in this unit.

▼ CONCEPTS REVIEW

Label each element of the Internet Explorer browser window shown in Figure A-20.

FIGURE A-20

Match each term with the statement that best describes it.

7. **Hyperlink**
8. **Quick Tabs button**
9. **Favorites Center**
10. **Address box**
11. **Uniform Resource Locator (URL)**

a. Click to view a new Web page
b. Displays the URL for the currently displayed page
c. Use to display all open Web pages as thumbnails
d. Displays a list of saved Web pages
e. A Web page's address

Select the best answer from the list of choices.

12. Software programs such as Internet Explorer and FireFox are called _____.
   a. Web companions
   b. Web browsers
   c. Web documents
   d. Web windows

13. Which of the following functions is NOT available on the status bar?
   a. Displays information about your connection progress
   b. Notifies you when you connect to another Web site
   c. Displays search results
   d. Displays "Done" when the page is loaded

14. Click the _____ button to view the links of pages you have visited and saved.
   a. Address
   b. Link
   c. Favorites Center
   d. Back

15. _____ browsing allows you to open more than one Web page at a time in a browser window.
   a. Tabbed
   b. Web
   c. Linked
   d. Favorites

16. You can search for Web sites by category by entering a keyword in the Address bar, then clicking the _____.
   a. Search button
   b. Refresh button
   c. Home button
   d. Link button

17. The letters following the dot after the domain name are called the _____ domain and tell you the type of site you are visiting.
   a. top-level
   b. home-level
   c. dot-com
   d. main-level

18. Which button on the Command bar should you click if you want to view the previous Web page on your computer?
   a. Home
   b. Last
   c. Back
   d. Link

19. Words or graphics on a Web page that, when clicked, enable you to navigate to another Web page location are called _____.
   a. Tabs
   b. Web browsers
   c. Hyperlinks
   d. Buttons

20. Using the Internet to gather personal information without the knowledge or permission of the person who's information is being collected is called _____.
   a. Phishing
   b. Linking
   c. Popping
   d. Spam

21. When viewing a Web page, what method for clicking a link will NOT open a new page on a new tab?
   a. Press and hold [Ctrl], then click
   b. Right-click, then click Open in New Tab
   c. Double-click the link
   d. Press and hold [Ctrl], then press T

▼ SKILLS REVIEW

1. Start Internet Explorer.
   a. Make sure your computer is connected to the Internet.
   b. Start Internet Explorer.

2. Explore the browser window.
   a. Identify the Command bar, menu bar, Address bar, Search box, Links bar, status bar, URL, browser window, and scroll bar.
   b. Identify the buttons for printing, searching, viewing favorites, and returning to the home page.
   c. Identify the complete URL of the current Web page.

3. View and navigate Web pages.

a. Open the Web page **www.llnl.gov** using the Address bar to open the Web page shown in Figure A-21.

b. Click a link on the Web page to view a new Web page.

c. Return to the default home page for your browser.

d. Click the Back button.

e. Follow another link to investigate the content.

f. Return to the default home page for your browser.

4. Use tabbed browsing.

a. Open the Web page **www.nytimes.com** using the Address bar.

b. Right-click a link on the Web page to open an article in a new tab.

c. Click the New Tab tab to open a third tab in the browser window, then open **www.cnn.com** in the new tab using the Address bar.

d. Press and hold [CTRL], then click a link on the CNN home page to open a fourth tab.

e. Click the Quick Tabs button to view all four Web pages as thumbnails.

f. Click the first thumbnail to view the Web page. Your screen should resemble Figure A-22.

g. Close all tabs except for the New York Times tab.

5. Save favorite Web pages.

a. Open the Web page **www.nasa.gov** using the Address bar.

b. Add the Web page to your Favorites Center.

c. Return to the default home page for your browser.

d. Using the Favorites Center, return to the NASA home page.

6. Print a Web page.

a. Click any link on the NASA home page that is interesting to you.

b. Use Print Preview to preview the Web page in printed form.

c. Verify that the Print Size is set to Shrink To Fit. If there is more than one page, look at 2 Page View, as shown in Figure A-23.

d. Print one copy of the first page only.

e. Close Print Preview.

FIGURE A-21

FIGURE A-22

FIGURE A-23

▼ SKILLS REVIEW (CONTINUED)

7. Search for information on the Web.

  a. Click the Search box in the Address bar.

  b. Type any keyword or phrase for which you would like to find information, then execute the search and review the results.

  c. Click any link in the Search results page and read the Web page.

  d. Enter the URL for a search engine in the Address Bar (you can use www.google.com, www.ask.com, www.live.com, or www.yahoo.com).

  e. Type any keyword or phrase for which you would like to find information, then start the search using the search engine.

  f. View the resulting list of links, then click a link and review the Web page.

  g. Return to the search results page, then explore some of the other hyperlinks you found.

8. Get Help.

  a. Open Microsoft Internet Explorer Help, then search for a topic of interest to you.

  b. Click any link for any topic you want to learn more about.

  c. Read the results.

  d. Close the Windows Internet Explorer Help window.

9. Exit Internet Explorer.

  a. Delete any Favorites you created using the Organize Favorites dialog box.

  b. Exit Internet Explorer.

▼ INDEPENDENT CHALLENGE 1

You are an aspiring journalist interested in understanding how different journalists approach the same story. You decide to use the Web to find some articles for comparison.

  a. Start Internet Explorer.

  b. Read and compare the coverage of a current international news story using two of the following sites:

  - CNN   www.cnn.com
  - MSNBC News   www.msnbc.com
  - National Public Radio   www.npr.org
  - ABC News   www.abcnews.com
  - CBS News   www.cbsnews.com

  c. Open each news story in its own tab in the browser window.

  d. Use the Page Setup dialog box to add your name as a footer to the printed page, then print one page of the same story from both sites that you chose using the Shrink to Fit option.

Advanced Challenge Exercise

You should be able to find many English-language versions of non-U.S. papers.

  - Use your favorite search engine to locate an online news media source from a country other than the United States. You can search on keywords such as "Asian newspapers" or "European newspapers."
  - See if you can find the news story you researched in Step b.
  - Read the article.
  - Use the Page Setup dialog box to add your name as a footer to the printed page, then print one page of the article from the site that you chose.

  e. Close all but one of the tabs, then exit Internet Explorer.

Internet

▼ INDEPENDENT CHALLENGE 2

You have been asked by your local community college to teach a short course on classic films from the 1940s and 1950s. The class will meet four times; each class will begin with a screening and be followed by a discussion. You decide to use the Web to research the material.

   a. Start Internet Explorer.

   b. Go to your favorite search engine, then use a keyword search to find a Web site that contains information about films made in the 1940s.

   c. Find two films from the 1940s that you want to show as part of the course. View the information about each film in a separate tab in the browser window.

   d. Click several links on the film site and review the online resources.

   e. Search the film site to find two films from the 1950s. View the information about each film in a separate tab in the browser window.

   f. Add the film site as a favorite to the Favorites Center.

   g. Use the Page Setup dialog box to add your name as a footer to the printed page, then print one page for each film from the site.

Advanced Challenge Exercise

   ■ Find one page that includes a link for media such as audio or video.

   ■ Click the link and listen to the audio or play the video.

   ■ After listening to or viewing the media file, close the window.

   h. Delete the film site from the Favorites Center, then exit Internet Explorer.

▼ INDEPENDENT CHALLENGE 3

As a student of American political history, you want to learn about your representatives in the U.S. government. You decide to use the Web to get information about this topic.

   a. Start Internet Explorer, then access the following government Web site: **www.thomas.gov**.

   b. Explore the site to find information about members of Congress. Use the Page Setup dialog box to add your name as a footer to the printed page, then print one page from that site.

   c. In a new tab, open the Web site **www.senate.gov**, the U.S. Senate home page, as shown in Figure A-24.

   d. Click the Senators link, then find a link to a Web site for a senator who represents the state that you would most like to visit. Click the link, then print one page from that site.

   e. Explore three links on the senator's Web site to learn more about those topics, opening each page in a new tab.

   f. Use the Quick Tabs feature to navigate between the Web pages.

   g. Use the Page Setup dialog box to add your name as a footer to the printed page, then print one page from one of the related sites.

   h. Exit Internet Explorer.

FIGURE A-24

▼ REAL LIFE INDEPENDENT CHALLENGE

You would like to select a search engine to use consistently when you search the Web. You decide to compare several search engines to determine which one you like the most.

a. Start Internet Explorer. Using two of the search engines listed below, type **nobel prize winners** in the Search text box, and then search for the topic.

- Yahoo!   www.yahoo.com
- Live Search   www.live.com
- Google   www.google.com
- Ask   www.ask.com

b. Add your name as a footer to the printed page, then print the first page of the results from each search. Circle the name of the search engine and the number of results it produced.

c. On a sheet of paper, write which search engine you think is better and include a few reasons for your preference.

Advanced Challenge Exercise

- Create a folder in the Favorites Center called **Search Results**.
- Add the home page for your favorite search engine to the Favorites Center, in the Search Results folder.
- Return to your home page, then use the Favorites Center to go to the search engine home page.
- Delete the Search Results folder and search engine home page from the Favorites Center.

d. Exit Internet Explorer.

▼ VISUAL WORKSHOP

Graphics you find as you view pages on the Web can be static images, video, or animated graphics. Find two Web sites that include a video. You may be given the option to watch the video using a player such as Windows Media Player, as shown in Figure A-25. Other viewing options may include other players or viewing the video directly through the Web page. View at least one video on a news site and one video on a topic-specific Web site such as an organization or tourism site. Write a brief summary of the videos you watched. Did you have to load a special program to watch the video? Identify the Web sites on which the videos were located.

FIGURE A-25

Creating Documents with Word 2007

Microsoft Office Word 2007 is a word processing program that makes it easy to create a variety of professional-looking documents, from simple letters and memos to newsletters, research papers, blog posts, business cards, résumés, financial reports, and other documents that include multiple pages of text and sophisticated formatting. In this unit, you will explore the editing and formatting features available in Word and create two documents. You have been hired to work in the Marketing Department at Quest Specialty Travel (QST), a tour company that specializes in cultural tourism and adventure travel. Shortly after reporting to your new office, Ron Dawson, the vice president of marketing, asks you to use Word to create a memo to the marketing staff and a fax to one of the tour developers.

OBJECTIVES

Understand word processing software

Explore the Word program window

Start a document

Save a document

Select text

Format text using the Mini toolbar

Create a document using a template

View and navigate a document

Understanding Word Processing Software

A **word processing program** is a software program that includes tools for entering, editing, and formatting text and graphics. Microsoft Word is a powerful word processing program that allows you to create and enhance a wide range of documents quickly and easily. Figure A-1 shows the first page of a report created using Word and illustrates some of the Word features you can use to enhance your documents. The electronic files you create using Word are called **documents**. One of the benefits of using Word is that document files can be stored on a hard disk, CD, flash drive, or other storage device, making them easy to transport, exchange, and revise. ▧▧▧ Before beginning your memo to the marketing staff, you explore the editing and formatting capabilities available in Word.

DETAILS

You can use Word to accomplish the following tasks:

- **Type and edit text**

  The Word editing tools make it simple to insert and delete text in a document. You can add text to the middle of an existing paragraph, replace text with other text, undo an editing change, and correct typing, spelling, and grammatical errors with ease.

- **Copy and move text from one location to another**

  Using the more advanced editing features of Word, you can copy or move text from one location and insert it in a different location in a document. You also can copy and move text between documents. Being able to copy and move text means you don't have to retype text that is already entered in a document.

- **Format text and paragraphs with fonts, colors, and other elements**

  The sophisticated formatting tools available in Word allow you to make the text in your documents come alive. You can change the size, style, and color of text, add lines and shading to paragraphs, and enhance lists with bullets and numbers. Formatting text creatively helps you highlight important ideas in your documents.

- **Format and design pages**

  The Word page-formatting features give you power to design attractive newsletters, create powerful résumés, and produce documents such as business cards, CD labels, and books. You can change the paper size and orientation of your documents, organize text in columns, and control the layout of text and graphics on each page of a document. For quick results, Word includes preformatted cover pages, pull quotes, and headers and footers, as well as galleries of coordinated text, table, and graphic styles that you can rely on to give documents a polished look.

- **Enhance documents with tables, charts, diagrams, and graphics**

  Using the powerful graphics tools available in Word, you can spice up your documents with pictures, photographs, lines, shapes, and diagrams. You also can illustrate your documents with tables and charts to help convey your message in a visually interesting way.

- **Use Mail Merge to create form letters and mailing labels**

  The Word Mail Merge feature allows you to send personalized form letters to many different people. You can also use Mail Merge to create mailing labels, directories, e-mail messages, and other types of documents.

- **Share documents securely**

  The Word Document Inspector feature makes it quick and easy to thoroughly remove comments, tracked changes, and unwanted personal information from your files before you share them with others. You can also add a digital signature to a document, convert a file to a format suitable for publishing on the Web, and easily recognize a document that might contain a potentially harmful macro.

FIGURE A-1: A report created using Word

Add headers to every page

Insert graphics

Format the size and appearance of text

Create columns of text

Create tables

Add lines

Add bullets to lists

Create charts

Align text in paragraphs evenly

Add page numbers in footers

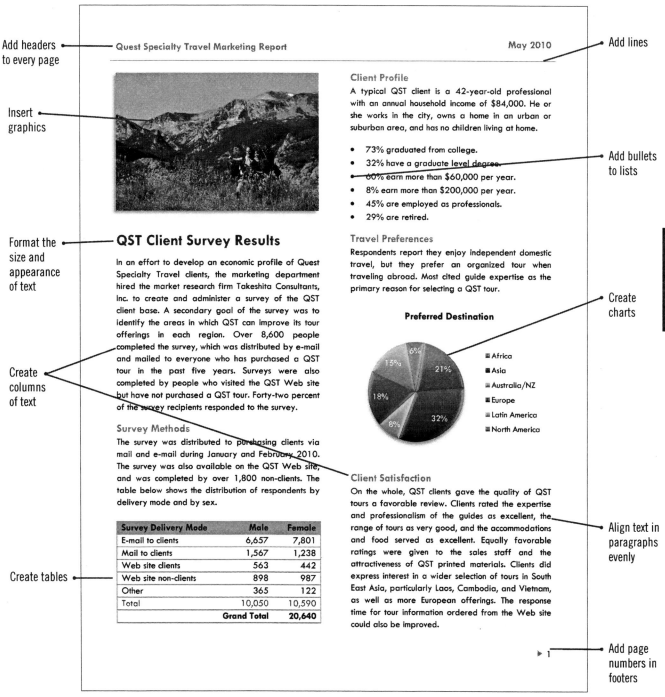

Quest Specialty Travel Marketing Report   May 2010

Client Profile

A typical QST client is a 42-year-old professional with an annual household income of $84,000. He or she works in the city, owns a home in an urban or suburban area, and has no children living at home.

- 73% graduated from college.
- 32% have a graduate level degree.
- 60% earn more than $60,000 per year.
- 8% earn more than $200,000 per year.
- 45% are employed as professionals.
- 29% are retired.

QST Client Survey Results

In an effort to develop an economic profile of Quest Specialty Travel clients, the marketing department hired the market research firm Takeshita Consultants, Inc. to create and administer a survey of the QST client base. A secondary goal of the survey was to identify the areas in which QST can improve its tour offerings in each region. Over 8,600 people completed the survey, which was distributed by e-mail and mailed to everyone who has purchased a QST tour in the past five years. Surveys were also completed by people who visited the QST Web site but have not purchased a QST tour. Forty-two percent of the survey recipients responded to the survey.

Survey Methods

The survey was distributed to purchasing clients via mail and e-mail during January and February 2010. The survey was also available on the QST Web site, and was completed by over 1,800 non-clients. The table below shows the distribution of respondents by delivery mode and by sex.

Travel Preferences

Respondents report they enjoy independent domestic travel, but they prefer an organized tour when traveling abroad. Most cited guide expertise as the primary reason for selecting a QST tour.

Preferred Destination

- Africa
- Asia
- Australia/NZ
- Europe
- Latin America
- North America

Client Satisfaction

On the whole, QST clients gave the quality of QST tours a favorable review. Clients rated the expertise and professionalism of the guides as excellent, the range of tours as very good, and the accommodations and food served as excellent. Equally favorable ratings were given to the sales staff and the attractiveness of QST printed materials. Clients did express interest in a wider selection of tours in South East Asia, particularly Laos, Cambodia, and Vietnam, as well as more European offerings. The response time for tour information ordered from the Web site could also be improved.

Survey Delivery Mode	Male	Female
E-mail to clients	6,657	7,801
Mail to clients	1,567	1,238
Web site clients	563	442
Web site non-clients	898	987
Other	365	122
Total	10,050	10,590
Grand Total		20,640

▶ 1

Planning a document

Before you create a new document, it's a good idea to spend time planning it. Identify the message you want to convey, the audience for your document, and the elements, such as tables or charts, you want to include. You should also think about the tone and look of your document—are you writing a business letter, which should be written in a pleasant, but serious tone and have a formal appearance, or are you creating a flyer that must be colorful, eye-catching, and

fun to read? The purpose and audience for your document determines the appropriate design. Planning the layout and design of a document involves deciding how to organize the text, selecting the fonts to use, identifying the graphics to include, and selecting the formatting elements that will enhance the message and appeal of the document. For longer documents, such as newsletters, it can be useful to sketch the layout and design of each page before you begin.

Creating Documents with Word 2007

Exploring the Word Program Window

When you start Word, a blank document appears in the document window. ███████ You examine the elements of the Word program window.

STEPS

1. **Start Word**

   The **Word program window** opens, as shown in Figure A-2. The blinking vertical line in the document window is the **insertion point**. It indicates where text appears as you type. The blank document opens in Print Layout view. **Views** are different ways of displaying a document in the document window.

2. **Move the mouse pointer around the Word program window**

   The mouse pointer changes shape depending on where it is in the Word program window. You use pointers to move the insertion point or to select text to edit. Table A-1 describes common pointers in Word.

3. **Place the mouse pointer over a button on the Ribbon**

   When you place the mouse pointer over a button or some other elements of the Word program window, a ScreenTip appears. A **ScreenTip** is a label that identifies the name of the button or feature, briefly describes its function, conveys any keyboard shortcut for the command, and includes a link to associated help topics, if any.

   Using Figure A-2 as a guide, find the elements described below in your program window.

   - The **title bar** displays the name of the document and the name of the program. Until you give a new document a different name, its temporary name is Document1. The title bar also contains resizing buttons and the program Close button. These buttons are common to all Windows programs.
   - Clicking the **Office button** opens a menu of commands related to managing and sharing documents, including opening, printing, and saving a document, creating a new document, and preparing a document for distribution. The Office button also provides access to the Word Options dialog box, which is used to customize the way you use Word.
   - The **Quick Access toolbar** contains buttons for saving a document and for undoing, redoing, and repeating a change. You can modify the Quick Access toolbar to include the commands you use most frequently.

   - The **Ribbon** contains the names of the Word tabs. Each **tab** includes buttons for commands, which are organized in **groups**. For example, the Home tab includes the Clipboard, Font, Paragraph, Styles, and Editing groups, each containing buttons related to editing and formatting text. The Ribbon also includes the **Microsoft Office Word Help button**, which you use to access the Word Help system.
   - The **document window** displays the current document. You enter text and format your document in the document window.

   - The rulers appear in the document window in Print Layout view. The **horizontal ruler** displays left and right document margins as well as the tab settings and paragraph indents, if any, for the paragraph in which the insertion point is located. The **vertical ruler** displays the top and bottom document margins.
   - The **vertical scroll bar** and the **horizontal scroll bar** are used to display different parts of the document in the document window. The scroll bars include **scroll boxes** and **scroll arrows**, which you can use to move easily through a document.
   - The **status bar** displays the page number of the current page, the total number of pages and words in the document, and the status of spelling and grammar checking. It also includes the view buttons, the Zoom level button, and the Zoom slider. You can customize the status bar to display other information.
   - The **view buttons** on the status bar allow you to display the document in Print Layout, Full Screen Reading, Web Layout, Outline, or Draft view.
   - The **Zoom level** button and the **Zoom slider** provide quick ways to enlarge and decrease the size of the document in the document window, making it easy to zoom in on a detail of a document or to view the layout of the document as a whole.

FIGURE A-2: Elements of the Word program window

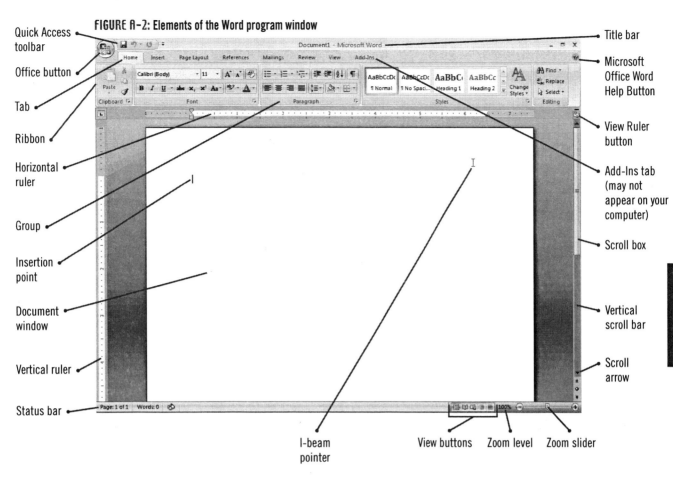

Quick Access toolbar

Office button

Tab

Ribbon

Horizontal ruler

Group

Insertion point

Document window

Vertical ruler

Status bar

Title bar

Microsoft Office Word Help Button

View Ruler button

Add-Ins tab (may not appear on your computer)

Scroll box

Vertical scroll bar

Scroll arrow

I-beam pointer

View buttons

Zoom level

Zoom slider

Word 2007

TABLE A-1: Common mouse pointers in Word

name	pointer	use to
I-beam pointer	I	Move the insertion point in a document or to select text
Click-and-type pointers: left-align click-and-type pointer; center-align click-and-type pointer	I≡ or I≡	Move the insertion point in a blank area of a document in Print Layout or Web Layout view; double-clicking with a Click and Type pointer automatically applies the paragraph formatting (alignment and indentation) required to position text or a graphic at that location in the document
Selection pointer	⟍	Click a button or other element of the Word program window; appears when you point to elements of the Word program window
Right-pointing arrow pointer	⟋	Select a line or lines of text; appears when you point to the left edge of a line of text in the document window
Hand pointer	🖑	Open a hyperlink; appears when you point to a hyperlink in a task pane or when you press [Ctrl] and point to a hyperlink in a document
Hide white space pointer	⊟	Hide the white space in the top and bottom margins of a document in Print Layout view
Show white space pointer	⊞	Show the white space in the top and bottom margins of a document in Print Layout view

Starting a Document

You begin a new document by simply typing text in a blank document in the document window. Word includes a **word-wrap** feature so that as you type Word automatically moves the insertion point to the next line of the document when you reach the right margin. You only press [Enter] when you want to start a new paragraph or insert a blank line. ▰▰▰ You type a quick memo to the marketing staff.

STEPS

1. Type Memorandum, then press [Enter] twice

Each time you press [Enter] the insertion point moves to the start of the next line.

2. Type TO:, then press [Tab] twice

Pressing [Tab] moves the insertion point several spaces to the right. You can use the [Tab] key to align the text in a memo header or to indent the first line of a paragraph.

3. Type QST Managers, then press [Enter]

The insertion point moves to the start of the next line.

4. Type: FROM: [Tab] [Tab] Ron Dawson [Enter]
        DATE: [TAB] [Tab] July 12, 2010 [Enter]
        RE: [Tab] [Tab] Marketing Meeting [Enter] [Enter]

Red or green wavy lines may appear under the words you typed, indicating a possible spelling or grammar error. Spelling and grammar checking is one of the many automatic features you will encounter as you type. Table A-2 describes several of these automatic features. You can correct any typing errors you make later.

5. Type The next marketing staff meeting will be held on the 16th of July at 1 p.m. in the conference room on the ground floor., then press [Spacebar]

As you type, notice that the insertion point moves automatically to the next line of the document. You also might notice that Word automatically changed "16th" to "16th" in the memo. This feature is called **AutoCorrect**. AutoCorrect automatically makes typographical adjustments and detects and adjusts typing errors, certain misspelled words (such as "taht" for "that"), and incorrect capitalization as you type.

6. Type Heading the agenda will be the launch of our new Mai Chau Mountain Tribal Trek, a ten-day walking and rafting tour of the sultry rivers, hidden villages, and misty forests of northern Vietnam, scheduled for February 2012.

When you type the first few characters of "February," the Word AutoComplete feature displays the complete word in a ScreenTip. **AutoComplete** suggests text to insert quickly into your documents. You can ignore AutoComplete for now. Your memo should resemble Figure A-3.

7. Press [Enter], then type Wim Hoppengarth is in Hanoi hammering out the details. A preliminary draft of the tour brochure is attached. Bring your creative ideas for launching this exciting new tour to the meeting.

When you press [Enter] and type the new paragraph, notice that Word adds more space between the paragraphs than it does between the lines within each individual paragraph. This is part of the default style for paragraphs in Word, called the Normal style.

8. Position the I pointer after for (but before the space) in the last line of the first paragraph, then click

Clicking moves the insertion point after "for."

9. Press [Backspace] three times, then type to depart in

Pressing [Backspace] removes the character before the insertion point.

10. Move the insertion point before staff in the first sentence, then press [Delete] six times to remove the word staff and the space after it

Pressing [Delete] removes the character after the insertion point. Figure A-4 shows the revised memo.

FIGURE A-3: Memo text in the document window

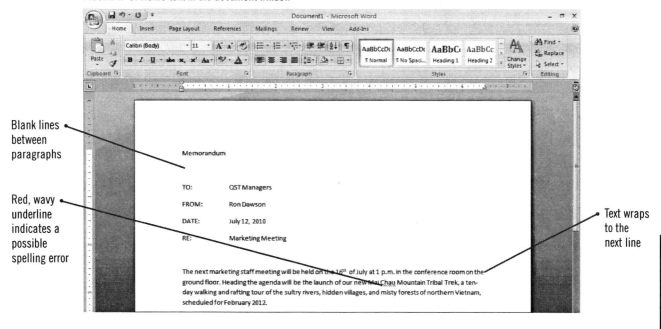

Blank lines between paragraphs

Red, wavy underline indicates a possible spelling error

Text wraps to the next line

FIGURE A-4: Edited memo text

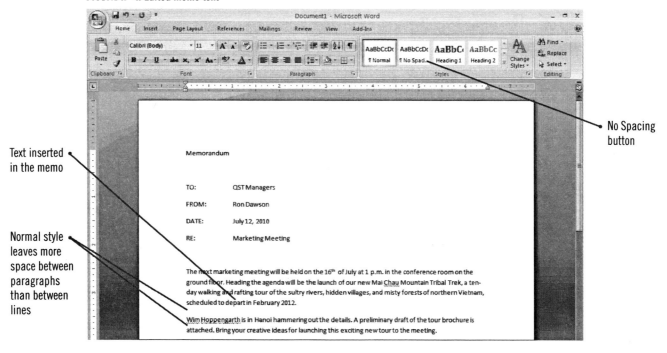

No Spacing button

Text inserted in the memo

Normal style leaves more space between paragraphs than between lines

TABLE A-2: Automatic features that appear as you type in Word

feature	what appears	to use
AutoComplete	A ScreenTip suggesting text to insert appears as you type	Press [Enter] to insert the text suggested by the ScreenTip; continue typing to reject the suggestion
AutoCorrect	A small blue box appears when you place the pointer over text corrected by AutoCorrect; an AutoCorrect Options button ⬚▾ appears when you point to the corrected text	Word automatically corrects typos, minor spelling errors, and capitalization, and adds typographical symbols (such as © and ™) as you type; to reverse an AutoCorrect adjustment, click the AutoCorrect Options list arrow, then click Undo or the option that will undo the action
Spelling and Grammar	A red wavy line under a word indicates a possible misspelling; a green wavy line under text indicates a possible grammar error	Right-click red- or green-underlined text to display a shortcut menu of correction options; click a correction to accept it and remove the wavy underline

Creating Documents with Word 2007

Saving a Document

To store a document permanently so you can open it and edit it in the future, you must save it as a **file**. When you **save** a document you give it a name, called a **filename**, and indicate the location where you want to store the file. Files created in Word 2007 are automatically assigned the .docx file extension to distinguish them from files created in other software programs, including previous versions of Word. Files created in previous versions of Word carry the .doc file extension. You can save a document using the Save button on the Quick Access toolbar or the Save command on the Office menu. Once you have saved a document for the first time, you should save it again every few minutes and always before printing so that the saved file is updated to reflect your latest changes. ██████ You save your memo using a descriptive filename and the default file extension.

STEPS

TROUBLE
If you don't see the extension .docx as part of the filename, Windows is set not to display file extensions.

1. **Click the Save button 🖫 on the Quick Access toolbar**

   The first time you save a document, the Save As dialog box opens, as shown in Figure A-5. The default filename, Memorandum, appears in the File name text box. The default filename is based on the first few words of the document. The default file extension, .docx, appears in the Save as type list box. Table A-3 describes the functions of some of the buttons in the Save As dialog box.

2. **Type Vietnam Tour Memo in the File name text box**

   The new filename replaces the default filename. Giving your documents brief descriptive filenames makes it easier to locate and organize them later. You do not need to type .docx when you type a new filename.

TROUBLE
Click Browse Folders in the Save As dialog box to display the Navigation pane and folder window.

3. **Navigate to the drive and folder where you store your Data Files**

   You can navigate to a different drive or folder either by clicking a location in the Address bar to go directly to that location, or by clicking an arrow next to a location in the Address bar to open a list of subfolders, and then selecting a new location from the list. Click the double arrow in the Address bar to navigate to the next highest level in the folder hierarchy. You can also double-click a drive or folder in the Navigation pane or the folder window to change the active location. When you are finished, the drive or folder where you store your Data Files appears in the Address bar. Your Save As dialog box should resemble Figure A-6.

QUICK TIP
To save a document so it can be opened in a previous version of Word, click the Save as type list arrow, then click Word 97-2003 Document (*.doc)

4. **Click Save**

   The document is saved to the drive and folder you specified in the Save As dialog box, and the title bar displays the new filename, Vietnam Tour Memo.docx.

5. **Place the insertion point before ten-day in the second sentence, type rugged, then press [Spacebar]**

   You can continue to work on a document after you have saved it with a new filename.

6. **Click 🖫**

   Your change to the memo is saved. Saving a document after you give it a filename saves the changes you make to the document. You also can press [Ctrl][S] to save a document.

Working with XML and binary files

The default x suffix in the .docx file extension indicates a file is saved in the Office **XML format**, which is new to Word 2007. Earlier versions of Word employed a binary file format, signified by the familiar .doc file extension. To facilitate file sharing between the different versions of Office, Word 2007 allows you to open, edit, and save files in either XML or binary format. When you open a binary file in Word 2007, the words Compatibility Mode appear in the title bar next to the filename. You can also turn on Compatibility Mode by saving a copy of an XML file in Word 97-2003 format. When you are working in Compatibility Mode, some Word 2007 document features, including built-in document themes, margins, text boxes, tures, including built-in document themes, margins, text boxes,

SmartArt, bibliographies, mail merge data, and certain theme colors, fonts, and effects will be permanently changed or behave differently.

Converting a binary file to XML format is simple: click the Office button, click Convert on the Office menu, and then click OK in the Microsoft Office Word dialog box that opens. This turns off Compatibility Mode. Once a file is converted to XML, you can save the converted file, which replaces the original .doc file with a .docx file of the same filename, by clicking the Save button, or you can use the Save As command on the Office menu to create a new .docx file, preserving the original binary .doc file.

FIGURE A-5: Save As dialog box

Click an arrow in the Address bar to change the active folder or drive

Active folder

Navigation pane

Click Folders button to display expandable list of folders in the Navigation pane

Default filename and file extension are selected

Click to hide the Navigation pane and folder window

Address bar

Search for an item in the active location

Folder window displays the folders and files in the active folder or drive (yours will differ)

Click to change the file type

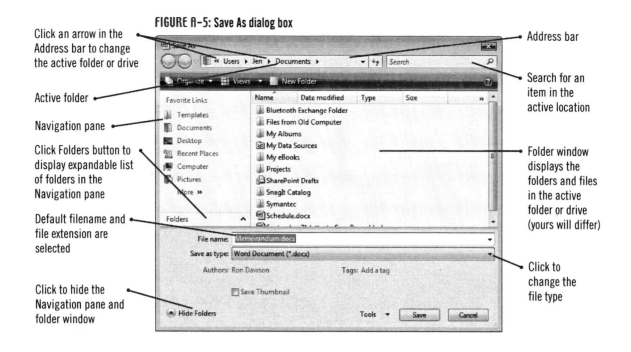

FIGURE A-6: File to be saved to the Unit A folder

Location of Data Files (yours might differ)

Your folder window might list the files and folders in the active location

New filename

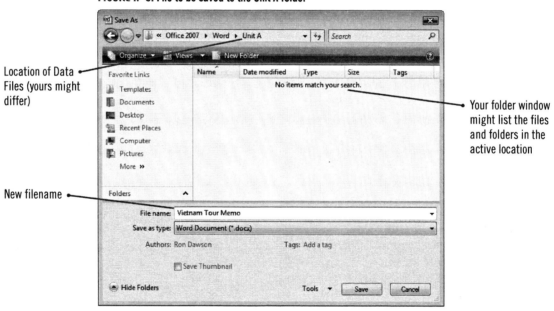

TABLE A-3: Save As dialog box buttons

button	use to
○ Back	Navigate to the next highest level in the folder hierarchy (to the drive or folder that contains the active folder)
○ Forward	Navigate to the subfolder that was previously shown in the Address bar
Organize ▾ **Organize**	Open a menu of commands related to organizing the selected file or folder, including Cut, Copy, Delete, Rename, and Properties
Views ▾ **Views**	Change the way folder and file information is shown in the folder window in the Save As dialog box; click the Views list arrow to open a menu of options
New Folder **New Folder**	Create a new folder in the current folder or drive

Selecting Text

Before deleting, editing, or formatting text, you must **select** the text. Selecting text involves clicking and dragging the I-beam pointer across text to highlight it. You also can click with the ⬧ pointer in the blank area to the left of text to select lines or paragraphs. Table A-4 describes the many ways to select text. You revise the memo by selecting text and replacing it with new text.

1. **Click the Show/Hide ¶ button ¶ in the Paragraph group**

   Formatting marks appear in the document window. **Formatting marks** are special characters that appear on your screen and do not print. Common formatting marks include the paragraph symbol (¶), which shows the end of a paragraph—wherever you press [Enter]; the dot symbol (•), which represents a space—wherever you press [Spacebar]; and the arrow symbol (→), which shows the location of a tab stop—wherever you press [Tab]. Working with formatting marks turned on can help you to select, edit, and format text with precision.

   TROUBLE

   If you make a mistake, you can deselect the text by clicking anywhere in the document window.

   ---

2. **Click before QST Managers, then drag the I pointer over the text to select it**

   The words are selected, as shown in Figure A-7. For now you can ignore the faint toolbar that appears over text when you first select it.

3. **Type Marketing Staff**

   The text you type replaces the selected text.

4. **Double-click Ron, type your first name, double-click Dawson, then type your last name**

   Double-clicking a word selects the entire word.

   QUICK TIP

   If you delete text by mistake, immediately click the Undo button ↺ on the Quick Access toolbar to restore the deleted text to the document.

   ---

5. **Place the pointer in the margin to the left of the RE: line so that the pointer changes to ⬧, click to select the line, then type RE: [Tab][Tab] Launch of new Vietnam trekking tour**

   Clicking to the left of a line of text with the ⬧ pointer selects the entire line.

6. **Select sultry in the third line of the first paragraph, type meandering, select misty forests, then type stunning limestone peaks**

7. **Select the sentence Wim Hoppengarth is in Hanoi hammering out the details., then press [Delete]**

   Selecting text and pressing [Delete] removes the text from the document.

   QUICK TIP

   Always save before and after editing text

   ---

8. **Click ¶, then click the Save button 🖫 on the Quick Access toolbar**

   Formatting marks are turned off and your changes to the memo are saved. The Show/Hide ¶ button is a **toggle button**, which means you can use it to turn formatting marks on and off. The edited memo is shown in Figure A-8.

TABLE A-4: Methods for selecting text

to select	use the pointer to
Any amount of text	Drag over the text
A word	Double-click the word
A line of text	Click with the ⬧ pointer to the left of the line
A sentence	Press and hold [Ctrl], then click the sentence
A paragraph	Triple-click the paragraph or double-click with the ⬧ pointer to the left of the paragraph
A large block of text	Click at the beginning of the selection, press and hold [Shift], then click at the end of the selection
Multiple nonconsecutive selections	Select the first selection, then press and hold [Ctrl] as you select each additional selection
An entire document	Triple-click with the ⬧ pointer to the left of any text, press [Ctrl][A], or click the Select button in the Editing group on the Home tab, and then click Select All

FIGURE A-7: Text selected in the memo

Selected text

Left document margin

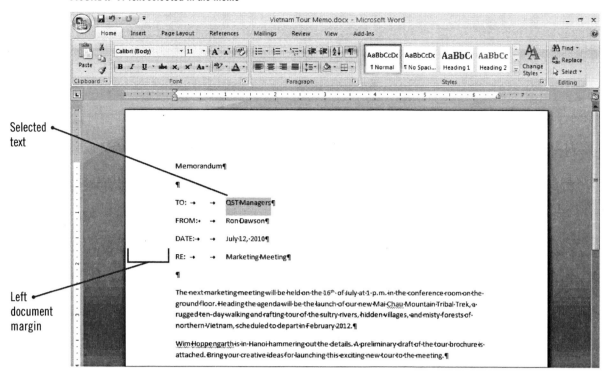

FIGURE A-8: Edited memo with replacement text

Replacement text

Formatting Text Using the Mini Toolbar

Changing the format of text is a fast and fun way to spruce up the appearance of a document and highlight important information. You can easily format text with fonts, colors, styles, borders, and other formatting options by selecting the text and clicking a command on the Home tab. The **Mini toolbar**, which appears faintly above text when you first select it, also includes the most commonly used text and paragraph formatting commands. Table A-5 describes the function of the buttons on the Mini toolbar. You enhance the appearance of the memo by formatting the text using the Mini toolbar. Before printing the finished memo, you preview it in Print Preview.

STEPS

1. **Double-click Memorandum**

   The Mini toolbar appears in ghosted fashion over the selected text. When you point to the Mini toolbar, it becomes solid, as shown in Figure A-9, and you can click a formatting option to apply it to the selected text.

2. **Click the Center button ☰ on the Mini toolbar**

   The word Memorandum is centered between the left and right document margins.

3. **Click the Grow Font button A⃗ on the Mini toolbar eight times, then click the Bold button B on the Mini toolbar**

   Each time you click the Grow Font button the selected text is enlarged. Applying **bold** to the text makes it thicker and darker.

4. **Select TO:, click B, select FROM:, click B, select DATE:, click B, select RE:, then click B**

   Bold is applied to the heading text.

5. **Click the blank line between the RE: line and the body text, then click the Bottom Border button ▦ in the Paragraph group**

   A single-line border is added between the heading and the body text in the memo.

6. **Click the Office button 🔘, point to Print, then click Print Preview**

   The document appears in Print Preview. Before you print a document, it's a good habit to examine it carefully in **Print Preview** so you can identify and correct any problems before printing.

7. **Move the pointer over the memo text until it changes to 🔍, then click the word Memorandum**

   Clicking with the 🔍 pointer magnifies the document in the Print Preview window and changes the pointer to 🔍. The memo appears as it will look when printed, as shown in Figure A-10. Clicking with the 🔍 pointer reduces the size of the document in the Print Preview window.

8. **Click the Magnifier check box in the Preview group**

   Deselecting the Magnifier check box turns off the magnification feature and allows you to edit the document in Print Preview. In edit mode, the pointer changes to I.

9. **Examine your memo carefully for errors, correct any mistakes, then click the Close Print Preview button in the Preview group**

   Print Preview closes and the memo appears in the document window.

10. **Save the document, click 🔘, click Print, click OK in the Print dialog box, click 🔘, then click Close**

    A copy of the memo prints using the default print settings. You can use the Print dialog box to change the current printer, change the number of copies to print, select what pages of a document to print, and modify other printing options. After printing, the document closes, but the Word program window remains open.

FIGURE A-9: Mini toolbar

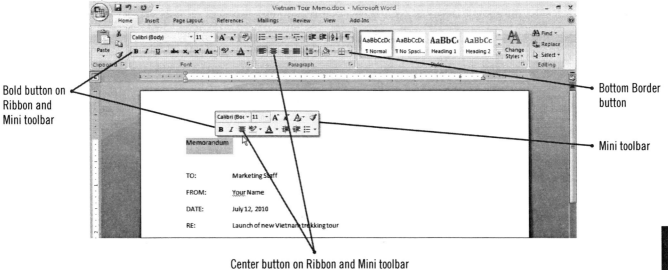

Bold button on Ribbon and Mini toolbar

Bottom Border button

Mini toolbar

Center button on Ribbon and Mini toolbar

FIGURE A-10: Completed memo in the Print Preview window

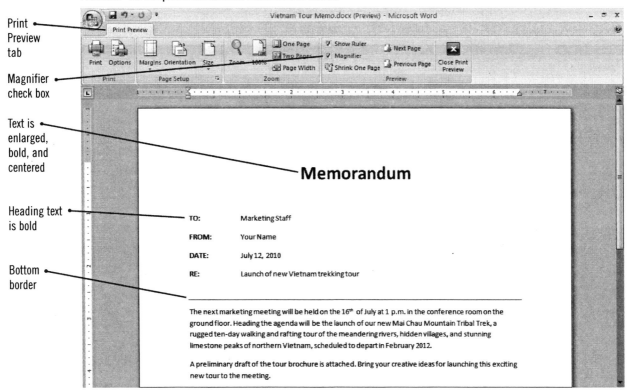

Print Preview tab

Magnifier check box

Text is enlarged, bold, and centered

Heading text is bold

Bottom border

TABLE A-5: Buttons on the Mini toolbar

button	use to	button	use to
Calibri (Boc ▼)	Change the font of text	*I*	Italicize text
11 ▼	Change the font size of text	≣	Center text between the margins
A˄	Make text larger	ab ▼	Apply colored highlighting to text
A˅	Make text smaller	A ▼	Change the color of text
A	Apply a style to text	達	Decrease the indent level of a paragraph
✓	Copy the formats applied to text to other text	達	Increase the indent level of a paragraph
B	Apply bold to text	≔ ▼	Format paragraphs as a bulleted list

Creating Documents with Word 2007

Creating a Document Using a Template

Word includes many templates that you can use to quickly create memos, faxes, letters, reports, brochures, and other professionally designed documents. A **template** is a formatted document that contains placeholder text, generic text that you replace with text specific to your needs. You use the New command on the Office menu to open a file that is based on a template. You then replace the placeholder text with your own text, and save the document with a new filename. You want to fax a draft of the Vietnam tour brochure to Wim Hoppengarth, the tour developer for Asia. You use a template to create a fax cover sheet.

1. Click the Office button 🔘, then click New

The New Document dialog box opens, as shown in Figure A-11.

To create a new blank document, make sure Blank document is selected, then click Create.

2. Click Installed Templates in the Templates Categories pane, scroll down the list of Installed Templates, then click Oriel Fax

A preview of the Oriel Fax template appears in the New Document dialog box.

Double-clicking an icon in the Templates dialog box also opens a new document based on the template.

3. Click Create

The Oriel Fax template opens as a new document in the document window. It contains placeholder text, which you can replace with your own information.

4. Click [Pick the date]

The placeholder text is selected and appears inside a content control. A **content control** is an interactive object that you use to customize a document with your own information. A content control might include placeholder text, a drop-down list of choices, or a calendar. To deselect a content control, you click a blank area of the document.

5. Click the Pick the date list arrow

A calendar opens below the content control. You use the calendar to select the date you want to appear on your document—simply click a date on the calendar to enter that date in the document. You can use the arrows to the left and right of the month and year to scroll the calendar and display a different month.

6. Click the Today button in the calendar

The current date replaces the placeholder text.

You can delete a content control by right-clicking it, and then clicking Remove Content Control on the Edit menu.

7. Click [TYPE THE RECIPIENT NAME], type Wim Hoppengarth, Guest, click [Type the recipient fax number], then type 1-84-4-555-1510

You do not need to drag to select the placeholder text in a content control, you can simply click it. The text you type replaces the placeholder text.

8. Click [Type the recipient phone number], press [Delete] twice, press [Backspace] seven times, then type HOTEL NIKKO HANOI, ROOM 1384

The recipient phone number content control is removed from the document.

9. If the text In the From line is not your name, drag to select the text, then type your name

When the document is created, Word automatically enters the user name identified in the Word Options dialog box in the From line. This text is not placeholder text, so you have to drag to select it.

10. Replace the remaining heading placeholder text with the text shown in Figure A-12, click 🔘, click Save As, then save the document as Wim Fax to the drive and folder where you store your Data Files

The document is saved with the filename Wim Fax.

FIGURE A-11: New Document dialog box

Installed templates

Types of templates available with an active Internet connection

Select to create a blank document

Your list of recently used templates will differ or may not appear at all

FIGURE A-12: Document created using the Oriel fax template

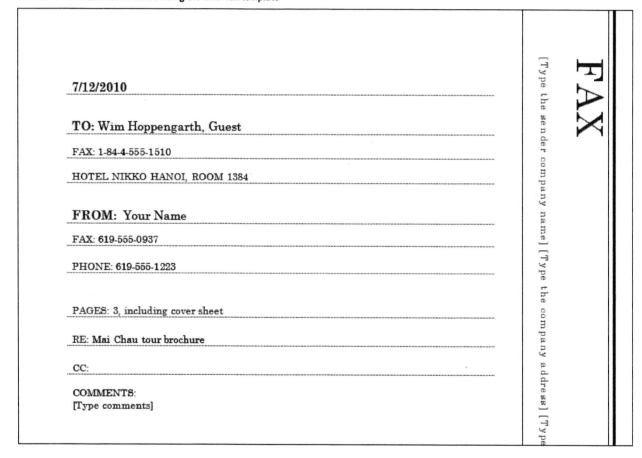

FAX

[Type the sender company name] [Type the company address] [Type

7/12/2010

TO: Wim Hoppengarth, Guest

FAX: 1-84-4-555-1510

HOTEL NIKKO HANOI, ROOM 1384

FROM: Your Name

FAX: 619-555-0937

PHONE: 619-555-1223

PAGES: 3, including cover sheet

RE: Mai Chau tour brochure

CC:

COMMENTS:
[Type comments]

Using the Undo, Redo, and Repeat commands

Word remembers the editing and formatting changes you make so that you can easily reverse or repeat them. You can reverse the last action you took by clicking the Undo button ⤺ on the Quick Access toolbar, or you can undo a series of actions by clicking the Undo list arrow ⤺ ▾ and selecting the action you want to reverse. When you undo an action using the Undo list arrow, you also undo all the actions above it in the list—that is, all actions that were performed after the action you selected. Similarly, you can keep the change you just reversed by using the Redo button ⤻ on the

Quick Access toolbar. The Redo button appears only immediately after clicking the Undo button to undo a change.

If you want to repeat an action you just completed, you can use the Repeat button ⟳ on the Quick Access toolbar. For example, if you just typed "thank you," clicking ⟳ inserts "thank you" at the location of the insertion point. If you just applied bold, clicking ⟳ applies bold to the currently selected text. You also can repeat the last action you took by pressing [F4].

Viewing and Navigating a Document

The Word Zoom feature lets you enlarge a document in the document window to get a close-up view of a detail, or reduce the size of the document in the document window for an overview of the layout as a whole. You zoom in and out on a document using the tools in the Zoom group on the View tab and the Zoom level button and Zoom slider on the status bar. ▆▆▆▆ You find it's helpful to zoom in and out on the document as you finalize the fax cover sheet.

STEPS

1. **Click the down scroll arrow at the bottom of the vertical scroll bar until COMMENTS: is at the top of your document window**

    The scroll arrows or scroll bars allow you to **scroll** through a document. You scroll through a document when you want to display different parts of the document in the document window. You can also scroll by clicking the scroll bar above and below the scroll box, or by dragging the scroll box up or down in the scroll bar. In longer documents, you can click the Previous Page button ▲ or the Next Page button ▼ on the scroll bar to display the document page by page.

2. **Click [Type comments], then type A draft copy of the Mai Chau tour brochure is attached. Please revise the text for accuracy. The photos are for placement only. Have you hired a photographer yet?**

3. **Click the Zoom level button `100%` on the status bar**

    The Zoom dialog box opens. You use the Zoom dialog box to select a zoom level for displaying the document in the document window.

    <div class="quick-tip">

    QUICK TIP

    You can also click the Zoom button in the Zoom group on the View tab to open the Zoom dialog box.

    </div>

4. **Click the Whole page option button, then click OK**

    The entire document is displayed in the document window.

5. **Click the text at the bottom of the page to move the insertion point to the bottom of the page, click the View tab, then click the Page Width button in the Zoom group**

    The document is enlarged to the width of the document window. When you enlarge a document, the area where the insertion point is located appears in the document window.

6. **Click in the Urgent box, type x, then click the One Page button in the Zoom group**

    The entire document is displayed in the document window.

7. **Click Fax to move the insertion point to the upper-right corner of the page, then move the Zoom slider to the right until the Zoom percentage is 100%, as shown in Figure A-13**

    Moving the Zoom slider to the right enlarges the document in the document window. Moving the zoom slider to the left allows you to see more of the page at a reduced size. You can also move the Zoom slider by clicking a point on the Zoom slider, or by clicking the Zoom Out and Zoom In buttons.

8. **Click the Zoom In button ⊕ three times, click the vertical placeholder [Type the sender company name], press [Delete] twice, click [Type the company address], press [Delete] twice, click [Type the company phone number], then type Quest Specialty Travel, San Diego, CA**

    The text you type replaces the vertical placeholder text. You do not always need to replace the placeholder text with the type of information suggested in the content control.

9. **Preview the document in Print Preview, correct any errors, close Print Preview, click `130%`, click 100%, click OK, save the document, print it, close the file, then exit Word**

    The completed fax coversheet is shown in Figure A-14.

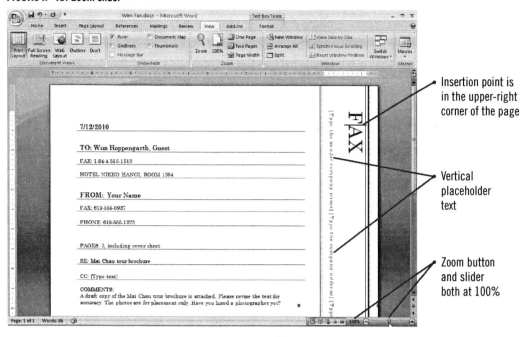

Insertion point is in the upper-right corner of the page

Vertical placeholder text

Zoom button and slider both at 100%

FIGURE A-14: Completed fax cover sheet

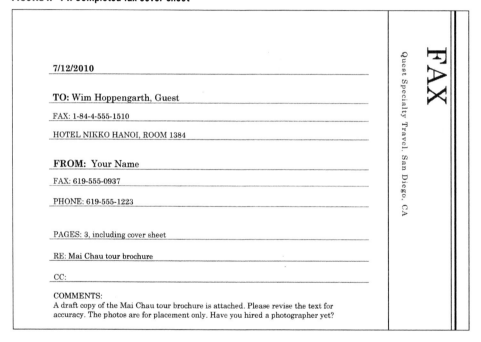

Using Word document views

Each Word view provides features that are useful for working on different types of documents. The default view, **Print Layout view**, displays a document as it will look on a printed page. Print Layout view is helpful for formatting text and pages, including adjusting document margins, creating columns of text, inserting graphics, and formatting headers and footers. Also useful is **Draft view**, which shows a simplified layout of a document, without margins, headers and footers, or graphics. When you want to quickly type, edit, and format text, it's often easiest to work in Draft view. Other Word views are helpful for performing specialized tasks. **Full Screen Reading view** displays document text so that it is easy to read and annotate. You can easily highlight content, add comments, and track and review changes in Full Screen Reading view. **Web Layout view** allows you to accurately format Web pages or documents that will be viewed on a computer screen. In Web Layout view, a document appears just as it will when viewed with a Web browser. Finally, **Outline view** is useful for editing and formatting longer documents that include multiple headings. Outline view allows you to reorganize text by moving the headings. You switch between views by clicking the view buttons on the status bar or by using the commands on the View tab. Changing views does not affect how the printed document will appear. It simply changes the way you view the document in the document window.

Practice

▼ CONCEPTS REVIEW

Label the elements of the Word program window shown in Figure A-15.

FIGURE A-15

Match each term with the statement that best describes it.

7. Template
8. Formatting marks
9. Status bar
10. Ribbon
11. AutoComplete
12. Horizontal ruler
13. AutoCorrect
14. Zoom slider

a. Enlarges and reduces the document in the document window
b. Special characters that appear on screen but do not print
c. Provides access to Word commands
d. Displays tab settings and paragraph indents
e. A formatted document that contains placeholder text
f. Fixes certain errors as you type
g. Displays the number of pages in the current document
h. Suggests text to insert into a document

Select the best answer from the list of choices.

15. Which of the following does not contain commands?
   a. The Mini toolbar
   b. The status bar
   c. The Ribbon
   d. The Office menu

16. Which tab includes buttons for formatting text?
   a. Home
   b. Insert
   c. Page Layout
   d. View

17. Which of the following is not included in a ScreenTip for a command?
   a. Keyboard shortcut for the command
   b. Alternative location of the command
   c. Description of the function of the command
   d. Link to a help topic on the command

18. Which element of the Word program window shows the settings for the top and bottom document margins?
   a. View tab
   b. Status bar
   c. Vertical scroll bar
   d. Vertical ruler

19. **What is the default file extension for a document created in Word 2007?**
   a. .doc
   c. .docx
   b. .dot
   d. .dotx

20. **Which view is best for annotating text with comments and highlighting?**
   a. Draft view
   c. Full Screen Reading view
   b. Outline view
   d. Print Layout view

▼ SKILLS REVIEW

1. **Explore the Word program window.**
   a. Start Word.
   b. Identify as many elements of the Word program window as you can without referring to the unit material.
   c. Click the Office button, then drag the pointer through the menu commands, pointing to the arrow when commands include an arrow.
   d. Click each tab on the Ribbon, review the groups and buttons on each tab, then return to the Home tab.
   e. Point to each button on the Home tab and read the ScreenTips.
   f. Click the view buttons to view the blank document in each view, then return to Print Layout view.
   g. Use the Zoom slider to zoom all the way in and all the way out on the document, then return to 100%.

2. **Start a document.**
   a. In a new blank document, type FAX at the top of the page, then press [Enter] two times.
   b. Type the following, pressing [Tab] as indicated and pressing [Enter] at the end of each line:
      To: [Tab][Tab] Joanna Card
      From: [Tab] [Tab] Your Name
      Date: [Tab] [Tab] Today's date
      Re: [Tab] [Tab] Reservation confirmation
      Pages: [Tab] [Tab] 1
      Fax: [Tab] [Tab] (603) 555-5478
   c. Press [Enter] again, then type Thank you for your interest in our summer festival weekend package, which includes accommodations for three nights in downtown Montreal, continental breakfast, and a festival pass. Rooms are still available during the following festivals: International Jazz Festival, Just for Laughs Festival, Montreal Fringe Festival, and Le Festival des Arts du Village. Please see the attached schedule for festival dates and details.
   d. Press [Enter], then type To make a reservation, please call me at (514) 555-7482. I will need payment in full by the 3rd of June to hold a room. No one knows how to celebrate summer like Montrealers!
   e. Insert Grand Prix Festival, before International Jazz Festival.
   f. Using the [Backspace] key, delete 1 in the Pages: line, then type 2.
   g. Using the [Delete] key, delete festival in the last sentence of the first paragraph.

3. **Save a document.**
   a. Click the Save button on the Quick Access toolbar.
   b. Save the document as Card Fax with the default file extension to the drive and folder where you store your Data Files.
   c. After your name, type a comma, press [Spacebar], then type Global Montreal
   d. Save the document.

4. **Select text.**
   a. Turn on formatting marks.
   b. Select the Re: line, then type Re: [Tab] [Tab] Summer Festival Weekend Package
   c. Select three in the first sentence, then type two.
   d. Select 3rd of June in the second sentence of the last paragraph, type 15th of May, select room, then type reservation.
   e. Delete the sentence No one knows how to celebrate summer like Montrealers!
   f. Turn off the display of formatting marks, then save the document.

5. Format text using the Mini toolbar.

  a. Select FAX, then click the Grow Font button on the Mini toolbar 11 times.

  b. Apply bold to the word FAX, then center it on the page.

  c. Apply a bottom border under the word FAX.

  d. Apply bold to the following words in the fax heading: To:, From:, Date:, Re:, Pages:, and Fax:.

  e. View the document in Print Preview.

  f. Click the word FAX to zoom in on the document, then proofread the fax.

  g. Switch to edit mode, then correct any typing errors in your document.

  h. Close Print Preview, then save the document. Compare your document to Figure A-16.

  i. Print the fax using the default print settings, then close the document.

FIGURE A-16

FAX

To:	Joanna Card
From:	Your Name, Global Montreal
Date:	April 14, 2010
Re:	Summer Festival Weekend Package
Pages:	2
Fax:	(603) 555-5478

Thank you for your interest in our summer festival weekend package, which includes accommodations for two nights in downtown Montreal, continental breakfast, and a festival pass. Rooms are still available during the following festivals: Grand Prix Festival, International Jazz Festival, Just for Laughs Festival, Montreal Fringe Festival, and Le Festival des Arts du Village. Please see the attached schedule for dates and details.

To make a reservation, please call me at (514) 555-7482. I will need payment in full by the 15th of May to hold a reservation.

6. Create a document using a template. This exercise requires an Internet connection.

  a. Click the Office button, then click New to open the New Document dialog box.

  b. Scroll down the list of Microsoft Office Online templates in the Templates pane, click Memos, select the Memo (Professional design) template, click Download, then click Continue. (*Note:* You must be working with an active Internet connection to download a template from Microsoft Office Online. Select a different memo template if the Professional design memo is not available to you.)

  c. Type Louis Philippe Ouellette to replace the To placeholder text, type your name to replace the From placeholder text, then type Sold out summer festival packages to replace the Re placeholder text.

  d. Select the Cc line, then press [Delete]. The date in the document should be the current date.

  e. Click the Office button, click Convert, click OK, then save the document with the filename Sold Out Memo to the drive and folder where you store your Data Files.

7. View and navigate a document.

  a. Scroll down until How to Use This Memo Template is at the top of your document window.

  b. Delete the text How to Use This Memo Template.

  c. Select the remaining placeholder body text, type Packages for the following summer festivals are sold out: First Peoples' Festival, Chamber Music Festival, and Dragon Boat Race Festival. We had expected these packages to be less popular than those for the bigger festivals, but interest has been high. Next year, we will increase our bookings for these festivals by 30%.

  d. Use the Zoom dialog box to view the Whole Page.

  e. Click Company Name Here to move the insertion point to the upper-right corner of the page, then use the Zoom slider to set the Zoom percentage at approximately 200%.

  f. Replace Company Name Here with Global Montreal, then reduce the zoom percentage to 100%.

  g. Preview the document in Print Preview, correct any errors, close Print Preview, save the document, print it, close the file, then exit Word. Compare your document to Figure A-17.

FIGURE A-17

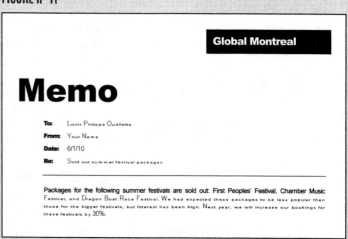

Global Montreal

Memo

To:	Louis Philippe Ouellette
From:	Your Name
Date:	6/1/10
Re:	Sold out summer festival packages

Packages for the following summer festivals are sold out: First Peoples' Festival, Chamber Music Festival, and Dragon Boat Race Festival. We had expected these packages to be less popular than those for the bigger festivals, but interest has been high. Next year, we will increase our bookings for these festivals by 30%.

▼ INDEPENDENT CHALLENGE 1

Yesterday you interviewed for a job as U.S. marketing director at Edo Design Services. You spoke with several people at Edo, including Mayumi Suzuki, chief executive officer, whose business card is shown in Figure A-18. You need to write a follow-up letter to Ms. Suzuki, thanking her for the interview and expressing your interest in the company and the position. She also asked you to send her some samples of your marketing work, which you will enclose with the letter.

a. Start Word and save a new blank document as **Edo Letter** to the drive and folder where you store your Data Files.

FIGURE A-18

b. Begin the letter by clicking the No Spacing button in the Styles group. You use this button to apply the No Spacing style to the document so that your document does include extra space between paragraphs.

c. Type a personal letterhead for the letter that includes your name, address, telephone number, and e-mail address. If Word formats your e-mail address as a hyperlink, right-click your e-mail address, then click Remove Hyperlink. (*Note:* Format the letterhead after you finish typing the letter.)

d. Three lines below the bottom of the letterhead, type today's date.

e. Four lines below the date, type the inside address, referring to Figure A-18 for the address information. Be sure to include the recipient's title, company name, and full mailing address in the inside address. (*Hint:* When typing a foreign address, type the name of the country in capital letters by itself on the last line.)

f. Two lines below the inside address, type the salutation.

g. Two lines below the salutation, type the body of the letter according to the following guidelines:
- In the first paragraph, thank her for the interview. Then restate your interest in the position and express your desire to work for the company. Add any specific details you think will enhance the power of your letter.
- In the second paragraph, note that you are enclosing three samples of your work and explain something about the samples you are enclosing.
- Type a short final paragraph.

h. Two lines below the last body paragraph, type a closing, then four lines below the closing, type the signature block. Be sure to include your name in the signature block.

i. Two lines below the signature block, type an enclosure notation. (*Hint:* An enclosure notation usually includes the word "Enclosures" or the abbreviation "Enc." followed by the number of enclosures in parentheses.)

j. Format the letterhead with bold, centering, and a bottom border.

k. Save your changes.

l. Preview and print the letter, then close the document and exit Word.

▼ INDEPENDENT CHALLENGE 2

Your company has recently installed Word 2007 on its company network. As the training manager, it's your responsibility to teach employees how to use the new software productively. Now that they have begun working with Word 2007, several employees have asked you about sharing Word 2007 documents with colleagues who are using an earlier version of Word. In response to their queries, you decide to write a memo to all employees explaining file compatibility issues between Word 2007 and previous versions of Word. Rather than write the memo from scratch, you revise a memo you wrote earlier on this topic to the department heads. That memo was written on your home office computer, which still has Word 2003 installed.

a. Start Word, open the file **WD A-1.doc** from the drive and folder where you store your Data Files, then read the memo to get a feel for its contents. The .doc file extension lets you know this file was created in a previous version of Word. Notice the words Compatibility Mode in the title bar. Compatibility Mode ensures that no new features in Word 2007 are available while you are working with the document so that the document will be fully accessible to people who use previous versions of Word.

b. Save the file in Word 97-2003 format as **XML Memo** to the drive and folder where you store your Data Files.

▼ INDEPENDENT CHALLENGE 2 (CONTINUED)

c. Replace the information in the memo header with the information shown in Figure A-19. Make sure to include your name in the From line and the current date in the Date line.

d. Apply bold to To:, From:, Date:, and Re:.

e. Increase the size of WORD TRAINING MEMORANDUM to match Figure A-19, center the text on the page, add a border below it, then save your changes.

FIGURE A-19

WORD TRAINING MEMORANDUM

To:	All employees
From:	Your Name, Training Manager
Date:	Today's date
Re:	File compatibility in Word 2007

f. In order to save the memo in XML format, click the Office button, click Convert, read the text in the Microsoft Office Word dialog box, then click OK. Notice the phrase Compatibility Mode no longer appears in the title bar. Compatibility Mode is turned off.

g. Click the Save button. Notice the file extension in the title bar changes to .docx if Windows is set to display file extensions on your computer.

Advanced Challenge Exercise

■ Using the Font list on the Mini toolbar, apply a different font to WORD TRAINING MEMORANDUM. Make sure to select a font that is appropriate for a business memo.

■ Using the Font Color button on the Mini toolbar, change the color of WORD TRAINING MEMORANDUM to an appropriate color.

■ Save a copy of the memo in Word 97-2003 format as XML Memo ACE to the drive or folder where you store your Data Files. (*Hint*: Click the Office button, point to Save As, then click Word 97-2003 Format.)

h. Preview and print the memo, then close the document and exit Word.

▼ INDEPENDENT CHALLENGE 3

You are an expert on global warming. The president of the National Park Association, Jeremy Moynihan, has asked you to be the keynote speaker at an upcoming conference on the impact of climate change on the national parks, to be held in Glacier National Park. You use one of the Word letter templates to write a letter to Mr. Moynihan accepting the invitation and confirming the details. Your letter to Mr. Moynihan should reference the following information:

• The conference will be held June 4–6, 2010, at the Many Glacier Hotel in the park.

• You have been asked to speak for an hour on Saturday, June 5, followed by one half hour for questions.

• Mr. Moynihan suggested the lecture topic "Melting Glaciers, Changing Ecosystems."

• Your talk will include a 45-minute slide presentation.

• The National Park Association will make your travel arrangements.

• Your preference is to arrive at Glacier Park International Airport in Kalispell on the morning of Friday, June 4 and to depart on Monday, June 7. You would like to rent a car at the airport for the drive to the Many Glacier Hotel.

• You want to fly in and out of the airport closest to your home.

a. Start Word, open the New Document dialog box, click Installed Templates, and then select an appropriate letter template. Save the document as Moynihan Letter to the drive and folder where you store your Data Files.

b. Replace the placeholders in the letterhead with your personal information. Include your name, address, phone number, and e-mail address. Delete any placeholders that do not apply. (*Hint*: Depending on the template you choose, the letterhead might be located at the top or on the side of the document. You can press [Enter] when typing in a placeholder to add an additional line of text. You can also change the format of text typed in a placeholder.)

c. Use the Pick the date content control to select the current date.

d. Replace the placeholders in the inside address. Be sure to include Mr. Moynihan's title and the name of the organization. Make up a street address and zip code.

e. Type **Dear Mr. Moynihan:** for the salutation.

f. Using the information listed previously, type the body of the letter:

- In the first paragraph, accept the invitation to speak and confirm the important conference details.
- In the second paragraph, confirm your lecture topic and provide any relevant details.
- In the third paragraph, state your travel preferences.
- Type a short final paragraph.

g. Type **Sincerely,** for the closing, then include your name in the signature block.

h. Adjust the formatting of the letter as necessary. For example, remove bold formatting or change the font color of text to a more appropriate color.

Advanced Challenge Exercise

- Zoom in and out on the document, looking for spelling, grammar, and formatting errors.
- Correct your spelling and grammar errors, if any, by right-clicking any red- or green-underlined text and then choosing from the options on the shortcut menu.
- View the letter in Full Screen Reading view, then click the Close button to return to Print Layout view.

i. Proofread your letter, make corrections as needed, then save your changes.

j. Preview the letter, print the letter, close the document, then exit Word.

▼ REAL LIFE INDEPENDENT CHALLENGE

This Independent Challenge requires an Internet connection.

The computer keyboard has become as essential an office tool as the pencil. The more adept you become at touch typing—the fastest and most accurate way to type—the more comfortable you will be working with computers and the more saleable your office skills to a potential employer. The World Wide Web is one source of information on touch typing, and many Web sites include free typing tests and online tutorials to help you practice and improve your typing skills. In this independent challenge, you will take an online typing test to check your typing skills. You will then research the fundamentals of touch typing and investigate some of the ergonomic factors important to becoming a productive keyboard typist.

a. Use your favorite search engine to search the Web for information on typing. Use the keywords **typing** and **typing ergonomics** to conduct your search.

b. Review the Web sites you find. Choose a site that offers a free online typing test, take the test, then print the Web page showing the results of your typing test.

c. Start Word and save a new blank document as **Touch Typing** to the drive and folder where you store your Data Files.

d. Type your name at the top of the document.

e. Type a brief report on the results of your research. Your report should answer the following questions:

- What are the URLs of the Web sites you visited to research touch typing and keyboard ergonomics? (*Hint*: A URL is a Web page's address. An example of a URL is www.course.com.)
- What are some of the benefits of using the touch typing method?
- In touch typing, on which keys should the fingers of the left and right hands rest?
- What ergonomic factors are important to keep in mind while typing?

f. Save your changes to the document, preview and print it, then close the document and exit Word.

Create the cover letter shown in Figure A-20. Before beginning to type, click the No Spacing button in the Styles group on the Home tab. Add the bottom border to the document after you finish typing. Save the document as Wong Cover Letter to the drive and folder where you store your Data Files, print a copy of the letter, then close the document and exit Word.

FIGURE A-20

Your Name

345 West 11th Avenue, Anchorage, AK 99501
Tel: 907-555-7283; Fax: 907-555-1445

June 28, 2010

Ms. Sylvia Wong
Wong Associates
2286 East Northern Lights Blvd.
Suite 501
Anchorage, AK 99514

Dear Ms. Wong:

I read of the opening for a public information assistant in the June 27 edition of adn.com, and I would like to be considered for the position. I am a recent graduate of Greater Anchorage Community College (GACC), and I am interested in pursuing a career in public relations.

My interest in a public relations career springs from my publicly acknowledged writing and journalism abilities. For example, at GACC, I was a reporter for the student newspaper and frequently wrote press releases for campus and community events.

I have a wealth of experience using Microsoft Word in professional settings. Last summer, I worked as an office assistant for the architecture firm Coleman & Greenberg, where I used Word to create newsletters, brochures, and financial reports. During the school year, I also worked part-time in the GACC Office of Community Relations, where I used the Word mail merge feature to create form letters and mailing labels.

My enclosed resume details my skills and experience. I welcome the opportunity to discuss the position and my qualifications with you. I can be reached at 907-555-7283.

Sincerely,

Your Name

Enc.

Editing Documents

The sophisticated editing features in Word make it easy to revise and polish your documents. In this unit, you learn how to revise an existing file by opening it, copying and moving text, and then saving the document as a new file. You also learn how to perfect your documents using proofing tools and how to quickly prepare a document for distribution to the public. You have been asked to edit and finalize a press release for a QST promotional lecture series. The press release should provide information about the series so that newspapers, radio stations, and other media outlets can announce it to the public. QST press releases are disseminated by fax and by e-mail. Before distributing the file electronically to your lists of press contacts and local QST clients, you add several hyperlinks and then strip the file of private information.

OBJECTIVES

Cut and paste text

Copy and paste text

Use the Office Clipboard

Find and replace text

Check spelling and grammar

Research information

Add hyperlinks

Prepare a document for distribution

Cutting and Pasting Text

The editing features in Word allow you to move text from one location to another in a document. The operation of moving text is often called **cut and paste**. When you cut text, it is removed from the document and placed on the **Clipboard**, a temporary storage area for text and graphics that you cut or copy from a document. To cut text, you select it and then click the Cut button in the Clipboard group on the Home tab. To insert the text from the Clipboard into the document, you place the insertion point where you want to insert the text, and then click the Paste button in the Clipboard group. You also can move selected text by dragging it to a new location using the mouse. This operation is called **drag and drop**. You open the press release that was drafted by a colleague, save it with a new filename, and then reorganize the information in the press release using the cut-and-paste and drag-and-drop methods.

STEPS

QUICK TIP

Use the Open button 📂 on the Quick Access toolbar if the toolbar has been customized to include this button.

1. **Start Word, click the Office button 🏢, click Open, navigate to the drive and folder where you store your Data Files, click WD B-1.docx, then click Open**

   The document opens. Once you have opened a file, you can edit it and use the Save or the Save As command to save your changes. You use the **Save** command when you want to save the changes you make to a file, overwriting the file that is stored on a disk. You use the **Save As** command when you want to leave the original file intact and create a duplicate file with a different filename, file extension, or location.

2. **Click 🏢, click Save As, type Wanderlust PR in the File name text box, then click Save**

   You can now make changes to the press release file without affecting the original file.

3. **Replace Ron Dawson with your name, scroll down until the headline Katherine Quoss to Speak... is at the top of your document window, then click the Show/Hide ¶ button ¶ in the Paragraph group on the Home tab to display formatting marks**

4. **Select Alaskan guide Gilbert Coonan, (including the comma and the space after it) in the third paragraph, then click the Cut button ✂ in the Clipboard group**

   The text is removed from the document and placed on the Clipboard. Word uses two different clipboards: the **system Clipboard** (the Clipboard), which holds just one item, and the **Office Clipboard**, which holds up to 24 items. The last item you cut or copy is always added to both clipboards. You'll learn more about the Office Clipboard in a later lesson.

QUICK TIP

You can also paste text by right-clicking where you want the text to be located, and then clicking Paste on the Edit menu.

5. **Place the insertion point before Serengeti (but after the space) in the first line of the third paragraph, then click the Paste button in the Clipboard group**

   The text is pasted at the location of the insertion point, as shown in Figure B-1. The Paste Options button 📋 appears below text when you first paste it in a document. You'll learn more about the Paste Options button in the next lesson. For now, you can ignore it.

6. **Press and hold [Ctrl], click the sentence Ticket prices include lunch. in the fourth paragraph, then release [Ctrl]**

   The entire sentence is selected.

TROUBLE

If you make a mistake, click the Undo button ↩ on the Quick Access toolbar, then try again.

7. **Press and hold the mouse button over the selected text until the pointer changes to ⬚**

   Notice the pointer's vertical line. You use this to indicate the location where you want the text to be inserted when you release the mouse button.

8. **Drag the pointer's vertical line to the end of the fifth paragraph (between the period and the paragraph mark) as shown in Figure B-2, then release the mouse button**

   The selected text is moved to the location of the insertion point. It is convenient to move text using the drag-and-drop method when the locations of origin and destination are both visible on the screen. Text is not placed on the Clipboard when you move it using drag-and-drop.

9. **Deselect the text, then click the Save button 💾 on the Quick Access toolbar**

FIGURE B-1: Moved text with Paste Options button

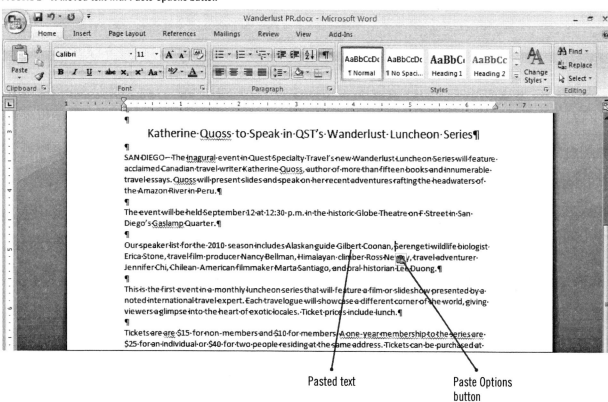

Pasted text

Paste Options button

FIGURE B-2: Text being dragged to a new location

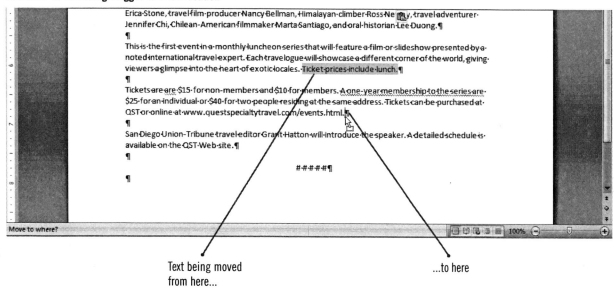

Text being moved from here...

...to here

Using keyboard shortcuts

Instead of using the Cut, Copy, and Paste commands to edit text in Word, you can use the **keyboard shortcuts** [Ctrl][X] to cut text, [Ctrl][C] to copy text, and [Ctrl][V] to paste text. A **shortcut key** is a function key, such as [F1], or a combination of keys, such as [Ctrl][S], that you press to perform a command. For example, you can press [Ctrl][S] to saves changes to a document instead of clicking the Save button on the Quick Access toolbar or clicking Save on the Office menu. Becoming skilled at using keyboard shortcuts can help you to quickly accomplish many of the tasks you perform frequently in Word. If a keyboard shortcut is available for a command, then it is listed in the ScreenTip for the command.

Copying and Pasting Text

Copying and pasting text is similar to cutting and pasting text, except that the text you copy is not removed from the document. Rather, a copy of the text is placed on the Clipboard, leaving the original text in place. You can copy text to the Clipboard using the Copy button in the Clipboard group on the Home tab, or you can copy text by pressing [Ctrl] as you drag the selected text from one location to another. You continue to edit the press release by copying text from one location to another.

QUICK TIP

You can also copy selected text by right-clicking it, and then clicking Copy on the Edit menu.

1. **Select Wanderlust Luncheon in the headline, then click the Copy button 📋 in the Clipboard group**

   A copy of the text is placed on the Clipboard, leaving the text you copied in place.

2. **Place the insertion point before season in the third body paragraph, then click the Paste button in the Clipboard group**

   "Wanderlust Luncheon" is inserted before "season," as shown in Figure B-3. Notice that the pasted text is formatted differently than the paragraph in which it was inserted.

QUICK TIP

If you don't like the result of a paste option, try another option or click the Undo button 🔄 and then paste the text again.

3. **Click the Paste Options button 📋, then click Match Destination Formatting**

   The Paste Options button allows you to change the formatting of pasted text. The formatting of "Wanderlust Luncheon" is changed to match the rest of the paragraph. The options available on the Paste Options menu depend on the format of the text you are pasting and the format of the surrounding text.

4. **Select www.questspecialtytravel.com in the fifth paragraph, press and hold [Ctrl], press and hold the mouse button until the pointer changes to 📋**

5. **Drag the pointer's vertical line to the end of the last paragraph, placing it between site and the period, release the mouse button, then release [Ctrl]**

   The text is copied to the last paragraph. Since the formatting of the text you copied is the same as the formatting of the paragraph in which you inserted it, you can ignore the Paste Options button. Text is not copied to the Clipboard when you copy it using the drag-and-drop method.

6. **Place the insertion point before www.questspecialtytravel.com in the last paragraph, type at followed by a space, then save the document**

   Compare your document with Figure B-4.

Splitting the document window to copy and move items in a long document

If you want to copy or move items between parts of a long document, it can be useful to split the document window into two panes so that the item you want to copy or move is displayed in one pane and the destination for the item is displayed in the other pane. To split a window, click the Split button in the Window group on the View tab, drag the horizontal split bar that appears to the location you want to split the window, and then click. Once the document window is split into two panes, you can drag the split bar to resize the panes and use the scroll bars in each pane to display different parts of the document. To copy or move an item from one pane to another, you can use the Cut, Copy, and Paste commands, or you can drag the item between the panes. When you are finished editing the document, double-click the split bar to restore the window to a single pane, or click the Remove Split button in the Window group on the View tab.

FIGURE B-3: Text pasted in document

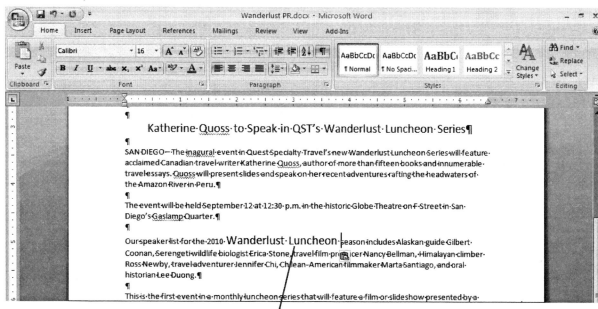

Formatting of the pasted
text matches the headline

FIGURE B-4: Copied text in document

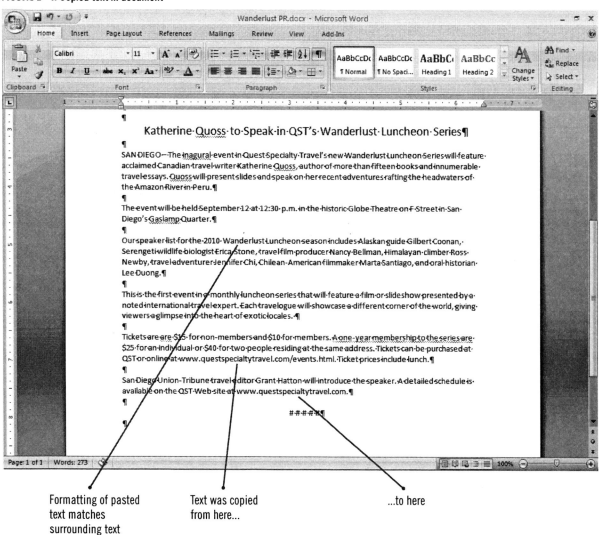

Formatting of pasted
text matches
surrounding text

Text was copied
from here...

...to here

Using the Office Clipboard

The Office Clipboard allows you to collect text and graphics from files created in any Office program and insert them into your Word documents. It holds up to 24 items and, unlike the system Clipboard, the items on the Office Clipboard can be viewed. To display the Office Clipboard, you simply click the launcher in the Clipboard group on the Home tab. You add items to the Office Clipboard using the Cut and Copy commands. The last item you collect is always added to both the system Clipboard and the Office Clipboard. You use the Office Clipboard to move several sentences in your press release.

QUICK TIP

You can set the Office Clipboard to open automatically when you cut or copy two items consecutively by clicking Options in the Clipboard task pane, and then selecting Show Office Clipboard Automatically.

QUICK TIP

An item remains on the Office Clipboard even after you paste it.

1. **Click the launcher ◨ in the Clipboard group**

   The Office Clipboard opens in the Clipboard task pane. It contains the Wanderlust Luncheon item you copied in the last lesson.

2. **Select the sentence San Diego Union-Tribune travel editor ... (including the space after the period) in the last paragraph, right-click the selected text, then click Cut on the Edit menu**

   The sentence is cut to the Office Clipboard.

3. **Select the sentence A detailed schedule is... (including the ¶ mark), right-click the selected text, then click Cut**

   The Office Clipboard displays the items you cut or copied, as shown in Figure B-5. The icon next to each item indicates the items are from a Word document. The last item collected displays at the top of the Clipboard task pane. As new items are collected, the first items collected move down the task pane.

4. **Place the insertion point at the end of the second paragraph (after Quarter. but before the ¶ mark), then click the San Diego Union-Tribune... item on the Office Clipboard**

   Clicking an item on the Office Clipboard pastes the item in the document at the location of the insertion point. Items remain on the Office Clipboard until you delete them or close all open Office programs. Also, if you add a 25th item to the Office Clipboard, the first item is deleted.

5. **Place the insertion point at the end of the third paragraph (after Duong.), then click the A detailed schedule is... item on the Office Clipboard**

   The sentence is pasted in the document.

6. **Select the fourth paragraph, which begins with the sentence This is the first event... (including the ¶ mark), right-click the selected text, then click Cut**

   The paragraph is cut to the Office Clipboard.

7. **Place the insertion point at the beginning of the third paragraph (before Our...), right-click, click Paste on the Edit menu, then press [Backspace]**

   The sentences from the "This is the first..." paragraph are pasted at the beginning of the "Our speaker list..." paragraph. You can paste the last item collected using either the Paste command or the Office Clipboard.

8. **Place the insertion point at the end of the third paragraph (after www.questspecialtytravel.com and before the ¶ mark), then press [Delete] twice**

   The ¶ symbols and the extra blank lines between the third and fourth paragraphs are deleted.

9. **Click the Show/Hide ¶ button ¶ in the Paragraph group**

   Compare your press release with Figure B-6. Note that many Word users prefer to work with formatting marks on at all times. Experiment to see which method you prefer.

QUICK TIP

To delete an individual item from the Office Clipboard, click the list arrow next to the item, then click Delete.

10. **Click the Clear All button on the Clipboard task pane to remove the items from the Office Clipboard, click the Close button on the Clipboard task pane, press [Ctrl][Home], then save the document**

    Pressing [Ctrl][Home] moves the insertion point to the top of the document.

FIGURE B-5: Office Clipboard in Clipboard task pane

Click to resize or move the Clipboard task pane

Clipboard task pane

Items stored on the Office Clipboard (yours may include additional items)

Click to change display options for the Office Clipboard

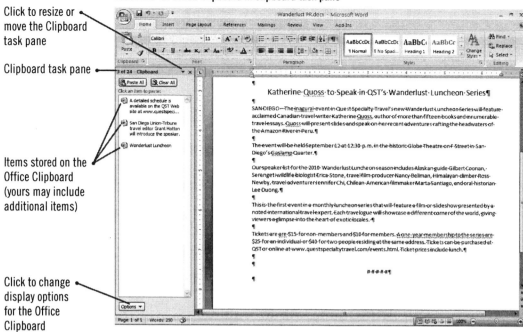

FIGURE B-6: Revised press release

Last item collected

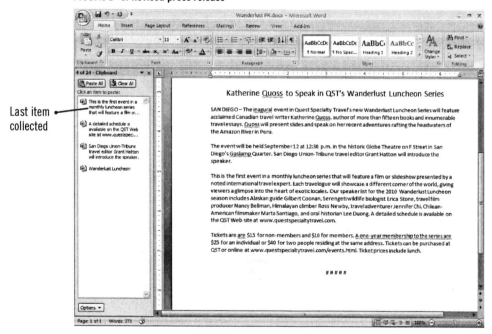

Copying and moving items between documents

The system and Office Clipboards also can be used to copy and move items between Word documents. To copy or cut items from one Word document and paste them into another, first open both documents and the Clipboard task pane in the program window. With multiple documents open, you can copy and move items between documents by copying or cutting the item(s) from one document and then switching to another document and pasting the item(s). To switch between open documents, click the button on the taskbar for the document you want to appear in the document window. You can also display both documents at the same time by clicking the Arrange All button or the View Side by Side button in the Window group on the View tab. The Office Clipboard stores all the items collected from all documents, regardless of which document is displayed in the document window. The system Clipboard stores the last item collected from any document.

Editing Documents

Finding and Replacing Text

The Find and Replace feature in Word allows you to automatically search for and replace all instances of a word or phrase in a document. For example, you might need to substitute "tour" for "trip," and it would be very time-consuming to manually locate and replace each instance of "trip" in a long document. Using the Replace command you can automatically find and replace all occurrences of specific text at once, or you can choose to find and review each occurrence individually. You also can use the Find command to locate and select every occurrence of a specific word or phrase in a document. ▓▓▓▓ QST has decided to change the name of the lecture series from "Wanderlust Luncheon Series" to "Wanderlust Travelogue Series." You use the Replace command to search the document for all instances of "Luncheon" and replace them with "Travelogue."

STEPS

TROUBLE

If any of the Search Options check boxes are selected in your Find and Replace dialog box, deselect them. If Format appears under the Find what or Replace with text box, click in the text box, then click No Formatting.

1. **Click the Replace button in the Editing group, then click More in the Find and Replace dialog box**

   The Find and Replace dialog box opens, as shown in Figure B-7.

2. **Type Luncheon in the Find what text box**

   "Luncheon" is the text that will be replaced.

3. **Press [Tab], then type Travelogue in the Replace with text box**

   "Travelogue" is the text that will replace "Luncheon."

4. **Click the Match case check box in the Search Options section to select it**

   Selecting the Match case check box tells Word to find only exact matches for the uppercase and lowercase characters you entered in the Find what text box. You want to replace all instances of "Luncheon" in the proper name "Wanderlust Luncheon Series." You do not want to replace "luncheon" when it refers to a lunchtime event.

QUICK TIP

To find, review, and replace each occurrence individually, click Find Next.

5. **Click Replace All**

   Clicking Replace All changes all occurrences of "Luncheon" to "Travelogue" in the press release. A message box reports three replacements were made.

6. **Click OK to close the message box, then click Close in the Find and Replace dialog box**

   Word replaced "Luncheon" with "Travelogue" in three locations, but did not replace "luncheon."

7. **Click the Find button in the Editing group**

   The Find and Replace dialog box opens with the Find tab displayed. The Find command allows you to quickly locate all instances of text in a document. You can use it to verify that Word did not replace "luncheon."

QUICK TIP

To highlight all instances of specific text in a document, click Reading Highlight on the Find tab, then click Highlight All.

8. **Type luncheon in the Find what text box, make sure the Match case check box is still selected, click Find in, click Main Document on the menu that opens, then click Close**

   The Find and Replace dialog box closes and "luncheon" is selected in the document, as shown in Figure B-8.

9. **Deselect the text, press [Ctrl][Home], then save the document**

Navigating a document using the Go To command

Rather than scrolling to move to a different place in a longer document, you can use the Go To command to quickly move the insertion point to a specific location. To move to a specific page, section, line, table, graphic, or other item in a document, click the Page number button on the status bar to open the Find and Replace dialog box with the Go To tab displayed. On the Go To tab in the Find and Replace dialog box, select the type of item you want to find in the Go to what list box, enter the relevant information about that item, and then click Go To or Next to move the insertion point to the item.

Replace only exact matches of upper-case and lowercase characters

Find only complete words

Use wildcards (*) in a search string

Find words that sound like the Find what text

Find and replace all forms of a word

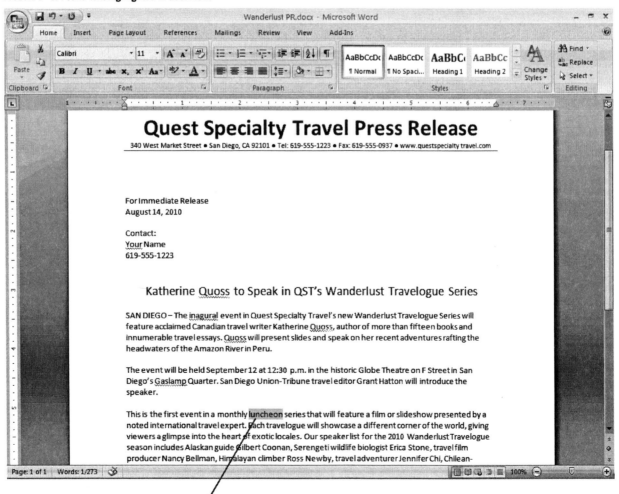

Found text is highlighted

Word 2007

Checking Spelling and Grammar

When you finish typing and revising a document, you can use the Spelling and Grammar command to search the document for misspelled words and grammar errors. The Spelling and Grammar checker flags possible mistakes, suggests correct spellings, and offers remedies for grammar errors such as subject-verb agreement, repeated words, and punctuation. ▆▆▆▆ You use the Spelling and Grammar checker to search your press release for errors. Before beginning the search, you set the Spelling and Grammar checker to ignore words, such as Quoss, that you know are spelled correctly.

STEPS

1. **Right-click Quoss in the headline**

   A shortcut menu that includes suggestions for correcting the spelling of "Quoss" opens. You can correct individual spelling and grammar errors by right-clicking text that is underlined with a red or green wavy line and selecting a correction. Although "Quoss" is not in the Word dictionary, it is spelled correctly in the document.

2. **Click Ignore All**

   Clicking Ignore All tells Word not to flag "Quoss" as misspelled.

3. **Press [Ctrl][Home], click the Review tab, then click the Spelling and Grammar button in the Proofing group**

   The Spelling and Grammar: English (United States) dialog box opens, as shown in Figure B-9. The dialog box identifies "inagural" as misspelled and suggests possible corrections for the error. The word selected in the Suggestions box is the correct spelling.

4. **Click Change**

   Word replaces the misspelled word with the correctly spelled word. Next, the dialog box identifies "Gaslamp" as a misspelled word and suggests the correction "Gas lamp". The proper name "Gaslamp Quarter" is spelled correctly in the document.

5. **Click Ignore Once**

   Word ignores the spelling. Next, the dialog box indicates that "are" is repeated in a sentence.

6. **Click Delete**

   Word deletes the second occurrence of the repeated word. Next, the dialog box flags a subject-verb agreement error and suggests using "is" instead of "are," as shown in Figure B-10. The phrase selected in the Suggestions box is correct.

7. **Click Change**

   Word replaces "are" with "is" in the sentence and the Spelling and Grammar dialog box closes. Keep in mind that the Spelling and Grammar checker identifies many common errors, but you cannot rely on it to find and correct all spelling and grammar errors in your documents. Always proofread your documents carefully.

8. **Click OK to complete the spelling and grammar check, press [Ctrl][Home], then save the document**

FIGURE B-9: Spelling and Grammar: English (United States) dialog box

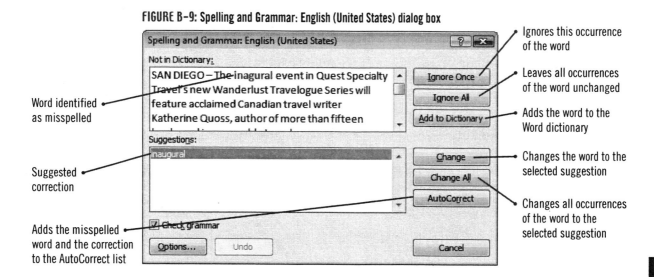

Word identified as misspelled

Suggested correction

Adds the misspelled word and the correction to the AutoCorrect list

Ignores this occurrence of the word

Leaves all occurrences of the word unchanged

Adds the word to the Word dictionary

Changes the word to the selected suggestion

Changes all occurrences of the word to the selected suggestion

FIGURE B-10: Grammar error identified in Spelling and Grammar dialog box

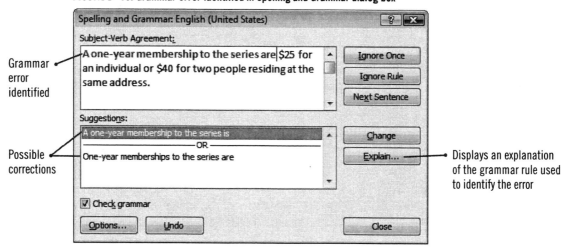

Grammar error identified

Possible corrections

Displays an explanation of the grammar rule used to identify the error

---

Inserting text with AutoCorrect

As you type, AutoCorrect automatically corrects many commonly misspelled words. By creating your own AutoCorrect entries, you can set Word to quickly insert text that you type often, such as your name or contact information, or to correct words you frequently misspell. For example, you could create an AutoCorrect entry so that the name "Ron Dawson" is automatically inserted whenever you type "rd" followed by a space. You create AutoCorrect entries and customize other AutoCorrect and AutoFormat options using the AutoCorrect dialog box. To open the AutoCorrect dialog box, click the Office button, click Word Options on the Office menu, click Proofing in the Word Options dialog box that opens, and then click

AutoCorrect Options. On the AutoCorrect tab in the AutoCorrect dialog box, type the text you want to be automatically corrected in the Replace text box (such as "rd"), type the text you want to be automatically inserted in its place in the With text box (such as "Ron Dawson"), and then click Add. The AutoCorrect entry is added to the list. Click OK to close the AutoCorrect dialog box, and then click OK to close the Word Options dialog box. Note that Word inserts an AutoCorrect entry in a document only when you press [Spacebar] after typing the text you want Word to correct. For example, Word will insert "Ron Dawson" when you type "rd" followed by a space, but not when you type "Mountain Rd."

Editing Documents

Researching Information

The Word Research feature allows you to quickly search reference sources for information related to a word or phrase. Among the reference sources available in the Research task pane is a Thesaurus, which you can use to look up synonyms for awkward or repetitive words. When you are working with an active Internet connection, the Research task pane provides access to dictionary, encyclopedia, translation, and other reference sources, as well as third-party research services, such as medical and legal dictionaries. ▰▰▰ After proofreading your document for errors, you decide the press release would read better if several adjectives were more descriptive. You use the Thesaurus to find synonyms.

QUICK TIP

You can also click the Research button in the Proofing group to open the Research task pane.

1. **Scroll down until the headline is displayed at the top of your screen**

2. **Select noted in the first sentence of the third paragraph, then click Thesaurus in the Proofing group**

   The Research task pane opens, as shown in Figure B-11. "Noted" appears in the Search for text box and possible synonyms for "noted" are listed under the Thesaurus: English (U.S.) heading in the task pane.

QUICK TIP

To look up synonyms for a different word, type the word in the Search for text box, then click the green Start searching button.

3. **Point to prominent in the list of synonyms**

   A box containing a list arrow appears around the word.

4. **Click the list arrow, click Insert on the menu that appears, then close the Research task pane**

   "Prominent" replaces "noted" in the press release.

5. **Right-click innumerable in the first sentence of the first paragraph, point to Synonyms on the Edit menu, then click numerous**

   "Numerous" replaces "innumerable" in the press release.

6. **Select the four paragraphs of body text (including the ¶ at the end of the last paragraph), then click the Word Count button 🔢 in the Proofing group**

   The Word Count dialog box opens, as shown in Figure B-12. The dialog box lists the number of pages, words, characters, paragraphs, and lines included in the selected text. Notice that the status bar also displays the number of words included in the selected text and the total number of words in the entire document. If you want to view the page, character, paragraph, and line count for the entire document, make sure nothing is selected in your document, and then click Word Count in the Proofing group.

QUICK TIP

To add or remove available reference sources, click Research options in the Research task pane.

7. **Click Close, press [Ctrl][Home], then save the document**

8. **Click the Office button 🔘, click Save As, type Wanderlust PR Public in the File name text box, then click Save**

   The Wanderlust PR file closes and the Wanderlust PR Public file is displayed in the document window. You will modify this file to prepare it for electronic release to the public.

FIGURE B-11: Research task pane

Word selected in the document

Click to select a different reference source

Possible meaning for the selected word

Synonyms for the active meaning of the word

Click to add or change reference sources

FIGURE B-12: Word Count dialog box

Publishing a blog directly from Word

A **blog**, which is short for weblog, is an informal journal that is created by an individual or a group and available to the public on the Internet. A blog usually conveys the ideas, comments, and opinions of the blogger and is written using a strong personal voice. The person who creates and maintains a blog, the **blogger**, typically updates the blog daily. If you have or want to start a blog, you can configure Word to link to your blog site, so that you can write, format, and publish blog entries directly from Word. To create a blog entry, click the Office button, click New, then double-click New blog post to open a predesigned blog post document that you can customize with your own text, formatting, and images. When you are ready to publish the entry to your blog, Word prompts you to log onto your personal blog account. To blog directly from Word, you must first obtain a blog account with a blog service provider. The Word Help system provides detailed information on obtaining and registering your personal blog account with Word.

Editing Documents

Adding Hyperlinks

A **hyperlink** is text or a graphic that, when clicked, "jumps" the viewer to a different location or program. When a document is viewed on screen, hyperlinks allow readers to link (or "jump") to a Web page, an e-mail address, a file, or a specific location in a document. When you create a hyperlink in a document, you select the text or graphic you want to use as a hyperlink and then specify the location you want to jump to when the hyperlink is clicked. You create a hyperlink using the Hyperlink button in the Links group on the Insert tab. Text that is formatted as a hyperlink appears as colored, underlined text. ▓▓▓▓▓ Hundreds of people on your lists of press and client contacts will receive the press release by e-mail or Internet fax. To make it easier for these people to access additional information about the series, you add several hyperlinks to the press release.

STEPS

QUICK TIP

By default, Word automatically creates a hyperlink to an e-mail address or URL when you type the address or URL in a document.

1. **Select your name, click the Insert tab, then click the Hyperlink button in the Links group**

   The Insert Hyperlink dialog box opens, as shown in Figure B-13. You use this dialog box to specify the location of the Web page, file, e-mail address, or position in the current document you want to jump to when the hyperlink—in this case, your name—is clicked.

2. **Click E-mail Address in the Link to section**

   The Insert Hyperlink dialog box changes so you can create a hyperlink to your e-mail address.

3. **Type your e-mail address in the E-mail address text box, type Wanderlust Travelogue Series in the Subject text box, then click OK**

   As you type, Word automatically adds mailto: in front of your e-mail address. After you close the dialog box, the hyperlink text—your name—is formatted in blue and underlined.

QUICK TIP

To remove a hyperlink, right-click it, then click Remove Hyperlink. Removing a hyperlink removes the link, but the text remains.

4. **Press and hold [Ctrl], then click the your name hyperlink**

   An e-mail message addressed to you with the subject "Wanderlust Travelogue Series" opens in the default e-mail program. People who receive the press release electronically can use the hyperlink to send you an e-mail message about the series.

5. **Close the e-mail message window**

   The hyperlink text changes to purple, indicating the hyperlink has been followed.

6. **Scroll down, select Gaslamp Quarter in the second paragraph, click the Hyperlink button, click Existing File or Web Page in the Link to section, type www.gaslamp.org in the Address text box, then click OK**

   As you type the Web address, Word automatically adds http:// in front of "www." The text "Gaslamp Quarter" is formatted as a hyperlink to the Gaslamp Quarter Association home page at www.gaslamp.org. When clicked, the hyperlink will open the Web page in the default browser window.

7. **Select detailed schedule in the last sentence of the third paragraph, click the Hyperlink button, type www.questspecialtytravel.com in the Address text box, then click OK**

   The text "detailed schedule" is formatted as a hyperlink to the QST Web site. If you point to a hyperlink in Word, the link to location appears in a ScreenTip. You can edit ScreenTip text to make it more descriptive.

QUICK TIP

You can also edit the hyperlink destination or the hyperlink text.

8. **Right-click Quarter in the Gaslamp Quarter hyperlink, click Edit Hyperlink, click ScreenTip in the Edit Hyperlink dialog box, type Map, parking, and other information about the Gaslamp Quarter in the ScreenTip text text box, click OK, click OK, save your changes, then point to the Gaslamp Quarter hyperlink in the document**

   The ScreenTip you created appears above the Gaslamp Quarter hyperlink, as shown in Figure B-14.

TROUBLE

If you are not working with an active Internet connection, skip this step.

9. **If you are working with an active Internet connection, press [Ctrl], click the Gaslamp Quarter hyperlink, close the browser window that opens, press [Ctrl], click the detailed schedule hyperlink, then close the browser window**

   Before distributing a document, it's important to test each hyperlink to verify it works as you intended.

Editing Documents

FIGURE B-13: Insert Hyperlink dialog box

Create a hyperlink to a Web page or file

Create a hyperlink to a location in the current file

Create a hyperlink to a new blank document

Create a hyperlink to an e-mail address

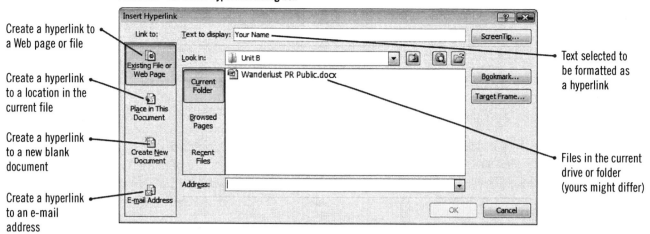

Text selected to be formatted as a hyperlink

Files in the current drive or folder (yours might differ)

FIGURE B-14: Hyperlinks in the document

Purple indicates the hyperlink has been followed

Hyperlinks are colored and underlined

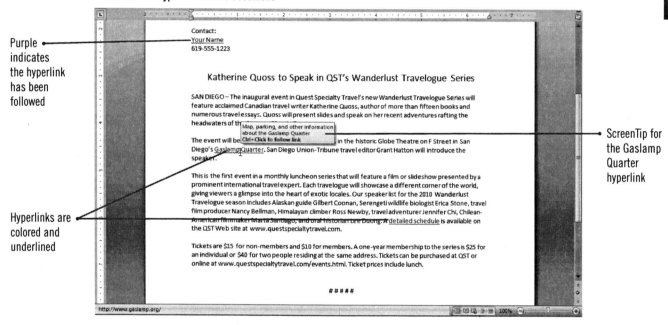

ScreenTip for the Gaslamp Quarter hyperlink

E-mailing and faxing documents directly from Word

Word includes several options for distributing and sharing documents over the Internet directly from within Word, including e-mailing and faxing documents. When you e-mail a document from within Word, the document is sent as an attachment to an e-mail message using your default e-mail program. To e-mail a file, open the file in Word, click the Office button, point to Send, and then click E-mail. A message window opens that includes the filename of the current file as the message subject and the file as an attachment. Type the e-mail address(es) of the recipient(s) in the To and Cc text boxes, any message you want in the message window, and then click Send on the message window toolbar to send the message. The default e-mail program sends a copy of the document to each recipient. It's also possible to fax a document directly from within Word, although faxing a document requires registration with a third-party Internet fax service. To fax a document, open it in Word, click the Office button, point to Send, click Internet Fax, click OK to find and select a fax service if you don't already have one, and then follow the on-screen instructions. Fax services generally charge a monthly or per page fee for sending and receiving faxes.

Editing Documents

Preparing a Document for Distribution

Before you distribute a document electronically to people outside your organization, it's wise to make sure the file does not include embedded private or confidential information. The Prepare command on the Office menu includes tools for stripping a document of sensitive information, for securing its authenticity, and for guarding it from unwanted changes once it is distributed to the public. See Table B-1. One of these tools, the Document Inspector, detects and removes unwanted private or confidential information from a document. Another tool, Mark as Final, allows you to make a document read-only so it cannot be modified by viewers. ▰▰▰ Before sending the press release to the public, you remove all identifying information from the file and mark it as final.

STEPS

1. **Press [Ctrl][Home], click the Office button 🔘, point to Prepare, then click Properties**

   The Document Information panel opens above the document window, as shown in Figure B-15. It shows the standard document properties for the press release. **Document properties** are user-defined details about a file that describe its contents and origin, including the name of the author, the title of the document, and keywords that you can assign to help organize and search your files.

2. **Click 🔘, point to Prepare, click Inspect Document, then click Yes**

   The Document Inspector dialog box opens. You use this dialog box to indicate which private or identifying information you want to search for and remove from the document.

3. **Make sure all the check boxes are selected, then click Inspect**

   After a moment, the Document Inspector dialog box changes to indicate that the file contains document properties. You might not want this information to be available to the public.

4. **Click Remove All next to Document Properties, then click Close**

   The standard document property information is removed from the press release document.

5. **Click 🔘, point to Prepare, then click Mark as Final**

   A dialog box indicating that the document will be marked as final opens.

6. **Click OK, then click OK if a second message box opens**

   The document is saved automatically, "Final" appears in the Status text box in the Document Information panel, and the commands on the Insert tab are disabled, indicating that the document is marked as final and cannot be changed. The Marked as Final icon also appears in the status bar.

7. **Click the Close button in the Document Information panel, click 🔘, point to Print, click Quick Print, close the file, then exit Word**

   The press release prints. The completed press release is shown in Figure B-16.

TABLE B-1: Prepare command options

feature	use to
Properties	View and modify the standard document properties and open the Properties dialog box
Inspect Document	Detect and remove unwanted private or proprietary information from a document, including document properties, comments, revisions, annotations, personal information, custom XML data, and hidden text
Encrypt Document	Add encryption to a document to make it more secure
Add a Digital Signature	Add an invisible digital signature to a document to verify its authenticity and integrity
Mark as Final	Indicate to readers that a document is read-only and cannot be edited
Run Compatibility Checker	Check the document for features that are not supported by previous versions of Microsoft Word

Editing Documents

FIGURE B-15: Document Information panel

Document properties assigned when the original file was created

Your file location will differ

Document Information panel

FIGURE B-16: Completed press release for electronic distribution

Quest Specialty Travel Press Release

340 West Market Street ● San Diego, CA 92101 ● Tel: 619-555-1223 ● Fax: 619-555-0987 ● www.questspecialty travel.com

For Immediate Release
August 14, 2010

Contact:
Your Name
619-555-1223

Katherine Quoss to Speak in QST's Wanderlust Travelogue Series

SAN DIEGO – The inaugural event in Quest Specialty Travel's new Wanderlust Travelogue Series will feature acclaimed Canadian travel writer Katherine Quoss, author of more than fifteen books and numerous travel essays. Quoss will present slides and speak on her recent adventures rafting the headwaters of the Amazon River in Peru.

The event will be held September 12 at 12:30 p.m. in the historic Globe Theatre on F Street in San Diego's Gaslamp Quarter. San Diego Union-Tribune travel editor Grant Hatton will introduce the speaker.

This is the first event in a monthly luncheon series that will feature a film or slideshow presented by a prominent international travel expert. Each travelogue will showcase a different corner of the world, giving viewers a glimpse into the heart of exotic locales. Our speaker list for the 2010 Wanderlust Travelogue season includes Alaskan guide Gilbert Coonan, Serengeti wildlife biologist Erica Stone, travel film producer Nancy Bellman, Himalayan climber Ross Newby, travel adventurer Jennifer Chi, Chilean-American filmmaker Marta Santiago, and oral historian Lee Duong. A detailed schedule is available on the QST Web site at www.questspecialtytravel.com.

Tickets are $15 for non-members and $10 for members. A one-year membership to the series is $25 for an individual or $40 for two people residing at the same address. Tickets can be purchased at QST or online at www.questspecialtytravel.com/events.html. Ticket prices include lunch.

# # # # #

Viewing and modifying advanced document properties

The Document Information panel includes summary information about the document that you enter to suit your needs. To view more detailed document properties, including those entered automatically by Word when the document is created, click the Document Properties list arrow in the Document Information panel, and then click Advanced Properties to open the Properties dialog box. The General, Statistics, and Contents tabs of the Properties dialog box display information about the file that is automatically created and updated by Word. The General tab shows the file type, location, size, and date and time the file was created and last modified; the Statistics tab displays information about revisions to the document along with the number of pages, words, lines, paragraphs, and characters in the file; and the Contents tab shows the title of the document. You can define other document properties using the Summary and Custom tabs of the Properties dialog box. The Summary tab shows information similar to the information shown in the Document Information panel. The Custom tab allows you to create new document properties, such as client, project, or date completed. To create a custom property, select a property name in the Name list box on the Custom tab, use the Type list arrow to select the type of data you want for the property, type the identifying detail (such as a project name) in the Value text box, and then click Add. When you are finished viewing or modifying the document properties, click OK to close the Properties dialog box, then click the Close button in the Document Information panel.

Editing Documents

Practice

▼ CONCEPTS REVIEW

Label the elements of the Word program window shown in Figure B-17.

FIGURE B-17

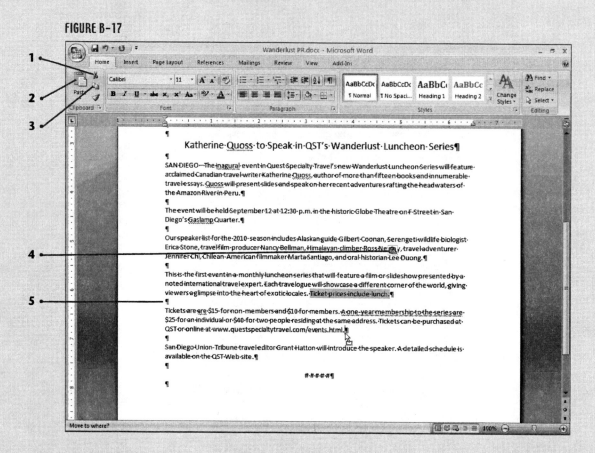

Match each term with the statement that best describes it.

6. **Hyperlink**

7. **Cut**

8. **Shortcut key**

9. **Document properties**

10. **Paste**

11. **Office Clipboard**

12. **System Clipboard**

13. **Blog**

14. **Thesaurus**

a. Command used to insert text stored on the Clipboard into a document

b. Temporary storage area for up to 24 items collected from Office files

c. Temporary storage area for only the last item cut or copied from a document

d. A function key or a combination of keys that perform a command when pressed

e. Text or a graphic that jumps the reader to a different location or program when clicked

f. An informal journal that is available to the public on the Internet

g. User-defined details about a file that describe its contents and origin

h. Feature used to suggest synonyms for words

i. Command used to remove text from a document and place it on the Clipboard

Editing Documents

Select the best answer from the list of choices.

15. What is the keyboard shortcut for the Paste command?

    a. [Ctrl][C]

    b. [Ctrl][V]

    c. [Ctrl][X]

    d. [Ctrl][P]

16. Which of the following statements is *not* true?

    a. The Office Clipboard can hold more than one item.

    b. You can view the contents of the Office Clipboard.

    c. When you move text by dragging it, a copy of the text you move is stored on the system Clipboard.

    d. The last item cut or copied from a document is stored on the system Clipboard.

17. To locate and select all instances of a word in a document, which command do you use?

    a. Highlight

    b. Replace

    c. Find

    d. Search

18. Which command is used to display a document in two panes in the document window?

    a. New Window

    b. Split

    c. Two Pages

    d. Arrange All

19. Which of the following is an example of a document property?

    a. Keyword

    b. Language

    c. URL

    d. Permission

20. A hyperlink *cannot* be linked to which of the following?

    a. Web page

    b. E-mail address

    c. ScreenTip

    d. New blank document

▼ SKILLS REVIEW

1. Cut and paste text.

    a. Start Word, click the Office button, then open the file WD B-2.docx from the drive and folder where you store your Data Files.

    b. Save the document with the filename **PAOS 2010 PR**.

    c. Select **Your Name** and replace it with your name.

    d. Display paragraph and other formatting marks in your document if they are not already displayed.

    e. Use the Cut and Paste buttons to switch the order of the two sentences in the fourth paragraph (which begins New group shows...).

    f. Use the drag-and-drop method to switch the order of the second and third paragraphs.

    g. Adjust the spacing if necessary so that there is one blank line between paragraphs, then save your changes.

2. Copy and paste text.

    a. Use the Copy and Paste buttons to copy **PAOS 2008** from the headline and paste it before the word **map** in the third paragraph.

    b. Change the formatting of the pasted text to match the formatting of the third paragraph, then insert a space between **2008** and **map** if necessary.

    c. Use the drag-and-drop method to copy **PAOS** from the third paragraph and paste it before the word **group** in the second sentence of the fourth paragraph, then save your changes.

3. Use the Office Clipboard.

    a. Use the launcher in the Clipboard group to open the Clipboard task pane.

    b. Scroll so that the first body paragraph is displayed at the top of the document window.

    c. Select the fifth paragraph (which begins Studio location maps...) and cut it to the Office Clipboard.

    d. Select the third paragraph (which begins Portsmouth is easily accessible...) and cut it to the Office Clipboard.

    e. Use the Office Clipboard to paste the Studio location maps... item as the new fourth paragraph.

    f. Use the Office Clipboard to paste the Portsmouth is easily accessible... item as the new fifth paragraph.

    g. Adjust the spacing if necessary so that there is one blank line between each of the six body paragraphs.

    h. Turn off the display of formatting marks, clear and close the Office Clipboard, then save your changes.

Editing Documents

4. Find and replace text.

    a. Using the Replace command, replace all instances of 2008 with 2010.

    b. Replace all instances of the abbreviation st with street, taking care to replace whole words only when you perform the replace. (*Hint*: Deselect Match case if it is selected.)

    c. Use the Find command to find all instances of st in the document and to make sure no errors occurred when you replaced st with street. (*Hint*: Deselect the Find whole words only check box.)

    d. Save your changes to the press release.

5. Check spelling and grammar and research information.

    a. Switch to the Review tab.

    b. Move the insertion point to the top of the document, then use the Spelling and Grammar command to search for and correct any spelling and grammar errors in the press release. (*Hint*: Jumpin' is not misspelled.)

    c. Use the Thesaurus to replace thriving in the second paragraph with a different suitable word.

    d. Check the word count of the press release.

    e. Proofread your press release, correct any errors, then save your changes.

6. Add hyperlinks.

    a. Save the document as PAOS 2010 PR Public, then switch to the Insert tab.

    b. Select your name, then open the Insert Hyperlink dialog box.

    c. Create a hyperlink to your e-mail address with the subject PAOS 2010.

    d. Test the your name hyperlink, then close the message window that opens. (*Hint*: Press [Ctrl], then click the hyperlink.)

    e. Select NEA in the last paragraph of the press release, then create a hyperlink to the URL www.nea.gov.

    f. Right-click the NEA hyperlink, then edit the hyperlink ScreenTip to become Information on the National Endowment for the Arts.

    g. Point to the NEA hyperlink to view the new ScreenTip, then save your changes.

    h. If you are working with an active Internet connection, press [Ctrl], click the NEA hyperlink, view the NEA home page in the browser window, then close the browser window.

7. Prepare a document for distribution.

    a. Click the Office button, point to Prepare, then view the document properties for the press release.

    b. Use the Prepare command to run the Document Inspector.

    c. Remove the document property data, then save your changes.

    d. Use the Prepare command to mark the document as final. The finished press release is shown in Figure B-18.

    e. Print the press release, close the file, then exit Word.

FIGURE B-18

PRESS RELEASE

FOR IMMEDIATE RELEASE
September 7, 2010

Contact:
Your Name
603-555-2938

PAOS 2010
Portsmouth Artists Open Their Studios to the Public

PORTSMOUTH, NH -- The fall 2010 Open Studios season kicks off with Portsmouth Artists Open Studios on Saturday and Sunday, October 13 and 14, from 11 a.m. to 6 p.m. More than 60 Portsmouth artists will open their studios and homes to the public for this annual event, now in its tenth year.

Portsmouth is an historic and diverse city, long home to a flourishing community of artists. Quiet residential streets lined with charming Victorians edge a vibrant commercial and industrial zone, all peppered with the studios of printmakers, sculptors, painters, glass and jewelry makers, illustrators, potters, photographers, watercolorists, and other artists working in a wide range of mediums.

Internationally celebrated sculptor Eva Russo will display her new work in the rotunda of City Hall. New PAOS group shows will open at the Atlantic Gallery and at Jumpin' Jay's Fish Café, both on Congress Street.

Studio location maps will be available prior to the opening at businesses and public libraries, and on the days of the event at Market Square. Market Square is located at the junction of Congress Street and Pleasant Street in downtown Portsmouth.

Portsmouth is easily accessible from all points in the Northeast by car or bus, and from Boston and Portland by train. On Saturday, non-Portsmouth residents may park in permit-only areas provided they display a copy of the PAOS 2010 map on the dashboard. There are no parking restrictions on Sundays in Portsmouth.

PAOS 2010 receives funds from participating artists and from the Portsmouth Arts Council, the New Hampshire Cultural Council, and the NEA, with valuable support from local universities and businesses.

#####

▼ INDEPENDENT CHALLENGE 1

Because of your success in revitalizing a historic theatre in Wellington, New Zealand, you were hired as the director of The Hobart Lyric Theatre in Hobart, Tasmania, to breathe life into its theatre revitalization efforts. After a year on the job, you are launching your first major fund-raising drive. You'll create a fund-raising letter for the Lyric Theatre by modifying a letter you wrote for the theatre in Wellington.

a. Start Word, open the file WD B-3.docx from the drive and folder where you store your Data Files, then save it as **Lyric Fundraising Letter**.

b. Replace the theatre name and address, the date, the inside address, and the salutation with the text shown in Figure B-19.

c. Use the Replace command to replace all instances of **Wellington** with **Hobart**.

d. Use the Replace command to replace all instances of **Town Hall** with **Lyric**.

e. Use the Replace command to replace all instances of **New Zealanders** with **Tasmanians**.

f. Use the Find command to locate the word **considerable**, then use the Thesaurus to replace the word with a synonym.

g. Move the fourth body paragraph so that it becomes the second body paragraph.

h. Create an AutoCorrect entry that inserts **Executive Director** whenever you type **exd**.

i. Replace Your Name with your name in the signature block, select Title, then type **exd** followed by a space.

j. Use the Spelling and Grammar command to check for and correct spelling and grammar errors.

FIGURE B-19

The Hobart Lyric Theatre
60-62 Macquarie Street, Hobart, Tasmania 7001, Australia

November 10, 2010

Ms. Natasha Campbell
450 Elizabeth Street
North Hobart, TAS 7004

Dear Ms. Campbell:

Advanced Challenge Exercise

- Open the Document Information panel, change the title to **Hobart Lyric Theatre**, then add the keyword **fund-raising**.
- Open the Properties dialog box, add your name as author on the Summary tab, then review the paragraph, line, word, and character count on the Statistics tab.
- On the Custom tab, add a property named **Project** with the value **Capital Campaign**, then close the dialog box and the Document Information panel.

k. Proofread the letter, correct any errors, save your changes, print a copy, close the document, then exit Word.

▼ INDEPENDENT CHALLENGE 2

An advertisement for job openings in Toronto caught your eye and you have decided to apply. The ad, shown in Figure B-20, was printed in last weekend's edition of your local newspaper. Instead of writing a cover letter from scratch, you revise a draft of a cover letter you wrote several years ago for a summer internship position.

a. Read the ad shown in Figure B-20 and decide which position to apply for. Choose the position that most closely matches your qualifications.

b. Start Word, open WD B-4.docx from the drive and folder where you store your Data Files, then save it as **Cover Letter**.

c. Replace the name, address, telephone number, and e-mail address in the letterhead with your own information.

d. Remove the hyperlink from the e-mail address.

e. Replace the date with today's date, then replace the inside address and the salutation with the information shown in Figure B-20.

f. Read the draft cover letter to get a feel for its contents.

g. Rework the text in the body of the letter to address your qualifications for the job you have chosen to apply for:

- Delete the third paragraph.
- Adjust the first sentence of the first paragraph as follows: specify the job you are applying for, including the position code, and indicate where you saw the position advertised.
- Move the first sentence in the last paragraph, which briefly states your qualifications and interest in the position, to the end of the first paragraph, then rework the sentence to describe your current qualifications.
- Adjust the second paragraph as follows: describe your work experience and skills. Be sure to relate your experience and qualifications to the position requirements listed in the advertisement. Add a third paragraph if your qualifications are extensive.
- Adjust the final paragraph as follows: politely request an interview for the position and provide your phone number and e-mail address.

h. Include your name in the signature block.

i. When you are finished revising the letter, check it for spelling and grammar errors and correct any mistakes. Make sure to remove any hyperlinks.

j. Save your changes to the letter, print a copy, close the document, then exit Word.

FIGURE B-20

*Global*Dynamics

Career Opportunities in Toronto

Global Dynamics, an established software development firm with offices in North America, Asia, and Europe, is seeking candidates for the following positions in its Toronto facility:

Instructor

Responsible for delivering software training to our expanding Canadian customer base. Duties include delivering hands-on training, keeping up-to-date with product development, and working with the Director of Training to ensure the high quality of course materials. Successful candidate will have excellent presentation skills and be proficient in Microsoft PowerPoint and Microsoft Word. **Position B12C6**

Administrative Assistant

Proficiency with Microsoft Word a must! Administrative office duties include making travel arrangements, scheduling meetings, taking notes and publishing meeting minutes, handling correspondence, and ordering office supplies. Must have superb multitasking abilities, excellent communication, organizational, and interpersonal skills, and be comfortable working with e-mail and the Internet. **Position B16F5**

Copywriter

The ideal candidate will have marketing or advertising writing experience in a high tech environment, including collateral, newsletters, and direct mail. Experience writing for the Web, broadcast, and multimedia is a plus. Fluency with Microsoft Word required. **Position C13D4**

Positions offer salary, excellent benefits, moving expenses, and career growth opportunities.

Send resume and cover letter referencing position code to:

Thomas Finlay
Director of Recruiting
Global Dynamics
330 University Avenue
Toronto, Ontario M5G 1R8
Canada

▼ INDEPENDENT CHALLENGE 3

As administrative director of continuing education, you drafted a memo to instructors asking them to help you finalize the course schedule for next semester. Today you'll examine the draft and make revisions before distributing it as an e-mail attachment.

a. Start Word, open the file WD B-5.docx from the drive and folder where you store your Data Files, then save it as **Business Courses Memo**.

b. Replace Your Name with your name in the From line, then scroll down until the first body paragraph is at the top of the screen.

Advanced Challenge Exercise

■ Use the Split command on the View tab to split the window under the first body paragraph, then scroll until the last paragraph of the memo is displayed in the bottom pane.

■ Use the Cut and Paste buttons to move the sentence **If you are planning to teach...** from the first body paragraph to become the first sentence in the last paragraph of the memo.

■ Double-click the split bar to restore the window to a single pane.

c. Use the [Delete] key to merge the first two paragraphs into one paragraph.

d. Use the Office Clipboard to reorganize the list of twelve-week courses so that the courses are listed in alphabetical order.

e. Use the drag-and-drop method to reorganize the list of one-day seminars so that the seminars are listed in alphabetical order, then clear and close the Office Clipboard.

f. Select Web site in the first paragraph, then create a hyperlink to the URL **www.course.com** with the ScreenTip **Spring 2011 Business Course**.

g. Select e-mail me in the last paragraph, then create a hyperlink to your e-mail address with the subject **Final Business Course Schedule**.

h. Use the Spelling and Grammar command to check for and correct spelling and grammar errors.

i. Use the Document Inspector to strip the document of document property information, ignore any other content that is flagged by the Document Inspector, then close the Document Inspector.

j. Proofread the memo, correct any errors, save your changes, print a copy, close the document, then exit Word.

▼ REAL LIFE INDEPENDENT CHALLENGE

This Independent Challenge requires an Internet connection.

Reference sources—dictionaries, thesauri, style and grammar guides, and guides to business etiquette and procedure—are essential for day-to-day use in the workplace. Much of this reference information is available on the World Wide Web. In this independent challenge, you will locate reference sources on the Web and use some of them to look up definitions, synonyms, and antonyms for words. Your goal is to familiarize yourself with online reference sources so you can use them later in your work.

a. Start Word, open the file WD B-6.docx from the drive and folder where you store your Data Files, then save it as **Web Reference Sources**. This document contains the questions you will answer about the Web reference sources you find. You will type your answers to the questions in the document.

b. Replace the placeholder text at the top of the Web Reference Sources document with your name and the date.

c. Use your favorite search engine to search the Web for grammar and style guides, dictionaries, and thesauri. Use the keywords **grammar, usage, dictionary, glossary,** and **thesaurus** to conduct your search.

d. Complete the Web Reference Sources document, then proofread it and correct any mistakes.

e. Save the document, print a copy, close the document, then exit Word.

▼ VISUAL WORKSHOP

Open WD B-7.docx from the drive and folder where you store your Data Files, then save the document as **Australian Visa Letter**. Replace the placeholders for the date, letterhead, inside address, salutation, and closing with the information shown in Figure B-21, then use the Office Clipboard to reorganize the sentences to match Figure B-21. Correct spelling and grammar errors, remove the document property information from the file, mark the document as final, then print a copy.

FIGURE B-21

Your Name

4637 Baker Street, Chicago, IL 60627; Tel: 630-555-2840

1/3/2010

Embassy of Australia
1601 Massachusetts Avenue NW
Washington, DC 20036

Dear Sir or Madam:

I am applying for a long-stay tourist visa to Australia, valid for four years. I am scheduled to depart for Sydney on March 13, 2010, returning to Chicago on September 8, 2010.

During my stay in Australia, I will be interviewing musicians and recording footage for a film I am making on contemporary Australian music. I would like a multiple entry visa valid for four years so I can return to Australia after this trip to follow up on my initial research. I will be based in Sydney, but I will be traveling frequently to film performances and to meet with musicians and producers.

Included with this letter are my completed visa application form, my passport, a passport photo, a copy of my return air ticket, and the visa fee. Please contact me if you need further information.

Sincerely,

Your Name

Enc: 5

UNIT
C
Word 2007

Formatting Text and Paragraphs

Files You Will Need:

WD C-1.docx
WD C-2.docx
WD C-3.docx
WD C-4.docx
WD C-5.docx
WD C-6.docx

Formatting can enhance the appearance of a document, create visual impact, and help illustrate a document's structure. The formatting of a document can also set the tone of the document, allowing readers to know at a glance if the document is business-like, serious, formal, informal, or fun. In this unit you learn how to format text using different fonts and font-formatting options. You also learn how to change the alignment, indentation, and spacing of paragraphs, how to spruce up documents with borders, shading, bullets, and other paragraph-formatting effects, and how to add footnotes and endnotes to a document. The Word live preview feature simplifies formatting by allowing you to quickly preview the different formatting options in your document before you apply them. You have finished drafting the text for a two-page flyer advertising last minute specials for October tours. Now, you need to format the flyer so it is attractive and highlights the significant information. The flyer will be distributed to clients with the quarterly newsletter.

OBJECTIVES

Format with fonts

Copy formats using the Format Painter

Change line and paragraph spacing

Align paragraphs

Work with tabs

Work with indents

Add bullets and numbering

Add borders and shading

Add footnotes and endnotes

Formatting with Fonts

Formatting text with different fonts is a quick and powerful way to enhance the appearance of a document. A **font** is a complete set of characters with the same typeface or design. Arial, Times New Roman, Comic Sans, Courier, Tahoma, and Calibri are some of the more common fonts, but there are hundreds of others, each with a specific design and feel. Another way to alter the impact of text is to increase or decrease its **font size**, which is measured in points. A **point** is ½ of an inch. ▰▰▰ You change the font and font size of the body text, title, and headings in the flyer, selecting fonts and font sizes that enhance the sales tone of the document and help to visually structure the report for readers.

STEPS

1. **Start Word, open the file** WD C-1.docx **from the drive and folder where you store your Data Files, then save it as** Last Minute Deals

   Notice that the name of the font used in the document, Calibri, is displayed in the Font list box in the Font group. The word "(Body)" in the Font list box indicates Calibri is the font used for body text in the current theme, the default theme. A **theme** is a related set of fonts, colors, styles, and effects that is applied to an entire document to give it a cohesive appearance. The font size, 11, appears next to it in the Font Size list box.

2. **Scroll the document to get a feel for its contents, press [Ctrl][Home], press [Ctrl][A] to select the entire document, then click the Font list arrow in the Font group**

   The Font list, which shows the fonts available on your computer, opens as shown in Figure C-1. The font names are formatted in the font and can appear in more than one location on the font list.

3. **Drag the pointer slowly down the font names in the Font list, use the scroll box to scroll down the Font list, then click Garamond**

   Dragging the pointer down the font list allows you to preview how the selected text will look if the highlighted font is applied. Clicking a font name applies the font. The font of the flyer changes to Garamond.

4. **Click the Font Size list arrow in the Font group, drag the pointer slowly up and down the Font Size list, then click 12**

   Dragging the pointer over the font sizes allows you to preview how the selected text will look if the highlighted font size is applied. The font size of the selected text increases to 12 points.

5. **Select the title** Quest Specialty Travel Last Minute Travel Deals, **click the Font list arrow, click Trebuchet MS, click the Font Size list arrow, click 22, then click the Bold button** **B** **in the Font group**

   The title is formatted in 22-point Trebuchet MS bold.

6. **Click the Font Color list arrow** **A▾** **in the Font group**

   A gallery of colors opens. It includes the set of theme colors in a range of tints and shades as well as a set of standard colors. You can point to a color in the gallery to preview it applied to the selected text.

7. **Click the Blue, Accent 1 color as shown in Figure C-2, then deselect the text**

   The color of the title text changes to blue. The active color on the Font Color button also changes to blue.

8. **Select the heading** Rajasthan Desert Safari, **then, using the Mini toolbar, click the Font list arrow, click Trebuchet MS, click the Font Size list arrow, click 14, click** **A▾**, **click the Dark Blue, Text 2 color, click** **B**, **then deselect the text**

   The heading is formatted in 14-point Trebuchet MS bold with a dark blue color. Notice that when you use the buttons on the Mini toolbar to format text, you cannot preview the formatting options in the document.

9. **Press [Ctrl][Home], then click the Save button** **🖫** **on the Quick Access toolbar**

   Compare your document to Figure C-3.

FIGURE C-1: Font list

Font list arrow

Fonts used in the default theme

Your list of recently used fonts will differ

Alphabetical list of all fonts on your computer

Font Size list arrow

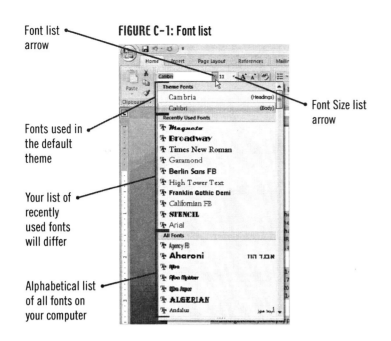

FIGURE C-2: Font Color gallery

Font Color list arrow

Name of color appears as a ScreenTip

Click to create a custom color

Live preview of Blue, Accent 1 color applied to text

FIGURE C-3: Document formatted with fonts

Title formatted in 22-point Trebuchet MS, bold, blue

Body text formatted in 12-point Garamond

Heading formatted in 14-point Trebuchet MS, bold, dark blue

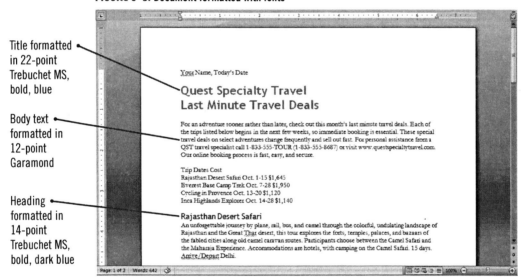

Adding a drop cap

A fun way to illustrate a document with fonts is to add a drop cap to a paragraph. A **drop cap** is a large initial capital letter, often used to set off the first paragraph of an article. To create a drop cap, place the insertion point in the paragraph you want to format, click the Insert tab, and then click the Drop Cap button in the Text group to open a menu of Drop cap options. Preview and select one of the options on the menu, or click Drop Cap Options to open the Drop Cap dialog box, shown in Figure C-4. In the Drop Cap dialog box, select the position, font, number of lines to drop, and the distance you want the drop cap to be from the paragraph text, and then click OK. The drop cap is added to the paragraph as a graphic object.

Once a drop cap is inserted in a paragraph, you can modify it by selecting it and then changing the settings in the Drop Cap dialog box. For even more interesting effects, enhance a drop cap with font color, font styles, or font effects, fill the graphic object with shading, or add a border around it. To enhance a drop cap, first select it, and then experiment with the formatting options available in the Font dialog box and in the Borders and Shading dialog box.

FIGURE C-4: Drop Cap dialog box

Copying Formats Using the Format Painter

You can dramatically change the appearance of text by applying different font styles, font effects, and character-spacing effects. For example, you can use the buttons in the Font group to make text darker by applying **bold** or to slant text by applying *italic*. You can also use the Font dialog box to apply font effects and character-spacing effects to text. When you are satisfied with the formatting of certain text, you can quickly apply the same formats to other text using the Format Painter. The **Format Painter** is a powerful Word feature that allows you to copy all the format settings applied to selected text to other text that you want to format the same way. ▆▆▆▆ You spice up the appearance of the text in the document by applying different font styles and effects. After formatting a heading and subheading, you use the Format Painter to apply the settings to other headings and subheadings.

STEPS

1. **Select immediate booking is essential in the first body paragraph, click the Bold button** B **on the Mini toolbar, select the entire paragraph, then click the Italic button** I **on the Mini toolbar**

   "Immediate booking is essential" is bold and the entire paragraph is formatted in italic.

QUICK TIP
To change the case of selected text from lowercase to uppercase — and visa versa — click the Change Case button **Aa▾** in the Font group, and then select the case style you want to use.

2. **Select Last Minute Travel Deals, then click the launcher** ▣ **in the Font group**

   The Font dialog box opens, as shown in Figure C-5. You can use options on the Font tab to change the font, font style, size, and color of text, and to add an underline and apply font effects to text.

3. **Scroll down the Size list, click 48, click the Font color list arrow, click the Red, Accent 2 color in the Theme Colors, click the Shadow check box, click OK, then deselect the text**

   The text is larger, red, and has a shadow effect.

4. **Select Last Minute Travel Deals, right-click, click Font on the Edit menu, click the Character Spacing tab, click the Scale list arrow, click 80%, click OK, then deselect the text**

   You use the Character Spacing tab in the Font dialog box to change the scale, or width, of the selected characters, to alter the spacing between characters, or to raise or lower the characters. Decreasing the scale of the characters makes them narrower and gives the text a tall, thin appearance, as shown in Figure C-6.

5. **Scroll down, select the subheading Camel Safari, then, using the Mini toolbar, click the Font list arrow, click Trebuchet MS, click** B**, click** I**, click the Font Color list arrow** A▾**, click the Red, Accent 2 color in the Theme Colors, then deselect the text**

   The subheading is formatted in Trebuchet MS, bold, italic, and red.

TROUBLE
Move the pointer over the document text to see the ▞I pointer.

6. **Select Camel Safari, then click the Format Painter button** ▞ **in the Clipboard group**

   The pointer changes to ▞I.

7. **Scroll down, select Maharaja Experience with the** ▞I **pointer, then deselect the text**

   The subheading is formatted in Trebuchet MS, bold, italic, and red, as shown in Figure C-7.

8. **Scroll up as needed, select Rajasthan Desert Safari, then double-click** ▞

   Double-clicking the Format Painter button allows the Format Painter to remain active until you turn it off. By keeping the Format Painter turned on you can apply formatting to multiple items.

QUICK TIP
You can also press [Esc] to turn off the Format Painter.

9. **Scroll down, select the headings Everest Base Camp Trek, Cycling in Provence, and Inca Highlands Explorer with the** ▞I **pointer, click** ▞ **to turn off the Format Painter, then save your changes**

   The headings are formatted in 14-point Trebuchet MS bold with a dark blue font color.

FIGURE C-5: Font tab in Font dialog box

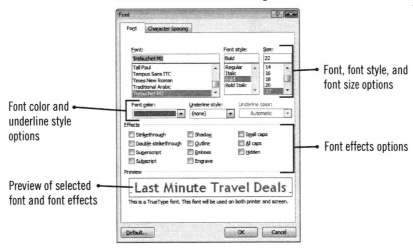

Font, font style, and font size options

Font color and underline style options

Font effects options

Preview of selected font and font effects

FIGURE C-6: Font and character spacing effects applied to text

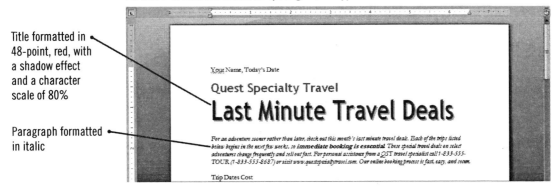

Title formatted in 48-point, red, with a shadow effect and a character scale of 80%

Paragraph formatted in italic

FIGURE C-7: Formats copied and applied using the Format Painter

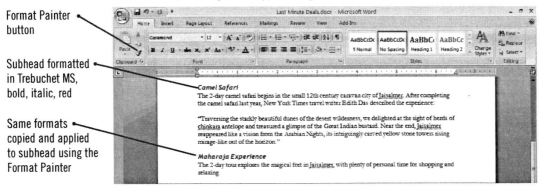

Format Painter button

Subhead formatted in Trebuchet MS, bold, italic, red

Same formats copied and applied to subhead using the Format Painter

Underlining text

Another creative way to call attention to text and to jazz up the appearance of a document is to apply an underline style to words you want to highlight. The Underline list arrow in the Font group displays straight, dotted, wavy, dashed, and mixed style underlines, along with a gallery of colors to choose from. To apply an underline to text, simply select it, click the Underline list arrow, and then select an underline style from the list. For a wider variety of underline styles, click More Underlines in the list, and then select an underline style in the Font dialog box. You can change the color of an underline at any time by selecting the underlined text, clicking the Underline list arrow, pointing to Underline Color, and then choosing from the options in the color gallery. If you want to remove an underline from text, select the underlined text, and then click the Underline button.

Formatting Text and Paragraphs

Changing Line and Paragraph Spacing

Increasing the amount of space between lines adds more white space to a document and can make it easier to read. Adding space before and after paragraphs can also open up a document and improve its appearance. You use the Line Spacing list arrow in the Paragraph group on the Home tab to quickly change line spacing. To change paragraph spacing, you use the Spacing options in the Paragraph group on the Page Layout tab. Line and paragraph spacing are measured in points. ▟▟▟ You increase the line spacing of several paragraphs and add extra space under each heading to give the report a more open feel. You work with formatting marks turned on, so you can see the paragraph marks (¶).

STEPS

1. **Press [Ctrl][Home], click the Show/Hide ¶ button ▟ in the Paragraph group, place the insertion point in the italicized paragraph under the title, then click the Line Spacing list arrow ▟ in the Paragraph group on the Home tab**

   The Line Spacing list opens. This list includes options for increasing the space between lines. The check mark on the Line Spacing list indicates the current line spacing.

2. **Click 1.15**

   The space between the lines in the paragraph increases to 1.15 lines. Notice that you do not need to select an entire paragraph to change its paragraph formatting; simply place the insertion point in the paragraph you want to format.

3. **Select the five-line list that begins with Trip Dates Cost, click ▟, then click 1.5**

   The line spacing between the selected paragraphs changes to 1.5. To change the paragraph-formatting features of more than one paragraph, you must select the paragraphs.

4. **Scroll down, place the insertion point in the heading Rajasthan Desert Safari, then click the Page Layout tab**

   The paragraph spacing settings for the active paragraph are shown in the Before and After text boxes in the Paragraph group on the Page Layout tab.

5. **Click the After up arrow in the Spacing section of the Paragraph group so that 6 pt appears**

   Six points of space are added after the Rajasthan Desert Safari heading paragraph.

6. **Scroll down, place the insertion point in the heading Everest Base Camp Trek, then press [F4]**

   Pressing [F4] repeats the last action you took, in this case, adding six points of space after the paragraph. Six points of space are added below the Everest Base Camp Trek heading.

7. **Scroll down, select Cycling in Provence, press and hold [Ctrl], select Inca Highlands Explorer, release [Ctrl], then press [F4]**

   When you press [Ctrl] as you select items, you can select and format multiple items at once. Six points of space are added after each heading.

8. **Press [Ctrl][Home], place the insertion point in Last Minute Travel Deals, click the Before up arrow in the Spacing section of the Paragraph group twice so that 12 pt appears**

   The second line of the title has 12 points of space before it. Compare your document with Figure C-8.

9. **Click the Home tab, click ▟, then save your changes**

FIGURE C-8: Line and paragraph spacing applied to document

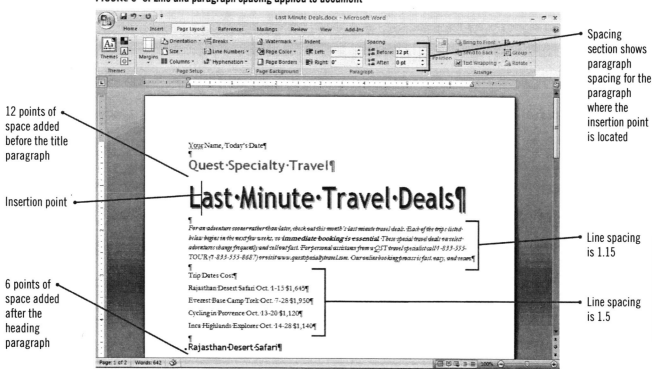

12 points of space added before the title paragraph

Insertion point

6 points of space added after the heading paragraph

Spacing section shows paragraph spacing for the paragraph where the insertion point is located

Line spacing is 1.15

Line spacing is 1.5

Formatting with Quick Styles

You can also apply multiple format settings to text in one step by applying a style. A **style** is a set of formats, such as font, font size, and paragraph alignment, that are named and stored together. Formatting a document with styles is a quick and easy way to give it a professional appearance. To make it even easier, Word includes sets of styles, called **Quick Styles**, that are designed to be used together in a document to make it attractive and readable. A Quick Style set includes styles for a title, several heading levels, body text, quotes, and lists. The styles in a Quick Style set use common fonts, colors, and formats, so that using the styles together in a document gives the document a cohesive look.

To view the active set of Quick Styles, click the More button in the Styles group on the Home tab to expand the Quick Styles gallery, shown in Figure C-9. As you move the pointer over each style in the gallery, a preview of the style is applied to the selected text. To apply a style to the selected text, you simply click the button for that style in the Quick Style gallery. To remove a style from selected text, you click the Clear Formatting button in the Font group or in the Quick Styles gallery.

If you want to change the active set of Quick Styles to a Quick Style set with a different design, click the Change Styles button in the Styles group, point to Style Set, and then select the Quick Style set that best suits your document's content, tone, and audience. Distinctive, Traditional, Modern, Fancy, and Formal are some examples of the Quick Style sets you can choose to apply. When you

change the Quick Style set, a complete set of new fonts and colors is applied to the entire document. You can also change the color scheme or font used in the active Quick Style set by clicking the Change Styles button, pointing to Colors or to Fonts, and then selecting from the available color schemes or font options.

FIGURE C-9: Quick Styles gallery

AaBbCcDc ¶ Normal	AaBbCcDc No Spacing	AaBbCc Heading 1	AaBbCc Heading 2
AaBbCcI Heading 3	AaB Title	AaBbCc. Subtitle	AaBbCcDc Subtle Em...
AaBbCcL Emphasis	AaBBCCDL Intense E...	AaBbCcDc Strong	AaBbCcD Quote
AaBbCcD Intense Q...	AaBBCCDL Subtle Ref...	AABBCCDL Intense R...	AABBCCDL Book Title
AaBbCcDc ¶ List Para...			

Save Selection as a New Quick Style...
Clear Formatting
Apply Styles...

Formatting Text and Paragraphs

Aligning Paragraphs

Changing paragraph alignment is another way to enhance a document's appearance. Paragraphs are aligned relative to the left and right margins in a document. By default, text is **left-aligned**, which means it is flush with the left margin and has a ragged right edge. Using the alignment buttons in the Paragraph group, you can **right-align** a paragraph—make it flush with the right margin—or **center** a paragraph so that it is positioned evenly between the left and right margins. You can also **justify** a paragraph so that both the left and right edges of the paragraph are flush with the left and right margins. ▰▰▰▰ You change the alignment of several paragraphs at the beginning of the report to make it more visually interesting.

STEPS

1. **Replace** Your Name, Today's Date **with your name, a comma, and the date**

2. **Select your name, the comma, and the date, then click the Align Text Right button** 🔳 **in the Paragraph group**

   The text is aligned with the right margin. In Page Layout view, the junction of the white and shaded sections of the horizontal ruler indicates the location of the left and right margins.

3. **Place the insertion point between your name and the comma, press [Delete] to delete the comma, then press [Enter]**

   The new paragraph containing the date is also right-aligned. Pressing [Enter] in the middle of a paragraph creates a new paragraph with the same text and paragraph formatting as the original paragraph.

4. **Select the two-line title, then click the Center button** 🔳 **in the Paragraph group**

   The two paragraphs that make up the title are centered between the left and right margins.

5. **Scroll down as needed, place the insertion point in the Rajasthan Desert Safari heading, then click** 🔳

   The Rajasthan Desert Safari heading is centered.

6. **Place the insertion point in the italicized paragraph under the title, then click the Justify button** 🔳 **in the Paragraph group**

   The paragraph is aligned with both the left and right margins, as shown in Figure C-10. When you justify a paragraph, Word adjusts the spacing between words so that each line in the paragraph is flush with the left and the right margins.

7. **Place the insertion point in Rajasthan Desert Safari, then click the launcher** 🔳 **in the Paragraph group**

   The Paragraph dialog box opens, as shown in Figure C-11. The Indents and Spacing tab shows the paragraph format settings for the paragraph where the insertion point is located. You can check or change paragraph format settings using this dialog box.

8. **Click the Alignment list arrow, click Left, click OK, then save your changes**

   The Rajasthan Desert Safari heading is left-aligned.

FIGURE C-10: Modified paragraph alignment

- Right margin on the ruler
- View Ruler button
- Right-aligned
- Center-aligned
- Justified
- Left-aligned

FIGURE C-11: Indents and Spacing tab in Paragraph dialog box

- Alignment options
- Line spacing options
- Spacing above and below paragraphs options
- Preview of selected settings

Formatting a document using themes

Changing the theme applied to a document is another powerful and efficient way to tailor a document's look and feel, particularly when a document is formatted with a Quick Style set. By default, all documents created in Word are formatted with the default Office theme—which uses Calibri as the font for the body text—but you can change the theme at any time to fit the content, tone, and purpose of a document. When you change the theme for a document, a complete set of new theme colors, fonts, and effects is applied to the whole document.

To preview how various themes look when applied to the current document, click the Themes button in the Themes group on the Page Layout tab, and then move the pointer over each theme in the gallery and notice how the document changes. When you click the theme you like, all document content that uses theme colors, all text

that is formatted with a style, including default body text, and all table styles and graphic effects change to the colors, fonts, and effects used by the theme. In addition, the gallery of colors changes to display the set of theme colors, and the active Quick Style set changes to employ the theme colors and fonts. Note that changing the theme does not affect the formatting of text to which font formatting has already been applied, nor does it change any standard or custom colors used in the document.

If you want to tweak the document design further, you can modify it by applying a different set of theme colors, heading and body text fonts, or graphic effects. To do this, simply click the Theme Colors, Theme Fonts, or Theme Effects button in the Themes group, move the pointer over each option in the gallery to preview it in the document, and then click the option you like best.

Working with Tabs

Tabs allow you to align text vertically at a specific location in a document. A **tab stop** is a point on the horizontal ruler that indicates the location at which to align text. By default, tab stops are located every ½" from the left margin, but you can also set custom tab stops. Using tabs, you can align text to the left, right, or center of a tab stop, or you can align text at a decimal point or insert a bar character. Table C-1 describes the different types of tab stops. You set tabs using the horizontal ruler or the Tabs dialog box. You use tabs to format the summary information on last minute tour deals so it is easy to read.

STEPS

1. **Scroll as needed, then select the five-line list beginning with Trip Dates Cost**

   Before you set tab stops for existing text, you must select the paragraphs for which you want to set tabs.

2. **Point to the tab indicator L at the left end of the horizontal ruler**

   The icon that appears in the tab indicator indicates the active type of tab; pointing to the tab indicator displays a ScreenTip with the name of the active tab type. By default, left tab is the active tab type. Clicking the tab indicator scrolls through the types of tabs and indents.

3. **Click the tab indicator to see each of the available tab and indent types, make Left Tab L the active tab type, click the 1" mark on the horizontal ruler, then click the 3½" mark on the horizontal ruler**

   A left tab stop is inserted at the 1" mark and the 3½" on the horizontal ruler. Clicking the horizontal ruler inserts a tab stop of the active type for the selected paragraph or paragraphs.

4. **Click the tab indicator twice so the Right Tab icon ⌐ is active, then click the 5" mark on the horizontal ruler**

   A right tab stop is inserted at the 5" mark on the horizontal ruler, as shown in Figure C-12.

5. **Place the insertion point before Trip in the first line in the list, press [Tab], place the insertion point before Dates, press [Tab], place the insertion point before Cost, then press [Tab]**

   Inserting a tab before Trip left-aligns the text at the 1" mark, inserting a tab before Dates left-aligns the text at the 3½" mark, and inserting a tab before Cost right-aligns Cost at the 5" mark.

6. **Insert a tab at the beginning of each remaining line in the list**

   The paragraphs left-align at the 1" mark.

7. **Insert a tab before each Oct. in the list, then insert a tab before each $ in the list**

   The dates left-align at the 3½" mark. The prices right-align at the 5" mark.

8. **Select the five lines of tabbed text, drag the right tab stop to the 5½" mark on the horizontal ruler, then deselect the text**

   Dragging the tab stop moves it to a new location. The prices right-align at the 5½" mark.

9. **Select the last four lines of tabbed text, click the launcher ◰ in the Paragraph group, then click Tabs in the Paragraph dialog box**

   The Tabs dialog box opens, as shown in Figure C-13. You can use the Tabs dialog box to set tab stops, change the position or alignment of existing tab stops, clear tab stops, and apply tab leaders to tabs. **Tab leaders** are lines that appear in front of tabbed text.

10. **Click 3.5" in the Tab stop position list box, click the 2 option button in the Leader section, click Set, click 5.5" in the Tab stop position list box, click the 2 option button in the Leader section, click Set, click OK, deselect the text, then save your changes**

    A dotted tab leader is added before each 3.5" and 5.5" tab stop in the last four lines of tabbed text, as shown in Figure C-14.

Formatting Text and Paragraphs

FIGURE C-12: Left and right tab stops on the horizontal ruler

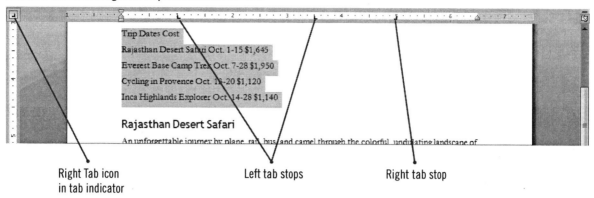

Right Tab icon in tab indicator

Left tab stops

Right tab stop

FIGURE C-13: Tabs dialog box

Select the tab stop you want to modify

Clears the selected tab stop

Clears all tab stops

FIGURE C-14: Tab leaders

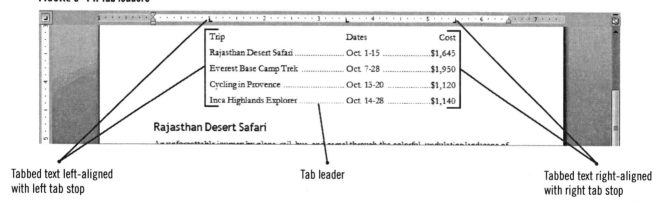

Tabbed text left-aligned with left tab stop

Tab leader

Tabbed text right-aligned with right tab stop

TABLE C-1: Types of tabs

tab	use to
⌊ Left tab	Set the start position of text so that text runs to the right of the tab stop as you type
⊥ Center tab	Set the center align position of text so that text stays centered on the tab stop as you type
⌋ Right tab	Set the right or end position of text so that text moves to the left of the tab stop as you type
⊥ Decimal tab	Set the position of the decimal point so that numbers align around the decimal point as you type
∣ Bar tab	Insert a vertical bar at the tab position

Working with Indents

When you **indent** a paragraph, you move its edge in from the left or right margin. You can indent the entire left or right edge of a paragraph, just the first line, or all lines except the first line. The **indent markers** on the horizontal ruler indicate the indent settings for the paragraph in which the insertion point is located. Dragging an indent marker to a new location on the ruler is one way to change the indentation of a paragraph; changing the indent settings in the Paragraph group on the Page Layout tab is another; and using the indent buttons in the Paragraph group on the Home tab is a third. Table C-2 describes different types of indents and some of the methods for creating each. ▰▰▰ You indent several paragraphs in the report.

Press [Tab] at the beginning of a paragraph to indent the first line ½".

1. **Press [Ctrl][Home], place the insertion point in the italicized paragraph under the title, then click the Increase Indent button ▦ in the Paragraph group on the Home tab**

   The entire paragraph is indented ½" from the left margin, as shown in Figure C-15. The indent marker ▟ also moves to the ½" mark on the horizontal ruler. Each time you click the Increase Indent button, the left edge of a paragraph moves another ½" to the right.

2. **Click the Decrease Indent button ▦ in the Paragraph group**

   The left edge of the paragraph moves ½" to the left, and the indent marker moves back to the left margin.

Take care to drag only the First Line Indent marker. If you make a mistake, click the Undo button, then try again.

3. **Drag the First Line Indent marker ▽ to the ¾" mark on the horizontal ruler**

   Figure C-16 shows the First Line Indent marker being dragged. The first line of the paragraph is indented ¾". Dragging the First Line Indent marker indents only the first line of a paragraph.

4. **Scroll to the bottom of page 1, place the insertion point in the quotation, click the Page Layout tab, click the Indent Left text box in the Paragraph group, type .5, click the Indent Right text box, type .5, then press [Enter]**

   The left and right edges of the paragraph are indented ½" from the margins, as shown in Figure C-17.

5. **Press [Ctrl][Home], place the insertion point in the italicized paragraph, then click the launcher ▣ in the Paragraph group**

   The Paragraph dialog box opens. You can use the Indents and Spacing tab to check or change the alignment, indentation, and paragraph and line spacing settings applied to a paragraph.

6. **Click the Special list arrow, click (none), click OK, then save your changes**

   The first line indent is removed from the paragraph.

TABLE C-2: Types of indents

indent type: description	to create
Left indent: The left edge of a paragraph is moved in from the left margin	Enter the position you want the left edge of the paragraph to align in the Indent Left text box in the Paragraph group on the Page Layout tab; or drag the Left Indent marker ▭ on the ruler right to the position where you want the left edge of the paragraph to align
Right indent: The right edge of a paragraph is moved in from the right margin	Enter the position you want the right edge of the paragraph to align in the Indent Right text box in the Paragraph group on the Page Layout tab; or drag the Right Indent marker △ on the ruler left to the position where you want the right edge of the paragraph to end
First line indent: The first line of a paragraph is indented more than the subsequent lines	Drag ▽ on the ruler right to the position where you want the first line of the paragraph to begin; or activate the First Line Indent marker ▽ in the tab indicator, and then click the ruler at the position where you want the first line of the paragraph to begin
Hanging indent: The subsequent lines of a paragraph are indented more than the first line	Drag the Hanging Indent marker ▟ on the ruler right to the position where you want the hanging indent to begin; or activate the Hanging Indent marker ▟ in the tab indicator, and then click the ruler at the position where you want the second and remaining lines of the paragraph to begin
Negative indent (or Outdent): The left edge of a paragraph is moved to the left of the left margin	Enter the negative position you want the left edge of the paragraph to align in the Indent Left text box in the Paragraph group on the Page Layout tab; or drag the Left Indent marker ▭ on the ruler left to the position where you want the negative indent to begin

FIGURE C-15: Indented paragraph

First Line Indent marker

Hanging Indent marker

Left Indent marker

Indented paragraph

Right Indent marker

Increase Indent button

Decrease Indent button

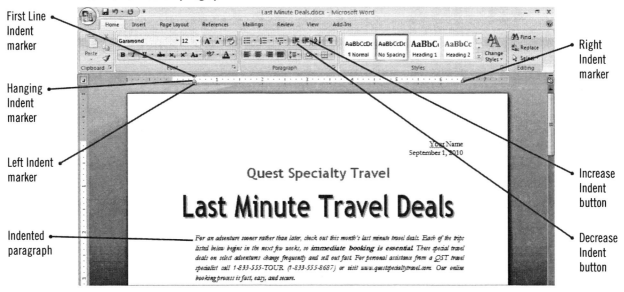

FIGURE C-16: Dragging the First Line Indent marker

First Line Indent marker being dragged

Dotted line shows the position of indent in the document

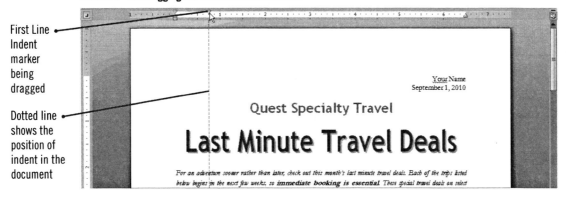

FIGURE C-17: Paragraph indented from the left and right

Paragraph indented ½" from left margin

Paragraph indented ½" from right margin

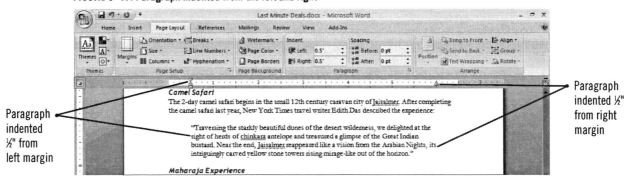

Clearing formatting

If you are unhappy with the way text is formatted, you can use the Clear Formatting command to return the text to the default format settings. The default format includes font and paragraph formatting: text is formatted in 11-point Calibri, and paragraphs are left-aligned with 1.15 point line spacing, 10 points of space below, and no indents. To clear formatting from text and return it to the default format, select the text you want to clear, and then click the Clear Formatting button in the Font group on the Home tab. If you prefer to return the text to the default font and remove all paragraph formatting, making the text 11-point Calibri, left-aligned, single spaced, with no paragraph spacing or indents, select the text and then simply click the No Spacing button in the Styles group on the Home tab.

Adding Bullets and Numbering

Formatting a list with bullets or numbering can help to organize the ideas in a document. A **bullet** is a character, often a small circle, that appears before the items in a list to add emphasis. Formatting a list as a numbered list helps illustrate sequences and priorities. You can quickly format a list with bullets or numbering by using the Bullets and Numbering buttons in the Paragraph group on the Home tab. ▰▰▰ You format the lists in your report with numbers and bullets.

STEPS

1. **Scroll until the Everest Base Camp Trek heading is at the top of your screen**

2. **Select the three-line list of 3-day add-ons, click the Home tab, then click the Numbering list arrow 📋 ▾ in the Paragraph group**

   The Numbering Library opens, as shown in Figure C-18. You use this list to choose or change the numbering style applied to a list.

3. **Drag the pointer over different numbering styles, then click the numbering style shown in Figure C-18**

   Dragging the pointer over the numbering styles allows you to preview how the selected text will look if the highlighted numbering style is applied. After clicking, the paragraphs are formatted as a numbered list.

4. **Place the insertion point after Pokhara — Valley of Lakes, press [Enter], then type Temples of Janakpur**

   Pressing [Enter] in the middle of the numbered list creates a new numbered paragraph and automatically renumbers the remainder of the list. Similarly, if you delete a paragraph from a numbered list, Word automatically renumbers the remaining paragraphs.

5. **Click 1 in the list**

   Clicking a number in a list selects all the numbers, as shown in Figure C-19.

6. **Click the Bold button B in the Font group**

   The numbers are all formatted in bold. Notice that the formatting of the items in the list does not change when you change the formatting of the numbers. You can also use this technique to change the formatting of bullets in a bulleted list.

7. **Select the list of items under Last minute participants in the Everest Base Camp trek..., then click the Bullets button 📋 in the Paragraph group**

   The four paragraphs are formatted as a bulleted list using the most recently used bullet style.

8. **Click a bullet in the list to select all the bullets, click the Bullets list arrow 📋 ▾ in the Paragraph group, click the check mark bullet style, then save your changes**

   The bullet character changes to a check mark, as shown in Figure C-20.

QUICK TIP

To change the style, font, number format, and alignment of the numbers in a list, right-click the list, point to Numbering, then click Define New Number Format.

QUICK TIP

To remove a bullet or number, select the paragraph(s), then click 📋 or 📋.

QUICK TIP

To use a symbol or a picture for a bullet character, click Define New Bullet in the Bullet list, and then select from the options in the Define New Bullet dialog box.

Creating multilevel lists

You can create lists with hierarchical structures by applying a multilevel list style to a list. To create a **multilevel list**, also called an outline, begin by applying a multilevel list style using the Multilevel List list arrow 📋▾ in the Paragraph group on the Home tab, then type your outline, pressing [Enter] after each item. To demote items to a lower level of importance in the outline, place the insertion point in the item, then click the Increase Indent button 📋 in the Paragraph group on the Home tab. Each time you indent a paragraph, the item is demoted to a lower level in the outline. Similarly, you can use the Decrease Indent button 📋 to promote an item to a higher level in the outline. You can also create a hierarchical structure in any bulleted or numbered list by using 📋 and 📋 to demote and promote items in the list. To change the multilevel list style applied to a list, select the list, click 📋▾, then select a new style.

Formatting Text and Paragraphs

FIGURE C-18: Numbering Library

Numbering list arrow

Number format will be applied to selected text

Choose this numbering style

Click to change the style, format, and alignment of the numbers in a list

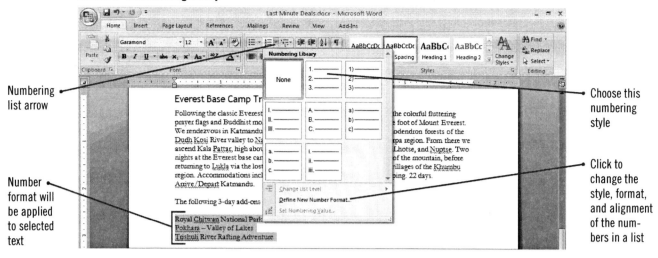

FIGURE C-19: Numbered list

Bullets button

Numbers selected in numbered list

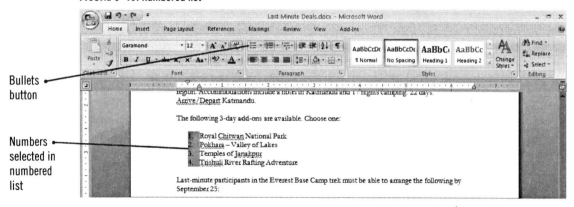

FIGURE C-20: Check mark bullets applied to list

Numbers are bold

Check mark bullets

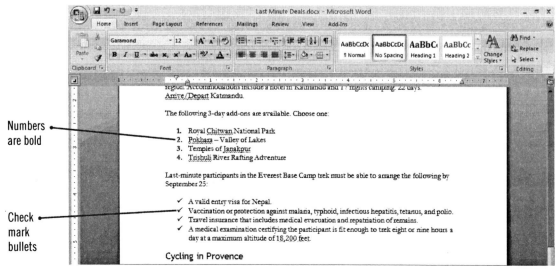

Adding Borders and Shading

Borders and shading can add color and splash to a document. **Borders** are lines you add above, below, to the side, or around words or paragraphs. You can format borders using different line styles, colors, and widths. **Shading** is a color or pattern you apply behind words or paragraphs to make them stand out on a page. You apply borders and shading using the Borders button and the Shading button in the Paragraph group on the Home tab. ▰▰▰ You enhance the tabbed text of the last minute tours schedule by adding shading to it. You also apply a border around the tabbed text to set it off from the rest of the document.

1. **Press [Ctrl][Home], then scroll down until the tabbed text is at the top of your screen**

2. **Select the five paragraphs of tabbed text, click the Shading list arrow ⬛▾ in the Paragraph group on the Home tab, click the Blue, Accent 1, Lighter 60% color, then deselect the text**

   Light blue shading is applied to the five paragraphs. Notice that the shading is applied to the entire width of the paragraphs, despite the tab settings.

3. **Select the five paragraphs, drag the Left Indent marker ⬛ to the ¾" mark on the horizontal ruler, drag the Right Indent marker ⬛ to the 5¾" mark, then deselect the text**

   The shading for the paragraphs is indented from the left and right, which makes it look more attractive, as shown in Figure C-21.

4. **Select the five paragraphs, click the Bottom Border list arrow ⬛▾ in the Paragraph group, click Outside Borders, then deselect the text**

   A black outside border is added around the selected text. You can use the Borders list arrow to add a border above, below, to the side of, or around the selected text, among other options. The style of the border added is the most recently used border style, in this case the default, a thin black line.

5. **Select the five paragraphs, click the Outside Borders list arrow ⬛▾, click No Border, click the No Border list arrow ⬛▾, then click Borders and Shading**

   The Borders and Shading dialog box opens, as shown in Figure C-22. You use the Borders tab to change the border style, color, and width, and to add boxes and lines to words or paragraphs.

When creating custom borders, it's important to select the style, color, and width settings before applying the borders in the Preview section.

6. **Click the Box box in the Setting section, scroll down the Style list, click the double line style, click the Color list arrow, click the Dark Blue, Text 2 color, click the Width list arrow, click 1½ pt, click OK, then deselect the text**

   A 1½-point dark blue double line border is added around the tabbed text.

7. **Select the five paragraphs, click the Bold button ⬛ in the Font group, click the Font Color list arrow ⬛▾ in the Font group, click the Dark Blue, Text 2 color, then deselect the text**

   The text changes to bold dark blue.

8. **Select the first line in the tabbed text, click the launcher ⬛ in the Font group, click the Font tab if it is not the active tab, click 14 in the Size list, click the Font Color list arrow, click the Red, Accent 2 color, click the Small caps check box in the Effects section, click OK, deselect the text, then save your changes**

   The text in the first line of the tabbed text is enlarged and changed to red small caps, as shown in Figure C-23. When you change text to small caps, the lowercase letters are changed to uppercase letters in a smaller font size.

FIGURE C-21: Shading applied to the tabbed text

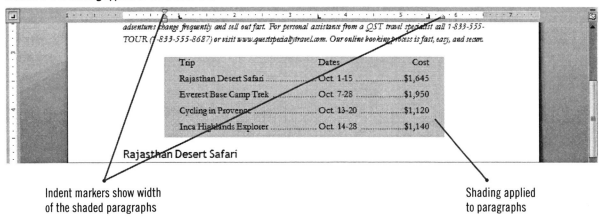

Indent markers show width
of the shaded paragraphs

Shading applied
to paragraphs

FIGURE C-22: Borders tab in Borders and Shading dialog box

Choose a line style

Preview of border
settings

Click buttons or edges of
preview to apply borders

Choose to apply the settings
to a paragraph or to
selected text

Click to change the
location of the border
relative to the text

Select border
formats before
applying them
in the Preview
area

Select Custom
to add a single
border

FIGURE C-23: Border and font formatting applied to tabbed text

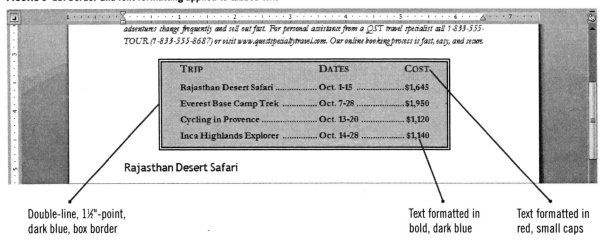

Double-line, 1½"-point,
dark blue, box border

Text formatted in
bold, dark blue

Text formatted in
red, small caps

Highlighting text in a document

The Highlight tool allows you to mark and find important text in a document. **Highlighting** is transparent color that is applied to text using the Highlight pointer ✏. To highlight text, click the Text Highlight Color list arrow 🖍 in the Font group on the Home tab, select a color, then use the I-beam part of the ✏ pointer to select the text. Click 🖍 to turn off the Highlight pointer. To remove highlighting, select the highlighted text, click 🖍, then click No Color. Highlighting prints, but it is used most effectively when a document is viewed on screen.

Formatting Text and Paragraphs

Adding Footnotes and Endnotes

Footnotes and endnotes are used in printed documents to provide further information, comment on, or supply references for text in a document. A **footnote** or **endnote** is an explanatory note that consists of two linked parts: the note reference mark that appears next to text to indicate that additional information is offered in a footnote or endnote, and the corresponding footnote or endnote text. Word places footnotes at the end of each page and endnotes at the end of the document. You insert and manage footnotes and endnotes in a document using the tools in the Footnotes group on the References tab. Before finalizing the document, you add several footnotes to expand upon the document information.

STEPS

1. **Place the insertion point after Cost in the top row of the tabbed text, click the References tab, then click the Insert Footnote button in the Footnotes group**

   A note reference mark, in this case a superscript 1, appears after Cost, and the insertion point moves below a separator line at the bottom of the page. A note reference mark can be a number, a symbol, a character, or a combination of characters.

2. **Type International flights, travel insurance, visas, and taxes are not included in the tour price.**

   The footnote text appears below the separator line at the bottom of page 1.

3. **Place the insertion point at the end of the quotation at the bottom of page 1, click the Insert Footnote button, then type April 12, 2009**

   The footnote text for the second footnote appears under the first footnote at the bottom of page 1, as shown in Figure C-24.

4. **Scroll to the middle of page 2, place the insertion point at the end of the second line in the bulleted list, click the Insert Footnote button, then type Vaccination requirements are subject to change and should be confirmed before departure.**

   The footnote text for the third footnote appears at the bottom of page 2.

5. **Scroll up, place the insertion point after the Everest Base Camp Trek heading, click the Insert Footnote button, then type Due to altitude, terrain, and distance walked, this trek is for strong mountain walkers only.**

   Notice that when you inserted a new footnote between existing footnotes, Word automatically renumbered the footnotes. The new footnote appears above the final footnote at the bottom of page 2.

6. **Press [Ctrl][Home], click the Next Footnote button in the Footnotes group**

   The insertion point moves to the first reference mark in the document.

7. **Click the Next Footnote button, press [Delete] to select the number 2 reference mark, then press [Delete] again**

   The reference mark and associated footnote are deleted from the document and the footnotes are automatically renumbered. You must select a reference mark to delete a footnote; you can not simply delete the footnote text itself.

8. **Scroll to the bottom of page 2, notice the remaining footnotes have been renumbered, press [Ctrl][Home], then save your changes**

   The completed document is shown in Figure C-25.

9. **Click the Office button , point to Print, click Quick Print, close the document, then exit Word**

   A copy of the flyer prints. Depending on your printer, colors might appear differently when you print. If you are using a black-and-white printer, colors will print in shades of gray.

FIGURE C-24: Footnotes in the document

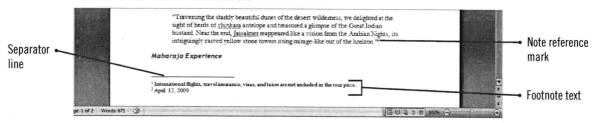

Separator line

"Traversing the starkly beautiful dunes of the desert wilderness, we delighted at the sight of herds of chinkara antelope and treasured a glimpse of the Great Indian bustard. Near the end, Jaisalmer reappeared like a vision from the Arabian Nights, its intriguingly carved yellow stone towers rising mirage-like out of the horizon."²

Maharaja Experience

¹ International flights, travel insurance, visas, and taxes are not included in the tour price.
² April 12, 2009

Note reference mark

Footnote text

Page: 1 of 2   Words: 671

FIGURE C-25: Completed document

Your Name
September 1, 2010

Quest Specialty Travel

Last Minute Travel Deals

For an adventure sooner rather than later, check out this month's last minute travel deals. Each of the trips listed below begins in the next few weeks, so **immediate booking is essential** *These special travel deals on select adventures change frequently and sell out fast. For personal assistance from a QST travel specialist call 1-833-555-TOUR (1-833-555-8687) or visit www.questspecialtytravel.com. Our online booking process is fast, easy, and secure.*

TRIP	DATES	COST¹
Rajasthan Desert Safari	Oct. 1-15	$1,645
Everest Base Camp Trek	Oct. 7-28	$1,950
Cycling in Provence	Oct. 13-20	$1,120
Inca Highlands Explorer	Oct. 14-28	$1,140

Rajasthan Desert Safari

An unforgettable journey by plane, rail, bus, and camel through the colorful, undulating landscape of Rajasthan and the Great Thar desert, this tour explores the forts, temples, palaces, and bazaars of the fabled cities along old camel caravan routes. Participants choose between the Camel Safari and the Maharaja Experience. Accommodations are hotels, with camping on the Camel Safari. 15 days. Arrive/Depart Delhi.

Camel Safari
The 2-day camel safari begins in the small 12th century caravan city of Jaisalmer. After completing the camel safari last year, New York Times travel writer Edith Das described the experience:

"Traversing the starkly beautiful dunes of the desert wilderness, we delighted at the sight of herds of chinkara antelope and treasured a glimpse of the Great Indian bustard. Near the end, Jaisalmer reappeared like a vision from the Arabian Nights, its intriguingly carved yellow stone towers rising mirage-like out of the horizon."

Maharaja Experience
The 2-day tour explores the magical fort in Jaisalmer, with plenty of personal time for shopping and relaxing.

¹ International flights, travel insurance, visas, and taxes are no included in the tour price.

Everest Base Camp Trek²

Following the classic Everest expedition route, this trek leads hikers past the colorful fluttering prayer flags and Buddhist monasteries of traditional Sherpa villages, to the foot of Mount Everest. We rendezvous in Katmandu, fly to Lukla, and traverse the pine and rhododendron forests of the Dudh Kosi River valley to Namche Bazaar, the bustling center of the Sherpa region. From there we ascend Kala Pattar, high above the tree line, for suburb views of Everest, Lhotse, and Nuptse. Two nights at the Everest base camp allows us ample time to explore the base of the mountain, before returning to Lukla via the lost valleys, high mountain passes, and remote villages of the Khumbu region. Accommodations include a hotel in Katmandu and 17 nights camping. 22 days. Arrive/Depart Katmandu.

The following 3-day add-ons are available. Choose one:

1. Royal Chitwan National Park
2. Pokhara – Valley of Lakes
3. Temples of Janakpur
4. Trishuli River Rafting Adventure

Last-minute participants in the Everest Base Camp trek must be able to arrange the following by September 25:

✓ A valid entry visa for Nepal.
✓ Vaccination or protection against malaria, typhoid, infectious hepatitis, tetanus, and polio.³
✓ Travel insurance that includes medical evacuation and repatriation of remains.
✓ A medical examination certifying the participant is fit enough to trek eight or nine hours a day at a maximum altitude of 18,200 feet.

Cycling in Provence

The fertile, rambling terrain of Provence provides the backdrop for this easy-going trip. Days are spent cycling between pleasant medieval towns and delightful villages, with ample time to linger at the sights along the way. At night, we relax in the comfort and warmth of small, local hotels. The average daily ride is 30 miles, but there are options for longer routes if you want to cycle more. 8 days. Arrive/Depart Nice.

Inca Highlands Explorer

This epic overland adventure combines the highlights of Inca civilization with an astonishing five-day Andean trek through cloud forests and snow-capped peaks to the ancient Inca site of Machu Picchu. We then travel by road to gorgeous Lake Titicaca, birthplace of the Inca legend, and on to La Paz, Bolivia, the world's highest capital city. Accommodations include camping and hotels. 15 days. Arrive Lima/Depart La Paz.

² Due to altitude, terrain, and distance walked, this trek is for strong mountain walkers only.
³ Vaccination requirements are subject to change and should be confirmed before departure.

Word 2007

Creating a bibliography

Many documents require a **bibliography**, a list of sources that you consulted or cited in creating the document. The Word bibliography feature allows you to quickly create sources, add citations to a document, and automatically generate a bibliography based on the source information you provide for the document. Each time you create a new source, the source information is saved on your computer so that it is available for use in any document.

To add a citation and source to a document, begin by selecting the style you want to use for the citation and source using the Style list arrow in the Citations & Bibliography group on the References tab. APA, Chicago, and MLA are commonly used styles. Next, place the insertion point at the end of the sentence where you want to add the citation, click the Insert Citation button in the Citations & Bibliography group, click Add New Source, and then enter the relevant information about the reference source in the Create Source dialog box. When you have finished adding citations to a document and are ready to create a bibliography, place the insertion point where you want the bibliography, usually at the end of the document, click the Bibliography button in the Citations & Bibliography group, and then click a built-in bibliography style from the gallery, or click Insert Bibliography. The bibliography is inserted in the document as a field, and can be formatted any way you choose.

Practice

▼ CONCEPTS REVIEW

Label each element of the Word program window shown in Figure C-26.

FIGURE C-26

Match each term with the statement that best describes it.

8. Footnote

9. Shading

10. Point

11. Style

12. Bibliography

13. Highlight

14. Bullet

15. Border

a. Color or pattern that is applied behind text to make it look attractive

b. A note placed at the bottom of a page that comments on part of the document text

c. A list of sources consulted or cited in creating a document

d. A line that can be applied above, below, or to the sides of a paragraph

e. Transparent color that is applied to text to mark it in a document

f. A unit of measurement equal to ½ of an inch

g. A character that appears at the beginning of a paragraph to add emphasis

h. A set of format settings

Select the best answer from the list of choices.

16. What is Garamond?
   a. A character format
   b. A style
   c. A font
   d. A text effect

17. What is the most precise way to increase the amount of white space between two paragraphs?
   a. Change the before paragraph spacing for the second paragraph
   b. Indent the paragraphs
   c. Change the line spacing of the paragraphs
   d. Insert an extra blank line between the paragraphs

18. In which type of indent are the subsequent lines of a paragraph indented more than the first line?
   a. Hanging indent
   b. Negative indent
   c. First Line indent
   d. Right indent

19. Which dialog box is used to change the scale of characters?
   a. Paragraph
   b. Borders and Shading
   c. Tabs
   d. Font

20. Which button is used to align a paragraph with both the left and right margins?
   a. ▤
   b. ▤
   c. ▤
   d. ▤

▼ SKILLS REVIEW

1. Format with fonts.
   a. Start Word, open the file WD C-2.docx from the drive and folder where you store your Data Files, save it as **Franklin EDA Report**, then scroll through the document to get a feel for its contents.
   b. Press [Ctrl][A], then format the text in 12-point Californian FB. Choose a different serif font if Californian FB is not available to you.
   c. Press [Ctrl][Home], format the report title **Town of Franklin Economic Development Authority Report Executive Summary** in 26-point Berlin Sans FB. Choose a different sans serif font if Berlin Sans FB is not available to you.
   d. Change the font color of the report title to Purple, Accent 4, Darker 25%, then press [Enter] after Franklin in the title.
   e. Place the insertion point in the first body paragraph under the title, then add a two-line drop cap to the paragraph using the Dropped position.
   f. Format the heading **Mission Statement** in 14-point Berlin Sans FB with the Purple, Accent 4, Darker 25% font color.
   g. Press [Ctrl][Home], then save your changes to the report.

2. Copy formats using the Format Painter.
   a. Use the Format Painter to copy the format of the Mission Statement heading to the following headings: **Guiding Principles, Issues, Proposed Actions**.
   b. Show formatting marks, then format the paragraph under the Mission Statement heading in italic.
   c. Format **Years Population Growth**, the first line in the four-line list under the Issues heading, in bold, small caps, with Purple, Accent 4, Darker 50% font color.
   d. Change the font color of the next two lines under Years Population Growth to Purple, Accent 4, Darker 50%.
   e. Format the line **Source: Office of State Planning** in italic.

    f. Scroll to the top of the report, then change the character scale of Town of Franklin Economic Development Authority Report to 90%.

    g. Change the character scale of Executive Summary to 150%, then save your changes.

3. Change line and paragraph spacing.

    a. Change the line spacing of the three-line list under the first body paragraph to 1.5 lines.

    b. Add 24 points of space before and 6 points of space after the Executive Summary line in the title.

    c. Add 12 points of space after the Mission Statement heading, then use the F4 key to add 12 points of space after each additional heading in the report (Guiding Principles, Issues, Proposed Actions).

    d. Add 6 points of space after each paragraph in the list under the Guiding Principles heading.

    e. Change the line spacing of the 4-line list under the Issues heading that begins with Years Population Growth to 1.15.

    f. Add 6 points of space after each paragraph under the Proposed Actions heading.

    g. Press [Ctrl][Home], then save your changes to the report.

4. Align paragraphs.

    a. Press [Ctrl][A] to select the entire document, then justify all the paragraphs.

    b. Center the three-line report title.

    c. Press [Ctrl][End], type your name, press [Enter], type the current date, then right-align your name and the date.

    d. Save your changes to the report.

5. Work with tabs.

    a. Scroll up and select the four-line list of population information under the Issues heading.

    b. Set left tab stops at the 2" mark and the 3¾" mark.

    c. Insert a tab at the beginning of each line in the list.

    d. In the first line, insert a tab before Population. In the second line, insert a tab before 4.5%. In the third line, insert a tab before 53%.

    e. Select the first three lines, then drag the second tab stop to the 3" mark on the horizontal ruler.

    f. Press [Ctrl][Home], then save your changes to the report.

6. Work with indents.

    a. Indent the paragraph under the Mission Statement heading ½" from the left and ½" from the right.

    b. Indent the first line of the paragraph under the Guiding Principles heading ½".

    c. Indent the first line of the three body paragraphs under the Issues heading ½".

    d. Press [Ctrl][Home], then save your changes to the report.

7. Add bullets and numbering.

    a. Apply bullets to the three-line list under the first body paragraph. Change the bullet style to small black circles if necessary.

    b. Change the font color of the bullets to Purple, Accent 4, Darker 25%.

    c. Scroll down until the Guiding Principles heading is at the top of your screen.

    d. Format the six-paragraph list under Guiding Principles as a numbered list.

    e. Format the numbers in 14-point Berlin Sans FB, then change the font color to Purple, Accent 4, Darker 25%.

    f. Scroll down until the Proposed Actions heading is at the top of your screen, then format the paragraphs under the heading as a bulleted list using check marks as the bullet style.

    g. Change the font color of the bullets to Purple, Accent 4, Darker 25%, press [Ctrl][Home], then save your changes to the report.

8. Add borders and shading.

    a. Change the font color of **Town of Franklin Economic Development Authority Report** to White, Background 1, then apply Orange, Accent 6 shading.

    b. Add a 1-point Orange, Accent 6 border below the Mission Statement heading.

    c. Use the F4 key to add the same border to the other headings in the report (Guiding Principles, Issues, Proposed Actions).

    d. Under the Issues heading, select the first three lines of tabbed text, which are formatted in purple, then apply Purple, Accent 4, Lighter 60% shading to the paragraphs.

    e. Select the first three lines of tabbed text again if necessary, then add a 1½ -point Orange, Accent 6 single line box border around the paragraphs.

    f. Indent the shading and border around the paragraphs 1¾" from the left and 1¾" from the right, then save your changes.

9. Add footnotes and endnotes.

    a. Place the insertion point at the end of item 5 under the Guiding Principles heading, insert an endnote, then type **A capital reserve fund was established in 2009.**

    b. Place the insertion point at the end of item 3, insert an endnote, then type **See the Downtown District EDA Report.**

    c. Place the insertion point at the end of the third item in the list under the Proposed Actions heading, insert an endnote, then type **Scheduled for February 2010.**

    d. Locate and delete the first endnote from the document. Scroll to the end of the document and verify the endnotes are correct.

    e. Press [Ctrl][Home], save your changes to the report, view the report in Print Preview, then print a copy. The formatted report is shown in Figure C-27.

    f. Turn off formatting marks, close the file and exit Word.

FIGURE C-27

▼ INDEPENDENT CHALLENGE 1

You are an estimator for Jermanok Construction in the Australian city of Wollongong. You have drafted an estimate for a home renovation job, and need to format it. It's important that your estimate have a clean, striking design, and reflect your company's professionalism.

a. Start Word, open the file WD C-3.docx from the drive and folder where you store your Data Files, save it as **Jermanok Construction**, then read the document to get a feel for its contents. Figure C-28 shows how you will format the letterhead.

FIGURE C-28

b. Select the entire document, change the style to No Spacing, then change the font to 12-point Times New Roman.

c. In the first paragraph, format **Jermanok** in 24-point Arial Black and change the case to All caps. Format **Construction** in 24-point Arial, apply italic, then delete the space between the two words. (*Hint*: Select a similar font if Arial Black is not available to you.)

d. Format the next line in 10-point Arial, then right-align the two-line letterhead.

e. Add a 2¼ -point dotted black border below the address line paragraph.

f. With the insertion point in the address line, open the Borders and Shading dialog box, click Options to open the Border and Shading Options dialog box, change the Bottom setting to 5 points, then click OK twice to adjust the location of the border relative to the line of text.

g. Format the title **Proposal of Renovation** in 14-point Arial Black, then center the title.

h. Format the following headings (including the colons) in 11-point Arial Black: **Date, Work to be performed for and at, Scope of work, Payment schedule**, and **Agreement.**

i. Select the 14-line list under **Scope of work** that begins with **Demo of all...,** then change the paragraph spacing to add 4 points of space after each paragraph in the list. (*Hint*: Select 0 pt in the After text box, type 4, then press Enter.)

j. With the list selected, set a right tab stop at the 6¼" mark, insert tabs before every price in the list, then apply dotted line tab leaders.

k. Format the list as a numbered list, then apply bold to the numbers.

l. Apply bold to the two lines, **Total estimated job cost...** and **Approximate job time...** below the list.

m. Replace Your Name with your name in the signature block, select the signature block (Respectfully submitted through your name), set a left tab stop at the 3¼" mark, then indent the signature block using tabs.

n. Examine the document carefully for formatting errors and make any necessary adjustments.

o. Save and print the document, then close the file and exit Word.

▼ INDEPENDENT CHALLENGE 2

Your employer, The Lange Center for Contemporary Arts in Halifax, Nova Scotia, is launching a membership drive. Your boss has written the text for a flyer advertising Lange membership, and asks you to format it so that it is eye catching and attractive.

a. Open the file WD C-4.docx from the drive and folder where you store your Data Files, save it as **Membership Drive 2010**, then read the document. Figure C-29 shows how you will format the first several paragraphs of the flyer.

FIGURE C-29

What we do for ARTISTS

Since 1982, the artist residency program at the Lange Center for Contemporary Arts has supported the work of more than 1500 artists from all over Canada and from 40 other nations. The residency awards include studio and living space, a monthly stipend to help artists with their expenses, and use of specialized equipment for all types of visual and performance art. Each artist gives a public lecture or performance at the Lange.

b. Select the entire document, change the style to No Spacing, then change the font to 11-point Arial Narrow.

c. Center the first line, **Membership Drive**, and apply shading to the paragraph. Choose a dark custom shading color of your choice for the shading color. (*Hint*: Click More Colors, then select a color from the Standard or Custom tab.) Format the text in 26-point Arial Narrow, bold, with a white font color. Expand the character spacing by 10 points.

d. Format the second line, **2010**, in 36-point Arial Black. Expand the character spacing by 25 points and change the character scale to 250%. Center the line.

e. Format each **What we do for...** heading in 12-point Arial, bold. Change the font color to the same custom color used for shading the title. (*Note*: The color now appears in the Recent Colors section of the Font Color gallery.) Add a single line ½-point black border under each heading.

f. Format each subheading (**Gallery, Lectures, Library, All members...**, and **Membership Levels**) in 10-point Arial, bold. Add 3 points of spacing before each paragraph. (*Hint*: Select 0 in the Before text box, type 3, then press Enter.)

g. Indent each body paragraph ¼", except for the lines under the **What we do for YOU** heading.

h. Format the four lines under the All members... subheading as a bulleted list. Use a bullet symbol of your choice and format the bullets in the custom font color.

i. Indent the five lines under the Membership Levels heading ¼". For these five lines, set left tab stops at the 1¼" mark and the 2" mark on the horizontal ruler. Insert tabs before the price and before the word All in each of the five lines.

j. Format the name of each membership level (**Artistic, Conceptual**, etc.) in 10-point Arial, bold, italic, with the custom font color.

k. Format the **For more information** heading in 14-point Arial, bold, with the custom font color, then center the heading.

l. Format the last two lines in 11-point Arial Narrow, and center the lines. In the contact information, replace Your Name with your name, then apply bold to your name.

Advanced Challenge Exercise

- ■ Change the font color of **2010** to a dark gray and add a shadow effect.
- ■ Add a shadow effect to each **What we do for...** heading.
- ■ Add a 3-point dotted black border above the **For more information** heading.

m. Examine the document carefully for formatting errors and make any necessary adjustments.

n. Save and print the flyer, then close the file and exit Word.

▼ INDEPENDENT CHALLENGE 3

One of your responsibilities as program coordinator at Solstice Mountain Sports is to develop a program of winter outdoor learning and adventure workshops. You have drafted a memo to your boss to update her on your progress. You need to format the memo so it is professional looking and easy to read.

a. Start Word, open the file WD C-5.docx from the drive and folder where you store your Data Files, then save it as **Solstice Winter Memo**.

b. Select the heading **Solstice Mountain Sports Memorandum**, apply the Quick Style Title to it, then center the heading. (*Hint*: Open the Quick Style gallery, then click the Title button.)

c. In the memo header, replace Today's Date and Your Name with the current date and your name.

d. Select the four-line memo header, set a left tab stop at the ¾" mark, then insert tabs before the date, the recipient's name, your name, and the subject of the memo.

e. Apply the Quick Style Strong to **Date:**, **To:**, **From:**, and **Re:**.

f. Apply the Quick Style Heading 2 to the headings **Overview**, **Workshops**, **Accommodations**, **Fees**, and **Proposed winter programming**.

g. Under the Fees heading, apply the Quick Style Emphasis to the words **Workshop fees** and **Accommodations fees**.

h. On the second page of the document, format the list under the **Proposed winter programming** heading as a multilevel list. Figure C-30 shows the hierarchical structure of the outline. (*Hint*: Apply a multilevel list style, then use the Increase Indent and Decrease Indent buttons to change the level of importance of each item.)

i. Change the outline numbering style to the bullet numbering style shown in Figure C-30, if necessary.

Advanced Challenge Exercise

■ Zoom out on the memo so that two pages display in the document window, then, using the Change Styles button, change the style set to Modern.

■ Using the Change Case button, change the title Solstice Mountain Sports Memorandum so that only the initial letter of each word is capitalized.

■ Using the Themes button, change the theme applied to the document.

■ Using the Theme Fonts button, change the fonts to a font set of your choice. Choose fonts that allow the document to fit on two pages.

■ Using the Theme Colors button, change the colors to a color palette of your choice.

■ Apply different styles and adjust other formatting elements as necessary to make the memo attractive, eye-catching, and readable.

j. Save and print the document, then close the file and exit Word.

FIGURE C-30

> Proposed winter programming
> ❖ Skiing, Snowboarding, and Snowshoeing
>   ➢ Skiing and Snowboarding
>   ▪ Cross-country skiing
>   • Cross-country skiing for beginners
>   • Intermediate cross-country skiing
>   • Inn-to-inn ski touring
>   • Moonlight cross-country skiing
>   ▪ Telemarking
>   • Basic telemark skiing
>   • Introduction to backcountry skiing
>   • Exploring on skis
>   ▪ Snowboarding
>   • Backcountry snowboarding
>   ➢ Snowshoeing
>   ▪ Beginner
>   • Snowshoeing for beginners
>   • Snowshoeing and winter ecology
>   ▪ Intermediate and Advanced
>   • Intermediate snowshoeing
>   • Guided snowshoe trek
>   • Above tree line snowshoeing
> ❖ Winter Hiking, Camping, and Survival
>   ➢ Hiking
>   ▪ Beginner
>   • Long-distance hiking
>   • Winter summits
>   • Hiking for women
>   ➢ Winter camping and survival
>   ▪ Beginner
>   • Introduction to winter camping
>   • Basic winter mountain skills
>   • Building snow shelters
>   ▪ Intermediate
>   • Basic winter mountain skills II
>   • Ice climbing
>   • Avalanche awareness and rescue

▼ REAL LIFE INDEPENDENT CHALLENGE

The fonts you choose for a document can have a major effect on the document's tone. Not all fonts are appropriate for use in a business document, and some fonts, especially those with a definite theme, are appropriate only for specific purposes. In this Independent Challenge, you will use font formatting and other formatting features to design a letterhead and a fax coversheet for yourself or your business. The letterhead and coversheet should not only look professional and attract interest; the design should say something about the character of your business or your personality. Figure C-31 shows an example of a business letterhead.

FIGURE C-31

jennifer**weizenbaum**communications

167 East 12th Street, 4th floor, New York, NY 10003   Tel: 212-555-9767   Fax: 212-555-2992   www.jweizenbaum.com

a. Start Word, and save a new blank document as **Personal Letterhead** to the drive and folder where you store your Data Files.

b. Type your name or the name of your business, your address, your phone number, your fax number, and your web site or e-mail address.

c. Format your name or the name of your business in a font that expresses your personality or says something about the nature of your business. Use fonts, font colors, font effects, borders, shading, paragraph formatting, and other formatting features to design a letterhead that is appealing and professional.

d. Save your changes, print a copy, then close the file.

e. Open a new blank document and save it as **Personal Fax Coversheet**. Type FAX, your name or the name of your business, your address, your phone number, your fax number, and your web site or e-mail address at the top of the document.

f. Type a fax header that includes the following: Date; To; From; Re; Number of pages, including cover sheet; and Comments.

g. Format the information in the fax coversheet using fonts, font effects, borders, shading, paragraph formatting, and other formatting features. Since a fax coversheet is designed to be faxed, all fonts and other formatting elements should be black. Format the fax header using tabs.

h. Save your changes, print a copy, close the file, then exit Word.

Open the file WD C-6.docx from the drive and folder where you store your Data Files. Create the menu shown in Figure C-32. (*Hints:* Use Harlow Solid Italic and Eras Light ITC or similar fonts. Change the font size of the heading to 48 points, the font size of Daily Specials to 20 points, the font size of the days and the specials to 16 points, and the font size of the descriptions to 12 points. Format the prices using tabs. Use paragraph spacing to adjust the spacing between paragraphs so that all the text fits on one page.) Save the menu as **Nina's Trackside**, then print a copy.

FIGURE C-32

Nina's Trackside Café

Daily Specials

Monday
    Chicken Cajun Bleu: Cajun chicken, chunky blue cheese, cucumbers, leaf lettuce, and tomato on our roasted garlic roll. $6.50

Tuesday
    Clam Chowder: Classic New England thick, rich, clam chowder in our peasant French bread bowl. Served with a garden salad. $5.95

Wednesday
    Veggie Chili: Hearty veggie chili with melted cheddar in our peasant French bread bowl. Topped with sour cream & scallions. $5.95

Thursday
    French Dip: Lean roast beef topped with melted cheddar on our roasted garlic roll. Served with a side of au jus and red bliss mashed potatoes. $6.95

Friday
    Turkey-Bacon Club: Double-decker roasted turkey, crisp bacon, leaf lettuce, tomato, and sun-dried tomato mayo on toasted triple seed. $6.50

Saturday
    Greek Salad: Our large garden salad with Kalamata olives, feta cheese, and garlic vinaigrette. Served with an assortment of rolls. $5.95

Sunday
    Hot Chicken and Gravy: Delicious chicken and savory gravy served on a thick slice of toasted honest white. Served with a garden salad. $6.95

Chef: Your Name

Formatting Documents

The page-formatting features of Word allow you to lay out and design the pages of your documents creatively. In this unit, you learn how to change the document margins, determine page orientation, add page numbers, and insert headers and footers. You also learn how to format text in columns and how to illustrate your documents with tables and clip art. You have written and formatted the text for the quarterly newsletter for QST clients. You are now ready to lay out and design the newsletter pages. You plan to organize the articles in columns and to enhance the visual appeal of the newsletter by adding a table and clip art.

OBJECTIVES

Set document margins

Divide a document into sections

Insert page breaks

Format columns

Insert page numbers

Add headers and footers

Edit headers and footers

Insert a table

Insert clip art

Setting Document Margins

Changing a document's margins is one way to change the appearance of a document and control the amount of text that fits on a page. The **margins** of a document are the blank areas between the edge of the text and the edge of the page. When you create a document in Word, the default margins are 1" at the top, bottom, left, and right sides of the page. You can adjust the size of a document's margins using the Margins command on the Page Layout tab, or using the rulers. ▰▰▰▰ The newsletter should be a four-page document when finished. You begin formatting the pages by reducing the size of the document margins so that more text fits on each page.

STEPS

1. **Start Word, open the file** WD D-1.docx **from the drive and folder where you store your Data Files, then save it as** Footprints

   The newsletter opens in Print Layout view.

2. **Scroll through the newsletter to get a feel for its contents, then press [Ctrl][Home]**

   The newsletter is currently five pages long. Notice that the status bar indicates the page where the insertion point is located and the total number of pages in the document.

3. **Click the Page Layout tab, then click the** Margins **button in the Page Setup group**

   The Margins menu opens. You can select predefined margin settings from this menu, or click Custom Margins to create different margin settings.

4. **Click Custom Margins**

   The Page Setup dialog box opens with the Margins tab displayed, as shown in Figure D-1. You can use the Margins tab to change the top, bottom, left, or right document margin, to change the orientation of the pages from portrait to landscape, and to alter other page layout settings. **Portrait orientation** means a page is taller than it is wide; **landscape orientation** means a page is wider than it is tall. This newsletter uses portrait orientation. You can also use the Orientation button in the Page Setup group on the Page Layout tab to change the orientation of a document.

5. **Click the Top down arrow three times until 0.7" appears, then click the Bottom down arrow until 0.7" appears**

   The top and bottom margins of the newsletter will be .7". Notice that the margins in the Preview section of the dialog box change as you adjust the margin settings.

6. **Press [Tab], type .7 in the Left text box, press [Tab], then type .7 in the Right text box**

   The left and right margins of the newsletter will also be .7". You can change the margin settings by using the arrows or by typing a value in the appropriate text box.

7. **Click OK**

   The document margins change to .7", as shown in Figure D-2. The location of each margin (right, left, top, and bottom) is shown on the horizontal and vertical rulers at the intersection of the white and shaded areas. You can also change a margin setting by using the ⟺ pointer to drag the intersection to a new location on the ruler.

8. **Click the View tab, then click the** Two Pages **button in the Zoom group**

   The first two pages of the document appear in the document window.

9. **Scroll down to view all five pages of the newsletter, press [Ctrl][Home], click the** Page Width **button in the Zoom group, then save your changes**

FIGURE D-1: Margins tab in Page Setup dialog box

Default margin settings

Select page orientation

Select part of document to apply settings to

Select gutter position

Set gutter margin

Set mirror margins and other page layout options

Preview of margin settings

FIGURE D-2: Newsletter with smaller margins

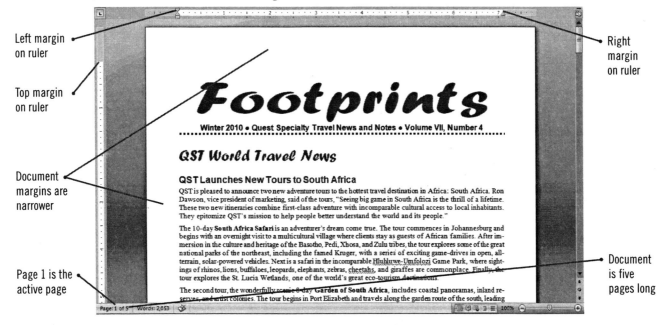

Left margin on ruler

Top margin on ruler

Document margins are narrower

Page 1 is the active page

Right margin on ruler

Document is five pages long

Changing orientation, margin settings, and paper size

By default, the documents you create in Word use an 8½" × 11" paper size in portrait orientation with the default margin settings. You can change the orientation, margin settings, and paper size to common settings using the Orientation, Margins, and Size buttons in the Page Setup group on the Page Layout tab. You can also adjust these settings and others in the Page Setup dialog box. For example, to change the layout of multiple pages, use the Multiple pages list arrow on the Margins tab to create pages that use mirror margins, that include two pages per sheet of paper, or that are formatted like a folded booklet. **Mirror margins** are used in a document with facing pages, such as a magazine, where the margins on the left page are a mirror image of the margins on the right page. Documents with mirror margins have inside and outside margins, rather than right and left margins. Another type of margin is a gutter margin, which is used in documents that are bound, such as books. A **gutter** adds extra space to the left, top, or inside margin to allow for the binding. Add a gutter to a document by adjusting the setting in the Gutter position text box on the Margins tab. To change the size of the paper used, use the Paper size list arrow on the Paper tab to select a standard paper size, or enter custom measurements in the Width and Height text boxes.

Word 2007

Formatting Documents

Dividing a Document into Sections

Dividing a document into sections allows you to format each section of the document with different page layout settings. A **section** is a portion of a document that is separated from the rest of the document by section breaks. **Section breaks** are formatting marks that you insert in a document to show the end of a section. Once you have divided a document into sections, you can format each section with different column, margin, page orientation, header and footer, and other page layout settings. By default, a document is formatted as a single section, but you can divide a document into as many sections as you like. █████ You insert a section break to divide the document into two sections, and then format the text in the second section in two columns. First, you customize the status bar to display section information.

STEPS

1. **Right-click the status bar, click Section on the Customize Status Bar menu that opens (if it is not already checked), then click the document to close the menu**

   The status bar indicates the insertion point is located in section 1 of the document.

2. **Click the Home tab, then click the Show/Hide ¶ button ¶ in the Paragraph group**

   Turning on formatting marks allows you to see the section breaks you insert in a document.

3. **Place the insertion point before the headline QST Launches New Tours to South Africa, click the Page Layout tab, then click the Breaks button in the Page Setup group**

   The Breaks menu opens. You use this menu to insert different types of section breaks. See Table D-1.

4. **Click Continuous**

   Word inserts a continuous section break, shown as a dotted double line, above the headline. The document now has two sections. Notice that the status bar indicates the insertion point is in section 2.

5. **Click the Columns button in the Page Setup group**

   The columns menu opens. You use this menu to format text in one, two, or three columns of equal width, or to create two columns of different widths, one narrow and one wider. To create columns with custom widths and spacing, you click More Columns on the Columns menu.

6. **Click Two**

   Section 2 is formatted in two columns of equal width, as shown in Figure D-3. The text in section 1 remains formatted in a single column. Notice that the status bar now indicates the document is four pages long. Formatting text in columns is another way to increase the amount of text that fits on a page.

7. **Click the View tab, click the Two Pages button in the Zoom group, scroll down to examine all four pages of the document, press [Ctrl][Home], then save the document**

   The text in section 2—all the text below the continuous section break—is formatted in two columns. Text in columns flows automatically from the bottom of one column to the top of the next column.

TABLE D-1: Types of section breaks

section	function
Next page	Begins a new section and moves the text following the break to the top of the next page
Continuous	Begins a new section on the same page
Even page	Begins a new section and moves the text following the break to the top of the next even-numbered page
Odd page	Begins a new section and moves the text following the break to the top of the next odd-numbered page

Formatting Documents

FIGURE D-3: Continuous section break and columns

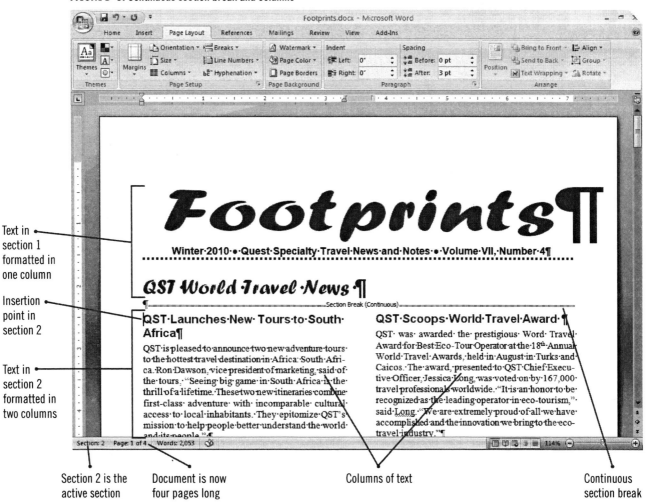

Text in section 1 formatted in one column

Insertion point in section 2

Text in section 2 formatted in two columns

Section 2 is the active section

Document is now four pages long

Columns of text

Continuous section break

Changing page layout settings for a section

Dividing a document into sections allows you to vary the layout of a document. In addition to applying different column settings to sections, you can apply different margins, page orientation, paper size, vertical alignment, header and footer, page numbering, footnotes, endnotes, and other page layout settings. For example, if you are formatting a report that includes a table with many columns, you might want to change the table's page orientation to landscape so that it is easier to read. To do this, you would insert a section break before and after the table to create a section that contains only the table, and then you would change the page orientation of the section that contains the table to landscape. Or, you might be creating a title page for a report, and want to center the text on the title page between the top and bottom margins. To do this you would insert a next page section break after the title page and then use the

Vertical alignment list arrow on the Layout tab of the Page Setup dialog box to change the **vertical alignment** of the section to Center. You can vertically align text on a page only when the text does not fill the page—for example, if you are creating a flyer or a title page.

To check or change the page layout settings for an individual section, place the insertion point in the section, then open the Page Setup dialog box. Select any options you want to change, click the Apply to list arrow, click This section, then click OK. When you select This section in the Apply to list box, the settings are applied to the current section only. If you select Whole document in the Apply to list box, the settings are applied to all the sections in the document. Use the Apply to list arrow in the Columns dialog box or the Footnote and Endnote dialog box to change those settings for a section.

Formatting Documents

Inserting Page Breaks

As you type text in a document, Word inserts an **automatic page break** (also called a soft page break) when you reach the bottom of a page, allowing you to continue typing on the next page. You can also force text onto the next page of a document by using the Break command to insert a **manual page break** (also called a hard page break). ▨▨▨▨ You insert manual page breaks where you know you want to begin each new page of the newsletter.

STEPS

1. **Place the insertion point before the headline Spotlight on Japan on page 2, click the Page Layout tab, then click the** Breaks button **in the Page Setup group**

   The Breaks menu opens. You also use this menu to insert page, column, and text-wrapping breaks. Table D-2 describes these types of breaks.

   > **QUICK TIP**
   >
   > Manual and automatic page breaks are always visible in Draft view.

2. **Click Page**

   Word inserts a manual page break before "Spotlight on Japan" and moves all the text following the page break to the beginning of the next page. The page break appears as a dotted line in Print Layout view when formatting marks are displayed. Page break marks are visible on the screen but do not print.

3. **Scroll down to pages 3 and 4, place the insertion point before the headline Language and Culture Immersion: Antigua, Guatemala, press and hold [Ctrl], then press [Enter]**

   Pressing [Ctrl][Enter] is a fast way to insert a manual page break. The headline is forced to the top of the fourth page, as shown in Figure D-4.

   > **QUICK TIP**
   >
   > You can also double-click a page break to select it, and then press [Delete] to delete it.

4. **Place the insertion point before the headline Traveler's Corner on page 4, then press [Ctrl][Enter]**

   The headline is forced to the top of the fifth page.

5. **Press [Ctrl][Home], click to the left of the** page break at the top of page 2 to select it, **then press [Delete]**

   The manual page break is deleted and the text from pages 2 and 3 flows together. You can also click to the left of a section or a column break to select it.

   > **QUICK TIP**
   >
   > To add line numbers in the margin to the left of each line on a page, in a section, or in a document, click the Line Numbers button in the Page Setup group, and then select an option.

6. **Click the Breaks button, then click** Next Page

   A next page section break is inserted at the top of page 2 and the text following the break is forced to the top of page 3, as shown in Figure D-5. The document now contains three sections.

7. **Place the insertion point in section 2 on page 1 (the body text), then save the document**

   The status bar indicates the insertion point is in section 2. In the next lesson you will format the columns in section 2 so that the entire section fits on the first page of the newsletter.

Controlling automatic pagination

Another way to control the flow of text between pages (or between columns) is to apply pagination settings to specify where Word positions automatic page breaks. For example, you might want to make sure an article appears on the same page as its heading, or you might want to prevent a page from breaking in the middle of the last paragraph of a report. To manipulate automatic pagination, simply select the paragraphs(s) or line(s) you want to control, click the launcher in the Paragraph group on the Home or Page Layout tab, click the Line and Page Breaks tab in the Paragraph dialog box, select one or more of the following settings from the Pagination section, and then click OK. Apply the Keep with next setting to any paragraph you want to appear together with the next paragraph on a single page, in order to prevent the page from breaking between the paragraphs. To prevent a page from breaking in the middle of a paragraph or between certain lines, select the paragraph or lines and apply the Keep lines together setting. Finally, to specify that a certain paragraph follows an automatic page break, apply the Page break before setting to the paragraph. Note that the Widow/Orphan control setting is turned on by default in the Pagination section of the dialog box. This setting ensures that at least two lines of a paragraph appear at the top and bottom of every page. In other words, it prevents a page from beginning with just the last line of a paragraph (a **widow**), and prevents a page from ending with only the first line of a new paragraph (an **orphan**).

FIGURE D-4: Manual page break in document

Hard page break

Text that follows break is forced onto the next page

FIGURE D-5: Next page section break in document

Text that follows break is forced onto the next page and is in a new section

Next page section break

TABLE D-2: Types of breaks

break	function
Page	Forces the text following the break to begin at the top of the next page
Column	Forces the text following the break to begin at the top of the next column
Text Wrapping	Forces the text following the break to begin at the beginning of the next line

Formatting Columns

Formatting text in columns often makes the text easier to read. You can apply column formatting to a whole document, to a section, or to selected text. The Columns command on the Page Layout tab allows you to quickly create columns of equal width and spacing, and to customize the width and spacing of columns. To control the way text flows between columns, you can insert a **column break**, which forces the text following the break to move to the top of the next column. You can also balance columns of unequal length on a page by inserting a continuous section break at the end of the last column on the page. You continue to format the newsletter using columns.

STEPS

1. **Make sure the insertion point is in section 2, click the Columns button in the Page Setup group, then click Right.**

   The text in section 2 is reformatted into two columns of unequal width. The formatting of the text in section 3 does not change. All the text now fits on four pages.

2. **Select the headline Spotlight on Japan: Visiting a Ryokan in the Land of the Shoguns and the paragraph mark below it, click the Columns button, then click One**

   A continuous section break is added below the headline. The headline is formatted as a single column in its own new section, section 3, where the insertion point is located. The newsletter now contains 4 sections, each with different column formatting.

3. **Scroll down, place the insertion point before Malaria: A Serious... on page 4, click the Zoom Level button 52% on the status bar, click the Page width option button, click OK, click the Breaks button in the Page Setup group, then click Continuous**

   A continuous section break is inserted before the Malaria headline, and the insertion point is in the new section, section 5.

4. **Click the Columns button, then click More Columns**

   The Columns dialog box opens, as shown in Figure D-6.

5. **Select Three in the Presets section, click the Spacing down arrow twice until 0.3" appears, select the Line between check box, then click OK**

   All the text in section 5 is formatted in three columns of equal width with a line between the columns, as shown in Figure D-7.

6. **Click the Zoom Level button 114% on the status bar, click the Whole page option button, then click OK**

   Page 4 would look better if the three columns were balanced—each the same length.

7. **Place the insertion point at the end of the third column (before the final paragraph mark), click the Breaks button, then click Continuous**

   The columns in section 5 adjust to become roughly the same length.

8. **Scroll up to page 3, place the insertion point before the heading Luxurious Adventure: Tunisia, click the Breaks button, then click Column**

   The text following the column break is forced to the top of the next column. The page looks cleaner when the Tunisia article does not break across the columns.

9. **Click the View tab, click the Two Pages button in the Zoom group, then save the document**

   The columns on pages 3 and 4 are formatted as shown in Figure D-8.

FIGURE D-6: Columns dialog box

Select a preset format for columns

Set custom widths and spacing for columns

Select to create columns of equal width

Change the number of columns

Select to add a line between columns

Preview of current settings

Select part of document to apply format to

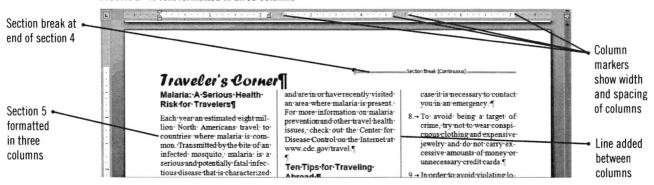

FIGURE D-7: Text formatted in three columns

Section break at end of section 4

Section 5 formatted in three columns

Column markers show width and spacing of columns

Line added between columns

FIGURE D-8: Columns on pages 3 and 4 of the newsletter

Text following column break forced to top of next column

Column break

Continuous section break

Columns in section 5 are balanced

Hyphenating text in a document

Hyphenating a document is another way to control the flow of text in columns. Hyphens are small dashes that break words that fall at the end of a line. Hyphenation diminishes the gaps between words in justified text and reduces ragged right edges in left-aligned text. If a document includes narrow columns, hyphenating the text can help give the pages a cleaner look. To hyphenate a document automatically, click the Hyphenation button in the Page Setup group on the Page Layout tab, and then click Automatic. To set the hyphenation zone—the distance between the margin and the end of the last word in the line—click the Hyphenation button and then click Hyphenation Options to open the Hyphenation dialog box. A smaller hyphenation zone results in a greater number of hyphenated words.

Formatting Documents

Inserting Page Numbers

If you want to number the pages of a multiple-page document, you can insert a page number field in the top, bottom, or side margin of each page. A **field** is a code that serves as a placeholder for data that changes in a document, such as a page number or the current date. When you use the Page Number button on the Insert tab to add page numbers to a document, you insert the page number field at the top, bottom, or side of any page and Word automatically numbers all the pages in the document for you. You insert a page number field so that page numbers will appear centered between the margins at the bottom of each page in the document.

STEPS

QUICK TIP

Point to Current Position to insert a page number field at the location of the insertion point.

1. **Click the Page Width button in the Zoom group on the View tab, press [Ctrl][Home], click the Insert tab, then click the Page Number button in the Header & Footer group**

   The Page Number menu opens. You use this menu to select the position for the page numbers. If you choose to add a page number field to the top, bottom, or side of a document, a page number will appear on every page in the document. If you choose to insert it in the document at the location of the insertion point, the field will appear on that page only.

2. **Point to Bottom of Page**

   A gallery of formatting and alignment options for page numbers located at the bottom of a page opens, as shown in Figure D-9.

QUICK TIP

To change the location or formatting of page numbers, click the Page Number button, point to a page number location, then select a format from the gallery.

3. **Drag the scroll box down the gallery to view the options, scroll to the top of the gallery, then click Plain Number 2 in the Simple section**

   The page number 1 appears centered in the Footer area at the bottom of the first page, as shown in Figure D-10. The document text is gray, or dimmed, because the Footer area is open. Text that is inserted in a Footer area appears at the bottom of every page in a document.

4. **Double-click the document text, then scroll to the bottom of page 1**

   Double-clicking the document text closes the Footer area. The page number is now dimmed because it is located in the Footer area, which is no longer the active area. When the document is printed, the page numbers appear as normal text. You will learn more about working with the Footer area in the next lesson.

QUICK TIP

To remove page numbers from a document, click the Page Number button, then click Remove Page Numbers.

5. **Scroll down the document to see the page number at the bottom of each page**

   Word automatically numbered each page of the newsletter, and each page number is centered at the bottom of the page. If you want to change the numbering format or to start page numbering with a different number, you can simply click the Page Number button, click Format Page Numbers, and then choose from the options in the Page Number Format dialog box.

6. **Press [Ctrl][Home], then save the document**

Moving around in a long document

Rather than scrolling to move to a different place in a long document, you can use the Browse by Object feature to quickly move the insertion point to a specific location. Browse by Object allows you to browse to the next or previous page, section, line, table, graphic, or other item of the same type in a document. To do this, first click the Select Browse Object button ⊙ below the vertical scroll bar to open a palette of object types. On this palette, click the button for the type of item by which you want to browse, and then click the Next ⬇ or Previous ⬆ buttons to scroll through the items of that type in the document.

FIGURE D-9: Gallery of options for page numbers located at the bottom of the page

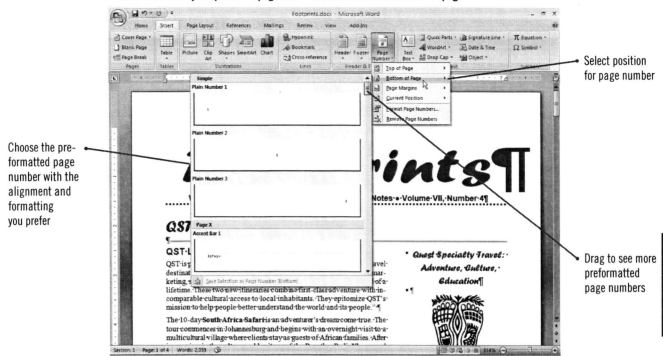

Choose the pre-formatted page number with the alignment and formatting you prefer

Select position for page number

Drag to see more preformatted page numbers

FIGURE D-10: Page number in document

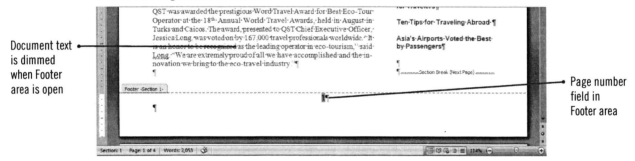

Document text is dimmed when Footer area is open

Page number field in Footer area

Inserting Quick Parts

The Word Quick Parts feature makes it easy to insert reusable pieces of content into a document quickly. The **Quick Parts** items you can insert include fields, such as for the current date or the total number of pages in a document; document property information, such as the author and title of a document; and building blocks, which are customized content that you create, format, and save for future use.

To insert a Quick Part into a document at the location of the insertion point, click the Quick Parts button in the Text group on the Insert tab (or, if headers and footers are open, click the Quick Parts button in the Insert group on the Header and Footer Tools Design tab), and then select the type of Quick Part you want to insert. To insert a field into a document, click Field on the Quick Parts menu that opens, click the name of the field you want to insert in the Field dialog box, and then click OK. Field information is updated automatically each time the document is opened or saved.

To insert a document property, point to Document Property on the Quick Parts menu and then click the property you want to insert. The property is added to the document as a content control and contains the document property information you entered in the Document Information panel. If you did not assign a document property, the content control contains a placeholder, which you can replace with your own text. Once you replace the placeholder text—or edit the document property information that appears in the content control—this text replaces the document property information in the Document Information panel.

To insert a building block, click Building Blocks Organizer on the Quick Parts menu, select the building block you want, and then click Insert. You will learn more about working with building blocks in later lessons.

Adding Headers and Footers

A **header** is text or graphics that appears at the top of every page of a document. A **footer** is text or graphics that appears at the bottom of every page. In longer documents, headers and footers often contain information such as the title of the publication, the title of the chapter, the name of the author, the date, or a page number. You can add headers and footers to a document by double-clicking the top or bottom margin of a document to open the Header and Footer areas, and then inserting text and graphics into them. You can also use the Header or Footer command on the Insert tab to insert predesigned headers and footers that you can modify to include your own information. ████ You create a header that includes the name of the newsletter and the current date, and add the word "Page" to the footer.

STEPS

1. **Click the Insert tab, then click the** Header **button in the Header & Footer group**

   A gallery of built-in header designs opens.

2. **Scroll down the gallery to view the header designs, scroll to the top of the gallery, then click Blank**

   The Header and Footer areas open and the document text is dimmed. When the document text is dimmed, it cannot be edited. The Header & Footer Tools Design tab also opens and is the active tab, as shown in Figure D-11. This tab is available whenever the Header and Footer areas are open. The Header and Footer areas of a document are independent of the document itself and must be formatted separately. For example, if you select all the text in a document and then change the font, the header and footer font does not change.

3. **Type Footprints in the content control in the Header area, press [Spacebar] twice, then click the Date & Time button in the Insert group**

   The Date and Time dialog box opens. You use this dialog box to select the format for the date or time and to indicate whether you want the date or time inserted in the document as a field that is updated automatically, or as static text. Word uses the clock on your computer to compute the date and time.

4. **Make sure the Update Automatically check box is selected, then click OK**

   A date field is inserted into the header using the default month/date/year (M/d/yyyy) format. The word "Footprints" and the current date will appear at the top of every page in the document.

5. **Select Footprints and the date, click the Font list arrow on the Mini toolbar, click Forte, click the Center button ▤ on the Mini toolbar, then click in the Header area to deselect the text**

   The text is formatted in Forte and centered in the Header area. In addition to the alignment buttons, you can use the Insert Alignment Tab button in the Position group on the Header & Footer Tools Design tab to left-, center-, and right-align text in the Header and Footer areas with the document margins.

6. **Click the Go to Footer button in the Navigation group**

   The insertion point moves to the Footer area, where a page number field is centered in the Footer area. You can use the buttons in the Navigation group to move quickly between the Header and Footer areas on the current page or to a header or a footer in the previous or next section of the document.

7. **Verify that the insertion point is before the page number field, type Page, press [Spacebar], select the text and the field in the footer, click the Font list arrow on the Mini toolbar, click Forte, then click in the Footer area to deselect the text and field**

   The footer text is formatted in Forte.

8. **Click the Close Header and Footer button in the Close group, save the document, then scroll down until the bottom of page 1 and the top of page 2 appear in the document window**

   The Header and Footer areas close and the header and footer text is dimmed, as shown in Figure D-12.

Formatting Documents

FIGURE D-11: Header area open

Header & Footer Tools Design tab

Header area is open

Content control

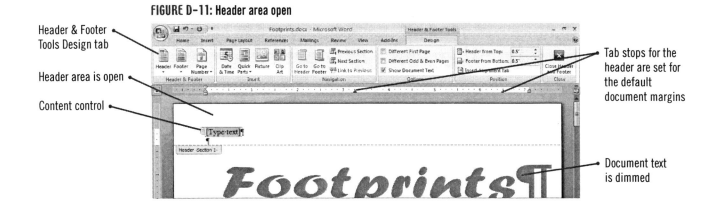

Tab stops for the header are set for the default document margins

Document text is dimmed

FIGURE D-12: Header and footer in document

Page number appears in footer on every page

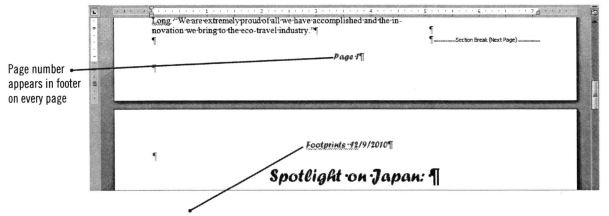

Header text appears centered in the header on every page (your date will differ)

Adding a custom header or footer to the gallery

When you design a header that you want to use again in other documents, you can add it to the Header gallery by saving it as a building block. **Building blocks** are reusable pieces of formatted content or document parts, including headers and footers, page numbers, and text boxes, that are stored in galleries. Building blocks include predesigned content that comes with Word, as well as content that you create and save for future use. For example, you might create a custom header that contains your company name and logo and is formatted using the fonts, border, and colors you use in all company documents.

To add a custom header to the Header gallery, select all the text in the header, including the last paragraph mark, click the Header button, and then click Save Selection to Header Gallery. In the

Create New Building Block dialog box that opens, type a unique name for the header in the Name text box, click the Gallery list arrow and select the appropriate gallery, verify that the Category is General, and then type a brief description of the new header design in the Description text box. This description appears in a ScreenTip when you point to the custom header in the gallery. When you are finished, click OK. The new header appears in the Header gallery under the General category.

To remove a custom header from the Header gallery, right-click it, click Organize and Delete, make sure the appropriate building block is selected in the Building Blocks Organizer that opens, click Delete, click Yes, and then click Close. You can follow the same process to add or remove a custom footer to the Footer gallery.

Formatting Documents

Editing Headers and Footers

To change header and footer text or to alter the formatting of headers and footers, you must first open the Header and Footer areas. You open headers and footers by using the Edit Header or Edit Footer command in the Header and Footer galleries, or by double-clicking a header or footer in Print Layout view. You modify the header by adding a small circle symbol between "Footprints" and the date. You also add a border under the header text to set it off from the rest of the page. Finally, you remove the header and footer text from the first page of the document.

STEPS

1. **Scroll down, place the insertion point at the top of page 2, position the pointer over the header text at the top of page 2, then double-click**

   The Header and Footer areas open. The insertion point is located in the Header area at the top of page 2.

QUICK TIP

To insert a character such as an em dash (—) or an ellipsis (...), select the character on the Special Characters tab in the Symbol dialog box, and then click Insert.

2. **Place the insertion point between the two spaces after Footprints, click the Insert tab, click the Symbol button in the Symbols group, then click More Symbols in the gallery of recently used symbols**

   The Symbol dialog box opens and is similar to Figure D-13. **Symbols** are special characters, such as graphics, shapes, and foreign language characters, that you can insert into a document. The symbols shown in Figure D-13 are the symbols included with the (normal text) font. You can use the Font list arrow on the Symbols tab to view the symbols included with each font on your computer.

TROUBLE

If you cannot locate the symbol, be sure the Font is (normal text) and then type 2022 in the Character code text box.

3. **Scroll the list of symbols if necessary to locate the bullet symbol shown in Figure D-13, select the bullet symbol, click Insert, then click Close**

   A bullet symbol is added at the location of the insertion point.

4. **With the insertion point in the header text, click the Home tab, click the Bottom Border list arrow [▦ ▾] in the Paragraph group, then click Borders and Shading**

   The Borders and Shading dialog box opens.

5. **Click the Borders tab if it is not already selected, click Custom in the Setting section, click the dotted line in the Style list box (the second line style), click the Width list arrow, click 2¼ pt, click the Bottom border button in the Preview section, make sure Paragraph is selected in the Apply to list box, click OK, double-click the document text to close the Header and Footer areas, then click the Show/Hide button [¶] in the Paragraph group**

   A dotted line border is added below the header text, as shown in Figure D-14.

QUICK TIP

To remove headers or footers from a document, click the Header or Footer button, and then click Remove Header or Remove Footer.

6. **Press [Ctrl][Home] to move the insertion point to the beginning of the document**

   The newsletter already includes the name of the document at the top of the first page, making the header information redundant. You can modify headers and footers so that the header and footer text does not appear on the first page of a document or a section.

7. **Position the pointer over the header text at the top of page 1, then double-click**

   The Header and Footer areas open. The Options group on the Header & Footer Tools Design tab includes options for creating a different header and footer for the first page of a document or a section, and for creating different headers and footers for odd- and even-numbered pages. For example, in a document with facing pages, such as a magazine, you might want the publication title to appear in the left-page header and the publication date to appear in the right-page header.

QUICK TIP

You can enter different text in the First Page Header and First Page Footer areas when the Different first page check box is selected.

8. **Click the Different First Page check box to select it, then click the Close Header and Footer button**

   The header and footer text is removed from the Header and Footer areas on the first page.

9. **Scroll to see the header and footer on pages 2, 3, and 4, then save the document**

FIGURE D-13: Symbol dialog box

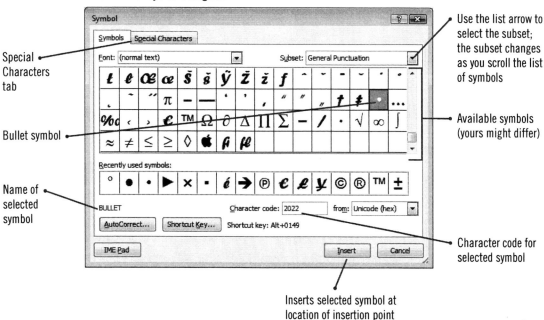

Special Characters tab

Bullet symbol

Name of selected symbol

Use the list arrow to select the subset; the subset changes as you scroll the list of symbols

Available symbols (yours might differ)

Character code for selected symbol

Inserts selected symbol at location of insertion point

FIGURE D-14: Symbol and border added to header

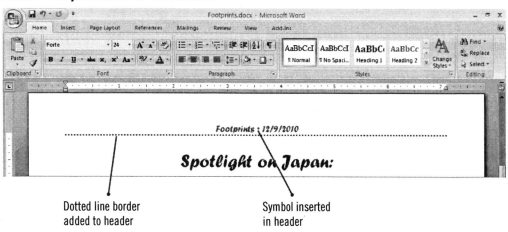

Dotted line border added to header

Symbol inserted in header

Creating an AutoText building block

AutoText is a type of building block that allows you to store text and graphics that you use frequently so that you can easily insert them in a document. AutoText entries are stored in the Building Blocks Organizer, and each AutoText entry has a unique name, so that you can find it when you need it. For example, you might want to store your company letterhead or a list of staff names and titles, so that you can easily insert them in a document without having to retype or reformat the information.

To create a custom AutoText entry, enter the text or graphic you want to store—such as a company letterhead or staff list—in a document, select it, click the Quick Parts button in the Text group on the Insert tab, and then click Save Selection to Quick Part Gallery. In the Create New Building Block dialog box that opens, enter a unique name for the new building block, select AutoText for the Gallery, enter any other relevant information, such as a description, and then click OK to save the text or graphic as an AutoText entry in the Building Blocks Organizer.

To insert an AutoText entry or any other building block into a document at the location of the insertion point, click the Quick Parts button, click Building Blocks Organizer, scroll the list of building blocks to find the building block you want, select it, and then click Insert.

Formatting Documents

Inserting a Table

Adding a table to a document is a useful way to illustrate information that is intended for quick reference and analysis. A **table** is a grid of columns and rows of cells that you can fill with text and graphics. A **cell** is the box formed by the intersection of a column and a row. The lines that divide the columns and rows of a table and help you see the grid-like structure of the table are called **borders**. A simple way to insert a table into a document is to use the Insert Table command on the Insert tab. This command allows you to determine the dimensions and format of a table before it is inserted. ▰▰▰ You add a table showing the details for the QST tours mentioned by name in the newsletter.

STEPS

1. **Click the Show/Hide button ¶ in the Paragraph group, then scroll until the heading Featured Tour Details on page 3 is at the top of your document window**

2. **Place the insertion point before the heading Featured Tour Details, click the Page Layout tab, click the Breaks button in the Page Setup group, then click Continuous**
   A continuous section break is inserted before the heading. The document now includes six sections, with the heading Featured Tour Details in the fifth section.

3. **Click the Columns button in the Page Setup group, then click One**
   Section 5 is formatted as a single column.

4. **Place the insertion point before the second paragraph mark below the heading, click the Insert tab, click the Table button in the Tables group, then click Insert Table**
   The Insert Table dialog box opens. You use this dialog box to create a blank table with a set number of columns and rows, and to choose an option for sizing the width of the columns in the table.

5. **Type 4 in the Number of columns text box, press [Tab], type 6 in the Number of rows text box, make sure the Fixed column width option button is selected, then click OK**
   A blank table with four columns and six rows is inserted in the document at the location of the insertion point. The insertion point is in the upper-left cell of the table, the first cell in the header row. When the insertion point is in a table, the Table Tools Design tab becomes the active tab.

6. **Type Tour in the first cell in the first row, press [Tab], type Season, press [Tab], type Length, press [Tab], type Cost, then press [Tab]**
   Pressing [Tab] moves the insertion point to the next cell in the row. At the end of a row, pressing [Tab] moves the insertion point to the first cell in the next row. You can also click in a cell to move the insertion point to it.

7. **Type the text shown in Figure D-15 in the table cells, pressing [Tab] to move from cell to cell**
   Don't be concerned if the text wraps to the next line in a cell as you type: you will adjust the width of the columns after you finish typing.

8. **Click the Table Tools Layout tab, click the AutoFit button in the Cell Size group, click AutoFit Contents, click the AutoFit button again, then click AutoFit Window**
   The width of the table columns is adjusted to fit the text and then the window. You modify the structure of a table using the commands on the Table Tools Layout tab. To edit the text in a table, simply place the insertion point in a cell and then type.

9. **Click the Table Tools Design tab, click the More button ▾ in the Table Styles group to expand the Table Styles gallery, click the Light List – Accent 2 style, then clear the First Column check box in the Table Style Options group**
   The Light List - Accent 2 style table style is applied to the table, as shown in Figure D-16. A **table style** includes format settings for the text, borders, and shading in a table.

10. **Click the View tab, click the Two Pages button, then save the document**
    Completed pages 3 and 4 are shown in Figure D-17.

Header row

Row

Cell

Column

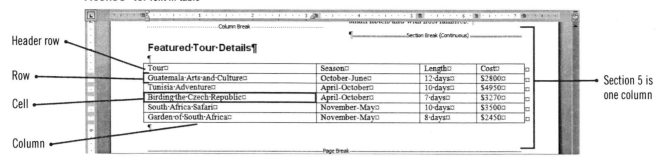

Section 5 is one column

FIGURE D-16: Completed table

First Column check box

Header row

Light List – Accent 2 table style

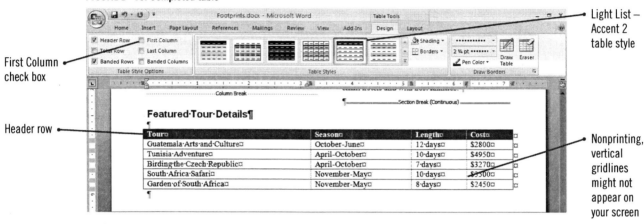

Nonprinting, vertical gridlines might not appear on your screen

FIGURE D-17: Completed pages 3 and 4

Section: 5   Page: 3 of 4   Words: 2,094

Word 2007

Inserting Clip Art

Clip art is a collection of graphic images that you can insert into a document. Clip art images are stored in the **Clip Organizer**, a library of the **clips**—media files such as graphics, photographs, sounds, movies, and animations—that come with Word. You can add a clip to a document using the Clip Art command on the Insert tab. Once you insert a clip art image, you can wrap text around it, resize it, enhance it, and move it to a different location. ▰▰▰▰ You illustrate the second page of the newsletter with a clip art image.

STEPS

QUICK TIP

If you are working with an active Internet connection, your search results will include clips from the Microsoft Office Online Web site.

1. **Click the Page Width button in the Zoom group, scroll to the top of page 2, place the insertion point before the second body paragraph, which begins With its blend..., click the Insert tab, then click the Clip Art button in the Illustrations group**

   The Clip Art task pane opens. You can use this task pane to search for clips related to a keyword.

2. **Select the text in the Search for text box if necessary, type pagoda, click the Search in list arrow, make sure Everywhere has a check mark, click the Results should be list arrow, make sure All media types has a check mark, then click Go**

   Clips that include the keyword "pagoda" appear in the Clip Art task pane, as shown in Figure D-18.

TROUBLE

Select a different clip if the clip shown in Figure D-18 is not available to you. If you are not working with an active Internet connection, use the keyword "Asia".

3. **Point to the clip called out in Figure D-18, click the list arrow that appears next to the clip, click Insert on the menu, then close the Clip Art task pane**

   The clip is inserted at the location of the insertion point. When a graphic is selected, the active tab changes to the Picture Tools Format tab. This tab contains commands used to adjust, enhance, arrange, and size graphics. Until you apply text wrapping to a graphic, it is part of the line of text in which it was inserted (an **inline graphic**). To move a graphic independently of text, you must wrap the text around it to make it a **floating graphic**, which can be moved anywhere on a page.

4. **Click the Position button in the Arrange group, then click Position in Middle Right with Square Text Wrapping**

   The photo is moved to the middle right side of the page and the text wraps around it. The white circles that appear on the square edges of the graphic are the **sizing handles**. Applying text wrapping to the photo made it a floating graphic.

5. **Click the Shape Width up arrow in the Size group until 3.8" appears**

   The photo is enlarged. Notice that when you increased the width of the photo, the height increased proportionally. You can also resize a graphic proportionally by dragging a sizing handle.

QUICK TIP

To crop a graphic or to change its scale using precise measurements, click the launcher in the Size group, then adjust the settings on the Size tab in the Size dialog box.

6. **Scroll to the top of page 2, position the pointer over the graphic, when the pointer changes to ⇖ drag the graphic up and to the left so it is centered on the page and its top is just under the second line of text as shown in Figure D-19, then release the mouse button**

   The graphic is moved up and is roughly centered between the margins.

7. **Click the Position button, click More Layout Options, click the Picture Position tab if necessary, click the Alignment option button in the Horizontal section, click the Alignment list arrow, click Centered, then click OK**

   The Advanced Layout dialog box allows you to position a graphic using precise measurements.

8. **Click the More button ⊽ in the Picture Styles group, select the Soft Edge Oval picture style, click the Text Wrapping button in the Arrange group, click Tight, then deselect the graphic**

   A picture style is applied to the photo and the text wraps tight to the oval shape.

TROUBLE

If page 3 is a blank page or contains text continued from page 2, reduce the size of the graphic on page 2.

9. **Click the View tab, then click the Two Pages button**

   The completed pages 1 and 2 are displayed, as shown in Figure D-20.

10. **Click the Page Width button, press [Ctrl][End], press [Enter], type your name, save your changes, print the document, then close the document and exit Word**

FIGURE D-18: Clip Art task pane

- Type search keyword here
- Select collections in which to search for clips
- Select type of clips
- Select this clip
- Clips with the keyword "pagoda"
- Open the Clip Organizer
- Search for clips online

FIGURE D-19: Graphic being moved to a new location

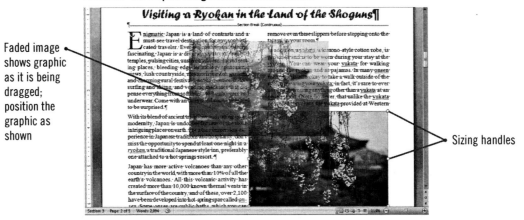

Faded image shows graphic as it is being dragged; position the graphic as shown

Sizing handles

FIGURE D-20: Completed pages 1 and 2 of newsletter

Graphic is centered on page

Text wraps around graphic

Practice

If you have a SAM user profile, you may have access to hands-on instruction, practice, and assessment of the skills covered in this unit. Log in to your SAM account (http://sam2007.course.com/) to launch any assigned training activities or exams that relate to the skills covered in this unit.

▼ CONCEPTS REVIEW

Label each element shown in Figure D-21.

FIGURE D-21

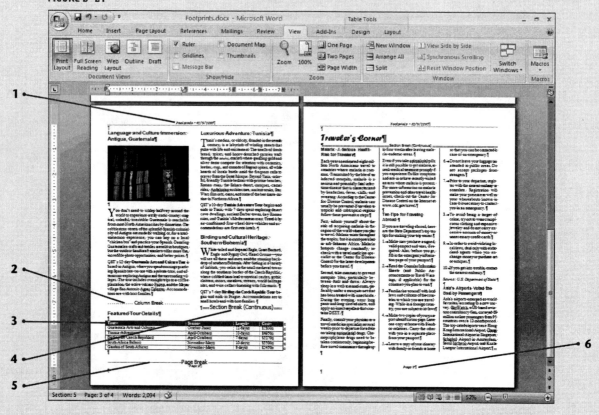

Match each term with the statement that best describes it.

7. Footer
8. Header
9. Manual page break
10. Section break
11. Field
12. Inline graphic
13. Floating graphic
14. Margin

a. An image that is inserted as part of a line of text
b. The blank area between the edge of the text and the edge of the page
c. A formatting mark that divides a document into parts that can be formatted differently
d. Text or graphics that appear at the bottom of every page in a document
e. A placeholder for information that changes
f. A formatting mark that forces the text following the mark to begin at the top of the next page
g. Text or graphics that appear at the top of every page in a document
h. An image to which text wrapping has been applied

Formatting Documents

Select the best answer from the list of choices.

15. Which type of break can you insert if you want to force text to begin on the next page?

   a. Automatic page break

   b. Continuous section break

   c. Text wrapping break

   d. Next page section break

16. Which type of break do you insert if you want to balance the columns in a section?

   a. Column break

   b. Continuous section break

   c. Manual page break

   d. Text wrapping break

17. Which of the following cannot be inserted using the Quick Parts command?

   a. AutoText building block

   b. Document property

   c. Page number field

   d. Page break

18. Which of the following do documents with mirror margins always have?

   a. Gutters

   b. Landscape orientation

   c. Inside and outside margins

   d. Different first page headers and footers

19. What name describes formatted pieces of content that are stored in galleries?

   a. Header

   b. Field

   c. Building Block

   d. Property

20. What must you do to change an inline graphic to a floating graphic?

   a. Apply text wrapping to the graphic

   b. Resize the graphic

   c. Anchor the graphic

   d. Move the graphic

▼ SKILLS REVIEW

1. Set document margins.

   a. Start Word, open the file WD D-2.docx from the drive and folder where you store your Data Files, then save it as **Greenwood Fitness**.

   b. Change the top and bottom margins settings to Moderate: 1" top and bottom, and .75" left and right.

   c. Save your changes to the document.

2. Divide a document into sections.

   a. Hide the white space in the document by moving the pointer to the top of a page, then double-clicking with the Hide White Space pointer that appears.

   b. Turn on the display of formatting marks, then customize the status bar to display sections if necessary.

   c. Scroll down, then insert a continuous section break before the **Facilities** heading.

   d. Format the text in section 2 in two columns, then save your changes to the document.

3. Insert page breaks.

   a. Insert a manual page break before the heading **Welcome to the Greenwood Fitness Center!**.

   b. Scroll down and insert a manual page break before the heading **Services**.

   c. Scroll down and insert a manual page break before the heading **Membership**.

   d. Show the white space in the document by moving the pointer over the thick black line that separates the pages, and then double-clicking with the Show White Space pointer that appears.

   e. Press [Ctrl][Home], then save your changes to the document.

4. Format columns.

   a. On page 2, select **Facilities** and the paragraph mark below it, use the Columns button to format the selected text as one column, then center **Facilities** on the page.

   b. Balance the columns on page 2 by inserting a continuous section break at the bottom of the second column.

   c. On page 3, select **Services** and the paragraph mark below it, format the selected text as one column, then center the text.

   d. Balance the columns on page 3.

   e. On page 4, select **Membership** and the paragraph mark below it, format the selected text as one column, then center the text.

   f. Insert a column break before the **Membership Cards** heading, press [Ctrl][Home], then save your changes to the document.

5. Insert page numbers.

    a. Insert page numbers in the document at the bottom of the page. Select the Plain Number 2 page number style from the gallery.

    b. Scroll through the document to view the page numbers on each page, then save your changes to the document.

6. Add headers and footers.

    a. Double-click the margin at the top of a page to open the Header and Footer areas.

    b. With the insertion point in the Header area, click the Quick Parts button in the Insert Group on the Header & Footer Tools Design tab, point to Document Property, then click Author.

    c. Replace the text in the Author content control with your name, press [End] to move the insertion point out of the content control, then press [Spacebar].

    d. Click the Insert Alignment Tab button in the Position group, select the Right option button and keep the alignment relative to the margin, then click OK in the dialog box to move the insertion point to the right margin.

    e. Use the Insert Date and Time command in the Insert group to insert the current date as static text.

    f. Move the insertion point to the Footer area.

    g. Double-click the page number to select it, then format the page number in bold italic.

    h. Close headers and footers, view the header and footer on each page, then save your changes to the document.

7. Edit headers and footers.

    a. Open headers and footers, then apply italic to the text in the header.

    b. Move the insertion point to the Footer area, then change the footer style to Plain Number 3. (*Hint*: Click the Page Number button, point to Bottom of Page, then click the new style.)

    c. Use the Symbol command on the Insert tab to open the Symbol dialog box, insert a black right-pointing triangle symbol (character code: 25BA), then close the Symbol dialog box. (*Note*: Select a different symbol if 25BA is not available to you.)

    d. Use the Header & Footer Tools Design tab to create a different header and footer for the first page of the document.

    e. Scroll to the beginning of the document, type your name in the First Page Header area, then apply italic to your name.

    f. Close headers and footers, preview the header and footer on each page in Print Preview, close Print Preview, then save your changes to the document.

8. Insert a table.

    a. On page 4, select the word Table at the end of the Membership Rates section, press [Delete], open the Insert Table dialog box, then create a table with two columns and five rows.

    b. Apply the green Light List - Accent 3 table style to the table.

    c. Press [Tab] to leave the first cell in the header row blank, then type Rate.

    d. Press [Tab], then type the following text in the table, pressing [Tab] to move from cell to cell.

Enrollment/Individual	$100
Enrollment/Couple	$150
Monthly membership/Individual	$35
Monthly membership/Couple	$60

    e. With the insertion point in the table, right-click the table, use the AutoFit command to AutoFit to Contents, and then AutoFit to Window.

    f. Save your changes to the document.

9. Insert clip art.

a. On page 1, place the insertion point in the second blank paragraph below A Rehabilitation and Exercise Facility. (*Hint:* Place the insertion point to the left of the paragraph mark.)

b. Open the Clip Art task pane. Search for clips related to the keyword fitness.

c. Insert the clip shown in Figure D-22. (*Note:* An active Internet connection is needed to select the clip shown in the figure. Select a different clip if this one is not available to you. If you are working offline, you might need to search using a keyword such as sports.)

d. Select the graphic, then drag the lower-right sizing handle down and to the right so that the graphic is about 3.75" wide and 3.1" tall. Size the graphic so that all the text and the manual page break fit on page 1. You can use the Shape Height and Shape Width text boxes in the Size group on the Format tab to size the graphic precisely if necessary.

e. Apply a Drop Shadow Rectangle picture style to the graphic.

f. Move the insertion point to page 3, search for clips related to the keyword massage, then insert an appropriate clip. Select a clip that works with the design of the document.

g. Use the Position command to position the clip at the bottom center of the document with square text wrapping.

h. Save your changes to the document. Preview the document, print a copy, then close the document and exit Word.

FIGURE D-22

The Greenwood Fitness Center

A Rehabilitation and Exercise Facility

Member Services

Hours of Operation

Monday – Friday:
6:00 a.m. to 10:00 p.m.

Saturday:
7:00 a.m. to 10:00 p.m.

Sunday:
1:00 p.m. to 5:00 p.m.

▼ INDEPENDENT CHALLENGE 1

You are the owner of a small business in White Horse, Yukon Territory, called Blue Chair Catering. You have begun work on the text for a brochure advertising your business and are now ready to lay out the pages and prepare the final copy. The brochure will be printed on both sides of an 8½" × 11" sheet of paper, and folded in thirds.

a. Start Word, open the file WD D-3.docx from the drive and folder where you store your Data Files, then save it as **Blue Chair**. Read the document to get a feel for its contents.

b. Change the page orientation to landscape, and change all four margins to .6".

c. Format the document in three columns of equal width.

d. Insert a next page section break before the heading **Catering Services**.

e. On page 1, insert column breaks before the headings **Sample Tuscan Banquet Menu** and **Sample Indian Banquet Menu**.

f. Change the column spacing on the first page to .4", add lines between the columns on the first page, then center the text in the columns.

g. Double-click the bottom margin to open the footer area, create a different header and footer for the first page, then type **Call for custom menus designed to your taste and budget** in the First Page Footer area.

h. Center the text in the footer area, format it in 20-point Papyrus, with a Blue, Accent 1 font color, then close headers and footers.

i. On page 2, insert a column break before Your Name. Press [Enter] as many times as necessary to move the contact information to the bottom of the second column. Be sure all five lines of the contact information are in column 2 and do not flow to the next column.

j. Replace Your Name with your name, then center the contact information in the column.

k. Insert a column break at the bottom of the second column. Then, type the text shown in Figure D-23 in the third column and apply the No Spacing style. Refer to the figure as you follow the instructions for formatting the text in the third column.

l. Format Blue Chair Catering in 30-point Papyrus, bold.

m. Format the remaining text in 12-point Papyrus. Center the text in the third column.

n. Insert the clip art graphic shown in Figure D-23 or another appropriate clip art graphic. Do not wrap text around the graphic.

o. Resize the graphic and add or remove blank paragraphs in the third column of your brochure so that the spacing between elements roughly matches the spacing shown in Figure D-23.

Advanced Challenge Exercise

- Insert a different appropriate clip art graphic at the bottom of the first column on page 2.
- Apply text wrapping to the graphic, then resize the graphic and position it so it enhances the design of the brochure.
- Apply a suitable picture style to the graphic.

p. Save your changes, preview the brochure in Print Preview, then print a copy. If possible, print the two pages of the brochure back to back so that the brochure can be folded in thirds.

q. Close the document and exit Word.

FIGURE D-23

Blue Chair Catering

Complete catering services available for all types of events. Menus and estimates provided upon request.

▼ INDEPENDENT CHALLENGE 2

You work in the Campus Safety Department at Pacific State College. You have written the text for an informational flyer about parking regulations on campus, and now you need to format the flyer so it is attractive and readable.

a. Start Word, open the file WD D-4.docx from the drive and folder where you store your Data Files, then save it as **Pacific Parking FAQ**. Read the document to get a feel for its contents.

b. Change all four margins to .7".

c. Insert a continuous section break before **1. May I bring a car to school?** (*Hint*: Place the insertion point before May.)

d. Scroll down and insert a next page section break before **Sample Parking Permit**.

e. Format the text in section 2 in three columns of equal width with .3" of space between the columns.

f. Hyphenate the document using the automatic hyphenation feature. (*Hint*: If the Hyphenation feature is not installed on your computer, skip this step.)

g. Add a 3-point dotted-line bottom border to the blank paragraph under Pacific State College. (*Hint*: Place the insertion point before the paragraph mark under Pacific State College.)

h. Open the Header area and insert your name in the header. Right-align your name and format it in 10-point Arial.

i. Add the following text to the footer, inserting symbols between words as indicated:
Parking and Shuttle Service Office • 54 Buckley Street • Pacific State College • 942-555-2227.

j. Format the footer text in 9-point Arial Black and center it in the footer. Use a different font if Arial Black is not available to you. If necessary, adjust the font and font size so that the entire address fits on one line.

k. Apply a 3-point dotted-line border above the footer text. Make sure to apply the border to the paragraph.

l. Balance the columns in section 2.

m. Add the clip art graphic shown in Figure D-24 (or another appropriate clip art graphic) to the upper-right corner of the document, above the border. Make sure the graphic does not obscure the border. (*Hint*: Apply text wrapping to the graphic before positioning it.)

n. Place the insertion point on page 2 (which is section 4). Change the left and right margins in section 4 to 1". Also change the page orientation of section 4 to landscape.

o. Change the vertical alignment of section 4 to center. (*Hint*: Use the Layout tab in the Page Setup dialog box.)

p. Apply a table style to the table similar to the style shown in Figure D-25.

q. Save your changes, preview the flyer in Print Preview, then print a copy. If possible, print the two pages of the flyer back to back.

r. Close the document and exit Word.

FIGURE D-24

> **Frequently Asked Questions (FAQ)**
> Department of Campus Safety
>
> **Parking & Shuttle Service Office**
> Pacific State College
> ·······································

FIGURE D-25

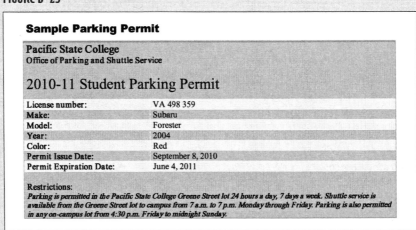

Formatting Documents

▼ INDEPENDENT CHALLENGE 3

A book publisher would like to publish an article you wrote on stormwater pollution in Australia as a chapter in a forthcoming book called *Environmental Issues for the New Millennium*. The publisher has requested that you format your article like a book chapter before submitting it for publication, and has provided you with a style sheet.

a. Start Word, open the file WD D-5.docx from the drive and folder where you store your Data Files, then save it as Chapter 9.

b. Change the font of the entire document to 11-point High Tower Text. If this font is not available to you, select a different font suitable for the pages of a book. Change the alignment to justified.

c. Change the paper size to 6" × 9".

d. Create mirror margins. (*Hint*: Use the Multiple Pages list arrow.) Change the top and bottom margins to .8", change the inside margin to .4", change the outside margin to .6", and create a .3" gutter to allow room for the book's binding.

e. Change the Zoom level to Page Width, open the Header and Footer areas, then apply the setting to create different headers and footers for odd- and even-numbered pages.

f. In the odd-page header, type Chapter 9, insert a symbol of your choice, then type Stormwater Pollution in the Fairy Creek Catchment.

g. Format the header text in 9-point High Tower Text italic, then right-align the text.

h. In the even-page header, type your name, insert a symbol of your choice, then insert a date field that updates automatically. (*Hint*: Scroll down or use the Next Section button to move the insertion point to the even-page header.)

i. Change the format of the date to include just the month and the year. (*Hint*: Right-click the date field, click Edit Field, then type MMMM yyyy in the Date Formats text box.)

j. Format the header text in 9-point High Tower Text italic. The even-page header should be left-aligned.

k. Insert a left-aligned page number field in the even-page footer area, format it in 10-point High Tower Text, insert a right-aligned page number field in the odd-page footer area, then format it in 10-point High Tower Text.

l. Format the page numbers so that the first page of your chapter, which is Chapter 9 in the book, begins on page 135. (*Hint*: Select a page number field, click the Page Number button, then click Format Page Numbers.)

m. Go to the beginning of the document, press [Enter] 10 times, type Chapter 9: Stormwater Pollution in the Fairy Creek Catchment, press [Enter] twice, type your name, then press [Enter] twice.

n. Format the chapter title in 16-point Calibri bold, format your name in 14-point Calibri, then left-align the title text and your name, as shown in Figure D-26.

FIGURE D-26

Chapter 9 • Stormwater Pollution in the Fairy Creek Catchment

Chapter 9: Stormwater Pollution in the Fairy Creek Catchment

Your Name

Australia's beaches are a key component of its cultural identity, but this symbol is not as clean as could be. Beach pollution is—or should be—an issue of great concern to the beach-going public. There are many reasons why beaches become polluted. Oil spills, industrial discharge of toxic waste, trash, and even unsafe levels of treated sewage are well-known and obvious sources of pollution. However, according to the Environmental Protection Agency (EPA), the most common cause of beach pollution is contaminated stormwater.

The environmental movement's concern about beach pollution has shifted from sewerage to stormwater. This change in focus is in large part due to increased water quality testing, which has revealed stormwater as the major culprit. In response, in 1997 the state government created the Waterways Package, a plan to improve the quality of the state's waterways. The state mandated that every council have a stormwater management plan aimed at achieving clean, healthy waterways, and allocated $60 million as part of a stormwater trust fund to improve water quality.

Stormwater causes beach pollution because it becomes contaminated with pollutants as it travels through the stormwater system. These pollutants can include dog droppings, automobile fluids, cigarette butts, litter, runoff from streets, and anything that is washed into the stormwater system. Stormwater is then piped into catchments (areas of land that drain to a common point) that empty unfiltered into the sea. This problem is exacerbated by land development, which alters

135

▼ INDEPENDENT CHALLENGE 3 (CONTINUED)

Advanced Challenge Exercise

- Scroll to page 4 in the document, place the insertion point at the end of the paragraph above the Potential health effects... heading, press [Enter] twice, type **Table 1: Total annual pollutant loads per year in the Fairy Creek Catchment**, format the text as bold, then press [Enter] twice.
- Insert a table with four columns and four rows.
- Type the text shown in Figure D-27 in the table. Do not be concerned when the text wraps to the next line in a cell.
- Apply the Light List Table style. Make sure the text in the header row is bold, then remove any bold formatting from the text in the remaining rows.
- AutoFit the table to fit the contents, then AutoFit the table to fit the window.

FIGURE D-27

Area	Nitrogen	Phosphorus	Suspended solids
Fairy Creek	9.3 tonnes	1.2 tonnes	756.4 tonnes
Durras Arm	6.2 tonnes	.9 tonnes	348.2 tonnes
Cabbage Tree Creek	9.8 tonnes	2.3 tonnes	485.7 tonnes

o. Save your changes, preview the chapter in Print Preview, print the first four pages of the chapter, then close the document and exit Word.

▼ REAL LIFE INDEPENDENT CHALLENGE

One of the most common opportunities to use the page layout features of Word is when formatting a research paper. The format recommended by the *MLA Handbook for Writers of Research Papers*, a style guide that includes information on preparing, writing, and formatting research papers, is the standard format used by many schools, colleges, and universities. In this independent challenge, you will research the MLA (Modern Language Association) guidelines for formatting a research paper and use the guidelines you find to prepare a sample research report.

a. Use your favorite search engine to search the Web for information on the MLA guidelines for formatting a research report. Use the keywords **MLA Style** and **research paper format** to conduct your search.

b. Look for information on the proper formatting for the following aspects of a research paper: paper size, margins, title page or first page of the report, line spacing, paragraph indentation, and page numbers. Print the information you find.

c. Start Word, open the file WD D-6.docx from the drive and folder where you store your Data Files, then save it as **Research Paper**. Using the information you learned, format this document as a research report.

d. Adjust the margins, set the line spacing, and add page numbers to the document in the format recommended by the MLA. Use **The Maori History of New Zealand** as the title for your sample report, use your name as the author name, and make up information about the course and instructor, if necessary. Make sure to format the title page exactly as the MLA style dictates.

e. Format the remaining text as the body of the research report. Indent the first line of each paragraph rather than use quadruple spacing between paragraphs.

f. Save the document, print a copy, close the document, then exit Word.

▼ VISUAL WORKSHOP

Open the file WD D-7.docx from the drive and folder where you store your Data Files, then modify it to create the article shown in Figure D-28. (*Hint*: Change all four margins to .6". To locate the flower clip art image, search using the keyword **dahlias**, and be sure only the Photographs check box in the Results should be in list box in the Clip Art task pane has a check mark. Select a different clip if the clip shown in the figure is not available to you.) Save the document with the filename **Gardener's Corner**, then print a copy.

FIGURE D-28

GARDENER'S CORNER

Putting a Perennial Garden to Bed

By Your Name

A certain sense of peace descends when a perennial garden is put to bed for the season. The plants are safely tucked in against the elements, and the garden is ready to welcome the first signs of life. When the work is done, you can sit back and anticipate the bright blooms of spring. Many gardeners are uncertain of how to close a perennial garden. This week's column demystifies the process.

Clean up

Garden clean up can be a gradual process—plants will deteriorate at different rates, allowing you to do a little bit each week.

- Edge beds and borders and remove stakes and other plant supports.
- Dig and divide irises, daylilies, and other early bloomers.
- Cut back plants when foliage starts to deteriorate, then rake all debris out of the garden and pull any weeds that remain.

Plant perennials

Fall is the perfect time to plant perennials! The warm, sunny days and cool nights provide optimal conditions for new root growth.

- Dig deeply and enhance soil with organic matter.
- Use a good starter fertilizer to speed up new root growth.
- Untangle the roots of new plants before planting.
- Water deeply after planting as the weather dictates, and keep plants moist for several days after planting.

Add compost

Organic matter is the key ingredient to healthy garden soil. Composting adds nutrients to the soil, helps the soil retain water and nutrients, and keeps the soil well aerated. If you take care of the soil, your plants will become strong and disease resistant. Before adding compost, use an iron rake to loosen the top few inches of soil. Spread a one to two inch layer of compost over the entire garden—the best compost is made up of yard waste and kitchen scraps—and then refrain from stepping on the area and compacting the soil.

To mulch or not to mulch?

Winter protection for perennial beds can only help plants survive the winter. Winter mulch prevents the freezing and thawing cycles, which cause plants to heave and eventually die. Here's what works and what doesn't:

- Always apply mulch after the ground is frozen.
- Never apply generic hay because is contains billions of weed seeds. Also, whole leaves and bark mulch hold too much moisture.
- Use a loose material to allow air filtration. Straw and salt marsh hay are excellent choices for mulch. If using leaves, use only stiff leaves such as Oak or Beech. Soft leaves, such as Maple, make it difficult for air and water to filtrate.
- Remove the winter mulch in the spring as soon as new growth begins.

For copies of earlier Gardener's Corner columns, call 1-800-555-3827.

UNIT A
Excel 2007

Getting Started with Excel 2007

Files You Will Need:

EX A-1.xlsx

EX A-2.xlsx

EX A-3.xlsx

EX A-4.xlsx

EX A-5.xlsx

In this unit, you will learn how spreadsheet software helps you analyze data and make business decisions, even if you aren't a math pro. You'll become familiar with the different elements of a spreadsheet and learn your way around the Excel program window. You will also work in an Excel worksheet and make simple calculations. You have been hired as an assistant at Quest Specialty Travel (QST), a company offering tours that immerse travelers in regional culture. You report to Grace Wong, the vice president of finance. As Grace's assistant, you create worksheets to analyze data from various divisions of the company, so you can help her make sound decisions on company expansion and investments.

OBJECTIVES

Understand spreadsheet software

Tour the Excel 2007 window

Understand formulas

Enter labels and values and use AutoSum

Edit cell entries

Enter and edit a simple formula

Switch worksheet views

Choose print options

Understanding Spreadsheet Software

Microsoft Excel is the electronic spreadsheet program within Microsoft Office. An **electronic spreadsheet** is an application you use to perform numeric calculations and to analyze and present numeric data. One advantage of spreadsheet programs over pencil and paper is that your calculations are updated automatically, so you can change entries without having to manually recalculate. Table A-1 shows some of the common business tasks people accomplish using Excel. In Excel, the electronic spreadsheet you work in is called a **worksheet**, and is contained in a file called a **workbook**, which has the file extension .xlsx. At Quest Specialty Travel, you use Excel extensively to track finances and manage corporate data.

When you use Excel, you have the ability to:

*   **Enter data quickly and accurately**

    With Excel, you can enter information faster and more accurately than with pencil and paper. Figure A-1 shows a payroll worksheet created using pencil and paper. Figure A-2 shows the same worksheet created using Excel. Equations were added to calculate the hours and pay. You can copy the payroll deductions that don't change from quarter to quarter, then use Excel to calculate the gross and net payroll by supplying unique data and formulas for each quarter. You can also quickly create charts and other elements to help visualize how the payroll is distributed.

*   **Recalculate data easily**

    Fixing typing errors or updating data is easy in Excel. In the payroll example, if you receive updated hours for an employee, you just enter the new hours and Excel recalculates the pay.

*   **Perform what-if analysis**

    The ability to change data and quickly view the recalculated results gives you the power to make informed business decisions. For instance, if you're considering raising the hourly rate for an entry-level tour guide from $12.50 to $15.00, you can enter the new value in the worksheet and immediately see the impact on the overall payroll as well as on the individual employee. Any time you use a worksheet to ask the question "what if?" you are performing **what-if analysis**. Excel also includes a Scenario Manager where you can name and save different what-if versions of your worksheet.

*   **Change the appearance of information**

    Excel provides powerful features for making information visually appealing and easier to understand. You can format text and numbers in different fonts, colors, and styles to make it stand out.

*   **Create charts**

    Excel makes it easy to create charts based on worksheet information. Charts are updated automatically in Excel whenever data changes. The worksheet in Figure A-2 includes a 3-D pie chart.

*   **Share information**

    It's easy for everyone at QST to collaborate in Excel, using the company intranet, the Internet, or a network storage device. For example, you can complete the weekly payroll that your boss, Grace Wong, started creating. You can also take advantage of collaboration tools such as shared workbooks, so that multiple people can edit a workbook simultaneously.

*   **Build on previous work**

    Instead of creating a new worksheet for every project, it's easy to modify an existing Excel worksheet. When you are ready to create next week's payroll, you can open the file for last week's payroll, save it with a new filename, and modify the information as necessary. You can also use predesigned, formatted files called **templates** to create new worksheets quickly. Excel comes with many templates, that you can customize.

FIGURE A-1: Traditional paper worksheet

Quest Specialty Travel
Tour Guide Payroll Calculator

Name	Hours	O/T Hrs	Hrly Rate	Reg Pay	O/T Pay	Gross Pay
Brueghel, Pieter	40	4	15—	600—	120—	720—
Cortona, Livia	35	0	10—	350—	0—	350—
Klimt, Gustave	40	2	12⁵⁰	500—	50—	550—
Le Pen, Jean-Marie	29	0	15—	435—	0—	435—
Martinez, Juan	37	0	12⁵⁰	462.50	0—	462.50
Mioshi, Keiko	39	0	20—	780—	0—	780—
Sherwood, Burton	40	0	15—	600—	0—	600—
Strano, Riccardo	40	8	15—	600—	240—	840—
Wadsworth, Alicia	40	5	12⁵⁰	500—	125—	625—
Yamamoto, Johji	38	0	15—	570—	0—	570—

FIGURE A-2: Excel worksheet

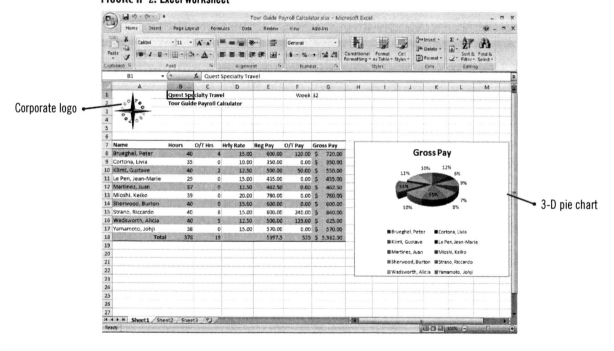

Corporate logo

3-D pie chart

Excel 2007

TABLE A-1: Business tasks you can accomplish using Excel

you can use spreadsheets to	by
Perform calculations	Adding formulas and functions to worksheet data; for example, adding a list of sales results or calculating a car payment
Represent values graphically	Creating charts based on worksheet data; for example, creating a chart that displays expenses
Generate reports	Creating workbooks that combine information from multiple worksheets, such as summarized sales information from multiple stores
Organize data	Sorting data in ascending or descending order; for example, alphabetizing a list of products or customer names, or prioritizing orders by date
Analyze data	Creating data summaries and short lists using PivotTables or AutoFilters; for example, making a list of the top 10 customers based on spending habits
Create what-if data scenarios	Using variable values to investigate and sample different outcomes, such as changing the interest rate or payment schedule on a loan

Touring the Excel 2007 Window

To start Excel, Microsoft Windows must be running. Similar to starting any program in Office, you can use the Start button on the Windows taskbar, or you may have a shortcut on your desktop you prefer to use. If you need additional assistance, ask your instructor or technical support person. 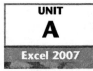 You decide to start Excel and familiarize yourself with the worksheet window.

QUICK TIP

For more information on starting a program or opening and saving a file, see the unit "Getting Started with Microsoft Office 2007."

1. **Start Excel, click the Microsoft Office button 🔘, then click Open**

2. **In the Open dialog box, navigate to the drive and folder where you store your Data Files, click EX A-1.xlsx, then click Open**

3. **Click 🔘, then click Save As**

TROUBLE

If you don't see the extension .xlsx on the filenames in the Open dialog box, don't worry; Windows can be set up to display or not to display the file extensions.

4. **In the Save As dialog box, navigate to the drive and folder where you store your Data Files if necessary, type Tour Guide Payroll Calculator in the File name text box, then click Save**

   Using Figure A-3 as a guide, identify the following items:
   - The **Name box** displays the active cell address. "A1" appears in the Name box.
   - The **formula bar** allows you to enter or edit data in the worksheet. The worksheet window contains a grid of columns and rows. Columns are labeled alphabetically and rows are labeled numerically. The worksheet window can contain a total of 1,048,576 rows and 16,384 columns.
   - The intersection of a column and a row is called a **cell**. Cells can contain text, numbers, formulas, or a combination of all three. Every cell has its own unique location or **cell address**, which is identified by the coordinates of the intersecting column and row.
   - The **cell pointer** is a dark rectangle that outlines the cell in which you are working. This cell is called the **active cell**. In Figure A-3, the cell pointer outlines cell A1, so A1 is the active cell. The column and row headings for the active cell are highlighted, making it easier to locate.
   - **Sheet tabs** below the worksheet grid let you switch from sheet to sheet in a workbook. By default, a workbook file contains three worksheets—but you can use just one, or have as many as 255, in a workbook. The Insert Worksheet button to the right of Sheet 3 allows you to add worksheets to a workbook. **Sheet tab scrolling buttons** let you navigate to additional sheet tabs when available.
   - You can use the **scroll bars** to move around in a document that is too large to fit on the screen at once.
   - The **status bar** is located at the bottom of the Excel window. It provides a brief description of the active command or task in progress. The **mode indicator** in the bottom-left corner of the status bar provides additional information about certain tasks.

5. **Click cell A4**

   Cell A4 becomes the active cell. To activate a different cell, you can click the cell or press the arrow keys on your keyboard to move to it.

6. **Click cell B5, press and hold the mouse button, drag ✛ to cell B14, then release the mouse button**

   You selected a group of cells and they are highlighted, as shown in Figure A-4. A selection of two or more cells such as B5:B14 is called a **range**; you select a range when you want to perform an action on a group of cells at once, such as moving them or formatting them. When you select a range, the status bar displays the average, count (or number of items selected), and sum of the selected cells as a quick reference.

FIGURE A-3: Open workbook

Add-Ins tab (may not appear on your computer)

Name box and current cell address

Cell pointer indicates active cell

Formula bar

Scroll bars

Insert Worksheet button

Status bar

Sheet tab scrolling buttons

Mode indicator

Sheet tabs

FIGURE A-4: Selecting a range

Selected cells

Average, Count, and Sum

Understanding Formulas

Excel is a truly powerful program because users at every level of mathematical expertise can make calculations with accuracy. To do so, you use formulas. **Formulas** are equations in a worksheet. You use formulas to make calculations as simple as adding a column of numbers, or as complex as profit-and-loss projections for a global corporation. To tap into the power of Excel, you should understand how formulas work. 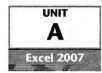 Managers at QST use the Tour Guide Payroll Calculator workbook to keep track of employee hours prior to submitting them to the Payroll Department. You'll be using this workbook regularly, so you need to understand the formulas it contains and how Excel calculates the results.

STEPS

1. **Click cell E5**

   The active cell contains a formula, which appears on the formula bar. All Excel formulas begin with the equal sign (=). If you wanted a cell to show the result of adding 4 plus 2, the formula in the cell would look like this: =4+2. If you wanted a cell to show the result of multiplying two values in your worksheet, such as the values in cells B5 and D5, the formula would look like this: =B5*D5, as shown in Figure A-5.

2. **Click cell F5**

   While you're entering a formula in a cell, the cell references and arithmetic operators appear on the formula bar. See Table A-2 for a list of common Excel arithmetic operators. When you're finished entering the formula, you can either click the Enter button on the formula bar, or press [Enter]. An example of a more complex formula is the calculation of overtime pay. At QST, overtime pay is calculated at twice the regular hourly rate times the number of overtime hours. The formula used to calculate overtime pay for the employee in row 5 is:

   O/T Hrs times (2 times Hrly Rate)

   In a worksheet cell, you would enter: =C5*(2*D5), as shown in Figure A-6.

   The use of parentheses creates groups within the formula and indicates which calculations to complete first—an important consideration in complex formulas. In this formula, the hourly rate is doubled, and that value is multiplied by the number of overtime hours. Because overtime is calculated at twice the hourly rate, managers are aware that they need to closely watch this expense.

DETAILS

In creating calculations in Excel, it is important to:

- **Know where the formulas should be**

  Excel formulas are created in the cell where they are viewed. This means that the formula calculating Gross Pay for the employee in row 5 will be entered in cell G5.

- **Know exactly what cells and arithmetic operations are needed**

  Don't guess; make sure you know exactly what cells are involved before creating a formula.

- **Create formulas with care**

  Make sure you know exactly what you want a formula to accomplish before it is created. An inaccurate formula may have far-reaching effects if the formula or its results are referenced by other formulas.

- **Use cell references rather than values**

  The beauty of Excel is that whenever you change a value in a cell, any formula containing a reference to that cell is automatically updated. For this reason, it's important that you use cell references in formulas, rather than actual values whenever possible.

- **Determine what calculations will be needed**

  Sometimes it's difficult to predict what data will be needed within a worksheet, but you should try to anticipate what statistical information may be required. For example, if there are columns of numbers, chances are good that both column and row totals should be present.

FIGURE A-5: Viewing a formula

Formula appears in formula bar

Result of formula appears in cell

FIGURE A-6: Formula with multiple operators

TABLE A-2: Excel arithmetic operators

operator	purpose	example
+	Addition	=A5+A7
-	Subtraction or negation	=A5-10
*	Multiplication	=A5*A7
/	Division	=A5/A7
%	Percent	=35%
^ (caret)	Exponent	=6^2 (same as 6^2)

Entering Labels and Values and Using AutoSum

To enter content in a cell, you can type on the formula bar or directly in the cell itself. When entering content in a worksheet, you should start by entering all the labels first. **Labels** are entries that contain text and numerical information not used in calculations, such as "2009 Sales" or "Travel Expenses." Labels help you identify data in worksheet rows and columns, making your worksheet easier to understand. **Values** are numbers, formulas, and functions that can be used in calculations. To enter a calculation, you type an equal sign (=) plus the formula for the calculation; some examples of an Excel calculation are "=2+2" and "=C5+C6." Functions are Excel's built-in formulas; you learn more about them in the next unit. You want to enter some information in the Tour Guide Payroll Calculator workbook, and use a very simple function to total a range of cells.

STEPS

1. **Click cell A15, then click in the formula bar**

   Notice that the **mode indicator** on the status bar now reads "Edit," indicating you are in Edit mode. You are in Edit mode any time you are entering or changing the contents of a cell.

2. **Type Totals, then click the Enter button ☑ on the formula bar**

   Clicking the Enter button accepts the entry. The new text is left-aligned. Labels are left-aligned by default, and values are right-aligned by default. Excel recognizes an entry as a value if it is a number or it begins with one of these symbols: +, -, =, @, #, or $. When a cell contains both text and numbers, Excel recognizes it as a label.

3. **Click cell B15**

   You want this cell to total the hours worked by all the tour guides. You might think you need to create a formula that looks like this: =B5+B6+B7+B8+B9+B10+B11+B12+B13+B14. However, there's an easier way to achieve this result.

QUICK TIP

If you change your mind and want to cancel an entry in the formula bar, click the Cancel button ☒ on the formula bar.

4. **Click the AutoSum button Σ in the Editing group on the Home tab of the Ribbon**

   The SUM function is inserted in your formula, and a suggested range appears in parentheses, as shown in Figure A-7. A **function** is a built-in formula; it includes the **arguments** (the information necessary to calculate an answer), as well as cell references and other unique information. Clicking the AutoSum button sums the adjacent range (that is, the cells next to the active cell) above or to the left, though you can adjust the range if necessary. Using the SUM function is quicker than entering a formula, and using the range B5:B14 is more efficient than entering individual cell references.

QUICK TIP

You can create formulas in a cell even before you enter the values to be calculated; the results will be recalculated as soon as the data is entered.

5. **Click ☑**

   Excel calculates the total contained in cells B5:B14 and displays the result, 378, in cell B15. The cell actually contains the formula =SUM(B5:B14), and the result is displayed.

6. **Click cell C13, type 6, then press [Enter]**

   The number 6 is right-aligned, the cell pointer moves to cell C14 and the value in cell F13 changes.

7. **Click cell C18, type Average Gross Pay, then press [Enter]**

   The new label is entered in cell C18. The contents appear to spill into the empty cells to the right.

QUICK TIP

You can also press [Tab] to complete a cell entry and move the cell pointer to the right.

8. **Click and hold cell B15, drag the mouse pointer to cell G15, click the Fill button 🔽 in the Editing group, then click Right in the Fill menu**

   Calculated values appear in the selected range, as shown in Figure A-8. Each filled cell contains a formula that sums the range of cells above. The Fill button fills cells based on the first number sequence in the range.

9. **Save your work**

FIGURE A-7: Creating a formula using the AutoSum button

Formula in selected cell

AutoSum button

Outline of cells included in formula

FIGURE A-8: Calculated values

Ribbon

Home tab

In cell C18, contents appear to spill into empty adjacent cells

Fill button

Formula in cell B15 is copied to selected adjacent cells

Navigating a worksheet

With over a million cells available in a worksheet, it is important to know how to move around in, or **navigate**, a worksheet. You can use the arrow keys on the keyboard [↑], [↓], [←], or [→] to move a cell at a time, or press [Page Up] or [Page Down] to move a screen at a time. To move a screen to the left press [Alt][Page Up]; to move a screen to the right press [Alt][Page Down]. You can also use the mouse pointer to click the desired cell. If the desired cell is not visible in the worksheet window, use the scroll bars or the Go To command by clicking the Find & Select button in the Editing group on the Home tab of the Ribbon. To quickly jump to the first cell in a worksheet press [Ctrl][Home]; to jump to the last cell, press [Ctrl][End].

Editing Cell Entries

You can change, or **edit**, the contents of an active cell at any time. To do so, double-click the cell, click in the formula bar, or just start typing. Excel switches to Edit mode when you are making cell entries. Different pointers, shown in Table A-3, guide you through the editing process. ▨▨▨▨ You noticed some errors in the worksheet and want to make corrections. The first error is in cell A5, which contains a misspelled name.

STEPS

QUICK TIP

Pressing [Enter] also accepts the cell entry, but moves the cell pointer down one cell.

1. **Click cell A5, then click to the right of P in the formula bar**

   As soon as you click in the formula bar, a blinking vertical line called the **insertion point** appears on the formula bar at the location where new text will be inserted. See Figure A-9. The mouse pointer changes to I when you point anywhere in the formula bar.

2. **Press [Delete], then click the Enter button ☑ on the formula bar**

   Clicking the Enter button accepts the edit, and the spelling of the employee's first name is corrected. You can also press [Enter] or [Tab] to accept an edit.

QUICK TIP

On some keyboards, you might need to press an "F Lock" key to enable the function keys.

3. **Click cell B6, then press [F2]**

   Excel switches to Edit mode, and the insertion point blinks in the cell. Pressing [F2] activates the cell for editing directly in the cell instead of the formula bar. Some people prefer editing right in the cell instead of using the formula bar, but it's simply a matter of preference; the results in the worksheet are the same.

QUICK TIP

The Undo button allows you to reverse up to 100 previous actions, one at a time.

4. **Press [Backspace], type 8, then press [Enter]**

   The value in the cell changes from 35 to 38, and cell B7 becomes the active cell. Did you notice that the calculations in cells B15 and E15 also changed? That's because those cells contain formulas that include cell B6 in their calculations. If you make a mistake when editing, you can click the Cancel button ☒ on the formula bar *before* pressing [Enter] to confirm the cell entry. The Enter and Cancel buttons appear only when you're in Edit mode. If you notice the mistake *after* you have confirmed the cell entry, click the Undo button ↺ on the Quick Access toolbar.

5. **Click cell A9, press [F2], press and hold [Shift], press [Home], then release [Shift]**

   Pressing and holding [Shift] lets you select text using the keyboard. Pressing [Home] moves the cursor to the beginning of the cell; pressing [End] would move the cursor to the end or the cell.

6. **Type Maez, Javier, then press [Enter]**

   When text is selected, typing deletes it and replaces it with the new text.

7. **Double-click cell C12, press [Delete], type 4, then click ☑**

   Double-clicking a cell activates it for editing directly in the cell. Compare your screen to Figure A-10.

8. **Save your work**

   Your changes to the workbook are saved.

Recovering a lost workbook file

Sometimes while you are using Excel, you may experience a power failure or your computer may "freeze," making it impossible to continue working. If this type of interruption occurs, Excel has a built-in recovery feature that allows you to open and save files that were open at the time of the interruption. When you restart Excel after an interruption, File Recovery mode automatically starts and tries to make any necessary repairs. If you need to use a corrupted workbook, you can try and repair it manually by clicking the Office button, then clicking Open. Select the workbook file you want to repair, click the Open list arrow, then click Open and Repair.

FIGURE A-9: Worksheet in Edit mode

Enter button

Active cell

Insertion point

Mode indicator

FIGURE A-10: Edited worksheet

Edited label

Edited value

TABLE A-3: Common pointers in Excel

name	pointer	use to
Normal	⊕	Select a cell or range; indicates Ready mode
Copy	▷⁺	Create a duplicate of the selected cell(s)
Fill handle	✛	Create an alphanumeric series in a range
I-beam	I	Edit contents of formula bar
Move	✛	Change the location of the selected cell(s)

Entering and Editing a Simple Formula

You use formulas in Excel to perform calculations such as adding, multiplying, and averaging. Formulas in an Excel worksheet start with the equal sign (=), also called the **formula prefix**, followed by cell addresses, range names, and values, along with calculation operators. **Calculation operators** indicate what type of calculation you want to perform on the cells, ranges or values. They can include **arithmetic operators**, which perform mathematical calculations such as adding and subtracting, **comparison operators**, which compare values for the purpose of true/false results, **text concatenation operators**, which join strings of text in different cells, and **reference operators**, which enable you to use ranges in calculations. 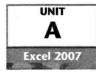 You want to create a formula in the worksheet that calculates gross pay for each employee.

STEPS

1. Click cell G5

This is the first cell where you want to insert the formula. To calculate gross pay, you need to add regular pay and overtime pay. For employee Peter Brueghel, regular pay appears in cell E5 and overtime pay appears in cell F5.

2. Type =, click cell E5, type +, then click cell F5

> **QUICK TIP**
> You can reference a cell in a formula either by typing the cell reference or clicking the cell in the worksheet; when you click a cell to add a reference, the Mode indicator changes to "Point."

Compare your formula bar to Figure A-11. The blue and green cell references in cell G5 correspond to the colored cell outlines. When entering a formula, it's a good idea to use cell references instead of values whenever you can. That way, if you later change a value in a cell (if, for example, Peter's regular pay changes to 615), any formula that includes this information reflects accurate, up-to-date results.

3. Click the Enter button ☑ on the formula bar

The results of the formula =E5+F5, 720, appear in cell G5. This same value appears in cell G15 because cell G15 contains a formula that totals the values in cells G5:G14, and there are no other values now.

4. Click cell F5

The formula in this cell calculates overtime pay by multiplying overtime hours (C5) times twice the regular hourly rate (2*D5). You want to edit this formula to reflect a new overtime pay rate.

5. Click to the right of 2 in the formula bar, then type .5 as shown in Figure A-12

The formula that calculates overtime pay has been edited.

6. Click ☑ on the formula bar

Compare your screen to Figure A-13. Notice that the calculated values in cells G5, F15, and G15 have all changed to reflect your edits to cell F5.

7. Save your work

Understanding named ranges

It can be difficult to remember the cell locations of critical information in a worksheet, but using cell names can make this task much easier. You can name a single cell or range of contiguous, or touching, cells. For example, you might name a cell that contains data on average gross pay "AVG_GP" instead of trying to remember the cell address C18. A named range must begin with a letter or an underscore. It cannot contain any spaces or be the same as a built-in name, such as a function or another object (such as a different named range) in the workbook. To name a range, select the cell(s) you want to name, click the name box in the formula bar, type the name you want to use, then press [Enter]. You can also name a range by clicking the Formulas tab, clicking the Define Name list arrow in the Defined Names group, then clicking Define Name. Type the new range name in the Name text box of the New Name dialog box, verify the selected range, then click OK. When you use a named range in a formula, the named range appears, rather than the cell address. You can also create a named range using the contents of a cell already in the range. Select the range containing the text you want to use as a name, then click Create from Selection button in the Defined Names group. The Create Names from Selection dialog box opens. Choose the location of the name you want to use, then click OK.

FIGURE A-11: Simple formula in a worksheet

Cell outline color corresponds to cell reference

Referenced cells are inserted in formula

Mode indicator changes to Point

FIGURE A-12: Edited formula in a worksheet

Edited value

FIGURE A-13: Edited formula with changes

Edited formula results in changes to these other cells

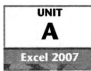
Switching Worksheet Views

You can change your view of the worksheet window at any time, using either the View tab on the Ribbon or the View buttons on the status bar. Changing your view does not affect the contents of a worksheet; it just makes it easier for you to focus on different tasks, such as entering content or preparing a worksheet for printing. The View tab includes a variety of viewing options, such as View buttons, zoom controls, and the ability to show or hide worksheet elements such as gridlines. The status bar offers fewer View options, but can be more convenient to use. You want to make some final adjustments to your worksheet, including adding a header so the document looks more polished.

STEPS

QUICK TIP

Although a work-sheet can contain more than a million rows and columns, the current docu-ment contains only as many pages as necessary for the current project.

1. **Click the** View tab **on the Ribbon, then click the** Page Layout View button **in the Workbook Views group**

   The view switches from the default view, Normal, to Page Layout view. **Normal view** shows the worksheet without including certain details like headers and footers or tools like rulers and a page number indicator; it's great for creating and editing a worksheet, but may not be detailed enough when you want to put the finishing touches on a document. **Page Layout View** provides a more accurate view of how a worksheet will look when printed, as shown in Figure A-14. The margins of the page are displayed, along with a text box for the header. A footer text box appears at the bottom of the page, but your screen may not be large enough to view it without scrolling. Above and to the left of the page are rulers. Part of an additional page appears to the right of this page, but it is dimmed, indicating that it does not contain any data. A page num-ber indicator on the status bar tells you the current page and the total number of pages in this worksheet.

2. **Drag the pointer ⌖ over the header** *without clicking*

   The header is made up of three text boxes: left, center, and right.

QUICK TIP

You can change header and footer information using the Header & Footer Tools Design tab that opens when a header or footer is active. For example, you can insert the date by clicking the Current Date button in the Header & Footer Elements group, or the time by clicking the Current Time button.

3. **Click the** left header text box, **type Quest Specialty Travel, click the** center text box, **type Tour Guide Payroll Calculator, click the** right header text box, **then type Week 32**

   The new text appears in the text boxes, as shown in Figure A-15.

4. **Select the range A1:G2, then press [Delete]**

   The duplicate information you just entered in the header is deleted from cells in the worksheet.

5. **Click the** Ruler checkbox **in the Show/Hide group on the View tab, then click the** Gridlines checkbox

   The rulers and the gridlines are hidden. By default, gridlines in a worksheet do not print, so hiding them gives you a more accurate image of your final document.

6. **Click the** Page Break Preview button 🖽 **on the status bar, then click OK in the Welcome to Page Break Preview dialog box, if necessary**

   Your view changes to **Page Break Preview**, which displays a reduced view of each page of your worksheet, along with page break indicators that you can drag to include more or less information on a page.

7. **Drag the bottom page break indicator to the bottom of row 21**

   See Figure A-16. When you're working on a large worksheet with multiple pages, sometimes you need to adjust where pages break; in this worksheet, however, the information all fits comfortably on one page.

QUICK TIP

Once you view a worksheet in Page Break Preview, the page break indica-tors appear as dot-ted lines after you switch back to Normal view.

8. **Click the** View tab if necessary, click Page Layout in the Workbook Views group, click the Ruler checkbox **in the Show/Hide group in the View tab, then click the Gridlines checkbox**

   The rulers and gridlines are no longer hidden. You can show or hide View tab items in any view.

9. **Save your work**

FIGURE A-14: Page Layout View

Ruler checkbox

Gridlines checkbox

Workbook Views group

Header text box

Vertical ruler

Current page and total number of pages

Horizontal ruler

Click

Additional dimmed page

FIGURE A-15: Header boxes

Header areas

Click

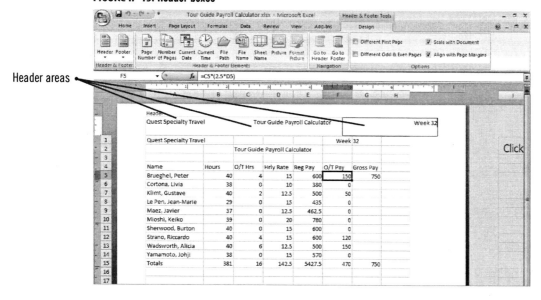

FIGURE A-16: Page Break Preview

Bottom page break indicator

Blue outline indicates print area

Getting Started with Excel 2007

Choosing Print Options

Before printing a document, you may want to review it using the Page Layout tab and Print Preview to fine-tune your printed output. You should also review your settings in the Print dialog box, to make sure you are printing the desired number of copies and using the correct printer. Tools on the Page Layout tab include a Page Setup group, where you can adjust print orientation (the direction in which the content prints across the page), paper size, and page breaks. The Scale to Fit group makes it possible to fit a large amount of data on a single page without making changes to individual margins. In the Sheet Options group, you can turn on and off gridlines and column/row headings. Reviewing your final worksheet in Print Preview shows you exactly how the worksheet will look when printed. ░░░░░ You are ready to prepare your worksheet for printing.

STEPS

1. **Click cell A21, type your name, then press [Enter]**

2. **Click the Page Layout tab on the Ribbon**

   Compare your screen to Figure A-17. The dotted line indicates the **print area**, the area to be printed.

QUICK TIP

You can use the Zoom slider at any time to enlarge your view of specific areas of your worksheet.

3. **Click the Orientation button in the Page Setup group, then click Landscape** 🖼

   The paper orientation changes to **landscape**, so the contents will print across the length of the page instead of across the width.

4. **Click the Orientation button in the Page Setup group, then click Portrait** 🖼

   The orientation returns to **portrait**, so the contents will print across the width of the page.

5. **Click the Gridlines View checkbox in the Sheet Options group on the Page Layout tab, click the Gridlines Print checkbox to select it if necessary, then save your work**

   Printing gridlines makes the data easier to read, but the gridlines will not print unless the Gridlines Print checkbox is checked.

QUICK TIP

You can print your worksheet using the default settings by clicking the Office button, pointing to Print, then clicking Quick Print.

6. **Click the Office button** 🔘**, point to Print, then click Print Preview**

   Print Preview shows exactly how your printed copy will look. You can print from this view by clicking the Print button on the Ribbon, or close Print Preview without printing by clicking the Close Print Preview button.

7. **Click the Zoom button in the Zoom group on the Print Preview tab**

   The image of your worksheet is enlarged. Compare your screen to Figure A-18.

QUICK TIP

To change the active printer, click the Name list arrow, then choose a different printer.

8. **Click the Print button in the Print group, compare your settings to Figure A-19, then click OK**

   One copy of the worksheet prints.

9. **Exit Excel**

Printing worksheet formulas

Sometimes you need to keep a record of all the formulas in a worksheet. You might want to do this to see exactly how you came up with a complex calculation, so you can explain it to others. You can do this by printing out the formulas in a worksheet rather than the results of those calculations. To do so, open the workbook containing the formulas you want to print. Click the Office button, then click Excel Options. Click Advanced in the left pane, scroll to the Display options for this worksheet section, click the list arrow and select the entire workbook or the sheet in which you want the formulas displayed, click the Show formulas in cells instead of their calculated results checkbox, then click OK.

FIGURE A-17: Worksheet with Portrait orientation

Page Layout tab

Scale field

Dotted line surrounds print area

Your name appears here

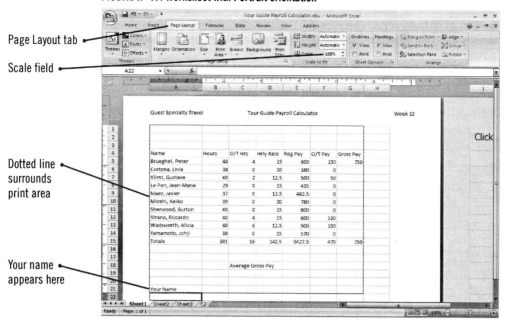

FIGURE A-18: Worksheet in Print Preview

Print button

Zoom button

Close Print Preview button

FIGURE A-19: Print dialog box

Active printer: yours will be different

Choose which pages to print

Number of copies field

Scaling to fit

If you have a large amount of data that you want to fit to a single sheet of paper, but you don't want to spend a lot of time trying to adjust the margins and other settings, use the Fit to option in the Page Setup dialog box. Open this dialog box by clicking the launcher in the Scale to Fit group in the Page Layout tab. Make sure the Page tab is selected, then click the Fit to option button. Select the number of pages you want the worksheet to fit on, then click OK. If you're ready to print, click Print and the Print dialog box will open. Select the pages you want to print and the number of copies you want, then click OK.

Practice

▼ CONCEPTS REVIEW

Label the elements of the Excel worksheet window shown in Figure A-20.

FIGURE A-20

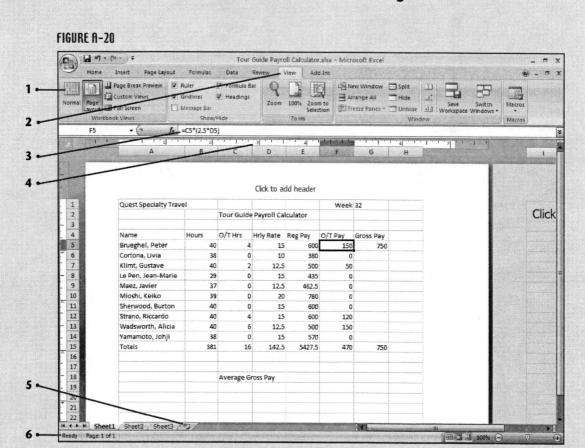

Match each term with the statement that best describes it.

7. **Cell**

8. **Normal View**

9. **Workbook**

10. **Name Box**

11. **Formula prefix**

12. **Orientation**

a. Direction in which contents of page will print

b. Equal sign preceding a formula

c. File consisting of one or more worksheets

d. Default view in Excel

e. Part of the Excel program window that displays the active cell address

f. Intersection of a column and a row

Select the best answer from the list of choices.

13. **In Excel, order of precedence determines:**
    a. The order in which worksheets are printed.
    b. The colors used to distinguish cell references.
    c. The order in which calculations are performed.
    d. How values are multiplied.

14. **The maximum number of worksheets you can include in a workbook is:**
    a. 3.
    b. 250.
    c. 255.
    d. Unlimited.

15. **A selection of multiple cells is called a:**
    a. Group.
    b. Range.
    c. Reference.
    d. Package.

16. **Using a cell address in a formula is known as:**
    a. Formularizing.
    b. Prefixing.
    c. Cell referencing.
    d. Cell mathematics.

17. **Which worksheet view shows how your worksheet will look when printed?**
    a. Page Layout
    b. Data
    c. Review
    d. View

18. **Which button should you click if you want to print formulas in a worksheet?**
    a. Save button
    b. Fill button
    c. Any button on the Quick Access Toolbar
    d. Office button

19. **Clicking the launcher in the Scale to Fit group on the Page Layout tab opens which dialog box?**
    a. Print
    b. Scale to Fit
    c. Width/Height
    d. Page Setup

20. **In which view can you see the header and footer areas of a worksheet?**
    a. Normal View
    b. Page Layout View
    c. Page Break Preview
    d. Header/Footer View

21. **Which key can you press to switch to Edit mode?**
    a. [F1]
    b. [F2]
    c. [F4]
    d. [F6]

▼ SKILLS REVIEW

1. **Understand spreadsheet software.**
   a. What is the difference between a workbook and a worksheet?
   b. Identify five common business uses for electronic spreadsheets.
   c. What is 'what-if' analysis?

2. **Tour the Excel 2007 window.**
   a. Start Excel.
   b. Open the file EX A-2.xlsx from the drive and folder where you store your Data Files, then save it as **Weather Statistics**.
   c. Locate the formula bar, the Sheet tabs, the mode indicator, and the cell pointer.

3. **Understand formulas.**
   a. What is the average high temperature of the listed cities? (*Hint*: Select the range B5:G5 and use the status bar.)
   b. What formula would you create to calculate the difference in altitude between Chicago and Phoenix?

4. **Enter labels and values and use AutoSum.**
   a. Click cell H7, then use the AutoSum button to calculate the total rainfall.
   b. Click cell H8, then use the AutoSum button to calculate the total snowfall.
   c. Save your changes to the file.

5. **Edit cell entries.**
   a. Use the [F2] key to correct the spelling of Sante Fe in a worksheet cell (the correct spelling is Santa Fe).
   b. Click cell A12, then type your name.
   c. Save your changes.

6. **Enter and edit a simple formula.**

   a. Change the value 41 in cell B8 to **52**.

   b. Change the value 35 in cell C7 to **35.4**.

   c. Select the range B10:G10, then use the Fill button in the Editing group on the Home tab to fill the formula to the remaining cells in the selection. (*Hint*: If you see a warning icon, click it, then click Ignore Error.)

   d. Save your changes.

7. **Switch worksheet views.**

   a. Click the View tab on the Ribbon, then switch to Page Layout view.

   b. Add the header **Average Annual Weather Statistics** to the center header box.

   c. Add your name to the right header box.

   d. Delete the contents of cell A1.

   e. Delete the contents of cell A12.

   f. Save your changes.

8. **Choose Print options.**

   a. Use the Page Layout tab to change the orientation to Portrait.

   b. Turn off gridlines by deselecting both the Gridlines View and Gridlines Print checkboxes in the Sheet Options group.

   c. View the worksheet in Print Preview, then zoom in to enlarge the preview. Compare your screen to Figure A-21.

   d. Open the Print dialog box, then print one copy of the worksheet.

   e. Save your changes, then close the workbook.

FIGURE A-21

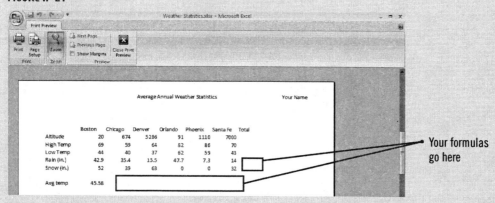

Your formulas go here

▼ **INDEPENDENT CHALLENGE 1**

A local real estate office has hired you to help them make the transition to using Excel in their office. They would like to list their properties in a worksheet. You've started a worksheet for this project that contains labels but no data.

a. Open the file EX A-3.xlsx from where you store your Data Files, then save it as **Real Estate Listings**.

b. Enter the data shown in Table A-4 in columns A, C, D, and E (the property address information should spill into column B).

TABLE A-4

Property Address	Price	Bedrooms	Bathrooms
1507 Cactus Lane	350000	3	2.5
32 California Lane	325000	3	4
60 Pottery Lane	475500	2	2
902 Fortunata Drive	295000	4	3
Total			

▼ INDEPENDENT CHALLENGE 1 (CONTINUED)

c. Use Page Layout View to create a header with the following components: a title in the center and your name on the right.

d. Create formulas for totals in cells C6:E6.

e. Save your changes, then preview your work and compare it to Figure A-22.

f. Print the worksheet.

g. Close the worksheet and exit Excel.

FIGURE A-22

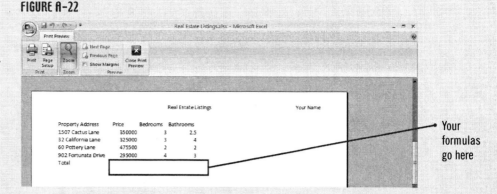

▼ INDEPENDENT CHALLENGE 2

FIGURE A-23

You are the General Manager for Hot Cars, a small auto parts supplier. Although the company is just three years old, it is expanding rapidly, and you are continually looking for ways to save time. You recently began using Excel to manage and maintain data on inventory and sales, which has greatly helped you to track information accurately and efficiently.

a. Start Excel.

b. Save a new workbook as **Hot Cars Sales** in the drive and folder where you store your Data Files.

c. Switch to an appropriate view, then add a header that contains your name in the left header text box and a title in the center header text box.

d. Using Figure A-23 as a guide, create labels for at least seven car manufacturers and sales for three months. Include other labels as appropriate. The car manufacturers should be in column A, and the months in columns B, C, and D. A Total row should be beneath the data, and a Total column should be in column E.

e. Enter values of your choice for the monthly sales for each manufacturer.

f. Add a formula in the Total column to calculate total monthly sales for each manufacturer. Add formulas at the bottom of each column of values to calculate the total for that column. Remember that you can use the SUM function to save time.

g. Save your changes, preview the worksheet, then print it.

▼ INDEPENDENT CHALLENGE 2 (CONTINUED)

Advanced Challenge Exercise

- Create a label two rows beneath the data in column A that says 15% increase.
- Create a formula in the row containing the 15% increase label that calculates a 15% increase in total monthly sales.
- Save the workbook.
- Display the formulas in the worksheet, then print a copy of the worksheet with formulas displayed.

h. Close the workbook(s) and exit Excel.

▼ INDEPENDENT CHALLENGE 3

FIGURE A-24

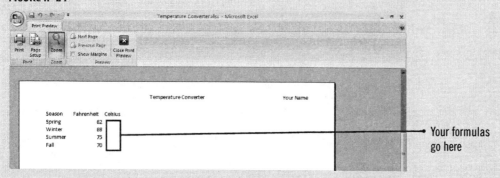

This Independent Challenge requires an Internet connection. Your office is starting a branch in Paris and you think it would be helpful to create a worksheet that can be used to convert Fahrenheit temperatures to Celsius, to help employees who are unfamiliar with this type of temperature measurement.

a. Start Excel, then save a blank workbook as **Temperature Converter** in the drive and folder where you store your Data Files.

b. Create column and row titles using Figure A-24 as a guide.

c. Create labels for each of the seasons.

d. In the appropriate cells, enter what you determine to be an ideal indoor temperature for each season.

e. Use your Web browser to find out the conversion rate for Fahrenheit to Celsius. (*Hint*: Use your favorite search engine to search on a term such as "temperature conversion.")

f. In the appropriate cells, create an equation that calculates the conversion of the Fahrenheit temperature you entered into a Celsius temperature.

g. Preview the worksheet in Page Layout View, adding your name to the header, as well as a meaningful title.

h. Save your work, then print the worksheet.

i. Close the file, then exit Excel.

▼ REAL LIFE INDEPENDENT CHALLENGE

FIGURE A-25

You've decided to quit your day job and turn your favorite hobby into a business. You've set up a small business selling the product or service of your choice. You want to use Excel to keep track of your many start-up costs.

a. Start Excel, open the file EX A-4.xlsx from the drive and folder where you store your Data Files, then save it as **Business Checkbook**.

b. Type check numbers (using your choice of a starting number) in cells A5 through A9.

c. Create sample data for the date, item, and amount in cells B5 through D9.

d. Save your work.

Advanced Challenge Exercise

- Use Help to find out about creating a series of numbers.
- Delete the contents of cells A5:A9.
- Create a series of numbers in cells A5:A9.
- In cell C15, type a brief description of how you created the series.
- Save the workbook.

e. Create formulas in cells E5:E9 that calculate a running balance. (*Hint*: For the first check, the running balance equals the starting balance minus a check; for the following checks, the running balance equals the previous balance value minus each check value.)

f. Create a formula in cell D10 that totals the amount of the checks.

g. Enter your name in cell C12, then compare your screen to Figure A-25.

h. Save your changes to the file, preview and print the worksheet, then exit Excel.

▼ VISUAL WORKSHOP

Open the file EX A-5.xlsx from the drive and folder where you store your Data Files, then save it as **Inventory Items**. Using the skills you learned in this unit, modify your worksheet so it matches Figure A-26. Enter formulas in cells D4 through D13 and in cells B14 and C14. Use the AutoSum button to make entering your formulas easier. Add your name in the left header text box, then print one copy of the worksheet once with the formulas not displayed, and one copy with the formulas displayed.

FIGURE A-26

Your formulas go here

241

Working with Formulas and Functions

Files You Will Need:

EX B-1.xlsx
EX B-2.xlsx
EX B-3.xlsx
EX B-4.xlsx

Using your knowledge of Excel basics, you can expand your worksheets to include more complex formulas and functions. To work more efficiently, you can copy and move existing formulas into other cells instead of manually retyping the same information. When copying or moving, you can also control how cell references are handled, so that your formulas always reference the intended cells. ▓▓▓ Grace Wong, vice president of finance at Quest Specialty Travel, needs to analyze tour revenue for the current year. She has asked you to prepare a worksheet that summarizes this revenue data and includes some statistical analysis. She would also like you to perform some what-if analysis, to see what quarterly revenues would look like with various projected increases.

OBJECTIVES

Create a complex formula

Insert a function

Type a function

Copy and move cell entries

Understand relative and absolute cell references

Copy formulas with relative cell references

Copy formulas with absolute cell references

Round a value with a function

Creating a Complex Formula

A **complex formula** is one that uses more than one arithmetic operator. You might, for example, need to create a formula that uses addition and multiplication. You can use arithmetic operators to separate tasks within a complex equation. In formulas containing more than one arithmetic operator, Excel uses the standard order of precedence rules to determine which operation to perform first. You can change the order of precedence in a formula by using parentheses around the part you want to calculate first. For example, the formula =4+2*5 equals 14, because the order of precedence dictates that multiplication is performed before addition. However, the formula =(4+2)*5 equals 30, because the parentheses cause 4+2 to be calculated first. ▰▰▰▰ You want to create a formula that calculates a 20% increase in tour revenue.

STEPS

1. **Start Excel, open the file EX B-1.xlsx from the drive and folder where you store your Data Files, then save it as** Tour Revenue Analysis

2. **Click cell B14, type =, click cell B12, then type +**
   In this first part of the formula, you are creating references to the total for Quarter 1.

3. **Click cell B12, then type *.2**
   The second part of this formula adds a 20% increase (B12*.2) to the original value of the cell. Compare your worksheet to Figure B-1.

4. **Click the Enter button ✓ on the formula bar**
   The result, 386122.344, appears in cell B14.

5. **Press [Tab], type =, click cell C12, type +, click cell C12, type *.2, then click ✓**
   The result, 410969.712, appears in cell C14.

6. **Drag the ✛ pointer from cell C14 to cell E14, click the Fill button ▦▾ in the Editing group on the Home tab of the Ribbon, then click Right**
   The calculated values appear in the selected range, as shown in Figure B-2.

7. **Save your work**

Reviewing the order of precedence

When you work with formulas that contain more than one operator, the order of precedence is very important because it affects the final value. For example, you might think the formula 4+2*5 equals 30, but because the order of precedence dictates that multiplication is performed before addition, the actual result is 14. If a formula contains two or more operators, such as 4+.55/4000*25, Excel performs the calculations in a particular sequence based on the following rules: Operations inside parentheses are calculated before any other operations. Reference operators (such as ranges) are calculated first. Exponents are calculated next, then any multiplication and division—progressing from left to right. Finally, addition and subtraction are calculated from left to right. In the example 4+.55/4000*25, Excel performs the arithmetic operations by first dividing 4000 into .55, then multiplying the result by 25, then adding 4. You can change the order of calculations by using parentheses. For example, in the formula (4+.55)/4000*25, Excel would first add 4 and .55, then divide that amount by 4000, then finally multiply by 25.

FIGURE B-1: Formula containing multiple arithmetic operators

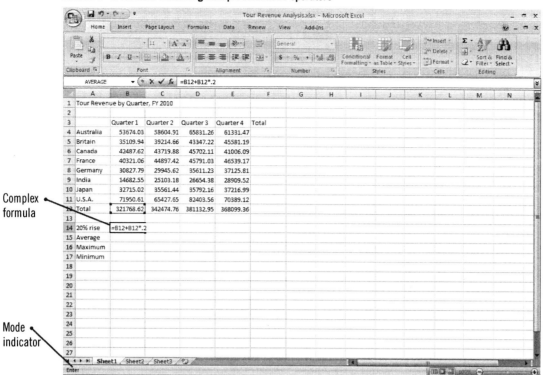

Complex formula

Mode indicator

FIGURE B-2: Complex formulas in worksheet

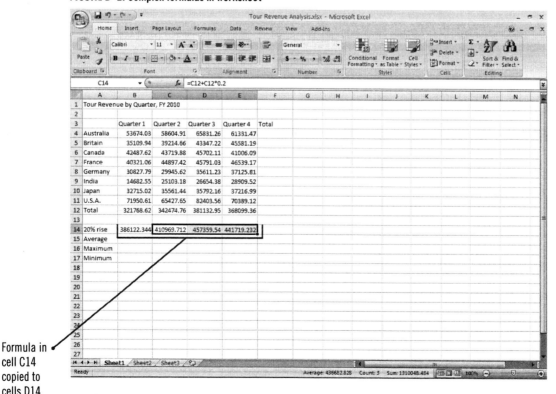

Formula in cell C14 copied to cells D14 and E14

Inserting a Function

Functions are predefined worksheet formulas that enable you to perform complex calculations easily. You can use the Insert Function button on the formula bar to choose a function from a dialog box. In addition to using the AutoSum button on the Ribbon to quickly insert the SUM function, you can click the AutoSum button list arrow to enter other frequently used functions, such as Average. Functions are organized into categories, such as Financial, Date & Time, and Statistical, based on their purpose. You can insert a function on its own, or as part of another formula. For example, you have used the SUM function on its own to add a range of cells. You could also use the SUM function within a formula that adds a range of cells and then multiplies the total by a decimal. If you use a function alone, it always begins with the formula prefix = (the equal sign). ▰▰▰ You need to calculate the average sales for the first quarter of the year, and decide to use a function to do so.

STEPS

QUICK TIP

When using the Insert Function button or the AutoSum button list arrow, it is not necessary to type the equal sign (=); Excel adds it as necessary.

1. **Click cell B15**

   This is the cell where you want to enter the calculation that averages revenue for the first quarter. You want to use the Insert Function dialog box to enter this function.

QUICK TIP

To learn about a function, click it in the Select a function list. Read the arguments and format required for the function.

2. **Click the Insert Function button 𝒇ₓ on the formula bar**

   An equal sign (=) is inserted in the active cell and in the formula bar, and the Insert Function dialog box opens, as shown in Figure B-3. In this dialog box, you specify the function you want to add by clicking it in the Select a function list. The Select a function list initially displays recently used functions. If you don't see the function you want, you can click the Or select a category list arrow to choose the desired category or, if you're not sure what category to choose, you can type the function name or a description in the Search for a function field. The AVERAGE function is a statistical function, but you don't need to open the Statistical category because this function appears in the Most Recently Used list.

3. **Click AVERAGE, if necessary, read the information that appears under the list, then click OK**

   The Function Arguments dialog box opens, where you define the range of cells you want to average.

QUICK TIP

When selecting a range, remember to select all the cells between and including the two references in the range.

4. **Click the Collapse button ▦ in the Number1 field of the Function Arguments dialog box, drag the ✛ pointer to select the range B4:B11, release the mouse button, then click the Expand button ▦**

   Clicking the Collapse button minimizes the dialog box so you can select cells in the worksheet. When you click the Expand button, the dialog box is restored, as shown in Figure B-4. You can also begin dragging in the worksheet to automatically minimize the dialog box; after you select the desired range, the dialog box is restored.

5. **Click OK**

   The Function Arguments dialog box closes and the calculated value displays in cell C15. The average revenue per country for Quarter 1 is 40221.0775.

6. **Click cell C15, click the AutoSum button list arrow Σ ▾ in the Editing group on the Home tab, then click Average**

   A ScreenTip beneath cell C15 displays the arguments needed to complete the function. The text number1 is shown in boldface type, telling you that the next step is to supply the first cell in the group you want to average. You want to average a range of cells.

7. **Drag ✛ to select the range C4:C11, then click the Enter button ✓ on the formula bar**

   The average revenue per country for the second quarter appears in cell C15.

8. **Select the range C15:E15, click the Fill button ▦ ▾ in the Editing group, then click Right**

   The formula in cell C15 is copied to the rest of the selected range, as shown in Figure B-5.

9. **Save your work**

FIGURE B-3: Insert Function dialog box

Search for a function field

Your list of recently used functions may differ

Or select a category list arrow

Description of selected function

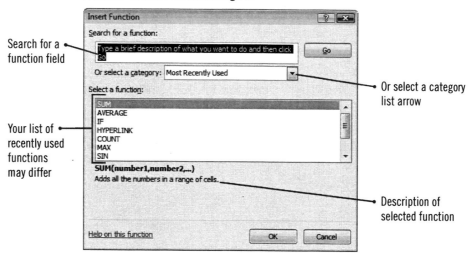

FIGURE B-4: Expanded Function Arguments dialog box

Function in formula bar

Insert Function button

Argument

Drag title bar of dialog box to move it if necessary

Description and argument format of selected function

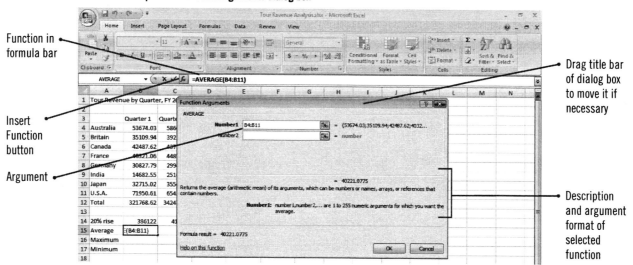

Excel 2007

FIGURE B-5: Average function in worksheet

Completed function appears in formula bar

Formula in cell C15 copied to cells D15 and E15

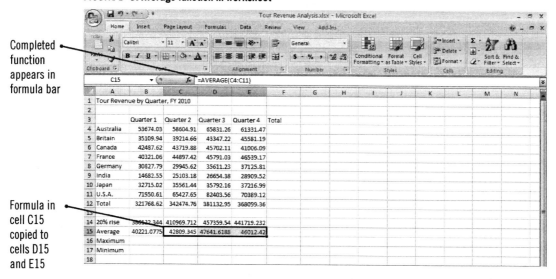

Working with Formulas and Functions

Typing a Function

In addition to entering a function using the Insert Function dialog box or the AutoSum button on the Ribbon, you can manually type the function into a cell and complete the arguments needed. This method requires that you know the name and initial characters of the function, but can be faster than opening several dialog boxes. Experienced Excel users often prefer this method, but it is only an alternative, not better or more correct than any other method. The AutoComplete feature makes it easier to enter function names because it suggests functions depending on the first letters you type. ▟▟▟▟▟ You want to calculate the maximum and minimum quarterly sales in your worksheet, and decide to manually enter these statistical functions.

STEPS

1. **Click cell B16, type =, then type m**

   Since you are manually typing this function, it is necessary to begin with the equal sign (=). The AutoComplete feature displays a list of function names beginning with M. Once you type an equal sign in a cell, each letter you type acts as a trigger to activate the AutoComplete feature. This feature minimizes the amount of typing you need to do to enter a function, and reduces typing and syntax errors.

QUICK TIP

You can single-click any function in the AutoComplete list to open a Screentip describing the selected function.

2. **Click MAX in the list**

   A Screentip appears, describing the function.

3. **Double-click MAX**

   The function is added to the cell and a Screentip appears beneath the cell to help you complete the formula. See Figure B-6.

4. **Select the range B4:B11, as shown in Figure B-7, then click the Enter button ☑ on the formula bar**

   The result, 71950.61, appears in cell B16. When you completed the entry, the closing parenthesis was automatically added to the formula.

5. **Click cell B17, type =, type m, then double-click MIN**

   The argument for the MIN function appears in the cell.

6. **Select the range B4:B11, then press [Enter]**

   The result, 14682.55, appears in cell B17.

7. **Select the range B16:E17, click the Fill button list arrow ▣▾ in the Editing group, then click Right**

   The maximum and minimum values for all of the quarters display in the selected range, as shown in Figure B-8.

8. **Save your work**

Using the COUNT and COUNTA functions

When you select a range, a count of cells in the range that are not blank appears in the status bar. For example, if you select the range A1:A5 and only cells A1 and A2 contain data, the status bar displays "Count: 2." To count nonblank cells more precisely, or to incorporate these calculations in a worksheet, you can use the COUNT and COUNTA functions. COUNT returns the number of cells that contain numeric data, including numbers, dates, and formulas. COUNTA returns the number of cells that contain any data at all, even text or a blank space. For example, the formula =COUNT(A1:A5) returns the number of cells in the range that contain numeric data, and the formula =COUNTA(A1:A5) returns the number of cells in the range that are not blank.

FIGURE B-6: MAX function in progress

13					
14	20% rise	386122.344	410969.712	457359.54	441719.232
15	Average	40221.0775	42809.345	47641.6188	46012.42
16	Maximum	=MAX(			
17	Minimum	MAX(**number1**, [number2], ...)			
18					

FIGURE B-7: Completing the MAX function

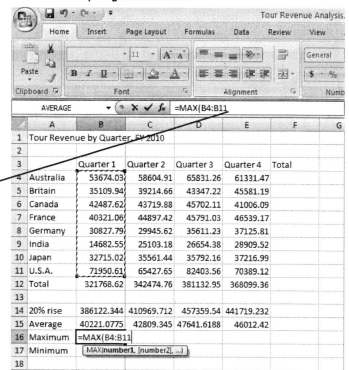

Closing parenthesis will be added automatically when you accept entry

FIGURE B-8: Completed MAX and MIN functions

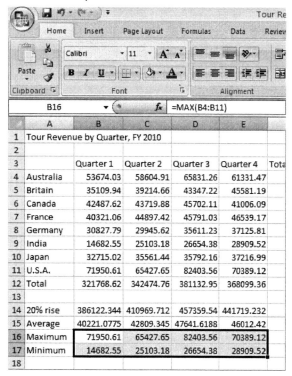

Working with Formulas and Functions

Copying and Moving Cell Entries

You can copy or move cells and ranges (or the contents within them) from one location to another using the Cut, Copy, and Paste buttons; the fill handle in the lower-right corner of the active cell; or the drag-and-drop feature. When you copy cells, the original data remains in the original location; when you cut or move it, the original data is deleted. You can also cut, copy, and paste cells or ranges from one worksheet to another. ▓▓▓▓ In addition to the 20% rise in tour revenue, you also want to show a 30% rise. Rather than retype this information, you copy and move the labels in these cells.

STEPS

1. **Select the range B3:E3, then click the Copy button 🖺 in the Clipboard group**

   The selected range (B3:E3) is copied to the **Office Clipboard**, a temporary storage area that holds the selections you copy or cut. A moving border surrounds the selected range until you press [Esc] or copy an additional item to the Clipboard. Notice that the information you copied remains in the selected range; if you had cut instead of copied, the information would have been deleted once it was pasted.

2. **Click the launcher 🖸 in the Clipboard group, click cell B19, then click the Paste button in the Clipboard group**

   The Office Clipboard pane opens, as shown in Figure B-9. Your Clipboard may contain additional items. When pasting an item from the Clipboard into the worksheet, you only need to specify the upper-left cell of the range where you want to paste the selection.

3. **Press [Delete]**

   The selected cells are empty. You have decided to paste the cells in a different row. You can repeatedly paste an item from the Office Clipboard as many times as you like, as long as the item remains in the Clipboard.

4. **Click cell B20 , click the first item in the Office Clipboard, then click the Close button on the Clipboard pane**

   Cells B20:E20 contain the copied labels.

5. **Click cell A14 , press and hold [Ctrl], point to any edge of the cell until the pointer changes to ▷⁺, drag ▷⁺ to cell A21, then release [Ctrl]**

   As you drag, the pointer changes to ▷⁺, as shown in Figure B-10.

6. **Click to the right of 2 in the formula bar, press [Backspace] , type 3, then press [Enter]**

7. **Click cell B21, type =, click cell B12 , type *1.3, then click ☑ on the formula bar**

   This new formula calculates a 30% increase of the revenue for Quarter 1, though using a different method from what you used previously. Anything you multiply by 1.3 returns an amount that's 130% of the original amount, or a 30% increase. Compare your screen to Figure B-11.

8. **Save your work**

FIGURE B-9: Copied data in Clipboard

Paste button

Copy button

Clipboard launcher

Item in Clipboard

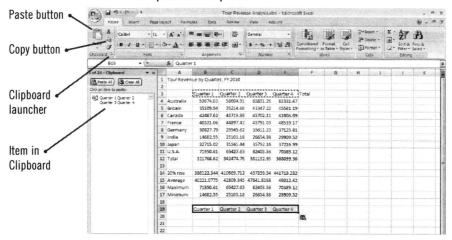

FIGURE B-10: Copying cell contents with drag-and-drop

Cell contents being copied

Plus (+) indicates copying in progress

Indicates new location of copy

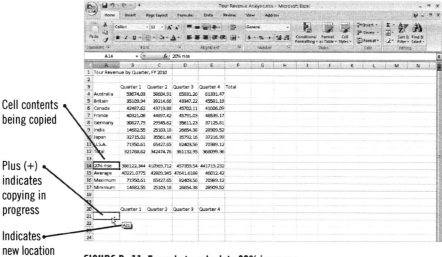

FIGURE B-11: Formula to calculate 30% increase

Formula calculates 30% increase

Inserting and deleting selected cells

As you add formulas to your workbook, you may need to insert or delete cells. When you do this, Excel automatically adjusts cell references to reflect their new locations. To insert cells, click the Insert button list arrow in the Cells group on the Home tab, then click Insert Cells. The Insert dialog box opens, asking if you want to insert a cell and move the selected cell down or to the right of the new one. To delete one or more selected cells, click the Delete button list arrow in the Cells group, click Delete Cells, and in the Delete dialog box, indicate which way you want to move the adjacent cells. When using this option, be careful not to disturb row or column alignment that may be necessary to maintain the accuracy of cell references in the worksheet. Click the Insert or Delete button to add/delete a single cell.

Working with Formulas and Functions

Understanding Relative and Absolute Cell References

As you work in Excel, you may want to reuse formulas in different parts of a worksheet to reduce the amount of data you have to retype. For example, you might want to include a what-if analysis in one part of a worksheet showing a set of sales projections if sales increase by 10%, and another analysis in another part of the worksheet showing projections if sales increase by 50%; you can copy the formulas from one section to another and just change the "1" to a "5". But when you copy formulas, it is important to make sure that they refer to the correct cells. To do this, you need to understand the difference between relative and absolute cell references. ▓▓▓▓ You plan to reuse formulas in different parts of your worksheets, so you want to understand relative and absolute cell references.

- **Use relative references when you want to preserve the relationship to the formula location**

    When you create a formula that references other cells, Excel normally does not "record" the exact cell address. Instead, it looks at the relationship that cell has to the cell containing the formula. For example, in Figure B-12, cell F5 contains the formula: =SUM(B5:E5). When Excel retrieves values to calculate the formula in cell F5, it actually looks for "the cell four columns to the left of the formula," which in this case is cell B5. This way, if you copy the cell to a new location, such as cell F6, the results will reflect the new formula location, and will automatically retrieve the values in cells B6, C6, D6, and E6. These are **relative cell references**, because Excel is recording the input cells *in relation to* or *relative to* the formula cell.

    In most cases, you want to use relative cell references when copying or moving, so this is the Excel default. In Figure B-12, the formulas in F5:F12 and in B13:F13 contain relative cell references. They total the "four cells to the left of" or the "eight cells above" the formulas.

- **Use absolute cell references when you want to preserve the exact cell address in a formula**

    There are times when you want Excel to retrieve formula information from a specific cell, and you don't want the cell address in the formula to change when you copy it to a new location. For example, you might have a price in a specific cell that you want to use in all formulas, regardless of their location. If you used relative cell referencing, the formula results would be incorrect, because Excel would use a different cell every time you copied the formula. Therefore you need to use an **absolute cell reference**, a reference that does not change when you copy the formula.

    You create an absolute cell reference by placing a $ (dollar sign) in front of both the column letter and the row number of the cell address. You can either type the dollar sign when typing the cell address in a formula (for example, "=C12*B16"), or you can select a cell address on the formula bar and then press [F4] and the dollar signs are added automatically. Figure B-13 show formulas containing both absolute and relative references. The formulas in cells B19 to E26 use absolute cell references to refer to a potential sales increase of 50%, shown in cell B16.

FIGURE B-12: Formulas containing relative references

Formula containing relative references

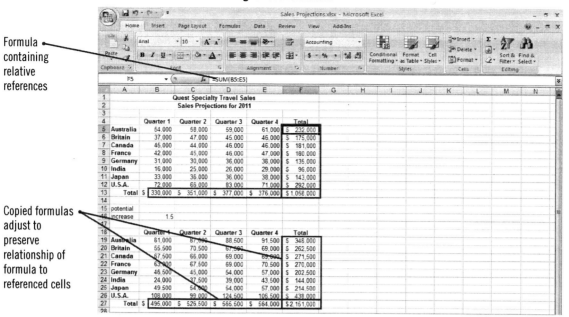

Copied formulas adjust to preserve relationship of formula to referenced cells

FIGURE B-13: Formulas containing absolute and relative references

Cell referenced in absolute formulas

Relative references in copied formulas adjust

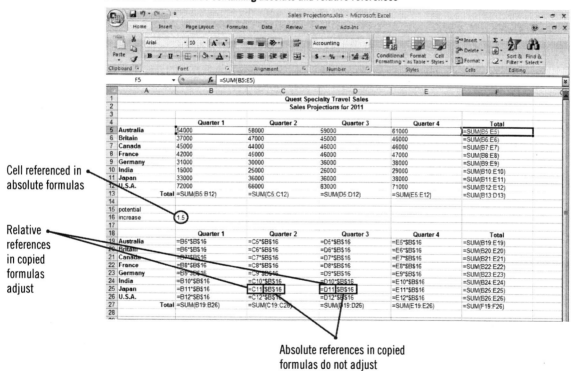

Absolute references in copied formulas do not adjust

Using a mixed reference

Sometimes when you copy a formula, you want to change the row reference, but keep the column reference the same. This type of cell referencing combines elements of both absolute and relative referencing and is called a **mixed reference**. For example, when copied, a formula containing the mixed reference C$14 would change the column letter relative to its new location, but not the row number.

In the mixed reference $C14, the column letter would not change, but the row number would be updated relative to its location. Like the absolute reference, a mixed reference can be created using the [F4] function key. With each press of the [F4] key, you cycle through all the possible combinations of relative, absolute, and mixed references (C14, C14, $C14, C14).

Copying Formulas with Relative Cell References

Copying and moving a cell allows you to reuse a formula you've already created. Copying cells is usually faster than retyping the formulas in them, and helps to prevent typing errors. You can use the Copy and Paste commands or the fill handle to copy formulas. The Fill button list arrow can also be used to fill cells containing formulas going left, right, up, down, and in series. If the cells you are copying contain relative cell references and you want to maintain the relative referencing, you don't need to make any changes to the cells before copying them. ~~[illegible]~~ You want to copy the formula in cell B21, which calculates the 30% increase in quarterly sales for quarter 1, to cells C21 through E21. You also want to create formulas to calculate total sales for each tour country.

STEPS

1. **Click cell B21, if necessary, then click the Copy button [icon] in the Clipboard group**

   The formula for calculating the 30% sales increase during Quarter 1 is copied to the Clipboard. Notice that the formula =B12*1.3 appears in the formula bar and a moving border surrounds the active cell.

2. **Click cell C21, then click the Paste button in the Clipboard group**

   The formula from cell B21 is copied into cell C21, where the new result of 445217.188 appears. Notice in the formula bar that the cell references have changed, so that cell C12 is referenced in the formula. This formula contains a relative cell reference, which tells Excel to substitute new cell references within the copied formulas as necessary. This maintains the same relationship between the new cells containing the formula and the cells within the formula. In this case, Excel adjusted the formula so that cell C12—the cell reference nine rows above C21—replaced cell B12, the cell reference nine rows above B21. You can drag the fill handle in a cell to copy cells or to continue a series of data (such as Quarter 1, Quarter 2, etc.) based on previous cells. This option is called **Auto Fill**.

3. **Point to the fill handle in cell C21 until the pointer changes to ✚, press and hold the left mouse button, drag ✚ to select the range C21:E21, then release the mouse button**

   See Figure B-14. A formula similar to the one in cell C21 now appears in the range D21:E21. After you release the mouse button, the **Auto Fill Options button** appears, so you can fill the cells with only specific elements of the copied cell if you wish.

4. **Click cell F4, click the AutoSum button Σ in the Editing group, then click the Enter button ✓ on the formula bar**

5. **Click [icon] in the Clipboard group, select the range F5:F6, then click Paste**

   See Figure B-15. After you release the mouse button, the **Paste Options button** appears, so you can paste only specific elements of the copied selection if you wish. The formula for calculating quarterly revenue for tours in Britain appears in the formula bar. You would like totals to appear in cells F7:F11. The Fill command in the Editing group can be used to copy the formula into the remaining cells.

6. **Select the range F6:F11**

7. **Click the Fill button list arrow [icon] in the Editing group, then click Down**

   The formulas are copied to each cell. Compare your worksheet to Figure B-16.

8. **Save your work**

FIGURE B-14: Copying a formula with the fill handle

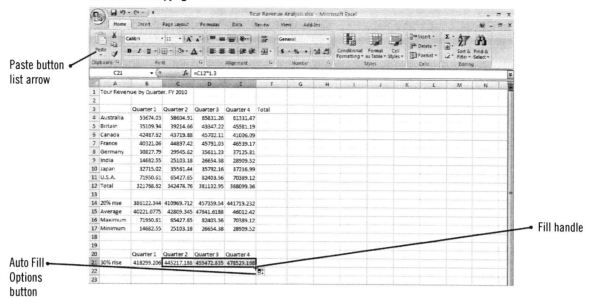

Paste button list arrow

Fill handle

Auto Fill Options button

FIGURE B-15: The results of using the Paste button

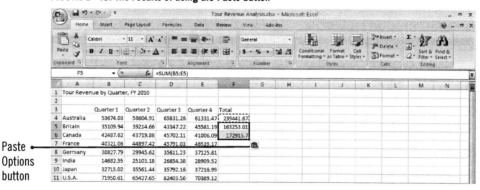

Paste Options button

FIGURE B-16: Copying cells using Fill Down

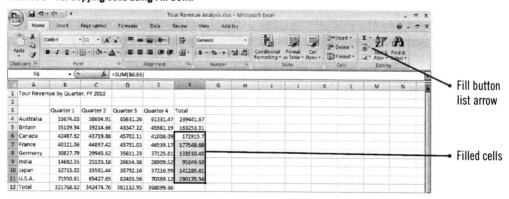

Fill button list arrow

Filled cells

Using Auto Fill options

When you use the fill handle to copy cells, the Auto Fill Options button appears. Auto Fill options differ depending on what you are copying. If you had selected cells containing a series (such as "Monday" and "Tuesday") and then used the fill handle, you would see options for continuing the series (such as "Wednesday" and "Thursday") or for simply pasting the copied cells. Clicking the Auto Fill Options button opens a list that lets you choose from the following options: Copy Cells, Fill Series (if applicable), Fill Formatting Only, or Fill Without Formatting. Choosing Copy Cells means that the cell and its formatting will be copied. The Fill Formatting Only option copies only the formatting attributes, but not the formula and its cell references. The Fill Without Formatting option copies the formula and its cell references, but no formatting attributes. Copy Cells is the default option when using the fill handle to copy a formula, so if you want to copy the cell, its references and formatting, you can ignore this button.

Copying Formulas with Absolute Cell References

When copying formulas, you might want one or more cell references in the formula to remain unchanged in relation to the formula. In such an instance, you need to apply an absolute cell reference before copying the formula, to preserve the specific cell address when the formula is copied. You create an absolute reference by placing a dollar sign ($) before the row letter and column number of the address (for example A1). ▓▓▓▓ You need to do some what-if analysis to see how various sales percentage increases might affect total revenues. You decide to add a column that calculates a possible increase in the total tour revenue, and then change the percentage to see various potential results.

STEPS

1. **Click cell H1, type Change, then press [→]**

2. **Type 1.1, then press [Enter]**
    You store the increase factor that will be used in the what-if analysis in this cell. The value 1.1 can be used to calculate a 10% increase; anything you multiply by 1.1 returns an amount that's 110% of the original amount, or a 10% increase.

3. **Click cell H3, type What if?, then press [Enter]**

4. **In cell H4, type =, click F4, type *, click cell I1, then click the Enter button ☑ on the formula bar**
    The result, 263385.8, appears in cell H4. This value represents the total annual revenue for Australia if there is a 10% increase. You want to perform a what-if analysis for all the tour countries.

5. **Drag the fill handle of cell H4 to extend the selection to cell H11**
    The resulting values in the range H5:H11 are all zeros, which is not the result you wanted. See Figure B-17. Because you used relative cell addressing in cell H4, the copied formula adjusted so that the formula in cell H5 is =F5*I2. Because there is no value in cell I2, the result is 0, an error. You need to use an absolute reference in the formula to keep the formula from adjusting itself. That way, it will always reference cell I1.

6. **Click cell H4, press [F2] to change to Edit mode, then press [F4]**
    When you press [F2], the range finder outlines the arguments of the equation in blue and green. When you press [F4], dollar signs are inserted in the cell address, changing the I1 cell reference to an absolute reference.

7. **Click ☑, then drag ＋ to extend the selection to range H4:H11**
    The formula correctly contains an absolute cell reference, and the value of H4 remains unchanged. The correct values for a 10% increase appear in cells H4:H11. You now want to see a 20% increase in sales.

8. **Click cell I1, type 1.2, then click ☑**
    The values in the range H4:H11 change to reflect the 20% increase. Compare your worksheet to Figure B-18.

9. **Save your work**

FIGURE B-17: Creating an absolute reference in formula

Absolute cell reference in formula

Incorrect values from relative referencing in copied formulas

FIGURE B-18: What-if analysis with modified change factor

Modified value

Using the fill handle for sequential text or values

Often, you need to fill cells with sequential text: months of the year, days of the week, years, or text plus a number (Quarter 1, Quarter 2,...). For example, you might want to create a worksheet that calculates data for every month of the year. Using the fill handle, you can quickly and easily create labels for the months of the year just by typing January in a cell. Drag the fill handle from the cell containing January until you have all the monthly labels you need. You can easily fill cells using sequences by dragging the fill handle. As you drag the fill handle, Excel automatically extends the existing sequence. (The content of the last filled cell appears in the ScreenTip.) Use the Fill button list arrow in the Editing group, then click Series to examine all the fill series options for the current selection.

Rounding a Value with a Function

The more you explore features and tools in Excel, the more ways you'll find to simplify your work and convey information more efficiently. For example, cells containing financial data are often easier to read if they contain fewer decimals than those that appear by default. You can achieve this result by using the ROUND function, to round down your results. ▨▨▨ In your worksheet, you'd like to round the cells showing the 20% rise in sales to show fewer digits; after all, it's not important to show cents in the projections, only whole dollars. You want Excel to round the calculated value to the nearest integer. You decide to edit cell B14 so it includes the ROUND function, and then copy the edited formula into the other formulas in this row.

STEPS

1. **Click cell B14, then click to the right of = on the formula bar**

   You want to position the function at the beginning of the formula, before any values or arguments.

2. **Type RO**

   AutoComplete displays a list of functions beginning with RO.

3. **Double-click ROUND in the AutoComplete list**

   The new function and an opening parenthesis are added to the formula, as shown in Figure B-19. A few additional modifications are needed to complete your edit of the formula. You need to indicate the number of digits to which the function should round numbers down, and you also need to add a closing parenthesis around the set of arguments that come after the ROUND function.

4. **Press [END], type ,0), then click the Enter button ☑ on the formula bar**

   The comma separates the arguments within the formula, and 0 indicates that you don't want any decimals to appear in the calculated value. When you complete the edit, the parenthesis at either end of the formula briefly become bold, indicating that the formula has the correct number of open and closed parentheses and is balanced.

5. **Click the fill handle of cell B14, then drag the ✚ pointer to cell E14**

   When you release the mouse button, the formula in cell B14 is copied to the selected range. All the values are rounded to display no decimals. Compare your worksheet to Figure B-20.

6. **Click cell A25, type your name, then click ☑ on the formula bar**

7. **Save your work, preview and print the worksheet, then exit Excel**

FIGURE B-19: Adding a function to an existing formula

ROUND function and opening parenthesis inserted in formula

Screentip indicates what information is needed

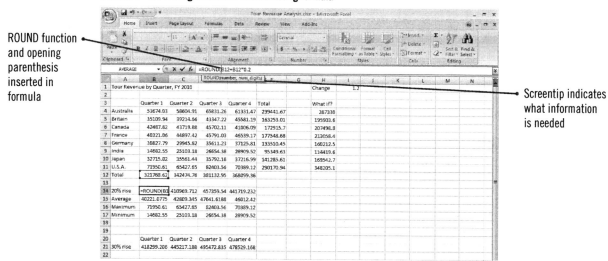

FIGURE B-20: Function added to formula

Function surrounds existing formula

Calculated values with no decimals

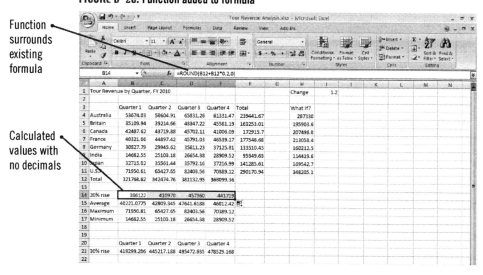

Creating a new workbook using a template

Excel **templates** are predesigned workbook files intended to save time when you create common documents such as balance sheets, expense statements, loan amortizations, sales invoices, or timecards. They contain labels, values, formulas, and formatting, so when you use a template all you have to do is customize it with your own information. Excel comes with many templates, and you can also create your own or find additional templates on the Web. Unlike a typical workbook, which has the file extension .xlsx, a template has the extension .xltx. To create a workbook using a template, click the Office button, then click New. The New Workbook dialog box opens. The Blank Workbook template is selected by default, because this is the template used to create a blank workbook with no content or special formatting. The left pane lists templates installed on your computer as well as many categories of templates available through Microsoft Office Online. Click a category, find the template you want, as shown in Figure B-21, click Download, then click Continue. A new workbook is created based on the template, so when you save the new file in the default format, it will have the

regular .xlsx extension. To save a workbook of your own as a template, open the Save As dialog box, then click the Save as type list arrow and change the file type to Excel Template.

FIGURE B-21: New Workbook dialog box

Working with Formulas and Functions

Practice

▼ CONCEPTS REVIEW

Label each element of the Excel worksheet window shown in Figure B-22.

FIGURE B-22

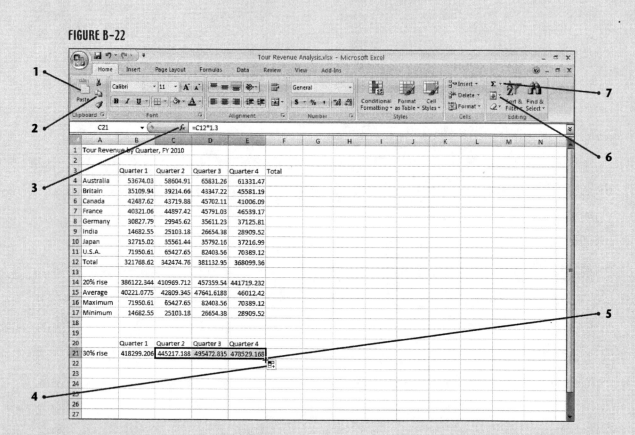

Match each term or button with the statement that best describes it.

8. **Launcher**

9. **Formula AutoComplete**

10. **Drag-and-drop**

11. **Fill handle**

12. **[Delete]**

a. Clears the contents of selected cells

b. Item on the Ribbon that opens a dialog box or task pane

c. Lets you move data from one cell to another without using the Clipboard

d. Displays an alphabetical list of functions from which you can choose

e. Lets you copy cell contents or continue a series of data into a range of selected cells

Select the best answer from the list of choices.

13. What type of cell reference changes when it is copied?
- **a.** Circular
- **b.** Absolute
- **c.** Relative
- **d.** Specified

14. What type of cell reference is C$19?
- **a.** Relative
- **b.** Absolute
- **c.** Mixed
- **d.** Certain

15. Which key do you press to convert a relative cell reference to an absolute cell reference?
- **a.** [F2]
- **b.** [F4]
- **c.** [F5]
- **d.** [F6]

16. You can use any of the following features to enter a function *except*:
- **a.** Insert Function button.
- **b.** Formula AutoComplete.
- **c.** AutoSum button list arrow.
- **d.** Clipboard.

17. Which key do you press to copy while dragging-and-dropping selected cells?
- **a.** [Alt]
- **b.** [Ctrl]
- **c.** [F2]
- **d.** [Tab]

▼ SKILLS REVIEW

1. Create a complex formula.

a. Open the file EX B-2.xlsx from the drive and folder where you store your Data Files, then save it as **Candy Supply Company Inventory**.

b. In cell B11, create a complex formula that calculates a 30% decrease in the total number of cases of Snickers bars.

c. Use the Fill button to copy this formula into cell C11 through cell E11, as shown in Figure B-23.

d. Save your work.

FIGURE B-23

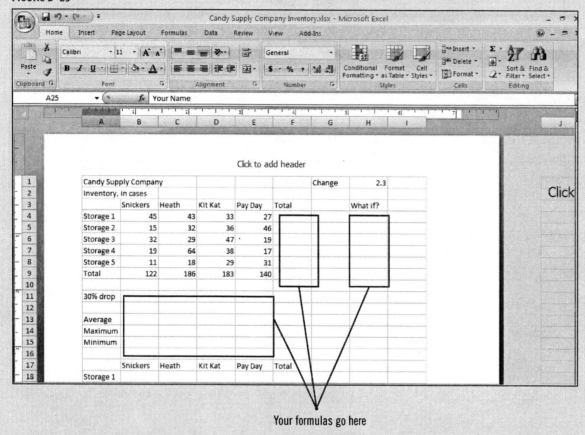

Your formulas go here

2. Insert a function.

a. Use the AutoSum button to create a formula in cell B13 that averages the number of cases of Snickers bars in each storage area. (*Hint*: Click the AutoSum button list arrow to open a list of available functions.)

b. Use the Insert Function button to create a formula in cell B14 that calculates the most cases of Snickers bars in a storage area.

c. Use the AutoSum button to create a formula in cell B15 that calculates the minimum number of cases of Snickers bars in a storage area.

d. Save your work.

3. Type a function.

a. In cell C13, type a formula that includes a function to average the number of cases of Heath bars. (*Hint*: Use AutoComplete to enter the function.)

b. In cell C14, type a formula that includes a function to calculate the maximum number of cases of Heath bars in a storage area.

c. In cell C15, type a formula that includes a function to calculate the minimum number of cases of Heath bars in a storage area.

d. Save your work.

4. Copy and move cell entries.

   a. Select the range B3:F3.

   b. Copy the selection into the Clipboard.

   c. Open the Clipboard task pane, then paste the selection into cell B17.

   d. Select the range A4:A9.

   e. Use the drag-and-drop method to copy the selection to cell A18. (*Hint*: The results should fill the range A18:A23.)

   f. Select the range H1:I1.

   g. Move the selection using the drag-and-drop method to cell G1.

   h. Save your work.

5. Understand relative and absolute cell referencess.

   a. Write a brief description of the difference between relative and absolute references.

   b. List at least three situations in which you think a business might use an absolute reference in its calculations. Examples can include calculations for different types of worksheets, such as timecards, invoices, and budgets.

6. Copy formulas with relative cell references.

   a. Select the range C13:C15.

   b. Use the fill handle to copy these cells to the range D13:E15.

   c. Calculate the total in cell F4.

   d. Use the Fill button to copy the formula in cell F4 down to cells F5:F9.

   e. Use the fill handle to copy the formula in cell E11 to cell F11.

   f. Save your work.

7. Copy formulas with absolute cell references.

   a. In cell H1, enter the value **1.575**.

   b. In cell H4, create a formula that multiplies F4 and an absolute reference to cell H1.

   c. Use the fill handle to copy the formula in cell H4 to cells H5 and H6.

   d. Use the Copy and Paste buttons to copy the formula in cell H4 to cells H7 and H8.

   e. Change the amount in cell H1 to **2.3**.

   f. Save your work.

8. Round a value with a function.

   a. Click cell H4.

   b. Edit this formula to include the ROUND function showing one digit.

   c. Use the fill handle to copy the formula in cell H4 to the range H5:H8.

   d. Enter your name in cell A25, then compare your work to Figure B-23.

   e. Save, preview, print, and close the workbook, then exit Excel.

▼ INDEPENDENT CHALLENGE 1

You are thinking of starting a small breakfast and lunch diner. Before you begin, you need to evaluate what you think your monthly expenses will be. You've started a workbook, but need to complete the entries and add formulas.

a. Open the file EX B-3.xlsx from the drive and folder where you store your Data Files, then save it as **Estimated Diner Expenses**.

b. Make up your own expense data and enter it in cells B4:B10. (Monthly sales are included in the worksheet.)

c. Create a formula in cell C4 that calculates the annual rent.

d. Copy the formula in cell C4 to the range C5:C10.

e. Move the label in cell A15 to cell A14.

f. Create a formula in cells B11 and C11 that totals the expenses.

g. Create a formula in cell C13 that calculates annual sales.

h. Create a formula in cell B14 that determines whether you will make a profit or loss, then copy the formula into cell C14.

i. Copy the labels in cells B3:C3 to cells E3:F3.

j. Type **Projection increase** in cell G1, then type **.2** in cell I1.

k. Create a formula in cell E4 that calculates an increase in the monthly rent by the amount in cell I1. You will be copying this formula to other cells, so you'll need to use an absolute reference.

l. Create a formula in cell F4 that calculates an annual increase based on the calculation in cell E4.

m. Create formulas in cells E13 and E14 and cells F13 and F14 that calculates monthly and annual sales and profit/loss based on the increase in cell E4.

n. Copy the formulas in cells E4:F4 in the remaining monthly and annual expenses.

o. Change the projection increase to **.15**, then compare your work to the sample in Figure B-24.

p. Enter your name in a cell in the worksheet.

q. Save your work, preview and print the worksheets, then close the workbook and exit Excel.

FIGURE B-24

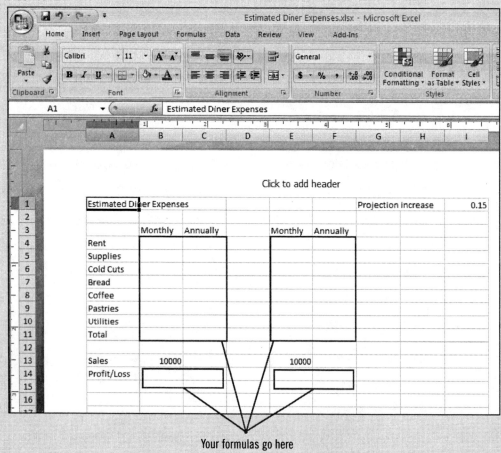

▼ INDEPENDENT CHALLENGE 2

The Pamper Yourself Salon & Day Spa is a small, growing spa that has hired you to organize its accounting records using Excel. The owners want you to track the company's expenses. Before you were hired, one of the bookkeepers began entering last year's expenses in a workbook, but the analysis was never completed.

a. Start Excel, open the file EX B-4.xlsx from the drive and folder where you store your Data Files, then save it as **Pamper Yourself Finances**. The worksheet includes labels for functions such as the Average, Maximum, and Minimum amounts of each of the expenses in the worksheet.

b. Think about what information would be important for the bookkeeping staff to know.

c. Create formulas in the Total column and row using the Sum function.

d. Create formulas in the Average, Maximum, and Minimum columns and rows using the method of your choice.

e. Save your work, then compare your worksheet to the sample shown in Figure B-25.

Advanced Challenge Exercise

- Create the label **Expense categories** in cell B19.
- In cell A19, create a formula using the COUNT function that determines the total number of expense categories listed per quarter.
- Save the workbook.

f. Enter your name in cell A25.

g. Preview the worksheet, then print it.

h. Save your work, then close the workbook and exit Excel.

FIGURE B-25

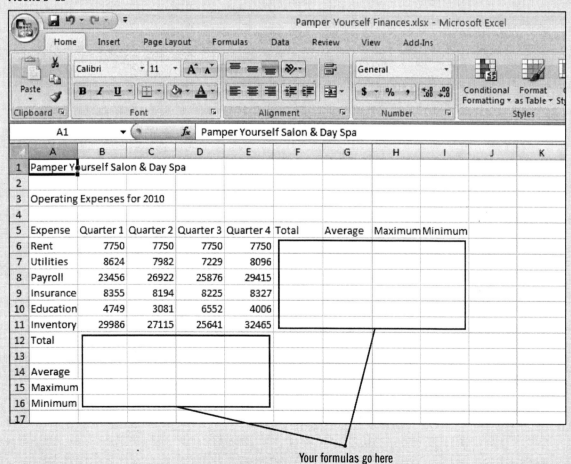

Your formulas go here

Working with Formulas and Functions

Excel 2007

▼ INDEPENDENT CHALLENGE 3

As the accounting manager of a locally-owned clothing store, it is your responsibility to calculate and submit accrued sales tax payments on a monthly basis to the state government. You've decided to use an Excel workbook to make these calculations.

a. Start Excel, then save a new, blank workbook to the drive and folder where you store your Data Files as **Sales Tax Calculations**.

b. Decide on the layout for all columns and rows. The worksheet will contain data for four stores, which you can name by store number, neighborhood, or another method of your choice. For each store, you will calculate total sales tax based on the local sales tax rate. You'll also calculate total tax owed for all four stores.

c. Make up sales data for at least four stores.

d. Enter the rate to be used to calculate the sales tax, using your own local rate.

e. Create formulas to calculate the sales tax owed for each store. If you don't know the local tax rate, use **6.5%**.

f. Create a formula to total all the owed sales tax, then compare your work to the sample shown in Figure B-26.

Advanced Challenge Exercise

■ Use the ROUND function to eliminate any decimals in the sales tax figures for each store and the total due.
■ Save the workbook.

g. Add your name to the header.

h. Save your work, preview and print each worksheet, then close the workbook and exit Excel.

FIGURE B-26

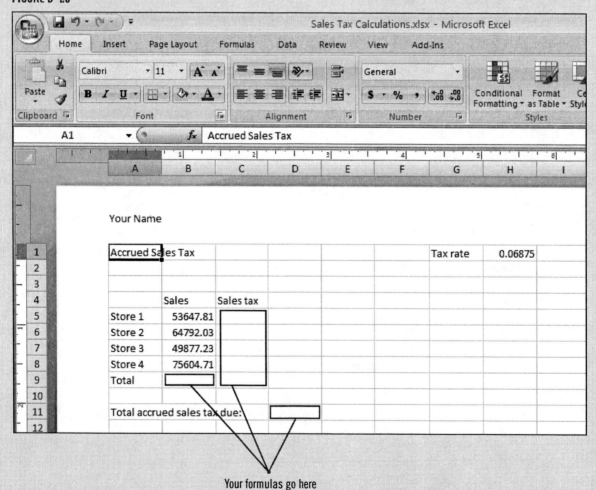

▼ REAL LIFE INDEPENDENT CHALLENGE

Many of your friends are purchasing homes, and you are thinking about taking the plunge yourself. As you begin the round of open houses and realtors' listings, you notice that there are many fees associated with buying a home. Some fees are based on a percentage of the purchase price and others are a flat fee; overall, they seem to represent a substantial amount above the purchase prices you see listed. You've seen three houses so far that interest you; one is moderately priced, one is more expensive, and the third is still more expensive. You decide to create an Excel workbook to figure out the real cost of buying each one.

a. Find out the typical cost or percentage rate of at least three fees that are usually charged when buying a home and taking out a mortgage. (*Hint*: If you have access to the Internet you can research the topic of home-buying on the Web, or you can ask friends about standard rates or percentages for items such as title insurance, credit reports, and inspection fees.)

b. Start Excel, then save a new, blank workbook to the drive and folder where you store your Data Files as **Home Purchase Fees**.

c. Create labels and enter data for three homes. If you enter this information across the columns in your worksheet, you should have one column for each house, with the purchase price in the cell below each label. Be sure to enter a different purchase price for each house.

FIGURE B-27

Your formulas go here

d. Create labels for the Fees column and for an Amount or Rate column. Enter the information on the three fees you have researched.

e. In each house column, enter formulas that calculate the fee for each item. The formulas (and use of absolute or relative referencing) will vary depending on whether the charges are a flat fee or based on a percentage of the purchase price.

f. Total the fees for each house, create formulas that add the total fees to the purchase price, then compare your work to the sample in Figure B-27.

g. Enter a title for the worksheet in the header.

h. Enter your name in the header, preview the worksheet, then print it.

i. Save your work, then close the file and exit Excel.

▼ VISUAL WORKSHOP

Create the worksheet shown in Figure B-28 using the skills you learned in this unit. Save the workbook as **Sales Analysis** to the drive and folder where you store your Data Files. Enter your name in the header as shown, then preview and print one copy of the worksheet. Print a second copy of the worksheet with the formulas showing.

FIGURE B-28

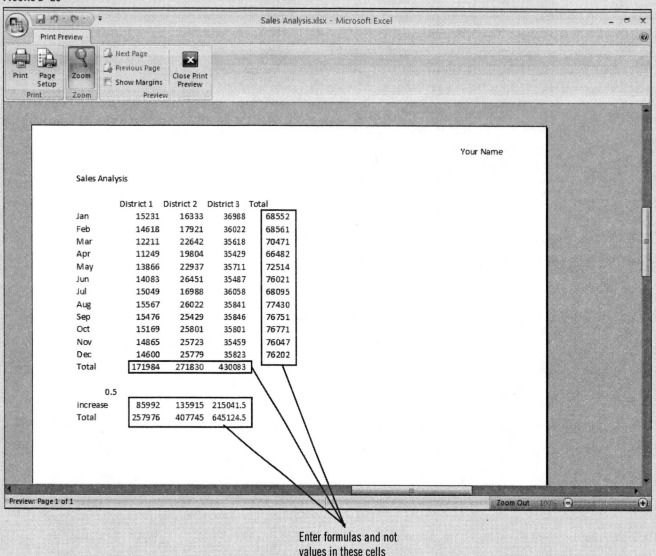

Enter formulas and not values in these cells

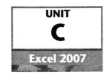

Formatting a Worksheet

You can use formatting features to make a worksheet more attractive or easier to read, and to emphasize key data. You can apply different formatting attributes such as colors, font styles, and font sizes to the cell contents, you can adjust column width and row height, and you can insert or delete columns and rows. You can also apply conditional formatting so that cells meeting certain criteria are formatted differently. This makes it easy to empha-size selected information, such as sales that exceed or fall below a certain threshold. The marketing managers at QST have requested information on advertising expenses for all QST locations during the past four quarters. Grace Wong has created a worksheet listing this information. She asks you to format the worksheet to make it easier to read and to call attention to important data.

OBJECTIVES

Format values

Change font and font size

Change attributes and alignment

Adjust column width

Insert and delete rows and columns

Apply colors, patterns, and borders

Apply conditional formatting

Name and move a sheet

Check spelling

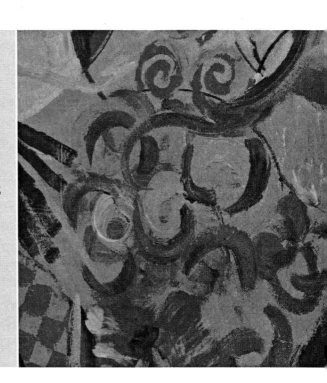

Formatting Values

The **format** of a cell determines how the labels and values look—for example, whether the contents appear boldfaced, italicized, or with dollar signs and commas. Formatting changes only the appearance of a value or label; it does not alter the actual data in any way. To format a cell or range, first you select it, then you apply the formatting using the Ribbon or a keyboard shortcut. You can apply formatting before or after you enter data in a cell or range. ▨▨▨ Grace has provided you with a worksheet that lists individual advertising expenses, and you're ready to improve its appearance and readability. You decide to start by formatting some of the values so they display as currency, percentages, and dates.

STEPS

1. **Start Excel, open the file EX C-1.xlsx from the drive and folder where you store your Data Files, save it as QST Advertising Expenses, click the View tab on the Ribbon, then click the Page Layout button**

   This worksheet is difficult to interpret because all the information looks the same. In some columns, the contents appear cut off because there is too much data to fit given the current column width. You decide not to widen the columns yet, because the other changes you plan to make might affect column width and row height. The first thing you want to do is format the data showing the cost of each ad.

2. **Select the range E4:E32, then click the Accounting Number Format button ▣ in the Number group on the Home tab**

   The default Accounting Number format adds dollar signs and two decimal places to the data, as shown in Figure C-1. Formatting this data in accounting format makes it easier to recognize. Excel automatically resizes the column to display the new formatting. The Accounting and Currency formats are both used for monetary values, but the Accounting format aligns currency symbols and decimal points of numbers in a column.

3. **Select the range G4:I32, then click the Comma Style button ▣ in the Number group**

   The values in columns G, H, and I display the Comma Style format, which does not include a dollar sign but can be useful for some types of accounting data.

4. **Select the range J4:J32, click the Number Format list arrow, click Percentage, then click the Increase Decimal button ▣ in the Number group**

   The data in the % of Total column is now formatted with a percent sign (%) and three decimal places. The Format list arrow lets you choose from popular number formats and shows an example of what the selected cell or cells would look like in each format (when multiple cells are selected, the example is based on the first cell in the range). Each time you click the Increase Decimal button, you add one decimal place; clicking the button twice would add two decimal places.

5. **Click the Decrease Decimal button ▣ in the Number group twice**

   Two decimal places are removed.

6. **Select the range B4:B31, click the launcher ▣ in the Number group**

   The Format Cells dialog box opens with the Date category already selected on the Number tab.

7. **Select the first 14-Mar-01 format in the Type list box as shown in Figure C-2, then click OK**

   The dates in column B appear in the 14-Mar-01 format. The second 14-Mar-01 format in the list displays all days in two digits (it adds a leading zero if the day is only a single-digit number), while the one you chose displays single-digit days without a leading zero. You can also open the Format Cells dialog box by right-clicking a selected range.

8. **Select the range C4:C31, right-click the range, click Format Cells on the shortcut menu, click 14-Mar in the Type list box in the Format Cells dialog box, then click OK**

   Compare your worksheet to Figure C-3.

9. **Press [Ctrl][Home], then save your work**

Formatting a Worksheet

FIGURE C-1: Advertising expense worksheet

Number Format list arrow

Accounting Number Format button

Commands in Number group change the appearance of numbers

Format as Table button

Decrease Decimal button

Increase Decimal button

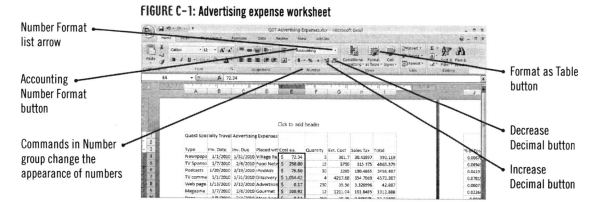

FIGURE C-2: Format Cells dialog box

Sample of selected type

Number format categories

This format looks similar to the one below it but displays single digit days without a leading zero

Date formats

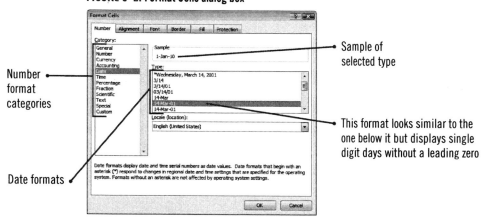

FIGURE C-3: Worksheet with formatted values

New format displays in the format box

Date formats appear without year

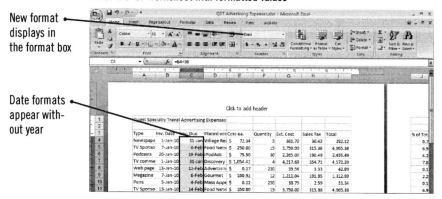

Formatting as a table

Excel includes 60 predefined table styles to make it easy to format selected worksheet cells as a table. You can apply table styles to any range of cells that you want to format quickly, or even to an entire worksheet, but they're especially useful for those ranges with labels in the left column and top rows, and totals in the bottom row or right column. To apply a table style, select the data to be formatted or click anywhere within the intended range (Excel can automatically detect a range of cells), click the Format as Table button in the Styles group on the Home tab, then click a style in the gallery, as shown in Figure C-4. Table styles are organized in three categories (Light, Medium, and Dark). Once you click a style, Excel confirms the range selection, then applies the style. Once you have formatted a range as a table, you can use Live Preview to preview with different choices by pointing to any style in the Table Styles gallery.

FIGURE C-4: Table Styles gallery

Changing Font and Font Size

A **font** is the name for a collection of characters (letters, numerals, symbols, and punctuation marks) with a similar, specific design. The **font size** is the physical size of the text, measured in units called points. A **point** is equal to 1/72 of an inch. The default font in Excel is 11-point Calibri. Table C-1 shows several fonts in different sizes. You can change the font and font size of any cell or range using the Ribbon, the Format Cells dialog box, or the Mini toolbar. You can open the Format Cells dialog box by clicking the launcher in the Font, Alignment, or Number group on the Home tab, or by right-clicking a selection, then clicking Format Cells in the shortcut menu. The Mini toolbar opens when you right-click a cell or range. ▓▓▓▓ You want to change the font and size of the labels and the worksheet title so that they stand out more from the data.

STEPS

QUICK TIP

To preview font and font size changes directly in selected cells, use the Font group on the Home tab; Live Preview shows font, font size, font color, and fill color when you hover the mouse pointer over selections in these lists and palettes.

1. **Right-click cell A1, click Format Cells on the shortcut menu, then click the Font tab in the Format Cells dialog box if necessary**
   See Figure C-5.

2. **Scroll down in the Font list to see an alphabetical listing of the fonts available on your computer, click Times New Roman in the Font list box, click 20 in the Size list box, preview the results in the Preview area, then click OK**
   The title appears in 20-point Times New Roman, and the Font group on the Home tab displays the new font and size information.

3. **Click the Increase Font Size button A˙ in the Font group twice**
   The size of the title increases to 24-point.

QUICK TIP

You can also format an entire row by clicking the row indicator button (or an entire column by clicking the column indicator button).

4. **Select the range A3:J3, right-click, then click the Font list arrow on the Mini toolbar**
   The Mini toolbar includes the most commonly used formatting tools, so it's great for making quick formatting changes. Notice that the font names on this font list are displayed in the font they represent.

QUICK TIP

Once you click the Font list arrow, you can quickly move to a font in the list by typing the first few characters of its name.

5. **Click Times New Roman, click the Font Size list arrow, then click 14**
   The Mini toolbar closes when you move the pointer away from the selection. Compare your worksheet to Figure C-6. Notice that some of the column headings are now too wide to appear fully in the column. Excel does not automatically adjust column widths to accommodate cell formatting; you have to adjust column widths manually. You'll learn to do this in a later lesson.

6. **Save your work**

TABLE C-1: Examples of fonts and font sizes

font	12 point	24 point
Calibri	Excel	Excel
Playbill	Excel	Excel
Comic Sans MS	Excel	Excel
Times New Roman	Excel	Excel

Formatting a Worksheet

FIGURE C-5: Font tab in the Format Cells dialog box

Currently selected font

Available fonts might differ on your computer

Effects options

Type a custom font size or select from the list

Font style options

Preview area shows sample of selected formatting

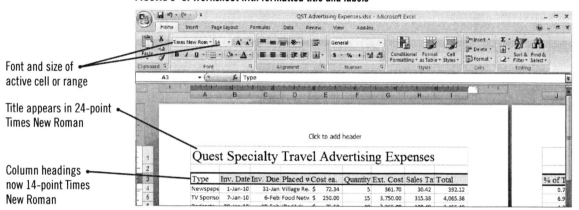

FIGURE C-6: Worksheet with formatted title and labels

Font and size of active cell or range

Title appears in 24-point Times New Roman

Column headings now 14-point Times New Roman

Inserting and adjusting clip art and other images

You can illustrate your worksheets using clip art and other images. A **clip** is an individual media file, such as art, sound, animation, or a movie. **Clip art** refers to images such as a corporate logo, a picture, or a photo. Microsoft Office comes with many clips available for your use. To add a clip to a worksheet, click Clip Art in the Illustrations group on the Insert tab. The Clip Art task pane opens. Here you can search for clips by typing one or more keywords (words related to your subject) in the Search for text box, then click Go. Clips that relate to your keywords appear in the Clip Art task pane, as shown in Figure C-7. (If you have a standard Office installation and an active Internet connection, you will see many clips available through Microsoft Office Online in addition to those on your computer.) Click the image you want, and it is inserted at the location of the active cell. You can also add your own images to a worksheet by clicking the Insert tab on the Ribbon, then clicking the Picture button. Navigate to the file you want, then click Insert Picture from File. To resize an image, drag any corner sizing handle. To move an image, point inside the clip until the pointer changes to ⬩, then drag it to a new location.

FIGURE C-7: Results of Clip Art search

Type keyword(s) here

Click to begin search

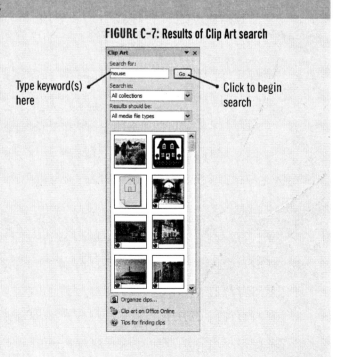

Formatting a Worksheet

Changing Attributes and Alignment

Attributes are styling formats such as bold, italic, and underlining that you can apply to affect the way text and numbers look in a worksheet. You can "paint" or copy a cell's format into other cells by using the Format Painter button in the Clipboard group on the Home tab of the Ribbon. This is similar to using copy and paste, but instead of copying cell contents, it copies only the cell's formatting. You can also change the **alignment** of labels and values in cells to be left, right, or center. You can apply attributes and alignment options using the Home tab, the Format Cells dialog box, or the Mini toolbar. See Table C-2 for a description of common attribute and alignment buttons that are available on the Home tab of the Ribbon and the Mini toolbar. ▓▓▓▓ You want to further enhance the worksheet's appearance by adding bold and underline formatting and centering some of the labels.

STEPS

1. **Press [Ctrl][Home], then click the Bold button B in the Font group**
   The title in cell A1 appears in bold.

2. **Click cell A3, then click the Underline button U in the Font group**
   The column heading is now underlined, though this may be difficult to see with the cell selected.

3. **Click the Italic button I in the Font group, then click B**
   The heading now appears in boldface, underlined, italic type. Notice that the Bold, Italic, and Underline buttons in the Font group are all selected.

4. **Click I**
   The italic attribute is removed from cell A3, but the bold and underline attributes remain.

5. **Click the Format Painter button ✓ in the Clipboard group, then select the range B3:J3**
   The formatting in cell A3 is copied to the rest of the labels in the column headings. You can turn off the Format Painter by pressing [Esc] or by clicking ✓. You decide the title would look better if it were centered over the data columns.

6. **Select the range A1:J1, then click the Merge & Center button ⊞ in the Alignment group**
   The Merge & Center button creates one cell out of the 10 cells across the row, then centers the text in that newly created large cell. The title "Quest Specialty Travel Advertising Expenses" is centered across the 10 columns you selected. You can change the alignment within individual cells using buttons on the Home tab; you can split merged cells into their original components by selecting the merged cells, then clicking the Merge & Center button.

7. **Select the range A3:J3, right-click, then click the Center button ≡ on the Mini toolbar**
   Compare your screen to Figure C-8. Although they may be difficult to read, notice that all the headings are centered within their cells.

8. **Save your work**

FIGURE C-8: Worksheet with formatting attributes applied

Formatting buttons selected

Merge & Center button

Center button

Title centered across columns

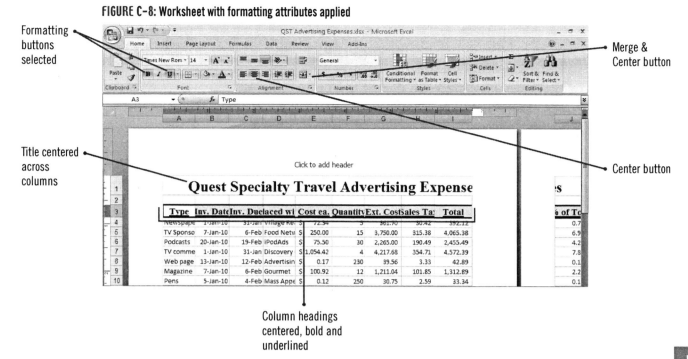

Column headings centered, bold and underlined

Rotating and indenting cell entries

In addition to applying fonts and formatting attributes, you can rotate or indent data within a cell to further change its appearance. You can rotate text within a cell by altering its alignment. To change alignment, select the cells you want to modify, then click the launcher in the Alignment group to open the Alignment tab of the Format Cells dialog box. Click a position in the Orientation box or type a number in the Degrees text box to change from the default horizontal alignment, then click OK. You can indent cell contents using the Increase Indent button on the Alignment group on the Home tab on the Ribbon, which moves cell contents to the right one space, or the Decrease Indent button, which moves cell contents to the left one space.

TABLE C-2: Common attribute and alignment buttons

button	description	button	description
B	Bolds text		Aligns text at the left edge of the cell
I	Italicizes text		Centers text horizontally within the cell
U	Underlines text		Aligns text at the right edge of the cell
	Adds lines or borders		Centers text across columns, and combines two or more selected, adjacent cells into one cell

Adjusting Column Width

As you format a worksheet, you might need to adjust the width of one or more columns to accommodate text or larger font size or style. The default column width is 8.43 characters wide, a little less than one inch. With Excel, you can adjust the width of one or more columns by using the mouse, the Ribbon, or the short-cut menu. Using the mouse, you can drag or double-click the right edge of a column heading. The Ribbon and shortcut menu include commands for making more detailed width adjustments. Table C-3 describes common column adjustment commands. ▧▧▧ You notice that some of the labels in column A don't fit in the cells. You want to adjust the widths of the columns so that the labels appear in their entirety.

STEPS

1. **Position the mouse pointer on the line between the column A and column B headings until it changes to ↔**

   See Figure C-9. The **column heading** is the box at the top of each column containing a letter. Before you can adjust column width using the mouse, you need to position the pointer on the right edge of the column you want to adjust. The entries for TV commercials are the widest in the column.

2. **Click and drag the ↔ to the right until the column displays the TV commercials entries fully**

3. **Position the pointer on the column line between columns B and C until it changes to ↔, then double-click**

   Column B automatically widens to fit the widest entry, in this case, the column label. Double-clicking activates the **AutoFit** feature, which automatically resizes a column so it accommodates the widest entry in a cell.

4. **Use AutoFit to resize columns C, D, and J**

5. **Select the range F5:I5**

   You can change the width of multiple columns at once, by first selecting either the column headings or at least one cell in each column.

6. **Click the Format button in the Cells group, then click Column Width**

   The Column Width dialog box opens. Column width measurement is based on the number of characters that will fit in the column when formatted in the Normal font and font size (in this case, 11 pt Calibri).

7. **Drag the dialog box by its title bar if its placement obscures your view of the worksheet, type 11 in the Column width text box, then click OK**

   The widths of columns F, G, H, and I change to reflect the new setting. See Figure C-10.

8. **Save your work**

Changing row height

Changing row height is as easy as changing column width. Row height is calculated in points, the same units of measure used for fonts. The row height must exceed the size of the font you are using. Normally, you don't need to adjust row heights manually, because row height adjusts automatically to accommodate other formatting changes. If you format something in a row to be a larger point size, Excel adjusts the row to fit the largest point size in the row. However, you have just as many options for changing row height as you do column width. Using the mouse, you can place the ↕ pointer on the line dividing the row heading from the heading below, and dragging to the desired height; double-clicking the line autofits the row height where necessary. You can also select one or more rows, then use the Row Height command on the shortcut menu, or the Row Height or AutoFit Row Height command on the Format button in the Cells group on the Home tab.

FIGURE C-9: Preparing to change the column width

Resize pointer

Row 2 heading

Column D heading

Click to change column or row formatting

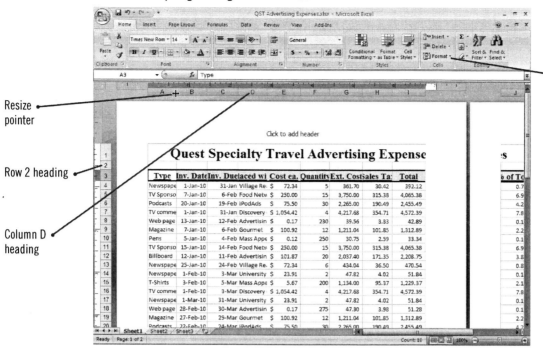

FIGURE C-10: Worksheet with column widths adjusted

Columns widened to display text

Columns widened to same width

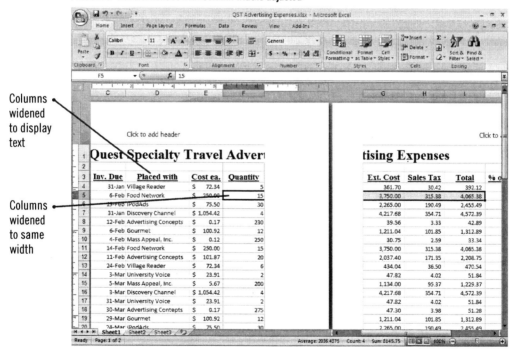

TABLE C-3: Common column formatting commands

command	description	available using
Column Width	Sets the width to a specific number of characters	Format button, shortcut menu
AutoFit Column Width	Fits to the widest entry in a column	Format button, mouse
Hide & Unhide	Hides or displays hidden column(s)	Format button, shortcut menu
Default Width	Changes the default column width for current worksheet	Format button

Formatting a Worksheet

Inserting and Deleting Rows and Columns

As you modify a worksheet, you might find it necessary to insert or delete rows and columns to keep your worksheet current. For example, you might need to insert rows to accommodate new inventory products or remove a column of yearly totals that are no longer necessary. When you insert a new row, the contents of the worksheet shift down from the newly inserted row. When you insert a new column, the contents of the worksheet shift to the right from the point of the new column. Excel inserts rows above the cell pointer and inserts columns to the left of the cell pointer. To insert multiple rows, drag across row headings to select the same number of rows as you want to insert. ███ You want to improve the overall appearance of the worksheet by inserting a row between the last row of data and the totals. Also, you have learned that row 27 and column J need to be deleted from the worksheet.

STEPS

1. Right-click cell A32, then click Insert on the shortcut menu

The Insert dialog box opens. See Figure C-11. You can choose to insert a column or a row, or you can shift the data in the cells in the active column right or in the active row down. An additional row between the last row of data and the totals will visually separate the totals.

2. Click the Entire row option button, then click OK

A blank row appears between the Billboard data and the totals, and the formula result in cell E33 has not changed. The Insert Options button ⬚ appears beside cell A33. Pointing to the button displays a list arrow, which you can click and then choose from the following options: Format Same As Above, Format Same As Below, or Clear Formatting. You want the default formatting, Same as Above.

3. Click the row 27 heading

All of row 27 is selected, as shown in Figure C-12.

4. Click the Delete button in the Cells group; *do not click the button arrow*

Excel deletes row 27, and all rows below this shift up one row. You must use the Delete button or the Delete command on the shortcut menu to delete a row or column; pressing [Delete] on the keyboard removes only the *contents* of a selected row or column.

5. Click the column J heading

The percentage information is calculated elsewhere and is no longer necessary in this worksheet.

6. Click the Delete button in the Cells group

Excel deletes column J. The remaining columns to the right shift left one column.

7. Save your work

Hiding and unhiding columns and rows

When you don't want data in a column or row to be visible, but you don't want to delete it, you can hide the column or row. To hide a selected column, click the Format button in the Cells group, point to Hide & Unhide, then click Hide Columns. A hidden column is indicated by a dark black vertical line in its original position. This black line disappears when you click elsewhere in the worksheet. You can display a hidden column by selecting the columns on either side of the hidden column, clicking the Format button in the Cells group, pointing to Hide & Unhide, and then clicking Unhide Columns. (To hide or unhide one or more rows, substitute Hide Rows and Unhide Rows for the Hide Columns and Unhide Columns commands.)

FIGURE C-11: Insert dialog box

Entire row
option
button

FIGURE C-12: Worksheet with row 27 selected

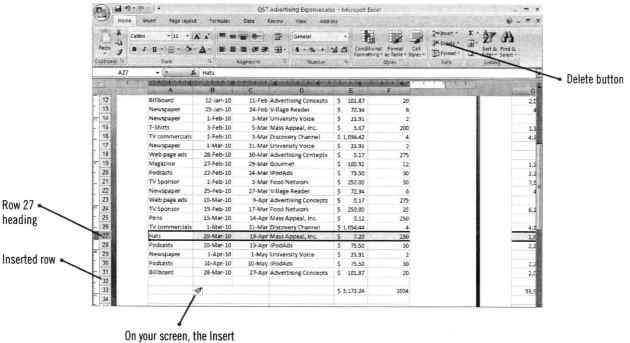

Delete button

Row 27
heading

Inserted row

On your screen, the Insert
Options button might appear
in a different location

Adding and editing comments

Much of your work in Excel may be in collaboration with teammates with whom you share worksheets. You can share ideas with other worksheet users by adding comments within selected cells. To include a comment in a worksheet, click the cell where you want to place the comment, click the Review tab on the Ribbon, then click the New Comment button in the Comments group. A resizable text box containing the computer user's name opens in which you can type your comments. A small, red triangle appears in the upper-right corner of a cell containing a comment. If comments are not already displayed in a workbook, other users can point to the triangle to display the comment. To see all worksheet comments, as shown in Figure C-13, click the Show All Comments button in the Comments group. To edit a comment, click the cell containing the comment, then click the Edit Comment button in the Comments group. To delete a comment, click the cell containing the comment, then click the Delete button in the Comments group.

FIGURE C-13: Comments in worksheet

18	Web page abs	28-Feb-10	30-Mar	Advertising Contepts	$ 0.17
19	Magazine	27-Feb-10	29-Mar	Gourmet	$ 100.92
20	Podcasts	22-Feb-10	24-Mar	iPodAds	$ 75.50
21	TV Sponsor	1-Feb-10	3-Mar	Food Networ	
22	Newspaper	25-Feb-10	27-Mar	Village Read	Grace Wong: Should we continue with this market, or expand to other publications?
23	Web page ads	10-Mar-10	9-Apr	Advertising C	
24	TV Sponsor	15-Feb-10	17-Mar	Food Networ	
25	Pens	15-Mar-10	14-Apr	Mass Appeal, Inc.	$ 0.12
26	TV commercials	1-Mar-10	31-Mar	Discovery Ch	
27	Podcasts	20-Mar-10	19-Apr	iPodAds	Grace Wong: I think this will turn out to be a very good decision.
28	Newspaper	1-Apr-10	1-May	University Vo	
29	Podcasts	10-Apr-10	10-May	iPodAds	
30	Billboard	28-Mar-10	27-Apr	Advertising Concepts	$ 101.87
31					
32					$5,166.04
33					
34					
35					
36					
37					
38					
39					

Sheet1 / Sheet2 / Sheet3

Ready

Applying Colors, Patterns, and Borders

You can use colors, patterns, and borders to enhance the overall appearance of a worksheet and to make it easier to read. You can add these enhancements by using the Border and Fill Color buttons in the Font group on the Home tab of the Ribbon and on the Mini toolbar, or by using the Fill tab and the Border tab in the Format Cells dialog box. You can apply a color to the background of a cell or a range, or to cell contents, and you can apply a pattern to a cell or range. You can apply borders to all the cells in a worksheet or only to selected cells to call attention to selected information. To save time, you can also apply **cell styles**, predesigned combinations of formatting attributes. ▟▟▟▟ You want to add a pattern, a border, and color to the title of the worksheet to give the worksheet a more professional appearance.

STEPS

1. **Select cell A1, click the Fill Color list arrow button [⬛▾] in the Font group, then hover the pointer over the Turquoise, Accent 2 color (first row, sixth column from the left)**
   See Figure C-14. Live Preview shows you how the color will look *before* you apply it.

> **QUICK TIP**
>
> When you change fill or font color, the color on the Fill Color and Font Color buttons changes to the last color you selected.

2. **Click the Turquoise, Accent 2 color (first row, sixth column from the left)**
   The color is applied to the background or fill of this cell. (Remember that cell A1 spans columns A through I because the Merge and Center command was applied.)

3. **Right-click cell A1, then click Format Cells on the shortcut menu**
   The Format Cells dialog box opens. Adding a pattern to cells can add to the visual interest of your worksheet. To format an entire row or column at once, click the row heading or column heading button.

> **QUICK TIP**
>
> Use fill colors and patterns sparingly. Too many colors can be distracting or make it hard to see which information is important.

4. **Click the Fill tab, click the Pattern Style list arrow, click the 6.25% Gray style (first row, sixth column from the left), then click OK**

5. **Click the Borders list arrow [⊞▾] in the Font group, then click Thick Bottom Border**
   Unlike underlining, which is a text-formatting tool, borders extend to the width of the cell, and can appear at the bottom of the cell, at the top, or on either side. It can be difficult to see a border when the cell is selected.

> **QUICK TIP**
>
> You can also create custom cell borders. Click the Borders list arrow in the Font group, click More Borders, then click the individual border buttons to create borders or boxes.

6. **Select the range A3:I3, click the Font Color list arrow [△▾] in the Font group, then click the Blue, Accent 1 color (first Theme color row, fifth column from the left) on the palette**
   The new color is applied to the selected range.

7. **Select the range J1:K1, click the Cell Styles button in the Styles group, then click the Neutral button (first row, fourth column from the left) on the palette**
   The font and color change in the range, as shown in Figure C-15.

8. **Save your work**

FIGURE C-14: Viewing fill color using LivePreview

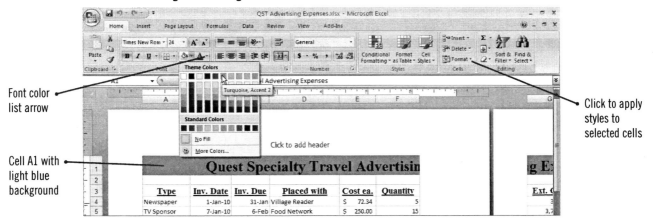

Font color list arrow

Cell A1 with light blue background

Click to apply styles to selected cells

FIGURE C-15: Worksheet with color, patterns, border, and style applied

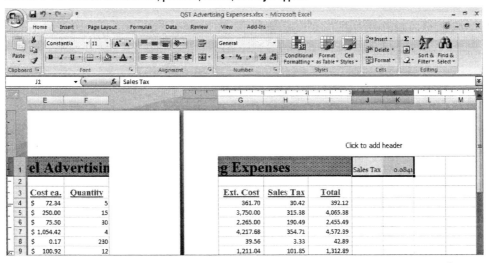

Saving time with themes and cell styles

You can save yourself time by formatting with themes and cell styles. A **theme** is a predefined set of attributes that gives your Excel worksheet a professional look. Formatting choices included in a theme are colors, fonts, and line and fill effects. A theme can be applied using the Themes button in the Themes group on the Page Layout tab on the Ribbon, as shown in Figure C-16. **Cell styles** are sets of attributes based on themes, so they are automatically updated if you change a theme. For example, if you apply the 20% - Accent1 cell style to cell A1 in a worksheet that has no theme applied, the fill color changes to light blue and the font changes to Constantia. If you change the theme of the worksheet to Metro, cell A1's fill color changes to light green and the font changes to Corbel, because these are the attributes that coordinate with the selected theme. Using themes and cell styles makes it easier to ensure that your worksheets are consistent and saves you from a lot of reformatting every time you make a change.

FIGURE C-16: Themes gallery

Applying Conditional Formatting

So far, you've used formatting to change the appearance of different types of data, such as dates, dollar amounts, worksheet titles, and column labels. But you can also use formatting to highlight important aspects of the data itself. For example, you can apply formatting that automatically changes the font color to red for any cells where ad costs exceed $100 and to green where ad costs are below $50. This type of formatting is called **conditional formatting** because Excel automatically applies different formats depending on conditions you specify. If the data meets your conditions, Excel applies the formats you specify. The formatting is updated if you change data in the worksheet. Data bars are a type of conditional formatting that visually illustrate differences among values. Grace is concerned about advertising costs exceeding yearly budget. You decide to use conditional formatting to highlight certain trends and patterns in the data, so it's easy to spot the most expensive expenditures.

STEPS

1. **Select the range I4:I30, click the Conditional Formatting button in the Styles group, point to Data Bars, then point to the Light Blue Data Bar (second row, second from left)**

   Live Preview shows how this formatting will appear in the worksheet, as shown in Figure C-17. Notice that the length of the bar in each cell reflects its value relative to other cells in the selection.

2. **Preview the Green Data Bar (first row, second from left), then click it**

3. **Select the range G4:G30, click the Conditional Formatting button in the Styles group, then point to Highlight Cells Rules**

   The Conditional Formatting menu displays choices for creating different types of formatting rules. For example, you can create a rule for values that are greater than a certain amount, less than a certain amount, or between two amounts.

4. **Click Between**

   The Between dialog box opens. Depending on the choice you made in the Highlight Cells Rules menu (such as "Greater Than" or "Less Than"), this dialog box displays different input boxes. You can define multiple different conditions and then assign formatting attributes to each one. You define the condition first. The default setting for the first condition is "Cell Value Is" "between." The value can be a constant, formula, cell reference, or date. The formatting default format is exactly what you want: Light Red Fill with Dark Red Text.

5. **Type 2000 in the first text box, type 4000 in the second text box, compare your settings to Figure C-18, then click OK**

   All cells with values between 2000 and 4000 in column G appear with a light red fill and dark red text.

6. **Click cell G7, type 3975.55, then press [Enter]**

   When the value in cell G7 changes, the formatting also changes, because the new value meets the condition to apply the format. Compare your results to Figure C-19.

7. **Press [Ctrl][Home] to select cell A1, then save your work**

Managing conditional formatting rules

If you create a conditional formatting rule and then want to change the conditions to reflect a different value or format, you don't need to create a new rule; instead, you can modify the rule using the Rule Manager. Select the cell(s) containing conditional formatting, click the Conditional Formatting button in the Styles group, then click

Manage Rules. The Conditional Formatting Rules Manager dialog box opens. Select the rules you want to edit or delete, click Edit Rule, modify the settings in the Edit the Rule Description area, click OK, then click OK again to close the dialog box. The rule is modified, and the new conditions are applied to the selected cells.

FIGURE C-17: Previewing a Data Bar

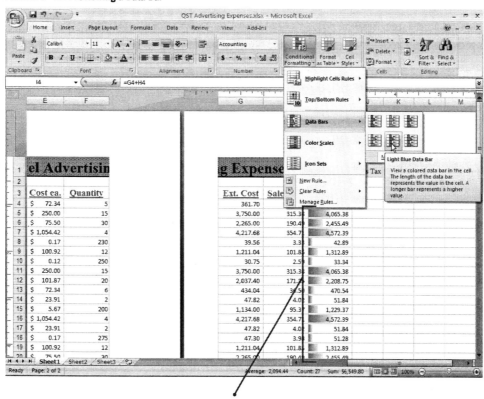

Data bars displayed
in sheet

FIGURE C-18: Setting conditions in Between dialog box

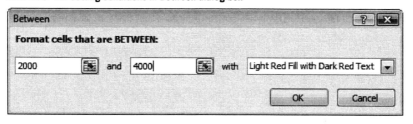

FIGURE C-19: Results of Conditional Formatting

Naming and Moving a Sheet

By default, an Excel workbook initially contains three worksheets, named Sheet1, Sheet2, and Sheet3. The sheet name appears on the sheet tab at the bottom of the worksheet. When you open a workbook, the first worksheet is the active sheet. To move from sheet to sheet, you can click any sheet tab at the bottom of the worksheet window. The sheet tab scrolling buttons, located to the left of the sheet tabs, are useful when a workbook contains too many sheet tabs to display at once. To make it easier to identify the sheets in a workbook, you can rename each sheet and add color to the tabs. You can also organize them in a logical way. For instance, to better track performance goals, you could name each workbook sheet for an individual salesperson, and you could move the sheets so they appeared in alphabetical order. ▨▨▨▨ In the current worksheet, Sheet1 contains information on advertising expenses. Sheet2 contains an advertising budget, and Sheet3 contains no data. You want to name the two sheets in the workbook to reflect their contents, add color to a sheet tab to easily distinguish one from the other, and change their order.

STEPS

1. **Click the Sheet2 tab**

   Sheet2 becomes active, appearing in front of the Sheet1 tab; this is the worksheet that contains the budgeted expenses. See Figure C-20.

2. **Click the Sheet1 tab**

   Sheet1, which contains the actual expenses, becomes active again.

> **QUICK TIP**
>
> You can also rename a sheet by right-clicking the tab, clicking Rename on the shortcut menu, typing the new name, then pressing [Enter].

3. **Double-click the Sheet2 tab, type Budget, then press [Enter]**

   The new name for Sheet2 automatically replaces the default name on the tab. Worksheet names can have up to 31 characters, including spaces and punctuation.

> **QUICK TIP**
>
> To delete a worksheet, select the worksheet you want to delete, click the Delete button list arrow in the Cells group, then click Delete Sheet. To insert a worksheet, click the Insert Worksheet button ▨ to the right of the sheet tabs.

4. **Right-click the Budget tab, point to Tab Color on the shortcut menu, then click the Bright Green, Accent 4, Lighter 80% color (second row, third column from the right) as shown in Figure C-21**

   The tab color changes to a bright green gradient.

5. **Double-click the Sheet1 tab, type Actual, then press [Enter]**

   Notice that the color of the Budget tab changes depending on whether it is the active tab; when the Actual tab is active, the color of the Budget tab changes to solid bright green. You decide to rearrange the order of the sheets, so that the Budget tab is to the left of the Actual tab.

6. **Click the Budget sheet tab, hold down the mouse button, drag it to the left of the Actual sheet tab, as shown in Figure C-22, then release the mouse button**

   As you drag, the pointer changes to ▨, the sheet relocation pointer, and a small, black triangle shows its position. The first sheet in the workbook is now the Budget sheet. See Figure C-23. To see hidden sheets, click the far left tab scrolling button to display the first sheet tab; click the far right navigation button to display the last sheet tab. The left and right buttons move one sheet in their respective directions.

7. **Click the Actual sheet tab, then enter your name in the left-side header box**

8. **Click the Page Layout tab on the Ribbon, click the Orientation button in the Page Setup group, then click Landscape**

9. **Press [Ctrl][Home], then save your work**

Formatting a Worksheet

FIGURE C-20: Sheet tabs in workbook

Sheet1 tab   Sheet2 tab

FIGURE C-21: Tab Color palette

Available colors

Excel 2007

FIGURE C-22: Sheet during move

Sheet relocation pointer   Sheet1 renamed   Indicates tab color

FIGURE C-23: Reordered sheets

Budget sheet comes before Actual sheet

Copying worksheets

There are times when you may want to copy a worksheet. For example, a workbook might contain a sheet with Quarter 1 expenses, and you want to use that sheet as the basis for a sheet containing Quarter 2 expenses. To copy a sheet within the same workbook, press and hold [Ctrl], drag the sheet tab to the desired tab location, release the mouse button, then release [Ctrl]. A duplicate sheet appears with the same name as the copied sheet followed by "(2)" indicating it is a copy. You can then rename the

sheet to a more meaningful name. To copy a sheet to a different workbook, both the source and destination workbooks must be open. Select the sheet to copy or move, right-click the sheet tab, then click Move or Copy in the shortcut menu. Complete the information in the Move or Copy dialog box. Be sure to click the Create a copy check box if you are copying rather than moving the worksheet. Carefully check your calculation results whenever you move or copy a worksheet.

Checking Spelling

Excel includes a spelling checker to help you ensure that the words in your worksheet are spelled correctly. The spelling checker scans your worksheet, displays words it doesn't find in its built-in dictionary, and suggests replacements when they are available. To check other sheets in a multiple-sheet workbook, you need to display each sheet and run the spelling checker again. Because the built-in dictionary cannot possibly include all the words that anyone needs, you can add words to the dictionary, such as your company name, an acronym, or an unusual technical term. Once you add a word or term, the spelling checker will no longer consider that word misspelled. Any words you've added to the dictionary using Word, Access, or PowerPoint are also available in Excel. Another feature, AutoCorrect, automatically corrects some spelling errors as you type. Before you distribute this workbook to Grace and the marketing managers, you check its spelling.

STEPS

1. **Click the Review tab on the Ribbon, then click the Spelling button in the Proofing group**

   The Spelling: English (U.S.) dialog box opens, as shown in Figure C-24, with "iPodAds" selected as the first misspelled word in the worksheet. For any word, you have the option to Ignore this case of the flagged word, Ignore All cases of the flagged word, or Add the word to the dictionary.

2. **Click Ignore All**

   Next, the spelling checker finds the word "Contepts" and suggests "Concepts" as an alternative.

3. **Verify that the word Concepts is selected in the Suggestions list, then click Change**

   When no more incorrect words are found, Excel displays a message indicating that all the words on the worksheet have been checked.

4. **Click OK**

5. **Click the Home tab, click Find & Select in the Editing group, then click Replace**

   The Find and Replace dialog box opens. You can use this dialog box to replace a word or phrase. It might be a misspelling that the Spelling Checker didn't recognize as wrong, such as a word that wasn't corrected with the spelling checker, or simply something you want to change. Grace has just told you that each instance of 'Billboard' in the worksheet should be changed to 'Sign'.

6. **Type Billboard in the Find what text box, press [Tab], then type Sign in the Replace with text box**

   Compare your dialog box to Figure C-25.

7. **Click Replace All, click OK to close the warning box, then click Close to close the Find and Replace dialog box**

   Excel has made two replacements.

8. **Save your work, view the Actual sheet in Print Preview, click the Page Setup button on the Ribbon, fit the worksheet to one page, then return to Print Preview**

   Compare your worksheet to Figure C-26.

9. **Print one copy of the worksheet, close it, then exit Excel**

E-mailing a workbook

You can send an entire workbook from within Excel using your installed email program, such as Microsoft Office Outlook or Outlook Express. To send a workbook as an e-mail message attachment, open the workbook, click the Office button, point to Send, then click E-mail. An email message opens with the workbook automatically attached; the filename appears in the Attached field. Complete the To and optional Cc fields, include a message if you wish, then click Send.

FIGURE C-24: Spelling: English dialog box

Misspelled word

Suggested replacements for misspelled word

Click to ignore all occurrences of misspelled word

Click to add word to dictionary

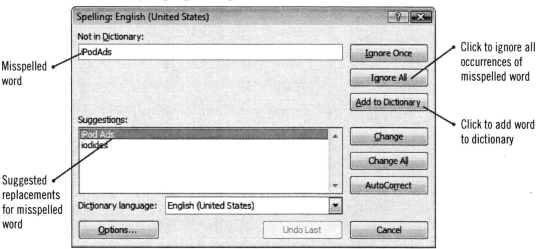

FIGURE C-25: Find and Replace dialog box

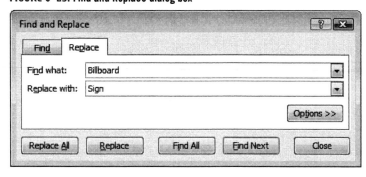

FIGURE C-26: Viewing worksheet in Print Preview

Practice

▼ CONCEPTS REVIEW

Label each element of the Excel worksheet window shown in Figure C-27.

FIGURE C-27

Match each command or button with the statement that best describes it.

8. **Spelling & Grammar button**
9. [2▾]
10. [⊞]
11. **[Ctrl][Home]**
12. **Conditional Formatting**
13. **[Delete]**

a. Erases the contents of a cell
b. Changes formatting of a cell based on cell contents
c. Moves cell pointer to cell A1
d. Checks for apparent misspellings in a worksheet
e. Displays options for erasing the contents of a cell
f. Centers cell contents over multiple cells

Select the best answer from the list of choices.

14. Which of the following is an example of an accounting number format?
   a. 5555   **c.** 55.55%
   b. $5,555.55   **d.** 5,555.55

15. What feature is used to delete a conditional formatting rule?
   a. Rule Reminder   **c.** Rule Manager
   b. Conditional Rule Manager   **d.** Format Manager

16. Which button removes boldface formatting from selected cells?
   a. *I*   **c.** [icon]
   b. **B**   **d.** **B**

17. Which button opens the Format Cells dialog box?
   a. [icon]   **c.** **B**
   b. [icon]   **d.** [icon]

18. What is the name of the feature used to resize a column to accommodate its widest entry?
   a. AutoFormat   **c.** AutoResize
   b. AutoFit   **d.** AutoRefit

19. Which button increases the number of decimal places in selected cells?
   a. [icon]   **c.** [icon]
   b. [icon]   **d.** [icon]

20. Which button applies multiple formatting styles to selected cells?
   a. [icon]   **c.** [icon]
   b. [icon]   **d.** [icon]

▼ SKILLS REVIEW

1. Format values.
   a. Start Excel, open the file EX C-2.xlsx from the drive and folder where you store your Data Files, then save it as **Health Insurance Premiums**.
   b. Enter a formula in cell B10 that totals the number of employees.
   c. Create a formula in cell C5 that calculates the monthly insurance premium for the accounting department. (*Hint*: Make sure you use the correct type of cell reference in the formula. To calculate the monthly premium, multiply the number of employees by the monthly premium.)
   d. Copy the formula in cell C5 to the range C6:C10.
   e. Format the range C5:C10 using the Accounting Number Format.
   f. Change the format of the range C6:C9 to the Comma Style.
   g. Reduce the number of decimals to 0 in cell B14, using a button in the Number group.
   h. Save your work.

2. Change fonts and font sizes.
   a. Select the range of cells containing the column labels (in row 4).
   b. Change the font of the selection to Times New Roman.
   c. Increase the font size of the selection to 12 points.
   d. Increase the font size of the label in cell A1 to 14 points.
   e. Save your changes.

3. Change attributes and alignment.
   a. Apply the bold and italic attributes to the worksheet title **QST Corporate Office**.
   b. Use the Merge & Center button to center the Health Insurance Premiums label over columns A through C.
   c. Apply the italic attribute to the Health Insurance Premiums label.
   d. Add the bold attribute to the labels in row 4.
   e. Use the Format Painter to copy the format in cell A4 to the range A5:A10.
   f. Apply the format in cell C10 to cell B14.

g. Change the alignment of cell A10 to Align Right.

h. Select the range of cells containing the column titles, then center them.

i. Remove the italic attribute from the Health Insurance Premiums label, then increase the font size to 14.

j. Move the Health Insurance Premiums label to cell A3, then add the bold and underline attributes.

k. Add a bottom double border to the last cell in the Employees column, above the total number of employees.

l. Save your changes.

4. **Adjust column width.**

a. Resize column C to a width of 10.71.

b. Use the AutoFit feature to resize columns A and B.

c. Clear the contents of cell A13 (do not delete the cell).

d. Change the text in cell A14 to **Monthly Insurance Premium**, then change the width of the column to **25**.

e. Resize any remaining columns as needed to view all the data.

f. Save your changes.

5. **Insert and delete rows and columns.**

a. Insert a new row between rows 5 and 6.

b. Add a new department—**Humanitarian Aid**—in the newly inserted row. Enter **5** for the Employees.

c. Copy the formula in cell C5 to C6.

d. Add the following comment to cell A6: **New department**. Display the comment, then drag to move it out of the way, if necessary.

e. Add a new column between the Department and Employees columns with the title **Family Coverage**, then resize the column using AutoFit.

f. Delete the Legal row.

g. Move the comment out of the way, if necessary.

h. Save your changes.

6. **Apply colors, patterns, and borders.**

a. Add an outside border around the range A4:D10.

b. Apply the Aqua, Accent 5, Lighter 80% fill color to the labels in the Department column (do not include the Total label).

c. Apply the Orange, Accent 6, Lighter 60% fill color to the range A4:D4.

d. Change the color of the font in the range A4:D4 to Red, Accent 2, Darker 25%.

e. Add a 12.5% Gray pattern style to cell A1.

f. Format the range A14:B14 with a pattern style of Thin Diagonal Stripes, a pattern color of White, Background 1, and a background color of Dark Blue, Text 2, Lighter 40%. Apply the bold attribute.

g. Save your changes.

7. **Apply conditional formatting.**

a. Select the range D5:D9, then create a conditional format that changes cell contents to green fill with dark green text if the value is between 4000 and 7000.

b. Select the range C5:C9, then create a conditional format that changes cell contents to red text if the number of employees exceeds 10.

c. Select the range C5:C9, then create a blue data bar.

d. Use the Rule Manager to modify the conditional format in cell C5 to display the cell contents in bold red text.

e. Copy the format in cell C5 to the range in C6:C9.

f. Merge and center the title over columns A-D.

8. **Name and move a sheet.**

a. Name the Sheet 1 tab **Insurance Data**.

b. Name the Sheet 3 tab **Employee Data**.

c. Change the Insurance Data tab color to Red, Accent 2, Lighter 40%.

d. Change the Employee Data tab color to Aqua, Accent 5, Lighter 40%.

▼ SKILLS REVIEW (CONTINUED)

e. Move the Employee Data sheet so it comes after (to the right of) the Insurance Data sheet.

f. Make the Insurance Data sheet active, enter your name in cell A20, then save your work.

9. **Check spelling.**

a. Move the cell pointer to cell A1.

b. Use the Find & Select feature to replace the Accounting label in cell A5 with Accounting/Legal.

c. Check the spelling in the worksheet using the spelling checker, and correct any spelling errors.

d. Save your changes.

e. Preview and print the Insurance Data sheet, compare your work to Figure C-28, then close the workbook and exit Excel.

FIGURE C-28

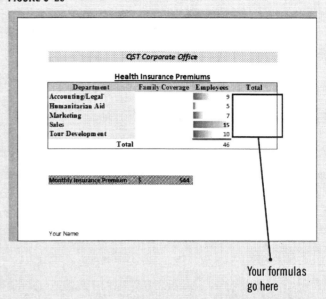

Your formulas go here

▼ INDEPENDENT CHALLENGE 1

You run a freelance accounting business, and one of your newest clients is Lovely Locks, a small beauty salon. Now that you've converted the salon's accounting records to Excel, the manager would like you to work on an analysis of the inventory. Although more items will be added later, the worksheet has enough items for you to begin your modifications.

a. Start Excel, open the file EX C-3.xlsx from the drive and folder where you store your Data Files, then save it as Lovely Locks Inventory.

b. Create a formula in cell E4 that calculates the value of the on-hand inventory, based on the price paid for the item, in cell B4. Format the cell in the Comma Style.

c. Use an absolute reference to calculate the sale price of the item in cell F4, using the markup value shown in cell I1.

d. Copy the formulas created above into the range E5:F14; first convert any necessary cell references to absolute so that the formulas work correctly.

e. Add the bold attribute to the column headings, and italicize the items in column A.

f. Make sure all columns are wide enough to display the data and headings.

g. Format the Sale Price column so it displays the Accounting Number Format with two decimal places.

h. Change the Price Paid column so it displays the Comma style with two decimal places.

i. Add a row under #2 Curlers for Nail files, price paid $0.31, sold individually (each), with 56 on hand.

j. Verify that all the formulas in the worksheet are correct. Adjust any items as needed, and check the spelling.

k. Use conditional formatting to call attention to items with a quantity of less than 20 on hand. Use yellow fill with dark yellow text.

l. Create an icon set for the range D4:D15 using the symbols of your choosing.

m. Add an outside border around the data in the Item column.

n. Delete the row containing the Pins item.

o. Enter your name in an empty cell below the data, then save the file.

p. Preview and print the worksheet, compare your work to the sample of page 1 shown in Figure C-29, close the workbook, then exit Excel.

FIGURE C-29

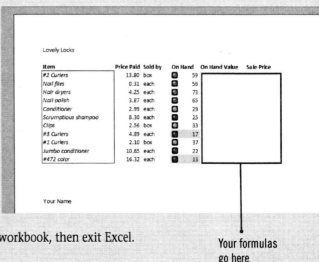

Your formulas go here

▼ INDEPENDENT CHALLENGE 2

You volunteer several hours each week with the Assistance League of South Bend, and are in charge of maintaining the membership list. You're currently planning a mailing campaign to members in certain regions of the city. You also want to create renewal letters for members whose membership expires soon. You decide to format the list to enhance the appearance of the worksheet and make your upcoming tasks easier to plan.

a. Start Excel, open the file EX C-4.xlsx from the drive and folder where you store your Data Files, then save it as South Bend Assistance League.

b. Remove any blank columns.

c. Create a conditional format in the Zip Code column so that entries greater than 46649 appear in light red fill with dark red text.

d. Make all columns wide enough to fit their data and headings.

e. Use formatting enhancements, such as fonts, font sizes, and text attributes, to make the worksheet more attractive.

f. Center-align the column labels.

g. Use conditional formatting so that entries for Year of Membership Expiration that are between 2011 and 2013 appear in a bold, contrasting color.

h. Adjust any items as necessary, then check the spelling.

i. Change the name of the Sheet 1 tab to one that reflects the sheet's contents, then add a tab color of your choice.

j. Enter your name in an empty cell, then save your work.

k. Before printing, preview the worksheet, make any final changes you think necessary, then print a copy. Compare your work to the sample shown in Figure C-30.

l. Close the workbook, then exit Excel.

FIGURE C-30

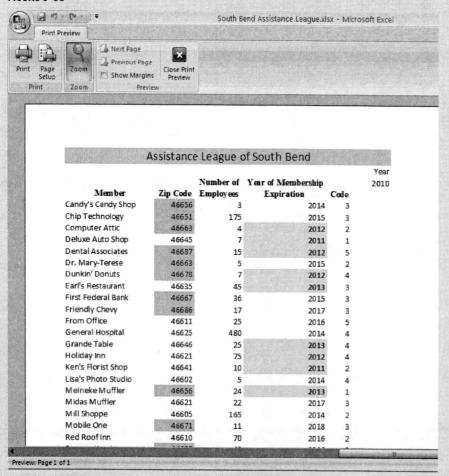

Member	Zip Code	Number of Employees	Year of Membership Expiration	Code	Year 2010
Candy's Candy Shop	46656	3	2014	3	
Chip Technology	46651	175	2015	3	
Computer Attic	46663	4	2012	2	
Deluxe Auto Shop	46645	7	2011	1	
Dental Associates	46687	15	2012	5	
Dr. Mary-Terese	46663	5	2015	2	
Dunkin' Donuts	46678	7	2012	4	
Earl's Restaurant	46635	45	2013	3	
First Federal Bank	46667	36	2015	3	
Friendly Chevy	46686	17	2017	3	
From Office	46611	25	2016	5	
General Hospital	46625	480	2014	4	
Grande Table	46646	25	2013	4	
Holiday Inn	46621	75	2012	4	
Ken's Florist Shop	46641	10	2011	2	
Lisa's Photo Studio	46602	5	2014	4	
Meineke Muffler	46656	24	2013	1	
Midas Muffler	46621	22	2017	3	
Mill Shoppe	46605	165	2014	2	
Mobile One	46671	11	2018	3	
Red Roof Inn	46610	70	2016	2	

▼ INDEPENDENT CHALLENGE 3

Fine Line Writing Instruments is a Chicago-based company that manufactures high-quality pens and markers. As the finance manager, one of your responsibilities is to analyze the monthly reports from your five district sales offices. Your boss, Joanne Bennington, has just asked you to prepare a quarterly sales report for an upcoming meeting. Because several top executives will be attending this meeting, Joanne reminds you that the report must look professional. In particular, she asks you to emphasize the company's surge in profits during the last month and to highlight the fact that the Northeastern district continues to outpace the other districts.

a. Plan a worksheet that shows the company's sales during the first quarter. Assume that all pens are the same price. Make sure you plan to include:

- The number of pens sold (units sold) and the associated revenues (total sales) for each of the five district sales offices. The five sales districts are: Northeastern, Midwestern, Southeastern, Southern, and Western.
- Calculations that show month-by-month totals for January, February, and March, and a three-month cumulative total.
- Calculations that show each district's share of sales (percent of Total Sales).
- Labels that reflect the month-by-month data as well as the cumulative data.
- Formatting enhancements and data bars that emphasize the recent month's sales surge and the Northeastern district's sales leadership.

b. Ask yourself the following questions about the organization and formatting of the worksheet: What worksheet title and labels do you need, and where should they appear? How can you calculate the totals? What formulas can you copy to save time and keystrokes? Do any of these formulas need to use an absolute reference? How do you show dollar amounts? What information should be shown in bold? Do you need to use more than one font? Should you use more than one point size?

c. Start Excel, then save a new, blank workbook as **Fine Line Writing Instruments** to the drive and folder where you store your Data Files.

d. Build the worksheet with your own price and sales data. Enter the titles and labels first, then enter the numbers and formulas. You can use the information in Table C-4 to get started.

e. Adjust the column widths as necessary.

f. Change the height of row 1 to 33 points.

g. Format labels and values, and change the attributes and alignment if necessary.

h. Resize columns and adjust the formatting as necessary.

i. Add data bars for the monthly Units Sold columns.

j. Add a column that calculates a 25% increase in sales dollars. Use an absolute cell reference in this calculation. (*Hint*: Make sure the current formatting is applied to the new information.)

TABLE C-4

Fine Line Writing Instruments										
1st Quarter Sales Report										
		January		February		March		Total	
Office	Price	Units Sold	Sales	Units Sold	Sales	Units Sold	Sales	Units Sold	Sales
Northeastern									
Midwestern									
Southeastern									
Southern									
Western									

Formatting a Worksheet

▼ INDEPENDENT CHALLENGE 3 (CONTINUED)

Advanced Challenge Exercise

- Use the Format as Table feature to add a table style of your choice to the data.
- Insert a clip art image related to pens in an appropriate location, adjusting its size and position as necessary.
- Save your work.

l. Enter your name in an empty cell.

m. Check the spelling in the workbook, then save your work.

n. Preview, compare your work to Figure C-31, then print the worksheet in landscape orientation.

o. Close the workbook file, then exit Excel.

FIGURE C-31

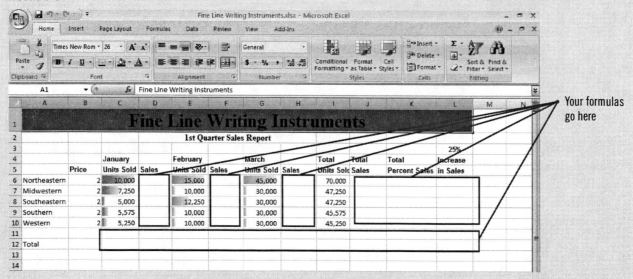

▼ REAL LIFE INDEPENDENT CHALLENGE

***Note*: This project requires an Internet connection.**

You are saving up to take an international trip you have always dreamed about. You plan to visit seven different countries over the course of two months, and budgeting an identical spending allowance in each country. To help work toward your goal, you want to create a worksheet that calculates the amount of native currency you will have in each country. You want the workbook to reflect the currency information for each country.

a. Start Excel, then save a new, blank workbook as **World Tour Budget** to the drive and folder where you store your Data Files.

b. Think of seven countries you would like to visit, then enter column and row labels for your worksheet. (*Hint*: You may wish to include row labels for each country, plus column labels for the country, the $1 equivalent in native currency, the total amount of native currency you'll have in each country, and the name of each country's monetary unit.)

c. Decide how much money you want to bring to each country (for example, $1000), and enter that in the worksheet.

d. Use your favorite search engine to find your own information sources on currency conversions for the countries you plan to visit.

e. Enter the cash equivalent to $1 in U.S. dollars for each country in your list. Also include the name of the currency used in each country.

f. Create an equation that calculates the amount of native currency you will have in each country, using an absolute cell reference in the formula.

g. Format the entries in column B with three decimal places and in column C with two decimal places, using the correct currency unit for each country. (*Hint*: Use the Number tab in the Format cells dialog box; choose the appropriate currency format from the Symbol list, using two decimal places.)

h. Create a conditional format that changes the font attributes of the calculated amount in the "$1,000 US" column to bold and red if the amount exceeds **500 units** of the local currency.

i. Merge and center the title over the column headings.

j. Add any formatting attributes to the column headings, and resize the columns as necessary.

k. Add a background color to the title.

Advanced Challenge Exercise

■ Modify the conditional format in the "$1,000 US" column so that entries between 1500 and 3999 display in red, boldface type, and entries above 4000 appear in blue, boldface type.

■ Delete all the unused sheets in the workbook.

■ Save your work as **World Tour Budget ACE** where you store your Data Files.

■ If you have access to an e-mail account, e-mail this workbook to your instructor as an attachment.

l. Enter your name in the header of the worksheet.

m. Spell check, save, preview and compare your work to Figure C-32, then print the worksheet.

n. Close the workbook and exit Excel.

FIGURE C-32

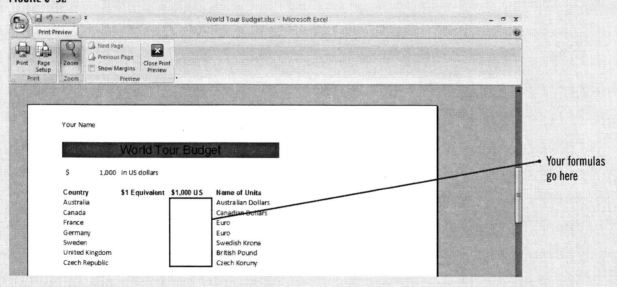

Open the file EX C-5.xlsx from the drive and folder where you store your Data Files, then save it as **Top Notch Personnel**. Use the skills you learned in this unit to format the worksheet so it looks like the one shown in Figure C-33. Create a conditional format in the Level column so that entries greater than 3 appear in red text. Create an additional conditional format in the Review Cycle column so that any value equal to 4 appears in green bold text. Replace the Accounting department label with Legal. (*Hint*: The only additional font used in this exercise is 16-point Times New Roman in row 1.) Enter your name in cell A25, check the spelling in the worksheet, then save and print your work.

FIGURE C-33

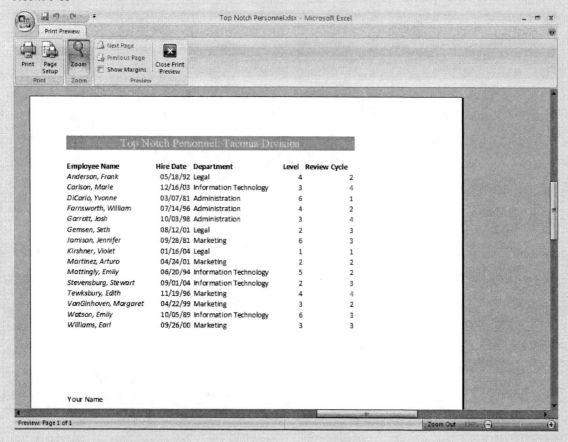

Working with Charts

Files You Will Need:

EX D-1.xlsx
EX D-2.xlsx
EX D-3.xlsx
EX D-4.xlsx
EX D-5.xlsx
EX D-6.xlsx

Worksheets provide an effective layout for calculating and organizing data, but the grid layout is not always the best format for presenting your work to others. To display information so it's easier to interpret, you can create a chart. **Charts**, often called graphs, present information in a pictorial format, making it easier to see patterns, trends, and relationships. In this unit, you learn how to create a chart, how to edit the chart and change the chart type, how to add text annotations and arrows, and how to preview and print the chart. At the upcoming annual meeting, Grace Wong wants to emphasize a growth trend at Quest Specialty Travel. She asks you to create a chart showing the increase in company revenues over the past four quarters.

OBJECTIVES

Plan a chart
Create a chart
Move and resize a chart
Change the chart design
Change the chart layout
Format a chart
Annotate and draw on a chart
Create a pie chart

Planning a Chart

Before creating a chart, you need to plan the information you want your chart to show and how you want it to look. Planning ahead helps you to decide what type of chart to create and how to organize the data. Understanding the parts of a chart makes it easier to format it and change specific elements so that the chart best illustrates your data. In preparation for creating the chart for Grace's presentation, you identify your goals for the chart and plan it.

DETAILS

Use the following guidelines to plan the chart:

* **Determine the purpose of the chart and identify the data relationships you want to communicate graphically**

  You want to create a chart that shows quarterly revenues throughout Quest Specialty Travel. This worksheet data is shown in Figure D-1. In the first quarter, the Marketing department launched an international advertising campaign. The campaign resulted in greatly increased sales starting in the second quarter. You want to create a chart for the annual meeting that illustrates the increase and compares sales across the quarters for each location.

* **Determine the results you want to see, and decide which chart type is most appropriate**

  Different chart types display data in distinctive ways. For example, a pie chart compares parts to the whole, so it's useful for showing what proportion of a budget amount was spent on print ads relative to what was spent on direct mail or radio commercials. A line chart, in contrast, is best for showing trends over time. To choose the best chart type for your data, you should first decide how you want your data displayed and interpreted. Table D-1 describes several different types of charts you can create in Excel and their corresponding buttons on the Insert tab of the Ribbon. Because you want to compare QST revenues in multiple locations over a period of four quarters, you decide to use a column chart.

* **Identify the worksheet data you want the chart to illustrate**

  Sometimes you use all the data in a worksheet to create a chart, while at other times you may need to select a range within the sheet. The worksheet from which you are creating your chart contains revenue data for the past year. You will need to use all the quarterly data contained in the worksheet.

* **Understand the elements of a chart**

  The chart shown in Figure D-2 contains basic elements of a chart. In the figure, QST locations are on the horizontal axis (also called the **x-axis**) and monthly sales are on the vertical axis (also called the **y-axis**). The horizontal axis is also called the **category axis** because it often contains the names of data groups, such as locations, months, or years. The vertical axis is also called the **value axis** because it often contains numerical values that help you interpret the size of chart elements. (3-D charts also contain a **z-axis**, for comparing data across both categories and values.) The area inside the horizontal and vertical axes is the **plot area**. The **tick marks** at the left edge of the vertical axis and **gridlines** (extending across the plot area) create a scale of measure for each value. Each value in a cell you select for your chart is a **data point**. In any chart, a **data marker** visually represents each data point, which in this case is a column. A collection of related data points is a **data series**. In this chart, there are four data series (Quarter 1, Quarter 2, Quarter 3, and Quarter 4), so you include a **legend** to make it easy to identify them.

FIGURE D-1: Worksheet containing revenue data

FIGURE D-2: Chart elements

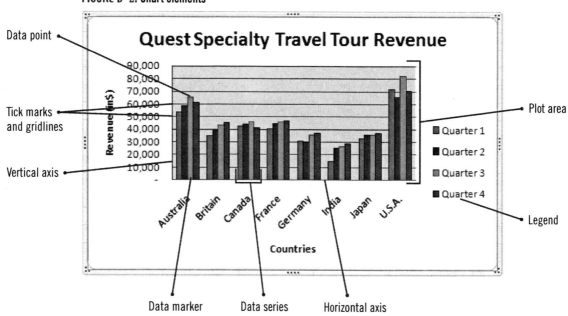

TABLE D-1: Common chart types

type	button	description
Column		Compares distinct object levels using a vertical format; the Excel default; sometimes referred to as a bar chart in other spreadsheet programs
Line		Compares trends over even time intervals; looks similar to an area chart, but does not emphasize total
Pie		Compares sizes of pieces as part of a whole; used for a single series of numbers
Bar		Compares distinct object levels using a horizontal format; sometimes referred to as a horizontal bar chart in other spreadsheet programs
Area		Shows how individual volume changes over time in relation to total volume
Scatter		Compares trends over uneven time or measurement intervals; used in scientific and engineering disciplines for trend spotting and extrapolation

Creating a Chart

To create a chart in Excel, you first select the range in a worksheet containing the data you want to chart. Once you've selected a range, you can use buttons on the Insert tab of the Ribbon to create and modify a chart. ▰▰▰▰ Using the worksheet containing the quarterly revenue data, you create a chart that shows the growth trend that occurred.

STEPS

QUICK TIP

When charting data for a particular time period, make sure all series are for the same time period.

1. **Start Excel, open the file EX D-1.xlsx from the drive and folder where you store your Data Files, then save it as Quarterly Tour Revenue**

   You want the chart to include the quarterly tour revenue figures, as well as quarter and country labels. You don't include the Total column and row because the quarterly figures make up the totals, and these figures would skew the chart.

QUICK TIP

To select nonadjacent cells, press and hold [Ctrl] while selecting each range.

2. **Select the range A4:E12, then click the Insert tab on the Ribbon**

   The Insert tab contains groups for inserting various types of objects, including charts. The Charts group includes buttons for each major chart type, plus an Other Charts button for additional chart types, such as stock charts for charting stock market data.

3. **Click the Column chart button, then click the Clustered Column button on the Column palette, as shown in Figure D-3**

   The chart is inserted in the center of the worksheet, and three contextual Chart Tools tabs open on the Ribbon: Design, Layout, and Format. On the Design tab, which is currently in front, you can quickly change the chart type, chart layout, and chart format and you can swap the data between the columns and rows. Currently, the countries are charted along the horizontal axis, with the quarterly revenues charted along the y-axis. This lets you easily compare quarterly revenues for each country.

4. **Click the Switch Row/Column button in the Data group on the Chart Tools Design tab**

   Clicking this button switches the data in the columns and rows, as shown in Figure D-4, so that the quarterly revenues are charted along the horizontal axis and the countries are plotted as the data points.

5. **Click the Undo button ↺ on the Quick Access toolbar**

   The chart returns to its original configuration.

6. **Click the Chart Tools Layout tab, click the Chart Title button in the Labels group, then click Above Chart on the palette**

   A title placeholder appears above the chart.

QUICK TIP

You can also triple-click to select a line of text.

7. **Click anywhere in the Chart Title text box, press [Ctrl][A] to select the text, type Quarterly Tour Revenue, then click anywhere in the chart to deselect the title**

   Adding a title helps identify the chart. This chart is known as an **embedded** chart because it's inserted directly in the current worksheet. The **sizing handles**, the small series of dots at the corners and sides of the chart's border, indicate that the chart is selected. See Figure D-5. Your chart might be in a different location on the worksheet and may look slightly different; you will move and resize it in the next lesson. Any time a chart is selected, as it is now, a blue border surrounds the worksheet data range, a purple border surrounds the row labels, and a green border surrounds the column labels. Embedding a chart in the current sheet is the default selection when creating a chart, but you can also place a chart on a different sheet in the workbook, or on a newly created chart sheet. A **chart sheet** is a sheet in a workbook that contains only a chart, which is linked to the workbook data.

8. **Save your work**

FIGURE D-3: Column chart palette

Clustered Column chart type

Column chart types

FIGURE D-4: Clustered Column chart with rows and columns switched

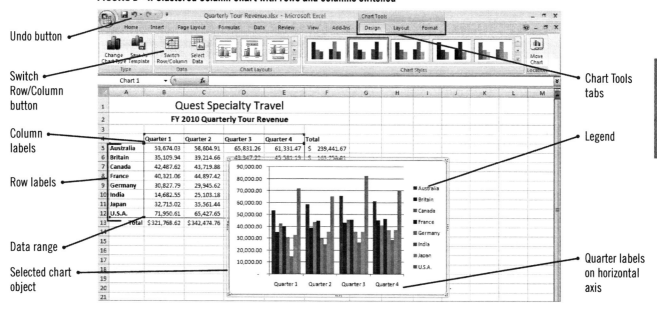

Undo button

Switch Row/Column button

Column labels

Row labels

Data range

Selected chart object

Chart Tools tabs

Legend

Quarter labels on horizontal axis

FIGURE D-5: Chart with rows and columns restored and title added

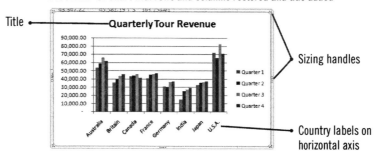

Title

Sizing handles

Country labels on horizontal axis

Using the contextual Chart Tools tabs

When a chart is selected, the three contextual Chart Tools tabs (Design, Layout, and Format) appear on the Ribbon. These tabs help guide you through developing and perfecting your chart. Using the Design tab, you can change overall color schemes and positioning of objects within the chart as well as the data range and configuration used for the chart. The Layout tab is used to add and modify chart elements, such as titles and labels, and for adding graphics, such as pictures, shapes, and text boxes. The Format tab lets you format objects such as shapes and text, arrange multiple objects so they are layered attractively, and resize any object to exact specifications. While these tabs organize chart tools in a logical order, it is not necessary to use them in the order in which they appear. In other words, you can jump from the Design tab to the Format tab, back to Design, then to Layout, if you wish.

Working with Charts

Moving and Resizing a Chart

Charts are graphics, or drawn objects, and are not located in a specific cell or at a specific range address. An **object** is an independent element on a worksheet. You can select an object by clicking within its borders; sizing handles around the object indicate it is selected. You can move a selected chart object anywhere on a worksheet without affecting formulas or data in the worksheet. However, any data changed in the worksheet is automatically updated in the chart. You can resize a chart to improve its appearance by dragging its sizing handles. You can even move a chart to a different sheet, and it will still reflect the original data. Chart objects contain other objects, such as a title and legend, which you can move and resize. In addition to repositioning chart elements to set locations using commands on the Layout tab, you can freely move any object using the mouse. Simply select it, then drag it or cut and paste it to a new location. When the mouse pointer hovers over any chart object, the name of the selected object appears on screen as a ScreenTip. You want to resize the chart, position it below the worksheet data, and move the legend.

STEPS

1. **Make sure the chart is still selected, then position the pointer over the chart**

   The pointer shape indicates that you can move the chart object or use a sizing handle to resize it. For a table of commonly used graphic object pointers, refer to Table D-2.

2. **Position on a blank area near the top left edge of the chart, press and hold the left mouse button, drag the chart until its upper left corner is at the upper left corner of cell A16, then release the mouse button**

   As you drag the chart, you can see an outline representing the chart's perimeter. The chart appears in the new location.

3. **Position the pointer on the right-middle sizing handle until it changes to ⇔, then drag the right edge of the chart to the right edge of column G**

   The chart is widened. See Figure D-6.

4. **Position the pointer over the upper-middle sizing handle until it changes to ⇔, then drag it to the top edge of row 15**

5. **Scroll down if necessary so row 26 is visible, position the pointer over the lower-middle sizing handle until it changes to ⇔, then drag the bottom border of the chart to the bottom border of row 26**

   You can move any object on a chart. You want to align the top of the legend with the top of the plot area.

6. **Click the legend to select it, press and hold [Shift], drag the legend up using so the dotted outline is approximately ¼" above the top of the plot area, then release [Shift]**

   When you click the legend, sizing handles appear around it and "Legend" appears as a ScreenTip when the pointer hovers over the object. As you drag, a dotted outline of the legend border appears. Pressing and holding the [Shift] key holds the horizontal position of the legend as you move it vertically.

7. **Click cell A12, type United States, click the Enter button ✔ on the formula bar, use AutoFit to resize column A, then press [Ctrl][Home]**

   The axis label changes to reflect the updated cell contents, as shown in Figure D-7. Changing any data in the worksheet modifies corresponding text or values in the chart. Because the chart is no longer selected, the Chart Tools tabs no longer appear on the Ribbon.

8. **Save your work**

Working with Charts

FIGURE D-6: Moved and resized chart

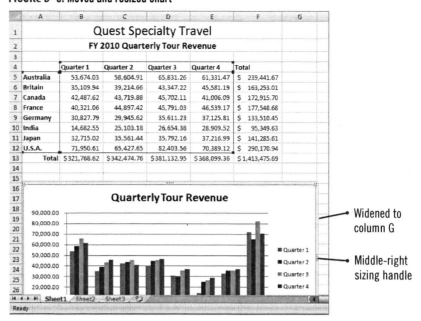

Widened to column G

Middle-right sizing handle

FIGURE D-7: Worksheet with modified legend and label

Modified text

Plot area

Label changes to match change in cell A12

TABLE D-2: Common graphic object pointers

name	pointer	use	name	pointer	use
Diagonal resizing	⤢ or ⤡	Change chart shape	I-beam	I	Edit chart text from corners
Draw	+	Create shapes	Move chart	⇖	Change chart location
Horizontal resizing	⇐	Change chart shape from left to right	Vertical resizing	↕	Change chart shape from top to bottom

Moving an embedded chart to a sheet

Suppose you have created an embedded chart that you decide would look better on a chart sheet. You can make this change without recreating the entire chart. To do so, first select the chart, click the Chart Tools Design tab, then click the Move Chart button in the Location group. The Move Chart dialog box opens. If the chart is embedded, click the New sheet option button, then click OK. If the chart is on its own sheet, click the Object in option button, then click OK.

Working with Charts

Changing the Chart Design

Once you've created a chart, it's easy to modify the design. You can change data values in the worksheet, and the chart is automatically updated to reflect the new data. Each of the Chart Tools tabs can be used to make specific changes in a chart. Using the Chart Tools Design tab, you can change the chart type in the Type group, modify the data range and configuration in the Data group, change the layout of objects in the Chart Layouts group, choose from coordinating color schemes in the Chart Styles group, and move the location of the chart in the Location group. The layouts in the Chart Styles group offer preconfigured arrangements of objects in your chart, such as a legend, title, or gridlines; these layouts offer an alternative to manually making formatting and design changes. ■■■■ You look over your worksheet and realize the data for the United States in Quarter 2 and Quarter 4 is incorrect. After you correct this data, you want to see how the same data looks using different chart layouts and types.

STEPS

1. **Click cell C12, type 75432.29, press [Tab] twice, type 84295.27, then press [Enter]**
   In the worksheet, the United States entries for Quarter 2 and Quarter 4 reflect the increased sales figures. See Figure D-8. The totals in column F and row 13 are also updated.

2. **Select the chart by clicking a blank area within the chart border, click the Chart Tools Design tab on the Ribbon, then click the Layout 3 button in the Chart Layouts group**
   The legend moves to the bottom of the chart. You prefer the original layout.

3. **Click the Undo button ⟲ on the Quick Access toolbar, then click the Change Chart Type button in the Type group**
   The Change Chart Type dialog box opens, as shown in Figure D-9, where you can choose from all available chart type categories and types. The left pane lists the available categories, and the right pane shows the individual chart types. An orange border surrounds the currently selected chart type.

4. **Click Bar in the left pane of the Change Chart Type dialog box, confirm that the Clustered Bar chart type is selected, then click OK**
   The column chart changes to a clustered bar chart. See Figure D-10. You look at the bar chart, then decide to see if the large increase in sales is more apparent if you use a three-dimensional column chart.

5. **Click the Change Chart Type button in the Type group, click Column in the left pane of the Change Chart Type dialog box, click 3-D Clustered Column (fourth from the left in the first row), then click OK**
   A three-dimensional column chart appears. You notice that the three-dimensional column format is more crowded than the two-dimensional format, but it gives you a sense of volume.

6. **Click the Change Chart Type button in the Type group, click the Clustered Column button (first from the left, first row), then click OK**

7. **Click the Style 3 button in the Chart Styles group**
   The columns change to shades of blue. You prefer the previous color scheme.

8. **Click ⟲ in the Quick Access toolbar, then save your work**

Creating a Combination Chart

You can apply a chart type to an existing data series in a chart, to create a combination chart. In the existing chart, select the data series that you want plotted on a secondary axis, then open the Format dialog box (use the shortcut menu, or click Format Selection in the Current Selection group of the Format tab on the Ribbon). In the Format dialog box, click Series Options, if necessary, click the Secondary Axis option button under Plot Series On, then click Close. Click the Layout tab on the Ribbon, click Axes in the Axes group, then click the type of secondary axis you want and where you want it to appear. To finish, click the Change Chart Type button in the Type group on the Design tab, then select a chart type for the secondary axis.

Working with Charts

FIGURE D-8: Worksheet with modified data

Modified data

Adjusted data points

FIGURE D-9: Change Chart Type dialog box

Currently selected chart type

Bar category

Chart type categories

FIGURE D-10: Column chart changed to bar chart

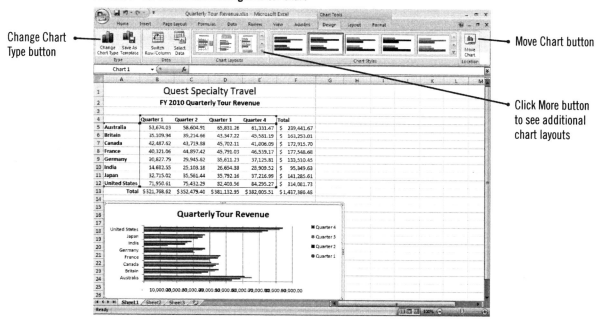

Change Chart Type button

Move Chart button

Click More button to see additional chart layouts

Working with a 3-D chart

Excel includes true 3-D chart types as well as chart types formatted in 3-D. In a true 3-D chart, a third axis, called the **z-axis**, lets you compare data points across both categories and values. The z-axis runs along the depth of the chart, so it appears to advance from the back of the chart. To create a true 3-D chart, look for chart subtypes that begin with "3-D," such as 3-D Column. Charts that are formatted in 3-D contain only two axes but their graphics give the illusion of three-dimensionality. For example, the Clustered Column in 3-D chart displays columns in a 3-D format, but does not include a z-axis that you can modify. To create a chart that is only formatted in 3-D, look for chart subtypes that end with "in 3-D." In a 3-D chart, other data series in the same chart can sometimes obscure columns or bars, but you can rotate the chart to obtain a better view. Right-click the chart, then click 3-D Rotation. The Format Chart Area dialog box opens, with the 3-D Rotation category active. This dialog box can also be used to modify fill, line, line style, shadow, and 3-D format. The 3-D Rotation options let you choose the orientation and perspective of the chart area, plot area, walls, and floor for a 3-D chart. You can use these rotation options to improve the appearance of plotted data within a chart. The 3-D Format options let you choose what three-dimensional effects you would like to apply to select chart elements. (Not all 3-D Format options are available on all charts.)

Changing the Chart Layout

Changing chart layout involves adding, removing, and modifying individual chart elements such as the chart title, plot area, gridlines, and data series. While the Chart Tools Design tab includes preconfigured chart layouts you can apply, the Chart Tools Layout tab makes it easy to create and modify individual chart objects. Using buttons on this tab, you can also add shapes and additional text to a chart, add and modify labels, change the display of axes, and modify the fill behind the plot area. You can also eliminate or change the look of gridlines. **Gridlines** are the horizontal and vertical lines in the chart that enable the eye to follow the value on an axis. You can create titles for the horizontal and vertical axes, add graphics, or add background color. You can even format the text you use in a chart. You want to make some layout changes in the chart, to make sure it's easy to interpret and improve its general appearance.

STEPS

QUICK TIP

The Chart Tools tabs appear on the Ribbon only when a chart or one of its objects is selected.

1. **With the chart still selected, click the Chart Tools Layout tab on the Ribbon, click the Gridlines button in the Axes group, point to Primary Horizontal Gridlines, then click None**

   The gridlines that extend from the value axis tick marks across the chart's plot area are removed from the chart, as shown in Figure D-11.

2. **Click the Gridlines button in the Axes group, point to Primary Horizontal Gridlines, then click Major & Minor Gridlines**

   Both major and minor gridlines now appear in the chart. **Minor gridlines** show the values between the tick marks. You can change the color of the columns to better distinguish the data series.

3. **Click the Axis Titles button in the Labels group, point to Primary Horizontal Axis Title, click Title Below Axis, triple-click the axis title, then type Tour Countries**

   Descriptive text on the category axis helps readers understand the chart.

QUICK TIP

You can also edit text in a chart element by positioning the pointer over the selected text box until it changes to I, click the text box, then edit the text.

4. **Click the Axis Titles button in the Labels group, point to Primary Vertical Axis Title, then click Rotated Title**

   A placeholder for the vertical axis title is added to the left of the vertical axis.

5. **Triple-click the vertical axis title, then type Revenue (in $)**

   The text "Revenue (in $)" appears to the left of the vertical axis, as shown in Figure D-12.

QUICK TIP

You can move any title to a new position by clicking an edge of the object then dragging it.

6. **Right-click the horizontal axis labels ("Australia", "Britain", etc.), click the Font list on the Mini toolbar, click Times New Roman, click the Font Size list on the Mini toolbar, then click 8**

   The font of the horizontal axis text changes to Times New Roman, and the font size decreases, making more of the plot area visible.

7. **Right-click the vertical axis labels, click the Font list on the Mini toolbar, click Times New Roman, click the Font Size list on the Mini toolbar, then click 8**

8. **Right-click the chart title ("Quarterly Tour Revenue"), click Format Chart Title on the shortcut menu, click Border Color in the left pane, then click the Solid line option button in the right pane**

   Adding a solid border is the first step to creating a shadow box that surrounds the title. You can only add a shadow to a text box that has a border.

9. **Click Shadow in the left pane, click the Presets list arrow, click the Offset Diagonal Bottom Right (first row, first from the left) style in the Outer group, click Close, then save your work**

   A border with a drop shadow surrounds the title. Compare your work to Figure D-13.

FIGURE D-11: Gridlines removed from chart

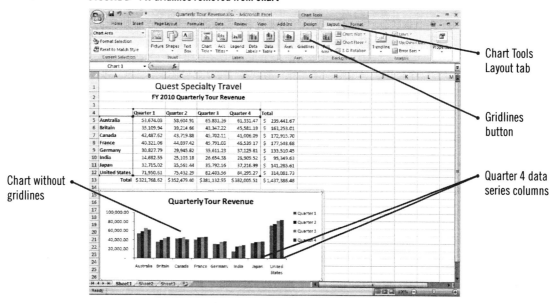

Chart Tools
Layout tab

Gridlines
button

Chart without
gridlines

Quarter 4 data
series columns

FIGURE D-12: Axes titles added to chart

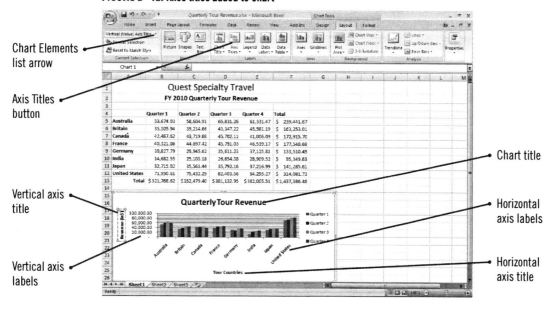

Chart Elements
list arrow

Axis Titles
button

Vertical axis
title

Vertical axis
labels

Chart title

Horizontal
axis labels

Horizontal
axis title

FIGURE D-13: Enhanced chart

Border and shadow
added to chart title

Modified axis
labels

Formatting a Chart

Formatting a chart can make it easier to read and understand. Many formatting enhancements can be made using the Chart Tools Format tab. You can change colors in a specific data series or you can apply a style to a series using the Shape Styles group. Styles make it possible to apply multiple formats, such as an outline, fill color, and text color, all with a single click. You can also make individual selections of fill color, outline, and other effects using the Shape Styles group. WordArt, which lets you create curved or stylized text, can be created using the WordArt Styles group. ▐▐▐▌ You want to improve the appearance of the chart by creating titles for the horizontal and vertical axes and adding a drop shadow to the chart title.

STEPS

1. **With the chart selected, click the Chart Tools Format tab on the Ribbon, then click any column in the Quarter 4 data series**

    The Chart Tools Format tab opens, and handles surround each column in the Quarter 4 data series, indicating that the entire series is selected.

2. **Click the Format Selection button in the Current Selection group**

3. **Click Fill in the left pane of the Format Data Series dialog box, then click the Solid fill option button**

4. **Click the Color list arrow** ▤▾**, click Orange, Accent 6 (first row, tenth from the left) as shown in Figure D-14, then click Close**

    All the columns for the series become orange, and the legend changes to match the new color. You can also change the color of selected objects by applying a shape style.

5. **Click any column in the Quarter 3 data series**

    Handles surround each column in the Quarter 3 data series.

6. **Click the More button** ▤ **on the Shape Styles gallery, then hover the pointer over the Moderate Effect – Accent 3 button (fifth row, fourth from the left) as shown in Figure D-15**

7. **Click the Subtle Effect – Accent 3 button (fourth row, fourth from the left) in the palette**

    The color for the data series changes, as shown in Figure D-16.

8. **Save your work**

Changing alignment in axis text and titles

The buttons on the Chart Tools Layout tab provide a few options for aligning axis text and titles, but you can customize the position and rotation to exact specifications using the Format dialog box. You can modify the alignment of axis text to make it fit better within the plot area. With a chart selected, right-click the axis text you want to modify, then click Format Axis on the shortcut menu. The Format Axis dialog box opens for the selected element. Click Alignment, then select the appropriate option. You can create a custom angle by clicking the Text direction list arrow, clicking Horizontal, then selecting the number of degrees from the Custom angle text box. When you have made the desired changes, click Close.

FIGURE D-14: Format Data Series dialog box

Click Border Color to control line display

Click Shadow to control shadow settings

Orange, Accent 6

FIGURE D-15: Chart with formatted data series

Subtle Effect – Accent 3

Moderate Effect – Accent 3

In Step 6, point to this style

Live Preview of current style

FIGURE D-16: Color of data series changed

Annotating and Drawing on a Chart

You can add text annotations and graphics to a chart to point out critical information. **Text annotations** are labels that further describe your data. You can also draw lines and arrows that point to the exact locations you want to emphasize. Shapes such as arrows and boxes can be added from the Illustrations group on the Insert tab or from the Insert group on the Chart Tools Layout group on the Ribbon. These groups are also used to Insert pictures and clip art. ▓▓▓▓ You want to call attention to the India tour revenue increases, so you decide to add a text annotation and an arrow to this information in the chart.

STEPS

1. **Make sure the chart is selected, click the Chart Tools Layout tab, click the Text Box button in the Insert group, then move the pointer over the worksheet**

   The pointer changes to ↓, indicating that you can begin typing text by clicking.

2. **Click to the right of the chart (anywhere *outside* the chart boundary)**

   A text box is added to the worksheet, and the Drawing Tools Format tab opens, so that you can format the new object. First you need to type the text.

3. **Type Great improvement**

   The text appears in a selected text box on the worksheet and the chart is no longer selected, as shown in Figure D-17. Your text box may be in a different location; this is not important, because you'll move the annotation in the next step.

4. **Point to an edge of the text box so that the pointer changes to ⁺⃛, drag the text box into the chart to the left of the chart title, as shown in Figure D-18, then release the mouse button**

   You want to add a simple arrow shape in the chart.

5. **Click the chart to select it, click the Chart Tools Layout tab, click the Shapes button in the Insert group, click the Arrow shape in the Lines category, then move the pointer over the chart**

   The pointer changes to ┼, and the status bar displays "Click and drag to insert an AutoShape." When you draw an arrow, the point farthest from where you start has the arrowhead. When ┼ is near the text box handles, the handles turn red. The red handles act as an anchor for the arrow.

6. **Position ┼ at the red square to the right of the t in the word "improvement" (in the text box), press and hold the left mouse button, drag the line to the Quarter 2 column in the India series, then release the mouse button**

   An arrow points to India's second quarter revenue, and the Drawing Tools Format tab displays options for working with this new object. You can resize, format, or delete it just like any other object in a chart.

7. **Click the Shape Outline list arrow in the Shape Styles group, point to Weight, then click 1½ pt**

   Compare your finished chart to Figure D-19.

8. **Save your work**

FIGURE D-17: Text box added

Drawing Tools
Format tab

Text
annotation

FIGURE D-18: Text annotation on chart

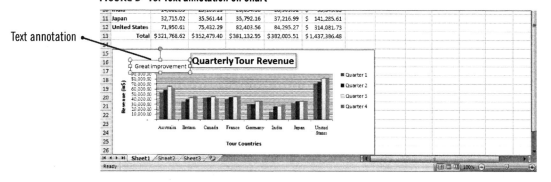

Text annotation

FIGURE D-19: Drawn object added to chart

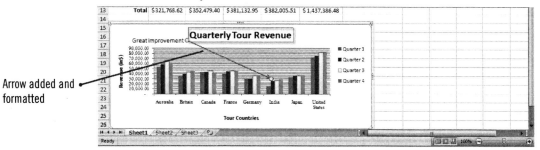

Arrow added and
formatted

Adding SmartArt graphics

In addition to charts, annotations, and drawn objects, you can create a variety of diagrams using SmartArt. Diagram types include List, Process, Cycle, Hierarchy, Relationship, Matrix, and Pyramid. To insert SmartArt, click the SmartArt button in the Illustrations group on the Insert tab on the Ribbon. Click the category of SmartArt you want to create from the left panel, then click the style from the center panel. The right panel shows a sample of the selection you've chosen, as shown in Figure D-20. The diagram appears on the worksheet as an embedded object with sizing handles. An additional window opens where you can enter the diagram text.

FIGURE D-20: Choose a SmartArt Graphic dialog box

Working with Charts

Creating a Pie Chart

You can create multiple charts based on the same worksheet data. While a column chart may illustrate certain important aspects of your worksheet data, you may find you want to create an additional chart to emphasize a different point. Depending on the type of chart you create, you have additional options for calling attention to trends and patterns. For example, if you create a pie chart, you can emphasize one data point by **exploding**, or pulling that slice away from, the pie chart. When you're ready to print a chart, you can preview it just as you do a worksheet, to check the output before committing it to paper. You can print a chart by itself or as part of the worksheet. ▰▰▰▰▰ At an upcoming meeting, Grace plans to discuss the total tour revenue and which countries need improvement. You want to create a pie chart she can use to illustrate total revenue. Finally, you want to print the worksheet and the charts.

STEPS

1. **Select the range A5:A12, press and hold [Ctrl], select the range F5:F12, click the Insert tab, click the Pie button in the Charts group, then click the Pie in 3-D button in the gallery**

   The new chart appears in the center of the worksheet. You can move the chart and quickly format it using a Chart Layout.

2. **Drag the chart so its top left corner is at the top left corner of cell G1, then click the Layout 2 button in the Chart Layouts group**

3. **Click the slice for the India data point, click again so it is the only data point selected, right-click, then click Format Data Point**

   The Format Data Point dialog box opens, as shown in Figure D-21. You can use the Point Explosion slider to control the distance a pie slice moves or you can type a value in the Point Explosion text box.

4. **Double-click 0 in the Point Explosion text box, type 40, then click Close**

   Compare your chart to Figure D-22. You decide to preview the chart and data before you print.

5. **Drag the bottom edge of the chart so it is close to the top of row 15, if necessary**

6. **Click cell A1, switch to Page Layout view, type Your Name in the left-hand header box, then click cell A1**

   You decide the chart and data would fit better on the page if they were printed in **landscape** orientation—that is, with the text running the long way on the page.

7. **Click the Page Layout tab, click the Orientation button in the Page Setup group, then click Landscape**

8. **Open the Print Preview window, click the Page Setup button on the Print Preview tab, click the Fit to option button, make sure the contents are set to fit to 1 page wide by 1 page tall, then click OK**

   The data and chart are positioned horizontally on a single page. See Figure D-23. The printer you have selected may affect the appearance of your preview screen, and if you do not have a color printer installed, the image will appear in black & white.

9. **Click the Print button on the Print Preview tab, print one copy of the page, save and close the workbook, then exit Excel**

FIGURE D-21: Format Data Point dialog box

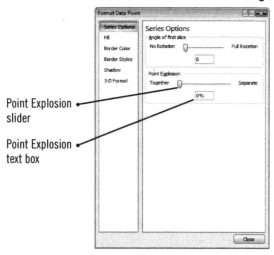

Point Explosion slider

Point Explosion text box

FIGURE D-22: Exploded pie slice

FIGURE D-23: Landscape view of completed charts

Using the Page Setup dialog box for a chart

When a chart is selected (or a chart sheet is active) and the Print Preview window is open, you can make modifications by clicking Page Setup in the Print group on the Print Preview tab. The Page Setup dialog box does not display all the options normally available. For example, the Center on page options (in the Margins tab) are not always available, and the Scaling options (in the Page tab) are grayed out.

You can also use the Show Margins checkbox in the Preview group of the Print Preview tab to accurately position a chart on the page. Margin lines appear on the screen and show you exactly how the margins appear on the page. The exact placement appears in the status bar when you press and hold the mouse button on the margin line. You can drag the lines to the exact settings you want.

Working with Charts

Practice

If you have a SAM user profile, you may have access to hands-on instruction, practice, and assessment of the skills covered in this unit. Log in to your SAM account (http://sam2007.course.com/) to launch any assigned training activities or exams that relate to the skills covered in this unit.

▼ CONCEPTS REVIEW

Label each element of the Excel chart shown in Figure D-24.

FIGURE D-24

Match each chart type with the statement that best describes it.

7. Line

8. Pie

9. Area

10. Column

11. Combination

a. Compares trends over even time intervals

b. Shows how volume changes over time

c. Compares data over time the Excel default

d. Displays a column and line chart using different scales of measurement

e. Compares data as parts of a whole

Working with Charts

313

Select the best answer from the list of choices.

12. Which tab on the Ribbon do you use to create a chart?

   a. Design   **c.** Page Layout

   b. Insert   **d.** Format

13. Which tab appears only when a chart is selected?

   a. Insert   **c.** Review

   b. Chart Tools Format   **d.** Page Layout

14. Which pointer do you use to resize a chart object?

   a. ╋   **c.** ↓

   b. I   **d.** ↕

15. How do you move an embedded chart to a chart sheet?

   a. Click a button on the Chart Tools Design tab.

   b. Drag the chart to the sheet tab.

   c. Delete the chart, switch to a different sheet, then create a new chart.

   d. Use the Copy and Paste buttons on the Ribbon.

16. The object in a chart that identifies patterns used for each data series is a(n):

   a. Data marker.   **c.** Organizer

   b. Data point.   **d.** Legend.

17. A collection of related data points in a chart is called a:

   a. Data series.   **c.** Cell address.

   b. Data tick.   **d.** Value title.

▼ SKILLS REVIEW

1. Plan a chart.

   a. Start Excel, open the Data File EX D-2.xlsx from the drive and folder where you store your Data Files, then save it as **Departmental Software Usage**.

   b. Describe the type of chart you would use to plot this data.

   c. What chart type would you use to compare total company expenses by department?

   d. What term is used to describe each value in a worksheet range selected for a chart?

2. Create a chart.

   a. In the worksheet, select the range containing all the data and headings.

   b. Click the Insert tab, if necessary.

   c. Create a clustered column chart, then add the chart title **Software Usage, by Department** above the chart.

   d. Save your work.

3. Move and resize a chart.

   a. Make sure the chart is still selected.

   b. Move the chart beneath the data.

   c. Resize the chart so it extends to the left edge of column I.

   d. Use the Chart Tools Layout tab to move the legend below the charted data.

   e. Resize the chart so its bottom edge is at the top of row 25.

   f. Save your work.

4. Change the chart design.

   a. Change the value in cell B3 to **25**. Observe the change in the chart.

   b. Select the chart.

   c. Use the Chart Layouts group on the Chart Tools Design tab to change to Layout 7, then undo the change.

   d. Use the Change Chart Type button on the Chart Tools Design tab to change the chart to a clustered bar chart.

   e. Change the chart to a 3-D clustered column chart , then change it back to a clustered column chart.

   f. Save your work.

5. Change the chart layout.

   a. Use the Layout tab to turn off the displayed gridlines in the chart.

   b. Change the font used in the horizontal and vertical axes labels to Times New Roman.

   c. Turn on the major gridlines for both the horizontal and vertical axes.

   d. Change the chart title's font to Times New Roman, with a font size of 20.

   e. Enter Departments as the horizontal axis title.

   f. Enter Number of Users as the vertical axis title. (*Hint*: Use a rotated title)

   g. Change the font size of the horizontal axis to 10, if necessary, and the font to Times New Roman.

   h. Change the font size of the vertical axis labels to 10, if necessary, and the font to Times New Roman.

   i. Change Personnel in the column heading to Human Resources. (*Hint*: Change the label in the worksheet, then resize the column.)

   j. Change the font size of the legend to 14.

   k. Add an offset diagonal bottom-right outer drop shadow to the chart title. (*Hint*: Use a solid line border in the default color.)

   l. Save your work.

6. Format a chart.

   a. Make sure the chart is selected, then select the Format tab, if necessary.

   b. Change the color of the Excel data series to Olive Green, Accent 3 Darker 50%.

   c. Change the shape effect of the Excel data series to Bevel – Circle.

   d. Save your work.

7. Annotate and draw on a chart.

   a. Make sure the chart is selected, then create the text annotation Needs more users.

   b. Position the text annotation so the 'N' in 'Needs' is positioned approximately below the 't' in 'Software'.

   c. Use the Shapes group on the Insert tab to create a 1½ pt weight arrow that points to the Excel users in the Design Department.

   d. Deselect the chart.

   e. Save your work.

8. Create a pie chart.

   a. Select the range A1:F2, then create a 3-D pie chart.

   b. Drag the 3-D pie chart beneath the existing chart.

   c. Change the chart title to Excel Users.

   d. Apply Chart Style 26 to the chart.

   e. Explode the Human Resources slice from the pie chart at 25%.

   f. In the worksheet, enter your name in the left section of the header.

▼ SKILLS REVIEW (CONTINUED)

g. View the worksheet and charts in the Print Preview window, make sure all the contents fit on one page, then compare your work to Figure D-25.

h. Save your work.

i. Close the workbook, then exit Excel.

FIGURE D-25

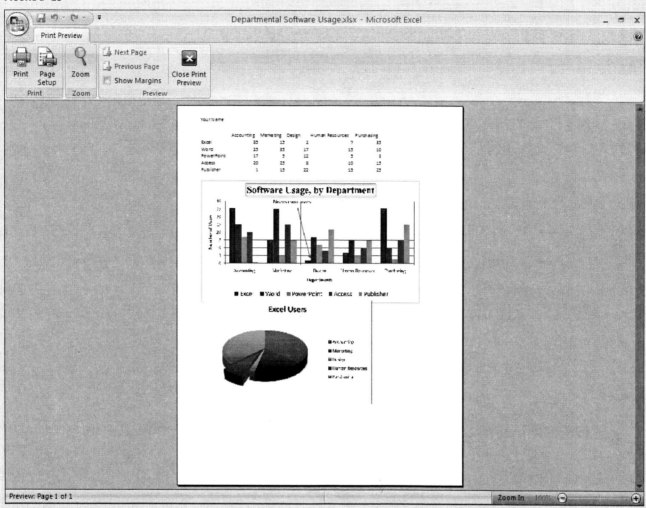

▼ INDEPENDENT CHALLENGE 1

You are the operations manager for the Springfield Theater Group in Massachusetts. Each year the group applies to various state and federal agencies for matching funds. For this year's funding proposal, you need to create charts to document the number of productions in previous years.

a. Start Excel, open the file EX D-3.xlsx from the drive and folder where you store your Data Files, then save it as **Springfield Theater Group**.

b. Take some time to plan your charts. Which type of chart or charts might best illustrate the information you need to display? What kind of chart enhancements do you want to use? Will a 3-D effect make your chart easier to understand?

c. Create a clustered column chart for the data.

d. If you wish, change at least one of the colors used in a data series.

e. Make the appropriate modifications to the chart to make it easy to read and understand, and visually attractive. Include chart titles, legends, and value and category axis titles, using the suggestions in Table D-3.

TABLE D-3

suggested chart enhancements for a column chart	
Title	Types and Number of Plays
Legend	Year 1, Year 2, Year 3, Year 4
Vertical axis title	Number of Plays
Horizontal axis title	Play Types

f. Create at least two additional charts for the same data to show how different chart types display the same data. Place each new chart on its own sheet in the workbook, and name the sheet according to the type of chart you created. One of the additional charts should be a pie chart; the other is up to you. Modify each new chart as necessary to improve its appearance and effectiveness. Compare your chart to the sample in Figure D-26.

FIGURE D-26

g. Enter your name in the worksheet header.

h. Save your work. Before printing, preview the workbook in Print Preview, then adjust any items as necessary.

i. Print the worksheet (charts and data).

j. Close the workbook, then exit Excel.

▼ INDEPENDENT CHALLENGE 2

FIGURE D-27

You work at Three Dog Bakery, a locally-owned bakery for dogs. One of your responsibilities at the bakery is to manage the company's sales and expenses using Excel. Another is to convince the current staff that Excel can help them make daily operating decisions more easily and efficiently. To do this, you've decided to create charts using the previous year's operating expenses, including rent, utilities, and payroll. The manager will use these charts at the next monthly meeting.

a. Start Excel, open the Data File EX D-4.xlsx from the drive and folder where you store your Data Files, then save it as **Three Dog Bakery Analysis**.

b. Decide which data in the worksheet should be charted. What type of chart or charts are best suited for the information you need to show? What kinds of chart enhancements are necessary?

c. Create a 3-D column chart (with the data series in rows) on the worksheet, showing the expense data for all four quarters. (*Hint*: Do not include the totals.)

d. Change the scale of the vertical axis (Expense data) so no decimals are displayed. (*Hint*: Right-click the scale you want to modify, click Format Axis, click Number category, change the number of decimal places, then click Close.)

e. Using the sales data, create two charts on this worksheet that illustrate trends in the data. (*Hint*: Move each chart to a new location on the worksheet, then deselect it before creating the next one.)

f. In one chart of the sales data, add data labels, then add chart titles as you see fit.

g. Make any necessary formatting changes to make the charts look more attractive, then enter your name in a worksheet cell.

h. Save your work.

i. Before printing, preview each chart, and adjust any items as needed. Fit the charts to a single page, then print one copy. Compare your work to the sample in Figure D-27.

j. Close the workbook, then exit Excel.

▼ INDEPENDENT CHALLENGE 3

FIGURE D-28

You are working as an account representative at the Inspiration Ad Agency. You have been examining the expenses charged to clients of the firm. The board of directors wants to examine certain advertising expenses and has asked you to prepare charts that can be used in this evaluation. In particular, you want to see how dollar amounts compare among the different expenses, and you also want to see how expenses compare with each other proportional to the total budget.

a. Start Excel, open the Data File EX D-5.xlsx from the drive and folder where you store your Data Files, then save it as **Ad Agency Expenses**.

b. Choose three types of charts that seem best suited to illustrate the data in the range A16:B24. What kinds of chart enhancements are necessary?

c. Create at least two different types of charts that show the distribution of advertising expenses. (*Hint*: Move each chart to a new location on the same worksheet.) One of the charts should be a 3-D pie chart.

d. Add annotated text and arrows highlighting important data, such as the largest expense.

e. Change the color of at least one data series in at least one of the charts.

f. Add chart titles and category and value axis titles where appropriate. Format the titles with a font of your choice. Place a drop shadow around the chart title in at least one chart.

g. Add your name to a section of the header, then save your work.

h. View the file in Print Preview. Adjust any items as needed. Be sure the charts are all visible on the page. Compare your work to the sample in Figure D-28.

Advanced Challenge Exercise

- Explode a slice from the 3-D pie chart.
- Add a data label to the exploded pie slice.
- Change the number format of labels in the non-pie charts so no decimals are displayed.
- Modify the scale of the vertical axis in one of the charts. (*Hint*: Right-click the vertical axis, click Format Axis, then click Axis Options.)
- Save your work, then view it in Print Preview.

i. Print the charts, close the workbook, then exit Excel.

FIGURE D-29

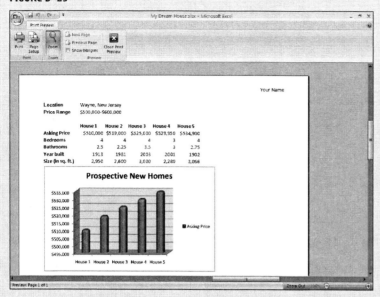

Note: This project requires an Internet connection.

A cash inheritance from a distant relative has finally been deposited in your bank account, and you have decided to quit your job and relocate to the town of your dreams. You have a good idea where you'd like to live and decide to use the Web to see what sort of houses are currently available.

a. Start Excel, then save a new, blank workbook as **My Dream House** to the drive and folder where you save your Data Files.

b. Decide on where you would like to live, and use your favorite search engine to find information sources on homes for sale in that area.

c. Determine a price range and features within the home. Find data for at least five homes that meet your location and price requirements, and enter them in the worksheet. See Table D-4 below for suggested data layout.

d. Format the data so it looks attractive and professional.

e. Create any type of column chart, using only the House and Asking Price data. Place it on the same worksheet as the data. Include a descriptive title.

f. Change the colors in the chart, using the Chart Style of your choice.

g. Enter your name in a section of the header.

TABLE D-4

location					
price range					
	House 1	House 2	House 3	House 4	House 5
Asking price					
Bedrooms					
Bathrooms					
Year built					
Size (in sq. ft.)					

h. Save the workbook. Preview the chart(s) and change margins and/or orientation as necessary. Compare your work to the sample chart shown in Figure D-29.

i. Print your worksheet(s), including the data and chart(s), making setup modifications as necessary.

Advanced Challenge Exercise

■ Change the chart type to a Clustered Column chart.

■ Create a combination chart that plots the asking price on one axis and the size of the home on the other axis. (*Hint*: Use Help to get tips on how to chart with a secondary axis.)

j. Close the workbook, then exit Excel.

▼ VISUAL WORKSHOP

Open the Data File EX D-6.xlsx from the drive and folder where you store your Data Files, then save it as **Projected Project Revenue**. Modify the worksheet data so it looks like Figure D-30, then create and modify two charts to match the ones shown in the figure. You will need to make formatting, layout, and design changes once you create the charts. Enter your name in the left section of the header, then save, preview, and print your results.

FIGURE D-30

Getting Started with Access 2007

In this unit, you will learn the purpose, advantages, and terminology of Microsoft Office Access 2007, the relational database program in Microsoft Office 2007. You will create and modify tables, the basic building blocks of an Access relational database. You'll also navigate, enter, update, preview, and print data. Mark Rock is the tour developer for United States group travel at Quest Specialty Travel (QST), a tour company that specializes in cultural tourism and adventure travel. Mark uses Access to store, maintain, and analyze customer and tour information.

OBJECTIVES

Understand relational databases

Open a database

Enter data

Edit data

Create a database

Create a table

Create primary keys

Relate two tables

Print a datasheet

Understanding Relational Databases

Microsoft Office Access 2007 is relational database software that runs on the Windows operating system. You use **relational database software** to manage data that is organized into lists, such as information about customers, products, vendors, employees, projects, or sales. Many small companies track customer, inventory, and sales information in a spreadsheet program such as Microsoft Office Excel. While Excel does offer some list management features, Access provides many more tools and advantages, mainly due to the "relational" nature of the lists that Access manages. Table A-1 compares the two programs. You and Mark Rock review the advantages of database software over spreadsheets for managing lists of information.

The advantages of using Access for database management include:

* ### Duplicate data is minimized

  Figures A-1 and A-2 compare how you might store sales data in a single Excel spreadsheet list versus three related Access tables. Note that with Access, you do not have to reenter information such as a customer's name and address or product description every time a sale is made, because lists can be linked, or "related," in relational database software.

* ### Information is more accurate, reliable, and consistent because duplicate data is minimized

  The relational nature of data stored in an Access database allows you to minimize duplicate data entry, which creates more accurate, reliable, and consistent information.

* ### Data entry is faster and easier using Access forms

  Data entry forms (screen layouts) make data entry faster and easier than entering data in a spreadsheet.

* ### Information can be viewed and sorted in many ways using Access queries, forms, and reports

  In Access, you can save queries (questions about the data), data entry forms, and reports, allowing you to use them over and over without performing extra work to re-create a particular view of the data.

* ### Information is more secure using Access passwords and security features

  Access databases can be password protected, and users can be given different privileges to view or update data.

* ### Several users can share and edit information simultaneously

  Unlike spreadsheets or word processing documents, Access databases are inherently multiuser. More than one person can be entering, updating, and analyzing data at the same time.

FIGURE A-1: Using a spreadsheet to organize sales data

	A	B	C	D	E	F	G	H	I	J	K	L	M	N	O	P
1	Cust No	First	Last	Street	City	State	Zip	Phone	Date	Invoice	Product No	Artist	Name	Format	Tracks	Cost
2	1	Kusong	Tse	222 Elm	Topeka	KS	66111	913-555-0000	8/1/2006	8111	11-222	Michael Smith	Always	CD	14	15
3	2	Paige	Denver	400 Oak	Lenexa	MO	60023	816-555-8877	8/1/2006	8112	11-222	Michael Smith	Always	CD	14	15
4	1	Kusong	Tse	222 Elm	Topeka	KS	66111	913-555-0000	8/2/2006	8113	22-333	Gold Flakes	Avalon	CD	13	14
5	3	Caitlyn	Baily	111 Ash	Ames	IA	50010	515-555-3333	8/3/2006	8114	22-333	Gold Flakes	Avalon	CD	13	14
6	2	Paige	Denver	400 Oak	Lenexa	MO	60023	816-555-8877	8/4/2006	8115	44-1111	Lungwort	Sounds	CD	15	13
7	3	Caitlyn	Baily	111 Ash	Ames	IA	50010	515-555-3333	8/4/2006	8116	44-1111	Lungwort	Sounds	CD	15	13
8	4	Max	Royal	500 Pine	Manilla	NE	55123	827-555-4422	8/5/2006	8117	44-1111	Lungwort	Sounds	CD	15	13
9																

Duplicate customer data is entered each time an existing customer makes an additional purchase

Duplicate product data is entered each time the same product is sold more than once

FIGURE A-2: Using a relational database to organize sales data

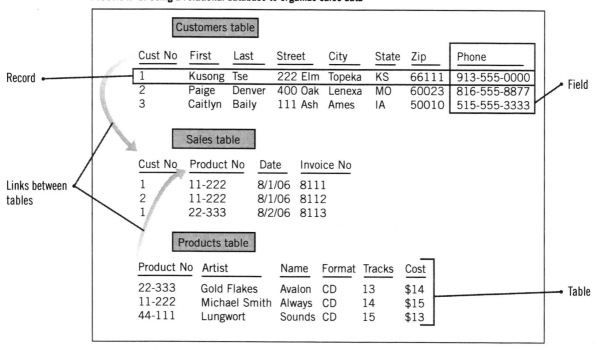

TABLE A-1: Comparing Excel to Access

feature	Excel	Access
Layout	Provides a natural tabular layout for easy data entry	Provides a natural tabular layout as well as the ability to create customized data entry screens
Storage	Limited to approximately 65,000 records per sheet	Stores any number of records up to 2 GB
Linked tables	Manages single lists of information	Allows links between lists of information to reduce data redundancy
Reporting	Limited to the current spreadsheet arrangement of data	Creates and saves multiple presentations of data
Security	Limited to file security options such as marking the file "read-only" or protecting a range of cells	Allows users to access only the records and fields they need
Multiuser capabilities	Does not easily allow multiple users to simultaneously enter and update data	Allows multiple users to simultaneously enter and update data
Data entry	Provides limited data entry screens	Provides the ability to create extensive data entry screens called forms

Opening a Database

You can start Access from the Start menu, which opens when you click the Start button on the Windows taskbar, or from an Access shortcut icon on the desktop. Access opens to the Getting Started with Microsoft Office Access page, which shows different ways to work with Access. To open a specific database in Access, you can click a database in the Open Recent Database list or click the More link to navigate to a different database. You can also start Access and open a database at the same time by opening the database directly from a My Computer or Windows Explorer window. ▓▓▓▓ Mark Rock has entered some tour information in a database called Quest-A. He asks you to start Access and review this database.

STEPS

1. **Start Access**

   Access starts and opens the Getting Started with Microsoft Office Access page, shown in Figure A-3, which helps you create a new database from a template, create a new blank database, or open an existing database.

TROUBLE

If a Security Warning bar appears below the Ribbon, click the Options button, click Enable this content, then click OK.

2. **Click the More link in the Open Recent Database list, navigate to the drive and folder where you store your Data Files, click the Quest-A.accdb database file, click Open, then click the Maximize button ▢ if the Access window is not already maximized**

   The Quest-A database contains two tables of data named States and Tours.

TROUBLE

If the Navigation Pane is not open, click the Shutter Bar Open/Close button ⟫ to open it and view database table names.

3. **In the Navigation Pane, double-click the Tours table to open it, then click ▢ on the Tours table**

   The Tours table opens in Datasheet View, as shown in Figure A-4. **Tables** are the fundamental building blocks of a relational database because they store all of the data. **Datasheet View** displays the data in a table in a spreadsheet-like view of fields and records called the **datasheet**. The Tours datasheet contains six fields and 21 records. **Field names** are listed at the top of each column. Important database terminology is summarized in Table A-2.

QUICK TIP

For more information on using features of the Access window that are new to Microsoft Office 2007, see the unit "Getting Started with Office 2007."

4. **In the Navigation Pane, double-click the States table to open it**

   The States table contains only two fields, StateAbbreviation and StateName, and four records. By using a separate States table, you only need to enter full state names such as Colorado and Florida once, rather than every time you enter a record for a particular state in the Tours table. The Tours and States tables are linked together via the common StateAbbreviation field. Later in this unit, you learn more about how multiple lists of information, defined as tables in Access, are linked to create relational databases.

FIGURE A-3: Getting Started with Microsoft Office Access page

Additional database template categories from Microsoft Office Online

Featured database templates

Open Recent Database list

More link

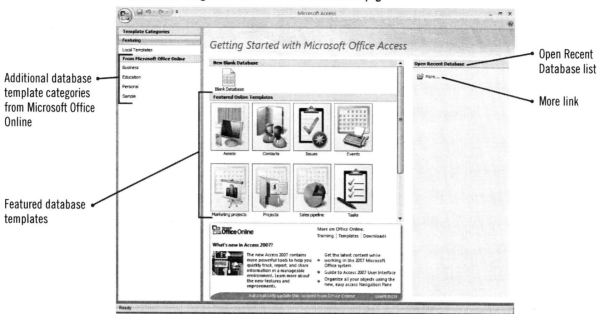

FIGURE A-4: Tours table

Shutter Bar Open/Close button

Navigation Pane showing tables

Each row is a record

Field names

Tours table open in Datasheet View

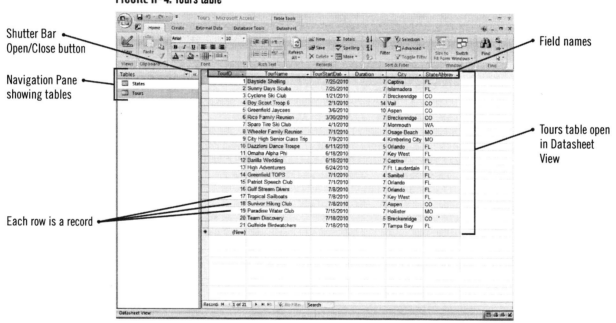

TABLE A-2: Important database terminology

term	description
Field	The smallest unit of data organization; consists of a specific category of data such as a customer's name, city, state, or phone number
Record	A group of related fields that describe a person, place, or thing
Key field	A field that contains unique information for each record, such as a customer number for a customer
Table	A collection of records for a single subject
Database	A collection of tables associated with a general topic
Relational database	An Access database with multiple tables that are linked together by a common field
Objects	The parts of an Access database that help you view, edit, manage, and analyze the data, such as **tables**, **queries**, **forms**, **reports**, **macros**, and **modules**

Entering Data

Your skill in navigating and entering data is a key to your success with a relational database. You use either mouse or keystroke techniques to navigate the data in the table's datasheet, which displays fields as columns and records as rows. 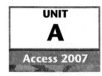 Mark Rock has developed some new tours for Quest Specialty Travel, and asks you to add this tour information by entering new records in the States and Tours tables of the Quest-A database.

STEPS

1. **Press [Tab] twice, then press [Enter] twice**

   Both the [Tab] and [Enter] keys move the focus to the next field. The **focus** refers to which data you would edit if you started typing. The field name and record selector button for the field and record that have the focus are highlighted with a different color. When you navigate to the last field of the record, pressing [Tab] or [Enter] advances the focus to the first field of the next record. You can also use the Next record ▶ and Previous record ◀ **navigation buttons** on the navigation bar in the lower-left corner of the datasheet to navigate the records. The **Current Record** text box on the navigation bar tells you the number of the current record as well as the total number of records in the datasheet.

2. **Click the StateAbbrev field below WA to position the insertion point to enter a new record**

   You can also use the New (blank) record button ▶✳ on the navigation bar to move to a new record. You enter new records at the end of the datasheet. You learn how to sort and reorder them later. A complete list of navigation keystrokes is shown in Table A-3.

3. **Type CA, press [Tab], then type California**

   Access saves data automatically as you move among records or within the database. With the California record entered in the States table, you're ready to enter a new tour record in the Tours table.

4. **Double-click the Tours table in the Navigation Pane, click (New) in the last row, press [Enter] to advance to the TourName field, type Perfect Waves, press [Enter], type 7/16/10, press [Enter], type 5, press [Enter], type Hunt Beach, press [Enter], type CA, then press [Enter]**

   The new tour record you entered is shown in Figure A-5. The TourID field is an **AutoNumber** field, which means that Access automatically enters the next consecutive number into the field as it creates the record.

Changing from Navigation mode to Edit mode

If you navigate to another area of the datasheet by clicking with the mouse pointer instead of pressing [Tab] or [Enter], you change from **Navigation mode** to Edit mode. In **Edit mode**, Access assumes that you are trying to make changes to the current field value, so

keystrokes such as [Ctrl][End], [Ctrl][Home], [←], and [→] move the insertion point *within* the field. To return to Navigation mode, press [Tab] or [Enter] (thus moving the focus to the next field), or press [↑] or [↓] (thus moving the focus to a different record).

FIGURE A-5: New record in the Tours table

Record selector box for TourID 16

Current focus

Navigation bar

New record added to the Tours table

Current Record text box

TABLE A-3: Navigation mode keyboard shortcuts

shortcut key	moves to the
[Tab], [Enter], or [→]	Next field of the current record
[Shift][Tab] or [←]	Previous field of the current record
[Home]	First field of the current record
[End]	Last field of the current record
[Ctrl][Home] or [F5]	First field of the first record
[Ctrl][End]	Last field of the last record
[↑]	Current field of the previous record
[↓]	Current field of the next record

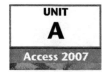

Editing Data

Updating existing information is another critical data management task. To change the contents of an existing record, click the field you want to change, then type the new information. You can delete unwanted data by clicking the field and using [Backspace] or [Delete] to delete text to the left or right of the insertion point. Other data-entry keystrokes are summarized in Table A-4. ▰▰▰▰▰ Mark Rock asks you to make some corrections to the records in the Tours table.

STEPS

1. **Double-click Dance in the TourName field of the TourID 10 record, and press the [Delete] key twice**

   You deleted both the word "Dance" and the extra space between "Dazzlers" and "Troupe." Access automatically saves new records and changes to existing data as soon as you move to another record or close the datasheet.

2. **Click after Barilla in the TourName field of TourID 12 record, and type -Cavuto**

   When you are editing a record, the **edit record symbol**, which looks like a small pencil, appears in the record selector box to the left of the current record, as shown in Figure A-6, to indicate you are in Edit mode.

3. **Double-click Speech in the TourID 15 record, and type Debate**

   You use the same editing techniques in an Access datasheet that you use in an Excel spreadsheet or Word document.

4. **Click the TourStartDate field in the TourID 22 record, click the Calendar icon 🔳, then navigate to and click August 27, 2010**

   The **calendar picker**, a pop-up calendar from which you can choose dates for a date field, is a new feature for Access 2007. You can also type the date directly into the field as 8/27/2010.

   QUICK TIP

   The ScreenTip for the Undo button displays the action you can undo.

5. **Press [Esc]**

   Pressing [Esc] once removes the current field's editing changes, so the TourStartDate changes back to 7/16/2010. Pressing [Esc] twice removes all changes to the current record. Once you move to another record, the edits are saved, you return to Navigation mode, and you can no longer use [Esc] to remove editing changes to the current record. You can, however, click the Undo button 🔄 on the Quick Access toolbar to undo the last change you made.

6. **Click the record selector for the TourID 16 record, click the Delete button in the Records group on the Home tab, then click Yes**

   A message warns that you cannot undo a record deletion operation. Notice that the Undo button is dimmed, indicating that it cannot be used now.

7. **Click the Close button ☒ on the title bar to close both the Quest-A.accdb database and Access 2007**

   Because Access saves data as you work in a database, you are not prompted to save data when you close the database or the Access itself.

Resizing and moving datasheet columns

You can resize the width of a field in a datasheet by dragging the **column separator**, the thin line that separates the field names to the left or right. The pointer changes to ↔ as you make the field wider or narrower. Release the mouse button when you have resized the field. To adjust the column width to accommodate the widest entry in the field, double-click the column separator. To move a column, click the field name to select the entire column, then drag the field name left or right.

FIGURE A-6: Edit mode

Edit record symbol

TABLE A-4: Edit mode keyboard shortcuts

editing keystroke	action
[Backspace]	Deletes one character to the left of the insertion point
[Delete]	Deletes one character to the right of the insertion point
[F2]	Switches between Edit and Navigation mode
[Esc]	Undoes the change to the current field
[Esc][Esc]	Undoes all changes to the current record
[F7]	Starts the spell check feature
[Ctrl][']	Inserts the value from the same field in the previous record into the current field
[Ctrl][;]	Inserts the current date in a Date field

Creating a Database

You can create a new database using an Access **template**, a sample database provided within the Microsoft Access program, or you can start with a blank database to create a database from scratch. Your decision depends on whether Access has a template that closely resembles the type of data you plan to manage. If it does, building your own database from a template might be faster than creating the database from scratch. Regardless of which method you use, you can always modify the database later, tailoring it to meet your specific needs. ▓▓▓▓ Mark Rock wants to organize Quest's clients, prospects, and vendors, and asks you to create an Access database to track contacts. You'll use the Contacts template to get started.

STEPS

QUICK TIP

To create a new blank database, use the Blank Database icon.

1. **Start Access**

   The "Getting Started with Microsoft Office Access" page opens, which you can use to create a database from a template. Some templates are stored on your computer when you install Access, and others are available from Microsoft Office Online.

TROUBLE

If an Access Help window or Security Warning bar opens, close it. If a Microsoft Office Genuine Advantage dialog box opens, click Continue.

2. **In the Featured Online Templates pane click Contacts, then click Download in the lower-right corner**

3. **Click the Watch This link on the left, then click the Watch this >> link to watch a short video on the Contact Management Database template**

   A short video plays explaining some of the features of the Microsoft Contact Management Database template. Note how to use the Options button to enable content.

4. **Close the Microsoft Office Online window, the Access Help window, and the Getting Started window**

   The Contact List form opens, as shown in Figure A-7.

5. **Click the Options button, click the Enable this content option button, click OK, close the Getting Started window if it opens again, enter your own name and e-mail address for the first record, use school information for the Business Phone and Company field, use Student for the Job Title field, then press [↓]**

   Although you are entering this record in an **Access form** (an easy-to-use data entry screen) instead of directly in a table, the data is stored in the underlying table. Forms and tables are database objects, and are displayed in the Navigation Pane. The **Navigation Pane** provides a way to move between objects (tables, queries, forms, and reports) in the database. Tables are the most important objects because they physically store all of the data. Table A-5 defines the four primary Access objects—tables, queries, forms, and reports—and the icon that identifies each in the Navigation Pane. When you created this database, the Contacts template not only created the Contact List form you used to enter your name, but also the Contact Details form and two reports, Directory and Phone Book.

TROUBLE

If the Phone Book report still shows your last name instead of "Johnson," close the report by right-clicking its tab and clicking Close, then double-click the report in the Navigation Pane to reopen it.

6. **Double-click the Contacts table in the Navigation Pane, double-click your last name in the Last Name field, type Johnson, then press [↓] to save the data**

   The Contacts table appears with the record you entered using the Contact List form. All data is physically stored in Access table objects when you move from record to record, even if the data is entered through a query or form.

7. **Double-click the Phone Book report in the Navigation Pane**

   All reports that depend on this data are automatically updated, as shown in Figure A-8.

8. **Click the Close button ☒ on the title bar to close both the Contacts database and Access 2007**

FIGURE A-7: Contact List form provided by the Contacts template

Shutter Bar Open/Close button

Form icon

Expand button

FIGURE A-8: Phone Book report provided by the Contacts template

Objects in the Contact database

Data edited in the Contacts table is updated in the Phone Book report

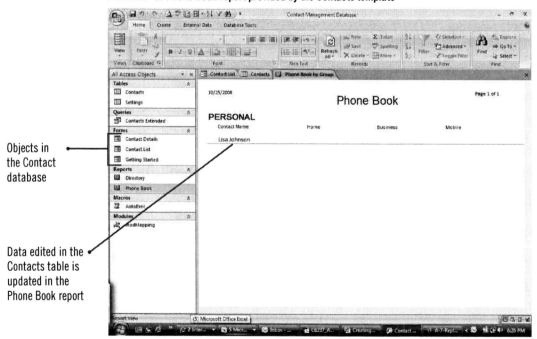

TABLE A-5: Access objects and their purpose

object	Navigation Pane icon	purpose
Table		Contains all of the raw data within the database in a spreadsheet-like view; tables are linked with a common field to create a relational database, which minimizes redundant data
Query		Allows the user to select a subset of fields or records from one or more tables; queries are created when a user has a question about the data
Form		Provides an easy-to-use data entry screen
Report		Provides a professional printout of data that can contain enhancements such as headers, footers, graphics, and calculations on groups of records

Getting Started with Access 2007

Creating a Table

After establishing your database, you often need to create a new table. You can use one of the table templates Access provides or you can create your own table from scratch. Creating a table consists of three essential tasks: meaningfully naming each field in the table, selecting an appropriate data type for each field, and naming the table itself. The **data type** determines what kind of data can be entered into a field, such as numbers, text, or dates. Data types are described in Table A-6. ▓▓▓▓ Mark Rock asks you to create a small table that lists the different types of tours Quest offers, such as Educational, Adventure, and Cultural. Because Access does not have a template for such a table, you'll create the table yourself.

STEPS

1. **Reopen the Quest-A.accdb database, enable content if prompted, click the Create tab on the Ribbon, click the Table button, then click the Maximize button** ▢

   A new, blank table datasheet appears, as shown in Figure A-9, with one sample field named ID that has an AutoNumber data type. You don't need this sample field in the table, so you can rename the first field and use it to identify tour categories.

2. **Click the ID field name, then click the Rename button on the Datasheet tab**

   ID in the column header is highlighted, allowing you to enter a new field name.

3. **Type Category, then press [↓]**

   The new field, renamed Category, is now the first field. With the field named appropriately, the next step is to choose the correct data type for the field. Currently, the field has an AutoNumber data type, but because this field will store the name of each tour category, you need to change its data type to Text.

4. **Click the Data Type list arrow (which currently displays AutoNumber) on the Datasheet tab, then click Text**

   For this table, you want to create one more field called TourDescription that also has a Text data type because it will store text descriptions of each tour.

5. **Double-click Add New Field, type TourDescription, then press [↓]**

   Because Text is the default data type for new fields, the TourDescription field has already been assigned with the correct data type.

6. **Click the blank cell below the Category field, type Adventure, then enter the remaining records as shown in Figure A-10**

   After naming the fields, assigning the data types, and entering the data, you save the table with an appropriate name. Table1 is the default name, but it is not very descriptive. You cannot rename a table that is open, so you'll close it and give it a descriptive name when prompted.

7. **Click the Close Window button** ☒ **for the new table, click Yes, type TourCategories, then click OK**

FIGURE A-9: New blank table in Datasheet View

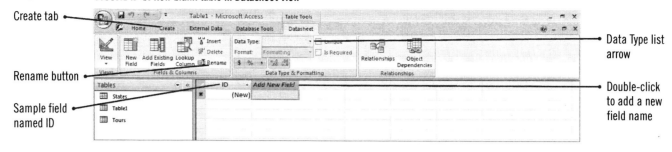

- Create tab
- Rename button
- Sample field named ID
- Data Type list arrow
- Double-click to add a new field name

FIGURE A-10: Complete datasheet

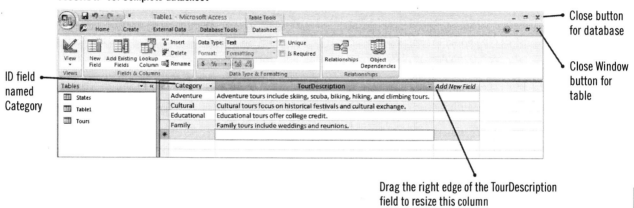

- ID field named Category
- Close button for database
- Close Window button for table
- Drag the right edge of the TourDescription field to resize this column

TABLE A-6: Data types

data type	description of data	size
Text	Text information or combinations of text and numbers, such as a street address, name, or phone number	Up to 255 characters
Memo	Lengthy text, such as comments or notes	Up to 65,535 characters
Number	Numeric information, such as quantities	Several sizes available to store numbers with varying degrees of precision
Date/Time	Dates and times	Size controlled by Access to accommodate dates and times across thousands of years (for example, 1/1/1850 and 1/1/2150 are valid dates)
Currency	Monetary values	Size controlled by Access; accommodates up to 15 digits to the left of the decimal point and four digits to the right
AutoNumber	Integers assigned by Access to sequentially order each record added to a table	Size controlled by Access
Yes/No	Only one of two values stored (Yes/No, On/Off, True/False)	Size controlled by Access
OLE Object	Office and Windows files that can be linked or embedded (OLE) such as pictures, sound clips, documents, or spreadsheets	Up to 2 GB
Attachment	Any supported file type including .jpg images, spreadsheets, and documents (new for Office 2007)	Up to 1 GB
Hyperlink	Web and e-mail addresses	Size controlled by Access

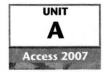
Creating Primary Keys

The **primary key field** of a table serves two important purposes. First, it contains data that uniquely identifies each record. No two records can have the exact same entry in the field designated as the primary key field. Secondly, the primary key field helps relate one table to another in a **one-to-many relationship**, where one record from one table is related to many records in the second table. For example, one state record in the States table might be related to many tours in the Tours table. In the States table, StateAbbreviation is the primary key field. This field is duplicated in the Tours table, providing the link between one state and many tours. The primary key field is always on the "one" side of a one-to-many relationship between two tables. ▓▓▓▓ Mark Rock asks you to check that a primary key field has been appropriately identified for each table.

STEPS

1. **Double-click Tours in the Navigation Pane, maximize the window, then click the Design View button on the Home tab**

   Design View, as shown in Figure A-11, is used to modify and define field properties that are not available in Datasheet View. You see many of a field's **properties** (characteristics that define a field) in the lower half of Design View. Some field properties, such as Field Name and Data Type, can be specified in either Datasheet View or Design View. Specifying the primary key field requires that you work in Design View.

2. **Click the TourID field if it is not already selected, then click the Primary Key button on the Design tab**

   A field designated as the primary key field for a table appears with the key icon, as shown in Figure A-12.

3. **Close and save the Tours table**

   Next, you'll use Design View to set the primary key fields for the other two tables.

4. **Double-click States in the Navigation Pane, click the Design View button, click StateAbbreviation if it is not already selected, click the Primary Key button, then close and save the States table**

   You'll use the Category field as the primary key field in the TourCategories table.

5. **Double-click TourCategories in the Navigation Pane, click the Design View button, make sure the Category field is the primary key, then close the TourCategories table**

   Now that each table has been modified to contain an appropriate primary key field, you no longer have to worry that two tour records in the Tours table could be assigned the same TourID, two states in the States table could be given the same StateAbbreviation, or two tour categories could be assigned to the same Category. In other words, assigning an appropriate primary key field to each table helps prevent you from entering incorrect and duplicate records. The second purpose of the primary key field is to help tie tables together in one-to-many relationships, which you learn about in the next lesson.

FIGURE A-11: Design View of the Tours table

Primary Key button

View button

Field Properties pane

FIGURE A-12: TourID is set as the primary key field

Save button

Primary key field symbol

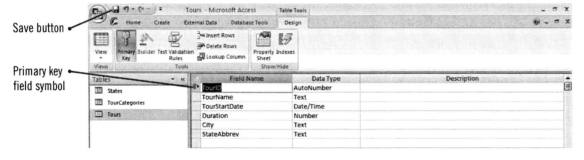

Learning about field properties

Properties are the characteristics that define the field. Two properties are required for every field: Field Name and Data Type. Many other properties, such as Field Size, Format, Caption, and Default Value, are defined in the Field Properties pane in the lower half of a table's Design View. As you add more property entries, you are generally restricting the amount or type of data that can be entered in the field, which increases data entry accuracy. For example, you might change the Field Size property for a State field to 2 in order to eliminate an incorrect entry such as FLL. Field properties change depending on the data type of the selected field. For example, there is no Field Size property for date fields, because Access controls the size of fields with a Date/Time data type.

Relating Two Tables

After you create tables and establish primary key fields, you must link the tables together in one-to-many relationships before you can build queries, forms, or reports that display fields from more than one table. A one-to-many relationship between two tables means that one record from the first table is related to many records in the second table. You use a common linking field, which is always the primary key field in the table on the "one" side of the relationship, to establish this connection. ▩▩▩▩ Mark Rock mentions that he plans to create reports that include tour, category, and state information. To help in creating the reports, you define the one-to-many relationships between the tables of the Quest-A database.

STEPS

1. **Click the Database Tools tab on the Ribbon, then click the Relationships button**

2. **Click the Show Table button on the Design tab, click States, click Add, click Tours, click Add, click TourCategories, click Add, then click Close**
   With all three tables visible in the Relationships window, you're ready to link them together. Each table is represented by a small **field list** window that displays the names of the fields in the table. The primary key field in each table is identified with the key symbol, as shown in Figure A-13.

3. **Drag StateAbbreviation in the States field list to the StateAbbrev field in the Tours field list**
   Dragging a field from one table to another in the Relationships window links the two tables by the selected fields and opens the Edit Relationships dialog box, as shown in Figure A-14. **Referential integrity**, a set of Access rules that govern data entry, helps ensure data accuracy.

4. **Click the Enforce Referential Integrity check box in the Edit Relationships dialog box, then click Create**
   The **one-to-many line** shows the link between the StateAbbreviation field of the States table (the "one" side) and the StateAbbrev field of the Tours table (the "many" side, indicated by the **infinity symbol**). Similarly, you need to create a one-to-many relationship between the TourCategories table and the Tours table, so that one category can be associated with many tours. However, because these tables do not have a common field, you must establish one before you can join the tables.

5. **Right-click the Tours field list, click Table Design, click the cell below StateAbbrev, type Category, then press [Tab] to specify the default Text data type**
   A field added to the "many" table to help establish a one-to-many relationship is called the **foreign key field**. Now that you created the foreign key field for the link between the Tours and TourCategories, you can join the tables in a one-to-many relationship.

6. **Close and save the Tours table, drag the Category field from the TourCategories table to the Category field of the Tours table, then click Create in the Edit Relationships dialog box**
   The final Relationships window should look like Figure A-15. The relationship line between the Tours and TourCategories tables is also a one-to-many relationship, but the "one" and "many" symbols do not appear because you did not establish referential integrity on this relationship. The primary key field for the Tours table is TourID, but because it participates on the "many" side of two different one-to-many relationships, it contains two foreign key fields, StateAbbrev and Category.

7. **Close and save the Relationships window**

FIGURE A-13: Relationships window

Show Table button

Primary key fields

Tables represented by field lists

FIGURE A-14: Edit Relationships dialog box

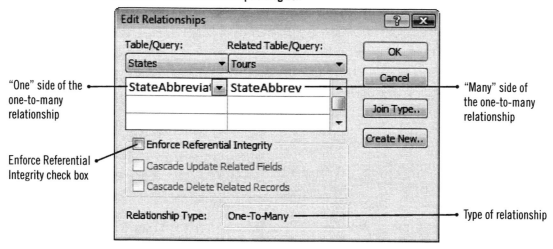

"One" side of the one-to-many relationship

Enforce Referential Integrity check box

"Many" side of the one-to-many relationship

Type of relationship

FIGURE A-15: Final Relationships window

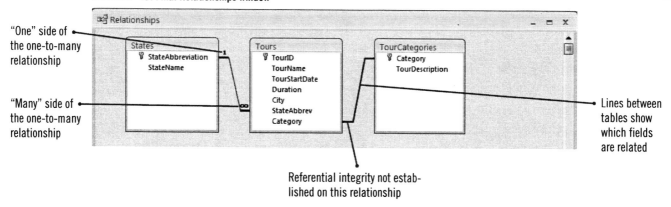

"One" side of the one-to-many relationship

"Many" side of the one-to-many relationship

Lines between tables show which fields are related

Referential integrity not established on this relationship

Enforcing referential integrity

Referential integrity is a set of rules that helps reduce invalid entries and orphan records. An **orphan record** is a record in the "many" table that doesn't have a matching entry in the linking field of the "one" table. With referential integrity enforced on a one-to-many relationship, you cannot enter a value in a foreign key field of the "many" table that does not have a match in the linking field of the "one" table. Referential integrity also prevents you from deleting a record in the "one" table if a matching entry exists in the foreign key field of the "many" table. You should enforce referential integrity on all one-to-many relationships if possible. If you are working with a database that already contains orphan records, you cannot enforce referential integrity on that relationship.

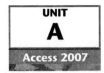

Printing a Datasheet

Printing and previewing Access data is similar to printing and previewing other types of Office documents. Previewing helps you see how the document will look when printed so you can make printing adjustments, such as changing the margins or page orientation, before printing it. ▟▟▚▚▘ Mark Rock asks you to print the Tours datasheet.

STEPS

1. **In the Navigation Pane, double-click the Tours table to open it in Datasheet View, then double-click each column separator to resize the columns to their best fit**
   One more new tour needs to be added to the list before you print it—a family reunion.

2. **Add a new record with your last name's Reunion in the TourName field, today's date in the TourStartDate field, 4 in the Duration field, your hometown in the City field, FL in the StateAbbrev field, and Family in the Category field**
   You decide to preview the datasheet before printing it to make sure it fits on one sheet of paper.

3. **Click the Office button ⊕, point to Print, then click Print Preview**
   The Tours table appears on a miniature page, as shown in Figure A-16, formatted as it will look when you print it. By previewing the datasheet, you realize that it is too wide to print on one page. (The Category and StateAbbrev fields do not appear on page 1.) You decide to try **landscape orientation** (11 inches wide by 8.5 inches tall) rather than the default **portrait orientation** (8.5 inches wide by 11 inches tall) to see if the printout fits on one page.

4. **Click the Landscape button on the Print Preview tab**
   The navigation buttons on the navigation bar in the lower-left corner in Figure A-17 are dim, indicating that the printout fits on one page.

QUICK TIP
Click the Close Print Preview button on the Print Preview tab to close the preview window and return to Datasheet View.

5. **Click the Print button on the Print Preview tab, then click OK**
   If you need to change printing options, you can use the Page Setup dialog box.

6. **Click the Close button ☒ on the title bar to close both the Quest-A.accdb database and Access 2007**

FIGURE A-16: Datasheet in print preview—portrait orientation

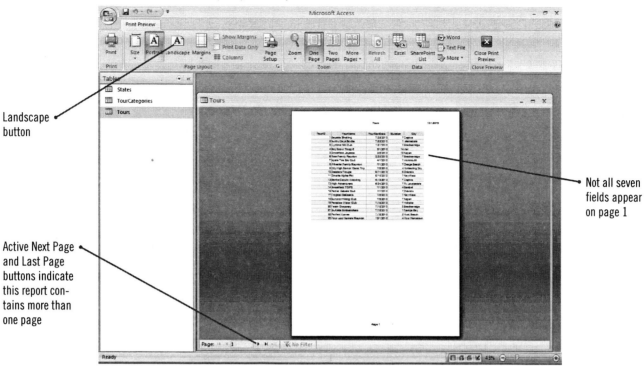

Landscape button

Not all seven fields appear on page 1

Active Next Page and Last Page buttons indicate this report contains more than one page

FIGURE A-17: Datasheet in print preview—landscape orientation

All fields now appear on page 1

Next Page and Last Page buttons are no longer active because the printout fits on one page

Practice

▼ CONCEPTS REVIEW

Label each element of the Access window shown in Figure A-18.

FIGURE A-18

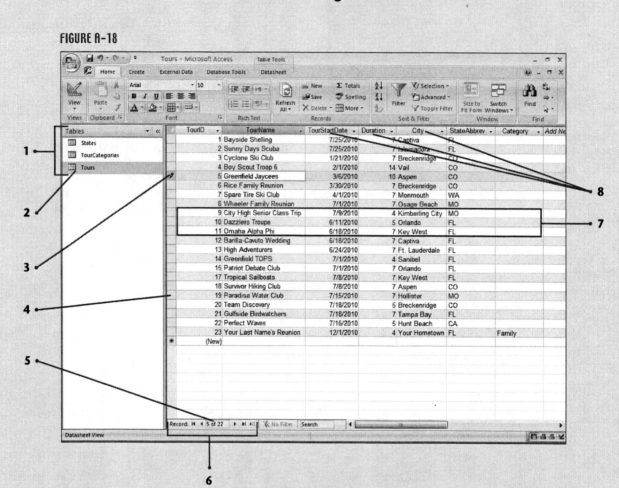

Match each term with the statement that best describes it.

9. Objects
10. Table
11. Record
12. Field
13. Datasheet
14. Form
15. Edit record symbol

a. Seven types of these are contained in an Access database and are used to enter, enhance, and use the data within the database

b. A collection of records for a single subject, such as all the customer records

c. A small pencil icon that appears in the record selector box

d. A spreadsheet-like grid that displays fields as columns and records as rows

e. A group of related fields for one item, such as all of the demographic information for one customer

f. A category of information in a table, such as a customer's name, city, or state

g. An Access object that provides an easy-to-use data entry screen

Select the best answer from the list of choices.

16. Which of the following is *not* a typical benefit of relational databases?

    a. More accurate data

    b. Automatic correction of data as it is entered

    c. Faster information retrieval

    d. Minimized duplicate data entry

17. Which of the following is *not* an advantage of managing data with relational database software such as Access versus spreadsheet software such as Excel?

    a. Uses a single table to store all data

    b. Reduces duplicate data entry

    c. Provides greater security

    d. Allows multiple users to enter data simultaneously

18. The object that creates a professional printout of data that includes headers, footers, and graphics is the:

    a. Query.

    b. Table.

    c. Report.

    d. Form.

19. The object that contains all of the database data is the:

    a. Report.

    b. Form.

    c. Page.

    d. Table.

20. What can you use to quickly create a new database?

    a. Template

    b. Object

    c. Module

    d. Form

▼ SKILLS REVIEW

1. Understand relational databases.

    a. Identify five advantages of managing database information in Access versus using a spreadsheet.

    b. Explain how a relational database organizes data to minimize redundant information. Use an example involving a database with two related tables, Customers and States, in your explanation.

2. Open a database.

    a. Explain the relationship between a field, a record, a table, and a database.

    b. Start Access.

    c. Open the **RealEstate-A.accdb** database from the drive and folder where you store your Data Files. Enable content if a Security Warning message appears.

    d. Open each of the three tables. On a sheet of paper, complete the following table:

table name	number of records	number of fields

3. Enter data.

    a. Enter the following records into the Agents table, then print it. Tab through the AgentNo field as it is defined with an AutoNumber data type and it automatically increments as you enter the rest of the data in the record.

AgentNo	AgentFirst	AgentLast	AgentPhone	AgencyNo
(10)	(Your first name)	(Your last name)	555-888-9999	1
(11)	(Your instructor's first name)	(Your instructor's last name)	555-888-5555	3

b. Enter the following record into the Agencies table, then print it. Tab through the AgencyNo field because it is an AutoNumber field.

AgencyNo	AgencyName	Street	City	State	Zip	AgencyPhone
(4)	(Your last name) Realty	(Your school's street address)	(Your school's city)	(Your school's state)	(Your school's zip code)	555-888-4444

4. Edit data.

a. Open the Listings table datasheet.

b. Change the Area field for ListingNo 7 from Shell Knob to **Ozark Mountain**.

c. Change the SqFt field for ListingNo 14 from 3500 to **5500**.

d. Delete the record for ListingNo 6. Resize the columns to their best fit. Your Listings table datasheet should look similar to the one in Figure A-19.

FIGURE A-19

e. Enter one new record, using your own last name in the Area field, then print the first page only of the datasheet in landscape orientation. (*Hint*: Click the Pages option button in the Print dialog box, then enter 1 in both the From and To boxes.)

f. Close the RealEstate-A.accdb database and Access 2007.

5. Create a database.

a. Open Access 2007, then use the Student database template in the Education category to create a new database. This requires you to be connected to the Internet. Close any windows that open before the database does.

b. In the Student List form that opens, enter your first and last names. Use any valid entries for the E-mail Address, Business Phone, Company, and Job Title fields.

c. Print the record.

d. Expand the Navigation Pane, then use it to complete the following table on a sheet of paper to identify the number and names of the objects that were automatically created by the Students database template. The first row is completed for you.

object type	number created	names of the objects
Tables	2	Students, Guardians
Queries		
Forms		
Reports		

6. **Create a table.**

 a. Create a new table called States with the following fields and data types:

 StateName   Text

 StateAbbreviation   Text

 b. Enter your own state in the first record.

 c. Close the States table, close the Students.accdb database, then exit Access 2007.

7. **Create primary keys.**

 a. Open the RealEstate-A.accdb database used in earlier steps. Enable content if prompted.

 b. Open the Agencies table in Design View, then set AgencyNo as the primary key field.

 c. Open the Agents table in Design View, then set AgentNo as the primary key field.

 d. Open the Listings table in Design View, then set ListingNo as the primary key field.

 e. Save all your changes.

 f. On another sheet of paper, answer the following questions:

 Why is a field with an AutoNumber data type a good candidate for the primary key field for that table?

 Why is a field with an AutoNumber data type *not* a good candidate for the foreign key field for a one-to-many relationship?

8. **Relate two tables.**

 a. In the Relationships window, set a one-to-many relationship between the Agencies and Agents table, using the common AgencyNo field. Apply referential integrity to this relationship.

 b. In the Relationships window, set a one-to-many relationship between the Agents and Listings table, using the common AgentNo field. Apply referential integrity to this relationship.

 c. Click the Relationship Report button on the Design tab, then print the report that is created.

 d. Close the Relationships report without saving changes, then close the Relationships window.

9. **Print a datasheet.**

 a. Preview and print the Agencies table datasheet in landscape orientation.

 b. Preview and print the Agents table datasheet in landscape orientation.

 c. Close the RealEstate-A.accdb database, and exit Access 2007.

▼ INDEPENDENT CHALLENGE 1

Review the following twelve examples of database tables:

- Telephone directory
- College course offerings
- Restaurant menu
- Cookbook
- Movie listing
- Islands of the Caribbean

- Encyclopedia
- Shopping catalog
- International product inventory
- Party guest list
- Members of the U.S. House of Representatives
- Ancient wonders of the world

For each example, write a brief answer for the following.

a. What field names would you expect to find in each table?

b. Provide an example of two possible records for each table.

Access 2007

▼ INDEPENDENT CHALLENGE 2

You are working with several civic groups to coordinate a community-wide cleanup effort. You have started a database called Recycle-A that tracks the clubs, their trash deposits, and the trash collection centers that are participating.

a. Start Access, then open the **Recycle-A.accdb** database from the drive and folder where you store your Data Files.

b. Open each table's datasheet, and write the number of records and fields in each of the tables.

c. In the Centers table datasheet, modify the ContactFirst and ContactLast names for the Trash Can record to your name.

d. Preview the Centers table datasheet in landscape orientation, print the datasheet if your instructor requests it, then close the table.

e. Open the Relationships window and complete the following table on a sheet of paper:

type of relationship	table on the "one" side of the relationship	table on the "many" side of the relationship	linking field name in the "one" table	linking field name in the "many" table
One-to-many				
One-to-many				

Advanced Challenge Exercise

- Open the datasheet for the Clubs table. Click the expand button to the left of each record (which looks like a small plus sign) to view related records from the Deposits table.
- Close the datasheet for the Clubs table. Open the datasheet for the Centers table. Click the expand button to the left of each record to view related records from the Deposits table.

f. Close the Centers table, close the Recycle-A.accdb database, then exit Access.

▼ INDEPENDENT CHALLENGE 3

You are working for an advertising agency that provides advertising media for small and large businesses in the Midwestern United States. You have started a database called Media-A which tracks your company's customers.

a. Start Access and open the **Media-A.accdb** database from the drive and folder where you store your Data Files. Enable content as needed.

b. Add a new record to the Customers table, using your own first and last names, **$7,788.99** in the YTDSales field, and any reasonable entry for the rest of the fields.

c. Edit the Rocket Laboratory record. The Company name should be **Johnson County Labs**, and the Street value should be **2145 College St**.

d. Preview the Customers datasheet in landscape orientation, print the datasheet if your instructor requests it, then close the table.

e. Create a States table with two fields, **StateName** and **StateAbbreviation**, both with a Text data type.

f. Enter at least three records into the States table, making sure that all of the states used in the Customers datasheet are entered in the States table. This includes Kansas KS, Missouri MO, and any other state you entered in previous steps.

g. In Design View, set the StateAbbreviation field as the primary key field, then save and close the States table.

▼ INDEPENDENT CHALLENGE 3 (CONTINUED)

Advanced Challenge Exercise

- Open the Relationships window, add both table field lists to the window, then expand the size of the Customers field list so that all fields are visible.
- Drag the StateAbbreviation field from the States table to the State field of the Customers table, to create a one-to-many relationship between the two tables. Enforce referential integrity on the relationship. If you are unable to enforce referential integrity, it means that there is a value in the State field of the Customers table that doesn't have a match in the StateAbbreviation field of the States table. Open both datasheets, making sure every state in the Customers table is also represented in the States table, close all datasheets, and reestablish the one-to-many relationship between the two tables with referential integrity.
- Click the Relationship Report button on the Design tab, then print the report that is created.
- Close the Relationships report without saving changes, then close the Relationships window.

h. Close the Media-A.accdb database, then exit Access 2007.

▼ REAL LIFE INDEPENDENT CHALLENGE

This Independent Challenge requires an Internet connection.

Now that you've learned about Microsoft Access and relational databases, brainstorm how you might use an Access database in your daily life or career. Start by visiting the Microsoft Web site, and explore what's new about Access 2007.

a. Connect to the Internet, and use your browser to go to your favorite search engine. Use the keywords "benefits of a relational database" or "benefits of Microsoft Access" to find articles that discuss the benefits of organizing data in a relational database.

b. Read several articles about the benefits of organizing data in a relational database such as Access, identifying three distinct benefits. As you read the articles, list all of the terminology unfamiliar to you as well, identifying at least five items.

c. Using a search engine or a Web site that provides a computer glossary such as *www.whatis.com* or *www.webopedia.com*, look up the definition of the five or more new terms you have identified.

d. Using the research you have conducted on the Web, create a one-page document that lists the three benefits of using a relational database you identified in Step b as well as the five or more technical terms that you researched in Step c. In order to document the original sources of your information, be sure to list the Internet Web page addresses (URLs such as *www.microsoft.com*) for each source you reference for benefits and definitions.

e. Apply this research to a job you have had or would like to secure in the future. In one paragraph, describe the job and give at least one example of how Access might be used to manage data important to that job. In a second paragraph, discuss how the benefits of using a relational database might apply to this example.

▼ VISUAL WORKSHOP

Open the **Basketball-A.accdb** database from the drive and folder where you store your Data Files, then open the Players table datasheet. Modify the first three records in the existing Players table to reflect the changes shown in the First, Last, and Height fields of Figure A-20. Note that your name should be entered in the First and Last fields of the first record. Resize all columns to show all data, print the first page of the datasheet in landscape orientation, close the Players table, close the Basketball-A.accdb database, then exit Access.

FIGURE A-20

First	Last	Height	PlayerNo	Year	Position	HomeTown	HomeState	Lettered?
Your First	Your Last	69	4	Jr	G	Cedar Rapids	IA	☐
Kelsey Ann	Douglas	70	5	So	G	Des Moines	IA	☑
Ellyse	Howard	71	12	So	G	Osseo	MN	☑
Amy	Hodel	72	21	Fr	F	Oakbrook	IL	☑
Theresa	Grant	73	22	Fr	F	McKinney	TX	☐
Sandy	Robins	65	23	So	G	Belmond	IA	☐
Ashley	Sydnes	75	30	Fr	F	Salina	KS	☐
Abbey	Walker	76	32	Fr	C	Fargo	ND	☐
Kristen	Czyenski	73	35	So	F	Omaha	NE	☐
Denise	Franco	72	42	Jr	F	Antigua	WI	☑
Megan	Hile	74	45	Jr	F	Vinton	IA	☑
Morgan	Tyler	71	51	So	G	Roseau	MN	☐
Jamie	Johnson	75	52	Fr	F	Belleville	IL	☐
*		0	0					☐

Building and Using Queries

Files You Will Need:

Quest-B.accdb

RealEstate-B.accdb

Vet-B.accdb

Membership-B.accdb

Recycle-B.accdb

Capitals-B.accdb

Basketball-B.accdb

You build queries in an Access database to ask "questions" about data, such as which adventure tours are scheduled for June or what types of tours take place in California. Queries present the answer in a datasheet, which you can sort, filter, and format. Because queries are stored in the database, they can be used multiple times. Each time a query is opened, it presents a current view of the latest updates to the database. Mark Rock, tour developer for U.S. group travel at Quest Travel Services, has several questions about the customer and tour information in the Quest database. You'll develop queries to provide Mark with up-to-date answers.

OBJECTIVES

Create a query

Use Query Design View

Modify queries

Sort and find data

Filter data

Apply AND criteria

Apply OR criteria

Format a datasheet

Creating a Query

A **query** allows you to select a subset of fields and records from one or more tables and then present the selected data as a single datasheet. A major benefit of working with data through a query is that you can focus on the information you need to answer your questions, rather than navigating the fields and records from many large tables. You can enter, edit, and navigate data in a query datasheet just like a table datasheet. However, keep in mind that Access data is physically stored only in tables, even though you can view and edit it through other Access objects such as queries and forms. Because a query doesn't physically store the data, a query datasheet is sometimes called a **logical view** of the data. Technically, a query is a set of **SQL** (Structured Query Language) instructions, but because Access provides several easy-to-use query tools, knowledge of SQL is not required to build or use Access queries. ▰▰▰ You use the Simple Query Wizard to build a query to display a few fields from the States and Tours tables in one datasheet.

1. **Start Access, open the Quest-B.accdb database, then enable content, if prompted**

   Access provides several tools to create a new query. One way is to use the **Simple Query Wizard**, which prompts you for information needed to create a new query.

2. **Click the Create tab on the Ribbon, click the Query Wizard button, then click OK to start the Simple Query Wizard**

   The first Simple Query Wizard dialog box opens, prompting you to select the fields you want to view in the new query.

3. **Click the Tables/Queries list arrow, click Table: Tours, double-click TourName, double-click City, then double-click Category**

   So far, you've selected three fields from the Tours table for this query. You also want to add the full state name, a field stored only in the States table.

   TROUBLE
   Click the Remove Single Field button `<` if you need to remove a field from the Selected Fields list.

4. **Click the Tables/Queries list arrow, click Table: States, then double-click StateName**

   You've selected three fields from the Tours table and one from the States table for your new query, as shown in Figure B-1. Because the Tours and States tables are linked together in this database by a common field (StateAbbrev), you can create queries by selecting individual fields from each of the linked tables to present a datasheet with a subset of desired fields.

5. **Click Next, select Tours Query, type ToursByState in the text box, click Finish, then maximize the datasheet**

   The ToursByState datasheet opens, displaying three fields from the Tours table and the StateName field from the States table, as shown in Figure B-2.

FIGURE B-1: Selecting fields in the Simple Query Wizard

Query Wizard button

Click to select other objects in the database

These fields will appear in the query

FIGURE B-2: ToursByState query datasheet

ToursByState query includes four fields, three from the Tours table and one from the States table

Using Query Design View

You use **Query Design View** to add, delete, or move the fields in an existing query, to specify sort orders, or to add **criteria** to limit the number of records shown in the resulting datasheet. (Criteria are limiting conditions you set in Query Design View.) You can also use Query Design View to create a new query from scratch. Query Design View presents the fields you can use for that query in small windows called **field lists**. If the fields of two or more related tables are used in the query, the relationship between two tables is displayed with a **join line** identifying which fields are used to establish the relationship. ▄▄▄▄▄ Mark Rock asks you to print a list of Adventure tours in Colorado. You use Query Design View to modify the existing ToursByState query to meet his request.

STEPS

1. **Click the** Home tab **on the Ribbon, then click the** Design View button **to switch to Query Design View for the ToursByState query**

   The Query Design View opens as shown in Figure B-3, showing the field lists for the States and Tours tables in the upper pane of the window, as well as the one-to-many relationship established between the two tables via the common StateAbbrev field. The four fields you previously requested for this query are displayed in the **query design grid** in the lower pane of the window.

   QUICK TIP
   Query criteria are not case sensitive.

2. **Click the first Criteria cell for the Category field, then type adventure**

   By adding the word "adventure" to the first Criteria cell for the Category field, only those records with this value in the Category field will be displayed in the datasheet.

3. **Click the Datasheet View button on the Design tab to switch to Datasheet View**

   The resulting datasheet lists the Adventure tours. To further narrow this list to tours in Colorado, you return to Query Design View and enter more criteria.

   TROUBLE
   If you see more than five records, return to Query Design View and make sure your criteria are on the same row.

4. **Click the Design View button on the Home tab, click the first Criteria cell for the StateName field, type Colorado, then click the Datasheet View button on the Design tab**

   Now only five records are displayed, as only five of the Adventure tours are in the state of Colorado, as shown in Figure B-4. You want to save this query with a different name.

5. **Click the Office button 🔘, click Save As, type ColoradoAdventures, then click OK**

   Now two queries are included in the Queries list on the Navigation Pane: ToursByState and ColoradoAdventures.

FIGURE B-3: Query Design View of the TourByState query

Datasheet View button

Field list for States table

Field list for Tours table

Query design grid

Criteria cell for Category field

FIGURE B-4: ColoradoAdventures datasheet

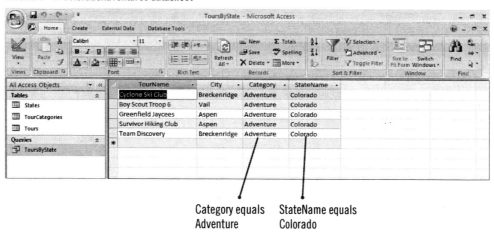

Category equals Adventure

StateName equals Colorado

Modifying Queries

To modify an existing query, you work in Query Design View. The upper pane of the Query Design View window shows the field lists for the tables used by the query. You use the lower pane of Query Design View to add, delete, or change the order of the fields shown on the datasheet. You also use the lower pane to add criteria to narrow the number of records selected, to define sort orders, and to build calculated fields. To delete or move a field in the query grid, you select it by clicking its field selector. The **field selector** is the thin gray bar above each field in the query grid. ▓▓▓▓▓ You want to add more fields and make other modifications to the ColoradoAdventures query. Use Query Design View to make the changes.

STEPS

1. **Click the Design View button on the Home tab**

   You want to move the StateName field to the third field position, immediately after the City field.

QUICK TIP

Drag the lower edge of a field list down to expand the number of fields displayed, and drag the split bar down to resize the two panes of Query Design View.

2. **Click the field selector for the StateName field to select it, then drag the StateName field selector one column to the left to position StateName between the City and Category fields**

   A black vertical line appears to help you visualize where you are repositioning the field. You also want to sort the records in ascending order based on the TourName field.

3. **Click the Sort cell for the TourName field, click the list arrow, then click Ascending**

   Defining the sort order in Query Design View allows you to permanently save the sort order with the query object so that every time you open the query, the specified sort is applied. Selecting an ascending sort order for the TourName field lists the query results in alphabetic order (A-Z) by TourName. You also want to add the TourStartDate and Duration fields to this query so they appear immediately after the TourName field.

QUICK TIP

To delete a field from a query, click its field selector button, then press [Delete]. Deleting a field from a query does not delete it from the underlying table; the field is only deleted from the query's logical view of the data.

4. **Drag the TourStartDate field from the Tours field list to the second column, then drag the Duration field from the Tours field list to the third column**

   The existing fields in the query grid move to the right to accommodate the addition of new fields to the grid, as shown in Figure B-5.

5. **Click the Datasheet View button on the Design tab to view the selected data**

   The datasheet is shown in Figure B-6. Note the order of the fields and sort order of the records.

6. **Change Discovery in the Team Discovery record to your last name, then save the ColoradoAdventures query**

7. **Click the Office button 🗐, point to Print, click Print Preview, click the Landscape button on the Print Preview tab, click the Print button, then click OK**

8. **Close Print Preview, then close the ColoradoAdventures query**

TourStartDate inserted as second field

Ascending sort order selected

Duration inserted as third field

Records sorted by TourName

TourStartDate and Duration fields added to the query

Adding or deleting a table to a query

You might want to add a table's field list to the upper pane of Query Design View in order to select fields from that table for the query. To add a new table to Query Design View, click the Design tab on the Ribbon, click the Show Table button, then add the desired table(s). To delete an unneeded table from Query Design View, click its title bar, then press [Delete].

Sorting and Finding Data

The Access sort and find features are handy tools that help you quickly organize and find data. Table B-1 describes the Sort and Find buttons on the Home tab. Besides using these buttons, you can also click the list arrow on a datasheet's column heading, and then click a sorting option. Sorting and finding data works exactly the same way in table and query datasheets. ▰▰▰▰ Mark Rock asks you to provide a list of tours sorted by TourStartDate, and then by Duration. He also asks you to correct two tours by changing the entry of "Site Seeing" to "Cultural" in the Category field.

QUICK TIP

Click the Navigation Pane list arrow, then make sure All Access Objects is checked to show all tables, queries, and other objects.

1. **Double-click Tours in the Navigation Pane to open the Tours datasheet, then maximize the window**

   By default, records in a table datasheet are sorted on the primary key field. For the Tours table, the primary key field is the TourID field.

QUICK TIP

A sort arrow appears next to the field name by which the datasheet is sorted.

2. **Click any value in the TourStartDate field, then click the Ascending button ⬆ on the Home tab**

   The records are re-sorted based on the TourStartDate field. Notice that some tours start on the same date. You can specify a second sort order to further sort the records that have the same date in the TourStartDate field.

TROUBLE

To clear the current sort order, click the Clear All Sorts button ⬇.

3. **Drag across the TourStartDate and Duration field selector buttons to select both columns, then click ⬆**

   The records are now listed in ascending order, first by TourStartDate, then by the values in the Duration field, as shown in Figure B-7. Sort orders always work left to right, so you might need to rearrange the fields before applying a sort order that uses more than one field. Your next task is to replace all occurrences of "Site Seeing" with "Cultural" in the Category field.

TROUBLE

If your find and replace did not work correctly, click the Undo button ↺ and repeat step 4.

4. **Click the Category column heading to select that field, click the Replace button ⬛ on the Home tab, type Site Seeing in the Find What box, press [Tab], type Cultural in the Replace With box, click Find Next to find the first occurrence of Site Seeing, click Replace, click Replace again to replace the next occurrence of "Site Seeing," then click Cancel**

   Access replaced two occurrences of "Site Seeing" with "Cultural" in the Category field, as shown in Figure B-8.

5. **Replace Rice in the TourID 26 record with your last name, then print the first page of the Tours datasheet**

6. **Save the Tours table**

   If you close a datasheet without saving the changes, the records return to the original sort order based on the values in the primary key field. If you close a datasheet and save layout changes, the last sort order is saved.

FIGURE B-7: Tours datasheet sorted by TourStartDate and Duration fields

Ascending button

Replace button

When records have the same TourStartDate, the records are sorted based on the Duration field

FIGURE B-8: "Site Seeing" replaced with "Cultural" in the Category field

"Cultural" replaces "Site Seeing" in two records

TABLE B-1: Sort and Find buttons

name	button	purpose
Ascending		Sorts records based on the selected field in ascending order (0 to 9, A to Z)
Descending		Sorts records based on the selected field in descending order (Z to A, 9 to 0)
Clear All Sorts		Removes the current sort order
Find		Opens the Find and Replace dialog box, which allows you to find data in a single field or in the entire datasheet
Replace		Opens the Find and Replace dialog box, which allows you to find and replace data
Go To		Helps you navigate to the first, previous, last, or new record
Select		Helps you select a single record or all records in a datasheet

Filtering Data

Filtering a table or query datasheet temporarily displays only those records that match given criteria. Recall that criteria are limiting conditions you set. For example, you might want to show only those tours in the state of Florida, or those tours with a duration of less than seven days. While filters provide a quick and easy way to display a subset of records in the current datasheet, they are not nearly as powerful or flexible as queries. For example, a query is a saved object within the database, whereas filters are temporary. Filters are removed when the datasheet is closed, but if you want to apply a filter over and over again, you can save it as a query. Table B-2 compares filters and queries. ▓▓▓▓ Mark Rock asks you to find all Adventure tours offered in the month of July. You can filter the Tours datasheet to provide this information.

QUICK TIP
You can also click the list arrow on a column heading, click the Select All check box to clear all the check boxes, then click the value to use as the filter.

1. **Click any occurrence of Adventure in the Category field, click the Selection button 🔽 on the Home tab, then click Equals "Adventure"**

Seventeen records are selected, as shown in Figure B-9. Filtering by a given field value, called **Filter By Selection**, is a fast and easy way to filter the records for an exact match. To filter for comparative data (for example, where TourStartDate is *equal to or greater than* 7/1/2010), you must use the **Filter By Form** feature. Filter buttons are summarized in Table B-3.

QUICK TIP
To save a filter permanently as a query object, click the Advanced button, then click Save As Query.

2. **Click the Advanced button 🖼 on the Home tab, then click Filter By Form**

The Filter by Form window opens. The previous Filter By Selection criterion, "Adventure" in the Category field, is still in the grid. Access distinguishes between text and numeric entries by placing quotation marks around text criteria.

QUICK TIP
If you need to clear previous criteria, click the Advanced button, then click Clear Grid.

3. **Click the TourStartDate cell, then type 7/*/2010 as shown in Figure B-10**

Filter by Form also allows you to apply two or more criteria at the same time. An asterisk (*) in the day position of the date criterion works as a wildcard, selecting any date in the month of July (the seventh month) in the year 2010.

4. **Click the Toggle Filter button 🔽 on the Home tab**

The datasheet redisplays all nine records that match both filter criteria, as shown in Figure B-11. Note that filter icons appear next to the TourStartDate and Category field names as both fields are involved in the filter.

QUICK TIP
Be sure to remove existing filters before applying a completely new filter, or you filter the current subset of records instead of applying the filter to the entire datasheet.

5. **Change Bayside in TourID 1 to your last name, then print the filtered datasheet**

To remove the current filter, you click the Toggle Filter button.

6. **Click 🔽 to remove the filter, then save and close the Tours datasheet**

Using wildcard characters

To search for a pattern, you can use a **wildcard** character to represent any character in the criteria entry. Use a ? (question mark) to search for any single character and an * (asterisk) to search for any number of characters. Wildcard characters are often used with the Like operator. For example, the criterion Like "12/*/10" would find all dates in December of 2010, and the criterion Like "F*" would find all entries that start with the letter F.

FIGURE B-9: Filtering for Adventure records

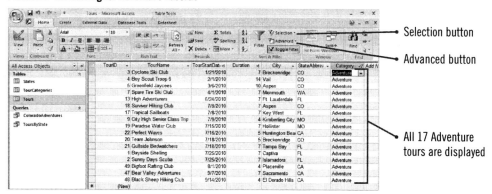

Selection button
Advanced button
All 17 Adventure tours are displayed

FIGURE B-10: Filter by Form window

Adding a criterion to display records with a TourStartDate in July, 2010

Toggle Filter button
"Adventure" criterion still in Category field

FIGURE B-11: Filtering for Adventure records in July, 2010

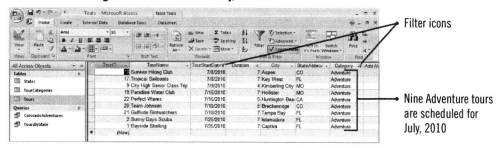

Filter icons
Nine Adventure tours are scheduled for July, 2010

TABLE B-2: Filters versus queries

characteristics	filters	queries
Are saved as an object in the database	No	Yes
Can be used to select a subset of records in a datasheet	Yes	Yes
Can be used to select a subset of fields in a datasheet	No	Yes
Resulting datasheet used to enter and edit data	Yes	Yes
Resulting datasheet used to sort, filter, and find records	Yes	Yes
Commonly used as the source of data for a form or report	No	Yes
Can calculate sums, averages, counts, and other types of summary statistics across records	No	Yes
Can be used to create calculated fields	No	Yes

TABLE B-3: Filter buttons

name	button	purpose
Filter		Provides a list of values in the selected field by which to customize a filter
Selection		Filters records that equal, do not equal, or are otherwise compared to the current value
Advanced		Provides advanced filter features such as Filter By Form, Save As Query, and Clear Grid
Toggle Filter		Applies or removes the current filter

Applying AND Criteria

As you have seen, you can limit the number of records that appear on a query datasheet by entering criteria into Query Design View. Criteria are tests, or limiting conditions, for which the record must be true to be selected for a datasheet. To create **AND criteria**, which means that *all* criteria must be true in order for the record to be selected, enter two or more criteria on the *same* Criteria row of the query design grid. Mark Rock asks you to provide a list of all educational tours in the state of California with a duration of greater than seven days. Use Query Design View to create the query with AND criteria to meet his request.

STEPS

QUICK TIP
Drag the bottom border of the Tours field list down to display all of the fields. The scroll bar disappears when all fields are displayed.

1. **Click the Create tab on the Ribbon, click the Query Design button, double-click Tours, click Close in the Show Table dialog box, then maximize the query window**
   You want to add four fields to this query.

2. **Double-click TourName, double-click Duration, double-click StateAbbrev, and double-click Category to add these fields to the query grid**
   Start by adding criteria to select only those records in California. Because you are using the StateAbbrev field, you need to use the two-letter state abbreviation for California, CA, as the Criteria entry.

3. **Click the first Criteria cell for the StateAbbrev field, type CA, then click the Datasheet View button on the Design tab**
   Querying for only those tours in the state of California selects 16 records. Next, you add criteria to select only those records in the Educational category.

4. **Click the Design View button on the Home tab to switch to Query Design View, click the first Criteria cell for the Category field, type Educational, then click the Datasheet View button on the Design tab**
   Criteria added to the same line of the query design grid are AND criteria. When entered on the same line, each criterion must be true for the record to appear in the resulting datasheet. Querying for both California and Educational tours selects six records. Every time you add AND criteria, you *narrow* the number of records that are selected because the record must be true for *all* criteria.

5. **Click the Design View button on the Home tab, click the first Criteria cell for the Duration field, then type >7, as shown in Figure B-12**
   Access assists you with **criteria syntax**, rules by which criteria need to be entered. Access automatically adds quotation marks around text criteria in Text fields and pound signs (#) around date criteria in Date/Time fields. The criteria in Number, Currency, and Yes/No fields are not surrounded by any characters. See Table B-4 for more information about comparison operators such as > (greater than).

TROUBLE
If your datasheet doesn't match Figure B-13, return to Query Design View and compare your criteria to that of Figure B-12.

6. **Click the Datasheet View button on the Design tab**
   The third AND criterion further narrows the number of records selected to three, as shown in Figure B-13.

7. **Click the Save button 🖫 on the Quick Access toolbar, type CaliforniaEducational as the query name, then click OK**
   The query is saved with the new name, CaliforniaEducational, as a new object in the Quest-B database.

Searching for blank fields

Is Null and **Is Not Null** are two other types of common criteria. The Is Null criterion finds all records where no entry has been made in the field. Is Not Null finds all records where there is any entry in the field, even if the entry is 0. Primary key fields cannot have a null entry.

FIGURE B-12: Query Design View with criteria on one row (AND criteria)

Datasheet View button

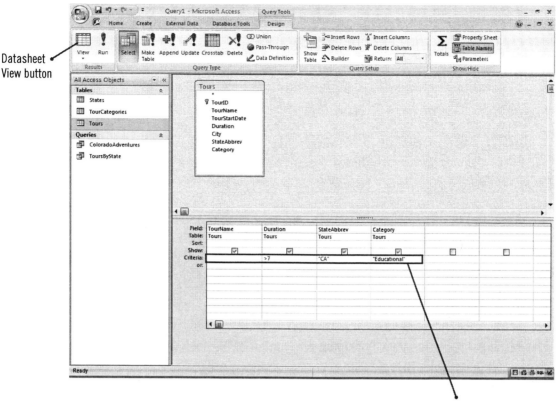

Criteria for displaying Educational tours in California that are longer than one week

FIGURE B-13: Datasheet of CaliforniaEducational query

Design View button

Three records meet the criteria you specified

TABLE B-4: Comparison operators

operator	description	expression	meaning
>	Greater than	>500	Numbers greater than 500
>=	Greater than or equal to	>=500	Numbers greater than or equal to 500
<	Less than	<"Braveheart"	Names from A to Braveheart, but not Braveheart
<=	Less than or equal to	<="Bridgewater"	Names from A through Bridgewater, inclusive
<>	Not equal to	<>"Fontanelle"	Any name except for Fontanelle

Applying OR Criteria

To create **OR criteria**, which means that *any one* criterion must be true in order for the record to be selected, enter two or more criteria on the *different* Criteria rows of the query design grid. To create OR criteria for the *same field*, enter the two criteria in the same Criteria cell separated by the OR operator. As you add rows of OR criteria to the query design grid, you *increase* the number of records selected for the resulting datasheet because the record needs to be true for *only one* of the criteria rows in order to be selected for the datasheet. Mark Rock asks you to add Cultural tours longer than seven days in duration from the state of California to the previous query. To do this, you can modify the query to employ OR criteria to add the records.

1. **Click the Design View button on the Home tab, click the second Criteria cell in the Category field, type cultural, then click the Datasheet View button on the Design tab**

   The query added all of the tours with "Cultural" in the Category field to the datasheet, as specified by the second row of the query grid in Query Design View. Because each row of the query grid is evaluated separately, the fact that three criteria were entered in the first row is of no consequence to the second row. In order for the second row to also apply three criteria—Cultural, California, and duration of greater than 7—three criteria must be entered in the second row. In other words, the criteria in one row have no effect on the criteria of other rows.

2. **Click the Design View button on the Home tab, click the second Criteria cell in the Duration field, type >7, click the second Criteria cell in the StateAbbrev field, then type CA**

   Query Design View should look like Figure B-14.

3. **Click the Datasheet View button on the Design tab**

   Five records were selected that meet all three criteria as entered in row one OR row two of the query grid, as shown in Figure B-15.

4. **Edit the Gold Country record to be your last name Country, then save, print, and close the datasheet**

   Because the CaliforniaEducational query now selects both educational and cultural records, you rename it.

5. **Right-click CaliforniaEducational in the Navigation Pane, click Rename on the shortcut menu, type CaliforniaEducationalCultural to rename the query, then press [Enter]**

FIGURE B-14: Query Design View with criteria on two rows (OR criteria)

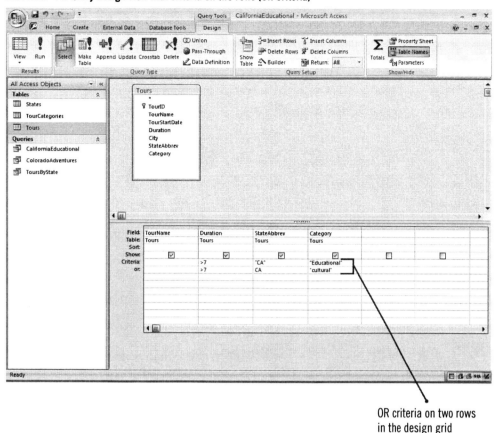

OR criteria on two rows
in the design grid

FIGURE B-15: Datasheet of CaliforniaEducationalCultural query

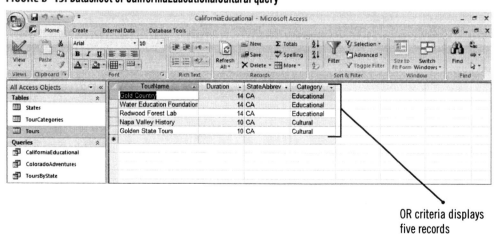

OR criteria displays
five records

Formatting a Datasheet

Although the primary Access tool to create professional printouts is the report object, you can print a datasheet as well. Although a datasheet printout does not allow you to add custom headers, footers, images, or subtotals as reports do, you can apply some formatting, such as changing the font size, font face, colors, and gridlines. 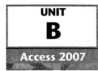 Mark Rock has asked you to create a printout of the different tour categories and their descriptions, which is stored in the TourCategories table. You can format the TourCategories datasheet before printing it for Mark.

STEPS

1. **Double-click TourCategories in the Navigation Pane**

   The TourCategories datasheet opens. Before applying new formatting enhancements, you preview the default printout.

2. **Click the Office button 🔘, point to Print, click Print Preview, then click the top edge of the paper to zoom in**

   The preview window displays the layout of the printout, as shown in Figure B-16. By default, the printout of a datasheet contains the object name and current date in the header. The page number is in the footer. You decide to increase the size of the font and data before printing.

3. **Click the Close Print Preview button on the Print Preview tab, click the Font Size list arrow, then click 12**

   A larger font size often makes a printout easier to read. You also need to adjust the width of the Description column to its best fit.

4. **Double-click the column separator to the right of the Description field**

   Double-clicking the column (field) separator automatically adjusts the width of the column to the widest entry in the datasheet.

5. **Click the Alternate Fill/Back Color button arrow 🔲 on the Home tab, then click Yellow**

   For datasheet printouts, alternating the background color of each row makes the printout easier to read, as shown in Figure B-17. You want to add one more new category, Sports, before printing the datasheet.

6. **Type Sports in the Category field for a new record, then type (any valid and unique description) for this category in the Description field**

7. **Preview the datasheet again, click the Print button on the Print Preview tab, then click OK in the Print dialog box**

8. **Save and close the TourCategories datasheet, close the Quest-B.accdb database, then exit Access**

FIGURE B-16: Default printout of a datasheet

Print Preview tab

Close Print Preview button

TourCategories datasheet in Print Preview

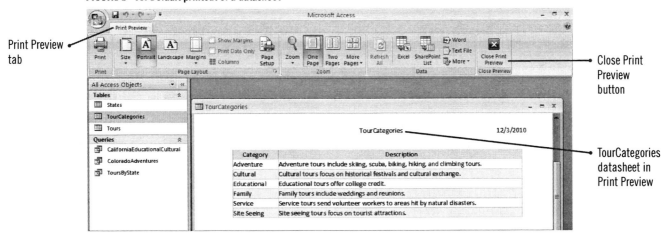

FIGURE B-17: Formatted datasheet

Font Size list arrow

Alternate Fill/Back Color button

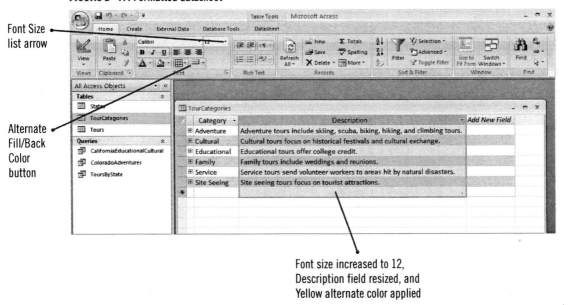

Font size increased to 12, Description field resized, and Yellow alternate color applied

Practice

▼ CONCEPTS REVIEW

Label each element of the Access window shown in Figure B-18.

FIGURE B-18

Match each term with the statement that best describes it.

8. **Query grid**
9. **Criteria**
10. **Filter**
11. **Syntax**
12. **Query**
13. **Sorting**
14. **Wildcard**
15. **Is Null**

a. Creates a datasheet of selected fields and records from one or more tables
b. Creates a temporary subset of records
c. Limiting conditions used to narrow the number of records that appear on a datasheet
d. Used to search for a pattern
e. Criterion that finds all records where no entry has been made in the field
f. The lower pane in Query Design View
g. Putting records in ascending or descending order based on the values of a field
h. Rules that determine how criteria is entered

Select the best answer from the list of choices.

16. The rules by which criteria need to be entered in the query grid are referred to as:

    a. Syntax.

    b. Hyperlink.

    c. Field lists.

    d. Formatting.

17. SQL stands for which of the following?

    a. Standard Query Language

    b. Structured Query Language

    c. Special Query Listing

    d. Simple Query Listing

18. A query is sometimes called a "logical view" of data because:

    a. You can create queries with the Logical Query Wizard.

    b. Queries contain logical criteria.

    c. Query naming conventions are logical.

    d. Queries do not store data, they only display a view of data.

19. Which of the following describes OR criteria?

    a. Using two or more rows of the query grid to select only those records that meet given criteria

    b. Selecting a subset of fields and/or records to view as a datasheet from one or more tables

    c. Reorganizing the records in either ascending or descending order based on the contents of one or more fields

    d. Using multiple fields in the query design grid

20. Which of the following is *not* true about a query?

    a. A query is the same thing as a filter.

    b. A query can be used to create calculated fields.

    c. A query can be used to create summary statistics.

    d. A query can be used to enter and edit data.

▼ SKILLS REVIEW

1. Create a query.

    a. Open the RealEstate-B.accdb database from the drive and folder where you store your Data Files. Enable content if you are prompted with a Security Alert message.

    b. Create a new query using the Simple Query Wizard. Select the AgentFirst and AgentLast names from the Agents table, and select the Type, SqFt, and Asking fields from the Listings table. Select all details, and title the query AgentListings.

    c. Choose any record with Michelle Litten's name and change it to your own. As soon as you save the changes by moving to another record, all three of Michelle's records update to your name. Although Michelle Litten was entered only once in the database, her agent number was linked to three different listings in the Listings table, which selects her name three times out of the Agents table for this query.

2. Use Query Design View.

    a. Open the AgentListings query in Query Design View.

    b. Enter criteria to display only homes with an Asking price of greater than $200,000. (*Hint*: Enter the value in the criterion as 200000 without a comma. Also, don't forget the greater than operator, >.) Display the datasheet.

    c. In Query Design View, sort the records in ascending order based on the AgentLast field, then display and print the datasheet.

    d. Save and close the AgentListings query.

3. Modify queries.

   a. Open the ListingsMasterList query in Datasheet View.

   b. Switch to Query Design View, then add the AgencyName field from the Agencies table to the first column in the query grid.

   c. Add the AgentFirst field to the third column.

   d. Add ascending sort orders to the AgentLast and AgentFirst fields, then display the datasheet.

   e. Print, save, and close the ListingsMasterList query.

4. Sort and find data.

   a. Open the Listings table datasheet.

   b. Select both the SqFt and LakeFt fields, then sort the records in descending order.

   c. In the Area field, find all occurrences of Shell Knob, replace them with **Shell City**, then close the Find and Replace dialog box.

   d. Enter your own last name in the Area field of the first record, then print only the first page of the datasheet.

5. Filter data.

   a. Filter the Listings datasheet for only those records where the Type field equals Two Story.

   b. Apply an advanced filter by form to further narrow the records so that only the Two Story listings with an Asking Price of greater than or equal to $194,500 are selected.

   c. Print the datasheet, then close the Listings datasheet without saving changes.

6. Apply AND criteria.

   a. Open the ListingsMasterList query in Query Design View.

   b. Enter criteria to select all of the listings in the Shell City area with three or more baths. Display the datasheet and save the changes.

   c. Print the ListingsMasterList datasheet in landscape orientation.

7. Apply OR criteria.

   a. Open the ListingsMasterList query in Query Design View.

   b. In addition to the existing criteria, include criteria to select all listings in Kimberling City with three or more baths, so that both Shell City and Kimberling City records with three or more baths are selected. Display the datasheet, compare it to Figure B-19, and save the changes.

FIGURE B-19

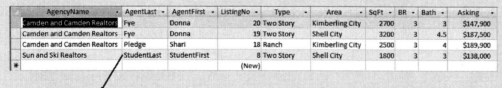

AgencyName	AgentLast	AgentFirst	ListingNo	Type	Area	SqFt	BR	Bath	Asking
Camden and Camden Realtors	Fye	Donna	20	Two Story	Kimberling City	2700	3	3	$147,900
Camden and Camden Realtors	Fye	Donna	19	Two Story	Shell City	3200	3	4.5	$187,500
Camden and Camden Realtors	Pledge	Shari	18	Ranch	Kimberling City	2500	3	4	$189,900
Sun and Ski Realtors	StudentLast	StudentFirst	8	Two Story	Shell City	1800	3	3	$138,000
*			(New)						

The order of the records might differ, depending on your name

   c. Print the ListingsMasterList datasheet in landscape orientation, then save and close the ListingsMasterList query.

8. Format a datasheet.

   a. Open the Agents table datasheet and apply the Arial Narrow font and a 14-point font size.

   b. Resize all columns so that all data and field names are visible.

   c. Apply a Light Gray 2 alternate fill/back color.

   d. Print the datasheet, then save and close the Agents datasheet.

   e. Close the RealEstate-B.accdb database, then exit Access.

▼ INDEPENDENT CHALLENGE 1

You have built an Access database to track the veterinarians and clinics where they work in your area.

a. Start Access, open the **Vet-B.accdb** database from the drive and folder where you store your Data Files, enable content if prompted, then open the Vets table datasheet.

b. Open the Clinics datasheet, review the data in both datasheets, then close them.

c. Using the Simple Query Wizard, select the Last and First fields from the Vets table, and select the ClinicName and Phone fields from the Clinics table. Title the query **ClinicListing**, then view and maximize the datasheet.

d. Sort the records in ascending order by Last name, then First name. Review the values in the Last field, and determine if the First sort order was needed.

e. Find Cooper in the Last field, and replace it with **Chen**.

f. Find any occurrence of Leawood Animal Clinic in the ClinicName field, and change Leawood to **Emergency**.

g. In Query Design View, add criteria to select only Emergency Animal Clinic or Animal Haven in the ClinicName field.

h. Display the datasheet, change Vicki Kowalewski's name to your own, then save and print the ClinicListing datasheet.

i. Close the ClinicListing datasheet and the Vet-B.accdb database, and exit Access.

▼ INDEPENDENT CHALLENGE 2

You have built an Access database to track membership in a community service club. The database tracks member names and addresses as well as their status in the club, which moves from rank to rank as the members contribute increased hours of service to the community.

a. Start Access, open the **Membership-B.accdb** database from the drive and folder where you store your Data Files, enable content if prompted, open the Members and Status table datasheets to review the data, then close them.

b. In Query Design View, build a query with the following fields: LName and FName from the Members table, and StatusLevel from the Status table.

c. View the datasheet, then return to Query Design View.

d. In Query Design View, add criteria to select only those members with a silver or gold StatusLevel. Apply an ascending sort order on the LName and FName fields, then view the datasheet.

e. Return to Query Design View, add an ascending sort order to StatusLevel, then rearrange the fields in the query grid so that the StatusLevel field is the first sort order, LName the second, and FName the third. View the datasheet.

f. Save the query with the name **GoldSilver**.

g. Return to Query Design View, then add the Phone field as the fourth field in the query. View the datasheet, shown in Figure B-20.

h. Enter your own name in the first record, widen all columns so that all data is visible, then print the datasheet.

i. Save and close the GoldSilver query, then close the Membership-B.accdb database, and exit Access.

FIGURE B-20

StatusLevel	LName	FName	Phone
Gold	Duman	Mary Jan	555-8844
Gold	Hammer	Mike	555-0365
Gold	Mullins	Jim	555-6434
Gold	Sinclaire	Connie	555-2277
Silver	Braven	Mary	555-7002
Silver	Cabriella	Jan	555-9871
Silver	Camel	Denise	555-8402
Silver	Custard	Gene	555-5102
Silver	Diverman	Barbara	555-0401
Silver	Dotey	Sylvia	555-4404
Silver	Eahlie	Andrea	555-0401
Silver	Eckert	Jay	555-7414
Silver	Garden	John	555-4344
Silver	Goode	Lois	555-1324
Silver	Hubert	Holly	555-6004
Silver	Maxim	Robert	555-4514
Silver	Mayberry	Mitch	555-0401
Silver	Nelson	Jenny	555-5084
Silver	Olson	Marcie	555-1388

Record: 1 of 19   No Filter   Search

▼ INDEPENDENT CHALLENGE 3

You have built an Access database to organize the deposits at a recycling center. Various clubs regularly deposit recyclable material, which is measured in pounds when the deposits are made.

a. Start Access, open the **Recycle-B.accdb** database from the drive and folder where you store your Data Files, then enable content if prompted.

b. Open the Clubs table datasheet to review this data, then close it. Open the Centers table datasheet to review this data, then close it.

c. Review the Deposits datasheet, then filter the datasheet for records where the Weight value is greater than or equal to 100.

d. Apply an alternate light gray fill/back color of your choice, print the datasheet, then save and close the Deposits datasheet.

e. Using either the Query Wizard or Query Design View, create a query with the following fields: Deposit Number, Deposit Date, and Weight from the Deposits table; Name from the Centers table; and Name from the Clubs table. Note that in the Simple Query Wizard's field list and in the query datasheet, when two fields from different tables have the same name, the fields are distinguished by adding the table name and a period before the field name.

f. Name the query **DepositList**. Sort the records in ascending order by Deposit Number.

g. Change any occurrence of "Adair" in the "Adair County Landfill" entry in the Centers.Name field to your last name, then print the datasheet.

h. Save and close the DepositList query.

Advanced Challenge Exercise

■ Compare the printout of the Deposits table datasheet and the DepositList query. In a document, answer the following questions:

- What common field links the Deposits table to the Centers table? (*Hint*: Use the Relationships window if the answer is not apparent from the printouts.)
- What common field links the Deposits table to the Clubs table? (*Hint*: Use the Relationships window if needed.)
- Why do you think that number fields are often used as the common field to link two tables in a one-to-many relationship, as opposed to text fields?
- How many times is each center name and each club name physically entered in the database?
- Why do many center names and club names appear many times on the DepositList query?

i. Close the Recycle-B.accdb database, then exit Access.

▼ REAL LIFE INDEPENDENT CHALLENGE

You can use an Access database to record and track your experiences, such as places you've visited. Suppose that your passion for travel includes a plan to visit the capitals of all 50 states. A database is provided with your Data Files that includes one table listing each state and capital, and another table of people from each state that you can contact for more information about state information.

a. Start Access, open the **Capitals-B.accdb** database from the drive and folder where you store your Data Files, then enable content if prompted.

b. Open both the Contacts and States datasheets to review their data, then close them.

c. In the States table, add a new field to track information about each state that you are personally interested in. Options include recording the current state population, state bird, primary tourist attraction, largest city, or any other fact about each state you choose.

d. Research and enter correct data for the new field you created in step c, for both your home state and another state that you are interested in, then print the States datasheet.

e. Using either Query Design View or the Simple Query Wizard, create a query with the following fields: StateName and Capital from the States table, and LName and FName from the Contacts table. Save the query as **StateContacts**, then display the datasheet.

▼ REAL LIFE INDEPENDENT CHALLENGE (CONTINUED)

   f. Use Query Design View to add three ascending sort orders on these fields—StateName, then LName, then FName—
      then display the datasheet.

   g. Use Query Design View to add a criterion to select only records from the state of New York, then display the datasheet.

   h. Edit Ablany to correct the spelling of New York's state capital, Albany. Navigate to a new record so that the edit is
      saved in the database.

   i. Format the datasheet to a 14-point font size, Times New Roman font face, and a Light Blue 1 alternate fill/back color.

   j. Save the revised query with the name **NewYorkContacts**.

   k. Change the name of the first record to your name, then print the datasheet.

Advanced Challenge Exercise

This Advanced Challenge Exercise requires an Internet connection.

■ Use the Web to research state mottos.

■ Create a Text field in the States table called Motto and enter the motto for at least five different states, including
  New York.

■ In Query Design View of the NewYorkContacts query, add the Motto field as the fifth column of the query.

■ View the datasheet, widen the motto field as necessary, as shown in Figure B-21, then print the
  NewYorkContacts query.

■ Close the NewYorkContacts query without saving changes.

   l. Close the Capitals-B.accdb database, then exit Access.

FIGURE B-21

StateName	Capital	LName	FName	Motto
New York	Albany	McCollum	Roman	Ever Upward!
New York	Albany	Oberstar	John	Ever Upward!
New York	Albany	Osborne	Mike	Ever Upward!
New York	Albany	Peterson	Hilda	Ever Upward!
New York	Albany	Pickering	Bob	Ever Upward!
New York	Albany	Porter	William	Ever Upward!
New York	Albany	Ramstad	Tammy	Ever Upward!
New York	Albany	Rehberg	Terry	Ever Upward!
New York	Albany	Sabo	Gary	Ever Upward!
New York	Albany	Schwarz	Paul	Ever Upward!
New York	Albany	Skelton	Randy	Ever Upward!
New York	Albany	Taylor	Corrine	Ever Upward!
New York	Albany	Terry	JoAnn	Ever Upward!
New York	Albany	Thompson	Ken	Ever Upward!
New York	Albany	Wicker	Luke	Ever Upward!

Record: 1 of 27   No Filter   Search

▼ VISUAL WORKSHOP

Open the **Basketball-B.accdb** database from the drive and folder where you store your Data Files, and enable content if prompted. Create a query based on the Players, Stats, and Games tables as shown in Figure B-22. Criteria has been added so that only those records where the Reb-O (offensive rebounds) and Reb-D (defensive rebounds) field values are equal to or greater than 1, and the 3P (three pointer) field values are equal to or greater than 2. The records are also sorted. A Light Gray 1 alternate fill/back color has been applied. Change the name of Kelsey Douglas to your own name before printing, save the query with the name HighPerformers, then close the query, the Basketball-B.accdb database, and Access.

FIGURE B-22

UNIT
A

PowerPoint 2007

Creating a Presentation in PowerPoint 2007

Files You Will Need:

No files needed.

Microsoft Office PowerPoint 2007 is a powerful computer software program that enables you to create visually dynamic presentations. With PowerPoint, you can create individual slides and display them as a slide show on your computer, a video projector, or over the Internet. ▰▰ Ellen Latsky is the European tour developer for Quest Specialty Travel (QST), an adventure tour company committed to providing travel experiences that immerse travelers into world cultures. One of Ellen's responsibilities is to present new tour ideas for the upcoming travel season at the annual sales meeting held at the company's corporate offices. As a newly hired summer intern, Ellen has asked you to get acquainted with PowerPoint and then start work on the new tour ideas presentation.

OBJECTIVES

Define presentation software

Plan an effective presentation

Examine the PowerPoint window

Enter slide text

Add a new slide

Apply a design theme

Compare presentation views

Print a PowerPoint presentation

Defining Presentation Software

Presentation software is a computer program you use to organize and present information to others. Whether you are explaining a new product or moderating a meeting, presentation software can help you effectively communicate your ideas. You can use PowerPoint to create presentations, as well as speaker notes for the presenter and handouts for the audience. Table A-1 explains how your information can be presented using PowerPoint. Ellen wants you to start work on the presentation that she will use to present the new European tour series. Because you are only somewhat familiar with PowerPoint, you get to work exploring its capabilities. Figure A-1 shows how a presentation looks printed as handouts. Figure A-2 shows how the same presentation might look printed as notes pages for a speaker.

DETAILS

You can easily complete the following tasks using PowerPoint:

- **Enter and edit text easily**

  Text editing and formatting commands in PowerPoint are organized by the task you are performing at the time, so you can enter, edit, and format text information simply and efficiently to produce the best results in the least amount of time.

- **Change the appearance of information**

  PowerPoint has many effects that can transform the way text, graphics, and slides appear. By exploring some of these capabilities, you discover how easy it is to change the appearance of your presentation.

- **Organize and arrange information**

  Once you start using PowerPoint, you won't have to spend much time making sure your information is correct and in the right order. With PowerPoint, you can quickly and easily rearrange and modify text, graphics, and slides in your presentation.

- **Incorporate information from other sources**

  Often, when you create presentations, you use information from a variety of sources. With PowerPoint, you can import text, photographs, numerical data, and facts from files created in such programs as Microsoft Word, Corel WordPerfect, Adobe Photoshop, Microsoft Excel, and Microsoft Access. You can also import graphic images from a variety of sources such as the Internet, other computers, a digital camera, or other graphics programs.

- **Present information in a variety of ways**

  With PowerPoint, you can present information using a variety of methods. For example, you can print handout pages or an outline of your presentation for audience members. You can display your presentation as an electronic slide show using your computer, or if you are presenting to a large group, you can use a video projector and a large screen. If you want to reach an even wider audience, you can publish the presentation to the Internet so people anywhere in the world can use a browser to view your presentation.

- **Collaborate on a presentation with others**

  PowerPoint makes it easy to collaborate with colleagues and coworkers to create a presentation using the Internet. You can use your e-mail program to send a presentation as an attachment to a colleague for feedback. If you have a large number of people that need to collaborate on a presentation, you can set up a shared workspace on the Internet so everyone in your group has access to the presentation.

+ Pacific means peaceful; named by Magellan in 1520.
+ Largest and deepest of the world's oceans.
+ Covers more than one-third of the earth's surface.
+ Contains more than 30,000 islands.

PowerPoint 2007

TABLE A-1: Presenting information using PowerPoint

method	description
On-screen presentations	Run a slide show from your computer or through a video projector to a large screen
Notes	Print a page with the image of a slide and notes about each slide for yourself or your audience
Audience handouts	Print handouts with one, two, three, four, six, or nine slides on a page
Online meetings	View or work on a presentation with your colleagues in real time
Outline pages	Print a text outline of your presentation to highlight the main points
Overheads	Print PowerPoint slides directly to transparencies using a standard printer

Planning an Effective Presentation

Before you create a presentation, you need to have a basic idea of the information you want to communicate. PowerPoint is a powerful and flexible program that gives you the ability to start a presentation simply by entering the text of your message. If you have a design or theme you want to use, you can start the presentation by working on the design. In most cases you'll probably enter the text of your presentation into PowerPoint first and then tailor the design to the message and audience. When preparing your presentation, you need to keep in mind not only to whom you are giving it, but also where you are giving it. It is important to know what equipment you will need, such as a sound system, computer, or projector. Use the planning guidelines below to help plan an effective presentation. Figure A-3 illustrates a storyboard for a well thought-out presentation.

DETAILS

In planning a presentation, it is important to:

- **Determine and outline the message you want to communicate**
  The more time you take developing the message and outline of your presentation, the better your presentation will be. A presentation with a clear message that reads like a story and is illustrated with visual aids will have the greatest impact on your audience. Start the presentation by describing the tour development goals, defining focus group data, and stating the tour strategy objectives. See Figure A-3.

- **Verify the audience and the delivery location**
  Audience and delivery location should be major factors in the type of presentation you create. For example, a presentation you develop for a staff meeting that is held in a conference room would not necessarily need to be as elaborate or detailed as a presentation that you develop for a large audience held in an auditorium. Room lighting, natural light, screen position, and room layout all affect how the audience responds to your presentation. This presentation will be delivered in a small auditorium to QST's management and sales team.

- **Determine the type of output**
  Output choices for a presentation include black-and-white or color handouts, on-screen slide show, or an online meeting. Consider the time demands and computer equipment availability as you decide which output types to produce. Because you are speaking in a small auditorium to a large group and have access to a computer and projection equipment, you decide that an on-screen slide show is the best output choice for your presentation.

- **Determine the design**
  Visual appeal, graphics, and design work to communicate your message. You can choose one of the professionally designed themes that come with PowerPoint, modify one of these themes, or create one of your own. You decide to choose one of PowerPoint's design themes to convey the new tour information.

- **Decide what additional materials will be useful in the presentation**
  You need to prepare not only the slides themselves but also supplementary materials, including speaker notes and handouts for the audience. You use speaker notes to help remember key details, and you pass out handouts for the audience to use as a reference during the presentation.

FIGURE A-3: Storyboard of the presentation

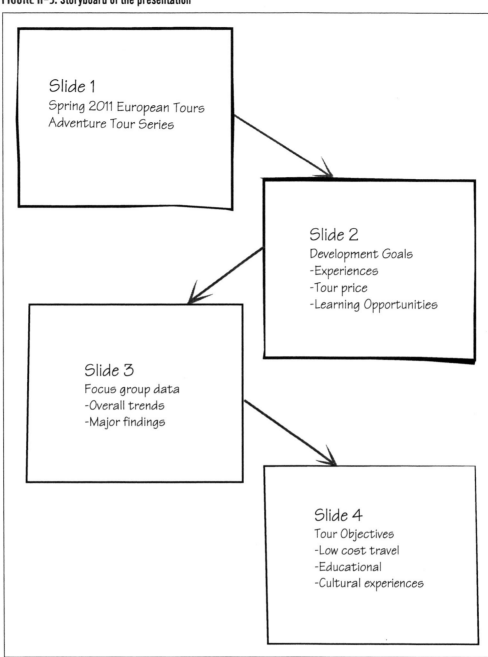

Slide 1
Spring 2011 European Tours
Adventure Tour Series

Slide 2
Development Goals
-Experiences
-Tour price
-Learning Opportunities

Slide 3
Focus group data
-Overall trends
-Major findings

Slide 4
Tour Objectives
-Low cost travel
-Educational
-Cultural experiences

Understanding copyright

Intellectual property is any idea or creation of the human mind. Copyright law is a type of intellectual property law that protects works of authorship, including books, Web pages, computer games, music, artwork, and photographs. Copyright protects the expression of an idea, but not the underlying facts or concepts. In other words, the general subject matter is not protected, but how you express it is, such as when several people photograph the same sunset. Copyright attaches to any original work of authorship *as soon* as it is created, you *do not* have to register it with the Copyright Office or display the copyright symbol, ©.

Fair use is an exception to copyright and permits the public to use copyrighted material for certain purposes without obtaining prior consent from the owner. Determining whether fair use applies to a work depends on its purpose, the nature of the work, how much of the work you want to copy, and the effect on the work's value. Unauthorized use of protected work (such as downloading a photo or a song from the Web) is known as copyright infringement, and can lead to legal action.

Examining the PowerPoint Window

When you first start PowerPoint, a blank slide appears in the PowerPoint window. PowerPoint has different **views** that allow you to see your presentation in different forms. By default, the PowerPoint window opens in **Normal view**, which is the primary view that you use to write, edit, and design your presentation. Normal view is divided into three areas called **panes**: the pane on the left contains the Outline and Slides tabs, the large pane is the Slide pane, and the small pane below the Slide pane is the Notes pane. You move around in each pane using the scroll bars. ▓▓▓▓ The PowerPoint window and the specific parts of Normal view are described below.

If you have trouble finding Microsoft PowerPoint 2007 on the All Programs menu, check with your instructor or technical support person.

1. **Click the** Start button ⊕ **on the taskbar, point to All Programs, click Microsoft Office, then click** Microsoft Office PowerPoint 2007

    PowerPoint starts and the PowerPoint window opens, as shown in Figure A-4.

Using Figure A-4 as a guide, examine the elements of the PowerPoint window, then find and compare the elements described below:

- The **Ribbon**—a wide (toolbar-like) band that runs across the entire PowerPoint window—is a new feature that organizes all of PowerPoint's primary commands. Each set of primary commands is identified by a **tab**; for example, the Home tab is selected by default as shown in Figure A-4. Commands are further arranged into **groups** on the Ribbon based on their function. So, for example, text formatting commands such as Bold, Underline, and Italic are located on the Home tab, in the Font group.

- The **Outline tab** displays the text of your presentation in the form of an outline, without showing graphics or other visual objects. Using this tab, it is easy to move text on or among slides by dragging text to reorder the information.

- The **Slides tab** displays the slides of your presentation as small images, called **thumbnails**. You can quickly navigate through the slides in your presentation by clicking the thumbnails on this tab. You can also add, delete, or rearrange slides using this tab.

- The **Slide pane** displays the current slide in your presentation.

- The **Notes pane** is used to type text that references a slide's content. You can print these notes and refer to them when you make a presentation or print them as handouts and give them to your audience. The Notes pane is not visible to the audience when you show a slide presentation in Slide Show view.

- The **Quick Access toolbar** provides immediate access to common commands that you use all the time, such as Save, Undo, and Redo. The Quick Access toolbar is always visible no matter which Ribbon tab you select. This toolbar is fully customizable. Click the Customize Quick Access Toolbar button to add or remove commands.

- The **View Shortcuts** on the status bar allow you to switch quickly between PowerPoint views.

- The **status bar**, located at the bottom of the PowerPoint window, shows messages about what you are doing and seeing in PowerPoint, including which slide you are viewing, and the design theme applied to the presentation. In addition, the status bar displays the Zoom slider controls, the **Fit slide to current window button** 🔳, and information on other functionality such as signatures and permissions.

- The **Zoom slider**, located in the lower-right corner of the status bar, allows you to zoom the slide in and out quickly.

FIGURE A-4: PowerPoint window in Normal view

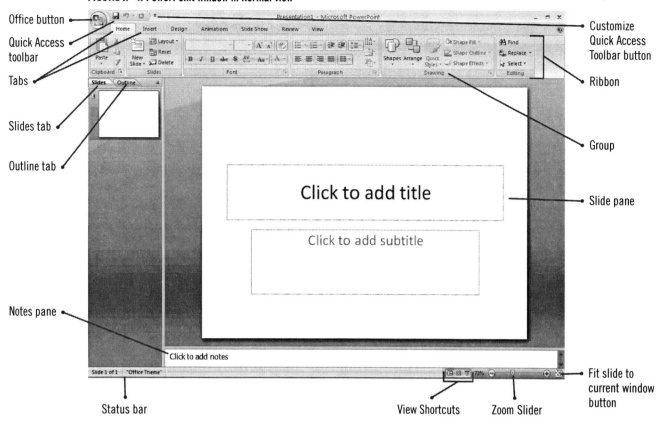

- Office button
- Quick Access toolbar
- Tabs
- Slides tab
- Outline tab
- Notes pane
- Status bar
- Customize Quick Access Toolbar button
- Ribbon
- Group
- Slide pane
- Fit slide to current window button
- View Shortcuts
- Zoom Slider

Click to add title

Click to add subtitle

Click to add notes

Slide 1 of 1   "Office Theme"

Viewing your presentation in grayscale or black and white

Viewing your presentation in grayscale (using shades of gray) or pure black and white is very useful when you are printing a presentation on a black-and-white printer and you want to make sure your presentation prints correctly. To see how your color presentation looks in grayscale or black and white, click the View tab, then click either the Grayscale or Pure Black and White button. Depending on which button you select, the Grayscale or the Black and White tab appears and the Ribbon displays different settings that you can customize. If you don't like the way an individual object looks in black and white or grayscale, you can change its color. Right-click the object, point to Black and White Setting or Grayscale Setting (depending on which view you are in), and choose from the options on the submenu.

Entering Slide Text

Each time you launch PowerPoint, a new presentation with a blank title slide appears in Normal view. The title slide has two **text placeholders**—boxes with dotted borders—where you enter text. The top text placeholder on the title slide is the **title placeholder**, labeled "Click to add title." The bottom text placeholder on the title slide is the **subtitle text placeholder**, labeled "Click to add subtitle." To enter text in a placeholder, click the placeholder and then type your text. After you enter text in a placeholder, the placeholder becomes a text object. An **object** is any item on a slide that can be modified. Objects are the building blocks that make up a presentation slide. ▓▓▓▓ Begin working on your presentation by entering text on the title slide.

STEPS

1. **Move the pointer over the title placeholder labeled "Click to add title" in the Slide pane**

   The pointer changes to I when you move the pointer over the placeholder. In PowerPoint, the pointer often changes shape, depending on the task you are trying to accomplish.

2. **Click the title placeholder in the Slide pane**

   The **insertion point**, a blinking vertical line, indicates where your text appears when you type in the placeholder. A **selection box** with a dashed line border and sizing handles appears around the placeholder, indicating that it is selected and ready to accept text. See Figure A-5.

<table>
<tr><td>

TROUBLE

If you press a wrong key, press [Backspace] to erase the character.

</td></tr>
</table>

3. **Type Spring 2011 European Tour Proposal**

   PowerPoint wraps and then center-aligns the title text within the title placeholder, which is now a text object. Notice that the text also appears on the slide thumbnail on the Slides tab.

4. **Click the subtitle text placeholder in the Slide pane**

   The subtitle text placeholder is ready to accept text.

5. **Type Adventure Tour Series, then press [Enter]**

   The insertion point moves to the next line in the text object.

6. **Type Your Name, press [Enter], type Tour Developer-Europe, press [Enter] then type Quest Specialty Travel**

   Notice that the AutoFit Options button ⊞ appears near the text object. The AutoFit Options button on your screen indicates that PowerPoint has automatically decreased the size of all the text in the text object so that it fits inside the text object.

7. **Click the Autofit Options button ⊞, then click Stop Fitting Text to This Placeholder on the shortcut menu**

   The text in the text object changes back to its original size and no longer fits in the text object.

8. **Position I to the right of Series, drag left to select the entire line of text, press [Backspace], then click outside the text object in a blank area of the slide**

   The Adventure Tour Series line of text is deleted and the Autofit Options button closes, as shown in Figure A-6. Clicking a blank area of the slide deselects all selected objects on the slide.

9. **Click the Save button ▣ on the Quick Access toolbar to open the Save As dialog box, then save the presentation as QuestA in the drive and folder where you store your Data Files**

FIGURE A-5: Title text placeholder ready to accept text

Selection box

Insertion point

Title text placeholder

I-beam pointer

Subtitle text placeholder

FIGURE A-6: Text on title slide

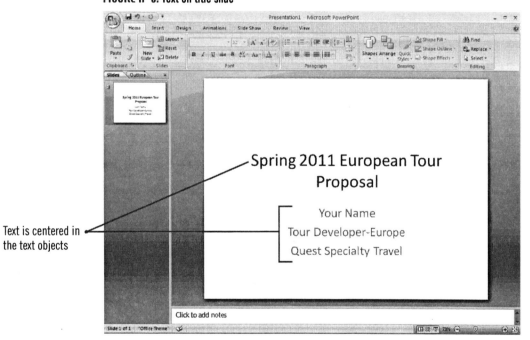

Spring 2011 European Tour Proposal

Your Name
Tour Developer-Europe
Quest Specialty Travel

Text is centered in the text objects

Saving fonts with your presentation

When you create a presentation, it uses the fonts that are installed on your computer. If you need to open the presentation on another computer, the fonts might look different if that computer has a different set of fonts. To preserve the look of your presentation on any computer, you can save, or embed, the fonts in your presentation. Click the Office button, then click the PowerPoint Options button. The PowerPoint Options dialog box opens. Click Save in the left pane, then click the Embed fonts in the file check box. Click the Embed all characters option button, then click OK to close the dialog box. Click Save on the Quick Access toolbar. Now the presentation looks the same on any computer that opens it. Using this option, however, significantly increases the size of your presentation, so only use it when necessary. You can freely embed any TrueType font that comes with Windows. You can embed other TrueType fonts only if they have no license restrictions.

Adding a New Slide

Ordinarily when you add a new slide to a presentation, you have a pretty good idea of what you want the slide to look like. For example, you may want to add a slide that has a title over bulleted text and a picture. To help you add a slide like this quickly and easily, PowerPoint provides nine standard slide layouts. A **slide layout** contains text and object placeholders that are arranged in a specific way on the slide. You have already worked with the Title Slide layout in the previous lesson. In the event that a standard slide layout does not meet your needs, you can modify an existing slide layout or create a brand new, custom slide layout. ▰▰▰ To continue developing the presentation, you create a slide that defines the QST development goals for the new tour series.

STEPS

1. **Click the New Slide button in the Slides group on the Home tab on the Ribbon**

   A new blank slide (now the current slide) appears as the second slide in your presentation as shown in Figure A-7. The new slide in the Slide pane contains a title placeholder and a content placeholder. A **content placeholder** can be used to insert text or objects such as clip art, tables, or charts. Table A-2 describes the content placeholder icons. Notice that the status bar indicates Slide 2 of 2 and that the Slides tab now contains two slide thumbnails. You can easily change the current slide's layout using the Layout button in the Slides group.

2. **Click the Layout button in the Slides group**

   The Layout gallery opens. Each layout is identified by a descriptive name.

3. **Point to the Two Content slide layout, then click the Two Content slide layout**

   A slide layout with a title placeholder and two content placeholders replaces the Title and Content layout for the current slide.

4. **Type Tour Development Goals, then click the left content placeholder**

   The text you type appears in the title placeholder and the insertion point appears at the top of the left content placeholder.

5. **Type Focus on significant experiences, then press [Enter]**

   A new first-level bullet automatically appears when you press [Enter].

6. **Press [Tab]**

   The new first-level bullet indents and becomes a second-level bullet.

7. **Type Preserve QST values, press [Enter], then click the Decrease List Level button ▤ in the Paragraph group**

   The Decrease List Level button changes the second-level bullet into a first-level bullet.

8. **Type Price tours reasonably, press [Enter], type Create learning opportunities, press [Enter], then click the Increase List Level button ▤ in the Paragraph group**

9. **Type Offer local guides, press [Enter], type Provide experts, then click the Save button ▤ on the Quick Access toolbar**

   The Increase List Level button creates a second-level bullet from a first-level bullet. The Save button saves all of the changes to the file. Compare your screen with Figure A-8.

FIGURE A-7: New blank slide in Normal view

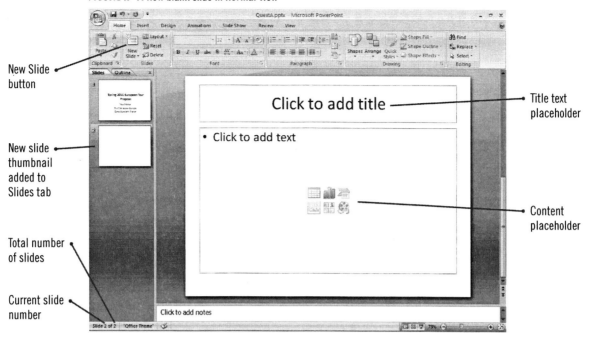

New Slide button

New slide thumbnail added to Slides tab

Total number of slides

Current slide number

Title text placeholder

Content placeholder

FIGURE A-8: New slide with Two Content slide layout

Decrease List Level button

Increase List Level button

First-level bullet

Second-level bullet

Two content placeholders based on the slide layout

Tour Development Goals
- Focus on significant experiences
  − Preserve QST values
- Price tours reasonably
- Create learning opportunities
  − Offer local guides
  − Provide experts

PowerPoint 2007

TABLE A-2: Content placeholder icons

click this icon	to insert a
	Table
	Graph chart
	Piece of clip art
	Picture from a file
	SmartArt graphic
	Movie or video clip

Applying a Design Theme

PowerPoint provides a number of design themes to help you quickly create a professional and contemporary looking presentation. A design **theme** incorporates sets of colors for fill, line, and shadow, called **theme colors**; fonts for titles and other text, called **theme fonts**; and effects for lines and fills, called **theme effects** to create a cohesive look. In most cases, you would apply one theme to an entire presentation; you can, however, apply multiple themes to the same presentation, or even a different theme on each presentation slide. You can use a design theme as is, or you can alter individual elements of the theme as needed. Unless you need to use a specific design theme, such as a company theme or product design theme, it is faster and easier to use one of the themes supplied with PowerPoint. If you design a custom theme, you can save it to use in the future. ▰▰▰ You decide to change the default design theme in the presentation to a new one.

STEPS

1. **Click the Slide 1 thumbnail on the Slides tab**

   Slide 1, the title slide, appears in the Slide pane.

2. **Click the Design tab on the Ribbon, then point to the Civic theme in the Themes group as shown in Figure A-9**

   The Design tab appears and a live preview of the Civic theme is displayed on the slide. A **live preview** allows you to see how your changes affect the slides before actually making the change. The live preview lasts about one minute and then your slide reverts back to its original state. The first (far left) theme thumbnail identifies the current theme applied to the presentation, in this case, the default design theme called the Office Theme. Depending on your monitor resolution and screen size, you can see between five and seven design themes visible in the Themes group. However, there are a total of 20 standard built-in themes available to use.

3. **Slowly move your pointer ▨ over the other design themes, then click the Themes group down scroll arrow once**

   A live preview of the theme appears on the slide each time you pass your pointer over the theme thumbnails, and a ScreenTip identifies the theme names.

4. **Move ▨ over the design themes, then click the Metro theme**

   The Metro design theme is applied to all the slides in the presentation. Notice the new slide background color, graphic elements, fonts, and text color. You decide that this theme isn't right for this presentation.

QUICK TIP

One way to apply multiple themes to the same presentation is to click the Slide Sorter button in the status bar, select a slide or a group of slides, then click the theme.

5. **Click the More button ▾ in the Themes group**

   The Themes gallery window opens. At the top of the gallery window in the This Presentation section are the current theme(s) applied to the presentation. Notice that just the Metro theme is listed here because when you changed the theme in the last step, you replaced the default theme with the Metro theme. The Built-In section identifies all of the standard themes that come with PowerPoint.

6. **Right-click the Solstice theme in the Themes group, then click Apply to Selected Slides**

   The Solstice theme is applied only to Slide 1. You like the Solstice theme better and decide to apply it to both slides.

7. **Right-click the Solstice theme in the Themes group, then click Apply to All Slides**

   The Solstice theme is applied to both slides. Preview the other slide in the presentation to see how it looks.

8. **Click the Next Slide button ▾ at the bottom of the vertical scroll bar**

   Compare your screen to Figure A-10.

9. **Click the Previous Slide button ▲ at the bottom of the vertical scroll bar, then save your changes**

FIGURE A-9: Slide showing a different design theme

Current theme applied

Office Theme

Civic Theme

New graphic elements

Themes group down scroll arrow

More button

New font type

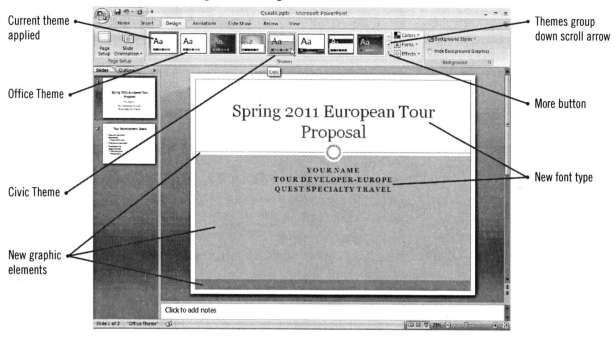

FIGURE A-10: Presentation with Solstice theme applied

Solstice theme

Solstice theme applied

Previous Slide button

Next Slide button

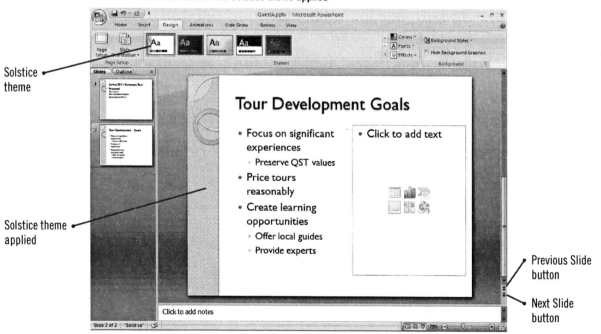

Customizing themes

You are not limited to using the standard themes PowerPoint provides; you can also modify a theme to create your own custom theme. For example, you might want to incorporate your company's colors on the slide background of the presentation or be able to type using fonts your company uses for brand recognition. To modify an existing theme, you can change the color theme, font theme, or the effects theme and then save it for future use by clicking the Themes group More button, then clicking Save Current Theme. You also have the ability to create a new font theme or a new color theme from scratch by clicking the Theme Fonts button or the Theme Colors button and then clicking Create New Theme Fonts or Create New Theme Colors. You work in the Create New Theme Fonts or Create New Theme Colors dialog box to define the custom theme fonts or colors.

Creating a Presentation in PowerPoint 2007

Comparing Presentation Views

PowerPoint has four basic views: Normal view, Slide Sorter view, Notes Page view, and Slide Show view. Each PowerPoint view displays your presentation in a different way and is used for different purposes. Normal view is the primary editing view where you add text, graphics, and other elements to the slides. Slide Sorter view is primarily used to rearrange slides, however, you can also add slide effects and design themes in this view. You use Notes Page view to type notes you want to remember about each slide. Slide Show view displays your presentation filling the computer screen and is the view used to give a presentation. To move easily among three of the PowerPoint views, use the View Shortcuts buttons located in the Status bar next to the Zoom slider. All PowerPoint views can be accessed using the View tab on the Ribbon. Table A-3 provides a brief description of the PowerPoint views. ▰▰▰▰ Examine each of the PowerPoint views, starting with Normal view.

STEPS

1. **Click the Outline tab, then click the small slide icon ▄ next to Slide 2 in the Outline tab**

   The text for Slide 2 is selected in the Outline tab and Slide 2 appears in the Slide pane as shown in Figure A-11. Notice that the status bar identifies the number of the slide you are viewing, the total number of slides in the presentation, and the name of the applied design theme.

2. **Click the Previous Slide button ⬆ at the bottom of the vertical scroll bar**

   Slide 1 appears in the Slide pane. The scroll box in the vertical scroll bar moves back up the scroll bar.

3. **Click the Slides tab**

   Thumbnails of the slides in your presentation appear again on the Slides tab. Since the Slides tab is narrower than the Outline tab, the Slide pane enlarges.

   > **QUICK TIP**
   > You can also switch between views using the commands in the Presentation Views group on the View tab.

4. **Click the Slide Sorter button ⊞ on the status bar**

   A thumbnail of each slide in the presentation appears as shown in Figure A-12. You can examine the flow of your slides and drag any slide or group of slides to rearrange the order of the slides in the presentation.

5. **Double-click Slide 1 in Slide Sorter view**

   Slide 1 appears in Normal view.

6. **Click the Slide Show button ⬔ on the status bar**

   The first slide fills the entire screen. In this view, you can practice running through your slides as they would appear in the slide show.

   > **QUICK TIP**
   > You can also press [Enter] or [Spacebar] to advance the slide show.

7. **Click the left mouse button to advance through the slides one at a time until you see a black slide, then click once more to return to Normal view**

   The black slide at the end of the slide show indicates that the slide show is finished. At the end of a slide show you automatically return to the slide and PowerPoint view you were in before you ran the slide show, in this case Slide 1 in Normal view.

8. **Click the View tab on the Ribbon, then click the Notes Page button in the Presentation Views group**

   Notes Page view appears, showing a reduced image of the current slide above a large text placeholder. You can enter text in this placeholder and then print the notes page for your own use.

9. **Click the Normal button in the Presentation Views group**

FIGURE A-11: Normal view with the outline tab displayed

Outline tab

Slides tab

Slide icon

Design theme name

Normal button

Slide Sorter button

Slide Show button

FIGURE A-12: Slide Sorter view

Slide 1

TABLE A-3: PowerPoint views

view name	button	button name	description
Normal	⊞	Normal	Displays the Outline and Slides tabs, the Slide pane, and the Notes pane at the same time; use this view to work on your presentation's content, layout, and notes concurrently
Slide Sorter	⊞⊞	Slide Sorter	Displays thumbnails of all slides in the order in which they appear in your presentation; use this view to rearrange and add special effects to your slides
Slide Show	▣	Slide Show	Displays your presentation as an electronic slide show
Notes Page	(no View Shortcut button)		Displays a reduced image of the current slide above a large text box where you can enter or view notes

Creating a Presentation in PowerPoint 2007

Printing a PowerPoint Presentation

You print your presentation when you want to review your work or when you have completed it and want a hard copy. Reviewing your presentation at different stages of development gives you a better perspective of the overall flow and feel of the presentation. You can also preview your presentation to see exactly how each slide looks before you print the presentation. When you are finished working on your presentation, even if it is not yet complete, you can close the presentation file and exit PowerPoint. ▰▰▰ You are done working on the tour presentation for now. You save and preview the presentation, then you print the slides and notes pages of the presentation so you can review them later. Before leaving for the day, you close the file and exit PowerPoint.

STEPS

1. **Click the Office button 🔘, point to Print, then click Print Preview**

   The Print Preview window opens as shown in Figure A-13. Notice the Print Preview tab appears on the Ribbon, which now displays associated commands for the Print Preview window.

2. **Click the Next Page button in the Preview group, then click the Print button in the Print group**

   You view Slide 2 before opening the Print dialog box. In the Print dialog box, you can specify what you want to print (slides, handouts, notes pages, or outline), the slide range, the number of copies to print, as well as other print options. The default options for the available printer are selected in the dialog box.

3. **Click the Slides option button in the Print range section of the dialog box to select it, type 2 to print only the second slide, then click OK**

   The second slide prints. To save paper when you are reviewing your slides, you can print in handout format, which lets you print up to nine slides per page.

4. **Click the Close Print Preview button in the Preview group, click the Office button 🔘, then click Print**

   The Print dialog box opens again. The options you choose in the Print dialog box remain there until you close the presentation.

5. **Click the All option button in the Print range section, click the Print what list arrow, click Handouts, click the Slides per page list arrow in the Handouts section, then click 3**

6. **Click the Color/grayscale list arrow, click Pure Black and White as shown in Figure A-14, then click OK**

   The presentation prints as handouts showing slide thumbnails next to blank lines. Using the Handouts with three slides per page printing option is a great way to print your presentation when you want to provide a way for audience members to take notes. Printing in pure black and white prints without any gray tones and can save printer toner.

7. **Click the Office button 🔘, then click Close**

   If you have made changes to your presentation, a Microsoft PowerPoint alert box opens asking you if you want to save changes you have made to your presentation file.

8. **Click Yes, if necessary, to close the alert box**

   Your presentation closes.

9. **Click the Office button 🔘, then click the Exit PowerPoint button**

   The PowerPoint program closes, and you return to the Windows desktop.

FIGURE A-13: Print Preview window

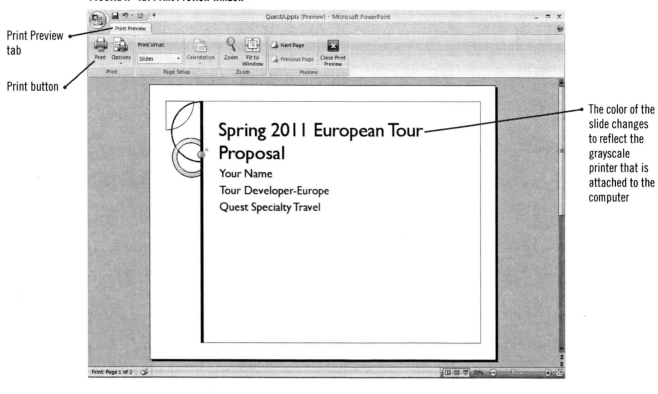

Print Preview tab

Print button

The color of the slide changes to reflect the grayscale printer that is attached to the computer

FIGURE A-14: Print dialog box with Handouts selected

Your printer name may be different

Slides option button

Click to select an item to print

Color/grayscale list arrow

Slides per page list arrow

Animating in PowerPoint

Providing emphasis to the information in your presentation can help your audience retain that information. Animating text and other objects is one dramatic way to provide emphasis. Animations make a presentation engaging and enjoyable to watch. You can animate text, shapes, diagrams, charts, and other objects, which provides you a wide variety of options to create a dynamic presentation. You can also add interesting effects to the way slides are presented or transition on the screen. Types of animation effects include flying in or out, fading, and changing color.

PowerPoint 2007

Creating a Presentation in PowerPoint 2007

388

Practice

If you have a SAM user profile, you may have access to hands-on instruction, practice, and assessment of the skills covered in this unit. Log in to your SAM account (http://sam2007.course.com/) to launch any assigned training activities or exams that relate to the skills covered in this unit.

▼ CONCEPTS REVIEW

Label each element of the PowerPoint window shown in Figure A-15.

FIGURE A-15

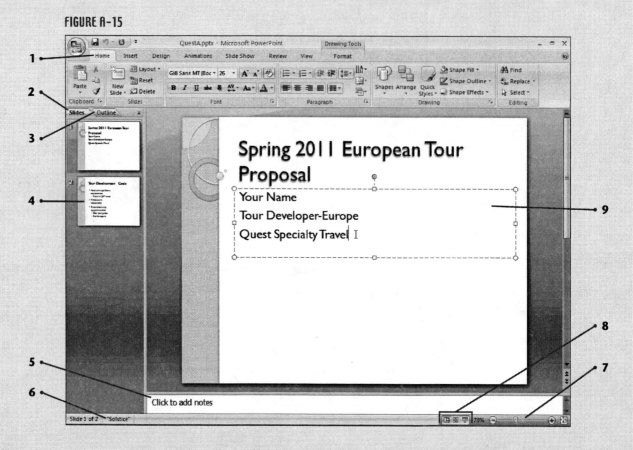

Match each term with the statement that best describes it.

10. **Ribbon**
11. **Normal view**
12. **Slide Sorter view**
13. **Zoom slider**
14. **Notes pane**

a. A view that displays slides as thumbnails
b. Used to organize all of PowerPoint's commands
c. Displays the Outline and Slides tabs, as well as the Slide and Notes panes
d. Used to type text that references slide content
e. Allows you to change the size of the slide in the window

Select the best answer from the list of choices.

15. When you type text in a placeholder, it becomes:

a. A label

b. A text object

c. A text processing object

d. A selection box

16. The buttons you use to switch between the PowerPoint views in the status bar are called:

a. Toolbar buttons

b. View buttons

c. PowerPoint buttons

d. View Shortcuts

17. All of the following are PowerPoint views, except:

a. Notes Page view

b. Outline Page view

c. Normal view

d. Slide Sorter view

18. What does the slide layout do in a presentation?

a. A slide layout defines how all the elements on a slide are arranged.

b. A slide layout automatically applies all the objects you can use on a slide.

c. The slide layout puts all your slides in order.

d. The slide layout enables you to apply a template to the presentation.

19. The view that fills the entire screen with each slide in the presentation is called:

a. Presentation view

b. Slide Sorter view

c. Slide Show view

d. Slide view

20. According to the unit, which of the following is not a guideline for planning a presentation?

a. Determine how much time you need to give the presentation.

b. Determine the purpose of the presentation.

c. Determine what you want to produce when the presentation is finished.

d. Determine which type of output you need to best convey your message.

21. Other than the Slide pane, where else can you enter slide text?

a. Slides tab

b. Outline tab

c. Tab Preview

d. Notes Page view

▼ SKILLS REVIEW

1. Start PowerPoint and examine the PowerPoint window.

a. Start PowerPoint, if necessary.

b. Identify as many elements of the PowerPoint window as you can without referring to the unit material.

c. Be able to describe the purpose or function of each element.

d. For any elements you cannot identify, refer to the unit.

2. Enter slide text.

a. In the Slide pane in Normal view, enter the text **Historic Middle Fork Land & Camps Protection Proposal** in the title placeholder. Refer to Figure A-16 as you complete the slide.

b. In the subtitle text placeholder, enter **Historic Lands Preservation Society**

FIGURE A-16: Slide 1 of the completed presentation

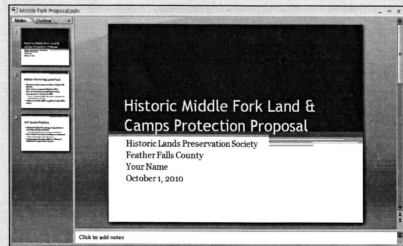

c. On the next line of the placeholder, enter Feather Falls County.

d. On the next line of the placeholder, enter Your Name.

e. On the next line of the placeholder, enter October 1, 2010. Let PowerPoint AutoFit the text in the text object.

f. Deselect the text object.

g. Save the presentation using the filename Middle Fork Proposal to the drive and folder where you store your Data Files.

3. **Add new slides.**

a. Create a new slide.

b. Using Figure A-17, enter text on the slide.

c. Create another new slide.

d. Using Figure A-18, enter text on the slide.

e. Save your changes.

4. **Apply a design theme.**

a. Click the Design tab.

b. Click the Themes group More button, then point to all of the themes.

c. Locate the Verve theme, then apply it to all the slides.

d. Move to Slide 1.

e. Locate the Urban theme, then apply it to Slide 1.

f. Apply the Urban theme to all of the slides in the presentation.

g. Use the Next Slide button to move to Slide 3, then save your changes.

5. **Compare presentation views.**

a. Click the View tab.

b. Click the Slide Sorter button in the Presentation Views group.

c. Click the Notes Page button in the Presentation Views group, then click the Previous Slide button twice.

d. Click the Normal button in the Presentation Views group, then click the Slide Show button.

e. Click until a black screen appears, then click to end the presentation.

f. Save your changes.

6. **Print and close a presentation, and exit PowerPoint.**

a. Print Slide 1 as slides in grayscale. (*Hint*: Click the Current slide option button in the Print dialog box.)

b. Print all the slides as handouts, 3 slides per page, in pure black and white.

c. Print the presentation outline.

d. Close the file, saving your changes.

e. Exit PowerPoint.

FIGURE A-17

Middle Fork Mining Lands Facts

- Covers over 360 acres in northern Feather Falls County
- First mining camps established in 1849
- Grew to be the largest established mining encampment in the state by 1861
  - In its prime, the Middle Fork camps included over 100 buildings and shops
- Took out over 80 million in gold ore (750 million today)

FIGURE A-18

HLP Society Positions

- Historic Middle Fork mining camps/lands are not being actively protected
  - Abandoned by federal and local governments
- Over 70% of the original buildings are destroyed
  - Human presence is harmful to area
- Need preservation plan ASAP or will lose all evidence of camps within 10 years

▼ INDEPENDENT CHALLENGE 1

You work for Resource Industries, a business that that offers environmental hazard clean up and project management. In an effort to expand the business, your boss has asked you to create a sales presentation that describes the services Resource Industries offers.

a. Start PowerPoint.

b. In the title placeholder on Slide 1, type **Resource Industries**

c. In the sub-title placeholder, type **Professional & Client Services**, press **[Enter]**, type **Your Name**, press **[Enter]**, then type **Today's Date**

d. Apply the Equity design theme to the slide.

e. Save your presentation with the filename **Resource Industries** to the drive and folder where you store your Data Files.

f. Use Figures A-19 and A-20 to add two more slides to your presentation. (*Hint*: Slide 2 uses the Comparison layout.)

g. Use the commands on the View tab to switch between all of PowerPoint's views.

h. Preview the presentation using the Print Preview command, print the presentation using the Slides option, save and close the file, then exit PowerPoint.

FIGURE A-19

Resource Industries Services

Professional Services
- Hazardous materials spills
- Drug lab contamination
- Environmental assessment
- Geotechnical drilling
- Underground storage tanks

Client Services
- 24-Hr Emergency Response Service
- Over 20 years of certification and company history
- Efficient project management
- Regulatory agency reporting
- Complete documentation

FIGURE A-20

Service Goals
- Prompt emergency service
- Superior project management
- Job done right the first time
- Job done on time and within budget
- Provide only the services needed to complete job
- Comply with all regulatory agencies
- Premier provider of environmental services

▼ INDEPENDENT CHALLENGE 2

You have recently been promoted to national sales manager at Windman Power Industries, which manufactures personal watercraft, including items such as paddle boats, canoes, kayaks, sail boats, and rafts. Part of your job is to present company sales figures at a yearly sales meeting. Use the following information as the basis for units sold nationally in your presentation: 797 canoes, 1302 kayaks, 421 paddle boats, 4219 sail boats, 230 rafts. Assume that Windman Power has five sales regions throughout the country: West, East, South, Midwest, and Northeast. Also, assume overall sales rose 22% during the last year and gross sales reached $230 million. The presentation should have at least five slides.

a. Spend some time planning the slides of your presentation. What is the best way to show the information provided? What other information could you add that might be useful for this presentation?

b. Start PowerPoint.

c. Give the presentation an appropriate title on the title slide and enter today's date and your name in the subtitle placeholder.

d. Add slides and enter appropriate slide text.

Creating a Presentation in PowerPoint 2007

▼ INDEPENDENT CHALLENGE 2 (CONTINUED)

e. On the last slide of the presentation, include the following information:

Windman Power Industries

PO Box 777

West Chester, IN 39022

f. Apply a design theme. A typical slide might look like the one shown in Figure A-21.

Advanced Challenge Exercise

- Open the Notes Page view.
- Add notes to three slides.
- Print the Notes Page view for the presentation.

g. Switch views. Run through the slide show at least once.

h. Save your presentation with the filename **Windman** where you store your Data Files.

i. Close the presentation and exit PowerPoint.

FIGURE A-21

An Overall View

Sales Figures
- This year's results!
  - $230 million gross sales
- Comparison to last year
  - $65 million increase in overall sales
- Region by region
  - West-up by 12%
  - East-down by 5%
  - Northeast-up by 6%
  - South-up by 11%
  - Midwest-up by 7%

National Sales
- Product Sales
  - Canoes- 797 units
  - Kayaks- 1302 units
  - Paddle boats- 421 units
  - Sail boats- 4219 units
  - Rafts- 230 units

▼ INDEPENDENT CHALLENGE 3

You work for ThaiMade Trade Co., an emerging company that exports goods from Thailand. The company wants to expand its business globally. The Internet marketing director has asked you to plan and create a PowerPoint presentation that he will use to convey an expanded Internet service that will target Western countries. This new Internet service will allow customers to purchase all kinds of Thai made goods. Sample items for sale include silver and turquoise jewelry, hand crafts, folk art, terra cotta kitchenware, wooden decorative items, and bamboo furniture. Your presentation should contain product information and pricing. Use the Internet, if possible, to research information that will help you formulate your ideas. The presentation should have at least five slides.

a. Spend some time planning the slides of your presentation. What information would a consumer need to have to purchase items on this Web site?

b. Start PowerPoint.

c. Give the presentation an appropriate title on the title slide and enter today's date and your name in the subtitle placeholder.

d. Add slides and enter appropriate slide text.

e. On the last slide of the presentation, type the following information:

ThaiMade Trade Co.

Satrani Condominium Room 214

36/980 Moo 5 Sethup Sub District, Muang district,

Chiangmai 50208 Thailand

Tel/Fax: +90-49-39850 Hotline: (03)249347

FIGURE A-22

Fine Jewelry Product List

Silver Jewelry	Turquoise Jewelry
☐ Bracelets	☐ Bracelets
☐ Necklaces	☐ Necklaces
☐ Rings	☐ Rings
☐ Earrings	☐ Earrings
☐ Watches	
☐ Pendants	

f. Apply a design theme. A typical slide might look like the one shown in Figure A-22.

g. Switch views. Run through the slide show at least once.

h. Save your presentation with the filename **ThaiMade** where you store your Data Files.

i. Close the presentation and exit PowerPoint.

▼ REAL LIFE INDEPENDENT CHALLENGE

Every year your college holds a large fund raising event to support a local charity. This year the Student Advisory Committee has chosen to help the East Hills Cerebral Palsy Center. To help them decide what kind of an event to hold this year, the Advisory Committee has appealed to the student body for fund raising ideas. Your idea is to host a regional Bar-B-Q cook off competition that includes local and professional cooking teams. Your idea was chosen as one of the finalist ideas and you need to present your proposal in a meeting of the Advisory Committee.

a. Spend some time planning the slides of your presentation. Assume the following: there are four competition categories (beef brisket, pork shoulder, pork ribs, and chicken); the competition is a two day event; event advertising will be city- and region-wide; local music groups will also be invited; there will be a kids section with games; the event will be held on the college football field. Use the Internet, if possible, to research information that will help you formulate your ideas.

b. Start PowerPoint.

c. Give the presentation an appropriate title on the title slide and enter your name and today's date in the subtitle placeholder.

d. Add slides and enter appropriate slide text. A typical slide might look like the one shown in Figure A-23.

e. View the presentation.

f. Save your presentation with the filename **Bar-B-Q Cookoff** where you store your Data Files.

g. Close the presentation and exit PowerPoint.

FIGURE A-23

Competition Structure

- **4 Judged Events**
  - Beef Brisket
  - Pork Shoulder
  - Pork Ribs
  - Chicken
- **Schedule**
  - Beef Brisket- judged at 12:30pm Sat
  - Pork Shoulder- judged at 4:30pm Sat
  - Pork Ribs- judged at 11:30am Sun
  - Chicken- judged at 3:30pm Sun

Create the presentation shown in Figures A-24 and A-25. Make sure you include your name on the title slide. Save the presentation as **PackJet Project Tests** where you store your Data Files. Print the slides.

FIGURE A-24

FIGURE A-25

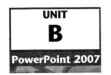

Modifying a Presentation

In the previous unit you learned how to enter slide text, add a new slide, and apply a design theme. Now, you are ready to take the next step in creating professional-looking presentations by learning to format text and work with drawn objects. In this unit, you'll enter text in the Outline tab, format text, draw and modify objects, add slide footer information, and check the spelling in the presentation. You continue working on the European tour proposal presentation for Ellen Latsky.

OBJECTIVES

Enter text in the Outline tab

Format text

Convert text to SmartArt

Insert and modify shapes

Edit and duplicate shapes

Align and group objects

Add slide headers and footers

Check spelling in a presentation

Entering Text in the Outline Tab

You can enter presentation text by typing directly on the slide in the Slide pane, or, if you'd rather focus on the presentation text without worrying about the layout, you can enter text in the Outline tab. The outline is organized so that the headings, or slide titles, appear at the top of the outline. Beneath the title, each subpoint, or each line of bulleted text, appears as one or more indented lines under the title. Each indent in the outline creates another level of bulleted text on the slide. ████ You switch to the Outline tab to enter text for two more slides in the European tour proposal presentation. Begin by entering more text using the Outline tab.

STEPS

QUICK TIP

To convert an older presentation to PowerPoint 2007 format, open the presentation in PowerPoint 2007, click the Office button, click Convert, then click OK in the dialog box.

1. **Start PowerPoint, open the presentation PPT B-1.pptx from the drive and folder where you store your Data Files, save it as QuestB, click the View tab on the Ribbon, then click the Arrange All button in the Window group**

   The Slide pane, Notes pane, and Slide and Outline tabs are now in their own window with the presentation title at the top.

2. **Click the Slide 2 thumbnail in the Slides tab, then click the Outline tab**

   The Outline tab enlarges to display the text that is on the slides. The slide icon and the text for Slide 2 are highlighted, indicating that it's selected. Notice the number 1 that appears to the left of the first-level bullet for Slide 2, indicating that there are multiple content placeholders on the slide.

3. **Click the Home tab on the Ribbon, click the New Slide button list arrow in the Slides group, then click Title and Content**

   A new slide, Slide 3, with the Title and Content layout appears as the current slide below Slide 2. A blinking insertion point appears next to the new slide in the Outline tab. See Figure B-1. Text that you enter next to a slide icon becomes the title for that slide.

4. **Type Focus Group Data Analyzed, press [Enter], then press [Tab]**

   When you first press [Enter] you create a new slide, but because you want to enter bulleted text on Slide 3 you press [Tab] so that the text you type is entered as bullet text on Slide 3.

5. **Type Trends, press [Enter], type Major Findings, press [Enter], type Conclusions, then press [Enter]**

   The last time you press [Enter], you create a bullet that has no text at the end of this slide.

6. **Press [Shift][Tab]**

   The last bullet that was created on Slide 3 becomes a new slide.

QUICK TIP

Pressing [Ctrl][Enter] while the cursor is in the text object creates a new slide with the same layout as the previous slide.

7. **Type Tour Strategy Objectives, press [Ctrl][Enter], then type the rest of the information on Slide 4 as shown in Figure B-2**

   Pressing [Ctrl][Enter] while the cursor is in the title text object moves the cursor into the content placeholder. Make sure you misspell the word "Utilze" as shown on the slide.

8. **Position the pointer on the Slide 4 icon in the Outline tab**

   The pointer changes to ✜. Slide 4 is out of order.

9. **Drag the Slide 4 icon up until a horizontal indicator line appears above the Slide 3 icon, then release the mouse button**

   The fourth slide moves up and switches places with the third slide.

10. **Click the Slides tab, then save your work**

    The Outline tab closes and the Slides tab is now visible in the window.

Modifying a Presentation

FIGURE B-1: Outline tab open showing new slide

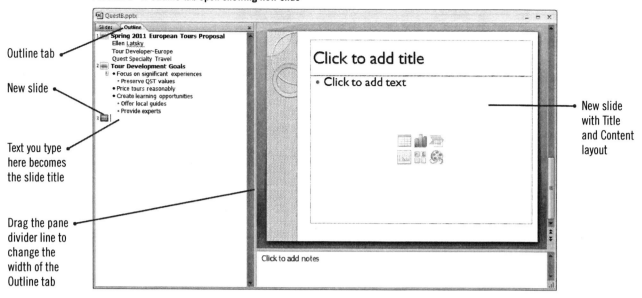

Outline tab

New slide

Text you type here becomes the slide title

Drag the pane divider line to change the width of the Outline tab

New slide with Title and Content layout

FIGURE B-2: Slide 4 with new information

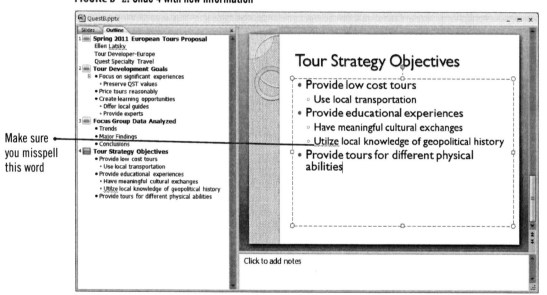

Make sure you misspell this word

Setting permissions

In PowerPoint, you can set specific access permissions for people who review or edit your work, so you have better control over your content. For example, you may want to give a user permission to edit or change your presentation but not allow them to print it. You can also restrict a user by permitting them to view the presentation, without the ability to edit or print the presentation, or you can give the user full access or control of the presentation. To use this feature, you first have to install the Windows Rights Management Services software using the Add or Remove Programs feature in the Control Panel, which installs the Restrict Permissions feature on the Office button. Then, to set user access permissions, click the Office button, point to Prepare, point to Restrict Permission, then click the appropriate option.

Formatting Text

Once you have entered and edited the text in your presentation, you can modify the way the text looks to emphasize your message. Important text should be highlighted in some way to distinguish it from other text or objects on the slide. For example, if you have two text objects on the same slide, you could draw attention to one text object by changing its color, font, or size. ▰▰▰▰ In order to enhance the European tour proposal presentation, you format text on Slide 4.

STEPS

1. **Click the Slide 4 thumbnail in the Slides tab, then double-click** Trends **in the text object**

   The word Trends is selected and a small semitransparent Mini toolbar appears above the text. The **Mini toolbar** contains basic text formatting commands, such as bold and italic, and appears when you select text using the mouse. This toolbar makes it quick and easy to format text, especially when the Home tab is not open.

2. **Move the pointer over the Mini toolbar, click the Font Color button list arrow** 🅰 ˙ **, then click the Dark Red color box under Standard Colors**

   The text changes color to dark red as shown in Figure B-3. As soon as you move the pointer over the Mini toolbar, the toolbar becomes clearly visible. When you click the Font Color button list arrow, the Font Color gallery appears showing the Theme Colors and Standard Colors. Notice that the Font Color button on the Mini toolbar and the Font Color button on the Home tab change color to reflect the new color choice.

3. **Click outside the text object in a blank area of the slide, press and hold [Shift], click the text object, then release [Shift]**

   A selection box with small circles and squares called **sizing handles** appears around the text object. The entire text object is selected, and changes you make now affect all of the text in the text object. If you click a text object without pressing [Shift], a dotted selection box appears, indicating that the object is active and ready to accept text, but the text object itself is not selected. When the whole text object is selected, you can change its size, shape, or other attributes. Changing the color of the text helps emphasize it.

4. **Click the Font Color button** 🅰 ˙ **in the Font group**

   All of the text in the text object changes to the dark red color.

5. **Click the Font list arrow in the Font group**

   A list of available fonts opens with Gill Sans MT, the current font used in the text object, selected at the top of the list with the Theme Fonts.

6. **Click Arial Narrow**

   The Arial Narrow font replaces the original font in the text object. Notice that as you move the pointer over the font names in the font list the text on the slide displays a live preview of the different font choices.

7. **Click the Text Shadow button** Ⓢ **in the Font group, click the Change Case button** Aa˙ **in the Font group, then click UPPERCASE**

   All of the text now displays a gray shadow and is uppercase.

8. **Click the Bullets button list arrow** ☰˙ **in the Paragraph group, click None, then click the Center button** ☰ **in the Paragraph group**

   The bullets no longer appear next to the text and the text moves to the center of the text box. Compare your screen to Figure B-4.

9. **Click a blank area of the slide outside the text object to deselect it, then save your work**

FIGURE B-3: Selected word with Mini toolbar open

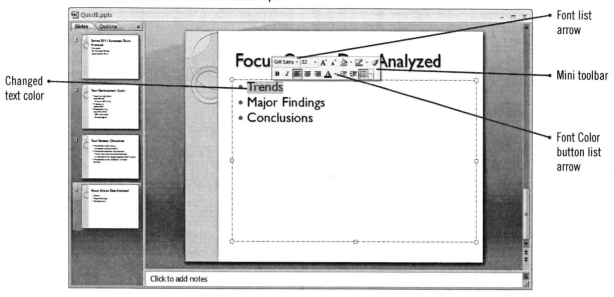

Font list arrow

Mini toolbar

Changed text color

Font Color button list arrow

FIGURE B-4: Formatted text

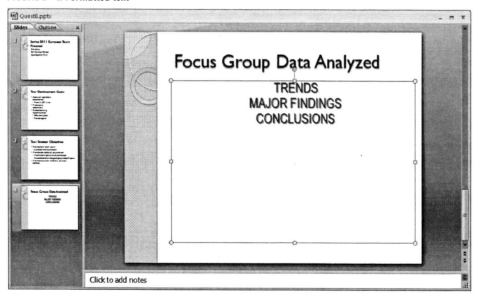

Replacing text and fonts

As you review your presentation, you may decide to replace certain text or fonts throughout the entire presentation using the Replace command. Text can be a word, phrase, or sentence. To replace specific text, click the Home tab on the Ribbon, then click the Replace button in the Editing group. In the Replace dialog box, enter the text you want to replace then enter the text you want to use as its replacement. You can also use the Replace command to replace one font for another. Simply click the Replace button list arrow in the Editing group, then click Replace Fonts to open the Replace Font dialog box.

Converting Text to SmartArt

Sometimes when you are working with text it just doesn't capture your attention, no matter how you dress it up with color or other formatting attributes. The introduction of the SmartArt graphic in PowerPoint 2007 increases your ability to create dynamic-looking text. A **SmartArt** graphic is a professional-quality diagram that visually illustrates text. There are seven basic categories, or types, of SmartArt graphics that illustrate text differently. For example, you can show steps in a process or timeline, show proportional relationships, or show how parts relate to a whole. You can create a SmartArt graphic from scratch or create one by converting existing text you have entered on a slide with a few simple clicks of the mouse. ▰▰▰▰ At QST, Ellen wants the text to appear visually dynamic so you convert the text on Slide 4 to a SmartArt graphic.

STEPS

1. **On Slide 4, click anywhere in the text object, then click the Convert to SmartArt Graphic button 🖾 in the Paragraph group**

   A gallery of SmartArt graphic layouts opens. As with many features in PowerPoint, you can preview how your text will look prior to applying the SmartArt graphic layout by using PowerPoint's Live Preview feature. You can review each SmartArt graphic layout and see how it changes the appearance of text.

2. **Move the pointer over the SmartArt graphic layouts in the gallery**

   Notice how the text becomes part of the graphic and the color and font changes each time you move the pointer over a different graphic layout. SmartArt graphic names appear as ScreenTips.

3. **Click the Basic Timeline layout in the SmartArt graphics gallery**

   A SmartArt graphic appears on the slide in place of the text object and a new SmartArt Tools Design tab opens on the Ribbon as shown in Figure B-5. A SmartArt graphic consists of two parts: the SmartArt graphic itself and a text pane where you type and edit text.

   > **QUICK TIP**
   >
   > The text objects in the SmartArt graphic can be moved and edited like any other text object in PowerPoint.

4. **If necessary, click the Text Pane button in the Create Graphic group to open the text pane, then click each bullet point in the text pane**

   Notice that each time you select a bullet point in the text pane, a selection box appears around the text objects in the SmartArt graphic.

5. **Click the Text Pane button, click the More button 🔽 in the Layouts group, then click the Alternating Flow layout**

   The text pane closes and the SmartArt graphic changes to the new graphic layout. You can radically change how the SmartArt graphic looks by applying a SmartArt Style. A **SmartArt Style** is a pre-set combination of simple and 3-D formatting options that follows the presentation theme.

   > **QUICK TIP**
   >
   > Click the Reset Graphic button in the Reset group to revert the SmartArt graphic to its original state.

6. **Move the pointer slowly over the styles in the SmartArt Styles group, then click the More button 🔽 in the SmartArt Styles group**

   A live preview of each style is displayed on the SmartArt graphic. The SmartArt styles are organized into sections; the top group offers suggestions for the best match for the document.

7. **Move the pointer over the styles in the 3-D section of the gallery, then click Powder**

   Notice how the new Powder style adds a bevel to the text boxes and makes them semi-transparent. Now move the SmartArt graphic more toward the center of the slide.

8. **Press [left-arrow key] twice, click a blank area of the slide outside the SmartArt graphic object to deselect it, then save your work**

   Compare your screen to Figure B-6.

FIGURE B-5: Text converted to a SmartArt graphic

Text Pane button

More button

Click to open the text pane

Contextual tabs for working with SmartArt graphics

FIGURE B-6: Final SmartArt graphic

Choosing SmartArt graphics

When choosing a SmartArt graphic to use on your slide, remember that you want the SmartArt graphic to communicate the message of the text effectively; not every SmartArt graphic layout achieves that goal. So, you must consider the type of text you want to illustrate. For example, does the text show steps in a process, does it show a continual process, or does it show non-sequential information? The answer to this question will dictate the type of SmartArt graphic layout you should choose. Also, the amount of text you want to illustrate will have an effect on the SmartArt graphic layout you choose. Most of the time key points will be the text you use in a SmartArt graphic. Finally, some SmartArt graphic layouts are limited by the number of shapes that they can accommodate. So, if you have four points you want to illustrate and you choose a graphic layout with only two shapes, you will not communicate your message correctly. Experiment with the SmartArt graphic layouts until you find the right one, and have fun in the process!

Modifying a Presentation

Inserting and Modifying Shapes

In PowerPoint you can insert many different types of shapes including lines, geometric figures, arrows, stars, callouts, and banners to enhance your presentation. You can create single shapes or combine several shapes together to make a more complex figure. You can modify many aspects of a shape including its fill color, line color, and line style, as well as add other effects like shadow, and 3-D effects. Instead of changing individual attributes, you can apply a Quick Style to a shape. A **Quick Style** is a set of formatting options, including line style, fill color, and effects. ~~█████~~ You decide to draw some shapes on Slide 3 of your presentation to complete the slide.

STEPS

1. **Click the Slide 3 thumbnail in the Slides tab**

   Slide 3 appears in the Slide pane.

2. **Press and hold [Shift], click the text object, then release [Shift]**

   The text object is selected.

3. **Position the pointer over the bottom-middle sizing handle, notice the pointer change to ↕, then drag the sizing handle up until the text object looks like Figure B-7**

   The text object decreases in size. When you position the pointer over a sizing handle, it changes to ↕. The pointer points in different directions depending on which sizing handle it is positioned over. When you drag a sizing handle, the pointer changes to ┼, and a faint gray outline appears, representing the size of the text object.

   TROUBLE

   If you see the Shapes gallery on the Ribbon, you are working at a higher resolution than the figures in this book, skip to step 5.

4. **Click the Shapes button in the Drawing group**

   A gallery of shapes organized by type opens. Notice that there is a section at the top of the gallery where all of the recently used shapes are placed.

5. **Click the Chevron shape ≫ in the Block Arrows section, position ┼ in the blank area of the slide below the text object, press and hold [Shift], drag down and to the right to create the chevron shape, as shown in Figure B-8, release the mouse button, then release [Shift]**

   A chevron arrow shape appears on the slide, filled with the default color. Pressing [Shift] while you create the object maintains the object's proportions as you change its size. To change the shape style apply a Quick Style from the Shape Styles group.

   TROUBLE

   If your shape is not approximately the same size as the one shown in Figure B-8, press [Shift] and drag one of the corner sizing handles to resize the object.

6. **Click the Drawing Tools Format tab, click the More button ▼ in the Shape Styles group, move the pointer over the styles in the gallery to review them, then click** Moderate Effect — Accent 3

   A red Quick Style with coordinated gradient fill, line, and shadow color is applied to the shape.

7. **Click the Shape Effects button in the Shape Styles group, then move the pointer over the effects to review them**

   The shape changes every time you move the pointer over a different effect.

8. **Point to Bevel, click Divot, then save your work**

FIGURE B-7: Resized text object

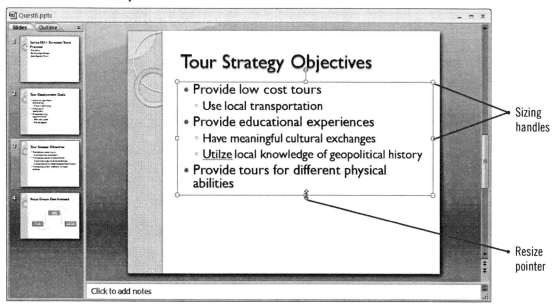

Sizing handles

Resize pointer

FIGURE B-8: Chevron arrow shape

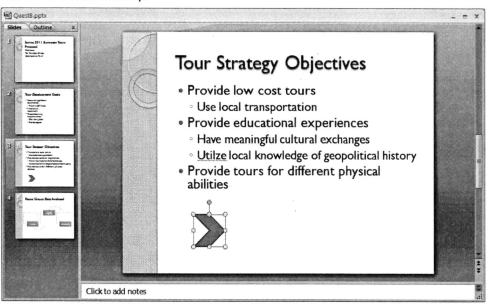

Changing the size and position of shapes

Usually when you resize a shape you can simply drag one of the sizing handles around the outside of the shape, but sometimes you may need to resize a shape more precisely. When you select a shape, the Drawing Tools Format tab appears on the Ribbon, offering you many different formatting options including some sizing commands located in the Size group. The Width and Height commands in the Size group allow you to change the width and height of a shape. You also have the option to open the Size and Position dialog box, which allows you to change the size of a shape, as well as the rotation, scale, and position of a shape on the slide.

Editing and Duplicating Shapes

Once you have created a shape you still have the ability to refine the aspects of the object. PowerPoint allows you to adjust various aspects of shapes to help change the look of them. For example, if you create a shape with an arrowhead but the head of the arrow does not look quite like you want it to look, you can change it. You can also add text to most PowerPoint shapes, and you can move or copy shapes. You want two identical arrows on Slide 4 to break up the look of the slide. You first change the shape of the arrow you've already created, and then you make a copy of it.

1. **Click the arrow shape on Slide 3 to select it, if it is not already selected**

    In addition to sizing handles, two other handles appear on the selected object. You use the **adjustment handle**—a small yellow diamond—to change the appearance of an object. The adjustment handle appears next to the most prominent feature of the object, like the head of an arrow in this case. You use the **rotate handle**—a small green circle—to manually rotate the object.

2. **Press and hold [Shift], drag the right-middle sizing handle on the arrow shape to the right approximately 1/2", release [Shift], then release the mouse button**

3. **Position the pointer over the middle of the selected arrow shape so that it changes to ⬥, then drag the arrow shape so that the arrow aligns with the left edge of the text in the text object as shown in Figure B-9**

    A semitransparent copy of the shape appears as you move the arrow shape to help you position it. PowerPoint uses a hidden grid to align objects; it forces objects to "snap" to the grid lines. Make any needed adjustments to the arrow shape position so it looks similar to Figure B-9.

4. **Position the pointer over the adjustment handle of the arrow shape so that it changes to ▷, then drag the adjustment handle to the right so it is halfway between the sizing handles**

    The arrow shape appearance changes.

5. **Position ⬥ over the arrow shape then press and hold [Ctrl]**

    The pointer changes to ⬥, indicating that PowerPoint makes a copy of the arrow shape when you drag the mouse.

6. **Holding [Ctrl], drag the arrow shape to the right until the arrow shape copy is in a blank area of the slide, release the mouse button, then release [Ctrl]**

    An identical copy of the arrow shape appears on the slide.

7. **Type Higher**

    The text appears in the selected arrow shape. The text is now part of the shape, so if you move or rotate the object, the text moves with it. Compare your screen with Figure B-10.

8. **Click the other arrow shape, type Aim, then click in a blank area of the slide**

    Clicking a blank area of the slide deselects all objects that are selected.

9. **Save your work**

FIGURE B-9: Slide showing resized shape

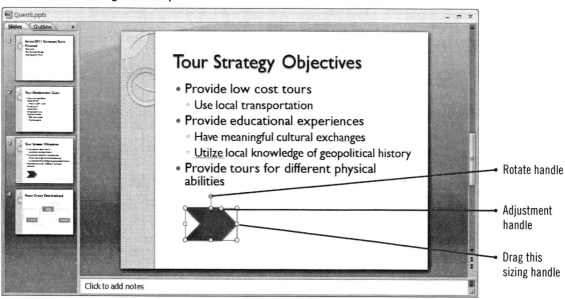

Rotate handle

Adjustment handle

Drag this sizing handle

FIGURE B-10: Slide showing duplicated shape

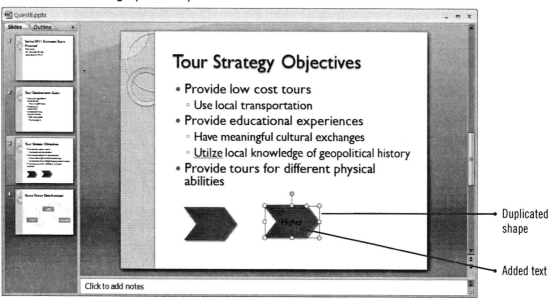

Duplicated shape

Added text

Understanding PowerPoint objects

Every object on a slide, whether it is a text object, a shape, a chart, a picture, or any other object, is stacked on the slide in the order it was created. So, for example, if you add three shapes to a slide, the first shape you create is on the bottom of the stack and the last shape you create is on the top of the stack. Each object, including Title and Content objects, can be moved up or down in the stack depending on how you want the objects to look on the slide. To move an object to the front of the stack, select the object, then click the Bring to Front button in the Arrange group on the Drawing Tools Format tab. To move an object to the back of the stack, click the Send to Back button in the Arrange group on the Drawing Tools Format tab. You can also open the Selection and Visibility pane by clicking the Selection Pane button in the Arrange group to view and rearrange all of the objects on the slide.

Aligning and Grouping Objects

After you are finished creating and modifying your objects, you can position them accurately on the slide to achieve the look you want. Using the Align commands in the Arrange group, you can align objects relative to each other by snapping them to a grid of evenly spaced vertical and horizontal lines. The Group command groups objects into one object, which secures their relative position to each other and makes it easy to edit and move them. The Distribute commands found with the Align commands evenly space objects horizontally or vertically relative to each other or the slide. ▰▰▰▰ You are ready to position and group the arrow shapes on Slide 3 to make the slide look consistent and planned.

STEPS

1. **Right-click a blank area of the slide, then click Grid and Guides on the shortcut menu**
   The Grid and Guides dialog box opens.

2. **Click the Display drawing guides on screen check box, then click OK**
   The PowerPoint guides appear as dotted lines on the slide and intersect at the center of the slide. They help you position the arrow shape.

3. **Position ⬚ over the vertical guide in a blank area of the slide, press and hold the mouse button until the pointer changes to a measurement guide, then drag the guide to the right until the guide position box reads 1.00**

4. **Position ⬚ over the Higher arrow shape (not over the text in the shape), then drag the arrow shape so that the left edge of the selection box touches the vertical guide as shown in Figure B-11**
   The arrow shape attaches or "snaps" to the vertical guide.

5. **With the Higher arrow shape selected, press and hold [Shift], click the Aim arrow shape, then release [Shift]**
   The two objects are now selected.

6. **Click the Drawing Tools Format tab on the Ribbon, click the Align button in the Arrange group, then click Align Bottom**
   The objects are now aligned horizontally along their bottom edges. Notice that the Higher arrow shape moves to align with the Aim arrow shape.

7. **Click the Group button in the Arrange group, then click Group**
   The objects group to form one object without losing their individual attributes. Notice that the sizing handles and rotate handle now appear on the outer edge of the grouped object, not around each individual object.

8. **Click the Align button, click Distribute Horizontally, then click a blank area of the slide**
   The objects are now distributed equally between the edges of the slide. Compare your screen with Figure B-12.

9. **Right-click a blank area of the slide, click Grid and Guides on the shortcut menu, click the Display drawing guides on screen check box, click OK, then save your work**
   The guides are no longer displayed on the slide.

FIGURE B-11: Repositioned shape

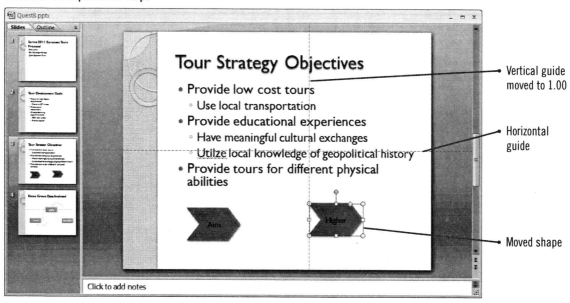

Vertical guide moved to 1.00

Horizontal guide

Moved shape

FIGURE B-12: Aligned and grouped shapes

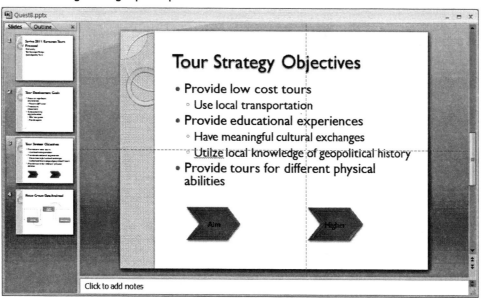

Distributing objects

There are two ways to distribute objects in PowerPoint: relative to each other and relative to the slide edge. If you choose to distribute objects relative to each other, PowerPoint evenly divides the empty space between all of the selected objects. When distributing objects in relation to the slide, PowerPoint evenly splits the empty space from slide edge to slide edge between the selected objects. To distribute objects relative to each other, click the Align button in the Arrange group on the Format tab, then click Align Selected Objects. To distribute objects relative to the slide, click the Align button in the Arrange group on the Format tab, then click Align to Slide.

Adding Slide Headers and Footers

Header and footer text, such as your company or product name, the slide number, and the date, can give your slides a polished look and make it easier for your audience to follow your presentation. On slides, you can add text to the footer; however, notes or handouts can include both header and footer text. Footer information that you apply to the slides of your presentation is visible in the PowerPoint views and when you print the slides. Notes and handouts header and footer text is visible when you print notes pages, handouts, and the outline. ▨▨▨▨ You add footer text to the slides of the European tour proposal presentation to make it easier for the audience to follow.

STEPS

1. **Click the Insert tab on the Ribbon, then click the Header & Footer button in the Text group**

   The Header and Footer dialog box opens, as shown in Figure B-13. The Header and Footer dialog box has two tabs: a Slide tab and a Notes and Handouts tab. The Slide tab is selected. There are three types of footer text, Date and time, Slide number, and Footer. The rectangles at the bottom of the Preview box identify the default position and status of the three types of footer text placeholders on the slides.

2. **Click the Date and time check box to select it**

   The date and time sub-options are now available and the far-left rectangle at the bottom of the Preview box has a dark border around it, signifying where the date and time information will appear on the slide. The Update automatically date and time option button is selected by default. This option updates the date and time every time you open or print the file.

3. **Click the Update automatically list arrow, then click the fourth option in the list**

   The date format changes to display the month spelled out, the date number, and the four-digit year.

4. **Click the Slide number check box, click the Footer check box, then type Your Name**

   The Preview box now shows that all three footer placeholders are selected.

5. **Click the Don't show on title slide check box**

   Selecting this check box prevents the footer information you entered in the Header and Footer dialog box from appearing on the title slide.

6. **Click Apply to All**

   The dialog box closes and the footer information is applied to all of the slides in your presentation except the title slide. Compare your screen to Figure B-14.

7. **Click the Slide 1 thumbnail in the Slides tab, then click the Header & Footer button in the Text group**

   The Header and Footer dialog box opens again. You want to show your company tag line in the footer on the title slide.

8. **Click the Don't show on title slide check box to deselect it, click the Footer check box, then select the text in the Footer text box**

9. **Type "Explore with us...learn from the world", click Apply, then save your work**

   Only the text in the Footer text box appears on the title slide. Clicking Apply applies the footer information to just the current slide.

FIGURE B-13: Header and Footer dialog box

Shows where footer text will appear on the slide

FIGURE B-14: Slide showing footer information

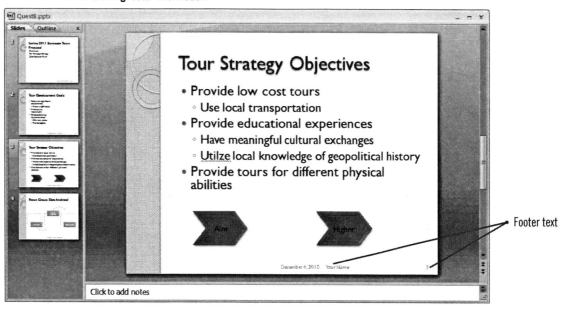

Footer text

Entering and printing notes

You can add notes to your slides when there are certain facts you want to remember during a presentation or when there is information you want to hand out to your audience. Notes do not appear on the slides when you run a slide show. Use the Notes pane in Normal view or Notes Page view to enter notes for your slides. To enter text notes on a slide, click in the Notes pane, then type. If you want to insert graphics as notes, you must use Notes Page view. To open Notes Page view, click the View tab on the Ribbon, then click the Notes Page button in the Presentation Views group. You can print your notes by clicking the Print what list arrow and then clicking Notes Pages in the Print dialog box. The notes page can be a good handout to give your audience to use during the presentation and then after as a reminder. If you don't enter any notes in the Notes pane, and print the notes pages, the slides print as thumbnails with blank lines to the right of the thumbnails to handwrite notes.

Checking Spelling in a Presentation

As your work on the presentation file nears completion, you need to review and proofread your slides thoroughly for errors. You can use the spellchecking feature in PowerPoint to check for and correct spelling errors. This feature compares the spelling of all the words in your presentation against the words contained in PowerPoint's electronic dictionary. You still must proofread your presentation for punctuation, grammar, and word-usage errors because the spellchecker recognizes only misspelled and unknown words, not misused words. For example, the spellchecker would not identify the word "lost" as an error, even if you had intended to type the word "cost." 🔖 Ellen wants to present a professional presentation, one without spelling errors. You're finished working with the European tour proposal presentation for now; this is a good time to check the spelling.

If your spellchecker doesn't find the word "Latsky," then a previous user may have accidentally added it to the custom dictionary. Skip Step 2 and continue with the lesson.

The spellchecker does not check the text in inserted pictures or objects.

1. **Click the Review tab on the Ribbon, then click the Spelling button in the Proofing group**

   PowerPoint begins to check the spelling in your presentation. When PowerPoint finds a misspelled word or a word it doesn't recognize, the Spelling dialog box opens, as shown in Figure B-15. In this case, PowerPoint does not recognize the name "Latsky" on Slide 1. It suggests that you replace it with the word "Lastly." You want the word to remain as you typed it.

2. **Click Ignore All**

   Clicking Ignore All tells the spellchecker not to stop at and question any more occurrences of this word in this presentation. The next word the spellchecker identifies as an error is the word "Utilze" in the text object on Slide 3. In the Suggestions list box, the spellchecker suggests "Utilize."

3. **Verify that Utilize is selected in the Suggestions list box, then click Change**

   If PowerPoint finds any other words it does not recognize, either change or ignore them. When the spellchecker finishes checking your presentation, the Spelling dialog box closes, and an alert box opens with a message that the spelling check is complete.

4. **Click OK**

   The alert box closes. You are satisfied with the presentation so far and you decide to print it. Compare your screen to Figure B-16.

5. **Click the Office button, then click the Print button**

   The Print dialog box opens.

6. **Make sure Slides is selected in the Print what list box, then click the Frame slides check box**

   The slides of your presentation print with a frame around each page.

7. **Click OK in the Print dialog box, then save your presentation**

8. **Click the Office button, then click Exit PowerPoint**

FIGURE B-15: Spelling dialog box

Selected word from Suggestions list

Suggestions list

Unrecognized word

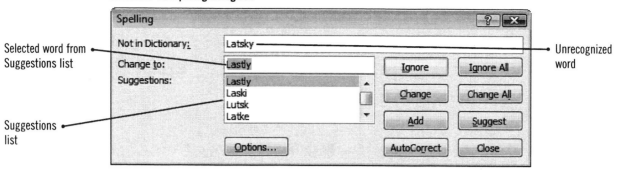

FIGURE B-16: Slide showing fixed spelling error

Fixed spelling error

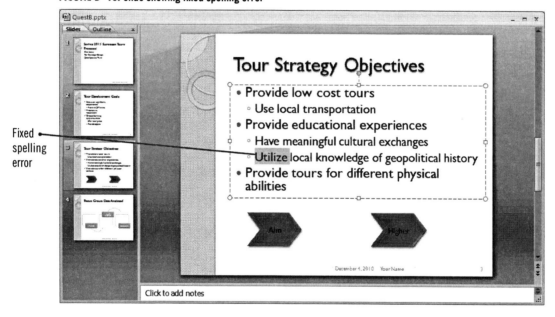

Checking spelling as you type

PowerPoint checks your spelling as you type. If you type a word that is not in the electronic dictionary, a wavy red line appears under it. To correct an error, right-click the misspelled word, then review the suggestions, which appear in the shortcut menu. You can select a suggestion, add the word you typed to your custom dictionary, or ignore it. To turn off automatic spellchecking, click the Office button, then click the PowerPoint Options button to open the PowerPoint Options dialog box. Click the Proofing button, then click the Check spelling as you type check box to deselect it. To temporarily hide the wavy red lines, click the Hide spelling errors check box to select it.

Modifying a Presentation

Practice

▼ CONCEPTS REVIEW

Label each element of the PowerPoint window shown in Figure B-17.

FIGURE B-17

Match each term with the statement that best describes it.

10. Mini toolbar
11. SmartArt graphic
12. Adjustment handle
13. Quick Style
14. Rotate handle
15. Sizing handle

a. A circle or square that appears around a selected object
b. A pre-set combination of formatting options that you apply to an object
c. A formatting toolbar
d. Changes the appearance of an object
e. Allows you to manually rotate an object
f. A diagram that visually illustrates text

Select the best answer from the list of choices.

16. Which of the following statements about the Mini toolbar is incorrect?
   a. It is semitransparent until you move the pointer over it.
   b. It is used to change the layout of a slide.
   c. It is used to format text.
   d. It appears when you select text.

17. Which statement about the PowerPoint spellchecker is true?
   a. PowerPoint only identifies spelling errors when you run the spellchecker.
   b. The spellchecker catches grammar problems.
   c. The spellchecker identifies misspelled and unknown words.
   d. Most misused words are caught by the spellchecker.

18. A professional-quality diagram that visually illustrates text best describes which of the following?
   a. A SmartArt graphic
   b. A shape
   c. A slide layout
   d. A content object

19. What does the adjustment handle do to a shape?
   a. Changes the shape to another
   b. Changes the rotation of a shape
   c. Changes the size of a shape
   d. Changes the appearance of a shape

20. How do you make a shape smaller?
   a. Drag the adjustment handle.
   b. Drag the sizing handle.
   c. Drag the rotate handle.
   d. Drag the shape edge.

21. What would you use to place a shape in a specific position on a slide?
   a. PowerPoint guides
   b. PowerPoint placeholders
   c. PowerPoint distribution angles
   d. PowerPoint anchor points

22. What is *not* true about grouped objects?
   a. Grouped objects have one rotate handle.
   b. Sizing handles appear around the grouped object.
   c. Grouped objects lose some of their individual characteristics.
   d. Grouped objects act as one object.

▼ SKILLS REVIEW

1. Enter text in the Outline tab.
   a. Open the presentation PPT B-2.pptx from the drive and folder where you store your Data Files, then save it as **TechJet**. The completed presentation is shown in Figure B-18.
   b. Create a new slide after Slide 3 with the Title and Content layout.
   c. Open the Outline tab, then type **Network Integration**.
   d. Press [Enter], press [Tab], type **Protocols and Conversions**, press [Enter], press [Tab], then type **Server codes and routing protocols**.
   e. Press [Enter], type **File transfer**, press [Enter], type **Data conversion**, press [Enter], then type **Platform functionality ratings**.
   f. Move Slide 4 to the Slide 3 position.

FIGURE B-18

    g. Switch back to the Slides tab.

    h. Save your changes.

2. Format text.

    a. Go to Slide 1.

    b. Select the name Joseph M. Sera, then move the pointer over the Mini toolbar.

    c. Click the Font Color list arrow, then click Orange under Standard Colors.

    d. Using [Shift] select the text object, then change all of the text to the color Orange.

    e. Click the Font Size list arrow, then click 24.

    f. Click the Bold button.

    g. Save your changes.

3. Convert text to SmartArt.

    a. Click the text object on Slide 4.

    b. Apply the Basic Cycle SmartArt graphic layout to the text object.

    c. Click the More button in the SmartArt Styles group, then apply the Inset style to the graphic.

    d. Reposition the diagram to the center of the slide, if necessary.

    e. Click outside the SmartArt graphic in an empty part of the slide.

    f. Save your changes.

4. Insert and modify shapes.

    a. Go to Slide 3.

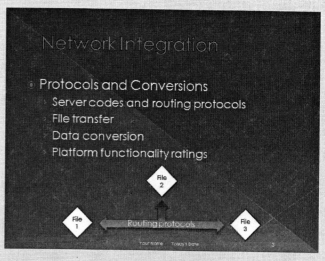

FIGURE B-19

    b. Using [Shift] select the text object, then drag the bottom-middle sizing handle up to decrease the size of the text object.

    c. Click the Insert tab on the Ribbon, then insert the Left-Right-Up Arrow shape from the Shapes gallery similar to the one in Figure B-19.

    d. Type **Routing protocols**, then click Moderate Effect – Accent 3 in the Shape Styles group.

    e. Click the Shape Effects button in the Shape Styles group, point to Shadow, then click Offset Bottom.

    f. Click the Shape Fill button in the Shape Styles group, point to Gradient, then click Linear Up.

    g. Click a blank area of the slide, then save your changes.

5. Edit and duplicate shapes.

    a. Insert a Diamond shape from the Shapes gallery to the left of the arrow shape.

    b. Click the More button in the Shape Styles group, click Colored Outline – Accent 4, then type **File 1**.

    c. Drag to select the text File 1, click the Home tab, click the Font Size button in the Font group, then click 14.

    d. Using [Ctrl] make two copies of the diamond shape, then change the text in one shape to **File 2** and the text in the other shape to **File 3**.

    e. Move the File 2 diamond shape to the top of the arrow shape and the File 3 diamond shape to the right of the arrow shape, as shown in Figure B-19.

    f. Click a blank area of the slide, then save your changes.

6. Align and group objects.

    a. Hold down [Shift], click the File 1 diamond shape, click the File 3 diamond shape, then release [Shift].

    b. Click the Drawing Tools Format tab if necessary, click Align, click Align Middle.

    c. Hold down [Shift], click the arrow shape, click the File 2 diamond shape, click the Group button in the Arrange group, then click Group.

    d. Click the Align button in the Arrange group, then click Distribute Horizontally.

    e. Save your work.

7. Add slide headers and footers.

   a. Open the Header and Footer dialog box.

   b. In the Slide tab, type today's date into the Fixed text box.

   c. Add the slide number to the footer.

   d. Type your name in the Footer text box.

   e. Apply the footer to all of the slides except the title slide.

   f. Open the Header and Footer dialog box again, then click the Notes and Handouts tab.

   g. Enter today's date in the Fixed text box.

   h. Type the name of your class in the Header text box, then click the Page number check box.

   i. Type your name in the Footer text box.

   j. Apply the header and footer information to all the notes and handouts.

   k. Save your changes.

8. Check spelling in a presentation.

   a. Perform a spelling check on the document and change any misspelled words. Ignore any words that are correctly spelled but that the spellchecker doesn't recognize. There is at least one misspelled word in the presentation.

   b. Save your changes, then close the file and exit PowerPoint.

▼ INDEPENDENT CHALLENGE 1

You are the Director of the Westminster Theater Arts Center in Kansas City, Missouri, and one of your many duties is to raise funds to cover operation costs. One of the primary ways you do this is by speaking to businesses, community clubs, and other organizations throughout the Kansas City region. Every year you speak to many organizations, where you give a short presentation detailing what the theater center plans to do for the coming season. You need to continue working on the presentation you started already.

   a. Start PowerPoint, open the presentation PPT B-3.pptx from the drive and folder where you store your Data Files, and save it as **WTAC 2011**.

   b. Use the Outline tab to enter the following as bulleted text on the Commitment to Excellence slide:
      Study
      Diligence
      Testing
      Excellence

   c. Apply the Verve design theme to the presentation.

   d. Change the font color of each play name on Slide 3 to Yellow.

   e. Change the bulleted text on Slide 5 to the Basic Cycle SmartArt graphic layout, then apply the Polished SmartArt Style.

Advanced Challenge Exercise

   ■ Open the Notes Page view.

   ■ To at least two slides, add notes that relate to the slide content that you think would be important when giving this presentation.

   ■ Save the presentation as **WTAC 2011 ACE** to the drive and folder where you store your Data Files, then print the Notes Page view for the presentation.

   f. Check the spelling in the presentation then view the presentation in Slide Show view.

   g. Add your name as a footer on the notes and handouts, print handouts (three slides per page), and then print the presentation outline.

   h. Save your changes, close your presentation, then exit PowerPoint.

PowerPoint 2007

▼ INDEPENDENT CHALLENGE 2

You are a manager for Schweizerhaus, Ltd., a Swiss mortgage loan company headquartered in Bern, Switzerland. You have been asked by your boss to develop a presentation outlining important details and aspects of the mortgage process for clients and investors. The focus of the presentation is the use of mortgage brokers to secure loans for clients.

a. Start PowerPoint, open the presentation PPT B-4.pptx from the drive and folder where you store your Data Files, and save it as **Loan Broker**.

b. Apply the Technic design theme to the presentation.

c. On Slide 4 select the three shapes, Banks, Mortgage Bankers, and Private Investors, then using the Align command distribute them vertically and align them to their left edges.

d. On Slide 4 select the three shapes, Borrower, Mortgage Broker, and Mortgage Bankers, then using the Align command distribute them horizontally and align them to their bottom edges.

e. Select all of the shapes, then apply Moderate Effect – Accent 2 from the Shape Styles group.

f. Using the Arrow shape from the Shapes gallery, draw a 3pt arrow between all of the shapes as shown in Figure B-20. (*Hint*: Draw one arrow shape, change the line weight to 3 pt using the Shape Outline button, then duplicate the shape.)

g. Create a sixth slide to end the presentation with the following information:
Schweizerhaus, Ltd.
Zieglerstrasse 765, Bern
TEL: 3937095, FAX: 9375719

h. Check the spelling in the presentation, view the presentation in Slide Show view, then view the slides in Slide Sorter view.

i. Add your name as a footer on the notes and handouts, print the presentation as handouts (two slides per page), then print the presentation outline.

j. Save your changes, close your presentation, then exit PowerPoint.

FIGURE B-20

▼ INDEPENDENT CHALLENGE 3

You are an independent distributor of natural foods in Bellingham, Washington. Your business, NorthWest Natural Foods, has grown progressively since its inception five years ago, but sales and profits have leveled off over the last nine months. In an effort to stimulate growth, you decide to acquire All Natural Inc., a major natural food dealer in California, which would allow your company to begin expanding into surrounding states. Use PowerPoint to develop a presentation that you can use to gain a financial backer for the acquisition. Create your own information for the presentation.

a. Start PowerPoint, create a new presentation, then apply the Concourse design theme to the presentation.

b. Enter **A Plan for Growth** as the main title on the title slide, and **NorthWest Natural Foods** as the subtitle.

c. Save the presentation as **NW Natural** to the drive and folder where you store your Data Files.

d. Add five more slides with the following titles: Slide 2-Background; Slide 3-Current Situation; Slide 4-Acquisition Goals; Slide 5-Our Management Team; Slide 6-Funding Required.

e. Enter text into the text placeholders of the slides. Use both the Slide pane and the Outline tab to enter text.

f. Convert text on one slide to a SmartArt graphic, then apply the SmartArt graphic style Subtle Effect.

▼ INDEPENDENT CHALLENGE 3 (CONTINUED)

Advanced Challenge Exercise

- Click the Replace button arrow in the Editing group on the Home tab, then click Replace Fonts.
- Replace the Eras Medium ITC font with the Arial font.
- Save the presentation as **NW Natural ACE** to the drive and folder where you store your Data Files.

g. Check the spelling in the presentation, view the presentation as a slide show, then view the slides in Slide Sorter view.

h. Add your name as a footer on the slides, save your changes, then print the slides.

i. Close your presentation, then exit PowerPoint.

▼ REAL LIFE INDEPENDENT CHALLENGE

Your computer professor at Central State University has been asked by the department head to convert his Applied Technology course into an accelerated course that both students and professional working people can take. Your professor has asked you to help him create a presentation for the class that he can post on the Internet and use as a promotional tool at local businesses. Most of the raw information is already on the slides, you primarily need to jazz it up by adding a theme, and some text formatting.

a. Start PowerPoint, open the presentation PPT B-5.pptx from drive and folder where you store your data files, and save it as **Applied Tech**.

b. Add a new slide after the Course Facts slide with the same layout, type **Course Details** in the title text placeholder, then enter the following as bulleted text in the Outline tab:
Unix/Information Systems
Networking
Applied Methods
Technology Solutions·
Software Design
Applications

c. Apply the Origin theme to the presentation.

d. Select the title text object on Slide 1 (*Hint*: Press [Shift] to select the whole object), then change the text color to Dark Red.

e. Change the font of the title text object to Bernard MT Condensed.

f. Change the text on Slide 4 to a SmartArt graphic. The text on this slide is a list so make sure the diagram type you choose is appropriate for the text.

g. Change the style of the SmartArt diagram using one of the SmartArt Styles, then view the presentation in Slide Show view.

h. Add the slide number and your name as a footer on the notes and handouts, print handouts (four slides per page), and then print the presentation outline.

i. Save your changes, close your presentation, then exit PowerPoint.

▼ VISUAL WORKSHOP

Create the presentation shown in Figures B-21 and B-22. Add today's date as the date on the title slide. Save the presentation as **Trade Analysis** to the drive and folder where you store your Data Files. Review your slides in Slide Show view, then add your name as a footer to the notes and handouts. Print the slides of your presentation, then print the outline. Save your changes, close the presentation, then exit PowerPoint.

FIGURE B-21

FIGURE B-22

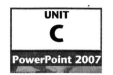

Inserting Objects into a Presentation

A good presenter will make use of visual elements, such as charts, graphics, and photographs, in conjunction with text to help communicate the presentation message. Visual elements keep the presentation interesting and help the audience focus on what the presenter is saying. ▟▛▞▞ In this unit, you continue working on the presentation for your boss Ellen Latsky by inserting visual elements, including clip art, a picture, and a chart, into the presentation. You format these objects using PowerPoint's powerful object editing features.

OBJECTIVES

Insert text from Microsoft Word

Insert clip art

Insert and style a picture

Insert a text box

Insert a chart

Enter and edit chart data

Insert a table

Insert and format WordArt

Inserting Text from Microsoft Word

PowerPoint makes it easy to insert text from other sources into a presentation. Documents saved in Microsoft Word format (.docx), Rich Text Format (.rtf), plain text format (.txt), and HTML format (.htm) can be inserted into a presentation. If you have an existing Word document or outline, you can import it into PowerPoint to create a new presentation or use it to insert additional slides in an existing presentation. When you import a Microsoft Word or a Rich Text Format document into a presentation, PowerPoint creates an outline structure based on the styles in the document. For example, a Heading 1 style in the Word document becomes a slide title in PowerPoint and a Heading 2 style becomes the first level of text in a bulleted list. If you insert a plain text format document into a presentation, PowerPoint creates an outline based on the tabs at the beginning of the document's paragraphs. Paragraphs without tabs become slide titles; paragraphs with one tab indent become first-level text in bulleted lists; paragraphs with two tabs become second-level text in bulleted lists; and so on. ▓▓▓▓ Ron Dawson, QST's Vice President of Marketing, sent you a Microsoft Word document with data from a focus group study QST held last spring. You use this information in the presentation.

STEPS

1. **Start PowerPoint, open the presentation PPT C-1.pptx from the drive and folder where you store your Data Files, save it as QuestC, click the** View tab **on the Ribbon, then click the Arrange All button in the Window group**

2. **Click the Outline tab, then click the Slide 4 icon in the Outline tab**

   Slide 4 appears in the Slide pane. Each time you click a slide icon in the Outline tab, the slide title and text are highlighted indicating the slide is selected. Before you insert information into a presentation, you must first designate where you want the information to be placed. In this case, the Word document will be inserted after Slide 4, the selected slide.

3. **Click the Home tab on the Ribbon, click the** New Slide button list arrow **in the Slides group, then click** Slides from Outline

   The Insert Outline dialog box opens.

4. **Select the Word document file PPT C-2.docx from the drive and folder where you store your Data Files, then click** Insert

   Four new slides (5, 6, 7, and 8) are added to the presentation. See Figure C-1.

5. **Read the text for the new Slide 5 in the Slide pane, then review the text on slides 6, 7, and 8 in the Outline tab**

   After reviewing the text on the new slides, you realize that the information on Slide 8 is not necessary for the presentation.

6. **Click the Slides tab, then right-click the Slide 8 thumbnail**

   A shortcut menu opens displaying a number of common commands. Right-clicking most objects in PowerPoint opens a shortcut menu.

7. **Click Delete Slide on the shortcut menu**

   Slide 8 is deleted from the presentation. The last slide in the presentation displaying a picture placeholder now appears in the Slide pane. You also notice that Slide 6 should come before Slide 5.

8. **Click Slide 6 in the Slides tab, then drag it above Slide 5**

   Slide 6 and Slide 5 change places. Compare your screen to Figure C-2.

9. **Click the Save button 🖫 on the Quick Access Toolbar**

FIGURE C-1: Outline tab showing imported text

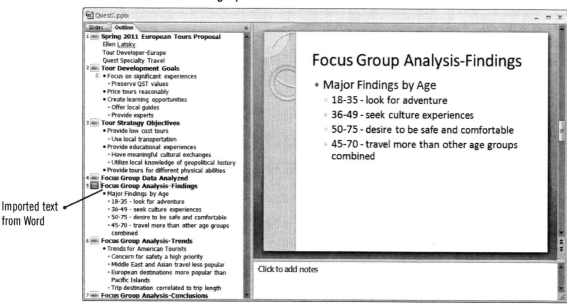

Imported text from Word

FIGURE C-2: Presentation after moving a slide

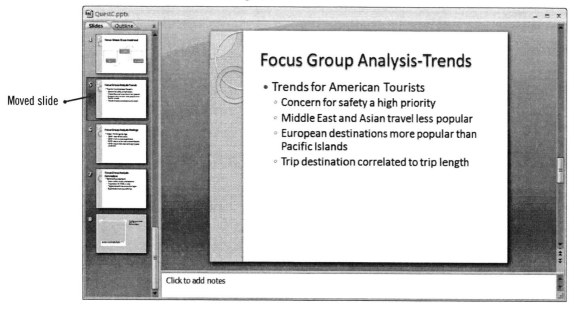

Moved slide

Inserting slides from other presentations

To insert slides from another presentation into the current presentation, click the New Slide button list arrow in the Slides group, then click Reuse Slides. The Reuse Slides task pane opens on the right side of the window. Click the Open a PowerPoint File link, locate the presentation you want to use, then click Open. Click the slide(s) to place them in the presentation. The new slides automatically take on the theme of the current presentation. You can also copy slides from one presentation to another. Open both presentations, change the view of each presentation to Slide Sorter view or use the Arrange All command to see both presentations, select the desired slides, then copy and paste them (or use drag and drop) into the desired presentation.

Inserting Clip Art

PowerPoint has access to many professionally designed graphics, called **clip art**, which you can place in your presentation. In Microsoft Office, clip art and other media files, including photographs, movies, and sounds, are stored in a file index system called the Microsoft Clip Organizer and are identified by descriptive keywords. The Clip Organizer sorts the clip art into groups, including My Collections, Office Collections, and Web Collections. The Office Collections group holds all the media files that come with Microsoft Office. You can customize the Clip Organizer by adding clips to a collection, moving clips from one collection to another, or creating a new collection. As with drawn objects, you can modify clip art images by changing their shape, size, fill, or shading. Clip art is available from many sources outside the Clip Organizer, including the Microsoft Office Online Web site and commercially available collections that you can purchase. ▓▓▓ To enhance the QST presentation, you add a clip from the Clip Organizer to one of the slides and then adjust its size and placement.

STEPS

1. **Click the up scroll arrow in the Slides tab until Slide 2 appears, click the Slide 2 thumbnail, then click the Clip Art icon 🖼 in the Content placeholder**

   The Clip Art task pane opens. At the top of the task pane in the Search for text box, you enter a keyword to search for clips that meet that description. You can search for a clip in a specific collection or in all collections. You can also search for a clip that is a specific media type, such as clip art, photographs, movies, or sounds. At the bottom of the task pane, you can click a hyperlink to organize clips, locate other pieces of clip art at the Office Online Web site, or read tips on how to find clip art.

2. **Select any text in the Search for text box, type travel, click the Results should be list arrow, then click the Photographs check box, the Movies check box, and the Sounds check box to remove the check marks**

   Since you are only interested in finding clip art, deselecting the Photographs, Movies, and Sounds check boxes significantly reduces the amount of media PowerPoint needs to search through to produce your results. PowerPoint searches for clips identified by the keyword "travel."

QUICK TIP

If an alert dialog box appears asking if you want to add additional images from Microsoft Office Online, click Yes

3. **Click the Go button, then click the clip art thumbnail shown in Figure C-3**

   The clip art object appears in the content placeholder and the Picture Tools Format tab appears on the Ribbon. If you don't see the clip shown in Figure C-3, select another one. Although you can change a clip's size by dragging a corner sizing handle, you can also **scale** it to change its size by a specific percentage.

4. **Click the Size and Position dialog box launcher in the Size group, in the Scale section make sure the Lock aspect ratio check box has a check mark, in the Scale section click the Height up arrow until the Height and Width percentages display 110%, then click Close**

   The clip proportionally increases in size.

5. **Click the Picture Border button in the Picture Styles group, then click the Aqua, Accent 1 color box in the top row**

   A light blue border appears around the object.

QUICK TIP

You can use the Reset Picture button in the Adjust group to reset the object formatting.

6. **Click the Picture Border button, point to Weight, then click the 3 pt solid line style**

   The clip now has a 3-point solid border. It appears to be framed.

7. **Drag the clip art object straight down even with the bottom line of text**

   You don't like the new placement of the clip.

8. **Click the Undo button 🔄 on the Quick Access toolbar, click a blank area of the slide, then save your changes**

9. **Click the Results should be list arrow in the Clip Art task pane, click the All media types check box, click Go, then click the task pane Close button**

   Now the next time you search for a clip, PowerPoint will search through all media types. Compare the slide on your screen to the slide shown in Figure C-4.

Inserting Objects into a Presentation

FIGURE C-3: Screen showing Clip Art task pane

Select this clip

Clip Art icon

Click to locate clips on the Office Online Web site

FIGURE C-4: Slide with formatted clip art object

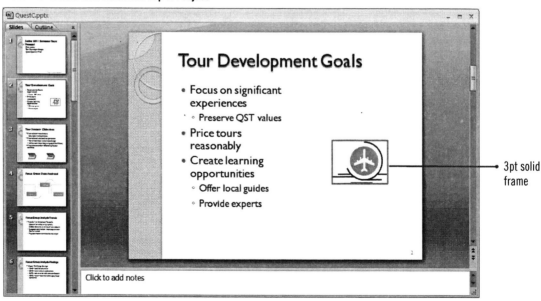

3pt solid frame

Finding more clips online

If you can't find exactly what you want in the Clip Organizer, you can easily download and use clips from the Clip Art and Media Web page in the Microsoft Office Online Web site. To get clips from the Clip Art Web page, click the Clip art on Office Online hyperlink at the bottom of the Clip Art task pane. If your computer is connected to the Internet, this will launch your Web browser and automatically connect you to the Microsoft Office Online Web site. You can search the site by keyword or browse by media type category. Each clip you download is automatically inserted into the Clip Organizer Web Collections folder and appears in the Clip Art task pane.

Inserting and Styling a Picture

In PowerPoint, a **picture** is defined as a digital photograph, a piece of line art or clip art, or other artwork that is created in another program and inserted into a PowerPoint presentation. PowerPoint gives you the ability to insert 17 different types of pictures including JPEG File Interchange Format and BMP Windows Bitmap. As with all objects in PowerPoint, you can format and style inserted pictures to help them fit the theme of your presentation. You can also hide a portion of the picture you don't want visible by **cropping** it. The cropped portion of a picture, unlike other objects such as clip art, is automatically deleted when the presentation is saved unless you change the setting in the Compression Settings dialog box. ▰▰▰ QST has a library of pictures from tours available to use in presentations. In this lesson, you insert a picture that has previously been saved to a file, and then you crop it and style it.

STEPS

QUICK TIP

You can also insert a picture by clicking the Picture button in the Illustrations group on the Insert tab.

1. **Click the down scroll arrow in the Slides tab until Slide 8 appears, click the Slide 8 thumbnail, then click the Insert Picture from File icon 🖼 in the content placeholder on the slide**

   The Insert Picture dialog box opens displaying the pictures available in the Pictures folder. The Pictures folder is the default folder.

2. **Select the picture file PPT C-3.jpg from the drive and folder where you store your Data Files, then click Insert**

   The picture appears in the Picture placeholder on the slide and the Picture Tools Format tab opens on the Ribbon. The picture would look better if you cropped some of the beach off the bottom.

3. **Click the Crop button in the Size group, then place the pointer over the bottom-middle sizing handle of the picture**

   The pointer changes to ⊤. When the Crop button is active, the sizing handles appear as straight black lines.

4. **Press and hold [Alt], drag the bottom edge of the picture up until the lower-left corner of the picture is at the water line as shown in Figure C-5, then click the Crop button**

   Pressing [Alt] while dragging or drawing an object in PowerPoint overrides the automatic snap-to-grid setting. PowerPoint has a number of picture formatting options, and you decide to experiment with some of them.

5. **Click the Picture Styles More button ▾, then click Bevel Rectangle (3rd row)**

   The picture changes shape. Notice that this particular style includes an adjustment handle so that you can adjust the shape of the picture.

6. **Click the Recolor button in the Adjust group, click Sepia in the Color Modes section, then click the Slide Show button 🖵 in the status bar**

   The slide fills your screen. After evaluating the slide you conclude that the shape and color changes you've made to the picture don't improve the look of the slide.

7. **Press [Esc], click the Undo button list arrow on the Quick Access toolbar, then click Format Picture**

   All of the formatting changes you made to the picture are removed. The cropped portion of the picture does not change and remains hidden.

8. **Click the Picture Styles More button, click Drop Shadow Rectangle (1st row), click a blank area on the slide, then save your changes**

   Compare your screen to Figure C-6.

FIGURE C-5: Using the cropping pointer to crop a picture

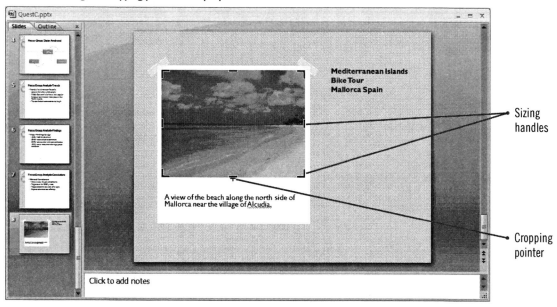

Sizing handles

Cropping pointer

FIGURE C-6: Cropped and styled picture

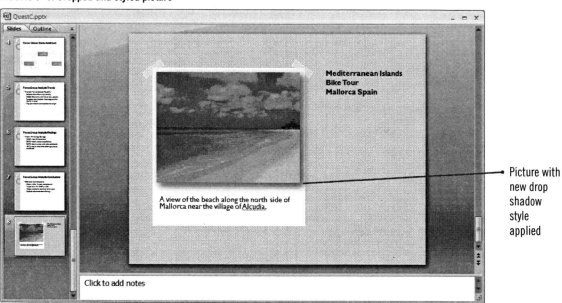

Picture with new drop shadow style applied

Picture compression

By default, all inserted pictures in PowerPoint 2007 are automatically compressed every time you save your presentation. If you want to prohibit the automatic compression of pictures or be able to choose individual pictures to compress, select a picture, then click the Picture Tools Format tab. Click the Compress Pictures button in the Adjust group, then click Options in the Compress Pictures dialog box. The Compression Settings dialog box opens. Notice that PowerPoint compresses pictures every time the presentation is saved and deletes cropped portions of pictures to save space. To compress individual pictures, make sure the top option in the Compression Settings dialog box is deselected, select a picture, click the Compress Pictures button, then click OK. To stop PowerPoint from automatically deleting cropped portions of pictures, deselect the check box next to the Delete cropped areas of pictures option in the Compression Settings dialog box.

Inserting a Text Box

As you've already learned, you enter text on a slide using a title or content placeholder that is arranged on the slide based on a particular slide layout. Every so often you need additional text on a slide where the traditional placeholder does not place text effectively for your message. You can create an individual text object by clicking the Text Box button in the Text group on the Insert tab on the Ribbon. There are two types of text objects that you can create: a text label, used for a small phrase where text doesn't automatically wrap to the next line inside the box; and a word processing box, used for a sentence or paragraph where the text wraps inside the boundaries of the box. Either type of text box can be formatted and edited just like any other text object. You decide to add a text object to Slide 8 to finish the information about the bike tour. You create a word processing box on the slide, enter text, edit text, and then format the text.

STEPS

1. **Click the Insert tab on the Ribbon, click the Text Box button in the Text group, then move the pointer to the blank area of the slide to the right of the picture**
   The pointer changes to ↓.

2. **Drag down and toward the right side of the slide about an inch and a half to create a word processing box**
   When you begin dragging, an outline of the text object appears, indicating how large a text object you are drawing. After you release the mouse button, an insertion point appears inside the text object, in this case a word processing box, which indicates that you can enter text. The font and font style appear in the Font group on the Ribbon.

3. **Type Travel from Palma to La Puebla for 135 miles over 6 days**
   Notice that the text object increases in size as your text wraps inside the text object. Your screen should look similar to Figure C-7. After entering the text you realize there is a mistake.

4. **Drag I over the phrase for 135 miles to select it**

5. **Position �ᵏ on top of the selected phrase and press and hold the mouse button**
   The pointer changes to ᵏ.

6. **Drag the selected words to the right of the word Travel in the text object, then release the mouse button**
   A light blue insertion line appears as you drag, indicating where PowerPoint places the text when you release the mouse button. The phrase "for 135 miles" moves after the word "Travel".

7. **Move ↕ to the edge of the text object, which changes to ᵏ, click the text object border, then click the Italic button 𝐼 in the Font group**
   All of the text in the text object is italicized.

8. **Drag the right-middle sizing handle of the text object to the right until the text is on two lines, position ᵏ over the text object edge, then drag it next to the picture caption**
   Your screen should look similar to Figure C-8.

9. **Click a blank area of the slide outside the text object, then save your changes**

FIGURE C-7: New text object

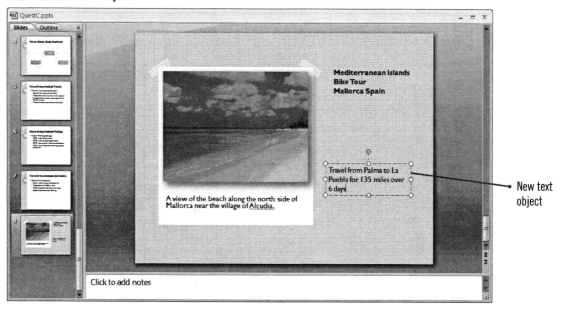

New text object

FIGURE C-8: Formatted text object

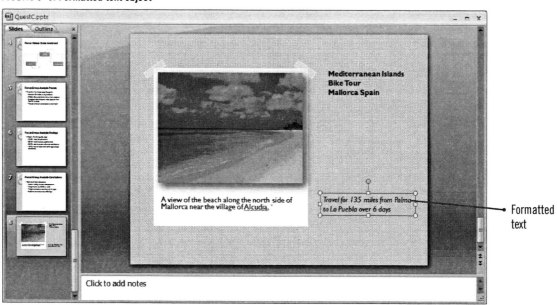

Formatted text

Sending a presentation using e-mail

You can send a copy of a presentation over the Internet to a reviewer for them to edit and add comments. You can use Microsoft Outlook, or any other compatible e-mail program, to send your presentation. Although your e-mail program allows you to attach files, you can send a presentation using Outlook from within PowerPoint. Click the Office button, point to Send, then click Email. Outlook opens and automatically creates an e-mail with the presentation attached to it. The recipient of the presentation can use PowerPoint 2007 or an earlier version of PowerPoint to edit the presentation or add comments. To open a PowerPoint 2007 file in an earlier version of PowerPoint, you must save the presentation as a PowerPoint 97-2003 presentation or install the Compatibility Pack for the Office 2007 Office system files from Microsoft's Web site. Once the presentation is back in your hands, you can view, edit, or delete the reviewer's comments.

Inserting a Chart

Often, the best way to communicate numerical information is with a visual aid such as a chart. If you have Microsoft Excel installed on your computer, PowerPoint uses Excel to create charts. If you don't have Excel installed, a charting program called **Microsoft Graph** opens that you can use to create charts for your slides. A **chart** is the graphical representation of numerical data. Every chart has a corresponding **worksheet** that contains the numerical data displayed by the chart. When you insert a chart object into PowerPoint, you are actually embedding it. An **embedded** object is one that is a part of your presentation (just like any other object you insert into PowerPoint) except that an embedded object's data source can be opened, in this case Excel, for editing purposes. Changes you make to an embedded object in PowerPoint using PowerPoint's features do not affect the data source for the data. ▓▓▓ You insert a chart on a new slide that graphically shows results from an online survey Ellen Latsky conducted.

STEPS

QUICK TIP
You can also add a chart to a slide by clicking the Insert Chart button in the Illustrations group on the Insert tab.

1. **Verify that Slide 8 is selected, click the** New Slide **button list arrow in the Slides group, then click** Title and Content

   A new slide is added to your presentation with the Title and Content slide layout.

2. **Click the Insert Chart icon 📊 in the Content placeholder**

   The Insert Chart dialog box opens as shown in Figure C-9. Each chart type includes a number of 2-D and 3-D styles. The Column chart type, for example, includes 19 different styles and the Line chart type includes 7 different styles. The Clustered Column chart is the default chart style. For a brief explanation of how each of these chart types graphs data, refer to Table C-1.

QUICK TIP
Microsoft Graph opens if Excel is not installed on your computer.

3. **Click OK**

   Excel opens in a split window sharing the computer screen with the PowerPoint window as shown in Figure C-10. The PowerPoint window displays the clustered column chart and the Excel window displays sample data in a worksheet. The Chart Tools Design tab on the Ribbon contains commands you use in PowerPoint to work with the chart. The worksheet consists of rows and columns. The intersection of a row and a column is called a **cell**. Cells are referred to by their row and column location; for example, the cell at the intersection of column A and row 1 is called cell A1. Cells in the first or left column contain **axis labels** that identify the data in a row for example, "Category 1" is an axis label. Cells in the first or top row are **legend** names and provide further information about the data. Cells below and to the right of the axis labels and legend names contain the data values that are represented in the chart. Each column and row of data in the worksheet is called a **data series**. Each data series has corresponding **data series markers** in the chart, which are graphical representations such as bars, columns, or pie wedges. The gray boxes with the numbers along the left side of the worksheet are called **row headings**, and the gray boxes with the letters along the top of the worksheet are called **column headings**.

TROUBLE
If the Excel window covers the slide in PowerPoint, click View on the PowerPoint Ribbon, click Window, then click Arrange All

4. **Move the pointer over the worksheet in the Excel window**

   The pointer changes to ✛. Cell A6 is the **active cell**, which means that it is selected. The active cell has a thick black border around it.

5. **Click cell C4**

   Cell C4 is now the active cell.

6. **Click the Excel Window Close button 🗙 on the title bar**

   The Excel window closes and the PowerPoint window fills the screen. A new chart object appears on the slide displaying the data from the Excel worksheet.

7. **Click in a blank area of the slide to deselect the chart object**

   The Chart Tools Design Ribbon is no longer active.

8. **Click the slide Title placeholder, type** On-line Survey Results, **then save your changes**

FIGURE C-9: Insert Chart dialog box

Default chart

FIGURE C-10: The PowerPoint and Excel split windows

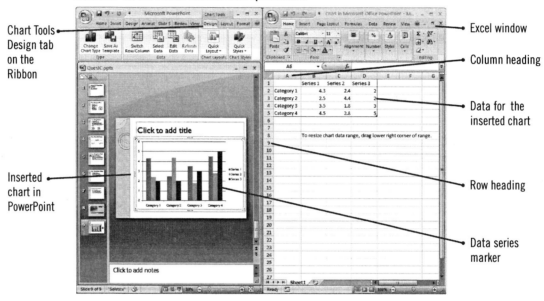

Chart Tools Design tab on the Ribbon

Inserted chart in PowerPoint

Excel window

Column heading

Data for the inserted chart

Row heading

Data series marker

TABLE C-1: Chart types

chart type	icon looks like	use to
Column		Track values over time or across categories
Line		Track values over time
Pie		Compare individual values to the whole
Bar		Compare values in categories or over time
Area		Show contribution of each data series to the total over time
XY (Scatter)		Compare pairs of values
Stock		Show stock market information or scientific data
Surface		Show value trends across two dimensions
Doughnut		Compare individual values to the whole with multiple series
Bubble		Indicate relative size of data points
Radar		Show changes in values in relation to a center point

Inserting Objects into a Presentation

Entering and Editing Chart Data

After you insert a chart into your presentation, you need to replace the sample data with the correct information. If you have data in an Excel worksheet or another source, you can import it into Excel; otherwise you can type your own information into the worksheet. As you enter data and make other changes in the Excel worksheet, the chart in PowerPoint automatically reflects the new changes. ████ You enter and format the survey data collected by Ellen.

STEPS

1. **Click the chart on Slide 9, click the Chart Tools Design tab on the Ribbon, then click the Edit Data button in the Data group**

   The chart is selected in PowerPoint and the worksheet opens in a separate Excel window. The data in the worksheet needs to be replaced with the correct information.

   QUICK TIP
   You can double-click the column divider lines between the column headings to automatically resize the column width to accommodate the widest entry.

2. **Click the Series 1 cell, type Safety, press [Tab], type Price, press [Tab], then type Experience**

   The Legend labels are entered. Pressing [Tab] in Excel moves the active cell from left to right one cell at a time in a row. Pressing [Enter] in the worksheet moves the active cell down one cell at a time in a column.

3. **Click the Category 1 cell, type 2 Years Past, press [Enter], type Last Year, press [Enter], then type This Year**

   The axis labels are entered and the chart in the PowerPoint window reflects all the changes.

   QUICK TIP
   Click the chart in the PowerPoint window, then move your pointer over each bar in the chart to see the data source values.

4. **Enter the remainder of the data shown in Figure C-11 to complete the worksheet, then press [Enter]**

   The sample information in Row 5 of the worksheet is not needed.

5. **Right-click the Row 5 row heading, then click Delete**

   Clicking a row heading selects the entire row. The chart currently shows the rows grouped by year, and the legend represents the columns in the datasheet. It would be more effective if the row data appeared in the legend so you could compare yearly results.

6. **Click the Switch Row/Column button in the Data group in the PowerPoint window**

   You have finished entering data in the Excel worksheet.

7. **Click the Excel window Close button** ⊠

   Notice that the height of each column in the chart, as well as the values along the vertical axis, adjust to reflect the numbers you typed. The vertical axis is also called the **Value axis**. The horizontal axis is called the **Category axis**. The column labels are now on the Category axis of the chart, and the row labels are listed in the legend.

8. **Click a blank area on the slide, then save the presentation**

   Compare your chart to Figure C-12.

FIGURE C-11: Worksheet showing chart data

New chart data

Delete this row

FIGURE C-12: Formatted chart

Value axis

Legend identifies the data series by rows

Category axis

Series in rows vs. series in columns

If you have difficulty visualizing what the Switch Row/Column command does, think about what is represented in the legend. **Series in Rows** means that the information in the datasheet rows will be on the Value or vertical axis and is the information shown in the legend.

The column labels will be on the Category or horizontal axis. **Series in Columns** means that the information in the columns becomes the information shown on the Value axis and in the legend; the row labels will be on the horizontal or Category axis.

Inserting Objects into a Presentation

Inserting a Table

As you create your presentation, you may have some information that would look best organized in rows and columns. For example, if you wanted to compare the basic details of three different cruise tours side by side, a table is ideal for this type of information. Once you have created a table, two new tabs, the Table Tools Design tab and the Table Tools Layout tab, appear on the Ribbon. You can use the Design tab to apply color styles, change cell borders and add cell effects. Using the Layout tab, you can add rows and columns to your table, adjust the size of cells, and align text in the cells. ▨▨▨▨ You decide that a table best illustrates the new adventure tour series being proposed by Ellen.

STEPS

1. **Verify that Slide 9 is selected, click the New Slide button list arrow in the Slides group, click Title Only, click the Insert tab on the Ribbon, then click the Table button in the Tables group**

   The Insert Table gallery opens where you can drag the mouse to specify the number of columns and rows you need in the table.

2. **Move the pointer over the grid to select a 4x3 cell area so that 4x3 Table appears in the gallery title bar, then click the lower right corner of the 4x3 grid**

   A table with four columns and three rows appears on the slide, and the Table Tools Design tab opens on the Ribbon. The table has 12 cells. The insertion point is in the first cell of the table and is ready to accept text.

3. **Type Self Guided, press [Tab], type Family, press [Tab], type Cruise, press [Tab], type Extreme, then press [Tab]**

   The text you typed appears in the top four cells of the table. Pressing [Tab] moves the insertion point to the next cell. Pressing [Enter] moves the insertion point to the next line in the cell. Pressing [Tab] in the last row, last column inserts a new row.

4. **Enter the rest of the table information shown in Figure C-13, then drag the right-middle sizing handle slightly to the right**

   The word Mediterranean now fits on one line. The table would look better if it were formatted differently.

5. **Click the Table Styles More button ▽ in the Table Styles group, scroll to the bottom of the gallery, then click Dark Style 1 – Accent 6**

   The background and text color change to reflect the table style you applied.

6. **Click the upper-left cell, click the Table Tools Layout tab, click the Select button in the Table group, click Select Row, then click the Center button ▤ in the Alignment group**

   The text in the top row is centered horizontally in each cell.

7. **Click the Select button in the Table group, click Select Table, then click the Center Vertically button ▤ in the Alignment group**

   The text in the whole table is centered vertically within each cell. The table would look better if all the rows were the same height.

8. **Click the Distribute Rows button ▥ in the Cell Size group, click the Table Tools Design tab, then click the Effects button ▨▾ in the Table Styles group**

   The Table Effects gallery opens. Apply a 3-D effect to the cells so that they stand out.

9. **Point to Cell Bevel, click Cool Slant, drag the table to the center of the blank area of the slide, click the slide title placeholder, type Adventure Series, click a blank area of the slide, then save the presentation**

   The effect makes the cells of the table stand out. Compare your screen with Figure C-14.

FIGURE C-13: The inserted table with data

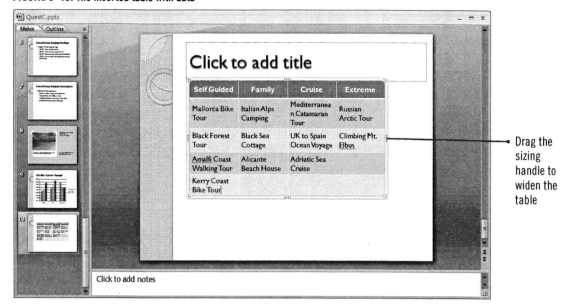

Drag the sizing handle to widen the table

FIGURE C-14: Formatted table

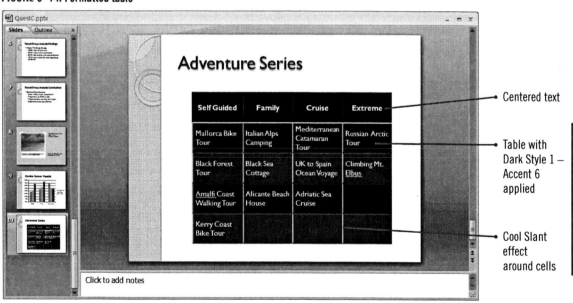

Centered text

Table with Dark Style 1 – Accent 6 applied

Cool Slant effect around cells

Saving slides as graphics

You can save PowerPoint slides as graphics and later use them in other presentations, in graphics programs, and on Web pages. Display the slide you want to save, click the Office button, then click Save As. In the Save As dialog box, click the Save as type list arrow, select the desired graphics format (for example, Web Page (*.htm;*.html), JPEG File Interchange Format (*.jpg), TIFF Tag Image Format (*.tif), or Device Independent Bitmap (*.bmp)), then name the file. Click Save, then click the desired option when the alert box appears asking if you want to save all the slides or only the current slide.

Inserting Objects into a Presentation

Insert and Format WordArt

As you work to create an interesting presentation, your goal should include making your slides visually appealing. Sometimes plain text can come across as dull and unexciting in a presentation. **WordArt** is a set of decorative text styles, or text effects, that you can apply to any text object to help direct the attention of your audience to a certain piece of information. You can use WordArt in two different ways: you can apply a WordArt text style to an existing text object that converts the text into WordArt, or you can create a new WordArt object. The WordArt text styles and effects include text shadows, reflections, glows, bevels, 3-D rotations, and transformations. ▨▨▨ Use WordArt to convert the QST tours tag line on Slide 1 so it is easier to see.

STEPS

1. **Click the Slide 1 thumbnail in the Slides tab, press [Shift], click the footer text object at the bottom of the slide, then drag the Zoom slider to the right until the Zoom percentage reaches 100%**

   Notice how the selected footer text object becomes the focal point as you zoom in. The footer text is hard to see and would look better with a WordArt style applied to it.

QUICK TIP

You can add a new WordArt object to a slide by clicking the Insert tab, then the WordArt button in the Text group.

2. **Click the Drawing Tools Format tab, click the WordArt Styles More button ▼, move your mouse over the WordArt styles in the gallery, then click Gradient Fill – Accent 6, Inner Shadow**

   The WordArt gallery displays all of the WordArt styles, and the Live Preview lets you see how each style would look if applied to the text.

3. **Click the Text Effects button 🄰▾ in the WordArt Styles group, point to Reflection, then click Tight Reflection, touching**

   The footer text object is now styled with a WordArt style and a reflection effect. You decide to increase the footer text font and give it a more prominent position on the slide.

4. **Click the Home tab on the Ribbon, click the Increase Font Size button 🄰 in the Font group twice, then drag the left-middle sizing handle to the left until the text is on one line**

   Now the footer text object is easier to read.

5. **Position ⬚ over the edge of the text object, drag to position the text object to match Figure C-15**

TROUBLE

Your zoom percentage may be different depending on your screen size and resolution.

6. **Click a blank area of the slide, click the Fit slide to current window button ▣ in the status bar**

   The slide returns to its original zoom percentage of 66%.

7. **Click the Slide Show button ▤ on the status bar, view the presentation, press [Esc] at the end of the slide show, then click the Slide Sorter button ▦ on the status bar**

   Figure C-16 shows the final presentation.

8. **Add your name as a footer to the notes and handouts, save your changes, print the presentation as handouts (four per page), then exit PowerPoint**

FIGURE C-15: Footer text converted to WordArt

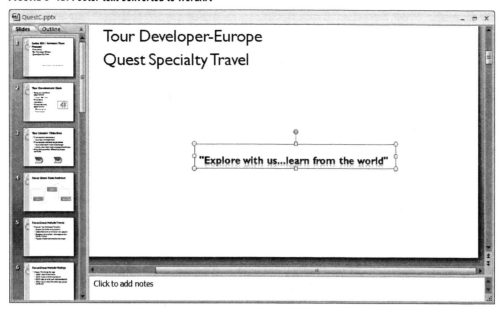

FIGURE C-16: Completed presentation in Slide Sorter view

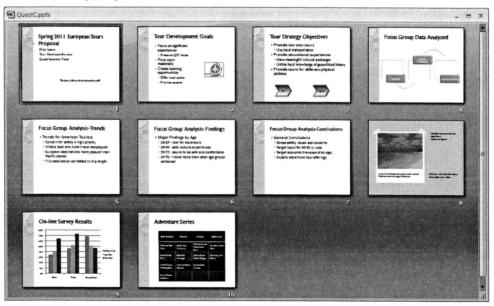

PowerPoint 2007

Using content templates from the Web

When you create a presentation, you have the option of using one of the many design themes supplied with PowerPoint, or you can use a template from the Microsoft Office Online Web site. These templates are designed and formatted with sample text, background and text colors, pictures, charts, and other graphic elements. To access a template from the Microsoft Office Online Web site, you need to be connected to the Internet, then click the Microsoft Office button. Click New to open the New Presentation dialog box. Click one of the template categories in the Microsoft

Office Online template list in the left pane, then download and save the template in PowerPoint. Some of the template categories have subcategories that you need to select to display the individual templates. If you don't have access to the Internet or if you want to view more template choices, you can select one of the installed PowerPoint templates. In the New Presentation dialog box, click Installed Templates in the Template Categories list to select one of the installed templates.

Inserting Objects into a Presentation

Practice

▼ CONCEPTS REVIEW

Label each element of the PowerPoint window shown in Figure C-17.

FIGURE C-17

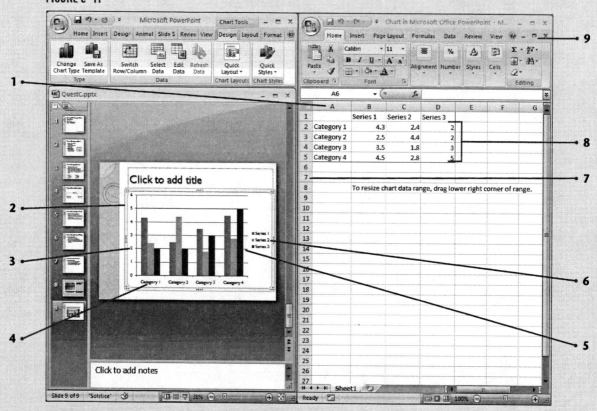

Match each term with the statement that best describes it.

10. Text label
11. Category axis
12. Value axis
13. Chart
14. WordArt

a. The graphical representation of numerical data
b. A set of decorative styles you can add to text
c. Another name for the vertical axis in a chart
d. A specific type of text object used to enter a small phrase
e. Another name for the horizontal axis in the chart

Select the best answer from the list of choices.

15. Which of the following statements about inserting text from Microsoft Word is *not* true?

  a. Each line of inserted text is placed onto separate slides.

  b. An outline structure is created in PowerPoint based on the Word styles used in the text.

  c. PowerPoint can insert text that has tabs at the end of paragraphs.

  d. You can create a new presentation based on inserted Word text.

16. What is the file index system that stores clip art, photographs, and movies called?

  a. Microsoft Clip Organizer   **c.** Clip Art Index

  b. Office Media Collections   **d.** WordArt Gallery

17. Hiding a portion of a picture or piece of clip art best describes which of the following actions?

  a. Adjusting   **c.** Styling

  b. Hiding   **d.** Cropping

18. Where is the numerical data located for a chart?

  a. Table   **c.** Worksheet

  b. Legend   **d.** Chart

19. An object that has its own data source and becomes a part of your presentation after you insert it best describes which of the following?

  a. A Word outline   **c.** A WordArt object

  b. An embedded object   **d.** A table

20. According to the book, which of the following objects is ideal to compare data side by side?

  a. Table   **c.** Outline

  b. Chart   **d.** Grid

21. A set of decorative text styles you apply to text describes which of the following items?

  a. Text labels   **c.** WordArt

  b. Illustrations   **d.** Gallery

22. What is a column of data in a worksheet called?

  a. Column headings   **c.** Data series markers

  b. Data series   **d.** Axis labels

▼ SKILLS REVIEW

1. Insert text from Microsoft Word.

  a. Open the file **PPT C-4.pptx** from the drive and folder where you store your Data Files, then save it as **Blue Moon**. You will work to create the completed presentation as shown in Figure C-18.

  b. Click Slide 3 in the Slides tab, then use the Slides from Outline command to insert the file **PPT C-5.docx** from the drive and folder where you store your Data Files.

  c. In the Slides tab, drag Slide 5 above Slide 4.

  d. In the Slides tab, delete Slide 7, Expansion Potential.

2. Insert clip art.

  a. Select Slide 4, then change the slide layout to the Two Content slide layout.

FIGURE C-18

b. Click the clip art icon in the right content placeholder, search for clip art using the keyword leadership, then insert the first clip in the Clip Art task pane.

c. In the Size group on the Picture Tools Format Ribbon, use the Shape Width up arrow to change the width to 2.4".

d. Click the Picture Border button, change the color of the clip art border to Gold, Accent 4.

e. Click the Picture Border button, change the weight of the clip art border to 4½ pt.

f. Click the Picture Effects button, point to 3-D Rotation, then click Off Axis 1 Right.

g. Drag the clip art so the bottom lines up with the bottom of the text object, then save your changes.

3. **Insert and style a picture.**

a. Select Slide 2, then insert the picture PPT C-6.jpg.

b. Completely crop the light blue section off the top of the picture, then crop the right side of the picture about ¼".

c. Drag the picture up so it is in the center of the blank area of the slide.

d. Click the Recolor button, then change the picture color to Grayscale.

e. Save your changes.

4. **Insert a text box.**

a. On Slide 2, insert a text box below the picture.

b. Type Private submissions for music up 19%.

c. Delete the word for, then drag the word music after the word Private.

d. Select the text object, then click the Shape Styles More button in the Shape Styles group on the Drawing Tools Format tab.

e. Point to Other Theme Fills, then click Style 11.

f. Center the text object under the picture.

5. **Insert a chart.**

a. Go to Slide 3, 2009 CD Sales by Quarter, apply the Title and Content slide layout, then insert a Clustered Bar chart.

b. Close Excel.

6. **Enter and edit chart data.**

a. Show the chart data.

b. Enter the data shown in Table C-2 into the worksheet.

c. Delete the data in Column D, then close Excel.

d. Change the chart style to Style 16 in the Chart Styles group.

e. Save your changes.

TABLE C-2

	U.S. Sales	Int. Sales
1st Qtr	290,957	163,902
2nd Qtr	429,840	125,854
3rd Qtr	485,063	135,927
4th Qtr	365,113	103,750

7. **Insert a table.**

a. Add a new slide after Slide 3 with the Title and Content layout.

b. Add the slide title New Subscription Plans.

c. Insert a table with 3 columns and 6 rows.

d. Enter the information shown in Table C-3, then change the table style to Light Style 2 – Accent 1. (*Hint*: Use the Copy and Paste commands to enter duplicate information in the table.)

e. Center the text in the top row.

TABLE C-3

Basic	Standard	Premium
$1.25 per download	$4.99 per month	$12.95 per month
Unlimited downloads	Max. 12 downloads	Max. 35 downloads
Limited access	Unlimited access	Unlimited access
Online registration	Online registration	Online registration
High-speed connection recommended	High-speed connection required	High-speed connection required

  f. In the Table Tools Layout tab, distribute the table rows.

  g. Save your changes.

8. Insert and format WordArt.

  a. Go to Slide 2, then select the bulleted list text object.

  b. Apply the WordArt style Fill – Accent 2, Warm Matte Bevel.

  c. View the presentation in Slide Show view, then save your changes.

  d. Add your name as a footer to the notes and handouts, print the slides as handouts (3 slides per page).

  e. Save your work, close the file, and exit PowerPoint.

▼ INDEPENDENT CHALLENGE 1

You are a financial management consultant for Casey Investments, located in St. Louis, Missouri. One of your responsibilities is to create standardized presentations on different financial investments for use on the company Web site. As part of the presentation for this meeting, you insert some clip art, add a text box, and insert a chart.

  a. Open the file PPT C-7.pptx from the drive and folder where you store your Data Files, then save it as **Casey**.

  b. Add your name as the footer on all notes and handouts, then apply the Oriel Design Theme.

  c. Insert a clustered column chart on Slide 6, then enter the data in Table C-4 into the worksheet.

  d. Format the chart using Style 27.

Advanced Challenge Exercise

- Click the Chart Tools Layout tab, click the Legend button, then click Show Legend at Top.
- Click the Chart Tools Format tab, then click the Current Selection list arrow in the Current Selection group, then click Series "3 Year."
- Click the Shape Fill button list arrow, then click the Orange color under Standard Colors.

TABLE C-4

	1 year	3 year	5 year	7 year
Bonds	4.2%	5.2%	7.9%	6.5%
Stocks	6.9%	8.2%	7.2%	9.6%
Mutual Funds	4.6%	6.0%	7.4%	11.4%

  e. Insert clip art of a set of scales on Slide 2, then format as necessary. (*Hint*: Use the keyword scales to search for clips.)

  f. On Slide 3, use the Align, and Distribute commands on the Drawing Tools Format tab in the Arrange group to align and distribute the objects so that the shapes are aligned on top and distributed horizontally.

  g. Spell check the presentation, then save it.

  h. View the slide show. Make changes if necessary.

  i. The final presentation should look like Figure C-19.

  j. Print the slides as handouts (6 slides per page), then close the presentation, and exit PowerPoint.

FIGURE C-19

▼ INDEPENDENT CHALLENGE 2

You work for Alcom Home Systems, a company based out of Colorado Springs, Colorado that provides integrated data, security, and voice command systems for homes. You have been asked to enhance a marketing presentation on a new product that the company is going to promote at a large trade fair in Las Vegas. You work on completing a presentation for the show. You insert some clip art, add a text box, and insert a chart.

a. Start PowerPoint, open the file PPT C-8.pptx from the drive and folder where you store your Data Files, and save it as **Alcom**.

b. Add your name and today's date to Slide 1 in the Subtitle text box.

c. Organize the objects on Slide 2 using the Align, Distribute, and Group commands. Add and format additional shapes to enhance the presentation.

d. On Slide 3, style the picture, recolor the picture, and use a picture effect.

e. Apply the Median theme to the presentation.

f. Insert the Word document file **PPT C-9.docx** to create additional slides from an outline after Slide 2.

g. Create a new slide after Slide 4, title the slide **Growth of Integrated Systems**, then insert a chart.

TABLE C-5

	Last Yr.	Current Yr.	Next Yr.
Traditional	91	85	74
Integrated	9	15	26

FIGURE C-20

h. Enter the data in Table C-5, then format the chart using at least two formatting commands. Be able to name which formatting commands you applied to the chart.

i. Insert a text box on the Alcom Home Systems slide (Slide 7). Create your own company contact and address information. Format the text box.

j. Spell check, then view the final slide show (refer to Figure C-20). Make any necessary changes.

k. Save the presentation, print the slides as handouts, close the file, and exit PowerPoint.

▼ INDEPENDENT CHALLENGE 3

You work for LearnSource Ltd., a company that produces instructional software to help people learn foreign languages. Once a year, LearnSource holds a meeting with their biggest client, the Department of State, to brief the government on new products and to receive feedback on existing products. Your boss has started a presentation and has asked you to look it over and add other elements to make it look better.

a. Start PowerPoint, open the file PPT C-10.pptx from the drive and folder where you store your Data Files, and save it as **LearnSource**.

b. Add an appropriate design theme to the presentation.

c. Insert the Word outline PPT C-11.docx after the Product Revisions slide.

d. Format the text so that the most important information is the most prominent.

e. Insert an appropriate table on a slide of your choice. Use your own information. (*Hint*: You can convert a bulleted list to a table.)

f. Add at least two appropriate shapes that emphasize slide content. Format the objects using shape styles. If appropriate, use the Align, Distribute, and Group commands to organize your shapes.

▼ INDEPENDENT CHALLENGE 3 (CONTINUED)

Advanced Challenge Exercise (*Internet connection required*)

- Open the Clip Art task pane, then click the Clip art on Office Online link to go to the Microsoft Office Online Web site.
- Insert an appropriate graphic.
- Format the graphic using Picture Tools Format tab.
- Be able to explain how you formatted the graphic object.

g. Spell check and view the final slide show (refer to Figure C-21). Make any necessary changes.

h. Add your name as footer text on the notes and handouts, save the presentation, then print the slides as handouts.

i. Save and close the file, and exit PowerPoint.

FIGURE C-21

▼ REAL LIFE INDEPENDENT CHALLENGE

You are on the Foreign Exchange Commission at your college and one of your responsibilities is to present information on past foreign student exchanges to different organizations on and off campus. You need to create a pictorial presentation that highlights a trip to a different country. Create a presentation using your own pictures or photographs given to you with permission by a friend.

Note: Three photographs (PPT C-12.jpg, PPT C-13.jpg, and PPT C-14.jpg,) from Dijon, France are provided, if necessary to help you complete this Independent Challenge.

a. Start PowerPoint, create a new blank presentation, and save it as Exchange to the drive and folder where you store your Data Files.

FIGURE C-22

b. Locate and insert the pictures you want to use. Place one picture on each slide using the Content with Caption slide layout.

c. Add information about each picture in the text placeholder and enter a slide title. If you use the pictures provided, research Dijon, France using the Internet for relevant information to place on the slides. (*Internet connection required*)

d. Apply an appropriate design theme.

e. Apply an appropriate title and your name to the title slide. Spell check, then view the final slide show (refer to Figure C-22).

f. Add a slide number to the slides and your name as footer text to the notes and handouts, save the presentation, then print the slides and notes pages (if any).

g. Save your work, close the file, and exit PowerPoint.

Inserting Objects into a Presentation

▼ VISUAL WORKSHOP

Create a one-slide presentation that looks like Figure C-23. The slide layout shown in Figure C-23 is a specific layout designed for pictures. Insert the picture file PPT C-6.jpg to complete this presentation. Add your name as footer to the slide, save the presentation as **Guitar Lessons** to the drive and folder where you store your Data Files, then print the slide.

FIGURE C-23

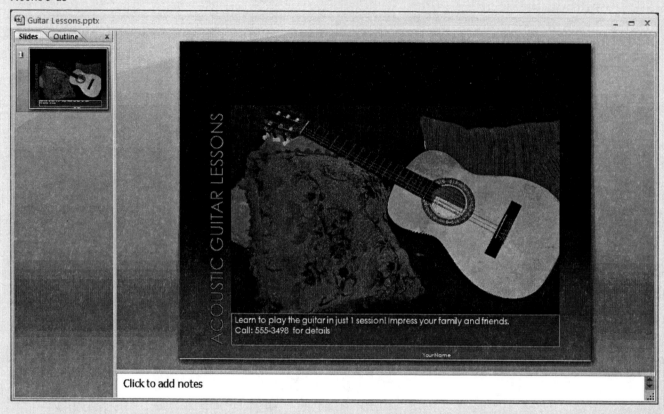

Finishing a Presentation

Though not required, having a consistent professional-looking theme throughout your presentation is optimal if you want to peak and retain your audience's interest in the subject matter you are presenting. PowerPoint helps you achieve a consistent look by providing ways to customize your slides' layout and background. Once you are finished working with the text and other objects of your presentation, you are ready to apply slide show effects, which determine the way the slides and objects on the slides appear in Slide Show view. ▰▰▰ Ellen has reviewed the presentation and is pleased with the slides you created for the Quest Specialty Travel presentation. You are ready to finalize the layouts and add effects to make the presentation interesting to watch.

OBJECTIVES

Understand masters

Customize background style

Use slide show commands

Set slide show transitions and timings

Set slide animation effects

Inspect a presentation

Evaluate a presentation

Create a design template

Understanding Masters

Each presentation in PowerPoint has a set of **masters**, which store information, including the position and size of text and content placeholders, text styles, background colors, effects, animations, and theme colors. There are three Master views: Slide Master view, Handout Master view, and Notes Master view. Changes made to the Slide Master are reflected on all the slides, changes made to the Notes Master are reflected in the Notes Page view, and changes made to the Handout Master are reflected when you print your presentation using one of the Handout print options. Design elements that you place on the Slide Master appear on every slide in the presentation. For example, you could insert a company logo in the upper-right corner of the slide master and that logo would then appear on every slide in your presentation. Each Slide Master has associated layouts. Changes made to a layout affect all slides that have that layout. ▰▰▰ You want to add the company logo to the presentation, so you open your presentation and examine the slide master.

STEPS

1. **Start PowerPoint, open the presentation PPT D-1.pptx from the drive and folder where you store your Data Files, save the presentation as QuestD, click the View tab on the Ribbon, then click the Arrange All button in the Window group**

   The title slide of the presentation appears.

QUICK TIP

You can press and hold [Shift] and click the Normal button on the status bar to display the slide master.

2. **Click the Slide Master button in the Presentation Views group, then click the Solstice Slide Master thumbnail (first thumbnail) in the left pane**

   The Slide Master view appears with the slide master displayed in the Slide pane as shown in Figure D-1. This master slide is the theme master slide (the Solstice theme in this case). Each master text placeholder identifies the font size, style, color, and position of text placeholders on the slide in Normal view. For example, the Master title placeholder, labeled "Click to edit Master title style," is positioned at the top of the slide and uses a brown, shadowed, 44 pt, Gill Sans MT font. Any objects you place on the slide master will appear on all slides in the presentation. The slide layouts located below the master slide thumbnail in the left pane follow the information in the master slide and changes you make to this master slide, including font changes, are reflected in all of the slide layouts. Each slide layout in the presentation can be modified independently. Each theme comes with its own associated slide masters.

QUICK TIP

When working with slide layouts, you can right-click the thumbnail to open a shortcut list of commands.

3. **Point to each slide layout in the left pane, then click the Title Only Layout thumbnail**

   As you point to each slide layout, a ScreenTip appears which identifies each slide layout by name and lists if any of the slides in the presentation are currently using the layout. Three slides are using the Title Only Layout, Slide 4, Slide 9, and Slide 10.

4. **Click the Solstice Slide Master thumbnail, click the Insert tab on the Ribbon, then click the Picture button in the Illustrations group**

   The Insert Picture dialog box opens.

5. **Select the picture file PPT D-2.jpg from the drive and folder where you store your Data Files, then click Insert**

   The QST graphic logo appears on the slide master and will appear on all slides in the presentation. The graphic is too large and needs to be repositioned on the slide so you reduce its size and move it to a better location on the slide.

6. **Click the Shape Width down arrow in the Size group until 1.1" appears, then drag the graphic to the upper left corner of the slide**

   Compare your screen to Figure D-2.

7. **Click the Normal button 🔳 on the status bar, then save your changes**

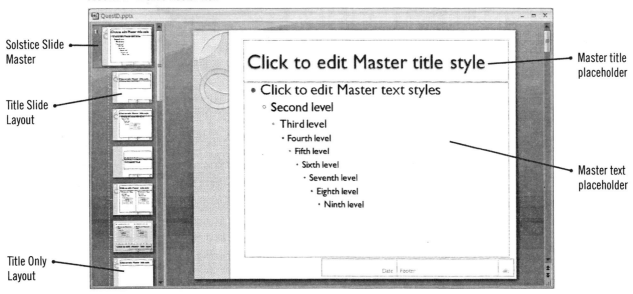

FIGURE D-1: Slide Master view

Solstice Slide Master

Title Slide Layout

Title Only Layout

Click to edit Master title style

- Click to edit Master text styles
  - Second level
    - Third level
      - Fourth level
        - Fifth level
        - Sixth level
          - Seventh level
            - Eighth level
              - Ninth level

Master title placeholder

Master text placeholder

Date | Footer

FIGURE D-2: Graphic added to the slide master

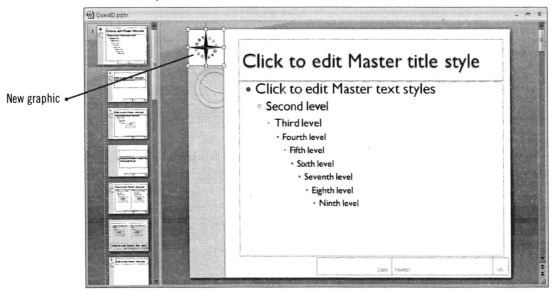

New graphic

Click to edit Master title style

- Click to edit Master text styles
  - Second level
    - Third level
      - Fourth level
        - Fifth level
        - Sixth level
          - Seventh level
            - Eighth level
              - Ninth level

Date | Footer

Create custom slide layouts

As you work with PowerPoint, you may find that you need to develop a customized slide layout. For example, you may need to create presentations for a client that has slides that display four pictures with a caption underneath each picture. To make everyone's job easier, you create a custom slide layout that includes only the placeholders needed for that particular slide layout. To create a custom slide layout, open Slide Master view, click the Insert Layout button in the Edit Master group. A new slide layout appears in the Slide pane. You can choose to add several different placeholders including Content, Text, Picture, Chart, Table, SmartArt, Media, and Clip Art. Click the Insert Placeholder button arrow in the Master Layout group, click the placeholder you want to add, drag ╋ to create the placeholder, then position the placeholder on the slide. In Slide Master view, you can add or delete placeholders in any of the slide layouts. You can rename a custom slide layout by clicking the Rename button in the Edit Master group and entering a descriptive name to better identify the layout.

Customizing the Background Style

Every slide in a PowerPoint presentation has a **background**, the area behind the text and graphics. You modify the background to enhance the slides using images and color. A **background graphic** is an object placed on the slide master. You can quickly change the background appearance by applying a background style, which is a set of color variations derived from the theme colors. **Theme colors** are a set of twelve coordinated colors that determine the colors for all slide elements in your presentation including: slide background, text and lines, shadows, title text, fills, accents, and hyperlinks. Every theme, such as Civic and Solstice, has its own set of theme colors. See Table D-1 for a description of the theme colors. ▄▄▄▄ The QST presentation needs some design enhancements. You decide to modify the background of the slides in the presentation by applying a background style.

STEPS

1. Click the Design tab on the Ribbon, then click the Background Styles button in the Background group

A gallery of background styles opens. Review the different backgrounds using Live Preview.

QUICK TIP

To apply a new background style to only selected slides, select the slides on the Slides tab or in Slide Sorter view, right-click the background style in the Background Styles gallery, then click Apply to Selected Slides.

2. Move the pointer over each style in the gallery, then click Style 6

Figure D-3 shows the new background on Slide 1 of the presentation. Even though you are working in Normal view, the new background style is applied to every slide in the presentation and to the master slide and master slide layouts. The new background style did not appear over the whole slide, which indicates there is a background graphic on the slide master that is preventing you from seeing the entire slide background.

3. Click the Hide Background Graphics check box in the Background group

For the selected slide, all the background graphics are hidden from view and only the text objects on the slide remain visible.

4. Click the Hide Background Graphics check box to display the background graphics, click the Background Styles button, then click Format Background

The Format Background dialog box opens.

QUICK TIP

You can also apply a gradient background style to a shape by right-clicking the shape, then clicking Format Shape in the shortcut menu.

5. Click the Type list arrow, click Linear, click the Direction button, click Linear Down, click Apply to All, then click Close

The gradient fill of the background style now progresses from dark to light starting at the bottom of the slide and moving to the top. You need to fix the background color of the QST logo graphic so it does not obstruct the slide background graphics.

6. Press [Shift], click the Normal button 🖳 on the status bar, click the Solstice Slide Master thumbnail in the left pane, then click the QST graphic

The graphic is selected in the Slide Master view.

7. Click the Picture Tools Format tab on the Ribbon, click the Recolor button in the Adjust group, click Set Transparent Color, then move the pointer over the slide

The pointer changes to the transparent pointer 🖌.

TROUBLE

If the white background does not become transparent, click the Undo button, then repeat the step.

8. Position 🖌 over the white background of the QST logo graphic, then click

The white background of the QST graphic becomes transparent and the slide background appears behind the graphic.

9. Click the Normal button 🖳 on the status bar, then save your work

Compare your screen to Figure D-4.

FIGURE D-3: Slide with new background style applied

New background style is applied to all the slides

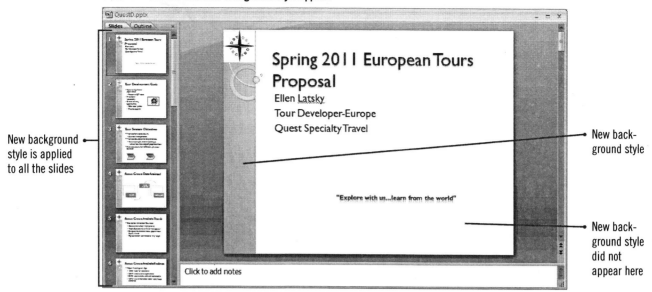

New background style

New background style did not appear here

FIGURE D-4: Finished slide

Graphic with transparent background

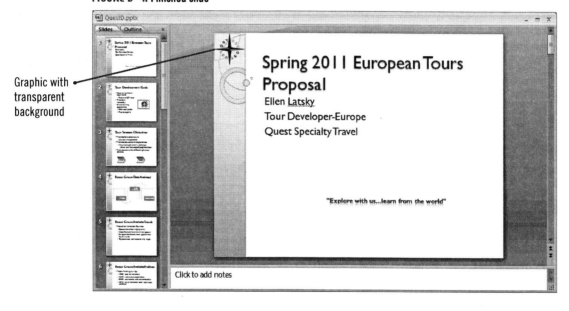

TABLE D-1: Theme colors

scheme element	description
Background color	Color of the slide's background; fills the slide
Text and lines color	Used for any typed characters and drawn lines; contrasts with the background color
Shadows color	The shadow color for text and other objects; generally a darker shade of the background color
Title text color	Used for slide title; like the text and line colors and contrasts with the background color
Fills color	Used to fill shapes and other objects with color. Contrasts with both the background and the text and line colors
Accent colors	Colors used for other objects on slides, such as bullets
Accent and hyperlink colors	Colors used for accent objects and for hyperlinks you insert
Accent and followed hyperlink color	Color used for accent objects and for hyperlinks after they have been clicked

Using Slide Show Commands

With PowerPoint, you can show a presentation on any compatible computer using Slide Show view. As you've seen, Slide Show view fills your computer screen with the slides of the presentation, showing them one at a time. Once the presentation is in Slide Show view, you can use a number of slide show options to tailor the show to meet your needs. For example, you can draw, or **annotate**, on slides or jump to different slides in other parts of the presentation. ▚▚▞▞ Ellen wants you to learn how to run a slide show and use the slide show options so you can help her when she gives the presentation. You run the slide show of the presentation and practice using some of the custom slide show options.

STEPS

1. **Click the View tab on the Ribbon, then click the Slide Show button in the Presentation Views group**

   The first slide of the presentation fills the screen.

2. **Press [Spacebar]**

   Slide 2 appears on the screen. Pressing [Spacebar] or clicking the left mouse button is the easiest way to move through a slide show. See Table D-2 for other Slide Show view key commands. You can also use the Slide Show shortcut menu for on-screen navigation during a slide show.

3. **Right-click anywhere on the screen, point to Go to Slide on the shortcut menu, then click 8 Mediterranean Islands Bike Tour**

   The slide show jumps to Slide 8. You can highlight or emphasize major points in your presentation by annotating the slide during a slide show using one of PowerPoint's annotation tools.

4. **Move the pointer to the bottom left corner of the screen to display the Slide Show toolbar, click the Pen Options menu button ✐, then click Highlighter**

   The pointer changes to the highlighter pointer ▮.

5. **Drag ▮ to highlight the text below the picture**

   Compare your screen to Figure D-5. While the annotation tool is visible, mouse clicks do not advance the slide show; however, you can still move to the next slide by pressing [Spacebar] or [Enter].

6. **Click the Pen Options menu button ✐ on the Slide Show toolbar, click Erase All Ink on Slide, then press [Ctrl][A]**

   The annotations on Slide 8 are erased and the pointer returns to ▷ when you press [Ctrl][A].

7. **Click the Slide Show menu button ▤ on the Slide Show toolbar, point to Go to Slide, then click 10 Adventure Series on the menu**

   Slide 10 appears.

8. **Press [Home], then press [Enter] to advance through the slide show, then when you see the black slide at the end of the slide show, press [Spacebar]**

   You are returned to Normal view. The black slide indicates the end of the slide show.

FIGURE D-5: Slide 8 in Slide Show view with highlight annotations

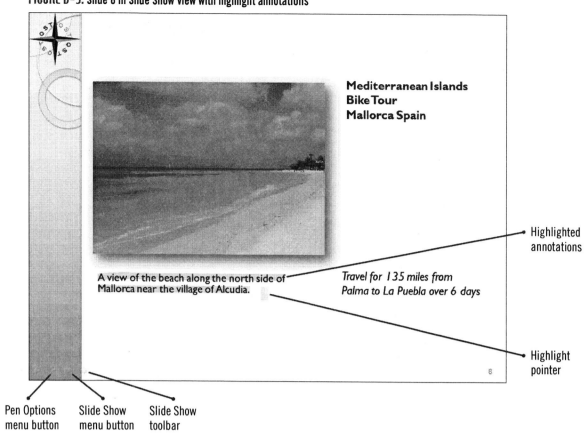

Mediterranean Islands
Bike Tour
Mallorca Spain

A view of the beach along the north side of
Mallorca near the village of Alcudia.

Travel for 135 miles from
Palma to La Puebla over 6 days

Highlighted
annotations

Highlight
pointer

Pen Options
menu button

Slide Show
menu button

Slide Show
toolbar

TABLE D-2: Basic Slide Show keyboard controls

control	description
[Enter], [Spacebar], [PgDn], [N], [down arrow key], or [right arrow key]	Advances to the next slide
[E]	Erases the annotation drawing
[Home], [End]	Moves to the first or last slide in the slide show
[H]	Displays a hidden slide
[up arrow key] or [PgUp]	Returns to the previous slide
[W]	Changes the screen to white; press again to return
[S]	Pauses the slide show; press again to continue
[B]	Changes the screen to black; press again to return
[Ctrl][M]	Shows or hides annotations on the slide
[Ctrl][A]	Changes pointer to ⟨
[Esc]	Stops the slide show

Setting Slide Show Transitions and Timings

In a slide show, you can specify how each slide advances in and out of view, and for how long each slide appears on the screen. **Slide transitions** are the special visual and audio effects you apply to a slide that determine how it moves in and out of view during the slide show. **Slide timing**, refers to the amount of time a slide is visible on the screen. Typically, you would set slide timings if you wanted the presentation to automatically progress through the slides during a slide show. Setting the correct slide timing, in this case, is important because it determines how long each slide is visible. Each slide can have a different slide timing. ▓▓▓▓ You decide to set slide transitions and 8 second slide timings for all the slides.

STEPS

1. **Make sure Slide 1 is selected, click the Animations tab on the Ribbon, then point to each of the transition options in the Transition to This Slide group**

   A Live Preview of each transition is displayed on the slide. Transitions are organized by type into five groups.

TROUBLE
You'll need to wait a few seconds until the Live Preview of the transition finishes to see the transition ScreenTip.

2. **Click the More button in the Transition to This Slide group, then click Box In in the Wipes section (3rd row)**

   The new slide transition plays on the slide and a transition icon appears next to the slide thumbnail in the Slides tab as shown in Figure D-6. The slide transition would have more impact if it were slowed down.

3. **Click the Transition Speed list arrow in the Transition to This Slide group, then click Medium**

   The Box In slide transition plays again at the slower speed. You can apply this transition to all of the slides in the presentation.

QUICK TIP
Click the transition icon under any slide in Slide Sorter view to see its transition play.

4. **Click the Apply To All button in the Transition to This Slide group, then click the Slide Sorter button ▦ on the status bar**

   All of the slides now have the Box In transition at the medium speed applied to them as identified by the transition icons located below each slide. The options under Advance Slide in the Transition to This Slide group determine how slides progress during a slide show—either by mouse click or automatically by slide timing.

5. **Click the Automatically After up arrow until 00.08 appears in the text box, then click the Apply To All button in the Transition to This Slide group**

   The timing between slides is 8 seconds as indicated by the time under each slide in Slide Sorter view. See Figure D-7. When you run the slide show, each slide will remain on the screen for 8 seconds. You can override a slide's timing and speed up the slide show by pressing [Spacebar], [Enter], or clicking the left mouse button during a slide show.

6. **Click Slide 8, click the Transition Sound list arrow in the Transition to This Slide group, then click Breeze**

   The Breeze sound will now play when Slide 8 appears during the slide show.

7. **Press [Home], click the Slide Show button ▣ on the status bar, then watch the slide show advance automatically**

8. **When you see the black slide at the end of the slide show, press [Spacebar], then save your changes**

   The slide show ends and returns to Slide Sorter view with Slide 1 selected.

FIGURE D-6: Applied slide transition

Box In slide transition

More button

Transition icon

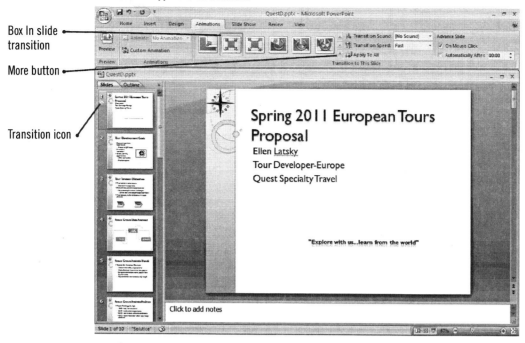

FIGURE D-7: Slide Sorter view showing applied transition and timing

Slide timing

Transition icon

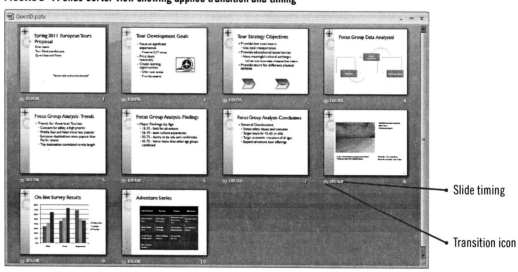

Rehearsing slide show timings

You can set different slide timings for each slide. For example, you can have the title slide appear for 20 seconds, the second slide for 1 minute, and so on. You can set timings by clicking the Rehearse Timings button in the Set Up group on the Slide Show tab. Slide Show view opens and the Rehearsal toolbar shown in Figure D-8 opens. It contains buttons to pause between slides and to advance to the next slide. After opening the Rehearsal toolbar, practice giving your presentation. PowerPoint keeps track of how long each slide appears and sets the timing accordingly. You can view your rehearsed timings in Slide Sorter view. The next time you run the slide show, you can use the timings you rehearsed.

FIGURE D-8: Rehearsal toolbar

Rehearsal

Total elapsed time for all slides

Move to the next slide

Click to pause

Time elapsed while viewing current slide

Click to reset the clock to zero for the current slide

PowerPoint 2007

Setting Slide Animation Effects

Animation effects let you control how the objects and main points in your presentation appear on the screen during a slide show. You can set custom animation effects or use one of several standard animation effects. For example, you can apply a Fade by 1st Level Paragraphs animation effect to bulleted text so that each first level bullet appears separately from the others. Using animation effects allows you to control how information flows and what information is emphasized. You can animate text, graphics, sounds, hyperlinks, SmartArt diagrams, charts and individual chart elements. The standard animation effects include Fade, Wipe, and Fly In and can be applied to any selected object. Custom animation effects are organized into four categories, which provide you a wide range of animation choices, such as Ease In and Flicker. ■■■■ Ellen wants you to animate the text and graphics of several slides in the presentation using animation effects.

STEPS

1. **Verify that the Animations tab is selected on the Ribbon, double-click Slide 2 to view it in Normal view, then click the body text object**

   The bullets in the text object can be animated to appear one at a time during a slide show.

   > **QUICK TIP**
   >
   > Animation effects can be serious and business-like or humorous. Choose appropriate effects for your presentation content and audience.

2. **Click the Animate list arrow in the Animations group, then click By 1st Level Paragraphs in the Fade section**

   As you click the animation option a Live Preview of the Box In transition and the Fade animation effect plays.

3. **Click the Slide Show button ▣ on the status bar, then press [Esc] when you see Slide 3**

   The Fade animation effect, which begins after the slide transition effect, is active on Slide 2. You can also animate other objects on a slide by setting custom animations.

4. **Make sure Slide 3 is selected, click the grouped arrow object on the slide, then click the Custom Animation button in the Animations group**

   The Custom Animation task pane opens.

   > **QUICK TIP**
   >
   > If you want the parts of a grouped object to animate individually, then you must ungroup the objects before you animate them.

5. **Click the Add Effect button in the Custom Animation task pane, then point to Entrance**

   A submenu of Entrance animation effects appears next to a menu of four animation categories, Entrance, Emphasis, Exit, and Motion Paths as shown in Figure D-9. An Entrance animation effect causes an object to enter the slide with an effect; an Emphasis animation effect causes an object already visible on the slide to have an effect; an Exit animation effect causes an object to leave the slide with an effect; and a Motion Paths animation effect causes an object to move on a specified path on the slide.

6. **Click More Effects**

   The Add Entrance Effect dialog box opens. All of the effects in this dialog box allow an object to enter the slide using a special effect.

   > **QUICK TIP**
   >
   > To change the order in which objects are animated on the slide, select the object in the Custom Animation task pane, then click the appropriate Re-Order arrow at the bottom of the pane.

7. **Scroll down to the Exciting section, click Glide, then click OK**

   The arrow object now has the glide effect applied to it as shown in Figure D-10. Notice that the arrow object now has an animation tag and is listed in the Custom Animation task pane as the first object to be animated on the slide. **Animation tags** identify the order in which objects are animated during slide show.

8. **Click the Custom Animation task pane Close button ⊠, click the Slide Show tab on the Ribbon, then click the From Beginning button in the Start Slide Show group to run the Slide Show from Slide 1**

   The special effects make the presentation more interesting to view.

9. **When you see the black slide, press [Spacebar], then save your changes**

FIGURE D-9: Custom Animation task pane open

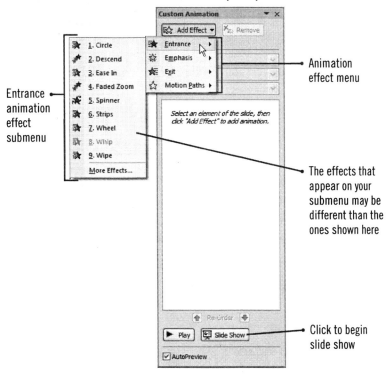

Entrance animation effect submenu

Animation effect menu

The effects that appear on your submenu may be different than the ones shown here

Click to begin slide show

FIGURE D-10: Screen showing animated arrow object

Click to preview Animation on the slide

Animation tag

Click to change animation options

Custom Animation list

Presentation checklist

You should always rehearse your slide show. If possible, rehearse your presentation in the room and with the computer that you will use. Use the following checklist to prepare for the slide show:

- Is **PowerPoint** or **PowerPoint Viewer** installed on the computer?
- Is your **presentation file** on the hard drive of the computer you will be using? Try putting a shortcut for the file on the desktop. Do you have a backup copy of your presentation file on a removable storage device?
- Is the **projection device** working correctly? Can the slides be seen from the back of the room?

- Do you know how to control **room lighting** so that the audience can see both your slides and their handouts and notes? You may want to designate someone to control the lights if the controls are not close to you.
- Will the **computer** be situated so you can advance and annotate the slides yourself? If not, designate someone to advance them for you.
- Do you have enough copies of your **handouts**? Bring extras. Decide when to hand them out, or whether you prefer to have them waiting at the audience members' seats when they enter.

Inspecting a Presentation

Reviewing your presentation can be an important step, not only to find and fix errors, but also to locate and delete private company or personal information and document properties you do not want to share with others. If you share presentations with others, especially over the Internet, it is a good idea to inspect the presentation file using the Document Inspector. The **Document Inspector** looks for hidden data and personal information that is stored in the file itself or in the document properties. Document properties, also known as **metadata**, includes specific data about the presentation, such as the author's name, subject matter, title, who saved the file last, and when the file was created. Other types of information the Document Inspector can locate and remove include: presentation notes, comments, ink annotations, invisible on-slide content, off-slide content, and custom XML data. ■■■ QST has strict rules about revealing personal and company information in documents. You decide to view and add some document properties, inspect your presentation file, and learn about the Mark as Final command.

STEPS

1. **Click the Office button 🔘, point to Prepare, then click Properties**

   The Document Properties pane opens showing the file location and the title of the presentation. Now enter some descriptive data for this presentation file.

2. **Enter the data shown in Figure D-11, then click the Properties pane Close button**

   This data provides detailed information about the presentation file that you can use to identify and organize your file. You can also use this information as search criteria to locate the file at a later time. You now use the Document Inspector to search for information you might want to delete in the presentation.

3. **Click 🔘, point to Prepare, click Inspect Document, click Yes to save the changes to the document, then read the dialog box**

   The Document Inspector dialog box opens. The Document Inspector searches the presentation file for six different types of information that you might want removed from the presentation before sending it.

4. **Make sure all of the check boxes are selected, then click Inspect**

   The presentation file is reviewed and the Document Inspector dialog box displays the results shown in Figure D-12. Notice that there are three items found: document properties in the Document Properties pane, an off slide object that you created and didn't use, and some reminder notes you wrote yourself in the Notes pane on Slides 8, 9, and 10. You decide to leave the document properties alone but delete the off-slide object, and the notes in the Notes pane for all of the slides.

5. **Click the Off-Slide Content Remove All button, click the Presentation Notes Remove All button, then click Close**

   All of those items are removed from the presentation.

6. **Click 🔘, point to Prepare, click Mark as Final, then click OK in the alert dialog box**

   A dialog box opens. Be sure to read the dialog box to understand what happens to the file and how to recognize a marked-as-final presentation. You decide to proceed with this operation.

7. **Click OK, click the Home tab on the Ribbon, click the Slide 1 thumbnail in the Slides pane, then click anywhere in the title text object**

   Notice that the commands on the Ribbon are dimmed as shown in Figure D-13. Because you marked the file as final, the file is read-only. A **read-only** file is one that can't be edited or modified in any way. Anyone who has received a read-only presentation can edit the presentation by removing the mark as final status. You still want to work on the presentation, so you remove the mark as final status.

8. **Click 🔘, point to Prepare, click Mark as Final, then save your changes**

   The commands on the Ribbon are active again, and the file can now be modified.

FIGURE D-11: Document Properties pane

Add this information

Your file location will be different

FIGURE D-12: Document Inspector dialog box

FIGURE D-13: Marked-as-final presentation

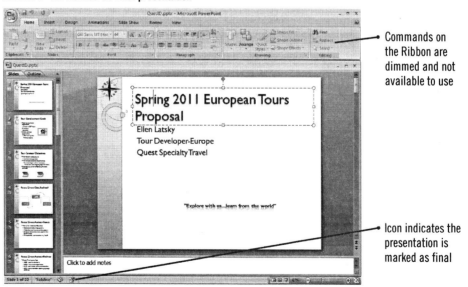

Commands on the Ribbon are dimmed and not available to use

Icon indicates the presentation is marked as final

Digitally sign a presentation

So what is a digital signature and why would you want to use one in PowerPoint? A digital signature is similar to a hand-written signature in that it authenticates your document; however, a digital signature, unlike a hand-written signature, is created using computer cryptography and is not visible within the presentation itself. There are three primary reasons you would add a digital signature to a presentation: one, to authenticate the signer of the document; two, to assure that the content of the presentation has not been changed since it was signed; and three, to assure the origin of the signed document. To add a digital signature, click the Office button, point to Prepare, click Add a Digital Signature, then follow the dialog boxes.

PowerPoint 2007

Finishing a Presentation

456

Evaluating a Presentation

As you create a presentation, keep in mind that a good design requires preparation. An effective presentation is focused and visually appealing—easy for the speaker to present and simple for the audience to understand. The visual elements (colors, graphics, and text) can strongly influence the audience's attention and interest and can determine the success of your presentation. See Table D-3 for general information on the impact a visual presentation has on an audience. ▉▉▉ You know Ellen will critique your presentation, so you take the time to evaluate your presentation's effectiveness.

STEPS

1. **Click the Slide Show button ▣ on the status bar, then press [Spacebar] when the slide show finishes**

2. **Click the Slide Sorter button ▦ on the status bar**
   You decide that Slide 8 should come after Slide 10.

3. **Drag Slide 8 to the right side of Slide 10, then save your changes**
   Slide 8 is moved to the end of the presentation. The final presentation is shown in Slide Sorter view. Compare your screen to Figure D-14.

4. **Double-click Slide 1, then evaluate your presentation according to the guidelines below**
   Figure D-15 shows a poorly designed slide. Contrast this slide with your presentation as you review the following guidelines.

When evaluating a presentation, it is important to:

- Keep your message focused

  Don't put every point you plan to say on your presentation slides. Keep the audience anticipating further explanations to the key points shown in the presentation.

- Keep your text concise

  Limit each slide to six words per line and six lines per slide. Use lists and symbols to help prioritize your points visually. Your presentation text provides only the highlights; use notes to give more detailed information. Your presentation focuses attention on the key issues and you supplement the information with further explanation and details during your presentation.

- Keep the design simple, easy to read, and appropriate for the content

  A design theme makes the presentation consistent. If you design your own layout, keep it simple and use design elements sparingly. Use similar design elements consistently throughout the presentation; otherwise, your audience may get confused.

- Choose attractive colors that make the slide easy to read

  Use contrasting colors for slide background and text to make the text readable. If you are giving an on-screen presentation, you can use almost any combination of colors that look good together.

- Choose fonts and styles that are easy to read and emphasize important text

  As a general rule, use no more than two fonts in a presentation and vary the font size, using nothing smaller than 24 points. Use bold and italic attributes selectively.

- Use visuals to help communicate the message of your presentation

  Commonly used visuals include clip art, photographs, charts, worksheets, tables, and movies. Whenever possible, replace text with a visual, but be careful not to overcrowd your slides. White space on your slides is OK!

FIGURE D-14: The final presentation in Slide Sorter view

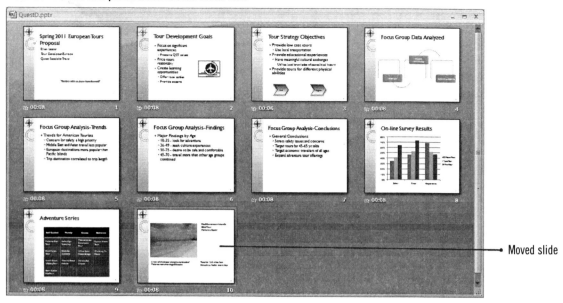

Moved slide

FIGURE D-15: A poorly designed slide

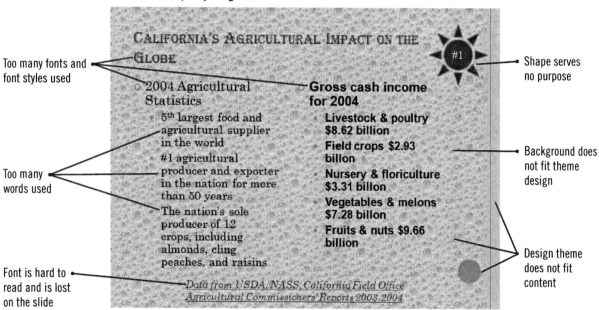

Too many fonts and font styles used

Too many words used

Font is hard to read and is lost on the slide

Shape serves no purpose

Background does not fit theme design

Design theme does not fit content

PowerPoint 2007

TABLE D-3: Audience impact from a visual presentation

impact	description
Visual reception	75% of all environmental stimuli is received through visual reception
Learning	55% of what an audience learns comes directly from visual messages
Retention	Combining visual messages with verbal messages can increase memory retention by as much as 30%
Presentation goals	You are twice as likely to achieve your communication objectives using a visual presentation
Meeting length	You are likely to decrease the average meeting length by 26% when you use a visual presentation

Source: *Presenters Online, www.presentersonline.com*

Finishing a Presentation

Creating a Design Template

When planning the design of your presentation, keep in mind that you are not limited to using just the standard themes PowerPoint provides or the ones you find on the Web. You can customize your presentation using a template. A **template** is a type of presentation file that contains custom design information made to the slide master, slide layouts, and theme. You can create a new template from a blank presentation, or you can modify an existing PowerPoint presentation that you have access to and save it as a template. If you modify an existing presentation, you can keep, change, or delete any color, graphic, or font as necessary. When you are finished creating a new presentation or modifying an existing presentation, you can save it as a template file, which adds the .potx extension to the filename. You can then use your template presentation as the basis for new presentations. ▰▰▰▰▰ You are finished working on your presentation for now. You want to save the presentation as a template so you and others can use it.

STEPS

QUICK TIP

Presentations saved to the Templates folder appear in the New Presentation dialog box under My Templates.

1. **Click the Office button 🏢, point to Save As, click Other Formats, click the Save as type list arrow, then click PowerPoint Template (*.potx)**

   Because this is a template, PowerPoint automatically opens the Templates folder on your hard drive as shown in Figure D-16.

2. **Use the Favorite Link or Folders pane to locate the drive and folder where you store your Data Files, click to select the filename (currently QuestD.potx) in the File name list box, type QuestD Template, then click Save**

   The presentation is saved as a PowerPoint template to the drive and folder where you store your Data Files, and the new template presentation appears in the PowerPoint window. The filename in the title bar has a .potx extension which identifies this presentation as a template.

3. **Click the Slide Sorter button 🔡 on the status bar, click Slide 3, press and hold [Shift], click Slide 10, release [Shift], then click the Cut button ✂ in the Clipboard group**

   Slides 3 through 10 are deleted.

4. **Double-click Slide 2, press and hold [Shift], click the body text object, click the title text object, right-click the clip art object, release [Shift], then click Cut**

   The clip art object and the text in the text objects are deleted. Sometimes templates have sample text.

5. **Type Slide Title Here, click the content placeholder, type Bulleted list, press [Enter], press [Tab], type Bulleted list, click the Layout button in the Slides group, then click Title and Content**

   Sample text replaces the text, and the slide layout changes to the Title and Content slide layout.

6. **Click the Slide 1 thumbnail in the Slides tab, press [Shift], select the three text objects on the slide, then press [Delete]**

   The WordArt object and the text in the text objects are deleted.

7. **Click the title text placeholder, type QST Template, click the subtitle placeholder, type Subtitle text here, then save your changes**

8. **Click the View tab, then click the Slide Sorter button in the Presentation Views group**

   Figure D-17 shows the final template presentation in Slide Sorter view.

9. **Save your work, print the template presentation as handouts (2 per page), close the presentation, then exit PowerPoint**

FIGURE D-16: Save As dialog box showing Templates folder

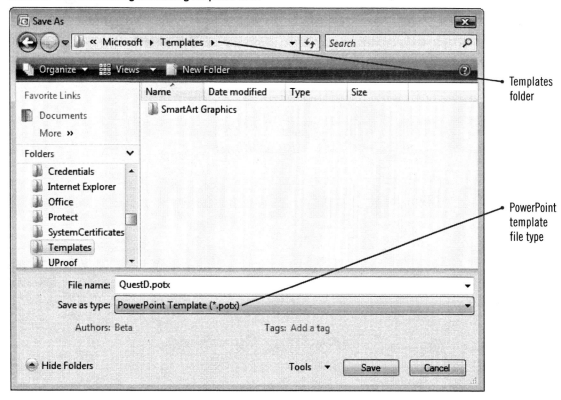

Templates folder

PowerPoint template file type

FIGURE D-17: Completed template presentation in Slide Sorter view

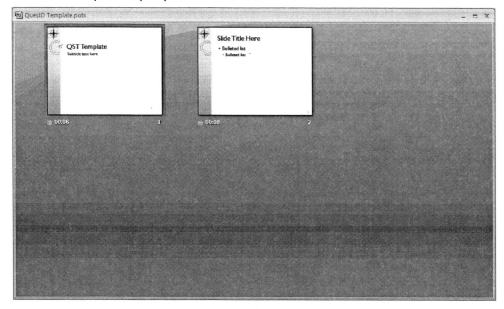

Applying a theme from another presentation

When you apply a theme from one presentation to another, you automatically apply the master layouts, colors and fonts over the existing presentation's theme. To apply a theme from another presentation, open the presentation you want to apply the theme to, click the Design tab, then click the Themes group More button.

Click Browse for Themes, use the Favorite Links or Folders pane to navigate to the presentation whose theme you want to apply. The presentation you select can be a regular presentation or a template with the .potx extension. Click the presentation name, then click Apply.

Finishing a Presentation

Practice

If you have a SAM user profile, you may have access to hands-on instruction, practice, and assessment of the skills covered in this unit. Log in to your SAM account (http://sam2007.course.com/) to launch any assigned training activities or exams that relate to the skills covered in this unit.

▼ CONCEPTS REVIEW

Label each element of the PowerPoint window shown in Figure D-18.

FIGURE D-18

Match each term with the statement that best describes it.

10. Animation tag
11. Background
12. Transitions
13. Masters
14. Metadata
15. Annotate

a. Visual effects that determine how a slide moves in and out of view during a slide show
b. Slides that store theme and placeholder information
c. To draw on a slide during a slide show
d. Includes document properties such as the author's name
e. Identifies the order in which objects are animated
f. The area behind text and graphics

Select the best answer from the list of choices.

16. Which of the following statements about masters is *not* true?

    a. Masters store information

    b. Changes made to the slide master are reflected in the handout and notes masters as well

    c. Each slide layout in the presentation has a corresponding slide layout in the Slide Master view

    d. The design theme is placed on the master slide

17. According to the book, an object placed on the slide master defines which item?

    a. A background graphic

    b. A logo

    c. A shape

    d. A master placeholder

18. What is the effect called that determines how a slide moves in and out of view during a slide show?

    a. Theme

    b. Animation

    c. Timing

    d. Transition

19. What is the effect called that controls how an object appears on the screen during a slide show?

    a. Transition

    b. Animation

    c. Path

    d. Template

20. The Document Inspector can do all of the following *except*,

    a. look for hidden data

    b. delete metadata

    c. remove on-slide content

    d. locate presentation notes

21. A PowerPoint file that *can't* be edited or modified defines what type of file?

    a. A marked as final file

    b. A template file

    c. An inspected file

    d. A file saved in another file format

22. According to the book, which standard should you follow to evaluate a presentation?

    a. Slides should include most of the information you wish to present

    b. The message should be outlined in a concise way.

    c. Use many different design elements to keep your audience from getting bored.

    d. Replace visuals with text as often as possible.

23. Which of the following statements about templates is *not* true?

    a. The file extension .potx is applied to the PowerPoint file when you save it as a template.

    b. You can create a template from a new presentation.

    c. A template is a type of presentation that contains custom design information.

    d. A template is designed to create custom slide layouts.

▼ SKILLS REVIEW

1. Understand masters.

    a. Open the presentation PPT D-3.pptx from the drive and folder where you store your Data Files, then save the presentation as **MediaCom**.

    b. Open the Slide Master view using the View tab, then click the Civic Slide Master thumbnail.

    c. Insert the picture PPT D-4.jpg, then resize the picture so it is 0.8" wide.

d. Drag the picture to the upper right corner of the slide within the design frame of the slide, then deselect the picture.

e. Switch to Normal view, then save your changes.

2. Customize the background style.

a. Switch to Slide 2, click the Design tab, then open the background styles gallery.

b. Change the background style to Style 3.

c. Open the Format Background dialog box.

d. Set the Transparency to 25%, then apply the background to all of the slides.

e. Close the dialog box, switch to Slide Master view, then open the Civic Slide Master slide.

f. Select the inserted picture, then use the Picture Tools Format tab to make its background transparent.

g. Switch to Normal view, then save your changes.

3. Use slide show commands.

a. Begin the slide show on Slide 1, then proceed to Slide 4.

b. Use the Felt Tip Pen to circle the words Early Adopters, Mass Adopters, and Late Adopters.

c. Use the Pen Options menu button to erase all ink on the slide, then change the pointer back to the Arrow.

d. Right-click the slide and go to Slide 8, use the Highlighter pointer to highlight each bullet on the slide.

e. Press [Home], then advance through the slide show, don't save any ink annotations, then save your work.

4. Set slide show transitions and timings.

a. Go to Slide 1, then apply the Wheel Clockwise, 8 Spokes transition in the Wipes group to all of the slides.

b. Change the transition speed to slow, then switch to Slide Sorter view.

c. Change the slide timing to 5 seconds, then apply to all of the slides.

d. Click Slide 10, then apply the Applause sound.

e. Click Slide 1, then switch to Normal view.

f. View the slide show, then save your work.

5. Set slide show animation effects.

a. Go to Slide 2, then open the Custom Animation task pane.

b. Apply the Emphasis Flash Bulb effect to the title text object, then apply the Entrance Unfold effect to both bulleted text objects.

c. On Slide 3 apply the Emphasis Shimmer effect to the title text object, then apply the Entrance Rise Up effect to the bulleted text object.

d. On Slide 4 apply the Entrance Flip effect to the title text object, then apply an Entrance animation effect of your choice from the Exciting group to the six individual objects in the graphic.

e. Apply animation effects to the rest of the slides in the presentation. Animate all of the text objects and the other objects.

f. Edit the animations effects as needed, then save your changes.

g. Compare your presentation to Figure D-19.

FIGURE D-19: Completed presentation

6. Inspect a presentation.

   a. Open the Document Properties pane, type **Internet Product** in the Subject text box, then type **Review** in the Status text box

   b. Close the Document Properties pane, then open the Document Inspector dialog box.

   c. Make sure the Off-Slide Content check box is selected, then inspect the presentation.

   d. Delete the off-slide content, and the presentation notes, then close the dialog box.

   e. Save your changes.

7. Evaluate a presentation.

   a. Go to Slide 1, then run a slide show.

   b. Evaluate the presentation using the points described in the lesson as criteria.

   c. Move Slide 6 below Slide 8.

   d. Save your work, then print the slides of your presentation.

8. Create a template.

   a. Save the presentation as a template (.potx) with the name **MediaCom Template** to the drive and folder where your Data Files are stored.

   b. Delete all slides except Slide 1 and Slide 2.

   c. Delete the picture and text on Slide 2, type **Slide Title Here** in the title text placeholder, type **Bulleted List 1** in the left content placeholder, then type **Bulleted List 2** in the right content placeholder.

   d. Delete the subtitle text object on Slide 1, then type **QST MediaCom Template** in the title text object in place of the current text.

   e. Delete the slide transitions and animations on both slides.

   f. Save your work, then print the presentation as handouts, two slides per page.

   g. Close the presentation, then exit PowerPoint.

▼ INDEPENDENT CHALLENGE 1

You are a travel consultant for Turner Travel, located in Portland, Oregon. You have been working on a sales presentation that is going to be accessed by customers on the company Web site. You need to finish up what you have been working on by adding transitions, timings, and animation effects to the sales presentation.

   a. Open the file PPT D-5.pptx from the drive and folder where you store your Data Files, and save the presentation as **TurnerTravel**.

   b. Add your name as the footer on all slides and handouts.

   c. Apply the Fade Through Black slide transitions to all of the slides.

   d. Apply the Entrance Glide animation to the title text on each slide.

   e. Apply the Emphasis Flicker animation to the bulleted text objects on each slide.

   f. Apply the Entrance Thread animation to the table on Slide 8.

   g. Apply a 10 second slide timing to each slide, then change the transition speed to Medium.

   h. Spell check the presentation, then save it.

   i. View the slide show, and evaluate your presentation. Make changes if necessary.

   j. Print the slides as handouts (six slides per page), then close the presentation, and exit PowerPoint.

▼ INDEPENDENT CHALLENGE 2

You are a development engineer at FarNorth Sports, Inc., an international sports product design company located in Winnipeg, Manitoba, Canada. FarNorth Sports designs and manufactures items such as bike helmets, bike racks, and kayak paddles, and markets these items primarily to countries in North America and Western Europe. You need to finish the work on a quarterly presentation that outlines the progress of the company's newest technologies by adding animations, customizing the background, and using the Document Inspector.

    a. Open the file PPT D-6.pptx from the drive and folder where you store your Data Files, and save the presentation as **FarNorth**.

    b. Apply an appropriate design theme, then apply a new slide background style. Make sure the new background style is appropriate for the design theme you have chosen.

    c. Apply the Box Out slide transition to all slides, then animate the following objects: the text on Slide 2, the clip art object on Slide 3, the table on Slide 4, and the chart on Slide 6. View the slide show to evaluate the effects you added and make adjustments as necessary.

    d. Run the Document Inspector with all options selected, identify what items the Document Inspector finds, close the Document Inspector dialog box, then review the slides to find the items.

    e. Add a slide at the end of the presentation that identifies the items the Document Inspector found.

    f. Run the Document Inspector again and remove all items except the document properties.

Advanced Challenge Exercise

- ■ Click the Rehearse Timings button on the Slide Sorter toolbar.
- ■ Set slide timings for each slide in the presentation.
- ■ Save new slide timings.

    g. Add your name as a footer to the handouts, save your work, then run a slide show to evaluate your presentation.

    h. Print the presentation as handouts (four slides per page), then close the presentation and exit PowerPoint.

▼ INDEPENDENT CHALLENGE 3

You work for JB & Associates Financial, a full service investment and pension firm. Your boss wants you to create a presentation on small business pension plan options to be published on the company Web site. You have completed adding the information to the presentation, now you need to add a design theme, format some information, add some animation effects, and add slide timings.

    a. Open the file PPT D-7.pptx from the drive and folder where you store your Data Files, and save the presentation as **SBPlans**.

    b. Apply an appropriate design theme.

    c. Apply animation effects to the following objects: the shapes on Slide 3 and the text and clip art on Slide 5. View the slide show to evaluate the effects you added and make adjustments as necessary.

    d. Convert the text on Slide 4 to a Basic Radial SmartArt graphic (Found in the Cycle category).

    e. Apply the Polished style to the SmartArt graphic, then change the colors of the graphic to Colorful Range – Accent Colors 2 to 3

    f. Switch to Slide 3, align the Sector and Quality arrow shapes to one another, then align the Allocation and Maturity arrow shapes to one another.

    g. Adjust the aligned arrow shapes so they are centered on the Buy/Sell oval shape, then apply a 15 second timing to Slides 3–7 and a 5 second timing to Slides 1 and 2.

Advanced Challenge Exercise

- Open the Slide Master view, select the last slide layout, then click the Insert Layout button.
- Click the Insert Placeholder button arrow, click Table, then drag a placeholder in the blank area of the master slide layout. (*Hint*: Draw the table placeholder so it takes up most of the blank space in the layout.)
- Return to Normal view, apply the new Custom Layout to Slides 6 and 7. Adjust the placeholder in Slide Master view if necessary.

h. Add your name as a footer to the handouts, save your work, then run a slide show to evaluate your presentation.

i. Print the presentation as handouts (four slides per page), then close the presentation and exit PowerPoint.

▼ REAL LIFE INDEPENDENT CHALLENGE

You work for the operations supervisor at the Southern State University student union. Create a presentation that you can eventually publish to the college Web site that describes all of the services offered at the student union.

a. Plan and create the slide presentation that describes the services and events offered at the student union. To help create content, use the student union at your school or use the Internet to locate information on college student unions. The presentation should contain at least six slides.

b. Use an appropriate design theme.

c. Add clip art and photographs available in the Clip Organizer to help create visual interest.

d. Save the presentation as **SSU Services** to the drive and folder where you store your Data Files. View the slide show and evaluate the contents of your presentation. Make any necessary adjustments.

e. Add transitions, animation effects, and timings to the presentation. View the slide show again to evaluate the effects you added.

f. Add your name as a footer to the handouts. Spell check, save, inspect, and print the presentation as handouts (four slides per page). Compare your finished presentation to Figure D-20.

g. Create a template from this presentation. Delete unnecessary slides and objects, type appropriate sample text if necessary, then save the presentation as **SSU Services Template** to the drive and folder where you store your Data Files.

h. Close the presentation and exit PowerPoint.

FIGURE D-20

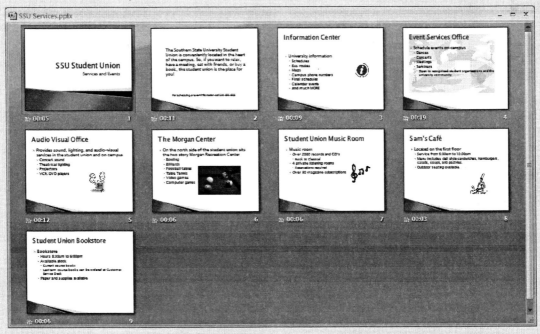

▼ VISUAL WORKSHOP

Open the file PPT D-8.pptx, then save the presentation as a template (.potx) with the filename **Island Travel Template** to the drive and folder where you store your Data Files. Change the presentation to look like Figures D-21 and D-22. Be sure to remove all unnecessary information, objects, and slides from the template presentation. Add your name as a footer to the slides.

FIGURE D-21

FIGURE D-22

Glossary

3½" disk *See* Floppy disk.

Absolute cell reference In a formula, a type of cell address that does not change when you copy the formula; indicated by a dollar sign before the column letter and/or row number. *See also* Relative cell reference.

Accessories Built-in programs that come with Windows Vista and XP, such as the Calculator for performing calculations.

Active The currently available document, program, or object; on the taskbar, the button of the active document appears in a darker shade while the buttons of other open documents are dimmed.

Active cell The cell in which you are currently working.

Active program The program that you are using, differentiated from other open programs by a highlighted program button on the taskbar and a differently colored title bar.

Active window The window that you are currently using, differentiated from other open windows by a differently colored title bar.

Address bar (Windows) A horizontal box near the top of a window (such as My Computer and Windows Explorer) that shows your current location in the computer's file hierarchy as a series of links separated by arrows, and that allows you to navigate to other locations on your computer. (Internet Explorer) The area below the toolbar that displays the address of the Web page currently opened.

Adjustment handle A small yellow diamond that changes the appearance of an object's most prominent feature.

Adware Software installed with another program that generates advertising revenue for the program's creator by displaying targeted ads to the program's user.

Align To place an objects' edges or centers on the same plane.

Alignment In Word, the position of text in a document relative to the margins; in Excel, the position of text in a cell relative to the cell edges, such as left, center, or right.

Alignment command In Access, a command used in Layout or Design View for a form or report to either left-, center-, or right-align a value within its control, or to align the top, bottom, right, or left edge of the control with respect to other controls.

American Standard Code for Information Interchange *See* ASCII.

Analog signal A continuous wave signal (sound wave) that can traverse ordinary phone lines.

AND criteria Criteria placed in the same row of the query design grid. All criteria on the same row must be true for a record to appear on the resulting datasheet.

Animation tag Identifies the order an object is animated on a slide during a slide show.

Annotate A freehand drawing on the PowerPoint screen made by using the Annotation tool. You can annotate only in Slide Show view.

Anti-spyware software Software that detects and removes spyware.

Antivirus software Software that searches executable files for the sequences of characters that may cause harm and disinfects the files by erasing or disabling those commands; *also called* virus protection software.

Application software Software that enables you to perform specific computer tasks, such as document production, spreadsheet calculations, database management, and presentation preparation.

Appointment In the Calendar in Outlook, an activity that does not involve inviting other people or scheduling resources.

Architecture The design and construction of a computer; *also called* configuration.

Argument Information that a function uses to create the final answer. Multiple arguments are separated by commas. All of the arguments for a function are surrounded by a single set of parentheses.

Arithmetic operators In a formula, symbols that perform mathematical calculations, such as plus (+), minus (–), multiply (*), divide (/), or exponentiation (^).

ASCII (American Standard Code for Information Interchange) The number system that personal computers use to represent character data.

Attachment A file, such as a picture, audio clip, video clip, document, worksheet, or presentation, that is sent in addition to an e-mail message composed by typing in the Message window.

Attributes Styling characteristics such as bold, italics, and underlining that you can apply to change the way text and numbers look in a worksheet or chart.

AutoComplete A feature that automatically suggests text to insert.

AutoCorrect A feature that automatically detects and corrects typing errors, minor spelling errors, and capitalization, and inserts certain typographical symbols as you type.

AutoFill Options button A feature that lets you fill cells with specific elements of the copied cell (such as formatting).

AutoFit A feature that automatically adjusts the width of a column or the height of a row to accommodate its widest or tallest entry.

Automatic page break A page break that is inserted automatically at the bottom of a page.

Autonumber A field data type in which Access enters a sequential integer for each record added into the datasheet. Numbers cannot be reused even if the record is deleted.

AutoText A feature that stores frequently used text and graphics so they can be easily inserted into a document.

Avg function Built-in Access function used to calculate the average of the values in a given field.

Axis label Text in a chart that identifies data.

.bmp The abbreviation for the bitmap graphics file format.

Back Color property A property that determines the background color of the selected control or section in a form or report.

Back up To save files to another location in case you have computer trouble and lose files.

Background The area behind the text and graphics on a slide.

Background graphic An object placed on the slide master.

Backward-compatible Software feature that enables documents saved in an older version of a program to be opened in a newer version of the program.

Bibliography A list of sources that you consulted or cited while creating a document.

Binary digit (bit) The representation of data as a 1 or 0.

Binding The field binding determines the field to which a bound control in a form or report is connected.

Bit *See* Binary digit.

Bits per second (bps) The unit of measurement for the speed of data transmission.

Blind courtesy copy (BCC) In e-mail, a way to send a message to a recipient who needs to be aware of the correspondence between the sender and the recipients, but is not the primary recipient of the message; used when the sender does not want to reveal who he or she has sent courtesy copies to.

Blog An informal journal that is created by an individual or a group and available to the public on the Internet; short for Weblog.

Blogger The person who creates and maintains a blog.

Bluetooth A wireless technology standard that allows electronic devices to use short range radio waves to communicate with one another or connect to the Internet; the radio waves can be transmitted around corners and through walls.

Bold Formatting applied to text to make it thicker and darker.

Boolean filter A word or symbol for locating programs, folders, and files by specifying or more criteria so that you have a greater chance of finding what you need.

Boot process The set of events that occurs between the moment you turn on the computer and the moment you can begin to use the computer.

Booting A process that Windows steps through to get the computer up and running.

Border A line that can be added above, below, or to the sides of a paragraph, text, or table cell; a line that divides the columns and rows of a table.

Bound control A control used in either a form or report to display data from the underlying field; used to edit and enter new data in a form.

bps *See* Bits per second.

Browser A program, such as Microsoft Internet Explorer, designed to access the Internet.

Browser window The specific area on the screen where the current Web page appears.

Building block Reusable piece of formatted content or a document part that is stored in a gallery.

Bullet A small graphic symbol used to identify items in a list.

Bullet mark A solid circle that indicates that an option is enabled.

Byte One character of storage space on disk or in RAM.

Cable Plastic-enclosed wires that attach a peripheral device to a computer port.

Cache memory Special high-speed memory chips on the motherboard or CPU that store frequently-accessed and recently-accessed data and commands; *also called* RAM cache *or* CPU cache.

Calculation A new value that is created by entering an expression in a text box on a form or report.

Calculation operators Symbols that indicate what type of calculation to perform on the cells, ranges, or values.

Calendar In Microsoft Outlook, provides a convenient way to manage your appointments and events.

Calendar icon An icon you can click to select a date from a pop-up calendar.

Calendar picker A pop-up calendar from which you can choose dates for a date field.

Capacity The amount of information a disk can hold, usually measured in megabytes (MB) or gigabytes (GB).

Card A removable circuit board that is inserted into a slot in the motherboard to expand the capabilities of the motherboard.

Cascading menu In Windows XP, a list of commands from a menu item with an arrow next to it; pointing to the arrow displays a submenu from which you can choose additional commands.

Categories In Outlook, a feature used to tag items so you can track and organize them by specific criteria.

Category axis Horizontal axis of a chart, usually containing the names of data groups; in a 2-dimensional chart, also known as the x-axis.

Cathode ray tube monitor *See* CRT monitor.

CD (compact disc) An optical storage device that can contain programs, music, movies, or your own personal files. A CD can store approximately 700 MB of data.

CD drive A drive that can read a CD (compact disc).

CD-R (compact disc recordable) A CD that on which you can record data with a laser that changes the reflectivity of a dye layer on the blank disk, creating dark spots on the disk's surface that represent the data; once the data is recorded, you cannot erase or modify it.

CD-ROM (compact disc read-only memory) A CD that contains software or music when you purchase it, but you cannot record additional data on it.

CD-RW (compact disc rewritable) A CD on which you can record data as on a CD-R, and then delete or re-record data on it as needed.

Cell The intersection of a column and a row in a worksheet, datasheet, or table.

Cell address The location of a cell, expressed by cell coordinates; for example, the cell address of the cell in column A, row 1 is A1.

Cell pointer A dark rectangle that outlines the active cell.

Cell styles Predesigned combinations of formatting attributes that can be applied to selected cells, to enhance the look of a worksheet.

Center Alignment in which an item is centered between the margins.

Central processing unit (CPU) *See* Microprocessor.

Channel The medium, such as telephone or coaxial cable, over which a message is sent in data communications.

Character spacing Formatting that changes the width or scale of characters, expands or condenses the amount of space between characters, raises or lowers characters relative to the line of text, and adjusts kerning (the space between standard combinations of letters).

Characters per second (cps) The unit of measurement for the speed of dot matrix printers.

Chart A graphical representation of numerical data from a worksheet that make it easier to see patterns, trends, and relationships. Types include 2-D and 3-D column, bar, pie, area, and line charts; *also called* graph.

Chart sheet A separate sheet in a workbook that contains only a chart, which is linked to the workbook data.

Check box A box that turns an option on when checked or off when unchecked.

Check mark A mark that indicates that a feature is enabled.

Chip An integrated circuit embedded in semiconductor material.

Circuit A path along which an electric current travels.

Circuit board A rigid piece of insulating material with circuits on it that control specific functions.

Classic style A Windows XP setting in which you single-click to select items and double-click to open them.

Click To quickly press and release the left button on the pointing device; *also called* single-click.

Click and Type A feature that allows you to automatically apply the necessary paragraph formatting to a table, graphic, or text when you insert the item in a blank area of a document in Print Layout or Web Layout view.

Click and Type pointer A pointer used to move the insertion point and automatically apply the paragraph formatting necessary to insert text at that location in the document.

Client A computer networked to and dependent on a server.

Client/server network A network with a server and computers dependent on the server.

Clip A media file, such as a graphic, photograph, sound, movie, or animation, that can be inserted into an Office document.

Clip art A collection of predesigned graphic images that can be inserted into documents, presentations, Web pages, spreadsheets, and other Office files to enhance their appearance.

Clip Organizer A library of art, pictures, sounds, video clips, and animations that all Office applications share.

Clipboard A temporary storage area on your computer's hard disk containing items that are cut or copied from any Office file and are available for pasting. *See also* Office Clipboard and System Clipboard.

Clock speed The pulse of the processor measured in megahertz or gigahertz.

Close To quit a program or remove a window from the desktop. The Close button is usually located in the upper-right corner of a window.

CMOS *See* Complementary metal oxide semiconductor memory.

Collapse button A button that shrinks a portion of a dialog box to hide some settings.

Column break A break that forces text following the break to begin at the top of the next column.

Column heading Shaded boxes located at the top of each column in a worksheet that contain letters identifying each column, such as A, B, etc.

Column separator The thin line that separates the Access field names to the left or right.

Combo box A bound control used to display a list of possible entries for a field in which you can also type an entry from the keyboard. It is a "combination" of the list box and text box controls.

Command An instruction to a program that causes it to perform a task.

Command bar Provides buttons for many options, such as printing Web pages, adding Favorites, and searching for information on the Internet.

Command button In a dialog box, a button that carries out or cancels an action. A command button usually has a label that describes its action, such as Cancel or Help. If the label is followed by an ellipsis (…), clicking the button displays another dialog box.

Compact disc *See* CD.

Compact disc read-only memory *See* CD-ROM.

Compact disc recordable *See* CD-R.

Compact disc rewritable *See* CD-RW.

Comparison operators In a calculation, symbols that compare values for the purpose of true/false results.

Compatible The capability of different programs to work together and exchange data.

Complementary metal oxide semiconductor (CMOS) memory A chip installed on the motherboard powered by a battery whose content changes every time you add or remove hardware on your computer system and that is activated during the boot process so it can identify where essential software is stored; *also called* semipermanent memory.

Compress To reduce the size of a file so that it takes up less storage space on a disk.

Computer An electronic device that accepts input, processes data, displays output, and stores data for retrieval later. (Windows Vista) A program that you use the manage the drives, folders, and files on your computer.

Computer network The hardware and software that makes it possible for two or more computers to share information and resources.

Computer system A computer, its peripheral devices, and software.

Computer window The window that shows the drives on your computer and as well as other installed hardware components.

Conditional format A type of cell formatting that changes based on the cell's value or the outcome of a formula.

Configuration *See* Architecture.

Contacts In Microsoft Outlook, enables you to manage all your business and personal contact information.

Content control An interactive object that is embedded in a document you create from a template and which expedites your ability to customize the document with your own information.

Content placeholder In PowerPoint, a slide area that is used to enter text or objects such as clip art, charts, or pictures.

Context-sensitive help Help that is specifically related to what you are doing.

Contextual tab A tab on the Ribbon that appears when needed to complete a specific task; for example, if you select a chart in an Excel workbook or a PowerPoint slide, three contextual Chart Tool tabs (Design, Layout, and Format) appear.

Control Any element on a form or report such as a label, text box, line, or combo box. Controls can be bound, unbound, or calculated.

Control Panel A set of Windows XP or Windows Vista tools used to change computer settings such as desktop colors or mouse settings.

Control Source property A property of a bound control in a form or report that determines the field to which the control is connected.

Controller card A card that plugs into a slot on the motherboard and connects to a port to provide an electrical connection to a peripheral device; *also called* expansion card *or* interface card.

Copy To place information onto the Clipboard in order to paste it in another location but also leave it in the original location.

Copy-and-paste operation The feature in document production software that allows you to duplicate selected words and objects somewhere else in the document.

Courtesy copy (CC) In e-mail, a way to send a message to a recipient who needs to be aware of the correspondence between the sender and the recipients, but is not the primary recipient of the message.

cps *See* Characters per second.

CPU *See* Microprocessor.

CPU cache *See* Cache memory.

Criteria Entries (rules and limiting conditions) that determine which records are displayed when finding or filtering records in a datasheet or form, or when building a query.

Criteria syntax Rules by which criteria need to be entered. For example, text criteria syntax requires that the criteria are surrounded by quotation marks (" "). Date criteria are surrounded by pound signs (#).

Crop To hide part of an object, such as clip art, using the Cropping tool or to delete a part of a picture.

CRT (cathode ray tube) monitor A monitor that uses gun-like devices to direct beams of electrons toward the screen to activate dots of color to form an image.

Current record The record that has the focus or is being edited.

Cut To remove information from a file and place it on the Clipboard, usually to be pasted into another location.

Cut and paste To move text or graphics using the Cut and Paste commands.

Cut-and-paste operation The feature in document production software that allow you to delete words and objects from one place in a document and place them somewhere else.

Data The words, numbers, figures, sounds, and graphics that describe people, events, things, and ideas.

Data bus The path between the microprocessor, RAM, and the peripherals along which communication travels.

Data communications The transmission of data from one computer to another or to a peripheral device via a channel using a protocol.

Data file A file created by a user, usually with software, such as a report that you write with a word processing program.

Data marker A graphical representation of a data point, such as a bar or column.

Data point An individual piece of data plotted in a chart.

Data series A column or row in a datasheet. Also, the selected range in a worksheet that Excel converts into a chart.

Data series marker A graphical representation of a data series, such as a bar or column.

Data type A required property for each field that defines the type of data that can be entered in each field. Valid data types include AutoNumber, Text, Number, Currency, Date/Time, OLE Object, and Memo.

Database A collection of information stored on one or more computers organized in a uniform format of records and fields.

Database designer The person responsible for building and maintaining tables, queries, forms, and reports.

Database management software Software you use to collect and manage data.

Datasheet A spreadsheet-like grid that displays fields as columns and records as rows.

Datasheet View A view that lists the records of the object in a datasheet. Tables, queries, and most form objects have a Datasheet View.

Date function A built-in Access function used to display the current date on a form or report; enter the Date function as Date( ).

Date Navigator A monthly calendar in the To-Do Bar that gives you an overview of the month and enables selection of a specific date to appear.

Default Settings preset by the operating system or program.

Delete (Office) To permanently remove an item from a document. (Windows) To place a file or folder in the Recycle Bin, where you can either remove it from the disk permanently or restore it to its original location.

Deleted Items folder The folder that stores items when you delete or erase a message from any mail folder, rather than being immediately, permanently deleted; *also called* trash folder.

Design View A view in which the structure of the object can be manipulated. Every Access object has a Design View.

Desktop The graphical user interface (GUI) displayed on your screen after you start Windows that you use to interact with Windows and other software on your computer.

Desktop computer A personal computer designed to sit compactly on a desk.

Destination file In integration, the file that receives copied information. A Word file that contains an Excel spreadsheet or chart is a destination file.

Details Pane A pane located at the bottom of a window that displays information about the selected disk, drive, folder, or file.

Device A hardware component in your computer system.

Device driver System software that handles the transmission protocol between a computer and its peripheral devices; *also called* driver.

Dialog box A window that opens when a program needs more information to carry out a command.

Dialog box launcher An icon available in many groups on the Ribbon that you can click to open a dialog box or task pane, offering an alternative way to choose commands. *Also called* Launcher.

Digital signal A stop-start signal that your computer outputs.

Digital signature A way to authenticate a computer user's files using computer cryptography. A digital signature is not visible in a file.

Digital subscriber line *See* DSL.

Diskette *See* Floppy disk.

Distribute To evenly divide the space horizontally or vertically between objects relative to each other or the slide edges.

Distribution list A collection of contacts to whom you want to send the same messages; makes it possible for you to send a message to the same group without having to select each contact in the group.

DNS server A computer responsible for directing Internet traffic.

Document An electronic file that you create using a program such as Word or WordPad.

Document Inspector An Office feature that examines a document for hidden data or personal information.

Document production software Software, such as word processing software, desktop publishing software, e-mail editors, and Web authoring software, that assists you in writing and formatting documents, including changing the font and checking the spelling.

Document properties Details about a file, such as author name or the date the file was created, that are used to describe, organize, and search for files.

Document window The portion of a program window that displays all or part of an open document.

Documents folder The folder on your hard drive used to store most of the files you create or receive from others.

Dot matrix printer A printer that transfers ink to paper by striking a ribbon with pins.

Dot pitch (dp) The distance between pixels on a monitor.

Double-click To press and release the left mouse button twice quickly.

dp *See* Dot pitch.

Draft view A view that shows a document without margins, headers and footers, or graphics.

Drag To point to an object, press and hold the left button on the pointing device, move the object to a new location, and then release the left button.

Drag and drop *See* Drag.

Drive A device that reads and saves files on a disk and is also used to store files; floppy drives read and save files on floppy disks, whereas hard drives read and save files on your computer's built-in hard disk.

Drive name A name for a drive that consists of a letter followed by a colon, such as C: for the hard disk drive.

Driver *See* Device driver.

Drop cap A large dropped initial capital letter that is often used to set off the first paragraph of an article.

Drop-down list button A button that opens a list with one or more options from which you can choose.

DSL (digital subscriber line) A high-speed connection over phone lines.

Dual-core processor A CPU that has two processors on the chip.

DVD An optical storage device that can store up to 15.9 GB of data; was originally an acronym for *digital video disc* and later *digital versatile disc*.

Edit To change the content or format of an existing file.

Edit mode The mode in which Access assumes you are trying to edit a particular field, so keystrokes such as [Ctrl][End], [Ctrl][Home], [], and [ ] move the insertion point within the field.

Edit record symbol A pencil-like symbol that appears in the record selector box to the left of the record that is currently being edited in either a datasheet or a form.

Electronic mail (e-mail) The technology that makes it possible for you to send and receive messages through the Internet.

Electronic spreadsheet A computer program that performs calculations and presents numeric data.

E-mail *See* Electronic mail.

E-mail message The message sent using e-mail technology.

E-mail software Enables you to send and receive e-mail messages over a network, within an intranet, and through the Internet.

Embed To place an object such as a text selection, value, or picture created in a source file into a destination file. An embedded object is edited by double-clicking it in the destination file and then using the tools of the source file to make changes. These changes appear only in the embedded object in the destination file, not in the source file.

Embedded chart A chart displayed as an object in a worksheet.

Embedded object An object that is created in one application and inserted to another. Embedded objects remain connected to the original program file in which they were created for easy editing.

Endnote Text that provides additional information or acknowledges sources for text in a document and that appears at the end of a document.

Ergonomic Designed to fit the natural placement of the body to reduce the risk of repetitive-motion injuries.

Ethernet port A port used to connect computers in a LAN or sometimes directly to the Internet; it allows for high-speed data transmission.

Event In the Calendar in Outlook, an activity that lasts 24 hours or longer.

Executable file A file that contains the instructions that tell a computer how to perform a specific task, such as the files that are used during the boot process.

Expand button A button that extends a dialog box to display additional settings.

Expansion card *See* Controller card.

Expansion slot An electrical connector on the motherboard into which a card is plugged; *also called* slot.

Exploding pie slice A slice of a pie chart that has been pulled away from the whole pie, in order to add emphasis.

Explorer Bar The pane on the left side of the screen in Windows Explorer that lists all drives and folders on the computer.

Expression A combination of values, functions, and operators that calculates to a single value. Access expressions start with an equal sign and are placed in a text box in either Form Design View or Report Design View.

Favorites Center Stores and organizes the links to the Web pages that you want to revisit often. To open the Favorites Center, you click the Favorites Center button on the Command bar.

Field (Word) A code that serves as a placeholder for data that changes in a document, such as a page number. (Access) A piece of information in a record.

Field list A list of the available fields in the table or query that the field list represents.

Field name The name given to each field in a table.

Field selector The button to the left of a field in Table Design View that indicates which field is currently selected. Also the thin gray bar above each field in the query grid.

File An electronic collection of stored data, such as text, a picture, video, or music, that has a unique name, distinguishing it from other files. Word creates word processing files; Excel creates spreadsheet files; Access creates database files; and PowerPoint creates presentation files.

File extension Additional characters assigned by a program added to the end of a filename to identify the type of file.

File hierarchy A logical structure for folders and files that mimics how you would organize files and folders in a filing cabinet.

File management The process of organizing and keeping track of files and folders.

Filename A unique, descriptive name for a file that identifies the file's content. A filename can be no more than 255 characters, including spaces, and can include letters, numbers, and certain symbols.

Filter Used to create a subset of a list, a filter lets you search for only specific information—for example, in Outlook Contacts, filter only for those contacts that live in New Jersey, or in an Access database or an Excel table, filter only for customers whose sales total over a certain amount.

Filter By Form A way to filter data that allows two or more criteria to be specified at the same time.

Filter By Selection A way to filter records for an exact match.

Firewall Hardware or software that prevents other computers on the Internet from accessing a computer or prevents a program on a computer from accessing the Internet.

First line indent A type of indent in which the first line of a paragraph is indented more than the subsequent lines.

Flash drive *See* USB flash storage device.

Flash memory Memory that is similar to ROM except that it can be written to more than once.

Flash memory card A small, portable card encased in hard plastic to which data can be written and rewritten.

Flash storage device A removable storage device that is plugged into a USB port to which data can be written and rewritten; know by other names, including USB drive, jump drive, thumb drive, and flash drive.

Flat panel monitor A lightweight monitor that takes up very little room on the desktop and uses LCD technology to create the image on the screen.

Floating graphic A graphic to which text wrapping has been applied, making the graphic independent of text and able to be moved anywhere on a page.

Floppy disk A flat circle of magnetic iron oxide-coated plastic enclosed in a hard plastic case that can store 1.44 MB of data; *also called* diskette or 3½" disk.

Focus The property that indicates which field would be edited if you were to start typing.

Folder An area on a disk that contains a group of related files. A folder may contain subfolders for organizing files into smaller groups.

Folder name A unique, descriptive name for a folder that identifies what you store in that folder.

Font The typeface or design of a set of characters (letters, numerals, symbols, and punctuation marks), such as Times New Roman.

Font effect Font formatting that applies a special effect to text, such as a shadow, an outline, small caps, or superscript.

Font size The size of text characters, measured in units called points (pts); a point is equal to 1/72 inch.

Footer Information, such as text, a page number, or a graphic, that appears at the bottom of every page in a document or a section.

Footnote Text that provides additional information or acknowledges sources for text in a document and that appears at the bottom of the page on which the note reference mark appears.

Foreign key field In a one-to-many relationship between two tables, the foreign key field is the field in the "many" table that links the table to the primary key field in the "one" table.

Form An Access object that provides an easy-to-use data entry screen that generally shows only one record at a time.

Form View The view of a form object that displays data from the underlying recordset and allows you to enter and update data.

Form Wizard An Access wizard that helps you create a form.

Format (n.) 1) The appearance of text and numbers, including color, font, attributes, borders, and shading. *See also* Number format. 2) The process of preparing a disk so it can store information. (v.) To enhance the appearance of a document by, for example, changing the font or font size or adding borders and shading to a document. Also refers to the process of preparing a disk so it can store information.

Format bar A toolbar in the WordPad window that displays buttons for formatting, or enhancing, the appearance of a document.

Format Painter A feature used to copy the format settings applied to the selected text to other text you want to format the same way.

Formatting marks Nonprinting characters that appear on screen to indicate the ends of paragraphs, tabs, and other formatting elements.

Formula A set of instructions used to perform one or more numeric calculations, such as adding, multiplying, or averaging, on values or cells.

Formula bar The area above the worksheet grid where you enter or edit data in the active cell.

Formula prefix An arithmetic symbol, such as the equal sign (=), used to start a formula.

Forwarding Sending an e-mail message you have received to someone else.

Full Screen Reading view A view that shows only the document text on screen, making it easier to read and annotate.

Function A built-in formula that provides a shortcut for a commonly used calculation, for example, SUM (for calculating a total) or COUNT (for counting items in a list).

Gadget A mini-program on the Windows Sidebar for performing an every day task, such as the Clock gadget for viewing the current time.

Gallery A collection of choices you can browse through to make a selection. Often available with Live Preview.

GB *See* Gigabyte.

GHz *See* Gigahertz.

Gigabyte (G or GB) 1,073,741,824 bytes, or about one billion bytes.

Gigahertz (GHz) One billion cycles per second.

Graph *See* Chart.

Graphic image *See* Image.

Graphical user interface (GUI) A computer environment in which the user manipulates graphics, icons, and dialog boxes to execute commands.

Graphics card The card installed on the motherboard that controls the signals the computer sends to the monitor; *also called* video display adapter or video card.

Graphics display A monitor that is capable of displaying graphics by dividing the screen into a matrix of pixels.

Graphics software Software that allows you to create illustrations, diagrams, graphs, and charts.

Gridlines Evenly spaced horizontal and/or vertical lines used in a worksheet or chart to make it easier to read.

Group 1) A collection of related commands on a tab on the Ribbon. 2) A combination of objects that has been changed into a single object so that when you move one of the objects, the others move with it.

Grouping To sort records in a particular order, plus provide a section before and after each group of records.

GUI *See* Graphical user interface.

Gutter Extra space left for a binding at the top, left, or inside margin of a document.

Hand-held computer A small computer designed to fit in the palm of your hand and that generally has fewer capabilities than personal computers.

Hanging indent A type of indent in which the second and subsequent lines of a paragraph are indented more than the first.

Hard copy A printed copy of computer output.

Hard disk A magnetic storage device that contains several magnetic oxide-covered metal platters that are usually sealed in a case inside the computer; used to store files and programs.

Hard page break *See* Manual page break.

Hardware The physical components of a computer.

Header Information, such as text, a page number, or a graphic, that appears at the top of every page in a document or a section.

Highlighting 1) Transparent color that can be applied to text to call attention to it. 2) When an icon is shaded differently, indicating it is selected. *See also* Select.

Home page The first Web page that opens every time you start Internet Explorer. Also applies to the main page that opens when you first go to a Web site.

Horizontal ruler A ruler that appears at the top of the document window in Print Layout, Draft, and Web Layout view.

Horizontal scroll bar *See* Scroll bar.

Hyperlink Text or a graphic that opens a file, Web page, or other item when clicked. Also known as a link.

I-beam pointer The pointer used to move the insertion point and select text.

Icon A small image on the desktop or in a window that represents a tool, resource, folder, or file you can open and use.

Image A nontextual piece of information such as a picture, piece of clip art, drawn object, or graph. Because images are graphical (and not numbers or letters), they are sometimes referred to as graphical images.

Inactive Describes a window or program that is open but not currently in use.

Inactive window An open window you are not currently using.

Inbox A mail folder that stores all incoming mail.

Indent The space between the edge of a line of text or a paragraph and the margin.

Indent marker A marker on the horizontal ruler that shows the indent settings for the active paragraph.

Infinity symbol The symbol that indicates the "many" side of a one-to-many relationship.

Information management software Software that keeps track of schedules, appointments, contacts, and "to-do" lists.

Infrared technology A wireless technology in which devices communicate with one another using infrared light waves; the devices must be positioned so that the infrared ports are pointed directly at one another.

Inkjet printer A printer that sprays ink onto paper and produces output whose quality is comparable to that of a laser printer.

Inline graphic A graphic that is part of a line of text.

Input The data or instructions you type into the computer.

Input and output (I/O) The flow of data from the microprocessor to memory to peripherals and back again.

Input device An instrument, such as a keyboard or a mouse, that you use to enter data and issue commands to the computer.

Insertion point A blinking vertical line that indicates where the next character will appear when text is entered in a Word document, an Excel cell or the formula bar, an Access record, a text placeholder in PowerPoint, or a filename in Windows.

Instant Search A Windows tool you use to quickly find a folder or file on your computer.

Integrate To incorporate a document and parts of a document created in one program into another program; for example, to incorporate an Excel chart into a PowerPoint slide, or an Access table into a Word document.

Integration The act of inserting and linking information among applications. *See also* Object Linking and Embedding.

Interface The look and feel of a program; for example, the appearance of commands and the way they are organized in the program window.

Interface card *See* Controller card.

Internet A network of connected computers and computer networks located around the world.

Intranet A computer network that connects computers in a local area only, such as computers in a company's office.

I/O *See* Input and output.

Is Not Null A criterion that finds all records in which any entry has been made in the field.

Is Null A criterion that finds all records in which no entry has been made in the field.

Italic Formatting applied to text to make the characters slant to the right.

Join line The line identifying which fields establish the relationship between two related tables.

Journal In Outlook, provides a trail of your activities within Microsoft Office by tracking all documents, spreadsheets, databases, presentations, or any Office file that you specify. When turned on, you can see a timeline of any calls, messages, appointments, or tasks.

Junk e-mail Unwanted mail that arrives from unsolicited sources. *Also called* spam.

Justify Alignment in which an item is flush with both the left and right margins.

K *See* Kilobyte.

KB *See* Kilobyte.

Keyboard The most frequently used input device; consists of three major parts: the main keyboard, the keypads, and the function keys.

Keyboard shortcut A combination of keys or a function key that can be pressed to perform a command (for example, [Ctrl][X] for Cut).

Keyword A descriptive word or phrase you enter to obtain a list of results that includes that word or phrase.

Kilobyte (KB or K) 1,024 bytes, or approximately one thousand bytes.

Labels Descriptive text or other information that identifies spreadsheet rows, columns, or chart data, but are not included in calculations.

LAN *See* Local area network.

Landscape orientation A print setting that positions a document so it spans the widest margins of the page, making the page wider than it is tall.

Laptop computer *See* Notebook computer.

Laser printer A printer that produces high-quality output quickly and efficiently by transferring a temporary laser image onto paper with toner.

Launch To open or start a program on your computer.

Launcher An icon available in many groups on the Ribbon that you can click to open a dialog box or task pane, offering an alternative way to choose commands. *Also called* dialog box launcher.

Layout view An Access view that lets you make some design changes to a form or report while you are browsing the data.

LCD (liquid crystal display) A display technology that creates images by manipulating light within a layer of liquid crystal.

Left-align Alignment in which the item is flush with the left margin.

Left function An Access function that returns a specified number of characters, starting with the left side of a value in a Text field.

Left indent A type of indent in which the left edge of a paragraph is moved in from the left margin.

Legend In a chart, an informative key that explains how information is represented by colors or patterns.

Line spacing The amount of space between lines of text.

Link (Office) A connection created between a source file and a destination file. When an object created in a source file is linked to a destination file, any changes made to the object in the source file also appear in the object contained in the destination file. (Windows) A shortcut for opening a Help topic or a Web site.

Linked object An object such as a text selection, value, or picture that is contained in a destination file and linked to a source file. When a change is made to the linked object in the source file, the change also occurs in the linked object in the destination file. *See also* Link.

Links bar A convenient place to store links to Web pages that you use often. Add a link to the Links bar by dragging the Internet Explorer icon that precedes the URL in the Address bar to the Links bar.

Liquid crystal display *See* LCD.

List box A box in a dialog box containing a list of items; to choose an item, click the list arrow, then click the desired item.

Live Preview A feature that lets you point to a choice in a gallery or palette and see the results in the document without actually clicking the choice.

Live taskbar thumbnails A Windows Aero feature that displays a small image of the content within open, but not visible windows, including live content such as video.

Live view In Windows Vista, a file icon that displays the actual content in a file on the icon.

Local area network (LAN) A network in which the computers and peripheral devices are located relatively close to each other, generally in the same building, and are usually connected with cables.

Lock To lock your user account, then display the Welcome screen.

Lock button A Start menu option that locks your computer.

Lock menu button A Start menu options that displays a list of shut-down options.

Log in To sign in with a user name and password before being able to use a computer.

Log Off To close all windows, programs, and documents, then display the Welcome screen.

Logical view The datasheet of a query is sometimes called a logical view of the data because it is not a copy of the data, but rather, a selected view of data from the underlying tables.

Macro An Access object that stores a collection of keystrokes or commands such as those for printing several reports in a row or providing a toolbar when a form opens.

Magnetic storage device A storage device that stores data as magnetized particles on mylar, a plastic, which is then coated on both sides with magnetic oxide.

Mainframe computer A computer used by larger business and government agencies that provides centralized storage, processing, and management for large amounts of data.

Malware A broad term that describes any program that is intended to cause harm or convey information to others without the owner's permission.

Manual page break A page break inserted to force the text following the break to begin at the top of the next page; *also called* hard page break.

Margin The blank area between the edge of the text and the edge of a page.

Masters In PowerPoint, one of three views that stores information about the presentation theme, fonts, placeholders, and other background objects. The three views are Slide Master view, Handout Master view, and Notes Master view.

Maximize To enlarge a window so it fills the entire screen. The Maximize button is usually located in the upper-right corner of a window.

MB *See* Megabyte.

Meeting In the Calendar in Outlook, an activity you invite people to or reserve resources for.

Megabyte (MB) 1,048,576 bytes, or about one million bytes.

Megahertz (MHz) One million cycles per second.

Memory A set of storage locations on the main circuit board that store instructions and data.

Memory capacity The amount of data that the device can handle at any given time; *also called* storage capacity.

Menu A list of related commands in a program (for example, the File menu).

Menu bar A bar near the top of a program window that provides access to most of a program's features through categories of related commands.

Message body In an e-mail message, where you write the text of your message.

Message header The area that contains the basic information about an e-mail message, including the sender's name and e-mail address, the names and e-mail addresses of recipients and CC recipients, a date and time stamp, and the subject of the message.

Metadata Another name for document properties that includes the author name, the document subject, the document title, and other personal information.

MHz *See* Megahertz.

Microprocessor A silicon chip, located on the motherboard, that is responsible for executing instructions to process data; *also called* processor *or* central processing unit (CPU).

Microsoft Graph A program that creates a chart to graphically depict numerical information when you don't have access to Microsoft Excel.

Microsoft Office Word Help button A button used to access the Word Help system.

Microsoft Windows Vista An operating system.

Microsoft Windows XP The operating system that preceded Windows Vista.

MIDI (musical instrument digital interface) card A sound card used to record and play back musical data.

Mini toolbar A toolbar that appears faintly above text when you first select it and includes the most commonly used text and paragraph formatting commands.

Minimize To reduce the size of a window; the Minimize button is usually located in the upper-right corner of a window.

Minimized window A window that shrinks to a button on the taskbar.

Mirror margins Margins used in documents with facing pages, where the inside and outside margins are mirror images of each other.

Mixed reference Cell reference that combines elements of both absolute and relative referencing.

Mode indicator An area in the lower-left corner of the status bar that informs you of a program's status. For example, when you are entering or changing the contents of a cell, the word 'Edit' appears.

Modem Stands for *mo*dulator-*dem*odulator; a device that converts the digital signals from your computer into analog signals that can traverse ordinary phone lines, and then converts analog signals back into digital signals at the receiving computer.

Module An Access object that stores Visual Basic programming code that extends the functions of automated Access processes.

Monitor The TV-like peripheral device that displays the output from the computer.

Motherboard The main circuit board of the computer on which processing tasks occur.

Mouse A pointing device that has a rolling ball or a laser on its underside and two or more buttons for clicking commands; some have a scroll wheel. You control the movement of the pointer by moving the entire mouse around on your desk or a special pad. *See also* Mouse pointer.

Mouse buttons The buttons on a mouse (right and left, and sometimes a middle button or wheel) that you use to make selections and issue commands in Windows or in an application program such as Microsoft Word.

Mouse pointer The typically arrow-shaped object on the screen that follows the movement of the mouse. The shape of the mouse pointer changes depending on the program and the task being executed. *See also* Mouse.

Move To change the location of a file by physically placing it in another location.

MP3 player A hand-held computer that is used primarily to play and store music, but that can also be used to watch digital movies and television shows.

Multilevel list A list with an hierarchical structure; an outline.

Multimedia authoring software Software that allows you to record digital sound files, video files, and animations that can be included in presentations and other documents.

Multi-tasking Working with more than one window or program at a time.

Musical instrument digital interface card *See* MIDI card.

My Computer In Windows XP, a program that you use to manage the drives, folders, and files on your computer. In Windows Vista, it is called simply Computer.

Name box Leftmost area of the formula bar that shows the cell reference or name of the active cell.

Named range A range of cells with a meaningful name such as "July Sales" instead of simply the range coordinates such as "C7:G7"; used to make it easier to reference data in a worksheet.

Navigate To move around in a worksheet; for example, you can use the arrow keys on the keyboard to navigate from cell to cell, or press [Page Up] or [Page Down] to move a screen at a time.

Navigation buttons Buttons in the lower-left corner of a datasheet or form that allow you to quickly navigate between the records in the underlying object as well as add a new record.

Navigation mode A mode in which Access assumes that you are trying to move between the fields and records of the datasheet (rather than edit a specific field's contents), so keystrokes such as [Ctrl][Home] and [Ctrl][End] move you to the first and last field of the datasheet.

Navigation Pane (Access) A pane in the Access program window that provides a way to move between objects (tables, queries, forms, reports, macros, and modules) in the database. (Outlook) In Normal view, it is typically on the left side of the screen, showing you the folder list in addition to the navigation shortcuts. (Windows) A pane on the left side of a window that contains links to your personal folders, including the Documents, Pictures, and Music folders.

Negative indent A type of indent in which the left edge of a paragraph is moved to the left of the left margin; *also called* outdent.

Network Two or more computers that share data and resources and which are connected to each other and to peripheral devices.

Network interface card (NIC) The card in a computer on a network that creates a communications channel between the computer and the network.

Network software Software that establishes the communications protocols that will be observed on the network and controls the "traffic flow" as data travels throughout the network.

NIC *See* Network interface card.

Node Any device connected to a network.

Nonvolatile memory *See* Read-only memory.

Normal view (PowerPoint) A presentation view that divides the presentation window into three sections: Slides or Outline tab, Slide pane, and Notes pane. (Excel) Default worksheet view that shows the worksheet without features such as headers and footers; ideal for creating and editing a worksheet, but may not be detailed enough when formatting a document.

Notebook computer A small, lightweight computer designed for portability; *also called* laptop computer.

Notes In Outlook, the electronic version of the sticky notes or Post-It™ notes you buy at your local stationery store; a convenient way to quickly jot down a reminder or an idea.

Notes Page view In PowerPoint, a presentation view that displays a reduced image of the current slide above a large text box where you can type notes.

Notes Pane In PowerPoint, the area in Normal view that shows speaker notes for the current slide; also in Notes Page view, the area below the slide image that contains speaker notes.

Notification area An area on the right side of the taskbar that displays the current time as well as icons for open programs, connecting to the Internet, and checking problems identified by Windows Vista.

Number format A format applied to values to express numeric concepts, such as currency, date, and percentage.

Object An item you place or draw in an Office document that can be modified. Objects include drawn lines and shapes, text, clip art, imported pictures, and charts.

Object Linking and Embedding (OLE) The term used to refer to the technology Microsoft uses to allow the integration of data between programs. Linking creates "live" connection between an object in a source file and a linked version in a destination file; embedding places an unconnected copy in the destination file.

Office button An element of Office 2007 program windows that provides access to commands for creating, opening, saving, printing, and sharing documents, and to options for personalizing the programs.

Office Clipboard A temporary storage area shared by all Office programs that can be used to cut, copy and paste multiple items within and between programs. The Office Clipboard can hold up to 24 items collected from any Office program. *See also* System Clipboard.

OLE *See* Object linking and embedding.

OLE object In Access, a field data type that stores pointers that tie files, such as pictures, sound clips, or spreadsheets, created in other programs to a record.

One-to-many line The line that appears in the Relationships window and shows which field is duplicated between two tables to serve as the linking field. The one-to-many line displays a "1" next to the field that serves as the "one" side of the relationship and displays an infinity symbol next to the field that serves as the "many" side of the relationship when referential integrity is specified for the relationship. Also called the one-to-many join line.

One-to-many relationship The relationship between two tables in an Access database in which a common field links the tables together. The linking field is called the primary key field in the "one" table of the relationship and the foreign key field in the "many" table of the relationship.

Online collaboration The ability to incorporate feedback or share information across the Internet or a company network or intranet.

Open To start a program or display a file.

Operating environment An operating system that provides a graphical user interface, such as Microsoft Windows and the MAC OS.

Operating system A computer program that controls the basic operation of your computer and the programs you run on it. Windows Vista and Windows XP are examples of operating systems. The operating system allocates system resources, manages storage space, maintains security, detects equipment failure, and controls basic input and output.

Optical storage device A polycarbonate disk coated with a reflective metal on which data is recorded using laser technology as a trail of tiny pits or dark spots in the surface of the disk; the data that these pits or spots represent can then be "read" with a beam of laser light.

Option button A small circle in a dialog box that you click to select an option.

OR criteria In Access, criteria placed on different rows of the query design grid. A record will appear in the resulting datasheet if it is true for any single row.

Orphan The first line of a paragraph when it appears alone at the bottom of a page.

Orphan record A record in the "many" table of a one-to-many relationship that doesn't have a matching entry in the linking field of the "one" table.

Outbox A temporary storage folder for e-mail messages that have not yet been sent.

Outdent *See* Negative indent.

Outline tab In PowerPoint, the section in Normal view that displays your presentation text in the form of an outline, without graphics.

Outline view In Word, view that shows the headings of a document organized as an outline.

Outlook Today Shows your day at a glance, like an electronic version of a daily planner book. When it is open, you can see what is happening in the Calendar, Tasks, and Messages for the day.

Output The result of the computer processing input.

Output device A device, such as a monitor or printer, that displays output.

Page Break Preview A worksheet view that shows page break indicators that you can drag to include more or less information on each page in a worksheet.

Page Layout View Provides an accurate view of how a worksheet will look when printed, including headers and footers.

Page orientation Printing or viewing a page of data in either a portrait (8.5 inches wide by 11 inches tall) or landscape (11 inches wide by 8.5 inches tall) direction.

Pages per minute (ppm) The unit of measurement for the speed of laser and inkjet printers.

Paint A graphics program that comes with Windows XP.

PAN *See* Personal area network.

Pane A section of a divided window.

Paragraph spacing The amount of space between paragraphs.

Parallel port A port that transmits data eight bits at a time.

Paste To insert items stored on the Clipboard into a document.

Paste Options button A button that appears next to a pasted object; it allows you to paste only specific elements of the copied selection, such as the formatting or values.

PDA (personal digital assistant) A hand-held computer that is generally used to maintain an electronic appointment book, address book, calculator, and notepad.

Peer-to-peer network A network in which all the computers essentially are equal, and programs and data are distributed among them.

Peripheral device The components of a computer that accomplish its input, output, and storage functions.

Permanent memory *See* Read-only memory.

Personal account In Outlook, identifies you as a user with information such as your e-mail address and password, the type of Internet service provider (ISP) you are using, and the incoming and outgoing mail server address for your ISP.

Personal area network (PAN) A network in which two or more devices communicate directly with each other.

Personal computer A computer typically used by a single user in the home or office for general computing tasks such as word processing, working with photographs or graphics, e-mail, and Internet access.

Personal digital assistant *See* PDA.

Pharm To break into a DNS server and redirect any attempts to access a particular Web site to a spoofed site.

Phish To send e-mails to customers or potential customers of a legitimate Web site asking them to click a link in the e-mail and then verify their personal information, which may then be used for illegal purposes; the link leads to a spoofed site.

Photo editing software Software that allows you to manipulate digital photos.

Picture A digital photograph, or a piece of line art or clip art that is created in another program and is inserted into an Office program.

Pin In Windows XP or Windows Vista, to place a program on the upper-left part of the Start menu for quick access.

Pixel (picture element) One of the small dots in a matrix into which a graphics display is divided.

Placeholder In PowerPoint, a dashed line box where you place text or objects.

Plot area In a chart, the area inside the horizontal and vertical axes.

Point 1) A unit of measure used for fonts and row height. One inch equals 72 points, or a point is equal to 1/72nd of an inch. 2) To position the mouse pointer in a particular location on your screen.

Pointer A small arrow or other symbol on the screen controlled by a pointing device.

Pointer trail A shadow of the mouse pointer that appears when you move the mouse (if you have the feature enabled); it helps you locate the pointer on your screen.

Pointing device A device, such as a mouse or trackball, that controls the pointer.

Pointing stick A small, eraser-like device embedded among the typing keys on a notebook computer that you push up, left, right, or down to move the pointer; buttons for clicking commands are located in front of the spacebar.

Pop-up A window that opens on your screen as you visit Web sites, generally to advertise products you may or may not want.

Port The interface between a cable and a controller card.

Portable computer card (PC card) A credit card–sized card that plugs directly into a slot in a notebook computer and that can contain additional RAM, a fax modem, or a hard disk drive (similar to a flash storage device).

Portrait orientation A print setting that positions the document on the page so the page is taller than it is wide.

Power button A Start menu option that puts your computer to sleep (your computer appears off and uses very little power).

PowerPoint Viewer A special application designed to run a PowerPoint slide show on any compatible computer that does not have PowerPoint installed.

Ppm *See* Pages per minute.

Presentation software A software program used to organize and present information.

Preview Prior to printing, to see onscreen exactly how the printed document will look.

Preview Pane A pane on the right side of a window that shows the actual contents of a selected file without opening a program. Preview may not work for some types of files.

Primary key field A field that contains unique information for each record. A primary key field cannot contain a null entry.

Print area The dotted line indicating the area to be printed.

Print Layout view A view that shows a document as it will look on a printed page.

Print Preview A view that displays how a document, spreadsheet, database object, or presentation will appear when printed.

Printer The peripheral computer component that produces a hard copy of the text or graphics processed by the computer.

Process To modify data in a computer.

Processor *See* Microprocessor.

Program Task-oriented software that you use for a particular kind of work, such as word processing or database management. Microsoft Access, Microsoft Excel, and Microsoft Word are all programs.

Program button A button on the taskbar that represents an open program or window.

Program tab A single tab on the Ribbon specific to a particular view, such as Print Preview.

Programming language Software used to write computer instructions.

Property (Windows) A characteristic of a specific computer element (such as the mouse, keyboard, or desktop display) that you can customize. (Access) A characteristic that further defines a field (if field properties), control (if control properties), section (if section properties), or object (if object properties).

Property sheet A window that displays an exhaustive list of properties for the chosen control, section, or object within the Form Design View or Report Design View.

Protocol The set of rules that establishes the orderly transfer of data between the sender and the receiver in data communications.

Query An Access object that provides a spreadsheet-like view of the data, similar tor with a subset of fields and/or records from one or more tables. Queries are created when the user has a "question" about the data in the database.

Query Design grid The bottom pane of the Query Design View window in which you specify the fields, sort order, and limiting criteria for the query.

Query Design View The window in which you develop queries by specifying the fields, sort order, and limiting criteria that determine which fields and records are displayed in the resulting datasheet.

Quick Access toolbar A small, customizable toolbar at the top of an Office program window that contains buttons for commonly used commands such as Save and Undo.

Quick Launch toolbar A toolbar located next to the Start button on the taskbar that contains buttons to start programs and to show the desktop.

Quick Part A reusable piece of content that can be inserted into a document, including a field, document property, preformatted building block.

Quick Style Determines how fonts, colors, and effects of the theme are combined and which color, font, and effect is dominant. A Quick Style can be applied to Smart Art, shapes, or text.

RAM *See* Random access memory.

RAM cache *See* Cache memory.

Random access memory (RAM) Chips on cards plugged into the motherboard that temporarily hold programs and data while the computer is turned on; *also called* volatile memory *or* temporary memory.

Range A selection of two or more cells, such as B5:B14.

Read-only An object property that indicates whether the object can read and display data, but cannot be used to change (write to) data.

Read-only memory (ROM) A chip on the motherboard that is prerecorded with and permanently stores the set of instructions that the computer uses when you turn it on; *also called* nonvolatile memory or permanent memory.

Really Simple Syndication (RSS) A format for feeding or syndicating news or any content from Web sites to your computer.

Receiver The computer or peripheral at the message's destination in data communications.

Record A collection of data items in a database.

Record Source property In a form or report, the property that determines which table or query object contains the fields and records that the form or report will display. It is the most important property of the form or report object. A bound control on a form or report has Control Source property. In this case, the Control Source property identifies the field to which the control is bound.

Recycle Bin A storage area on your computer's hard disk for deleted files, which remain in the Recycle Bin until you empty it. An icon on the desktop provides quick access to the Recycle Bin.

Reference operators Mathematical calculations which enable you to use ranges in calculations.

Referential integrity A set of Access rules that govern data entry and help ensure data accuracy.

Relational database software Software such as Access that is used to manage data organized in a relational database.

Relative cell references In a formula, a type of cell addressing that automatically changes column or row references when cells are copied or moved, to reflect the new location; default type of referencing used in Excel worksheets.

Removable storage Storage media that you can easily transfer from one computer to another, such as DVDs, CDs, or flash drives.

Report An Access object that creates a professional printout of data that may contain such enhancements as headers, footers, and calculations on groups of records.

Report View An Access view that maximizes the amount of data you can see on the screen.

Report Wizard An Access wizard that helps you create a report.

Resizing button A button that you use to adjust the size of a window, such as Maximize, Restore Down, and Minimize.

Resolution The number of pixels that a monitor displays.

Restart To shut down your computer, then start it again.

Restore To reduce the window to its size before it was maximized. The Restore button is usually located in the upper-right corner of a window.

Ribbon A bar near the top of an Office 2007 program window that contains the names of tabs, which contain the most frequently-used Office program commands.

Right-alignment Alignment in which an item is flush with the right margin.

Right-click To press and release the right mouse button once.

Right indent A type of indent in which the right edge of a paragraph is moved in from the right margin.

ROM *See* Read-only memory.

Rotate handle A green circular handle at the top of a selected object that you can drag to rotate the object.

Router A device that controls traffic between network components and usually has a built-in firewall.

Row heading The gray box containing the row number to the left of the row in a worksheet.

Row selector The small square to the left of a field in Table Design View or the Tab Order dialog box. Called the record selector in Datasheet View and Form View.

Rule In Outlook, enables you to organize your mail by setting parameters for incoming mail. For example, you can specify that all mail from a certain person goes into the folder for a specific project.

Ruler (Access) A vertical or horizontal guide that both appear in Form and Report Design View to help you position controls. (Word, WordPad) A horizontal guide at the top of a document window that marks a document's width in 1/8ths of an inch.

Sans serif font A font (such as Calibri) whose characters do not include serifs, which are small strokes at the ends of letters.

Save To store a file permanently on a disk or to overwrite the copy of a file that is stored on a disk with the changes made to the file.

Save As A command used to save a file for the first time or to create a new file with a different filename, leaving the original file intact.

Scale To change the size of a graphic to a specific percentage of its original size.

Scanner A device that transfers the content on a piece of paper into memory; you place a piece of paper on the glass, a beam of light moves across the glass, similar to a photocopier, and stores the image or words on the piece of paper as digital information.

Screen capture A virtual snapshot of your screen, as if you took a picture of it with a camera, which you can paste into a document.

Screen size The diagonal measurement from one corner of the screen to the other.

ScreenTip A label that appears on the screen when you position the mouse pointer over a button or an icon, to identify and provide information about the item or feature.

Scroll To use the scroll bars or the arrow keys to display different parts of a document in the document window.

Scroll arrow The arrow at the end of a scroll bar that is clicked to scroll a document one line at a time, or to scroll a document left and right in the document window.

Scroll arrow button A button at each end of a scroll bar for adjusting your view in small increments in that direction.

Scroll bar A bar on the right edge (vertical scroll bar) and bottom edge (horizontal scroll bar) of a window that allows you to move around to see features that are not visible or that are too large to fit on the screen at once. *See also* Scroll box.

Scroll box A rectangle located in the vertical and horizontal scroll bars that indicates your relative position in a file or window and that you can drag to view other parts of the file or window. *See also* Scroll bar.

Scroll wheel A wheel on a mouse that you roll to scroll the page on the screen.

SCSI (small computer system interface) port A port that provides an interface for one or more peripheral devices at the same port.

SDRAM *See* Synchronous dynamic RAM.

Search box A screen area used along with the Address bar to help you search for Web sites about a particular topic. Enter a keyword or words in the Search box, then click the Search button to activate the search.

Search criteria One or more pieces of information that helps Windows identify the program, folder, or file you want to locate.

Search engine A special Web site that searches the Internet for Web sites based on words or phrases that you enter.

Section (Access) A location of a form or report that contains controls. The section in which a control is placed determines where and how often the control prints. (Word) A portion of a document that is separated from the rest of the document by section breaks.

Section break A formatting mark inserted to divide a document into sections.

Security The steps a computer owner takes to prevent unauthorized use of or damage to the computer.

Select To highlight an item in order to perform some action on it. *See also* Highlighting.

Selection box A dashed border that appears around a text object or placeholder, indicating that it is ready to accept text.

Semipermanent memory *See* Complementary metal oxide semiconductor memory.

Sender The computer that originates the message in data communications.

Sent Items folder When you send an e-mail message, a copy of the message is stored in this folder to help you track the messages that you send out.

Serial port A port that transmits data one bit at a time.

Series in Columns The information in the columns of a worksheet that are on the Value axis; the row labels are on the Category axis.

Series in Rows The information in the rows of a worksheet that are on the Value axis; the column labels are on the Category axis.

Serif font A font (such as Times New Roman) whose characters include serifs, which are small strokes at the ends of letters.

Server A computer on a network that acts as the central storage location for programs and provides mass storage for most of the data used on the network.

Service provider The organization or company that provides e-mail or Internet access.

Shading A background color or pattern that can be applied to text, tables, or graphics.

Sheet tab Identifies sheets in a workbook and lets you switch between sheets; located below the worksheet grid.

Shortcut A link that you can place in any location that gives you quick access to a file, folder, or program located on your hard disk or network.

Shortcut key *See* Keyboard shortcut.

Shortcut menu A menu that appears when you right-click an item.

Shut down The action you perform when you have finished working with your computer; after you shut down it is safe to turn off your computer.

Sidebar A Windows Vista desktop component that displays gadgets. *See also* Gadget.

Single-click *See* Click.

Single-core processor A CPU with one processor on the chip.

Sizing handles Small squares or dots at each corner of a selected Access control, Excel chart, a graphic, or other object in an Office program. Dragging a sizing handle resizes the object. *Also called* handles.

Sleep To save your work, turn off the monitor, then reduce power consumption to all the hardware components in your computer so it appears off; press any key to use your computer again.

Slide layout This determines how all of the elements on a slide are arranged, including text and content placeholders.

Slide Pane The section of Normal view that contains the current slide.

Slide Show view A view that shows a presentation as an electronic slide show; each slide fills the screen.

Slide Sorter view A view that displays a thumbnail of all slides in the order in which they appear in your presentation; used to rearrange slides and slide transitions.

Slide timing The amount of time a slide is visible on the screen during a slide show.

Slide transition The special effect that moves one slide off the screen and the next slide on the screen during a slide show. Each slide can have its own transition effect.

Slider An item in a dialog box that you drag to set the degree to which an option is in effect.

Slides tab The section in Normal View that displays the slides of your presentation as small thumbnails.

Slot *See* Expansion slot.

Small computer system interface port *See* SCSI port.

SmartArt A professional quality graphic diagram supplied with Office 2007 programs that illustrates text using the following structures: List Process, Cycle, Hierarchy, Relationship, Matrix, and Pyramid.

SmartArt Style A pre-set combination of formatting options that follows the design theme that you can apply to a SmartArt graphic.

Soft page break *See* Automatic page break.

Software The intangible components of a computer system, particularly the programs that the computer needs to perform a specific task.

Source file In integration, the file from which information is copied or used. An Excel file inserted into a Word report is a source file. *See also* Destination file.

Spam Unwanted mail that arrives from unsolicited sources. Also called junk e-mail.

Spamming The sending of identical or near-identical unsolicited messages to a large number of recipients. Many e-mail programs have filters that identify this mail and place it in a special folder.

Specifications The technical details about a hardware component.

Spell check The feature in document production software that helps you avoid typographical and grammatical errors.

Spin box A box with two arrows and a text box; allows you to scroll in numerical increments or type a number.

Spoof To create a Web site that looks exactly like another legitimate site on the Web but steals the information people enter.

Spreadsheet software Software that helps you analyze numerical data.

Spyware Software that track a computer user's Internet usage and sends this data back to the company or person that created it, usually without the computer user's permission or knowledge.

SQL (Structured Query Language) A language that provides a standardized way to request information from a relational database system.

Standalone computer A personal computer that is not connected to a network.

Start button A button on the taskbar that you use to start programs, find and open files, access Windows Help and Support Center, and more.

Status bar (Excel) The bar at the bottom of the Excel window that provides information about various keys, commands, and processes.

Status bar (IE7) Located at the bottom of the IE7 window, it displays information about your connection progress whenever you open a new Web page or connect to another Web site, and displays the Web addresses of any links on the Web page when you move your mouse pointer over them.

Status bar (PowerPoint) The bar at the bottom of the PowerPoint window that contains messages about what you are doing and seeing in PowerPoint, such as the current slide number or the current theme.

Status bar (Windows) A horizontal bar at the bottom of a window that displays simple Help information and tips.

Status bar (Word) The bar at the bottom of the Word program window that shows information about the document, including the current page number, the total number of pages in a document, the document word count, and the on/off status of spelling and grammar checking, and contains the view buttons, the Zoom level button and the Zoom slider.

Status indicator Located towards the right side of the status bar, it is animated while a new Web page loads.

Storage capacity *See* Memory capacity.

Store-and-forward technology Technology used in electronic mail wherein messages are stored on a service provider's computer until a recipient logs on to a computer and requests his or her messages. At that time, the messages are forwarded to the recipient's computer.

Strong password A string of at least eight characters of upper and lowercase letters and numbers.

Style A named collection of character and paragraph formats that are stored together and can be applied to text to format it quickly.

Subfolder A folder within another folder for organizing sets of related files into smaller groups.

Subscript A font effect in which text is formatted in a smaller font size and placed below the line of text.

Subtitle text placeholder A box on a PowerPoint title slide reserved for subpoint text.

Suite A group of programs that are bundled together and share a similar interface, making it easy to transfer skills and program content among them.

Sum function A mathematical function that totals values in a field.

Supercomputer The largest and fastest type of computer used by large corporations and government agencies for processing a tremendous volume of data.

Superscript A font effect in which text is formatted in a smaller font size and placed above the line of text.

Switch User To lock your user account and display the Welcome screen so another user can log on.

Symbols Special characters that can be inserted into a document using the Symbol command.

Synchronous dynamic RAM (SDRAM) RAM that is synchronized with the CPU to allow faster access to its contents.

System Clipboard A clipboard that stores only the last item cut or copied from a document. *See also* Clipboard and Office Clipboard.

System resource Any part of the computer system, including memory, storage devices, and the microprocessor, that can be used by a computer program.

System software A collection of programs and data that helps the computer carry out its basic operating tasks.

Tab 1) In Office 2007 programs, a part of the Ribbon that includes groups of buttons for related commands. 2) In Windows and in application programs, a place in a dialog box where related commands and options are organized.

Tab leader A line that appears in front of tabbed text.

Tab order The sequence in which the controls on an Access form receive the focus when the user presses [Tab] or [Enter] in Form view.

Tab stop (Word) A location on the horizontal ruler that indicates where to align text. (Access) This refers to whether you can tab into a control when entering or editing data; in other words, whether the control can receive the focus.

Tabbed browsing Allows you to open more than one Web page at a time in a browser window. Click the tab for a Web page to display that Web page in front.

Table (Access) A collection of records for a single subject, such as all of the customer records. (Word, Excel, and PowerPoint) A grid made up of rows and columns of cells that you can fill with text and graphics.

Table style A named set of table format settings that can be applied to a table to format it all at once.

Tablet PC A computer designed for portability that includes the capability of recognizing ordinary handwriting on the screen.

Tabs Identify the current Web page or pages open in the browser; click a tab to view the Web page.

Tag A word or phrase assigned to a file that reminds you of a file's content.

Tape A magnetic storage media that provides inexpensive archival storage for large quantities of data.

Task Pane A separate section of a window that contains sets of menus, lists, options, and hyperlinks that are used to customize objects.

Taskbar A strip at the bottom of the screen that contains the Start button, Quick Launch toolbar, and clock that shows buttons for the programs that are running.

Tasks In Outlook, the electronic to-do list, whereby each task has a subject, a start and end date, priority, and a description.

TB *See* Terabyte.

Telecommunications The transmission of data over a comparatively long distance using a phone line.

Template An Office file whose content and/or formatting serves as the basis for new files. Each Office application has a special template file extension: .xltx (Excel), .dotx (Word), or .potx (PowerPoint). An Access template must be named Blank.accdb.

Temporary memory *See* Random access memory.

Terabyte (TB) 1,024 GB, or approximately one trillion bytes.

Terminal A computer connected to a network that uses mainframes as a server; it has a keyboard for input and a monitor for output, but processes little or no data on its own.

Terminal emulator A personal computer, workstation, or server that uses special software to imitate a terminal so that it can communicate with a mainframe or supercomputer for complex data processing.

Text annotations Labels added to a chart to draw attention to a particular area.

Text box A rectangular area in a dialog box in which you type text.

Text concatenation operators Mathematical calculations that join strings of text in different cells.

Text label A text box you create using the Text Box button, where the text does not automatically wrap inside the box. Text box text does not appear in the Outline tab.

Text placeholder A box with a dotted border and text that you replace with your own text.

Theme A predefined set of colors, fonts, and line and fill effects that can easily be applied to an Office document a give it a consistent, professional look.

Theme colors The set of 12 coordinated colors in an Office document a color scheme assigns colors for text, lines, fills, accents, hyperlinks, and background.

Thumbnail (PowerPoint) A small image of a slide. Thumbnails are visible on the Slides tab and in Slide Sorter view. (Windows) A smaller image of the actual contents of a file.

Tick marks Notations of a scale of measure on a chart axis.

Title The first line or heading on a slide.

Title bar The bar at the top of the program window that indicates the program name and the name of the current file.

Title placeholder A box on a slide reserved for the title of a presentation or slide.

Title slide The first slide in a presentation.

Toggle button A button that turns a feature on and off.

Toner A powdery substance used by laser printers to transfer a laser image onto paper.

Toolbar A strip with buttons that allow you to activate a command quickly.

Touch pad A touch-sensitive device on a laptop computer that you drag your finger over to control the pointer; buttons for clicking commands are located in front of the touch pad.

Touch pointer A pointer on the screen for performing pointing operations with a finger if touch input is available on your computer.

Trackball A pointing device with a rolling ball on the top side and buttons for clicking commands; you control the movement of the pointer by moving the ball.

Translucency The transparency feature of Windows Aero that enables you to locate content by seeing through one window to the next window.

Trash folder *See* Deleted Items folder.

Unbound Describes a group of controls that do not display data.

Unbound control A control that does not change from record to record and exists only to clarify or enhance the appearance of the form, using elements such as labels, lines, and clip art.

Uniform Resource Locator (URL) The Web page's address; appears in the Address box on the Address bar after you open (or load) the page.

Universal Serial Bus port *See* USB port.

URL (Uniform Resource Locator) A Web address.

USB connector A small, rectangular plug attached to a peripheral device and that you connect to a USB port.

USB drive *See* USB flash storage device.

USB flash drive (also called a pen drive, jump drive, keychain drive, and thumb drive) A popular, removable storage device for folders and files that provides ease of use and portability.

USB flash storage device A popular type of flash memory; *also called* USB drive *or* flash drive *or* flash storage device.

USB (Universal Serial Bus) port A high-speed port to which you can connect a device with a USB connector to have the computer recognize the device and allow you to use it immediately.

User The person primarily interested in entering, editing, and analyzing the data in the database.

User interface A collective term for all the ways you interact with a software program.

Username The first part of an e-mail address that identifies the person who receives the mail that is sent to this e-mail address.

Utility A type of system software that augments the operating system by taking over some of its responsibility for allocating hardware resources.

Value axis In a chart, vertical axis that contains numerical values; in a 2-dimensional chart, also known as the y-axis.

Values Numbers, formulas, and functions used in calculations.

VCards The Internet standard for creating and sharing virtual business cards.

Vertical alignment The position of text in a document relative to the top and bottom margins.

Vertical ruler A ruler that appears on the left side of the document window in Print Layout view.

Vertical scroll bar Appears along the right side of a page window if the page is longer than the window's viewable area; allows you to move the current Web page up or down in the browser window. *See also* Scroll bar.

Video card *See* Graphics card.

Video display adapter *See* Graphics card.

View A way of displaying a document in the document window; each view provides features useful for editing and formatting different types of documents.

View buttons Buttons on the status bar that are used to change document views.

View Shortcuts The buttons at the bottom of the PowerPoint window that you click to switch among views.

Virtual memory Space on the computer's storage devices that simulates additional RAM.

Virus A harmful program that instructs a computer to perform destructive activities, such as erasing a disk drive; variants are called worms and Trojan horses.

Virus protection software *See* Antivirus software.

Volatile memory *See* Random access memory.

Wallpaper The image that fills the desktop background.

WAN *See* Wide area network.

Web Layout view A view that shows a document as it will look when viewed with a Web browser.

Web page A document located on another computer that you can view over the Internet and that often contains words, phrases, and graphics that link to other documents.

Web site A group of Web pages focused on a particular subject.

Web site creation and management software Software that allows you to create and manage Web sites and to see what the Web pages will look like as you create them.

Welcome screen An initial startup screen that displays icons for each user account on the computer.

What-if analysis A decision-making tool in which data is changed and formulas are recalculated, in order to predict various possible outcomes.

Wi-Fi *See* Wireless fidelity.

Wide area network (WAN) A network that connects one or more LAN.

Widow The last line of a paragraph when it is carried over to the top of the following page, separate from the rest of the paragraph.

Wildcard A special character used in criteria to find, filter, and query data. The asterisk (*) stands for any group of characters. For example, the criterion I* in a State field criterion cell would find all records where the state entry was IA, ID, IL, IN, or Iowa. The question mark (?) wildcard stands for only one character.

WiMAX (Worldwide Interoperability for Microwave Access) A standard of wireless communication defined by the IEEE that allows computers to communicate wirelessly over many miles; signals are transmitted from WiMAX towers to a WiMAX receiver in a device.

Window A rectangular frame on a screen that can contain icons, the contents of a file, and/or other usable data.

Windows *See* Microsoft Windows Vista, Microsoft Windows XP.

Windows 3-D Flip A Windows Aero feature that allows you to display stacked windows at a three-dimensional angle to see even more of the content of all open windows and select the window you want to use.

Windows Aero A Windows Vista feature supported in some editions (or versions) of Windows Vista that enhances the transparency (or translucency) of the Start menu, taskbar, windows, and dialog boxes; enables live taskbar thumbnails, Windows Flip, and Windows 3-D Flip.

Windows Explorer A program that you use to manage files, folders, and shortcuts.

Windows Flip A Windows Aero feature that allows you to display a set of thumbnails, or miniature images, of all open windows so that you can select and switch to another window.

Windows Help and Support Center A resource that contains information about Windows XP and that includes an index, a table of contents, and links to useful Web pages.

Wireless fidelity The term created by the nonprofit Wi-Fi Alliance to describe networks connected using a standard radio frequency established by the Institute of Electrical and Electronics Engineers (IEEE); frequently referred to as *Wi-Fi*.

Wireless local area network (WLAN) A LAN connected using high frequency radio waves rather than cables.

WLAN *See* Wireless local area network.

Word processing box A text box you create using the Text Box button, where the text automatically wraps inside the box.

Word processing program A software program that includes tools for entering, editing, and formatting text and graphics.

Word size The amount of data that is processed by a microprocessor at one time.

Word-wrap A feature that automatically moves the insertion point to the next line as you type.

WordArt A set of decorative styles or text effects that is applied to text.

WordPad A word-processing program that comes with Windows XP and Windows Vista.

Workbook A collection of related worksheets contained within a single Excel file.

Worksheet In spreadsheet software, a page composed of columns and rows that create cells at their intersection; you type data and formulas into cells.

Worksheet window An area of the Excel program window that displays part of the current worksheet; the worksheet window displays only a small fraction of the worksheet, which can contain a total of 1,048,576 rows and 16,384 columns.

Workstation A computer that is connected to the network.

World Wide Web Part of the Internet that consists of Web pages located on different computers around the world.

Worldwide Interoperability for Microwave Access *See* WiMAX.

X-axis The horizontal axis in a chart; because it often shows data categories, such as months, *also called* the category axis.

XML format An acronym that stands for eXtensible Markup Language, which is a language used to structure, store, and send information. Also, the new Word 2007 file format.

Y-axis The vertical axis in a chart; because it often shows numerical values in a 2-dimensional chart, *also called* the value axis.

Z-axis The third axis in a true 3-D chart, lets you compare data points across both categories and values.

Zip disk A portable disk that can contain up to 750 MB, far more than a regular floppy disk.

Zip drive A drive that can read Zip disks.

Zoom level button A button on the status bar that is used to change the zoom level of the document in the document window.

Zoom slider An adjustment on the status bar that is used to enlarge or decrease the display size of the document in the document window.

Zooming in A feature that makes a document appear bigger, but shows less of it on screen at once; does not affect actual document size.

Zooming out A feature that lets you see more of a document on screen at once, but at a reduced size; does not affect actual document size.